Gilberto Perez

The

Material

Ghost

FILMS AND THEIR MEDIUM

The Johns Hopkins University Press
Baltimore

Johns Hopkins Paperbacks edition, 2000
9 8 7 6 5 4 3 2 1

The Johns Hopkins University Press
2715 North Charles Street
Baltimore, Maryland 21218-4363
www.press.jhu.edu

Library of Congress Cataloging-in-Publication Data will be found at
the end of this book.
A catalog record for this book is available from the British Library.

Most of the illustrations are frame enlargements made
photographically by Francene Keery; some were made electronically
by George Nicholas; some are from the Museum of Modern Art Film
Stills Archive.

Information on previous publication of parts of the book will be
found on page 449.

ISBN 0-8018-6523-9 (pbk.)

The

Material

Ghost

For my dear father

Gilberto Pérez Castillo

1911–1967

Contents

Illustrations

Acknowledgments

My greatest debt is to Diane Stevenson, my loving and beloved wife, my intellectual and sentimental companion, my best friend and my best critic. This book is the fruition of the work of many years, but acknowledgments are better brief. To list all my debts would take too long. One's own kin one should not have to acknowledge, but my dear mother, Edenia Guillermo, deserves mention for love and support above and beyond the call of motherhood. And let me also mention a few friends who have been of particular help to my work: Emilio Ambasz, Claudia Bell, Roberta Books, Jack Farrell, Ernie Gehr, Jeremy Gilbert-Rolfe, Alfred Guzzetti, Clara Hemphill, Juana Amelia Hernández, Victoria Rowe Holbrook, Dan Kleinman, Priscilla and Wolfgang Langewiesche, Angela Moger, William Park, William Pechter, Kevin Scott, David Shapiro, Arthur Szathmary, Susana Torre, Melinda Ward. My students over the years, at Princeton in the seventies and at Sarah Lawrence since the mid-eighties, have taught me as much as I have them. I am grateful to the institutions that have employed me and to the periodicals that have published me. A Mellon Faculty Fellowship at Harvard supported the writing of a book that was never written but in time transformed itself into this book. Sarah Lawrence gave me a Hewlett-Mellon grant for a reduced teaching load one semester and a small grant to help prepare the illustrations. Parts of this book have appeared in *Artforum,* the *Hudson Review,* the *Nation, Raritan, Sight and Sound,* and the *Yale Review.*

Film and Physics

People are incorrect to compare a director to an author.
If he's a creator, he's more like an architect. And an architect
conceives his plans according to precise circumstances.

JOHN FORD

The moviegoer watches the images on the screen in a dreamlike state. So he can be supposed to apprehend physical
reality in its concreteness.

SIEGFRIED KRACAUER, *Theory of Film*

The Havana where I grew up was a great town for going to the movies. It was Havana in the fifties, under the dictator Batista, so it was not the best of times. But it was a good time and place for a kid to become a moviegoer. On the screens of my city movies from all over the world unfolded: we got all the movies from Hollywood and we also got, not just a few for the presumed cognoscenti, but a good many movies from Italy and France and Russia, Mexico and Spain and South America, Japan and India and Scandinavia. My favorite movie theater, the Capri, regularly featured an international mix, so that in one program I might see together *Il Bidone* and *The Killing,* or *Gold of Naples* and *An American in Paris,* or *Madame de...* and *The Criminal Life of Archibaldo de la Cruz.* With negligibly few exceptions, the movies were all foreign, which is to say that none of them were: they all took place in the spellbinding elsewhere of the screen. Thankfully, movies were not dubbed for Cuban audiences but always shown in the original language; at an early age I got used to subtitles, which for me became part of the language of cinema. Moreover, I grew up in a time when movies were as often done in black and white as in color, which led to my having no color prejudice before the images on the screen. My movie upbringing was very liberal. Although naturally I liked some movies better than others, and naturally I noted differences in subject and style, temper and approach, I was raised not to discriminate on account of language or color or national origin.[1]

"If it has subtitles, it's art," says, only partly in jest, a friend whose persuasion is literary and whose formative moviegoing dates from the New York of the forties. For me, whose formative moviegoing normally entailed subtitles, the movies have always been a medium of art—no different from literature or painting in their small yield of good art among the middling and the bad. I first went to the movies with my father, and all through my childhood and adolescence he was my abiding moviegoing companion. The author of a book called *Nuestro Siglo* (Our Century), my father was a doctor with an avid interest in literature and the arts, and he imparted to me an ungainsayable sense that the movies belong in their company. "We generally become interested in movies because we *enjoy* them," wrote Pauline Kael, "and what we enjoy them for has little to do with what we think of as art."[2] The first part of her statement certainly fits me, but not the second. I grew up with the movies as art and with art not as something stuffy and affected but as something vital, like the movies.

The first criticism of the arts that seriously engaged me, even before my teens, was the movie criticism that was appearing in *Carteles*. The weekly *Carteles* was rather like a Cuban *Collier's* or *Saturday Evening Post;* the movie column was simply called "Cine," and for a while it didn't carry a byline. Yet it carried a distinctive critical voice. Subsequently that voice gained the name G. Caín, a pseudonym, it transpired, for the Cuban writer Guillermo Cabrera Infante, who later won acclaim with his splendid novel of nighttime Havana, *Tres tristes tigres* (a tongue-twisting title rendered in English as *Three Trapped Tigers*). To Cabrera Infante I owe my first attentive appreciation of what makes a movie move, what goes into the art of putting it together, my excited first awareness of the ways of the camera in shaping our view of the world pictured on the screen. His movie reviews gave me an education in seeing and in thinking with my eyes. Under the name G. Caín they were collected into a book, *Un oficio del siglo XX*, published in 1963 by Ediciones Revolución in Havana; in 1965 Cabrera Infante left Cuba. With few changes and no additions—nothing to update it—the book came out in English three decades later as *A Twentieth Century Job*.[3]

Of Antonioni's *Le Amiche*, for example, a reticently amazing film made in 1955 and all but unknown in this country even after its director became famous in the sixties, Cabrera Infante wrote a review perceptive of the film's accomplishment and responsive to its promise. Like Clement Greenberg's early reviews of Jackson Pollock, this was criticism whose awareness of the present put it in touch with the future, criticism with eyes to see both what was there in the work and what the work had in store, both what Antonioni had succeeded in doing with quiet originality and where he was tending to lead the practice of his art.

Film in the fifties seemed to many an art in decline if not downright fall. Classic Hollywood was dying, French cinema had mostly succumbed to academicism, and the neorealism that had vitalized Italian cinema in the postwar years was passing away too. Yet despite the apparent impoverishment, the fifties were actually a time of riches in the art of film. Cabrera Infante was among the few who recognized the cinematic achievement of the time: of Antonioni and Fellini in Italy, filmmakers who came out of neorealism and wielded the mirror it held up to nature in their own newly reflective ways; of Becker and Bresson in France, the one gripping the tangible with passion, the other reaching with precision for the unrepresentable; of Buñuel in Mexico, where the old surrealist, commercially employed, yet made some of his most incisive and arresting films; of the serenely eerie Mizoguchi and the restlessly sturdy Kurosawa in Japan and the corporeal and contemplative Satyajit Ray in India; of Hitchcock and Hawks and Minnelli in Hollywood and of such American mavericks as the expatriate Orson Welles and the young (later expatriate) Stanley Kubrick. And—unlike James Agee in the United States, for example, a film critic who mainly yearned for past glories—Cabrera Infante was a film critic animated by a sense of expectation and possibility, a spirited looking forward to the coming attractions of an art in the making.

My own posture today is similar to Agee's: as he looked back to the movies of his teens and twenties and in the cinema of Griffith and Chaplin, Eisenstein and Dovzhenko, saw the art's great era, so I look back to the movies of my teens and twenties and see an efflorescence of the art that peaked in the sixties and has not been matched since. Is such a posture—uncommon neither in Agee's time nor in mine—merely subjective, merely a matter of our being most impressed when at our most impressionable? Subjectivity necessarily informs our response to art, but that does not necessarily render our judgment devoid of objectivity. Surely it is significant, in any case—not just subjectively but aesthetically significant—that we should respond to the movies of our youth with something like the feelings of first love. Cabrera Infante's collected reviews take me back to the time of my first falling in love with the art of film.

Soon after I came to this country in the early sixties I found that matters already familiar to me from Cabrera Infante's reviews, which kept up with foreign criticism and partook of the spirit of the yellow-covered *Cahiers du cinéma* of the fifties, were for American film critics a hot new topic of controversy they called the *auteur* theory. The auteur theory has meant different things to different people. If it is taken to mean that film is the director's art—that the shaping hand specific to film and governing most of the best films is the director's—then it is a notion as old as the proposition that film is an art.

Orson Welles, a director with an immediately recognizable style if there ever was one, gallantly stands up for the actor in his interviews, conducted two decades ago when the auteur theory was at the height of its fashion, with auteur proponent and would-be auteur Peter Bogdanovich.[4] Most people go to the movies for the actors; most of the pleasure I get from movies these days comes from the actors; certainly the actors are a much better reason for going to the movies than anything most movie reviewers have to say. Opponents of the auteur theory have shown a literary partiality, however, and rather than the actor they have tended to promote the writer in their demotion of the director—unless they rest content with the assertion that movies are made by many hands. Many hands are sometimes viewed approvingly (as in the selfless group artistry of a medieval cathedral) but more often disapprovingly (as in the soulless fabrication on an assembly line). When the auteur theory fell into disfavor, not so much among film critics as among the growing ranks of film academics, it was not an appreciation of the actor or the writer that gained ascendancy but a repudiation of all individuality as a false consciousness inculcated by bourgeois ideology.

Late in 1913 D. W. Griffith, breaking with the Biograph Company, took out a full-page ad in the *New York Dramatic Mirror* declaring his authorship of the films he had been making since 1908 in Biograph's employ. Movie companies in that early period, and Biograph more doggedly than the others, kept the names of players and filmmakers unknown to the public; movies were to be seen as company products. Against this policy of company impersonality Griffith was asserting his authorship and his artistry. His work at Biograph had been momentously innovative. Rather than the company, his ad proclaimed, it was he who was responsible for "revolutionizing Motion Picture drama and founding the modern technique of the art."[5]

Long before the auteur theory was proposed, film critics and historians endorsed Griffith's claim to authorship. For several years now, however—years in which the study of film has established itself academically—dominant thinking in the field of film studies has in effect come down on the side of Biograph. The auteur theory, imported from France in the early sixties, has long been out of fashion; a newer bit of imported French theory has pronounced the author dead. The view of art as the creation or expression of individual genius is out of favor. Instead, thinking corporately, we are to admire the "genius of the system"[6] or, on the other side of the same coin, we are to decry the manipulations of a system that, it is believed, serves the purposes of an oppressive ideology and allows little room for deviation either in the making or in the viewing of a film.

Opponents of the auteur theory have charged it with being ahistorical, and the charge has some justice. "If directors and other artists cannot be wrenched from their historical environments," wrote Andrew Sarris in the early days of his influential advocacy of the auteur theory, "aesthetics is reduced to a subordinate branch of ethnography."[7] "What does he think it is?" retorted Pauline Kael.[8] And Christopher Faulkner takes a stand "for ethnography" in the introduction to his *Social Cinema of Jean Renoir*, where he maintains as others have that the auteur theory with its emphasis on individual creation and its tendency to play down historical circumstance is but a form of bourgeois ideology.[9] That may be, but it must also be recognized that, no less than an emphasis on individual creation, an emphasis on historical circumstance is a bourgeois way of thinking. Faulkner appears to believe that the idea of wrenching the artist from history has reigned unbrokenly since the Renaissance, but Sarris (following the American New Critics in this respect) was reacting against a historicism that had long been a dominant critical approach. Faulkner's charge of ahistoricism is itself ahistorical.

The trend of postmodern thinking has been against ideas of unity and wholeness. These are taken to be bourgeois fabrications, constructs of the ruling ideology, though they have a much longer history and, even as we call them into question, our thinking seems to require them. We think in terms of parts and wholes even if our parts don't exactly fit into our wholes. Faulkner's study of Renoir calls into question the unity of Renoir's authorship over the years but assumes the unity of determinant historical situations that produced one Renoir in the thirties and another Renoir in the fifties. The unity traditionally valued in a work of art, or in an artist's body of work, is currently discounted as a false consciousness promoting that other supposed figment of bourgeois ideology, the unity of the self. The perceived unity of an object is thought to endorse one's sense of one's own unity as a perceiving subject. My impression of *The Battleship Potemkin* (1925) as a unified work presumably fosters in me the idea that I am a unified self. But *Potemkin* encourages a different sense of unity in the spectator, a sense not of individuality but of class consciousness, of collective solidarity, a kind of unity at odds with the individualism of bourgeois ideology. What about Eisenstein as an *auteur*, the unity of his body of work? Supposedly my seeing *Potemkin* and *Ivan the Terrible* (1944–46) as works of the same individual, rather than as products of different historical circumstances, confirms me in my sense of my own individuality. But surely the question of Eisenstein's individuality in relation to his historical circumstances, and of my own in relation to mine, ought not to be decided in the abstract but examined in the concrete, for not all individuals, and not all historical circumstances, are the same. Wrenching the individual from historical circumstance may be ideological, but no more so than positing the individual as a figment of ideology and a puppet of history. Even if it were true that the self in our postmodern times is irreparably fragmented, that any notion of its unity merely clings to an illusion, surely this doesn't entitle us to decide that the same is true of all other times and places.

From the auteur theory, which brought the romantic cult of the artist into the upstart art of film, the winds of our fashions have blown to a view of the artist as the pawn of history and culture and society. Allegedly unpolitical yet originally a *politique*—a politics championing the author as the individual spirit resisting the conformities of the system—the auteur theory aggrandized the author but it better allowed for a dialectic between the author and the system, between the individual and his or her situation, than does a theory that aggrandizes the system into a virtually absolute rule. To be sure, the filmmaker is, even if not in the employ of a studio, under the sway of the social and political order, the culture and circumstance in which he or she works; but that will not in every way determine, though it will in many ways affect, the film he or she will make or the response a spectator will have to it. There is a margin of freedom when making a film and when viewing one, a margin for making the kind of film that invites the viewer's freedom of response; and that edge of freedom may make all the difference.

Academics who criticize bourgeois individualism think they are bucking the establishment. They seem not to recognize that the individualist model of capitalism has mostly given way to a corporate model and that a critique of individualism suits the corporate capitalism now reigning. The director as auteur certainly does not suit corporate Hollywood. The individual auteur never suited the Hollywood studio system, it may be argued, and that's the problem with the auteur theory in the first place: it doesn't fit the facts of movie production. But this argument shifts the ground from the ideology of individualism to the conditions of the movie industry: it is one thing to say that the individual artist is a figment of bourgeois ideology and quite another to say that the working conditions of Hollywood are inimical to the individual artist. The auteur theory values individual artistry and claims that it exists in the movies: it is one thing to argue that it doesn't exist in Hollywood and quite another to maintain that it doesn't exist anywhere and that only a false consciousness can lead us to value it. The auteur theory is the application to film of the genius theory of art. The genius theory may be all wrong, wrong about Beethoven and Michelangelo as about Vincente Minnelli and Frank Borzage; or it may be wrong in its application to film, or wrong in its application to Hollywood film. It should be kept straight where its wrongness is supposed to lie.

The main area of contention in the auteur controversy of the sixties was not whether film is the director's art but which directors are to be considered artists. Nobody disputed the individual artistry of Eisenstein or Renoir. Hollywood directors were the ones particularly in dispute. Where the auteur policy at *Cahiers du cinéma* broke new ground was in putting forward the artistry and the authorship of directors working in a commercial entertainment industry deemed inhospitable to personal artistic expression. Howard Hawks is a case in point, a director whose considerable achievement received scant critical attention before the French took him up. Alfred Hitchcock is an interesting case, a director whose authorship was singularly well publicized ("the master of suspense") while his artistry nonetheless remained insufficiently recognized until the French saw him as a true master.

Hitchcock himself devised the publicity through which his directorial signature (and his spryly deployed obese figure with its trademark intrusions into the world of his films) got to be known everywhere. He sold himself as director and sold his films as his creation. In *Hitchcock: The Making of a Reputation*, a study not of Hitchcock's films but of how they have been regarded, Robert E. Kapsis traces the lifelong promotion Hitchcock conducted in behalf of the director as a film's maker—the actors he characterized as "cattle"—and of himself as a stellar director.[10] Back in England in 1927 Hitchcock had his first hit, *The Lodger*, where he made his first cameo appearance in his own work. Already that year he started circulating the profile self-caricature that became another trademark. And in a London newspaper that year he said that "film directors live with their pictures while they are being made. They are their babies just as much as an author's novel is the offspring of his imagination. And that seems to make it all the more certain that when moving pictures are really artistic they will be created entirely by one man."[11] Asking whether Hitchcock's self-promotion had more to do with commerce or with art misses the intertwinement of the two in a director's career. Just as surely as he wanted to make money, Hitchcock required money in order to make art.

Hitchcock in the fifties showed his tamest commercial side and he also showed remarkable artistry and audacity. The first Hitchcock film I saw seemed to me entertaining but unimpressive: the glossy and shallow *To Catch a Thief* (1955) was decidedly on the commercial side. But then there was the breathtaking *Vertigo* (1958): no film in those years made more of an impression on me. All the moviegoing kids I knew in Havana loved it too, and Cabrera Infante hailed it as a masterpiece. Opinion ran otherwise in the United States, I was surprised to find, and keepers of the common wisdom would shake their heads and discountenance a liking for *Vertigo* as an inexplicable aberration of esoteric French taste. "Alfred Hitchcock, who produced and directed the thing," wrote John McCarten in his review of the film in the *New Yorker* (7 June 1958), "has never before indulged in such farfetched nonsense." Opinion has certainly changed. Most observers today would concur that *Vertigo* is a masterpiece, though they may not call it by that currently unfashionable term. Hitchcock's reputation rose with the auteur theory but did not decline with it. The feminist theory that next took hold in film studies privileged Hitchcock no less—and made *Vertigo* no less central in the canon.

Vertigo tells the story of a man (Jimmy Stewart, whose persona of the boyish regular guy here acquires a shading of disorder) in the grip of love beyond grasp. A figure of identification for the movie spectator—and especially for the spectator I was as an adolescent boy—this protagonist becomes enthralled by a woman (Kim Novak) as beautiful and as ghostly as the image of a movie star shimmering up close on the screen yet impossibly far away. Driven like the protagonist in his pursuit of this potent apparition of a woman, Cabrera Infante went to see the film "on three successive, obsessive nights" under the pull of "its complete immersion in the sea of magic" and pronounced it "the first romantic work of the twentieth century."[12] My sentiments exactly, at the time. Not, by and large, the way the film is regarded now. According to Kapsis, whose book is not about what he thinks but about what others think and thus presumably expresses the consensus of opinion, *Vertigo* is an "uncompromising indictment of romantic love."[13] Immersion in the sea of magic is not good for you. The first wave of feminist film theory saw the romanticism of *Vertigo* as enemy territory, a mesmerizing epitome of male desire and the male gaze; but those unable to let go either of *Vertigo* or of the theory that posits and reprehends the male gaze have endeavored to "save the film for feminism" by construing it as a condemnation of romanticism.

To the initial objection of many but to the subsequent admiration of most, in *Vertigo* Hitchcock goes against the rules of the well-made mystery and reveals the solution halfway through, when he unexpectedly shifts the point of view away from the entranced protagonist who so far has been the film's center of consciousness. By this bold move the film demystifies its ro-manticism. The protagonist's inamorata has been an imposture, not merely an idealized but a sheerly fictitious woman, we now learn from the woman herself who impersonated the figment that is the man's romantic obsession. We watch with a kind of horror as the unknowing protagonist singlemind-edly presses her and she misgivingly consents to play again the part of his romantic dream. And yet, even though we know better, something in us irresistibly responds all the same to the vision of beauty that eventually materializes before his eyes. Cabrera Infante's view is more nearly right than Kapsis's consensus. *Vertigo* demystifies its romanticism but it does not defuse it. In this it is like another great romantic film, Max Ophuls's *Letter from an Unknown Woman* (1948), whose protagonist is not a man but a woman in love with an illusion that no reality can dispel.

Does Hitchcock deserve his reputation? He deserves high praise, and among those reluctant to recognize the art of film he still needs cham-pioning. Within film circles, however, the answer to this question must be no, for he would have to be incomparably the greatest of all filmmakers to merit the amount of critical and academic attention bestowed on him, well in excess of any other director's share and giving no signs of diminution after many years and reams of articles and books. The best work is the best measure of an artist, and at his best Hitchcock is a great artist. His drafts-manship with the movie camera—what the French like to call *écriture*, writ-ing in the language of film—is extraordinary. But the no less extraordinary cinematic dexterity of Frank Capra, for example, has received far less atten-tion. "Capra has a touch of genius with a camera: his screen always seems twice as big as other people's, and he cuts as brilliantly as Eisenstein," wrote Graham Greene (who didn't much like Hitchcock) in one of his movie reviews of the thirties.[14] The attention Capra gets today goes mainly to the blend of sentiment and humor that has made viewing *It's a Wonderful Life* (1946) on television a national Christmas ritual. "No one else can balance the ups and downs of wistful sentiment and corny humor the way Capra can," wrote Pauline Kael, "but if anyone else should learn to, kill him."[15] The "Capracorn" that many warm to puts others off. "Enormous skill," said Orson Welles when Bogdanovich asked him about Capra, "but always that sweet *Saturday Evening Post* thing about him."[16]

If Hitchcock is a consummate camera draftsman, Capra is a master of texture and light, of texture as the play of light projected on the screen. Applying to film the duality proposed by Heinrich Wölfflin in art history, one may call Hitchcock linear, a leader of the eye along the exactly determined line of his camera angles and movements, and Capra painterly, a colorist in black-and-white film with a palette of luster and sparkle, glimmer and glow, light subdued and diffused and resplendent. The distinctive look and light of a Capra film owe much to the work of Joseph Walker, Capra's cameraman all through the thirties. In a perceptive appreciation of *It Happened One Night*, the 1934 sleeper that was Capra's first big hit—a memorable screwball comedy and a Depression romance of enduring enchantment, with Claudette Colbert as the fugitive heiress and Clark Gable as the newspaperman—James Harvey wrote: "Joseph Walker's photography gives the world of the film a consistent refulgent, glowing-from-within quality—especially the night world, from the rain on the auto camp windows, to the rushing, glittering stream Gable carries Colbert across, to the overarching haystacks, moonstruck and sagging, that the couple find themselves sleeping under after they leave the bus."[17]

In the rainy night Colbert and Gable spend together in the auto camp, separated by the blanket he hangs between their two beds and calls the "walls of Jericho," there is a moment of eloquent glimmer that Harvey aptly singles out, a dark close-up of Colbert in which, as she shifts a little in her bed, the camera briefly catches a moist reflection of light in her eyes: "a gleam slight but clear" that distills the "atmosphere of yearning" suffusing the whole movie.[18] And Capra crowns this with a cut that resonantly rhymes the inside and the outside: from the gleam in the close-up of the heroine to a long shot in which, through two cabin windows like eyes moist with the world's yearning, the rain falling outside gleams.

Capra's *It Happened One Night*, Leo McCarey's *The Awful Truth* (1937), and Hawks's *His Girl Friday* (1940) seem to me the three best screwball comedies, or comedies of remarriage as Stanley Cavell calls them,[19] the three best instances of a genre that represents classical old Hollywood at its best. Joseph Walker photographed all three. He was one of the world's great cinematographers. He has generally not gotten the recognition he deserves, and the failure of Capra himself to give him that recognition seems especially unjust. Like Hitchcock, Capra boosted his own authorship. It was fine that he asserted it in the face of an industry that would treat the director as mere hired help, but he also asserted it by minimizing the work of his collaborators. Beginning with *It Happened One Night*, which swept the Academy Awards for 1934, Capra won three Oscars for best director within five years; in 1938 he made the cover of *Time*. His was to be "the name above the title," as he called the autobiography he published in 1971—during the vogue of the auteur theory—a book that won him back some of the fame he had lost in years of decline and inactivity.[20] Telling the story of the poor Sicilian immigrant who rises to success in the movies, the book is informed by a cheery self-aggrandizement that plays down what anybody else did to assist the rise or contribute to the success. Capra does not properly acknowledge his debt to Walker's camera or to Robert Riskin's scripts for several of his films, including all three that won him directing Oscars.

In *Frank Capra: The Catastrophe of Success,* an unauthorized biography that reads like a lengthy rebuttal of the untrustworthy autobiography, Joseph McBride takes to task not just Capra's account but more generally the story of self-made success in the land of opportunity.[21] McBride begrudges Capra his success and gloats over his decline (even over his failure as a farmer), but he has a point: what Capra did depended on what others did; a Capra film was certainly not made by one man. Without Joseph Walker, without the work of other collaborators, without the artistic and historical circumstance in which he found himself, Capra would not have been Capra. But this doesn't mean that Capra was nothing. *It Happened One Night, The Awful Truth,* and *His Girl Friday* may be regarded as Joseph Walker films, or as films made at Columbia Pictures, or as instances of a genre of comedy, or as expressions of a time and place, a culture and society. But they may also be regarded as the work of their directors: we may not be interested in the personalities of Capra, McCarey, and Hawks as the auteur theory prescribes, but their art is on the screen.

Capra's politics is another issue McBride raises. Usually associated with the New Deal, Capra actually voted Republican, which leads McBride to charge him with political hypocrisy. But recognizing that Capra's films were not made by him alone ought to keep us from confusing the man's personal politics with the politics of his films. The scriptwriter who worked with Capra on *Mr. Smith Goes to Washington* (1939) was Sidney Buchman, who later was among those blacklisted in Hollywood for their leftist affiliation, and the "sweet *Saturday Evening Post* thing" combines in this film with a bitter indictment of the corruption of power in the American political system: Mr. Smith (Jimmy Stewart) may win in the end, but he wins at the very last minute by a kind of miracle, and the film makes painfully manifest that such an idealist would have been crushed in reality by the entrenched political machinery Mr. Smith was up against. In the seventies, at a talk Capra was giving on a tour of college campuses after his autobiography came out, I asked him why he had pushed Mr. Smith so far into the depths of defeat before rescuing him in an improbable happy ending. Surely, if he had wanted, he could easily have made the happy ending more probable? Capra took my question as hostile—which was not my intention—and then said something about Christ on the cross and victory won in defeat.

Mr. Smith Goes to Washington followed *Mr. Deeds Goes to Town* (1936) and was followed by *Meet John Doe* (1941) and *It's a Wonderful Life*: a series of Capra films enacting what Richard Griffith called a "fantasy of goodwill" and characterized as "a blend of realistic problem and imaginary solution epitomiz[ing] the dilemma of the middle-class mind in the New Deal period." Compared with Riskin's script for *Mr. Deeds*, Buchman's script for *Mr. Smith* treats the problem more realistically, which makes the solution a more evident fantasy: "Individual idealism is no solution for any practical problem," commented Griffith, "but it is the totem people worship when every other way out cuts across their thinking habits."[22] In *Meet John Doe*, however, which Riskin again scripted, the problem grows realistic to the point of not admitting a satisfactory solution, not even in fantasy. In *It's a Wonderful Life*, with a script by many hands (including such uncredited ones as Clifford Odets, Dorothy Parker, and Dalton Trumbo), the solution, built into the story from the beginning, becomes the ultimate fantasy of an angel from heaven.

Capra—I speak not of the man himself but of what comes across in the films, with all the factors and collaborators that went into their making—was an idealist who would not falsify reality to suit his ideas and so was led to have his fantasies literally take wing. He was not the populist he is often taken to be. His portrayal of the "little people" he purportedly loves tends to sentimentality and condescension. His politics are no sort of New Deal populism but a kind of middle-class noblesse oblige. George Bailey (Jimmy Stewart) in *It's a Wonderful Life* is not a figure of the common man but of the superior one, idealistically devoted to the common good and individually responsible, as the nightmare vision of what his hometown would have been like without him demonstrates, for fending off capitalist greed. And he is a figure that fails, that in reality would have been dead at the bottom of that river: Capra was an idealist who believed enough in his ideals not to take as their measure the world as it exists.

In a brilliant essay on Capra entitled "American Madness" after one of his films, William S. Pechter argued that Capra was aware, maybe not consciously but at some intuitive level, of the imaginary nature of his solutions, the unlikelihood of his happy endings.[23] The happy endings of comedy are often ironic endings, frankly contrived and intended to evoke a smile of disbelief. "Beaumarchais' *Marriage of Figaro* ends with the kind of improbability which we are to recognize as such and take ironically," wrote Eric Bentley in the course of drawing a contrast with another vein of comedy: "In Mozart's *Marriage of Figaro,* as in *Twelfth Night,* love and happiness have their reality in art, while the question of their reality in life is left in uncynical abeyance."[24] Love and happiness in *It Happened One Night* have their reality in just that way, the way of romantic comedy. But *Mr. Smith Goes to Washington* and *It's a Wonderful Life* are not exactly romantic comedies (*Mr. Deeds Goes to Town* comes closer). They reach their happy endings through the kind of improbability that could have easily been smoothed over but is instead—as when that angel must intervene in *It's a Wonderful Life* to save the hero from suicide—made difficult for us not to recognize as such. But these happy endings are not exactly ironic either. Things would not happen this way in real life, we know, and yet we smile in tense and wishful suspension of disbelief.

The career of Frank Capra offers a good refutation of the auteur theory. If he was a genius, the genius was all gone after *It's a Wonderful Life,* so dependent was it on the talents of others, on the factors and the themes, the energies and the conditions of a time and place. Yet for several years something like genius was there, not the genius of an individual if by that is meant a self-sufficient individual, not the genius of the system if by that is meant the studio system—it was Capra that made Columbia a major studio, not Columbia that made Capra a major director—but a genius of some kind that brought it all together and put it on the screen. The pieces he may have owed to others, but the ensemble, the way a Capra film hangs together on the screen, is unmistakably his. More like an architect than an author, as John Ford said of the job of a film director.

I came to the United States after high school, and I thought I was coming to study engineering. I went to M.I.T. There I started writing movie reviews for the campus newspaper. By the time I was a senior I wrote a regular column for *The Tech.* It was not a widely *liked* column—the humor magazine twice parodied it and ridiculed its pretensions—but it was widely *read.* Everybody on campus knew who I was; I had a taste of fame. Although I didn't know it at the time, I was on the path that has led to this book.

I didn't last long in engineering; in my sophomore year I switched my major to something less practical that I found more attractive—physics. Others may have thought of physics as the study of galaxies and subatomic particles, the outer realms of our experience, but what attracted me to physics was its ability to explain the world around me. It was thrilling to learn why it is that, thanks to the law of conservation of angular momentum and the stability it confers on rotating bodies, a moving bicycle doesn't tip over. It was exciting to take in Newton's explanation of the tides and to grasp how it comes about that the moon, though much smaller, has a larger effect on them than the sun. Some of my classmates would make fun of the nerd who talks physics rather than romance in the moonlight by the waterside with a girl, but for me the beauty of the ocean was enhanced rather than diminished by a knowledge of its physics. Around this time I had a dream that, while I was dreaming it, seemed irrefutably to prove the existence of God. The sun and the moon are celestial bodies of vastly different sizes, this dream proof went, and yet from the earth looking up at the sky they appear to be exactly the same size: hence God exists. Until I woke up I was quite convinced I had found the proof the philosophers had sought.

Physicists divide themselves into two camps, theoretical and experimental. The theoreticians tend to look down on the experimenters. Modern physics, since Galileo refuted Aristotle by dropping weights from the Leaning Tower of Pisa and seeing how they fall, has been based on empirical observation; but theoretical physics, in some kind of holdover from scholastic thinking, still enjoys greater prestige. I was a theoretical physicist, like Einstein, like Maxwell, like Heisenberg. A scientist friend from England, more aware of matters of class, would call me a "gentleman mathematician" who didn't want to get his hands dirty. I protested; a mathematician, to the Cuban middle class I was born to, was someone who taught school, assuredly lesser than an engineer; but my friend was not wrong to discern something snobbish in my theoretician's posture. I nearly failed the doctoral general examination because I did so badly in the experimental questions; I didn't bother to prepare for questions I didn't think belonged on the exam. The examiners passed me but demanded that, in penance, I do an experiment over the summer; I carried out the experiment successfully but in the course of it I accidentally broke an expensive piece of equipment that took weeks to replace. I was not cut out for empirical science. And yet the theory that attracted me was not a pure abstraction removed from concrete reality but the theory that explained to me why a bicycle doesn't tip over.

Film theory is to film criticism as theoretical physics is to experimental physics. A quarter-century ago—a quarter of the century it has been in existence—film began to be studied as an academic discipline. Film studies wanted theory. The theory academically fashionable in the humanities at that time and for years after was structuralist and poststructuralist theory. That's what's known as "theory" in film studies; that is the kind of theory that has shaped the field in the years of its academic existence. It is a theory largely detached from criticism and often disdainful of it, a theory presuming to know the answers ("always already" knowing the answers, to use one of its favorite phrases) and averse to getting its hands dirty with the evidence—the theoretician's snobbery augmented, as snobbery commonly is, by the insecurity of the parvenu, the newcomer to the academy anxious to gain status. It is decidedly an idealist theory—idealist in the sense that it gives primacy to ideas and expects reality to behave accordingly—but it considers itself materialist and thinks that it is exposing the idealism, the ideology, of others.

I am drawn to film theory as I was drawn to theoretical physics; I believe that film criticism and experimental physics—whether they know it or not, and better if they know it—alike depend on theory to guide and make sense of their practice, theory with the focus and structure it provides, the scheme of assumptions it constructs about what to look for and what to make of it. But I also believe that theory that applies to experience in its turn rests on experience; it must not take off into a realm of its own but must instead construct its schemes in vital give and take with concrete reality. I cannot go along with a film theory that eschews such a give and take with criticism, a theory that will not negotiate but just wants to dictate terms. This is a book of film criticism consistently drawn to theory but as consistently skeptical of what these days is called "theory."

Structuralist theory followed the linguistics of Ferdinand de Saussure and attempted to extend it beyond language proper to other forms of communication. Christian Metz made the most sustained effort to apply it to film. He concluded that film is not a language in any strict sense.[25] But the linguistic bent of film theory has persisted. One of its consequences is that, though the ordinary moviegoer naturally remains interested in the actors and other dramatic aspects of the medium, the film scholar seldom invokes theater any longer and instead considers film a form of narration. The distinction between narrative and drama goes back to Aristotle: narrative is told, recounted in the words of a storyteller; drama is enacted, performed by actors on a stage. Film may look like a medium of enactment, with actors and props and scenery, but the language-minded theoretician looks upon it as a narrative medium that tells stories much in the manner of words on a page. John Ellis, for example, maintains that films are told in a "historic mode of narration" that dissembles the mediation of a storyteller and conveys a "sense of reality narrating itself."[26] Entrenched within the linguistic model of cinema, Ellis seems unaware that what he is describing, and characterizing as a delusive endeavor to pass off fiction as reality, is the normal operation of drama, where indeed no storyteller figures but no one fails to recognize the proceedings as a fiction performed for an audience. My own theory of film narrative, set forth in chapter 2 of this book, takes film to be a medium poised between drama and narrative, between enactment and mediation.

The linguistic sign, for Saussure, consists of two parts joined together, a signifier and a signified. The signifier is a word, the word *tree*, for example, and the signified is a concept, the picture of a tree the word evokes in the mind. Saussure reversed the old model in which abstract words would refer to concrete things: the word, the signifier, is for him the sensory part of the sign, the more material part, while the signified, the picture the word evokes, is the more abstract part.[27] In Saussure's scheme words are what make an impression on the senses, pictures are conjured up in the mind. This was fine for a linguist—words were his material—but transferred to the study of visual images it gets things wrong.[28] Jacques Lacan, who worked over Freudian psychoanalysis on the model of Saussurean linguistics, put images in the province of the imaginary, which for him means the illusory plenitude of primary narcissism when the child seemed to possess the mother and the self seemed to possess the world. Metz, who turned to Lacanian psychoanalysis after his attempt at a more direct linguistic approach to film theory, pronounced the film image "the imaginary signifier."[29] What can an "imaginary signifier" be? Metz impossibly joined Saussure's term for the sensory part of the sign with Saussure's allocation of pictures to the realm of the mind. A signified can be imaginary, but a signifier cannot, for the signifier is precisely the part of the sign present to the senses, there to be registered; but for Metz the cinematic signifier is absent. What he means is that the film image, in his view, seems to show us a plenitude such as Lacan ascribes to the imaginary but actually it brings nothing before us, nothing but a shadow. The illusion of plenitude, the fact of absence: watching a film, the Lacanian supposes, one moment we feel in possession of the world and the next moment we feel the whole world lost to us. One problem with this theory, as Noël Carroll has observed, is that it assumes that we want the representation on the screen to be reality.[30] This is a mistake. The pleasure we take in film is the pleasure of representation.

So badly do we want reality on the screen, according to the Lacanian, that we deny to ourselves the evident fact that it is not there: instead of a willing suspension of disbelief, this theory proposes a clinging to illusion for fear of castration. Castration? The absence of the penis, Freud thought, terrifies the child who catches sight of the female genitals, and the fetish, usually an object seen just before—underwear the woman takes off, pubic hair that becomes velvet or fur, a foot or shoe if the child peers up the woman's legs—serves as a substitute for the missing penis that enables the fetishist to deny its absence. For the Lacanian we are all fetishists at the movies who fasten on the image to deny the absence of reality. *I Lost It at the Movies* was the title of Pauline Kael's first book. For the Lacanian we all lost it—we are all forever kept from the object of desire by the law of the father, all irreparably cut off from the world's body by the castrating intervention of language—and the movies are the fetish by which we fool ourselves that we have it.

Medusa's head was for Freud a symbol of the terrifying female genitals. Athena warned Perseus never to look at Medusa directly, but only at her reflection, and gave him a polished shield that would enable him to face the monster. "Of all the existing media the cinema alone holds up a mirror to nature," wrote Siegfried Kracauer in his *Theory of Film*. "The film screen is Athena's polished shield."[31] For Kracauer as for the Lacanian the screen is a mirror: for Kracauer a reproduction, a mirror that enables us to see the face of reality as normally we would not; for the Lacanian an illusion, a reenactment of the primal mirror Lacan posits where the child misperceives the self and the world. Neither Kracauer nor the Lacanian takes proper cognizance of the screen as a space of representation. The images on the screen are neither a reproduction of reality nor an illusion of it: rather they are a construction, derived from reality but distinct from it, a parallel realm that may look recognizably like reality but that nobody can mistake for it. Their picture of reality may be convincing, but in the way fiction is convincing; we respond to the picture not as we would to reality but as we respond to the constructs of representation. The images on the screen are a representation of reality—an imitation or mimesis in the Aristotelian sense—as a novel or a play or a painting is a representation.[32]

Nobody understands Lacan very well. It may be that he is difficult to understand because he is profound—he is so obscure that it's hard to tell—but it seems to have been his intention to make himself difficult to understand. In his youth he was associated with the surrealists and all his life he seems to have kept up the surrealist program of bafflement on purpose.[33] He may have been an important thinker or he may have been a charlatan and it's indeed surreal that it should be hard to tell; he was probably a bit of both. His vogue among American academics he no doubt enjoyed as part of the surrealist joke. The purpose of academics in making themselves difficult to understand is to stake out a field of specialized expertise to which outsiders will defer. They set up a jargon impenetrable to outsiders that they themselves may not understand very well, and after a while they may not even know that they don't know whereof they speak because they speak what has become the idiom of their field, the language in which they talk to one another by common consent.

Lacan had great influence on the academic film theory that emerged in the seventies but his influence came mostly from just one of his papers, the 1949 essay on the mirror stage. And his influence was amalgamated with that of his analysand Louis Althusser, who endeavored to recast Marxism on the linguistic model Lacan used on psychoanalysis. Like Lacan's, Althusser's influence came mostly from just one essay, the one on ideology and state apparatuses. Lacan on the imaginary and Althusser on ideology were the theory's two founding texts: no knowledge of film was necessary, those two essays and the requisite vocabulary were enough to set up shop as a film theoretician. The Lacanian imaginary got conflated with the Althusserian notion of ideology; the mirror stage and the movie screen theorized as its adult replication were construed as apparatuses of ideology, bourgeois, patriarchal, whatever was deemed to be the ruling ideology. What Lacan may have thought of this is not known. While academic film theory was laboring over the relation between the Lacanian imaginary and the Lacanian symbolic, Lacan himself, worried perhaps that he was being too easily (even if wrongly) understood, moved on to a still more obscure notion, the Lacanian real.[34]

The time of Lacanian-Althusserian theory is past. But its legacy still lingers. Its feminist legacy, for one thing: the feminist film theory of the seventies and eighties was cast largely in Lacanian-Althusserian terms. Those were the terms current at the time and they served their purpose, but they are not the necessary terms of feminism. The main thrust of Laura Mulvey's landmark essay of 1975, "Visual Pleasure and Narrative Cinema," was not to advance a film theory but to call for a film practice that would contest the joint dominance of Hollywood and patriarchy.[35] But it is mainly as theory that Mulvey's essay has been taken, and moreover theory taken as proven, Lacanian-Althusserian theory positing the film image, no matter what its content, no matter what its point of view, as the medium of a visual pleasure that only the male can enjoy, a pleasure made to the measure of the male gaze. The evidence, however, is that ever since the nickelodeon replaced the saloon as the chief entertainment of the people, women have been going to the movies as much as men and enjoying them as much as men, though they may not have always enjoyed the same movies. It is the task of a newer feminism to sort out the valid from the unwarranted in this Lacanian-

Althusserian phase, secure the insights gained into our situation, and move on to a better understanding of it.

"Visual Pleasure and Narrative Cinema" has been more cited and argued over than any other essay on film, but the disputes concerning it have for the most part been in the vein of argumentations within shared doctrine rather than critical examinations of the theory and the evidence. Hardly anyone has called into question the founding premise, skimpily argued in Mulvey's essay yet taken for granted since, that the film spectator is always in the position of a voyeur. The voyeur's pleasure comes from furtively watching something he (or she—except that the voyeur is theorized as male) is not supposed to be watching, a sight he is not invited to see; but what is on the screen is surely something we are being invited to watch, a sight meant for us to see. In certain cases it may be part of the fiction of a film that we are to assume the furtive position of a voyeur, but surely most of the time films don't take place in bedrooms or peep into sights normally concealed from view. And even if one grants the voyeur premise, there is the further largely unquestioned assumption that the voyeur position belongs solely to the male. In *Babel and Babylon,* her study of spectatorship in American silent film, Miriam Hansen brings up the interesting case of the film made in 1897 of the heavyweight championship bout between James Corbett and Robert Fitzsimmons: although prizefighting was a male preserve, the film of the prizefight was attended not only by men but also, in large numbers, by women.[36] Unexpected at the time and unaccountable by current feminist film theory, this female turnout must have had something to do with women taking pleasure in the sight of male bodies exhibited on the screen. The visual pleasure women take no doubt differs from men's; this doesn't mean that they take none.

Not only Lacanian-Althusserian film theory, but postmodern theory more generally, proceeds on the assumption that there is something fundamentally wrong with film, wrong across the board with the practice and the enjoyment of art, and takes as the principal concern of theory what is wrong with art as purveyor of illusion, handmaiden of the patriarchy and the bourgeoisie, instrument of the ruling order. It is ironic that since film began to be taught in the academy, which would seem to have announced that the art of film was starting to be institutionally recognized, the study of film has been governed largely by an emphasis on what is wrong with art. Neither the theory nor the criticism of art should be confined to praising its beauties. But if all that interested me about art, about film, were what is wrong with it, I would not be spending much time with film or with art. It is because I like film—not all of it, of course, but enough of it to make it worth my while to spend so much of my life with it—that I have written this book. And I have mostly written about films that I like.

Post-Theory is the title of a collection of essays edited by David Bordwell and Noël Carroll with the declared intention of "reconstructing film studies" after the deconstructions of Lacanian-Althusserian and other postmodern theory.[37] I concur with several of Bordwell and Carroll's criticisms of the theory they are anxious to leave behind; I especially concur with their objection to the theory's disdain for empirical evidence, to its haughty undertaking to render itself unassailable by dismissing as "empiricism" any attempt to put its propositions to the test of experience. But the "cognitivism" that Bordwell and Carroll would promote as a better theory, a more fruitful approach to the study of film, suffers, if not from empiricism, from what may be called "commonsensism," an unchallenged rule of the commonsensical that would have kept Galileo from ever discovering that all bodies, feathers as well as lead, fall to the earth at the same rate. To Judith Mayne's comment that Bordwell and Carroll's cognitivism takes no account of the unconscious and would leave psychoanalysis out of consideration, Carroll replies that cognitivism covers everything normal, explains everything explicable, and that psychoanalysis is only called for when the normal unaccountably breaks down, only applies when all else fails.[38] I tend to be skeptical of psychoanalysis, whether Freudian or Lacanian, but I am more skeptical of commonsensical explanations that would lay claim to everything. Psychoanalysis may have gone too far in its inroads into the psychopathology of everyday life, but Carroll's commonsensism would confine it to the ghetto of the otherwise inexplicable.

One cannot base a theory on the normal because one must already have a theory in order to decide what the normal is. Taking issue with Bordwell and Carroll on the matter of the norm, psychoanalysis as the abnormal and cognitivism as the norm, Judith Mayne writes that

> psychoanalysis puts radically into question the very notion of a norm. One could say also that it is through the exceptional, the extreme case, that psychoanalysis reads the norm, from the assumption that it is only in so-called deviance that anything resembling the "norm"—which is a concept that is meaningless *without* deviance—is readable. For the insight central to the most radical forms of psychoanalysis is that any notion of the norm is fragile indeed.[39]

One need not agree that psychoanalysis is the best way to call our ruling beliefs into question to see that a theory erecting our beliefs as the norm is no way to call them into question, that such a theory can only ratify the way things are. Neither psychoanalytic nor cognitivist, my own approach to the study of film often focuses on works in deviance from the norm not only because these are often the most interesting films but because they are often the ones that reveal the most about the workings of film, the properties and possibilities of the medium.

Film offers us representations that we mistake for perceptions of reality, says the Lacanian-Althusserian, who sees no need to attend to particulars, for in that general illusion of reality all the deceptions of ideology are supposed to lie.[40] I disagree: film offers us representations of perceptions, representations that may be convincing but convincing as fiction, as representations of reality, not as reality perceived firsthand. And we do need to attend to particulars not only for their intrinsic interest but for what they may have to tell us about the general. Bordwell and Carroll rightly contest the overweening generalizations of Lacanian-Althusserian theory, but they too seem to believe that theory has not much business with particulars. According to Carroll,

> Film theory speaks of the general case, whereas film interpretation deals with problematic or puzzling cases, or with the highly distinctive cases of cinematic masterworks. Film theory tracks the regularity and the norm, while film interpretation finds its natural calling in dealing with the deviation, with what violates the norm or with what exceeds it or what re-imagines it.[41]

What Carroll calls film interpretation is what I have been calling film criticism. I don't believe that theory should be divided from criticism or interpretation in this or any other way. Problematic or puzzling cases, highly distinctive works, are precisely what lead to the questioning of old theory and the formulation of new. The deviation, what violates the norm or exceeds it or reimagines it, is just what this book, in its combination of criticism and theory, often deals with.

Representation depends on convention. *Convention* is a problematic but necessary term for an often problematic but always necessary practice. A convention is something accepted, agreed upon, established. The term *conventional*, as Raymond Williams has discussed, has been used unfavorably since the romantics emphasized the artist's right to break the established rules of art. But an artist, as Williams wrote, "only leaves one convention to follow or create another."[42] For a convention in art is not just an established rule—that red at a traffic light means stop, for example—but an agreement on the part of the audience, a consent to what the work is doing, to a way of doing things the work proposes. Whether this is a well-established way or a bold new departure, it must gain an audience's agreement—it must be accepted as a convention—if the work is to get across to that audience. Even the most "conventional" work cannot just assume that its conventions have already been settled but must once again make them function for its audience; even the most innovative work cannot just disregard convention but must negotiate its audience's acceptance of its innovations—even if it is an unsure acceptance, an acceptance forever renegotiated. Theories that would have the spectator stepping into a prearranged position inscribed in the film neglect the fact that the spectator need not go along with the film, may even walk out of the film—that the film proposes a transaction to which it must win the spectator's consent.

Saussure said that the linguistic sign is arbitrary. "I say it is not arbitrary but conventional," answered Raymond Williams, "and that the convention is the result of a social process."[43] But all convention, even when socially or humanly motivated, was for Saussure essentially arbitrary, fixed by rule; and language was for him the most characteristic, the ideal system of expression because he saw it as totally arbitrary.[44] The arbitrariness of the sign, the view of all convention and expression as a matter of "codes" fixed by rule, has been an article of faith with structuralists and poststructuralists. Any attempt to bring forward the sign's motivation—the fact that a visual image, for example, is a sign motivated by resemblance to the object it represents—they look upon as a dissembling of its arbitrariness. The recognition of arbitrariness will supposedly lead to the realization that things can be changed. But changed toward what? Not changed for the better, for there can be nothing better, only more arbitrariness, if all our conventions and systems of expression, all our human transactions, can only be arbitrary.

The romantics revolted against convention in the name of nature. A classical thinker such as Aristotle saw no opposition between nature and culture and nothing wrong with convention, which was for him a natural because a human thing. The romantics opposed nature and culture but they saw the individual, and the artist above all, as a bridge between the two, a bringer of nature into culture. The structuralists and poststructuralists take over with a vengeance the romantic opposition between nature and culture and the romantic view of convention as arbitrary. But they see no bridge, no remedy, no alternative. They extend the arbitrariness to all human things. Certainly they do not see the individual as a carrier of nature, and the artist least of all: rather they see him or her as wholly the product of a wholly arbitrary culture.

To contest the arbitrariness of the sign it is important to distinguish between code and convention. A code is a rule to be followed, a convention is an agreement to be secured; a code is always a convention but a convention is not always a code. Art's conventions are sometimes codes—the halo designating sainthood in religious painting, the dark mustache designating villainy in old-fashioned melodrama—but more often they are not. Carroll fails to make this distinction; a critic of the structuralists and poststructuralists, he nonetheless shares their view of convention as something wholly arbitrary. Linear perspective is not a convention, he maintains, because

> a convention is something adopted in the context where there are alternative ways of achieving the same effect and it is a matter of indifference as to which of these alternatives is adopted, such as driving on the left or right hand side of the road. But if perspective is more accurate spatially, then it is not the case that it is one among numerous, indifferent alternatives for depicting the appearance of spatial layouts.[45]

A soliloquy in the theater is plainly a convention. But it is not arbitrary: it is motivated by its resemblance to the way someone we know might take us aside in life to confide his or her thoughts. And it is not a matter of indifference whether Hamlet's thoughts are expressed in the soliloquy Shakespeare gives him or written in Morse code at the back of the stage. Similarly, perspective is not arbitrary: it is motivated by its resemblance to the way we perceive things in life from the particular position in space we occupy at each moment. But this does not mean that perspective is not a convention. A soliloquy is easier to recognize as a convention because it is no longer current. Perspective was devised in the Renaissance but remains in force as a convention, and so seems natural, to this day.

The rule that we are to stop at a red light, or drive on the right side of the road, is enforced by the police. But art has no police to enforce its rules: it asks us to accept them as conventions, and it motivates them so as to win our acceptance. A picture done according to the rules of perspective asks the viewer to accept a representation of things from the perspective of a single point in space. Why should acceptance be required? Isn't that just the way things look in life? But a picture is not life. In life we may be limited to the view from where we stand but a picture can represent things in many other ways: a picture chooses to limit itself to an individual's perception and it must win our acceptance of that choice. Perspective won acceptance in the Renaissance because it expressed the outlook of a confident humanism: from a single viewing point the picture would offer a commanding view of the scene, conveying a sense of the world being revealed, yielding its meaning, to an individual human gaze. Later uses of perspective have stressed the sense of a limitation, a partial view. Either way the use of perspective seeks our agreement to look at nothing else but what an individual eye would see. Whether perspective is a pictorial convention or an accurate rendering of what we see has been much debated; such personages as Erwin Panofsky and E. H. Gombrich have taken opposite sides in this debate. Both sides are right: perspective is accurate—not a perfect rendering of what we see but a close enough approximation—and it is a convention. Its very accuracy in representing an individual's point of view—rather than some other way of viewing things—bespeaks the slant that makes it a convention.

In his *Theory of the Film* Béla Balázs wrote about the "silent soliloquy" enacted on the screen by the human face in close-up:

> The modern stage no longer uses the spoken soliloquy, although without it the characters are silenced just when they are the most sincere . . . when they are alone. The public of today will not tolerate the spoken soliloquy, allegedly because it is "unnatural." Now the film has brought us the silent soliloquy, in which a face can speak with the subtlest shades of meaning without appearing unnatural and arousing the distaste of the spectators. In this silent monologue the solitary human soul can find a tongue more candid and uninhibited than in any spoken soliloquy, for it speaks instinctively, subconsciously.[46]

No less than the stage soliloquy, the movie close-up is a convention. A close-up may imitate the way we look at the face of someone in life who draws our attention. But in life we focus our attention, and in a movie the camera focuses it for us: the camera looks at the face and we agree to look where the camera is looking. Moreover, in a movie the camera can come as close as it wants for as long as it wants: we agree to look in the way the camera looks, which is not the same as life.

The close-up is a special case of what may be called the convention of the shot. Theater asks its audience to accept the stage as the world: that is its basic convention. D. W. Griffith broke away from the staginess of early movies in which a whole scene would unfold before a camera fixed in its position like a spectator at the theater. Griffith—he wasn't the only one but he was the boldest and most systematic—broke a movie down into shots, now here and now there, now far and now near. As film historians have often said, he made the shot rather than the scene the basic unit of film construction. His basic innovation was the convention of the shot: if the theater asks its audience to take the stage as a whole world, the movies after Griffith have asked their audience to agree, for as long as each shot lasts on the screen, to look at just the piece of the world framed within that shot.

The convention of the shot entails our agreement not only to look at what is being shown on the screen but also not to look at what is not being shown. Moreover, it entails our agreement about what it is that is not being shown. If we see a long shot of Rio de Janeiro, for example, followed by a closer view of Ingrid Bergman and Cary Grant—I'm thinking of Hitchcock's *Notorious* (1946)—we are to agree that Ingrid Bergman and Cary Grant are in a Rio de Janeiro that is not being shown. The Rio de Janeiro in *Notorious* is a fictional Rio de Janeiro even if it includes some views of the real city. *Notorious* was shot mostly in the studio; Ingrid Bergman and Cary Grant weren't really in Rio de Janeiro. But even if they had been, even in a movie shot entirely on location, the relation between the actors and the setting, between what we see on the screen and the unseen surrounding space that each shot implies, is a fiction put together in the arrangement of the shots. The piece of the world we agree to look at in each shot on the screen is not a piece of our world—though it may look very much like one—but a piece of the fictional world the movie proposes for our acceptance.

Cinematic representation depends on our acceptance of absence: the absence of Rio de Janeiro when we see Ingrid Bergman and Cary Grant, the absence of most of the world from each image on the screen. It is curious that Lacanian film theory should have supposed that we "misrecognize" the image as a plenitude when the film image since Griffith has been something we are to accept as a fragment. On the model of the baby before the mirror, the Lacanian postulates a movie spectator who hasn't learned the first thing about watching movies, which is the convention of the shot: we are to accept the fragment we are seeing on the screen as just what we should be seeing at the moment, and to accept the absence of the implied rest of the world as something we don't need to see for now. That what we are seeing on the screen is not Ingrid Bergman and Cary Grant but merely their shadow is a condition of our seeing Ingrid Bergman and Cary Grant at all, a condition of cinematic representation just as it is a condition of painterly representation that we're not seeing God creating Adam on the ceiling of the Sistine Chapel but only paint applied on a surface. Except perhaps for babies, nobody watching a movie believes reality to be present on the screen or feels deprived by its absence. The play of presence and absence is central to the movies, but presence and absence in the realm of representation. Whereas a painting or a theater stage represents a whole, a bounded space containing all that can be seen, a movie represents only a piece at a time and implies an indefinitely larger space extending unseen beyond the boundaries of the image. Presence is not an illusion in the movies, nor absence a fact: presence and absence are conventions of cinematic representation.

Still photography too depends on our acceptance of the fragment. But not the fragment for now, the fragment forever: the art of still photography consists in making the fragment—the piece of space, the moment in time— stand on its own as all that can be seen. Like any fragment, a still photograph implies a larger whole that is not there; but it can only suggest that larger whole, it cannot construct it as a movie can, it cannot make it into a full-blown fiction. What lies beyond the image in the space out of frame is a suggestion in still photography that the movies make into a convention.

No one grasped better than André Bazin the extension of cinematic space beyond the boundaries of the image. "The screen is a mask," he wrote, "whose function is no less to hide reality than it is to reveal it. The significance of what the camera discloses is relative to what it leaves hidden."[47] But Bazin took cinematic space to be essentially the same as the space of reality, which always extends beyond what we can see. He did not recognize that the space off screen is a convention, a fiction, as much a construction as a stage setting and as amenable to different kinds of construction.

Whether the reproduction of reality or the imitation of dreams, the imaginary signifier or the realism of space, most theorists have attempted to define the nature of film as something given, something essential and unchanging; this book treats it as something variable and amenable to different kinds of construction, something to be defined through the concrete work of filmmaking and the conventions it develops in transaction with the audience. This book is a study, historical, critical, and theoretical, of the film medium not in the abstract but as it has been variously defined in the concrete; it focuses on several notable films and filmmakers whose expressive constructions of their medium have brought forward its properties and possibilities in significantly different ways.

Kracauer and Bazin were theorists who saw film as an extension of photography and saw photography as a record of reality. Kracauer was a purist; like Clement Greenberg, he believed that a medium should be confined to what defines it, what it alone can do; and as flatness defined painting for Greenberg, so for Kracauer photographic realism defined the film medium. Bazin had a more complex sense of the medium and even called for an *im*pure cinema, but a cinema nonetheless governed and informed by its peculiar closeness to reality. To this emphasis on reality the structuralists and poststructuralists opposed their emphasis on the sign; they thought the likes of Kracauer and Bazin naive to take the image for reality; but it was they who were naive to suppose that anyone would take for reality the light and shadows projected on the screen. The question is what kind of image the screen holds, what kind of representation of reality.

It is, Bazin said, an image that partakes of the reality it represents, an image that receives a "transference of reality" from the thing it pictures.[48] A painting is a handmade image and it carries in it something of the hand that made it, the hand of the painter. A photographic image is made by light and it carries in it something of the light that made it, the light the camera received from the reality before its open shutter. If a Gothic cathedral enshrines a metaphysics of light, light as a spiritual, transcendent element, the camera employs a physics of light, light as a material element of representation; and if the paint that goes into a painting is a material that belongs to the painter, the light that goes into a photograph is a material that belongs to the thing represented. Something of the thing itself comes through in its photographic representation.

The laws of physics are not indifferent to scale: a world twice as large would not be the same world twice as large but qualitatively a different world. In art too scale makes a difference. Still photographs are smaller than life; the movie screen is bigger than life. It is fitting that photographs are small, for they are small traces of life, residual little bits captured from life by means of optics and chemistry. It is fitting that the movie screen is big, for it proposes to take over from life and put in its place a world of the movie. The tendency to enlargement in certain recent photography reflects a changed conception of the photograph no longer as the record of anything real but as something made up. The tendency to watch movies on the small screen of television makes for a changed experience of the movie no longer as a world that takes us over but one we peer into and catch glimpses of.

Perhaps the most interesting chapter of Kracauer's *Theory of Film* is the one on the spectator, which combines his emphasis on photographic realism, the lifelike nature of the film image, with what might seem a contrary emphasis on the dreamlike nature of the spectator's experience, the "trancelike condition in which we find ourselves when looking at the screen."[49] Films, for Kracauer, present reality as a dream that makes us see reality as we would not otherwise see it, a dream that reclaims reality for us who have lost touch with it in our normal waking state. The more lifelike the film image is, the more dreamlike it looks:

> Perhaps films look most like dreams when they overwhelm us with the crude and unnegotiated presence of natural objects—as if the camera had just now extricated them from the womb of physical existence and as if the umbilical cord between image and actuality had not yet been severed. There is something in the abrupt immediacy and shocking veracity of such pictures that justifies their identification as dream images.[50]

Bazin said something similar when he wrote that photography is a "privileged technique of surrealist creation" because the image it produces is a "hallucination that is true."[51] The images of still photography, however, may be true, but they don't convey the feeling of hallucinations. The film image is the true hallucination, the material ghost.

If Einstein taught us that light falls like any other body, Bazin taught us that light leaves a track like any other body, an imprint the camera makes into an image. But the camera is not the only machine that makes the film image. The projector, the magic lantern, animates the track of light with its own light, brings the imprint of life to new life on the screen. The images on the screen carry in them something of the world itself, something material, and yet something transposed, transformed into another world: the material ghost. Hence both the peculiar closeness to reality and the no less peculiar suspension from reality, the juncture of world and otherworldliness distinctive of the film image.

1 :   The Documentary Image

> No film ever quite disappears into abstraction: what
> the camera reproduces has almost always on the most literal
> level the appearance of reality; that is one reason why the
> movies can afford to be so much more banal than the
> theater: when we complain of their "unreality" we do not
> mean exactly that they fail to carry conviction, but more
> probably that they carry conviction all too easily. In the
> blankest moments of [the film of] *Death of a Salesman* one
> sees, if not Willy Loman, who is always more a concept than
> a human being, at least the actor Fredric March, brought so
> close and clear that his own material reality begins to assert
> itself outside the boundaries that are supposed to be set
> by his role. On the stage, this would be a fault, for it would
> mean that the actor was seeking to impose himself on the
> play; here there is no need for him to put himself forward:
> he need only be present, a passive object merely available to
> the camera's infinite appetite for the material.
>
> ROBERT WARSHOW, "The Movie Camera
> and the American"

Microphone in hand, the television reporter stands in front of the White House or in the streets of Beirut, addressing us from the scene of the news. This lends an aura of truth to the newscast. That reliable witness, the camera, testifies to the reporter's presence on the spot and thereby abets the impression that the reporter too is a reliable witness. A painted backdrop of the scene wouldn't be nearly as persuasive in soliciting our trust, which is why the networks go to the trouble and expense of shooting on location when the news report could more easily have been delivered from a studio. But the camera's visual testimony, though presented as being of a piece with the verbal report, is extrinsic to it and little relevant to its content, a factual garnish to the words that carry the newscast's meaning. Words are what the newscast is about, words capable of bias or falsehood regardless of their place of delivery: spoken from a studio, printed on a page, those words the reporter speaks from the scene of the news would evidently be saying the same thing. It's a specious credibility that the news report gains from the location, an aura of truth without warrant, itself a sort of falsehood. Although intended to seem so, the reporter's words do not become more trustworthy by virtue of the camera-reproduced White House or Beirut streets we glimpse in back; such visual signs of actuality may as well have been painted backdrops, since they add nothing of substance to the words, the signs that count in the message being conveyed. The camera's claim to truth, the direct record it supplies of actual appearances, serves here to foster what amounts to a visual lie.

So much for the simplistic notion that the camera doesn't lie: lying or telling the truth is not the province of cameras but of the human beings who use them, put them to a purpose. In a way the camera deceives us, by its very directness, whenever its depictions seem so immediate that we take them as reality plain and simple, forgetting the artifice that goes into them, the slant of which they are capable. "Photography affects us like a phenomenon in nature, like a flower or a snowflake," wrote André Bazin,[1] thus laying himself open to the charge of "naturalization"—taking as natural what is in fact cultural, a human construction—though he didn't say photography *was* a phenomenon in nature, only that it affects us that way. Precisely because it affects us that way photography is a prime instrument of naturalization. Kracauer's *Theory of Film* concludes with praise for the most encompassing photographic naturalization ever attempted, the "Family of Man" exhibition organized by Edward Steichen, in which the camera's particulars, marshaled to serve the grandest universalization, were made to tell us that human beings are "naturally" the same everywhere. If the city was natural to Aristotle, photography is natural to our civilization. Better perhaps than any other of our constructions, the photographic image enacts what our culture thinks of as nature.

Leni Riefenstahl denies she was a Nazi propagandist. *Triumph of the Will,* her film of the 1934 rally of the Nazi Party at Nuremberg, was just a record of what happened, she maintains, just the facts as the camera registered them. And what's more, with no voice-over narration, no words to tell us what to think, just the facts speaking for themselves. It's easy to refute this rationalization. Normally, in a documentary of an ongoing event, the camera captures what it can of an event not being staged for its benefit, but in *Triumph of the Will,* which was produced by the Nazi Party and made with its full cooperation, the rally was staged as much for the camera, for the many cameras that were deployed, as for the people in attendance, so that the film could freely avail itself of the techniques of staged fiction, where the camera is conventionally empowered to capture not what it can but what it wants. *Triumph of the Will* was that rare thing, a documentary superproduction.

As many have observed, the opening of *Triumph of the Will* makes Hitler seem like a god descending from the clouds into the city of Nuremberg below. Yet Riefenstahl repeatedly shows us the airplane in which Hitler travels: this is a deus ex machina, a god owing his presence in the clouds to a machine that flies. Certainly this opening sequence aims to evoke wonder, and in 1934 the airplane doubtless was a wonder. But the airplane does something else. It keeps the film from taking off too far into the clouds of fantasy: it tells us that these clouds are a reality, a documented fact, and it implies that a superhuman Hitler is no fantasy either. *Triumph of the Will* is a fantasy seeking authentication in photographed reality. Over the pretty medieval city of Nuremberg, representing the German past, flies Hitler's airplane, representing the German future. The city and the airplane, both documented facts, are there to lend credence to the fiction of Hitler as the leader carrying the great spirit and inheritance of the German nation forward into the twentieth century. Riefenstahl says she is a documenter, not a propagandist, but *Triumph of the Will* conveys its most mendacious propaganda through its documentary quality.

Documentary is always a deceit, some have concluded; there is no such thing as a documentary film, they say. "Every film is a fiction film," wrote Christian Metz. "What is characteristic of the cinema is not the imaginary that it may happen to represent, but the imaginary that it *is* from the start."[2] On the screen nothing is real, he thought, not even the signifier: a chair on the stage is there before us, a chair we can sit on, but on the screen a chair is only a mirage. Bazin took a different view. "There is no such thing as a 'slice of life' in the theater," he wrote, for anything put on the stage is removed from life and turned into a show, made part of a performance.[3] On the stage nothing is real, everything is playing a part for an audience. Even a tree actually planted on the stage is still a kind of signpost for a tree; a chair on the stage is a chair we in the audience can*not* sit on for the duration of the performance. The stage is a demarcated area that stands for the world and stands apart from the world. It is on the screen, Bazin thought, that trees and chairs, the world's things, can be what they are in the world. Documentary is foreign to the theater and native to the movies.

Bazin erred when he opposed "cinematic realism" to "theatrical convention." Whatever realism is, cinematic or otherwise, it is a matter of convention, theatrical or otherwise. The trees and chairs we see on the screen are not the trees and chairs we encounter in the world: they are a representation of trees and chairs, one might even say a performance. But the performance is peculiarly close to the trees and chairs themselves: one might call it a documentary.

 In his book on photography, Roland Barthes wrote:

> It is often said that it was the painters who invented Photography (by bequeathing it their framing, the Albertian perspective, and the optic of the *camera obscura*). I say: no, it was the chemists. [For it was the chemists who] made it possible to recover and print directly the luminous rays emitted by a variously lighted object. The photograph is literally an emanation of the referent. From a real body, which was there, proceed radiations which ultimately touch me, who am here; the duration of the transmission is insignificant; the photograph of the missing being, as Sontag says, will touch me like the delayed rays of a star.[4]

A photograph, as Charles Sanders Peirce himself noted, is both an icon and an index in his sense of these terms. It is an icon because it gives an image, a likeness, of the subject it represents. It is an index because it has a direct connection with that subject, as a footprint has with a foot or a seismograph with movements of the ground. As icon the photograph was invented by the painters; as index, by the chemists. Crediting the chemists rather than the painters with photography's invention credits the index rather than the icon with photography's definition. In this view—the view set forth by Bazin in his well-known essay "Ontology of the Photographic Image," which opens *What Is Cinema?*—it is its being an imprint of light, a trace left by a real body whose appearance reaches us like the delayed rays of a star, that makes the photograph distinctively what it is.

Because it is an index, the photograph has been taken to be a trustier icon. Not that photography necessarily gives a better likeness than painting: what counts, as Bazin stressed, is not so much the resulting image as its genesis. A painting may be more vividly observed and more accurately detailed, but the photographic image affects us as a peculiarly believable icon because we know it to be an imprint received directly from life. Not having been fashioned by human hands, the photograph is supposedly unencumbered by human subjectivity. "All the arts are based on the presence of man," Bazin wrote; "only photography derives an advantage from his absence."[5]

A painting gains in value on account of its signature; a photograph gains in credence on account of its lack of a signature. What counts in either case is not so much the picture before our eyes as the unseen agency that brought it into being. As a unique handmade object, the original in painting traditionally possesses what Walter Benjamin called an "aura." In photography there is no original image, only copies, and thus, according to Benjamin, no aura. Yet a photographic image has its own kind of aura—the aura of a remnant, of a relic—stemming from the uniqueness, the original particularity, not of the picture but of the referent whose emanation it captures. In photography the original is the bit of reality that was there when the shutter was opened. Its retaining a trace of that original reality gives the photograph its special quality of authenticity. Authenticity, whether that of a signature marking a human presence or that derived from human absence, depends on origins. Origins are buried in the past, however, and apt to be called into question. Origins, many believe these days, are an illusion.

How do we know, when we look at a photograph, that the image we see is indeed a photograph, not an image human hands fabricated but an imprint a camera received of the light of the real? We know by the look of the photograph. It is because the image looks like a photograph, has the distinctive look photographs have—because we recognize it, iconically, as a photograph—that we take it to be a photograph rather than some other kind of picture. If the photograph as index lends credence to the icon, it is the look of the icon that convinces us to take it as an index. The icon loses its credence when we can see that it has been retouched or otherwise tampered with, when its look betrays the signs of contrivance or manipulation. If the photograph as index bears witness to the reality of its subject, the photograph as icon is what gives testimony to its being an index of that reality.

It is not the index rather than the icon, the imprint rather than the image, but the marriage of index and icon, imprint and image, that makes the photograph distinctively what it is.

Advocates of photography as art often feel that they must uphold the photograph as pictorial object, as icon rather than as index. Ordinarily we take pictures or have our pictures taken, but in photography circles pictures are made, not taken: humanly made, not mechanically taken. In response to detractors of the art of photography, who say that mechanical reproduction cannot be art,[6] defenders tend to slight the fact that the art is founded on mechanical reproduction. The photography they regard as art they generally see as an invention of the painters rather than of the chemists. Bent on establishing that there is no essential—no ontological— difference between photography and painting, Joel Snyder makes his case by dividing the photograph as icon, in which capacity it has no better claim than painting to an exact likeness of its subject, from the photograph as index, in which capacity it may yield an imprint of light blurred or overexposed to the point of being unrecognizable as an image of reality.[7] But the photograph is an imprint that is an image and an image that is an imprint, an imprint that bears likeness and an image that bears witness.

An imprint gives evidence of what has been; an image gives presence to what it depicts. A photograph gives evidence of what it depicts and gives presence to what has been. It is a documentary image as a painting can never be, not because it is necessarily more realistic than a painting but because it has a necessary material connection with reality.

What a photograph depicts has been; what a painting depicts comes into being in the picture. What a movie depicts can, in each of its details, be said to have been: each thing we see must have been there before the camera, which has no imagination and "infinite appetite for the material." But the movie as a whole, the world of the movie, comes into being on the screen. What has been is documentary, what comes into being is fiction; a movie is a fiction made up of documentary details. The camera doesn't make things up, it receives their light from reality; but the projector has its own light. One camp of film theory, the camp that stresses photographic realism, subordinates the projector to the camera's documentary image; the other camp, the camp that stresses fantasy and the imaginary, subordinates the camera to the projector's illusory image. But the film image is both the camera's and the projector's: the material ghost.

A still from the Lumière movie of a train arriving at a station gives presence to what has been. Projected on the screen, the movie animates that presence, brings it to life, we say; and many would say that it brings it into a present, a now rather than a then. The early spectators who got out of the train's way seem to have taken the movie as the present. But we don't get out of the way. We don't take a movie as the present, for the present is where we are, and a movie, even if it is a world animated into a now, is a world elsewhere. Hence Stanley Cavell has disputed that a movie is a present and maintained that it is a world past. But Cavell, like other theorists, confounds the photographic and the cinematic image. Still photographs are clearly of the past. The tense of the movies is not so clear.

Documentary is what has been, and yet it is often the more documentary movies that seem to give the stronger impression of the present. The newsreel immediacy of Roberto Rossellini's movies in the pioneer years of neorealism won praise from James Agee for "giving the illusion of the present tense."[8] The death of the Anna Magnani character in *Open City* (1945) is justly famous for its moving immediacy. It is a death designedly not pre-pared for. The dramatic tension in the scene Rossellini had cunningly di-verted in another direction, and it seemed to have subsided when suddenly the woman rushes out into the street as her boyfriend is taken prisoner and the Nazis shoot her dead. The tragedy bursts upon us unexpectedly, with the force of something real that the camera itself had not anticipated and pho-tographed as best it could in the rough manner of a newsreel. But the urgency of a newsreel is the urgency of the right then and there, not the right here and now: the camera may speak in the present, but it is a present now past when we watch it on the screen. The poignancy of such a scene—even if it is not a death scene it is always the poignancy of death—is the poignancy of what reaches us from the past with the urgency of the present.

Vittorio de Sica and Cesare Zavattini's brand of neorealism does not adopt the look of a newsreel; it does not look at the kind of thing that appears in the news but at the ordinary things of everyday life. And yet its closeness, its transparency to the ordinary has also been taken as a present-ness; its attention to the time of everyday life led Bazin to call Zavattini "something like the Proust of the indicative present."[9] Bazin specifically had in mind *Umberto D.* (1952), one of the last and perhaps the finest of the neorealist films, written by Zavattini, directed by De Sica, with the great G. R. Aldo as cinematographer. Umberto D. is an old man, a retired govern-ment clerk living alone on a meager pension and owing back rent on the room where he has long resided to a landlady who now wants to evict him. Nobody will help him out. His few friends back away; aside from his dog, only the landlady's housemaid, a young woman from the country with troubles of her own, shows any concern for him. But then there is De Sica's camera. It is a camera that, as Bazin said, shows affection for the characters as no other means of representation can, for no other means can represent human beings so concretely, so particularly, with such exact attention to their singularity. De Sica's camera loves his characters not because they are good or beautiful or admirable but because they are. The love it shows is not eros, the love of the desirable, but agape, the kind of love God bestows on his creatures. And it shows this love by staying with the characters through the details of ordinary experience, savoring the time of daily existence like a Proust delving into the present.

Umberto D. is a picture of alienation, alienation countered by affection. The affection of the portrayal, the camera's and ours, counters the alienation portrayed, the breach Umberto D. feels between himself and just about everyone and everything around him. The world is distant but we feel close;

the world is cold but there is warmth that may kindle it. Yet when the old man at last despairs of life and, intending to do himself in, leaves the room where he is not wanted, says good-bye to the maid, gets on a streetcar and sees her receding from him at an upstairs window, something remarkable happens: suddenly the whole world seems to recede irretrievably, suddenly what had seemed close at hand seems far away, suddenly the illusion of presentness gives way to a vertiginous pastness. No other work so chillingly conveys the mood of suicide. If the materiality of the film image, its closeness to concrete reality, enables De Sica to express love as no other medium can, the ghostliness of the image on the screen enables him to express death as no other medium can.

The lifelike image is also the ghostlike image: the vivid harbors the vanished. The vivid that at any moment may vanish, all the more vivid because we fear it may vanish, is the theme of Humphrey Jennings's great documentary of Britain at war, *Listen to Britain* (1942). "Humphrey Jennings worked best," wrote Eric Rhode, "when the things he loved were most under threat."[10] *Listen to Britain* focuses not on the war but on the everyday life of a people in wartime, the ordinary manifestations of existence made extraordinary under threat of destruction. Like *Umberto D.*, Jennings's documentary depends for its tenderness and its pathos on the combination of presentness and pastness peculiar to the film image. Perhaps the most eloquent moments in his cinematic orchestration of the "music of Britain at war" are moments of synchronized sound: the comedians Flanagan and Allen singing into a microphone at a factory workers' playtime, the pianist Myra Hess striking

Umberto D. The receding maid at the upstairs window.

the keyboard at a lunchtime concert at the National Gallery. The image with synchronized sound feels more present, more attached to the concrete, a more vivid affirmation of life not yet vanished.

A photograph is past, a painting is present; a play is present, a novel is past. The tense of the film image is dual, one might say: sometimes it acts like the present, sometimes like the past. Is light a wave or a stream of particles? Sometimes it acts like a wave, sometimes like particles, as modern physics has discovered: particle and wave, matter and energy, are not two different things but two different aspects of the same thing, two different ways in which the thing behaves. Present and past, icon and index, fiction and documentary, drama and narrative: these are different aspects of the film medium, different ways in which it can behave.

Jean-Luc Godard said that every film is a documentary of its actors. For Robert Warshow the abstraction of Willy Loman in *Death of a Salesman* was made concrete in the film, and invested with a power it did not have in the play, by the documentary of the actor Fredric March playing Willy Loman. In his own films Godard purposely brings forward the documentary of the actor as something distinct from the character being played. If an actor's performance is an icon of the character, the documentary of the actor is an index of the person giving the performance. Neorealism liked to use nonprofessional actors, who look more real and who look the part, so that the part would look more real, the index would provide the icon, the documentary would go a long way toward giving the performance. The kind of gap Godard sets up between the actor and the character was not for De Sica: he was the best of the neorealists at directing nonprofessionals, getting a performance out of the documentary.

The performance is a fiction—the man who played Umberto D. was no impoverished pensioner but an esteemed university professor—but a fiction so grounded in documentary particulars that the actor is unimaginable as any other character. The neorealist nonprofessional becomes identified with the character he or she plays. With a movie star it is the other way around: each character he or she plays becomes identified with the movie star. The movie star and the neorealist nonprofessional are icons that alike arise from the index, alike depend on the camera's documentary image—a documentary of Garbo's face or of the no less arresting face of Maria Pia Casilio as the maid in *Umberto D.* But the particulars of Casilio's face take their place among other documentary particulars in a world of everyday reality, whereas the particulars of Garbo's face inhabit from movie to movie a world of

Hollywood make-believe. Barthes was not wrong to say that Garbo's face (which in a well-known essay he compared not with Casilio's but with Audrey Hepburn's) is "an Idea" (Hepburn's is "an Event"),[11] but the Idea is not in the face alone but in the world where it comes into being. No doubt a face, to take hold of the screen, must find a world that suits it. No doubt a world must find faces that suit it. The faces of the great movie stars, their ways of being on the screen, all have the distinctive particularity of the documentary image. But out of the documentary image the screen makes a fiction, a world of the movie—of many movies, in the case of a star—and the documentary particulars become part of that fiction.

Spellbound by the mirage of movies, theorists like Kracauer and Bazin tend to slight the difference between watching a film and our experience of reality, as if no artifice came between us and the sea being shown on the screen, the trees going by in a traveling shot, as if that sea and those trees weren't pictures, projected images made up of light and shadows, flimsier in fact than any props on a theater stage. And yet this phantom medium can carry a charge of reality unattainable in the theater because derived by the camera from its involvement with actual things. All the world, because of the camera's access to it, may be enlisted as a stage for films. Neither real nor a mere fakery, the sea we watch on the screen bears the informing mark, set down on film by light received into the camera, of the sea's actual appearance. Even though Bazin neglected the contrivance that comes into play, he was right to feel that in the camera's pictures a reality stemming from the depicted things themselves is preserved. Something of the sea itself remains on the strip of film running through the projector.

There is reality in the film image, but reality at a remove. While the reality contributes impact and conviction, it's the remove that allows form and meaning to work their artifice on the things represented. It's because on film the sea becomes something other than itself, apart from the tangle of actual experience, that it can be arranged into a structure, a theme, a figure of expression. "Things are there . . . why manipulate them?"[12] Thus Rossellini declared his humility before the world's particulars, his "faith in reality," as Bazin admiringly called such an attitude. Bazin distinguished between "those directors who put their faith in the image and those who put their faith in reality."[13] By *image* he meant all the artifice of films, all that representation adds to the thing represented, and he preferred the faith in reality Rossellini avowed, the deference to things that are. But a filmmaker, respect though he or she may the reality before the camera, must rely on the image, on the artifice of representation, to express any sort of attitude, including a humble respect for things as they are. Much though it may profit from the camera's directness, a film could express nothing, signify nothing, were it not for the distance separating it from immediate experience, the remove that enables the arranging hand of meaning to put together articulate forms.

No film ever quite disappears into abstraction, but no film exactly plunges us into concrete reality either. The theatrical production Sergei Eisenstein staged in an actual factory, only to find the play overwhelmed by a factory present in full force before the spectators, made him see why the stage is kept apart from reality and led him to the screen, where, meeting reality not on its own ground but at the remove of images bearing its imprint, he could better deal with the unwieldy presences of the material world. Reality on film is always at a remove, but to a greater or lesser degree, and with a different quality of impact, depending on how it's treated. Every film may be a documentary of its actors, but most films are documentaries of little else; they may be shot on location yet they take place nowhere near the real world. Just as a real tree planted on the stage turns into a kind of signpost for a tree, so in most films a real location will be relegated, like the White House behind the television reporter, to the function of signpost for the place, a signpost adorned with camera naturalism to lend the proceedings a semblance of reality. The way scenes on location are done most of the time, the locations, though real, make no real difference. A typical scene will start by giving us, in a long shot or two, a brief introduction to the place; then, getting down to the point, a succession of closer views, dimming the place into a background little different from stage scenery, will concentrate our attention on the actors and their dramatic business, their facial expressions, lines of dialogue or pregnant pauses, exchange of loving glances or violent blows; after which, for conclusion, there will be another long shot or two, in case we've forgotten this is supposed to be the real world. Treated like a set, the place virtually becomes one on the screen, its actuality thinned into a naturalistic veneer, its role strictly subordinate to the actors and the drama. Just as the reporter's words carry the meaning of a newscast, so in most films the drama carries the meaning; and like those words, that drama, as usually conceived and enacted, means the same thing on location that it would in a studio.

Instead of doing a scene on location, Hollywood in the old days would regularly employ, as a shorthand metonymy, stock footage of the locale—the Eiffel Tower, palm trees by the sea, that sort of thing—and then go on to a studio enactment, often with the assistance of additional metonymical footage in the form of back projection. Although widely accepted at the time, such practices are no longer viable with audiences whose suspension of disbelief requires a stronger dose of "realism." Audiences nowadays will promptly detect and look askance at the fakery of back projection—the actors pretending to be out there in actual terrain, riding in a car along city streets or in a stagecoach across a Western wilderness, without in fact having left the studio. Surely this fakery didn't pass undetected in the old days, however: it was accepted, as a convention, by audiences who went to the movies for the actors and the story and were content to have back-projected footage standing in for the place. We mustn't condescendingly think that those audiences knew no better; as can be seen from W. C. Fields's hilarious parody in *The Fatal Glass of Beer* (1933), they weren't fooled by back projection; better probably than audiences who want more "realism," they knew what movies are predominantly about. Then and now, whether faked with back projection or shot on location, the place in most cases counts for little, even if now audiences expect the slicker veneer of actuality that shooting on location provides. Reality is as commonly attenuated, and as rarely confronted, in films now as it was then.

The call to confront it, however, has recurred throughout the history of cinema. Taking the camera out into the world, into the thick of concrete things, has been a vitalizing impulse, at different times and places since the Lumière beginnings, for such various filmmakers as Flaherty and Vertov, Keaton and Eisenstein, Dovzhenko and Vigo, Buñuel and Renoir, Jennings and Rossellini, De Sica and Satyajit Ray, Rouch and Pennebaker, Ford and Nunez and Burnett, Kurosawa and Gutiérrez Alea and Pereira dos Santos, Godard and Sembène and Kiarostami, Antonioni and Straub and Huillet. Not satisfied with a veneer, these filmmakers have sought from reality something richer and stranger, of more potency and consequence, but also, in just that measure, harder to deal with coherently, more resistant to articulate arrangement. For there lies the problem reality poses to the filmmaker seriously aiming to engage it: the closer the engagement with reality, the more difficult the task of giving it form and meaning. The remove of the film image makes the things of reality easier to handle, more amenable to the workings of art, and by keeping things at a far enough remove incoherence may be avoided, but so will any genuine engagement with reality. The risk of incoherence must be run, unruly reality met on a ground close enough to its own for its energies and its resistance to come into play. Only by contending with its resistance can a filmmaker derive from its energies, and arrange into expressive structures, a vividness and force that tell on the screen.

The problem reality poses to the filmmaker is exemplified in the work of Rossellini, who broke new ground in his grappling with the problem but more often than not failed to solve it. It is the problem of form, or the problem of fiction: the problem of giving form to the observed facts, the documentary details; the problem of making fiction out of the facts, making a fiction that does justice rather than violence to the documentary image. "I detested Rossellini's *Open City*," wrote Luis Buñuel in his autobiography. "The facile contrast between the tortured priest in the next room and the German officer drinking champagne with a woman in his lap seemed to me disgusting."[14] Buñuel put his finger on the kind of cheap manipulation to which this filmmaker who was against all manipulation on principle often resorted in practice. Rossellini at his best was a cinematic equivalent of the street photography of Robert Frank or Garry Winogrand (which he surely influenced): the picture snatched from life with the rough edges of life, the uncomposed look of something that was there rather than something arranged into a statement. This may seem easy to do—just open the shutter and let reality make the picture—but it is difficult to do well, and more difficult to do in a film than in a still photograph. A still photograph snatches the moment without having to worry about the complications of before and after; it has its own formal problems to solve but not the problem of time, the problem of story, the problem of fiction. Aptly characterized by one critic (Pauline Kael, in conversation) as "a great filmmaker who never made a great film," Rossellini achieved great moments but didn't manage so well the before and after.

Kracauer wants films to be as little as possible like dramatic stories and as much as possible like photographs that move. He considers stories uncinematic unless they are "permeable to the flow of life," which in effect means slight stories ever ready to give over to an interesting bit of life the camera may capture. He criticized the Roman episode in Rossellini's *Paisan* (1946) for being "a highly contrived story, not the kind of sketchy and nervous reportage in which most of *Paisan* excels."[15] But the trouble with this episode, as with other parts of *Paisan*, is not that it is highly but that it is badly contrived. Rossellini did better in *Germany Year Zero* (1947), a film as clumsy as *Open City* and *Paisan* and as often unconvincing and yet one that stays in the memory not just in bits and pieces but as a sustained whole. For the story he tells this time, highly contrived though it is—the story of a thirteen-year-old boy, a kind of Oedipus of fallen Germany, who kills his ailing father out of a misguided sense of duty—is so appropriate to the concrete setting that it affects us as the essential story of postwar Berlin, the dramatic action that best belongs in its ruin. The same setting, as treated by Billy Wilder in *A Foreign Affair* (1948)—Hollywood at that time, under the influence of Italian neorealism, began to go out on location much more often—makes for some striking views but remains little more than a backdrop, an added touch of local color. Rossellini (though he used back projection at times) gives the place central place, and his film is impossible to conceive apart from the specific detail and circumstance of its setting, like a piece of architecture built in intimate accordance with the site. Kracauer insists that tragedy is foreign to the cinema, but *Germany Year Zero* is a tragedy of a kind foreign to the theater, for the boy who is its protagonist exists as a character only in relation to the observed particulars of an actual environment. When, after an extended passage in which the camera watches him with the same puzzled stare it turns on his shattered city, the boy throws himself from one of the half-destroyed buildings down to his death amid the rubble, the raw power of graphically presented devastation has been transmuted into the enduring power of tragedy. It is in relation to this protagonist, to the action having him at its center, that the particulars of Rossellini's film are aligned into meaning and made to embody a general proposition.

Lumière made home movies for the world. He didn't have to have a story, he didn't have to have a vision, he could simply record the utterly unremarkable details of daily life—the arrival of a train, the feeding of a baby—and expect the public to be interested. He didn't think the interest would last, not in the movies as public entertainment; he seems to have thought his movie camera would, like Eastman's still camera, find its market in the home, where the family and friends would remain interested in watching the unremarkable moving on the screen, without a story, without a vision.

If Lumière has been proved wrong by the continuing success of the public movie, he has been proved right by the continuing success of the home movie, now more popular than ever because made more cheaply and quickly on video. The public movie after Lumière has been predominantly a staged fiction. The documentary movie that would reach a public beyond the home has tapped the interest of what's news and the interest of what's different: other than the home movie, the newsreel and the travelogue have been the two main types of documentary film. Of the two main founders of the documentary film as art, Dziga Vertov and Robert Flaherty, one came out of the newsreel and the other came out of the travelogue.

Vertov began as an editor of newsreels in Soviet Russia after the 1917 revolution. His work, and especially *The Man with a Movie Camera* (1929), has been been much admired in recent years as a kind of avant-garde cinema. But it is also very much a documentary cinema, not in the sense that it shows life as it is—no film does that, and least of all a film as emphatically arranged as *The Man with a Movie Camera*—but in the sense that it takes its materials directly from real life. It was important to Vertov that he was working with the materials of life, making them into a new order just as the Communist revolution was making life into a new order. His films are emphatically a construction but as emphatically not a figment of the imagination: a construction made out of pieces of reality. He insisted on representing unrehearsed life and he also insisted on the contrivance of cinematic representation. His two-edged stress on reality and on artifice eschewed the fiction of actors and concocted dramas at the same time that it embraced the fiction of arranged images projected on the screen.

Every film has an aspect of documentary and an aspect of fiction. How, then, can we talk about documentary as a kind of film distinct from fiction? The category eludes definition, as the various attempts to provide one have demonstrated, but this doesn't make it meaningless. All films may be documentary and all films may be fictional, but some are more documentary, and some are more fictional, than others. The term *nonfiction film*, though often used, is not to be preferred. Documentary film doesn't mean avoiding fiction, for no film can avoid fiction: it means establishing a certain relationship, a certain interplay, between the documentary and the fictional aspects of film so that the documentary aspect may come forward in some significant way.

Another documentary that declares the contrivance of its representation is Buñuel's *Land without Bread* (1932). Like Vertov's work, Buñuel's film has been much admired of late because it calls attention to its artifice and has been considered not really documentary for that reason. *Land without Bread* is the terrible reverse of *Nanook of the North*, the film that ten years before launched Flaherty's career and the art of the documentary. Whereas Flaherty celebrates the Eskimos—the Inuits—for their ability to contend successfully with inhospitable nature, Buñuel portrays a group of people—the inhabitants of Las Hurdes, a pocket of stagnant backwardness in the mountains of Spain—who are miserably defeated in their attempts to deal with an adverse environment. And whereas Flaherty refines the travelogue to serve his purposes, Buñuel, with a shocking irony that serves his, takes the travelogue where it was never intended to go.

Toward that wretched region of Spain *Land without Bread* adopts the tone, the mode of depiction, of the sort of documentary that visits some faraway land and gazes at its picturesque sights, noting unusual details of the flora and fauna and architecture; the unfortunate Hurdanos are presented in the manner of some inane travelogue that takes a casual interest in the curious customs of these exotic people. The form is at odds with the content. The style of representation is purposely inappropriate. The film calls itself into question. Buñuel introduced a showing of his earlier *Un Chien andalou* (1929) by telling the spectators that he hoped they wouldn't like it. *Land without Bread* not only doesn't want us to like it, it doesn't want us to trust it either. It disowns the conventional documentary posture that asks us to accept this as the truth.

Whether travelogue or newsreel, documentary film usually relies on a voice-over narration that tells us what we should make of what the camera shows us. An unreliable narrator is not uncommon in fiction: a variant of the convention that asks us to accept the story as filtered through a narrator's perceptions. An unreliable narrator in documentary, such as Buñuel gives us in *Land without Bread,* is something else: a challenge to the authority of documentary itself, a blatant move from documentary into fiction. And so those who think that every film is a fiction film love *Land without Bread* for exposing its own fictionality. A parody travelogue, the film has been called: a surreal joke. But merely as a parody, merely as a joke, the film wouldn't be very interesting. The condition of fiction it exposes takes on significance, incisive and unsettling significance, by being set against the condition of documentary. We may laugh at the Hurdanos, laugh at the way they keep trying to make things better and keep making them worse, but our laughter is troubled and complicated, is finally stopped, by the fact that the Hurdanos are real. We recognize that the travelogue is quite inadequate to represent their situation, but what form would be adequate to the terrible reality of their situation? *Land without Bread* defines itself as a documentary, as the kind of documentary it is, by declaring itself a fiction.

Why don't they get out? we ask as we watch the Hurdanos go on living from day to day the bad dream their life has been for generations. Some of them are cretins born of inbreeding, but most of them are as normal as we are. Why don't they get out? the film tacitly yet insistently asks. Although the region is isolated, it wouldn't be so difficult for them physically to leave. Some of them do leave, looking for work elsewhere, but then they come back, not having found it. They are not trapped by the geography but by deep-seated habits of life, entrenched communal traditions that, as if enacting some grotesque parody of human society corresponding to Buñuel's parody travelogue, have reduced them to utter misery.

Normally such misery would be represented with pity, but Buñuel's representation curbs our pity as it curbs any other ready outlet for our emotions. Not allowed simply to feel sorry for those unfortunates, we are brought to reflect on our own situation: a film that puts itself in question puts us viewers in question too. Why don't *we* get out, we may well ask ourselves, of the entrapments in our own lives? We are surely not exempt, the film leads us to recognize, from the habitual inhibition of the best human possibilities, the crippling implanted patterns of behavior, the pathology of human culture and society that the Hurdanos represent in the extreme. If the humanitarian film solicits our pity for others (we're OK, they're not OK), if the usual travelogue takes a rather condescending interest in the exotic (we're OK, they may be OK) and the more serious anthropological film tells us that the traditions and practices of another culture are as good as our own (we're OK, they're OK) or even superior (they're OK, we may not be OK), *Land without Bread* presses us to the realization that the trouble with them is but an aggravated case of our own trouble: they're not OK and neither are we. Curbing our pity, Buñuel arouses our fear, and in the tempered way of irony his parody travelogue engages the pity and fear of tragedy: an irony that disallows the release, the closure of catharsis, and makes for a sense of tragedy without end.

Whereas the fiction in Vertov's and Buñuel's documentaries wins approval nowadays as an acknowledgment of artifice, the fiction in Flaherty's documentaries tends to elicit disapproval as romantic escapism if not outright cheating. Flaherty was indeed an American Rousseauan who went to distant places looking for the essence of humanity in the encounter with nature and, not exactly finding what he sought, fabricated it in his films. Rather than recording what was there, Flaherty reconstructed what had been there, what, as he saw it, ought to have been there. The Inuits in *Nanook of the North* had known guns for a long time but in the film we only see them use the knife and spear and harpoon; the South Sea islanders in *Moana* (1926) had long abandoned the painful ritual of tattooing they perform at the film's climax; the islanders in *Man of Aran* (1934) had to be taught for the film how their ancestors used to hunt shark. Flaherty began as an explorer and he remained one in his films, not the cursory tourist who makes the usual travelogue but an unhurried visitor responsive to the place and its people and getting to know them well; his art has been likened to Inuit carving, which tries to discover a shape in the material, to bring it out from within rather than imposing it from without. But the shape Flaherty would bring out in his material was, for all the local differences and his attentive rendering of them, pretty much the same everywhere he went: a cinematic version of the universalizing "Family of Man."

Unlike a still photographer, however, Flaherty couldn't just snatch the moment that suited him; he couldn't even, as Steichen did in his exhibition, assemble a bunch of moments that suited him. To convey his view of things, Flaherty had to see them through time, to enact them in movement: the life he would reconstruct for us he had to bring to life on the screen. And he reconstructed that life, he enacted its movement, in the very place where that life would have been lived and with the very people who would have lived it. The Inuits in *Nanook of the North*—the Eskimos as Flaherty and most people called them—were knowing actors in the movie and active collaborators in its making. They made many suggestions—the walrus hunt, for example, done the old-fashioned way for the movie and, as they foresaw, an exciting movie scene—and they regularly saw the rushes, which were processed and projected right there. "It has always been most important for me to see my rushes," Flaherty said. "But another reason for developing the film in the north was to project it to the Eskimos so that they would accept and understand what I was doing and work together with me as partners."[16] And that partnership comes across in the finished film, as Andrew Sarris has noted:

> By involving himself in his material, [Flaherty] established a cinematic principle that parallels Werner Heisenberg's Uncertainty Principle in physics, namely, that the mere observation of nuclear (and cinematic) particles alters the properties of these particles. One of the most beautiful moments in the history of the cinema was recorded when Nanook smilingly acknowledged the presence of Flaherty's camera in his igloo. The director was not spying on Nanook or attempting to capture Nanook's life in the raw. He was collaborating with Nanook on a representation rather than a simulation of existence. What Flaherty understood so well was the potential degeneration of the documentary into voyeurism when the images of the camera were not reprocessed in the mind of the artist.[17]

The moment singled out by Sarris is a special moment in a partnership we feel throughout the whole movie. Having built an igloo with sure skill, and aware that in so doing he has provided a good scene for Flaherty to put in his movie, Nanook cuts out a window from inside the igloo and through that window smilingly peers at the camera, at the man peering at him through that other window which is the viewfinder. The subject of the picture and the maker of the picture, the two men with their two artifacts, igloo and camera, are seen here to come together in a joint venture. *Nanook of the North* makes its own acknowledgment of artifice. And that acknowledgment gives it its own validation as a documentary: like *Land without*

Bread, like *The Man with a Movie Camera, Nanook of the North* defines itself as the kind of documentary it is by declaring itself a fiction. It's apparent on the screen that Nanook, the real Eskimo whom we see in his environment, hunting or fishing or building an igloo, was at the same time consciously executing a self-portrait, performing for an audience that he knew would be curious to learn about him. This is Nanook's life, maybe not as it actually was, but as he demonstrated it for us.

For some it is a flaw that Nanook shows his awareness of the camera in his company. The actors in a dramatic film conventionally pretend that the camera is not there, and Flaherty reputedly made the documentary into art by infusing it with the techniques of dramatic filmmaking. In his history of the documentary Erik Barnouw commends *Nanook of the North* for its dramatic qualities but regrets those moments when Nanook and his family acknowledge the camera: "These seem holdovers from travelogue—characters posing for the camera, demonstrating their quaintness."[18] The travelogue before Flaherty was an attraction in what Tom Gunning calls a "cinema of attractions":[19] not a storytelling cinema but one that would address the spectators more baldly, seizing them with a bit of comedy, a bit of magic, a bit of sex, an action thrill—a series of turns as in a variety show. The travelogue was a bit of the exotic in that cinema's variety show. *Nanook of the North* retains something of the attraction, the spectacle frankly aimed at the spectator; Flaherty didn't let Nanook and his family grimace for the camera as an older travelogue would have, but neither did he dissemble the fact of

Nanook of the North. Nanook at the igloo window.

their performance for the camera as a dramatic film would have. Object though Barnouw and others may, the more direct engaging of the spectator works much to the film's benefit. Flaherty lessened the element of attraction in his later films, and this tends to lessen their impact: none of the people who act as if the camera didn't exist in *Moana* or *Man of Aran* exists as vividly on the screen as does Nanook of the North.

Opposing the cinema of attractions to the storytelling cinema, Gunning sets up an either/or: either a film openly addresses its viewers or it tells them a story. But *Nanook of the North* does both at once. The film is fortunate to have Nanook, a protagonist who can do both at once effortlessly. Possessing a rare spontaneous rapport with the camera—the kind of rapport that distinguishes a movie star—Nanook can show himself conscious of the film in the making without appearing self-conscious, can perform for an audience as if he were on a stage and at the same time perform an action in the real world. He welcomes the camera in his environment, welcomes us, in the fashion of a man no less himself as he entertains a guest. Whereas a dramatic film tells a story by performing it, without a storyteller, *Nanook of the North* has Nanook both as performer and as storyteller: teller of his own story who addresses it to us as he performs it for the camera. But Flaherty, the man behind the camera, is also the storyteller, and when Nanook happily faces him from the igloo window the two storytellers meet as one.

It is Flaherty's film, however: he had the upper hand, the final say in telling the story. He has been accused of exploiting the people he filmed: accused of colonialism, of imperialism. Already as an explorer and prospector Flaherty was not a loner in the wilderness but an employee of those who would colonize and exploit that wilderness; and as a filmmaker he certainly remained implicated in the colonial and imperial enterprise. It was not only as the wielder of the camera but as a white man that he had the upper hand over Nanook. But his identification of himself with Nanook, of the camera with the igloo, is not therefore to be dismissed as sham. Flaherty genuinely identified his work with Nanook's; he always identified his activity as a filmmaker with the activity of the people he filmed, the people he saw as holding their own with their courage and their craft. And through that identification he defined himself as an artist, he saw himself as someone whose work was his own rather than someone doing alienated labor. He may have been a colonialist but he was also a populist in his felt kinship with the people before his camera.

"*Nanook of the North* seems poised between documentary and fiction," writes William Rothman; "it marks a moment before the distinction between fiction and documentary is set."[20] Rothman means the distinction between fiction and documentary as genres, kinds of film. Every film is in some way poised between the documentary and the fictional aspects of its medium, between the documentary image the camera captures and the fiction projected on the screen. The films that stress their documentary aspect are especially called upon to deal with the problem of fiction, of negotiating that uncertain frontier where documentary and fiction meet. Between documentary and fiction, camera and projector, index and icon, absence and presence, past and present, narrative and drama, material and ghost, the film medium seeks its poise.

2 : The Narrative Sequence

"Begin at the beginning," the King said, very gravely, "and go
on till you come to the end: then stop."

LEWIS CARROLL, *Alice's Adventures in Wonderland*

Really, universally, relations stop nowhere, and the exquisite
problem of the artist is eternally but to draw, by a geometry
of his own, the circle within which they shall happily *appear*
to do so.

HENRY JAMES, Preface to *Roderick Hudson*

When he appears on the stage, besides what he is actually
doing he will at all essential points discover, specify, imply
what he is not doing; that is to say he will act in such a
way that the alternative emerges as clearly as possible, that
his acting allows the other possibilities to be inferred and
only represents one out of the possible variants.

BERTOLT BRECHT, "Short Description of a New Technique
of Acting Which Produces an Alienation Effect"

That telling a story and counting things are related acts is suggested by the words we have for them. To tell can also mean to count; a teller
can be one who tells or one who counts. To recount means to tell as well as to
count again; an account can be a computation or a narrative. The same
word, *contar*, means in Spanish both to count and to tell; *compter* and *conter*
are almost the same in French, as are *zählen* and *erzählen* in German. Telling
is indeed like counting, not in content, of course, but in form: a story is told
in succession, one thing and then another and then another, as things are
counted. It may be that we tell about things that happened one after another,
with the succession of the telling corresponding to the order of events in
time, as we count a row of objects following their order in place. It may be
that we describe a landscape, or the contents of a room, telling in succession
about things that were all there together, giving them an order nevertheless
in the act of describing them, as we would in that of counting them. When
we count things, one, two, three, we mentally put them in a row even if they

are not in any particular order themselves. We perform the same operation when we tell about things: we put them in sequence.

We look in the things we count for an order we can follow in the counting, beginning here and going on this way to end up there, but usually this order is more or less arbitrary, our choice of a sequence where none is unmistakably present. In telling a story we may likewise want to follow the natural succession of events. But it is not in the nature of things that they always come one after another in time; it is owing to the artificiality of language that they have to come one after another in the telling. There may be some order, even if not a succession in time, that seems natural to follow: describing first, for example, what strikes us as the dominant feature of a landscape. But someone else describing the same landscape might be struck by a different feature, or think it better to tell about other things first and save the most impressive for last. A narrative sequence, what is told first and what next and what next up to the end, is always to some extent an order of our making. The succession we make of things when we tell about them marks the artifact that is a narrative. A narrative is not just a story, something that happened or is imagined to have happened, but a story told: not a sequence that happened but a sequence made.[1]

A painting is the opposite of a narrative: it is there all at once. It may contain a story—any painting does that depicts an ongoing event, a battle, say, or a young woman reading a letter next to a window—but the story is put in simultaneous form. Narrative makes life into a sequence; painting makes life into a simultaneity. Lessing's argument in the *Laocoon* was that narrative is an art of time and painting an art of space, that narrative deals properly with what is sequential in life and painting with what is simultaneous. This argument neglects the artifice, the artificiality of art, the rendering of things as they do not occur in life that marks a work of art as a thing made. Viktor Shklovsky called *Tristram Shandy* "the most typical novel" because Sterne's continual intrusions on the story he is telling, the liberties he takes with the time of events, call attention to what is true of every novel, that the narrative sequence is not a fact of the story, the life recounted, but an arrangement given to that life in the process of recounting it.[2] The simultaneity of a painting is equally an arrangement—not necessarily the way things are, or could be, but the way they are made to be.

A sequence is an open-ended arrangement, admitting of indefinite addition; a simultaneity is conclusive. A narrative can go on and on, coming to an end at some point but even then potentially continuable; a painting is all there before us. A narrative continued is still a narrative, whereas to imagine a painting continued, what comes after it in time or what lies outside it in space, is no longer to think of a painting but of a different kind of thing, a comic strip perhaps, or a movie. A painting is a thing complete in itself, with no more to come, no more to see. A narrative is an additive thing and always subject to further addition—of more that happened in the story, of more and more that, as Sterne demonstrates in *Tristram Shandy* by his dwelling at inordinate length on some brief event, can be told about anything that happened. Counting stops when every item in the set being counted has been covered; but in telling a story it is impossible to cover everything in the life being recounted. Any account given of that life, however thorough, is of necessity partial, incomplete in time and in space, an enumeration of items in a set (the world) that is not denumerable, since it is inexhaustibly large and capable of being inexhaustibly detailed.

In a photograph, like a painting a simultaneous presentation of things, what is presented is but the fact of a simultaneity, reproduced by the camera: the things we see in a photograph happened to be together in the world, they were not put together in the picture. A painter starts with a surface on which he or she makes a picture; what the painter puts together on that surface is all there is to see. A photographer starts with something in the world of which he or she takes a picture; what appears in that picture may be all we can see but not all that could be seen of the things before the camera, only a section of space captured at a certain time from a certain perspective. A photograph is there all at once but it's not *all* there; like a narrative, it is an incomplete presentation, a partial view. It's always legitimate to ask how a photograph may continue, what more could be seen from a different perspective or at a different time or in a different section of space. A photograph is not a sequence but it is a fragment of a potential sequence; it invites being continued, continued by a caption, as happens with news photographs, or continued by other photographs, as happens in the movies, twenty-four times a second.

The movie camera automatically provides a sequence. Back in 1895, the first movie ever made—the first movie made by the Lumière brothers, not the first moving picture but the first picture made for the movie screen—gave the audience a nice sequence to see. From the fixed position where Louis Lumière put the camera he had just invented we see the gates of a factory being opened, the workers leaving for their lunch hour, the gates being closed—a beginning, a middle, and an end to please Aristotle, or the King in *Alice*. But this is the mere fact of a sequence, an event passively recorded by the camera, not the arrangement of a sequence that would be made in telling about the same event, with a narrator choosing what to tell about it and in what order. The movie camera, left to itself, does not put things one after another like a narrator: it merely records them that way.

Lumière chose where to begin, where to end, and where to place the camera; everything else in his movie was done automatically. Already these three choices are something like the choices of a narrator, but Lumière made them in such a way that his movie is as little as possible like a narrative. He begins at the point where the event begins, with the gates being opened; if he had begun with a held view of the gates before they were opened, that would have had the effect of making us wonder what comes next, a narrative strategy. He ends at the point where the event ends, with the gates being closed; if he had held for a little while a view of the gates after they were closed, that would have led us to expect something more to happen, and his film would have been less the simple record of an event and more like a narrative to be continued. His choice of where to place the camera could not help but make something like a narrative arrangement: the sequence of the workers leaving the factory is a fact, but the sequence of them entering and leaving the frame is an arrangement brought about by the placement of the camera. Lumière, however, placed his camera at a window across the street, in a position to give us an encompassing view of the scene. A closer view would have made the entering and leaving frame a more emphatic arrangement; showing us less of the scene, it would have made us wonder what else could have been shown. A view from farther away, showing us more than just that scene, perhaps the window frame or some other object in the room where the camera was, would similarly have made us wonder what else was there in that room. We may still wonder what else, or what next, for Lumière's movie, like any photographic record, could have been continued; but he sought to give it as far as possible the completeness of a painting.

At one point in *Moana* (1926), Flaherty's documentary about Samoa, we see a native boy starting to climb a coconut tree. We don't see the whole tree, only the bottom part of it, and that view is held, as the boy climbs up, until he disappears at the top of the frame. Then the camera moves upward to take in the boy climbing up another section of the tree, no longer the bottom and not yet the top, and that view is held until the boy again disappears at the top of the frame. Again the camera moves upward, to take in now the top part of the tree and the boy still climbing until finally he reaches the coconuts he was after. Like the workers leaving a factory, the climb is an event with a built-in beginning, middle, and end that could simply have been recorded in the manner of Lumière, from a fixed camera position sufficiently far back to take in, all in one view, the whole tree and the boy climbing it from the bottom to the top. But Flaherty chooses his own beginning, middle, and end, which are not simply those of the event. Like a narrator, he makes a sequence of something that is not: he shows us the tree a piece at a time, this and then that and then that, as if he were telling us about it. Deliberately he only shows us so much, which makes us curious to find out what more there is and surprised at how very tall the tree turns out to be. The climb, unlike the tree, is itself sequential, but Flaherty's rendering of it is sequential in a way that the climb is not. Deliberately he allows the boy to leave our view, which draws our interest to where the boy has gone, the space we are yet to see above the frame; if the camera had moved up the tree along with the boy, closely following the sequence of the climb, then the boy climbing, something continuously on screen, would have been the chief object of our interest. Like a man telling a story, Flaherty plays upon our expectations of more to come, our sense that the information he has given us is incomplete, and to be continued.

The way the camera here twice pauses and then moves is something we register as a gesture of looking, an act of seeing. It is our awareness of this gesture, this act, that most of all invests this sequence with the sense of a telling. In narrative theory telling and showing are often opposed, but the telling in this sequence is a way of showing.

Some recent film theory, borrowing terms from the linguist Émile Benveniste, would be disposed to call this way of showing "discourse," this gesture of looking "enunciation." Benveniste distinguished between *story,* by which he meant narration where no speaker intervenes, and *discourse,* by which he meant "every utterance assuming a speaker and a hearer, and in the speaker, the intention of influencing the other in some way."[3] *Discourse* is the kind of utterance *(énoncé)* marked by the act of uttering *(énonciation),* a speaker's act of saying this in this situation; such words as the pronoun *I* and the adverb *here* are marks of the enunciation found in the utterance. In like manner, some would maintain, the pause and movement of Flaherty's camera in this sequence are marks of his enunciation found in his utterance.

Benveniste's distinction is fine as long as "story" is a written text and "discourse" an oral exchange. But once "discourse" enters into written texts there is a problem: surely every "story" assumes a speaker and a hearer and an intention of influencing even if these are not expressly set forth. Film theorists borrowing Benveniste's terms have failed to recognize this problem. Taking film to be "story" because it has no express speaker, to be "discourse" because it has an intention of influencing, they imagine a kind of conspiracy effacing the enunciation in most films and, as Christian Metz put it, having discourse masquerade as story. And there are other problems with the attempt to apply Benveniste to film. On the one hand, the film image has no pronouns that would designate a speaker and a hearer; on the other hand, the image has always a *here*, for, unlike the speaker of a written utterance, the camera is always explicitly somewhere. While it cannot enunciate in the first or second person—an actor of course can, or a voice-over narrator, but that is another matter—the camera enunciates automatically that it is here looking at this from this angle and distance. The notion that the film image is an utterance, and that the camera as speaker of that utterance performs an enunciation usually effaced and sometimes made explicit, is a loose analogy masquerading as rigorous theory.

The camera is an observer, not a speaker; the boy climbing the coconut tree is something the camera sees, not something it says, not an utterance. Our sense of a telling in Flaherty's sequence comes not from an act of saying but from an act of seeing, from a way of directing our seeing. Rather than an enunciator, the camera is an indicator, an instrument for pointing our attention to things in the world before its gaze. If Lumière is a painter, Flaherty may be called a pointer.[4]

Like telling and showing, narration and description are often opposed. But as the telling in Flaherty's sequence is a way of showing, so is the narration a mode of description. Narration is opposed to description as action is to contemplation, but here the action of climbing the tree and the way of rendering that action on the screen—what feels like a narration— serve principally to give a striking description of that very tall coconut tree. Here as in *Nanook of the North*, Flaherty organizes our curiosity into a structure of discovery; he parcels out the world's sights in a strategy of gradual revelation, arousing and then satisfying our wish to see more of the world. His use of the camera is mainly descriptive, in an old narrative tradition of which he was perhaps the last major exponent, that of the traveler who has been to faraway places and comes back to tell us about them.

Of American filmmakers before Griffith the most notable was Edwin S. Porter, best known for *The Life of an American Fireman* and *The Great Train Robbery,* both from 1903. Porter began his career as a projectionist, and in those early days of movies, as Charles Musser has argued, the projectionist was an editor of sorts, in charge of arranging the sequence of views, the order in which the audience would see the varied and very short films that composed the program.[5] The art of film editing began with that sort of film projecting.

Groundbreaking at first and by the end of his career recalcitrantly old-fashioned, Porter's editing developed and remained in the style of the projectionist stringing together different views from different provenances, each allowed to run its course before the next would go on the screen. The climactic scene of *The Life of an American Fireman* depicts a rescue from a fire. Evidently feeling that more was needed than the single camera position for the entire scene that was standard practice in those days, Porter took the bold step of using two camera positions, inside and outside the house on fire. But he didn't cut back and forth between these two perspectives as Griffith in a few years would have done (and as in fact was done in a reedited version of the film that was long mistaken for the original). Instead he showed the whole scene twice over, first from inside a room where a woman and her child are in danger and then from the street outside, for a look at the rescue as it would appear to a witnessing bystander. The view from inside and the view from outside are treated like different views from different provenances shown one after the other in a projectionist's sequence. Inside we get the perspective of a spectator at the theater, outside we get the perspective of a news cameraman, and Porter lets each view stand separately rather than attempting to blend them together.

Is this a narrative sequence? Going back in time, going over the same event from a different point of view, is a narrative prerogative, and Porter may be thought of as a narrator relating the same event twice, or as an author giving us the viewpoints of two different narrators on the same event. But the event, we must not forget, is not related to us but staged for us, enacted before our eyes. Enacted twice: the first time on something that looks very much like a theater stage, the second time on a larger and rather more lifelike stage that suggests a newsreel (and in those days it was common practice to stage newsreels). It would be more accurate to think of Porter as an innovator in staging—staging for the screen—who gives us two consecutive versions of the same scene so that we can better apprehend its two principal aspects: the woman and child in danger, the fireman going to the rescue.

Narrative recounts a story as something that happened in the past; drama enacts a story and makes it present before an audience. Isn't representing the same event a second time, it may be asked, representing something that happened in the past? Isn't that second enactment a kind of recounting? It depends on how the audience takes it: if the audience accepts it as drama, if it accepts the conventions of its performance—which would include its being a second representation of the same event—then it takes it as present, as something made present. We can go back to a play or watch a movie again and get caught up in the drama the second time as much as the first. If he entertained the option, Porter no doubt thought that cutting back and forth between inside and outside would have been disconcerting for the audience, that showing one side at a time was more involving. But the style of representation he adopted is foreign to an audience watching his movie today, and insofar as we feel that foreignness, insofar as we hold back from the conventions he was asking his audience to accept, his enactment will recede from the present into the past and turn into a kind of recounting.[6]

It may be argued that, taken separately, each staging of the rescue functions as drama but that the sequence of the two, the editing of the scene, makes a narrative sequence. The argument applies as well to the cutting back and forth Griffith would have done and to any other editing technique by which the scene may be rendered on the screen as a sequence of views. That the art of film is in the editing used to be an article of faith: the scene belongs in the theater, in a film we must talk of the sequence. And it is still commonly thought that the art of film narrative is in the editing: the camera shows, the editing tells. Even André Bazin, who more than anyone else challenged the supremacy of editing in film theory, thought so: Griffith's development of editing, he maintained, "taught the cinema that it was not just capable of *showing* but of *telling*."[7] This is from an essay on Stroheim, whom Bazin praised as the negation of Griffith and the restorer of cinema to its "main function" of showing, and whose editing, brisker in fact than Griffith's, Bazin seems not to have seen: evidence of how well editing can perform the function of showing. Further evidence is the fact that while theorists and critics may prefer to discourse on the sequence, the ordinary moviegoer keeps talking about the scene.

Whatever else it may do, editing enables showing: the sequence can give us a fuller picture of the scene. Close-ups show us the details; angle and reverse angle show us both sides of the scene. The projectionist's sequence of inside and outside views may not bring us into the drama, but it certainly gives us a more rounded picture of Porter's rescue scene. Showing is not the same thing as dramatizing; dramatic involvement takes more than our seeing something, it takes the feeling of a story being made present before our eyes. And more than a means of showing, editing is a dramatic means: the sequence can give us a more vivid rendering of the action taking place in the scene. At our distance from Porter we can't be sure whether his second view of the rescue was intended to dramatize or to elucidate (the way the instant replay we get in a sports broadcast looks again at the event for purposes of elucidation); probably both. When it comes to Griffith's crosscutting we can be sure of the intention to dramatize. The cutting back and forth in his rescue scenes serves not just to show but to make present in dramatic fashion: the action is unfolding in two places at once, and Griffith's crosscutting keeps abreast of it in both places, makes it present on the screen in both places at once. This is clearly a dramatic rather than a narrative procedure. Try to imagine such a rescue scene, with all the excitement crosscutting can build up, accompanied by voice-over narration, whether from a character or any other narrator: it would not work, the scene would not admit narrated accompaniment, the presentness of the action would not tolerate the pastness of a narrative voice.

The notion that the camera shows and the editing tells is linked to the distinction between scene and summary in literary study. Strictly speaking, a novel has no scenes, only words; but when it depicts at some length what was happening at a particular time, usually with lines of dialogue, it is said to represent a scene. Summary is when it tells us in a few pages about what happened over a considerable stretch of time. "When the imagined duration of a story event is approximately 'equal' to the time of its telling/reading," writes Edward Branigan, "the result is a 'scene.' "[8] The quotes around *equal* and *scene* are operative. Scene is something a novel is said to show, to dramatize, whereas summary is something told, narrated. Editing in a film is thought to speed up time like summary in a novel. But of course editing can also slow down time. Porter's rescue scene lasts twice as long in his projectionist's sequence. Griffith's crosscutting is as apt to extend time as to compress it, and in any case it is nothing like a summary.

Editing is indeed a means of manipulating time, but that doesn't make it a narrative means. It is often supposed that, unedited, a scene unfolds before the camera in the time the event would take in real life—that a film like Hitchcock's *Rope* (1948), which almost entirely does without editing, takes place in real time. But time is manipulated not only in the editing but also in the writing and in the staging of a scene. Scenes in the theater surely don't take place in real time. "A clock that is working will always be a disturbance on the stage," wrote Walter Benjamin. "Even in a naturalistic play, astronomical time would clash with theatrical time."[9] All that happens in *Rope* (which was based on a play) couldn't possibly have happened in the time the film takes on the screen: *Rope* takes place not in real time but in theatrical time. Drama arranges its own time, and film editing is a means, regularly employed, of that dramatic arrangement.

Of itself a sequence of film shots is not a narrative sequence. But it can be, depending on the way the shot arrangement goes. Many film sequences function as narrated summary, with or without voice-over narration. And a narrative arrangement of shots can take various other forms besides the summary. Perhaps the most assiduous practitioner of narration by film editing has been Robert Bresson. "Form in Bresson's films is anti-dramatic, though strongly linear," wrote Susan Sontag. "It is, above all, a distinctive form of narration."[10] When people speak of "linear narrative" they usually mean a chain of events, a succession of scenes, a dramatic plot. Bresson's linear narrative is something different and more strictly deserving of the name. It is a chain of shots, not events but bits of events, fragments picked out from the world and put in a row like so many items being counted: not scenes but pieces of scenes taken out of a dramatic context and arranged in precise narrative order. Bresson called himself not a *metteur en scène* but a *metteur en ordre*, not a director, not one who sets things out on a stage, but one who puts things in order. "Each shot is like a word," he said, and with him this isn't mere theory but a rigorous filmmaking practice.[11] Each shot is like a word, and the arrangement of shots one after another is like an articulated sentence: not a dramatic succession but a narrative sequence.

"The poet may imitate by narration—in which case he can either take another personality as Homer does, or speak in his own person, unchanged—or he may present all his characters as living and moving before us." Thus Aristotle distinguishes between narrative and drama.[12] It is a distinction between telling and enacting. It is not, as people think, tantamount to the distinction between telling and showing. Drama for Aristotle is not about showing but about speaking, enacting speech. The medium of imitation, words, is the same in narrative and in drama, and the distinction is between the words of a narrator, sometimes given over to a character, and words wholly given over to dramatic characters and spoken by actors in performance. Tragedy, said Aristotle, is the imitation of an action "in the form of action, not of narrative."[13] But in Greek tragedy not much happens on the stage that an audience today would call action: the action imitated is the action of speaking. What was made present on the Greek stage was not primarily a visual scene but the speech of human beings.

More recent drama has been more about showing. But the distinction between telling and showing comes from the theory of narrative, where only telling is possible. Like Aristotle's distinction between narrative and drama, it is a distinction between things done with words: between words that tell us something and words that make us see it. But Aristotle's distinction is clear and precise and has to do with the material means of representation—the words on a page, the actors on a stage—whereas the distinction between telling and showing has to do with a kind of wishful thinking that the words on a page will evoke the actors on a stage.

"Aristotle's conception of *mimesis* applies primarily to theatrical performance," says David Bordwell.[14] This is a common error. *Mimesis,* or imitation, is Aristotle's term for representation, and it applies to all representation, pictorial or musical, narrative or dramatic. Bordwell, like other theorists, wants to contrast mimesis with diegesis. This is again an error. *Diegesis* is a term often used in recent theory to designate the world of a story, the world where the characters exist and the events unfold. *Diegesis* in this sense cannot be opposed to *mimesis,* for it refers to the world the mimesis brings into being. But the term is also used in a different sense. In book 3 of the *Republic* Plato distinguishes between *haplê diêgêsis,* or simple narrative in the poet's own words, and narrative through *mimêsis,* in which the poet imitates the words of another. Here *diegesis* means narrative or narration, and Plato does not oppose it to mimesis but distinguishes between a simple diegesis, a straight narration, and a diegesis employing mimesis, mixed with imitation of the characters' speech. This is akin to Aristotle's distinction between narrative and drama, and even more a matter of representation in words, even less a matter of telling versus showing as Bordwell and others take it to be. In book 10 of the *Republic* Plato uses *mimêsis* to mean representation generally in the same way Aristotle uses it. So much for the contrast between mimesis and diegesis.

It used to be assumed that film is a dramatic medium. Film would be talked about as narrative, of course, but that just meant a story, and it was taken for granted that film tells a story by enacting it, rendering it in dramatic form. No distinction was made between drama and narrative in the film medium. Thinking has changed among students of film. Nowadays the prevalent assumption is that film is a narrative medium. What else can it be, when the model of language is imposed and the images on the screen are theorized into the condition of words? The fact that film usually tells a story without a storyteller leads people to conclude, not that film is a dramatic medium, but that the enunciation has been effaced, the narrator suppressed, and to impute the effacement and suppression to the workings of a controlling ideology. Before it was all drama, now it is all narrative. Still no distinction is made between drama and narrative in film.

In his theory of film narration Bordwell doesn't adopt a linguistic model. He rightly criticizes those who look for a narrator in every film, who would ascribe to a narrator every sequence of film images. But even without a narrator he posits every film as a narration. He takes the kind of approach to narrative that stresses the construction, the articulation of a story irrespective of the medium of representation. Drama then is as much narrative as narrative is. The distinction between drama and narrative evaporates, and showing versus telling takes over, a showing and a telling irrespective of the medium that can as well occur on the page as on the stage, in words as in images.

"No purpose is served by assigning every film to a *deus absconditus*," writes Bordwell,[15] and his theory is all the better for doing without a hidden god, without an alleged narrator allegedly suppressed. In a study of Griffith's early years at Biograph and the origins of narrative film, Tom Gunning argues with Bordwell, however, and insists on putting the narrator back in the picture. Not that in Griffith's case Gunning posits a hidden or suppressed narrator: he posits in effect an auteur. His argument for the narrator boils down to the unexceptionable claim that we experience a film not as an object in nature but as a product of human making, "an intentional object, designed to have certain effects on us."[16] Where we see an intention we recognize an intelligence—that was the old argument from design for the existence of God—and Gunning calls that intelligence the narrator. He really means the implied author, the auteur.[17] A car or a pair of scissors, a building or a stage production, is also something we experience as an intentional object, but that doesn't make it the work of a narrator. If *narrator* is just a term for the fact that a film is a work, a product of human intention and human labor, then we are apt to lose sight of all about a film that may be specifically like a narrative, the product of a telling.

In a play, where there is no narrator, the implied author is the writer—implied because not there on the stage, not the speaker of the words that are the medium of imitation. But theater is also a visual medium; it presents us with something to see, what Aristotle called *opsis*, or spectacle. As theater becomes more visual, as showing on the stage makes more of a difference, another implied author may be recognized in the work: the author of the staging, the figure that rose to prominence in the nineteenth century as the stage director. In *The Winter's Tale* as staged by Ingmar Bergman the author is still Shakespeare, but the director is another governing intelligence that comes across in the performance. The notion that the director is the author of a film—the auteur theory—rests on the assumption that film is primarily a visual medium, a medium where seeing gains the upper hand, where showing governs meaning. Whether or not an implied author is inscribed in a film, whether or not this is the director, is not a matter of narration. What Griffith did that Gunning wants to call *narrativization*—showing as a means of telling, visual representation put to the purpose of unfolding a story—is better called *dramatization:* showing as a means of enacting, of making an action present on the screen, unfolding a story in the form of action, not of narrative. Griffith dramatized showing, made visual representation into a vehicle for dramatic action.

A much greater innovator than Porter, Griffith was like Porter an innovator in staging for the movie screen. Like Porter he devised a technique for switching stages in the picture show. Crosscutting was to Griffith what the projectionist's sequence was to Porter—his characteristic form of editing, his preferred way of putting different views together into a picture. And like Porter, Griffith held on stubbornly to his preferred way and stood aloof from further change, so that like Porter he ended up in early retirement from the industry he helped found. It was crosscutting above all, the technique of parallel editing and its various expressive possibilities, that Griffith developed in his pioneering years at Biograph (1908–13). He is famous for his use of the close-up, but that came later and with a certain curious reluctance: cutting *within* a scene rather than *between* scenes was something Griffith tended to resist even after other filmmakers were doing it all the time. Why? Gunning's narrator model has no answer to this question. Let the narrator give way to the director staging for the movies, and Griffith can be understood as a director faithful to a conception of the movie screen as a theater stage, a space presented whole before the spectator for the performance of each scene. The performance may be broken up by cutting to another scene, but the stage, the space of each scene within the proscenium arch of the frame, would remain whole for the spectator to see. Griffith was a director ready to cut quickly from one stage to another but reluctant to fracture the integrity of each stage on the screen. Even when he does cut within a scene, he usually keeps the same frontal perspective in the closer view, the perspective of a spectator at the theater who has the whole stage before his eyes and wields opera glasses for the significant detail.

Crosscutting is not foreign to the theater. Something of the kind occurs in Shakespeare, who wrote for a theater that did not pursue scenic realism or any elaborate form of staging and could shift with ease from one scene to another. The nineteenth-century theater, whose pursuit of scenic realism often took elaborate forms, also pursued effects of crosscutting, and it wasn't so easy to change scenes quickly on a stage laden with the appurtenances of realistic spectacle. In his valuable book *Stage to Screen*, A. Nicholas Vardac shows how the pursuit of both those goals, scenic realism and mobility of action, put the nineteenth-century theater on a road that led to the movies. One theatrical innovator Vardac discusses, Steele MacKaye, devised various movable stages—an elevator stage, a sliding stage, a floating stage, stages mounted on railroad tracks—that came close to making possible in the theater just the kind of switching back and forth between scenes that Griffith would soon start doing in the movies.[18]

Movable stages brought into place on cue and then ushered out of sight are a great deal more cumbersome than cutting, however, and even if they could be made to run with perfect smoothness they wouldn't work as well. On the stage the actors are right there; their actual presence before us helps make the action they perform present to us dramatically. On a movable stage the actors are right there moving in and out of sight, so that the illusion of our moving from one place to another, the illusion the movies do so well, is undermined by the evident fact that it is the actors doing the moving on their stage. Cutting works better because the actors we watch on the screen are not actually there before us, because the action they make present is not quite as present on the screen as an action performed on the stage: because the film image comes short of full dramatic immediacy and puts a certain mediation between us and the action, something like the mediation of narrative.

Drama presents, narrative reports. Aristotle's word for narrative in the *Poetics* is *apaggelia*, from the verb *apaggello*, to report, to bring tidings. Drama is here, narrative brings tidings from elsewhere. The movie camera, we like to say, takes us elsewhere, makes us feel that we are there. But there is not quite here, not quite present before us: the camera can as well be said to be reporting from elsewhere, to be bringing us tidings in the form of images. Film is both a dramatic and a narrative medium, and its narrative properties enabled Griffith to exploit its dramatic possibilities.

A Corner in Wheat (1909) depicts three stories: the story of the farmers who grow wheat, the story of a speculator who corners the market in wheat, and the story of the urban poor faced with the increasing price of bread. Here Griffith's crosscutting does not serve to dramatize. The three stories are kept separate and have no characters in common. Rather than linking them dramatically, the cutting back and forth between them makes the connections of a line of argument. It constructs a case rather than a plot. Griffith's crosscutting makes him felt here, not exactly as a narrator, but as a commentator seeking to win us over to his point of view. Unlike the crosscutting in a rescue scene, this would readily admit narrated accompaniment; it exploits more the narrative possibilities of the film medium. It is interesting that this crosscutting, not serving to unfold a story, should function more like a narrative.

Why distinguish between drama and narrative in film, it may be asked, if film is both a dramatic and a narrative medium? For a better understanding of how the thing works. For the same reason one distinguishes between a particle and a wave even if the kind of thing that skips around in quantum physics behaves like both.[19]

Words in a narrative mediate between us and the world they tell us about. They are someone's words, giving us not what happened but an account of what happened, someone's choice of what to tell. A play enacted on the stage is not an account: a play is what is happening in the only place where things can happen, the stage before us. Of course someone made the choice of what to put there, but once it is actually there, before us without mediation, it becomes a fact, excluding all other possibilities, no longer a matter of choice. Narrative is always a matter of choice, because the world is larger than anyone's account of it; but in a play the world is the stage. The sequence a narrator makes is an operation performed on the world, an enumeration of certain things in it; the sequence we get in a play is a presented fact. It is there on the stage and it is all there is; a play is complete like a painting.

Like the words of a narrator, the camera mediates between us and the world. But the camera is much more direct than words: its mediation is peculiarly immediate. What is on the screen is what is happening, not there before us directly, like a play, but there before the camera, directly reproduced by it. The camera makes no choices: it gives us whatever is there before it. What is on the screen is a fact, not an account. It is through our awareness of what is not on the screen, our sense of a larger world of which we are only being shown so much, that a film gets to be like a narrative.

A scene in *Pépé le Moko* (1937), a French gangster movie directed by Julien Duvivier with Jean Gabin in the lead, has Pépé and a woman reminiscing about Paris in an Algerian café. With mounting rapport they recite to each other names of metro stations in the city they both miss; we see him as he mentions a station, then her as she mentions another, back and forth, until, at the same time, they both mention the Place Blanche, and then we see them together in the same shot. Imagine this scene as Lumière would have done it: that last shot of Pépé and the woman together would have been held throughout, a shot framing squarely in one view all the elements of the scene, no less and no more, closing it off in space as beginning at the beginning and ending at the end would have closed it off in time. Lumière's scene, presented from a single encompassing point of view, closed off as if it were all there was, wouldn't have been much different from a scene on the stage. Duvivier's technique, his cutting back and forth, is certainly not stagy. Yet he does in each of his shots the same thing Lumière would have done in his one shot: have the duration and the framing match as nearly as possible the action being shown. Each of the shots in Duvivier's scene begins at the beginning and ends at the end of a line of dialogue, and it frames the person saying that line, the two persons in the last shot. The effect, as in Lumière, is a closing off: we are meant to be concerned with just this, the action there on the screen, not to consider what else might have been shown.

Duvivier's cutting doesn't make a sequence that is not in the scene; what it does is give a finer matching of the exchange between the two characters, the rapport of recollected metro stations, than would have been possible in a single static shot. It does what would have been done in *Moana* if a continuous camera movement had followed the movement of the boy up the tree: closely direct our attention to a sequence that is there. This kind of film technique is a refinement, a narrowing down, of what is done on the stage: presenting the fact of a sequence to the exclusion of all other possibilities. Of course we know that we are not being shown everything, that Pépé is there when we only see the woman and that the woman is there when we only see Pépé; but we get the feeling that we are being shown all that matters, the right thing at the right time. Duvivier's technique is an example of the dramatic, as opposed to the narrative, approach to film construction.

Imagine Duvivier's scene as his compatriot and contemporary Jean Renoir would have done it: all in one fixed shot, maybe, but not a self-contained shot in the manner of Lumière. Typically Renoir would have given us an off-center view of the scene, maybe even leaving out most of Pépé's body and having him hover at the edge of the screen, lean forward into frame and lean back out of it, or maybe showing us a section of another table in the café and letting us overhear part of another conversation; and Renoir typically might have begun his shot before Pépé and the woman sit down at their table, or ended it after they get up and leave. Renoir, in any case, would have opened up the scene, calling attention to what is not on the screen: that too may matter, we are always made to feel in his films, not just this being shown. In a Renoir film of the thirties—less so in his work since then—the action continually overflows our view of it, entering and leaving on all sides, pointing to what is left out, making us conscious that it could have been brought in but for a matter of choice.

At one point in *The Rules of the Game* (1939), Renoir's tragicomedy of love in a society "dancing on a volcano," the marquis de la Chesnaye and his wife and guests are preparing to retire for the night at his chateau. From a close view of the marquis the camera pulls back to show us the group in the kind of encompassing long shot—called a "master shot"—that sets the stage for a scene. Dramatic film technique often relies on such a master shot for laying out the space in which the action is to unfold and from which the camera is to pick out the successively significant details. But Renoir doesn't cut to any details: he holds the long shot as the various characters say good night to one another and leave frame, some going off toward the left and some toward the right, the marquis lingering for a moment at the edge of the screen before following his mistress toward the left. When only two minor characters remain, the camera moves in for a closer view of their brief exchange, and we may expect the scene to end with their going off to bed. But the camera pans with one of them, and its offhanded movement to the left suddenly opens up space in that direction, showing us a deep corridor we hadn't thought was there, a much larger stage lying unsuspected off to one side of the one we had been watching. Now this view is held, and it exhibits the deep focus Renoir has been noted for. Way in the background we can see the marquis and his mistress, and at closer range guests come in and out of their bedrooms, one carrying a suitcase, one blowing a horn, one throwing a pillow, while a female servant walks straight down the corridor toward the rear and the marquis wends his way among all his guests toward the front. When he comes close the camera pans with him, to the right this time, and in that other direction another deep space opens up to our view, another corridor variously populated that had been lying unsuspected off screen. Now this view is held and from a door in the rear a male servant walks stiff and straight toward the front, while guests say good night to the marquis's wife, Christine, at the door of her bedroom, and the marquis finds his way to that door and wants to speak with her—at which point a cut inside her bedroom brings to an end this uncommonly long take.

It is not his using deep focus and long takes but the way he uses them that makes Renoir's film technique a narrative technique. Directors like Orson Welles or William Wyler use deep focus and long takes dramatically, as a way of creating on the screen an enclosed space of dramatic representation, what we call a stage. The master shot followed by cutting to the

The Rules of the Game.
Three frames from the
same long take: the
marquis and his wife
and guests preparing
to retire for the night,
pan to the corridor to
the left, pan to the
corridor to the right.

significant things within the space it defines, the right thing at the right time, is another way of treating the screen as a stage. Renoir may often set up the screen as a stage but then he will break up the enclosure, he will open up a space beyond. Typically he uses deep focus not to bind front and back into a dramatic whole but to call attention to something else going on in back not directly related to the action in front and maybe just as important. And typically he uses long takes, as in the bedtime scene at the chateau, to open up space, to bring to our awareness all that lies outside our view, to activate the space off screen as an area where things take place with no less claim on our attention than those appearing on screen. First we see something like a stage, but then a little movement to the left and then a little movement to the right reveal in the wings of that stage a world extending deep and wide. The space of representation is twice unexpectedly redrawn. Any camera movement reframes our view, but Renoir's reframing changes our bearings in the space of our viewing, unsettles our sense of where we should be looking, what may be significant.

A party is being held at the chateau, with amateur theatricals. After the curtain closes on one of the acts, we cut behind it and see the marquis and Christine and other performers in costume. Christine has learned about her husband's affair and in a talk with his mistress pretended to have been condoning it, but when the mistress now hugs the marquis, Christine grabs the hand of another man and takes off with him, the marquis vainly calling after her and we, from our different perspective, feeling as bemused as he by her hasty departure. Cut to a frontal view of the audience from the stage, pan to the woman playing the piano, and then, in the background of the shot, we see Christine and the other man, a guest named St. Aubin, swiftly entering frame and as swiftly leaving it. We expect a closer view of them, a clearer picture of this important turn in the plot, but Renoir allows this to happen at the edges of our view, giving us the feeling that we could easily have missed it.

Another act is a danse macabre, a skeleton masquerade in which the performers invade the audience and points of light move about the darkened room. In the intermittently illuminated darkness we see the gamekeeper, Schumacher, looking for his wife, Christine's maid Lisette, whom we have just seen kissing Marceau, a flirtatious servant who has been pursuing her. Like an interested bystander the camera spots Schumacher at a doorway and starts following him in his search, picking him up at another doorway after he goes behind a wall, but at the next wall blocking him from view the camera movement comes upon Christine and St. Aubin on a couch, a couple not seen since they left the stage together and now found on the track of another couple. The camera pauses on them but continues moving and picks up Schumacher at yet another doorway, where he finds Lisette and Marceau. After pausing on this triangle the camera continues a little farther and comes upon André Jurieu, the pilot who flew the Atlantic for love of Christine and cares not at all about Schumacher and Lisette and Marceau but, configuring another triangle, directs an angry gaze at Christine and the man she's with. Having come to a halt at the corner where Jurieu stands, the camera now turns back in the direction of his gaze, and this reverse movement, pausing on Marceau as he sneaks away and Schumacher as he keeps Lisette from following, continues to Christine and St. Aubin as they get up from their couch and, glancing back at Jurieu, walk out of the room.

As in the scene showing the boy climbing the coconut tree in *Moana*, the way the camera here moves and pauses and keeps moving is something we register as a gesture of looking, a distinctive way of directing our seeing. We sense a mediating gaze between us and the scene, and the arrangement this makes on the screen is a narrative sequence. Our awareness of what is not on the screen is in Renoir as in Flaherty central to our response: the boy who disappears at the top of the screen and points to the unseen rest of the tree, the characters who enter and leave our view in Renoir's shot and give us the feeling of catching only glimpses of the action. But the stance of the mediating gaze, the style of the visual narration, is different in each case. Whereas in Flaherty we sense an observer who knows how tall the tree is and wants to surprise us, in Renoir we sense an observer who is himself surprised to find Christine and St. Aubin sitting there along the way to Lisette and Marceau, surprised to find an angry Jurieu standing there in the corner. Of course Renoir staged the scene and knew what he would find there, but the observer we sense in the scene is not Renoir himself—neither the actual nor the implied author—but the visual narrator he has chosen in his telling of the story, his narrative sequence.

Two actions—two love triangles—are going on at once in Renoir's shot. A parallel is being made between the two—between Schumacher and Jurieu as jealous men, between Lisette and Christine as amorous women, the love play among the servants and the love play among the masters—and this parallel could have been made by parallel editing. But cutting between Schumacher and Jurieu, between Lisette and Christine, would have pressed the parallel more than Renoir wants to. It is not, as his admirers often say, that he lets us make out the parallel for ourselves: this is a parallel he makes, not one we make out. But he makes it through a visual narrator who seems to be making it out, to be discovering it by happenstance. And so Schumacher and

The Rules of the Game.
Three frames from the
same long take:
Schumacher looking
for his wife, finding
her with Marceau, the
camera moving on to
André Jurieu.

Jurieu, Lisette and Christine, are not simply similar in this juncture but surprisingly similar. Lisette we had known to be coquettish, but not Christine. If we had been asked to compare Schumacher to another character, surely it wouldn't have been Jurieu but the marquis, another husband with a straying wife; and if we had been asked to compare Jurieu to another character, surely it wouldn't have been Schumacher but Marceau, another pursuer of someone else's wife. Renoir's way of making the parallel brings all these complexities into play. And it is by the play of such complexities that Schumacher, even though he hardly interacts with Jurieu throughout the film, ends up shooting him dead.

Whether by parallel editing or in some other way, most directors would have broken down into several shots this scene Renoir shows in a long uninterrupted take. Most directors would have shown us one thing at a time: Schumacher going after Lisette and Marceau would have been one thing to focus on, and once we'd taken that in, Christine and St. Aubin and Jurieu would have been another. We would have known that both things were occurring simultaneously, but we would have focused on one thing at a time and for the time being kept the other in abeyance. Renoir wants us to keep both things fully in mind at the same time, to be aware of what we're not seeing, not as something we don't need to see for now, but as a piece of the world missing from our view and quite as important as what we happen to be seeing. Going after Lisette and Marceau, Schumacher leads us to Christine and St. Aubin, but while we watch these two we remain fully aware of him, just as we remain fully aware of them while we watch him and his wife and her seducer. As one love triangle comes into view the other leaves: that we cannot see both at once is a limitation of our vision, but as Renoir presents them, both at once make equal claim on our interest.[20]

In *The Rules of the Game* the action is complicated, and in the extended sequence of the party at the chateau it reaches its culmination, with masters and servants chasing back and forth, lovers coupling and uncoupling, things going on all over the place and intruding on one another: too much, we feel, for the camera to cover it all. But more than the complications and impingements of the action, it is the posture of Renoir's camera, the way it looks at the world, that gives us the feeling of a partial view. Consider a scene in his earlier *Boudu Saved from Drowning* (1932) where the action is simple: the tramp Boudu, having lost his dog, walks morosely along a street by the Seine. Even here Renoir shows this in such a way—from a distance across the busy street, our view of Boudu obscured by the traffic coming between, the camera panning with him but not keeping pace with his movement and eventually allowing him to leave frame—that we register the incompleteness of what we see.

At the time people thought that, compared with a director like Duvivier, Renoir was technically rather clumsy: the camera, they believed, ought to keep up with the action. Dramatic film technique aims for a perfect fit between action and picture, between what is happening in the scene—the exchange of recollected metro stations in *Pépé le Moko*—and the views rendering it on the screen. But in a Renoir film, as in a narrative, the world is larger than any rendering can cover. There is always more to tell that a narrative leaves untold, and with Renoir we feel there is always more to see: the camera can only keep up with so much of the action and must leave the rest out of view. A shot doesn't show just the right thing because there is no right thing, only someone's choice of what to show; a cut isn't made at just the right time because there is no right time, only someone's choice of when to cut; we don't get a perfect fit between action and picture because no action is the right one to picture. Like a man telling a story, Renoir gives us a sequence that is his arrangement, his account of the world; Duvivier, like a dramatist, gives us a sequence that is there, set apart from the rest of the world and closed off from it.

There has been much talk about "narrative closure," and some theorists have even attempted to define narrative in terms of closure. But if closure is an issue for narrative, it is precisely because narrative is an additive thing that can go on and on without closure. Closure is something a narra-

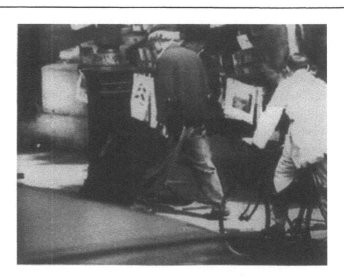

Boudu Saved from Drowning. Boudu across the street.

tive has to work for. A painting or a play has closure from the start: the space of representation, the canvas or the stage, is an enclosed space. The painting or the play may make a mess of it and end up without closure, but it starts with it. A narrative starts without it and it may strive toward it, but it can never gain the kind of completeness and containment that a painting or a play can have. Aristotle thought tragedy a higher form than epic because it was more of a piece.

Narrative is an open-ended arrangement, without the unity of a thing whole or an action complete. One way it aspires to unity is by focusing on one hero. But unity of the hero, as Aristotle warned, does not in itself make for unity of the work: "Infinitely various are the incidents in one man's life which cannot be reduced to unity." In narrative as in drama, Aristotle prescribed, the plot should imitate one action, not one person. Narrative ought "to be constructed on dramatic principles. It should have for its subject a single action, whole and complete, with a beginning, a middle, and an end. It will thus resemble a living organism in all its unity, and produce the pleasure proper to it."[21]

Henry James agreed that narrative should be constructed on dramatic principles, but rather than the unity of a single action, he sought for narrative the unity of a single consciousness. The unity proper to narrative was for James not the unity of what happened but the unity of the perception, the consciousness of what happened, the point of view from which it is recounted. If narrative is a messenger that brings tidings, let its unity and cohesion reside not in the tidings but in the messenger that brings them. If telling is always partial, let its partiality be part of the tale, let it be dramatized as the viewpoint of a participant. A narrative cannot be complete, James recognized, but it can be satisfyingly contained and made cohesive, he prescribed, by dramatizing its incompleteness, imputing it to the perspective of a character in the story. In his own work James managed a kind of dramatic unity by bringing the narrative point of view inside the action, presenting the story through the perceptions of a character in it, so that the account itself becomes part of the story, the way one character saw things. The plot imitates neither one hero nor one action but one consciousness. We are confined, in James, to a kind of stage, what one participant in a given situation was in a position to tell.

Imagine the shot of Boudu walking by the river preceded, or followed, by a shot of another character who is across the street looking on at the tramp from the same position as the camera. That would lead us to take our distant and unclear view of Boudu as just what that other character can see of him, to attribute the incompleteness of what is shown, the account given of the action, to the point of view of a participant. That would have the effect of dramatizing Renoir's shot, making its partial view of the scene itself part of the scene, turning his choice of what to show into the fact that a character saw it. The shot would become what is called a "point-of-view shot," a device rarely used by Renoir but of course a staple of dramatic film technique.

Actually the shot of Boudu walking (a panning shot taken with a telephoto lens) is followed by a shot of the maid dusting a telescope (as if to acknowledge that we have just seen Boudu through the lens of a telescope) in the apartment of a bourgeois bookseller. The bookseller comes into the room and starts looking out the window through the telescope, and now we get point-of-view shots from his perspective—the only point-of-view shots in the film. Through the telescope he espies Boudu—beautiful, he says, a perfect tramp—but when he sees the tramp jumping into the river he drops the telescope and rushes to the rescue. A crucial moment in the story, the attempted suicide of the main character, has been presented in a daringly partial way that makes us aware of the limitation in our view of Boudu and leaves obscure his motive for wanting to take his own life. And that limitation is not imputed to the point of view of the bourgeois bookseller: we feel it first in our telephoto perspective, and then we share it with him as he looks through his telescope. This is not his individual point of view but that of the class he belongs to; we feel the limitation not of an individual's perspective but of a class outlook. Boudu remains opaque throughout the film, opaque in our eyes as in the eyes of the bourgeoisie. The narrative point of view in *Boudu Saved from Drowning*, the limitation in our view of things, is not one character's perspective on the story but the way a whole social class sees the world.

Here as elsewhere Renoir tells a social story. His standpoint as the implied author is critical of the bourgeois, but his film adopts the narrative point of view, a socialized rather than individualized point of view, of the class under criticism. He tells the story of a disruptive individual, a tramp who will not fit into the bourgeois order of things, through the collective eyes of the bourgeoisie. A work of art expressing the outlook of a class is nothing unusual, but the class outlook expressed here is not an ideology we are to accept but a limitation we are to recognize. A more dramatic representation of the story—as in the play on which the film was based—would not have made us so aware of the slant of a point of view and the challenge to that slant in the person of Boudu.

A point-of-view shot, something a character sees, may be compared to a line of dialogue, something a character says. But it's a mistake to suppose that a character "enunciates" a point-of-view shot the way he or she enunci-ates a line of dialogue. A line of dialogue is something the character chooses to say, but having the camera assume a character's perspective at a certain moment is not something the character chooses. The character has no say in a point-of-view shot. A line of dialogue gives the character a voice in the proceedings; dialogue imitates the character's speech, the way someone talks, the words this particular person uses to express his or her thoughts and feelings. But a point-of-view shot merely imitates the perspective of a point in space: anybody else standing at that point would see the same thing.

The camera is an observer conventionally empowered to go everywhere and gain access anywhere, to see all that needs to be seen and at each moment to pick out the thing that matters. But the camera's being em-powered does not mean that a character is empowered when the camera takes that character's place in a point-of-view shot. Laura Mulvey and other theorizers of the male gaze in films assume that the male hero is empowered by point-of-view shots taken from his perspective; but the Jimmy Stewart character in *Vertigo* (1958), to use an example Mulvey adduces, is being manipulated rather than empowered when he follows the Kim Novak char-acter around San Francisco, as are we when we share his perspective in Hitchcock's entrancing point-of-view shots. And such celebrated purveyors of the male action film as John Ford and Howard Hawks are sparing in their use of the point-of-view shot; if John Wayne is empowered in their films, it is not because we often see through his eyes. No doubt it is true that films in our patriarchal culture represent things from a point of view predominantly male, but this male point of view is not predominantly expressed through the point-of-view shot. It is not the gaze so much as the stance that is male.

The point-of-view shot is a dramatic rather than a narrative technique. Although it may assist in establishing a narrative point of view—as in the first half of *Vertigo*, where the Jimmy Stewart character leads us through the narrative as its Jamesian center of consciousness—usually it is just part of the dramatic scene, like the dialogue. A point-of-view shot gives us merely a glimpse, a bit of someone's consciousness we share for a moment; a narrative point of view gives us our compass in the world of the story. For establishing the narrative point of view of a character, a center of consciousness deter-mining our perspective and perceptions, the point-of-view shot is neither sufficient nor necessary.

Using few point-of-view shots, *Letter from an Unknown Woman* (1948) nonetheless brings us into the point of view of its protagonist, Lisa Berndle (Joan Fontaine), the unknown woman whose deathbed letter to the man she loved all her life we hear on the soundtrack in her voice-over narration. The scarcity of point-of-view shots in Ophuls's film leads some to conclude that the images are not in the first person as the narration is and that they do not represent Lisa's consciousness as the narration does. Images have no grammatical person, and it's only loosely, figuratively, that one can speak of first-person images. But even loosely it cannot be said that point-of-view shots are in the first person: they show what a character sees but they do not issue from the character and are not intended by the character. A point-of-view shot can in no way be construed as the character's own statement. The images in *Letter from an Unknown Woman* may not be what one would call first-person images, but not because they are seldom point-of-view shots. And no matter what the person, they express the consciousness of the character; even if they are not Lisa's own statement, they are confined to her horizon and aligned with her standpoint. Henry James believed in telling a story through a character's consciousness but he was wary of telling it in the character's first person. *The Age of Innocence* (1993), Martin Scorsese's film version of the Edith Wharton novel, establishes the central consciousness of its protagonist, the narrative point of view of Newland Archer, even while using voice-over narration in the third person.

At one memorable moment in *Letter from an Unknown Woman* the camera may seem to stand back from Lisa's consciousness and to view the scene from a perspective incongruous with her own. On the one night Lisa spends with the man she loves, a handsome, philandering pianist (Louis Jourdan), when the two arrive at his place after a romantic evening together and go up the curving stairway to his apartment, the camera takes a position farther up the stairs and through the sinuous railing observes them from a steep high angle; losing them from view at the bottom of the frame, it pans a little to the right and picks them up again as they reach the landing. That arriving couple going up the stairs, that steep high angle and that bit of panning to the right strikingly repeat an earlier scene in which the adolescent Lisa, already irrevocably infatuated with the pianist, stood at that very spot on the stairway years before and covertly watched him arrive with another woman, one of the many he has taken on that amorous path to his apartment. In the earlier scene the camera viewed the arriving couple from a position behind Lisa; now the position and movement of the camera are just the same as before but Lisa, rather than watching from above, is down there in the place of the other woman. Earlier the camera's point of view was aligned with hers, and now it seems at odds with hers. Now Lisa herself, on that same amorous path with the pianist, is viewed in precisely the same way as that other unknown woman of years ago—which implies that, on her one night of love with the man she loves, Lisa is merely one more of the many, that this night so special to her is actually nothing special. Surely this is not the way Lisa views herself in the scene.[22]

And yet it is a point of view associated with her, with her point of view in the earlier scene. In the earlier scene the camera looked with her, not through her eyes in a point-of-view shot but from a position behind her, alongside her. The voice we hear in the voice-over narration is the voice of the older Lisa, the retrospective voice of the woman writing the letter, and the perspective alongside the adolescent Lisa suggests the point of view of the

Letter from an Unknown Woman. The adolescent Lisa watching the pianist arrive with another woman, Lisa herself in the other woman's place arriving with the pianist years later.

older woman looking back on her younger self. Point-of-view shots tend to be in the present tense, in the here and now of what the character is seeing: hence their scarcity in this film told in a retrospective narrative mode. If in the earlier scene the point of view was that of the retrospective Lisa, the point of view in the later scene, not just the physical but the narrative point of view, is the same. The difference is that now there is a greater discrepancy between the perspective of the Lisa we see in the scene and that of the retrospective Lisa, the perspective the camera assumes. This may not be the way Lisa views herself in the scene, but it is the way the Lisa writing the letter would look back on herself and her experience on that enchanted evening. She would recognize that she was but one more of the pianist's many women and at the same time she would hold on to the memory of that evening as something enchanted nonetheless. The adolescent girl who watched the pianist arrive with another woman dreamed of being in that other woman's place, and now the dream has come true. The older woman looking back knows full well that it was but a dream and yet cherishes it as the dream that gave meaning to her life. It is the narrative point of view Ophuls adopts, not only in the voice-over narration but in the images, that allows him to present this moment as something at once wonderful and paltry, everything and nothing. A woman prone to romantic fantasies, Lisa is a character some think incapable of such complexity of consciousness. But Lisa is a romantic of the same kind Ophuls is, a romantic quite aware of the illusion that sustains her, a romantic of the truest kind.[23]

Diegesis through mimesis of an individual consciousness, the Jamesian method of narration by imitation of a character's point of view, has been a preferred narrative method in film as in prose fiction. Film is both a dramatic and a narrative medium, and the Jamesian center of consciousness enables film to marry drama and narrative by dramatizing the narrative point of view. *The Thirty-nine Steps* (1935) is a classic example, the first of Hitchcock's films to set up its central character as its central consciousness, our hero as also our point of view. Carl Dreyer's *Vampyr* (1932) does something more unusual, setting up as central consciousness a character marginal to the story and in no position to follow it well, a protagonist who is mostly an observer, and a baffled observer at that. That other observer, the camera, follows this protagonist around the mysterious territory he explores, itself in no better position to follow the story. The path of Dreyer's camera, the narrative path we follow, is not quite the same as the protagonist's path but weaves in and out of it, departing far enough from his perspective to assert the camera's own but not so far as to break with his point of view. We

become aware of the camera as another consciousness in the same predicament as the protagonist, a predicament we recognize as not peculiar to him
but one each of us faces at the edge of that "undiscover'd country from
whose bourn no traveller returns." *Vampyr* is a narrative about death whose
point of view can only be unknowing.

In the main cinema is drama, drama shading into narrative and at
times punctuated with passages of narrative, and when it is not drama it is
usually dramatized narrative with a character as central consciousness. But
there is a narrative cinema that is not centered on a character. There is epic
cinema, for example, epic not in the sense of cast of thousands—which as a
rule means neither narrative nor drama but sheer spectacle—but in the sense
of telling national stories that everyone knows and that the narrator, speaking for everyone, relates from a stance of sure knowledge. It is this storytelling stance, not the stance of the dramatic camera, which may have access
everywhere but merely furthers the plot, that alone deserves the name "omniscient narrator." Such a godlike stance cannot be willed; the epic narrator
can assume it only because the public already knows what happened, only
because the people vest the storyteller with the authority to tell their story.
The American John Ford,[24] the Japanese Kenji Mizoguchi, and the African
Ousmane Sembène are among the few filmmakers who have assumed with
conviction such a stance of godlike omniscience.

Mizoguchi's *Sansho the Bailiff* (1954) begins with flashbacks. A boy,
Zushio, asks his mother about his father and, as the boy runs in the sunlit
woods, a dissolve to the boy running when he was younger takes us into the
past. The flashback ends with a camera movement that, in a storyteller's
gesture, settles on the mother and, as she turns her head, leads to a dissolve
bringing us back to the mother in the present. We have gone into the past by
way of the son and returned by way of the mother, and in a second flashback
we go by way of the mother and return by way of the son. No other flashbacks in film are framed in this shared manner: this is a memory that does
not belong to an individual but to the mother and son together and beyond
them to the public that knows their story.

Zushio and his sister are separated from their mother, and all are sold
into slavery. Years pass; the children have grown up as slaves. With his sister's
help—and, unknown to him, at the cost of her life—Zushio succeeds in
escaping from their enslavement under the bailiff Sansho. Seeking to redress
the wrongs that have been perpetrated, Zushio heads for Kyoto hoping to see
the prime minister. The camera is at the top of a hill and, imperturbable, it
holds a distant long shot as it watches the fugitive coming into view. Then, in

another storyteller's gesture characteristic of Mizoguchi, as Zushio starts walking down the slope of the hill the camera starts to move, not down the hill with him but upward, in an ascending movement delicately calculated to keep him in view right at the edge of the slope as he moves down it. The camera remains detached; it does not follow the character's movement but moves up as he moves down and watches him from above at a great distance. And yet it watches him, it purposely changes its position so that it can keep watching him; it moves in response to his movement, like the eye of a god imperturbable yet caring, a god whose superior vantage is nonetheless attentive to this frail tiny figure of suffering humanity.[25]

Hitchcock's *Shadow of a Doubt* (1943) begins with a suspicious character, Charles, lying in bed in a rooming house, a cigar in his hand and money dumped carelessly on his bedside table and on the floor beside him. Two men have come asking for him; he rises and pulls up the shade and from his upstairs window sees them down in the street, the camera taking his point of view on them as he mutters to himself, "What do you know? You're bluffing. You've nothing on me." Deciding to call their bluff, he goes down to the front door, and from his perspective we get another point-of-view shot of the two men standing at a corner, and then another point-of-view shot from a bit closer and then another, this last one a moving point-of-view shot as he moves toward them. But now, as he walks right past them, the point of view switches and we stay with the two men as Charles turns the corner and recedes into the background; they start following him and we stay in place as they recede. Cut to an overhead long shot of a stretch of urban wasteland where we see the tiny figures of the man pursued and his two pursuers. Cut to another godlike perspective on another barren stretch, but now the two pursuers have lost their quarry and the man pursued is nowhere to be seen until, in a stunning narrative move, the camera pans to Charles puffing on his cigar and watching them from high above.[26] The godlike perspective is revealed to be the point of view of the devil.

Here Hitchcock shows his narrative hand less in the point of view he adopts at any given moment—the point-of-view shots through Charles's eyes, the overhead perspectives on the chase—than in his shifts in point of view, and especially in the shift back to Charles when we least expect it. Charles here is not exactly the central consciousness but something more like the central mystery. The overhead perspectives suggest a godlike view, the high angle of knowledge, but there is much here that we don't know: this high angle is not omniscient. Pursued by the law, Charles runs away to paradise, to the idyllic small town where his sister and his niece Charlie and their family live—though paradise from the point of view of the devil looks rather comical and confining. When Charlie finds something in a paper at the local library that, together with a ring he has given her, incriminates her uncle Charles, the camera, in another striking narrative move, rises from a close-up of the ring to an extreme overhead long shot, the high angle of knowledge. *Shadow of a Doubt* may be taken as a story of the Garden of Eden, a kind of allegory in which the godlike high angle functions as the tree of knowledge. Biting into the fruit of that tree does not so much bring knowledge as bring on the loss of innocence, the recognition of what there is to know and what it means to know it, and so this high angle is not omniscient but expresses the position of knowledge, knowledge of good and evil associated with the devil. To rise to this high angle is to fall from grace; Charles is the fallen angel who assumes a godlike posture. Hitchcock's knowing camera cannot identify itself with god but only with the devil.

Neither omniscient like god nor knowing like the devil, Renoir's camera takes a human point of view. But it does not take an individual's point of view. To be human is to have limited knowledge, but not, with Renoir, knowledge limited to an individual consciousness. If his is not an epic camera that tells stories everybody knows, neither is it a Jamesian camera that limits itself to what one character knows. Renoir's style of narrative is singular in that it stays with no one character but ranges everywhere, and yet everywhere it makes us feel the limitation of our view. The point of view is multiple but the view is partial nonetheless.

If Henry James was a novelist who sought to dramatize, Bertolt Brecht was a dramatist who sought to narrate. Consider the scene in *The Caucasian Chalk Circle* in which Grusha, hesitant about rescuing the abandoned baby, is drawn to it, goes over and stays with it through the night, until in the morning she picks up the baby and takes it with her. Brecht has this played in pantomime, with a singer alongside telling about it in the words of a song, which refer to Grusha in the third person and to what is happening in the past tense: "As if it was stolen goods she picked it up. / As if she was a thief she crept away." Here the song is plainly a narrative, but it is also a performance by the singer, a kind of representation of the action; juxtaposed with the other representation, the performance in pantomime by the actress who plays Grusha, it has the effect of turning that too into a kind of narrative, an alternative account of the same action. The action, what happens in the scene, is not to be identified with either way of playing it on the stage, the song or the pantomime, two different versions calling each other into question, throwing open in our minds the possibility of other ways in which that action could have been played. We are, by an "alienation effect," distanced from the played scene, as the played scene is distanced, made distinct, from what happens in the scene being played. We are prevented, in Brecht, from taking the enactment for the action: the action is not performed, no longer there on the stage, but referred to by the performance. The convention of performance, the convention that the stage is to stand for the world, is undone by the alienation effect, and the stage made to refer to the world, turned into a medium of narrative.

Brecht's alienation effect is often construed as merely a counter to realism in the theater, a way of discarding the familiar room with a missing fourth wall, the convention that the stage is to present before us a duplicate piece of the real world—certainly not what Aristotle had in mind but what many think mimesis is. To be sure, Brecht was against the illusion of reality on the stage, but more generally he was against, in whatever mode of performance, the self-sufficiency of the stage as a substitute reality. This amounts to, as he insisted himself, a rejection of dramatic form, not just of realistic methods but of the dramatic principles Aristotle set down in the *Poetics*, the very convention that the stage is to present before us a played action whole and complete.

A model Brecht proposed for his "epic theater"—and by *epic* he meant a narrative as opposed to a dramatic theater—is a street scene where an eyewitness to a traffic accident demonstrates to others how it happened, acting out what he can to give a picture. No one watching his demonstration will take it for the action—not for the accident itself, of course, but not for an acceptable substitute either, a complete picture. Clearly we have here a narrative situation, an account given of what happened by acting it out: a model for a theater where the playing functions as a means of reporting the action rather than presenting it. What makes the street scene function as narrative is not anything it contains, not any particular way it is performed, but the spectator's awareness of what it is not—that it is not the accident, that it is only a partial enactment of it, that another eyewitness to the same event would give a different enactment. The sense of incompleteness, of what is not being played, that the spectator has in the street scene, Brecht sought to induce in the theater: a sense of the play not as a presented whole but as a series of fragments, a narrative sequence, someone's choice of what to play to give an account of the action. Brecht's practice of staging with vivid concreteness some things in a scene while other things are markedly left out; his use of interruption and incongruity to break the consistency of a presentation; the discontinuous construction of his plays, the gaps left open between scenes that are discrete, "each for itself" rather than each leading to the next—all these are ways of calling attention to what is not on the stage, making us notice where the playing comes short of a full portrayal and leaves room for an alternative. The alienation effect is not a style of performance but the negation of the performance by making the spectator aware of what it is not.

The song alongside the pantomime of Grusha and the baby is like a voice-over narration accompanying a silent scene. In order to have that narration Brecht had to turn off the sound and have the scene played silent; if Grusha had spoken, the scene would have been more dramatic, more present on the stage, and less amenable to the narrative past tense of the words being sung. Aristotle was right: what drama makes present on the stage is primarily the speech of human beings. The visual scene, however vividly presented, will always tolerate the pastness of a narration; but the moment a character speaks, the action comes to life before us. Brecht's characters speak, of course—speak words given them by a great poet of the theater—and the action their speech brings to life must be pushed away from us, by interruption and incongruity and various other methods of theatrical alienation, so that we may respond to it as a kind of played narrative.

Crosscutting, the close-up, the arsenal of film techniques Griffith and others developed in the silent era, served mainly to dramatize the visual scene, and at times make it present on the screen with such intensity that no narration could tolerably accompany it. But even after all these techniques were introduced, many silent films remained, for long stretches, mere illustrations, like animated picture books, to the narrative provided between the images by the written intertitles. Sound is often said to have brought greater realism to film. In an elementary sense this is true: sound is a part of reality that sound films are able to imitate. But whether they imitate it realistically is quite another matter. What sound brought to film, sound synchronized with the images, was not necessarily greater realism but greater dramatic presence. Most film images will admit voice-over narration—maybe not for the better, but they will admit it—except those images in which the human voice is seen to issue from the human body and heard to utter what a character has to say, those images making present on the screen the speech of human beings.

Like the surface of a painting, the stage is an area traditionally set apart from the world we inhabit. It is, by convention, set apart as an area of performance, which for the play's duration the audience is to take not as a piece of this world but as a realm of its own, separate and self-contained, a space of representation closed off from the surrounding space of reality. The equivalent in film to this convention of performance is the convention of the shot. That was what Griffith's technical innovations basically amounted to: the convention by which we grant the filmmaker license to frame on the screen just a part of things, not the whole area where things may be happening but a certain part where things are happening now. Big or small, here or there, whatever or wherever it may be, this is designated as the significant part, the part that need now concern us. If the stage is marked out as the area where from beginning to end the dramatic action is played, the shot marks out the area where the dramatic action is being played at the moment: though the area is variable from moment to moment rather than set for the duration, moment by moment the shot sets the stage. In a film we are to take the area framed in each shot, the particular piece of things we see represented on the screen, as the piece that matters for now, to the exclusion of everything else. The screen then becomes, like the stage, a space of representation closed off from the rest of the world. Since Aristotle, it has been a prevalent view that all art is otherworldly in that way, marking off a territory of its own, setting up its medium of imitation as an ideal realm parallel to reality where the work of art can come into being as a self-sufficient whole.

Brecht was a materialist who did away with the stage as an ideal realm. Not that, like Artaud and other challengers of theatrical convention, he sought to break down the boundaries between the stage and the audience; on the contrary, he wanted those boundaries clearly drawn so that the spectator could sit back and watch the performance with detachment. He made the demarcations clear: the spectator is not where the actor is and the actor is not where the character is; the spectator is not to become identified with the actor and the actor is not to become identified with the character. Brecht brought the stage back into the realm of our reality not by blurring its boundaries but by making plain the work of representation. The negation of the performance by the alienation effect is a dialectical negation of a negation: an undoing of the convention that we are to shut out of our minds, while the performance goes on, all reality outside the stage. That piece of the world set apart from it to produce drama is reinstated in it to produce narrative: brought back into this world, Brecht's stage is back as a narrative space.

There are those who believe that a materialist approach to film must so insist on the material implements of the medium—the camera, the film, the projector, the screen—as to renounce both drama and narrative, to renounce all representation as mere illusion. Its exponents may claim otherwise, but this sort of materialism has little to do with the historical materialism of the Marxist tradition; its products may be quite interesting, but even more than the ordinary movie they set up their medium—no longer of imitation—as a self-sufficient realm of its own, closed off from the rest of the world. Materialists of this sort tend to think of Renoir as a "realist," meaning a fosterer of the illusion of reality on the screen, no different in their book from the ordinary movie illusionist. Renoir was indeed a realist—as by his own account was Brecht, though not a realist in the line of Ibsen and Chekhov or in the party line of "socialist realism"—and if an illusionist is one who uses the medium to represent reality, then Renoir and Brecht were both illusionists and the ordinary movie should rather be called fantasist.[27] André Bazin was the first to recognize form and style in Renoir's practice, form and style rather than faltering technique offset by humane sentiments, but Bazin confused the issue somewhat by seeing Renoir's distinctive treatment of space in his films as an intrinsic attribute of the medium, the open space of film as opposed to the closed space of theater.[28] What Renoir was doing was challenging the space of film as it had in the main been constructed, challenging the convention of the shot as Brecht challenged the convention of performance.

For Bazin the space of theater was artificial, conventional, and the space of film was the same as the space of real life. Just as in real life we focus on something while the rest of the world lies unseen, so in a film the camera focuses on something while the rest of the world lies implied in the space off screen. Bazin wasn't the simpleminded realist some imagine: he didn't say that film is the same as real life, only that its space is the same as that of real life. But even so he was mistaken. The space of film is as artificial, as conventional, as the space of theater. If it seems more real to us, it is only because we find its artifice more familiar, its conventions easier to accept. Film imitates the way that in real life we focus on something always in the context of something larger, but in a film both what we focus on at each moment and the larger context of our attention, both what we see on the screen and what we take to be there in the space off screen, are arranged for us, a fiction arranged for us and asking us to go along with it.

It is a convention—as much a convention as anything in the theater—to show us this and not show us that, to have us agree we should be looking at what is being shown and not looking at what is being left out while keeping in mind what is being left out as a context for what is being shown. We are to go along with having our perception confined, while each shot is on the screen, to just so much of the world as the shot brings into view; we are to grant the existence of the rest, lying out of view in the space off screen, and consent to our not seeing what we grant to be there. The convention asking us to accept the existence of that unseen larger context asks us at the same time to accept its omission from view; as we agree that it is there we also agree we don't need to see it. All that lies in the space off screen is to be relegated to a background, an implied background to the action on screen, not very different in function from a stage backdrop except that it will change from one moment to the next. Like the convention of performance, this convention of the shot is a negation of the world outside a space of representation; like the scenes in a play, the succession of shots in a film can present an action whole and complete.

Jean Renoir was Brecht's friend and one of the intended members (Eisenstein was another) of the Diderot Society, the group of artists working in theater and film toward a "newer, anti-metaphysical and social art" that Brecht wanted to bring together under the name of the materialist philosopher.[29] Usually Renoir is described as warm and accepting, Brecht as cool and critical. One may want to describe them otherwise, one may want to point out the compassion in *Mother Courage* and the detachment in *Rules of the Game,* but one cannot dispute that Brecht and Renoir are artists of quite different temperaments. Yet they have in common the undoing of that ideal space where everything significant is supposed to be presented; both insist that we pay attention to what we are not being shown, both bring about a negation of that negation of the surrounding space of reality.

If Griffith, more than anyone else in his time, worked to establish the convention of the shot, more than anyone else in his time Renoir worked to disestablish it. The convention of the shot sets up a hierarchy of attention, asking us to accept this as the thing we should now attend to and take the rest as something less important. Renoir's use of deep focus, making the background as important as the foreground, denies the usual hierarchy of foreground and background within the image. Making what is left out of view as important as the image in view, Renoir's treatment of the space off screen— what Bazin called "lateral depth of field"—likewise denies the usual hierarchy of attention that privileges the space on screen and relegates the rest to an implied background off screen. Renoir denies his shots any of the special status the convention would grant them, any claim of their ideal adequacy to the things they depict for us, and reinstates them to their place in our world as fragments of a larger reality. Like Brecht's stage, Renoir's screen is undone as a dramatic space and brought back to our reality as a narrative space.[30]

Although the camera may go out into the space of reality, the screen, like the stage, is a space of fiction, whether dramatic or narrative fiction. But dramatic fiction sets itself apart from our reality in order to make its own reality present to us, whereas narrative fiction reports to us from the world we inhabit. The report may be a fiction and so may the reporter, but narrative sets up the fiction of reporting to us from a place in our world. The teller of a story does not stand apart from us like an actor on the stage; the story is told to us from the space where we stand. Here in this world no one's words can claim an ideal adequacy to the things they refer to: any account they give will leave a remainder of things untold. By our awareness of that remainder, what is left out of the account, where it comes short of Aristotle's norm of completion, we recognize the mediation characteristic of narrative, the presence of a teller between us and the tale. Unlike the accident reported in the street scene, what is represented on Brecht's stage or Renoir's screen is a fiction; but like the street scene, it is a representation that does not suspend itself from our reality but comes visibly from a place in it.

Drama is a social thing, something done in public, a performance before a public. Narrative since the rise of the novel has been mainly a private thing, something the writer writes alone and each of us readers reads alone. In this as in other respects, film lies between drama and narrative: going to the movies is something more private than the theater and more public than reading a novel. A film is shown in public, a performance for a public, but the performers are not exactly there before the public, we are not exactly in their company. Nor are we exactly alone: going to the movies is, or can be, a more social experience than those who carry on about the isolate spectator in the darkened auditorium usually allow. Certain spectators like their movie experience isolate, and others like it more communal—communal with the other spectators, however, not with the actors as in the theater.

Drama is a social thing, and behind the conventions of drama stand the conventions of society. We accept the rightness, the fittingness, the inevitability, of the played action on stage as we accept the rightness, the fittingness, the inevitability, of our social structures. It is not an individual's choice to have the story enacted this way: it is a social choice. If it seems to be the right thing rather than a matter of choice, it is because this is a choice socially sanctioned. Certainly drama can be critical of society, but its criticism can only come from within established social structures: drama rests on an acceptance of the assumptions its society makes about life—enough of an acceptance to hold an audience in their seats and secure their agreement to this stage that stands for the world, this played action and this way of playing it, this form of dramatic necessity.

The form of Jamesian narrative, its individual center of consciousness, is founded on communication from one individual to another, from the writer who writes alone to the reader who reads alone. Jamesian cinematic narrative, the camera's perspective confined to a character's, dramatized as an individual's point of view, likewise engages the viewer as an individual who sits alone in the darkened movie theater. Epic cinematic narrative descends from a mode of storytelling—and has given that mode renewed authority on the screen at a time when literature is no longer able to sustain it—in which stories are not what one individual tells another but what a people, "we" rather than "I," tell about their shared experience, their collective memory and imagination. Brecht's "epic theater" is not epic in that sense. It is a theater that denies drama's traditional acceptance of its society's assumptions and through that denial becomes a narrative theater: a kind of narrative in which the point of view is social rather than individual but socially subversive rather than socially cohesive in the epic manner. Renoir's cinematic narrative is of a similar kind.[31]

Renoir's narrative, like Brecht's, arises dialectically out of the undoing of drama, the negation of drama's negation of the world we inhabit. Drama is set up and subverted, drama with its conventions and constructions and behind them the conventions and constructions of society. Drama would normally ask us to accept these conventions and agree to these constructions, but as drama turns into narrative we recognize the incompleteness of its representations, the partiality of its assumptions. Drama turns into narrative because we cannot consent to the way things are, the way they have been set up, because we cannot go along with the rightness, the fittingness, the inevitability, of the prevailing order of things. If in Jamesian narrative we share the limitation of an individual's point of view, in Renoir's and in Brecht's kind of narrative we recognize the limitation of a social point of view. Usually society is not seen to have a point of view as an individual has: a point of view is merely one among other possibilities, while society is the proposed field of possibilities. The dialectic that makes drama into narrative makes us see the slant rather than the appropriateness of society's conventions and constructions, makes us see that they indeed constitute a point of view rather than just the way things are done, the way they must be.

A scene in *Cronaca di un amore* (1950), Michelangelo Antonioni's first feature film, has the two main characters, Paola and Guido—the wife of a Milanese industrialist and the man who had been before her marriage and is now again her lover—discussing in a hotel room what to do about her husband. We see them in a held mid-shot as Paola suggests that her husband could die and puts her hands around her lover's neck to simulate strangling; repelled by the idea of murder, Guido pushes her away from him, and as she moves toward the back wall the camera starts to move, not following her movement but in the opposite direction, away from the two of them until we see them in long shot. With this shot now held, Guido remains standing, mostly silent, while Paola paces toward the camera and back toward the wall, talking about the husband she dislikes and the money she doesn't want to give up. Before long, even though they are still undecided about what to do, the two lovers embrace and kiss, and at this point the camera again starts to move, again not toward them but in the opposite direction, further away from the kissing couple as the scene fades out.

Like Flaherty's camera showing us the boy and his climb up the coconut tree, like Renoir's camera following Schumacher as he looks for his wife during the danse macabre at the chateau, Antonioni's camera here frames and reframes our view, pauses and moves and pauses and moves again, in a way that makes us register, coming between us and the scene, its autonomous mediating gaze. Rather than a dramatic camera put at the service of the action being played, giving us what we are to take as the best view of the action, this is a narrative camera giving us what we take note of as its own view of the action. Its way of seeing, of rendering things on the screen, is in noticeable discrepancy with the things occurring before it. Its mediating presence in the scene is established by that discrepancy—a conflict, as Eisenstein would have called it—between action and picture, incident and image, between what is happening in the scene and what we are seeing on the screen.

In Flaherty's and in Renoir's scenes, we feel that what we are seeing is not enough: the discrepancy is primarily between the section of space being shown and the larger area claiming our interest. In Antonioni's scene it isn't primarily a matter of how much we are seeing of the world but of the position from which we are seeing it: the camera moves away from Paola and Guido not in order to show us more of the hotel room but so as to present the two lovers from a different perspective that modifies our response to their situation. The discrepancy we notice in Antonioni's scene is between action and point of view, between the drama being enacted in the scene and the perspective being adopted by the camera. We are pulled back from the characters at the very moments of emotional intensity, moments when we would have expected the camera to dramatize that intensity with a closer view: a close-up of Guido's face when he pushes Paola away, a camera movement following her toward the wall, an intimate two-shot when the two lovers make up and kiss—a view corresponding to what the characters are feeling. As in the words of a narrator, in the positioning of Antonioni's camera we recognize a point of view distinct from the action and able to give it a changed connotation. Rather than chiming in with the action as a dramatic camera would have, this camera not only keeps its distance, its moves run counter to the emotions acted out in the scene, holding back our involvement with the characters, inducing with regard to them, not the usual emotional identification, but a stance of critical detachment. This is an alienation effect, achieved by means different from Brecht's but still based, like many of his devices, on a deliberate incongruity, a camera positioning at odds with the action.

Unlike a sentence, unlike a painting, a photographic image always has a point of view—literally a point of view, for the camera is always positioned somewhere and the image it produces shows things as they appear from that particular point in space. But dramatic film technique makes the perspective of that point in space, the angle and distance from which we are viewing the scene, seem motivated by dramatic necessity: the convention of the shot asks us to accept that angle and distance as perfectly appropriate to the action, the best possible view of it at this point rather than a point of view among others equally possible. The point-of-view shot is a special case of the convention of the shot. It gives us the perspective of one character rather than another, but we are to take that as the perspective called for dramatically at this point, what best furthers the plot just as a character's line of dialogue is what best furthers the plot. For the camera's perspective to function as a narrative point of view we cannot just accept the appropriateness, we must register the particularity of that point in space. We must note how that angle and distance, the choice to show us one aspect of appearances rather than another, modifies our impression of things that would look different from a different perspective.

A kind of alienation effect is required, a dissociation of the camera from the things taking place before it so that it can assume a point of view distinct from the action, an independent position in the unfolding scene. This is the effect Antonioni achieves by lingering over an image, holding a view we might have just accepted until it begins to seem strange; by a mobile camera continually redirecting our attention, turning from one aspect to another along a course of its own; by suddenly cutting to a disorienting angle, a new perspective on things from which they appear unexpectedly different. Although Antonioni's portrayal of alienation in modern life has been much discussed, it has not been sufficiently noted that he treats it less as a subject of empathy than of critical scrutiny—that we are alienated from the alienated by the operation of his camera. In his study of Antonioni, Lorenzo Cuccu put forward the notion of *visione straniata,* "estranged vision," vision detached from the action, autonomous from the drama taking place in the scene, as opposed to *visione aderente,* "adherent vision," vision attached to the drama being enacted, bound up with its unfolding. Cuccu's *visione aderente* and *visione straniata* make a distinction rather similar to the distinction I have been making between dramatic and narrative camera technique.[32] *Visione straniata* is certainly a good term for the "alienation effect" of Antonioni's camera technique: the point of view of a stranger.

The dramatic camera knows exactly what to show us, knows the extent of what matters. The epic camera of Mizoguchi, the devil's camera Hitchcock employs, not only knows what to show us but makes palpable to us its stance of knowledge. The explorer's camera Flaherty employs has scouted the territory for us, has discovered what to show us. Renoir's camera is another kind of explorer, one who hasn't gone ahead of us into the territory and can't presume to know exactly what to show us. Antonioni's camera is like Renoir's in this respect, an inquiring rather than a knowing camera, though Renoir's camera takes the point of view of a friend rather than a stranger. Always in Antonioni we are made to sense what the photographer in *Blow-Up* (1966) is brought up against: the incompleteness of any view of appearances, the inconclusiveness of any perspective. We recognize a mediating point of view, in the position of a camera as in a narrator's words, by our awareness that other points of view could have been taken—that the account given leaves a remainder.

3 : The Bewildered Equilibrist

Amid the seeming confusion of our mysterious world,
individuals are so nicely adjusted to a system, and systems to
one another and to a whole, that, by stepping aside for a
moment, a man exposes himself to a fearful risk of losing his
place forever.

Nathaniel Hawthorne, "Wakefield"

Nothing in the strange world of Buster Keaton's comedy is stranger than the ending of *College* (1927). In that picture Buster plays a bookworm who strives to become a jock. The top student in his high-school class, and so averse to sports that he makes his graduation speech into a diatribe against athletics, he yet arrives at college the next fall with suitcases full not of books but of athletic equipment. With the dauntless determination characteristic of the Keaton hero, the little scholar involves himself in a pursuit for which he's quite unsuited but which is, under circumstances equally characteristic of Keaton, what's expected of him in his courtship of the girl he loves. Outraged like all his other classmates by his diatribe at graduation, she'll see no more of him, as she promptly informs him after the speech, unless he changes his attitude and takes up sports. And so he changes his attitude, neglecting all his studies at college and instead spending most of his time on the sports field. Although he seems inept beyond hope at the various athletic activities he doggedly tries out, he succeeds in winning her in the end, for he summons up unexpected abilities when she's in danger and he comes to the rescue, running much faster and jumping much farther than he ever could before, managing with no trouble now an obstacle race over the hedges in his path and a high pole-vault into the window of her room. With undiminished momentum, he quickly disposes of the villain, a brawny dolt who has been his rival for the girl's affections, and proceeds with her to church forthwith, not even pausing to change his athletic clothes before they are married. Then follows a very peculiar epilogue. No sooner are the newlyweds out of church than a dissolve transports us many years later to the middle-aged couple in their home, sitting among their several children; this in turn swiftly gives way to the couple in their advanced years, abidingly sitting at home beside each other; this in turn to the closing shot of their adjacent graves.

The element of sadness in Keaton's comedy has often been noted, and it certainly emerges in that brisk final depiction of aging and death. Coming on the heels of the triumphant happy ending, the sudden sadness of the epilogue takes us by surprise; but I don't think it constitutes such a break with the rest of the film as some believe. "What is this abrupt slap in the face doing at the end of an otherwise unquestioning love story?" wrote Walter Kerr in *The Silent Clowns*. "It takes no more than eleven seconds of playing time to deliver its chill, and yet it undoes on the spot all of the yearning, the struggle and the victory, of the narrative."[1] Evidently perturbed by the chill, Kerr misrepresents the epilogue as portraying a disappointed, even embittered couple, when nothing of the sort is suggested: all that we get is a brief summary of a long, uneventful marriage. It seems to me wrong, or only half-right, to view the epilogue as a brusque reversal of a hitherto romantic story. Although the hero is unquestioning in his devotion to the girl, the romanticism of the story has been tacitly called into question all along by the conveyed sense that the girl is as unreasonable in her peremptory demands as is the hero in his stubborn pursuit. If Keaton is a romantic, he's a singularly unsentimental one. Granted, we'd have expected the story to end with Buster's getting the girl, but the epilogue merely shows us that he gets to keep her:

Caricature of Buster Keaton by Gilberto Perez.

surely not the undoing but the exact fulfillment of his wishes. If the epilogue brings about a reversal of the happy ending, it does so by way of being a logical continuation of it, indeed a visual equivalent of those famous romantic last words: and they lived happily ever after.

Seeing the couple's whole life together go by on the screen in so short a time has, of course, none of the reassuring effect of those words. Yet even the disconcerting briskness of those final eleven seconds carries forward unbrokenly the haste of the climactic rescue and ensuing wedding, as if confirming Buster's aim to get things settled once and for all. *College* is not the only one of Keaton's films to conclude with the grave. In *Cops* (1922), a short film in which he's surreally chased by every cop in the city, "The End" appears inscribed on a tombstone capped with Buster's porkpie hat. The plot of *Cops*, however—unlike that of any of his full-length movies—has an unhappy outcome. Rejected by the girl he loves even after he manages to elude all the cops who have been after him, Buster suicidally puts himself back in their midst: an unusual ending for a comedy, to be sure, but not so strange as the way that in *College* the romance turns sad, in spite of its triumph, by being literally carried out to its conventional conclusion in the couple's staying together for the remainder of their lives.

"He has left the world without ever being quite in it," wrote Hugh Kenner on the occasion of Keaton's death in 1966. "Only saints and a few classic madmen have put forth a comparable power to suggest that this place where we all catch trains so deftly is yet not wholly the place for which we were made."[2] Unlike a saint or a madman, Buster proposes no defiance of the world's ways: on the contrary, he strives for a compliance with them. When in Rome, he goes to great lengths to do as the Romans do: to become an athlete if that is what the girl expects, to get married, have children, live happily ever after, if that is the prescribed happy ending. "As though dropped to this earth from some obscure cataclysm," wrote Kenner in his Keaton obituary (echoing Mallarmé's sonnet on the tomb of Edgar Poe), "he coped with this earth's systems as he could."[3] While on earth, he tried his best to do as earthlings do, and thereby made us aware of the peculiar systems by which we rule our lives.

Although not quite in the class of Keaton's very best—*Our Hospitality* (1923), *Sherlock Junior* (1924), *The Navigator* (1924), *The General* (1927), *Steamboat Bill, Jr.* (1928)—*College* seems to me a splendid film that has been generally underrated. It surpasses, I believe, Harold Lloyd's better-known college comedy, *The Freshman* (1925), which preceded it and no doubt influenced it. The hero of *The Freshman* is also an incompetent athlete who redeems himself in the end by performing unexpected feats, in his case by winning the decisive football game of the season. (Apparently to avoid too close a comparison with the Lloyd picture, football is one sport omitted from *College*.) In giving such prominence to athletics, however, both comedians were merely reflecting a fact of campus life—in which sports are often more important than studies—and making use of material naturally befitting the physical comedy of the silent screen. Their comic conceptions, in any case, are fundamentally different. For Lloyd, athletics are part of the image of the big man on campus his ambitious but unknowing hero wants to become, whereas Buster only wants the girl, a more realistic goal as well as a more romantic one. Lloyd's hero is a thoroughgoing incompetent, a classic fool, whereas Keaton's is only a fool for love, a bookworm out of his element on the sports field and quite aware of his problem. When, after knocking over every other hurdle along the racing track, he succeeds in clearing the last one, Buster, instead of deriving any satisfaction from that success, gravely appraises it as a fluke, and then tips over that last hurdle too, feeling that it might as well conform to the pattern of the others. Such disdain for flukes is inconceivable in the Lloyd hero, who'd get nowhere without them. Unlike Lloyd, Keaton never plays the kind of comic character who is preposterously deluded about himself and what's going on around him.

Buster usually has a good grasp of his situation, as good a grasp as one can expect from, as Kenner put it, "a visitor, not native."[4] He is a visitor to the sports field in *College* who knows that the odds are against him there but nonetheless keeps trying because he also knows that the girl won't have him any other way, because he is a compliant visitor desiring to participate in a situation in which a girl's ideal boyfriend must be a jock. The situation of being out of one's element recurs throughout Keaton's films. In *Steamboat Bill, Jr.* he plays a college student from Boston who seems to have done pretty well in that environment but whose father, a steamboat captain down South whom he goes to visit after a long separation, regards him as a sissy. Here again Buster finds himself having to cope with demands he hasn't encountered before. In *Steamboat Bill, Jr.* his predicament is compounded by the coincidental presence in the Southern river town of his girlfriend from Boston, whose notions of what he should be like run exactly counter to his father's. The overriding demands of a cyclone that sweeps the town are easier for Buster to meet than those of his father and his girl, and enable him to vindicate himself in their eyes by rescuing them both from drowning. Yet it takes those tempestuous circumstances for him to gain the approval they both denied him under normal conditions. Perhaps more vividly than in any other Keaton film, we get the sense in *Steamboat Bill, Jr.* that it's a difficult business to live up to what's expected of one.

As soon as he's done with the rescuing, Buster wordlessly dives back into the river, and for a moment both the father and the girl suppose, to their chagrin, that he wants no more to do with either of them. We are amused by their reaction, thinking that it would serve them right if he just got away. Although he promptly returns, bringing with him a clergyman in a life preserver to conduct a wedding on the spot, we've been led to question why he should stick by a girl and a father who've made such trouble for him. As in the ending of *College,* Buster here, in his eagerness to settle his triumph, entertains no second thoughts; but *we* do. And as in *College,* those final second thoughts only point up a question that has been implicit throughout what came before: why should Buster umprotestingly comply with the undue requirements laid upon him by others?

One answer is provided in *College* by the figure of a dean, friendly to the promising young scholar and built small like him, who may be regarded as an embodiment of what his scholarly future would be like. Disappointed that Buster has been doing poorly in his studies, the older man, when he hears the explanation, tearfully reveals that he himself loved a girl once but lost her to an athlete. Buster would rather take on the alien territory of sports than end up alone like the dean. If all comedians are outsiders, Keaton is the outsider who will not give up the attempt to join in, to connect with others. Chaplin's Tramp, by contrast, is more or less self-sufficient, "an aristocrat," as Robert Warshow put it, "fallen on hard times."[5] Lloyd's bespectacled democrat is a blundering free enterpriser, motivated by self-interest, patently inferior to his fellow men but aspiring to rise above them in the land of opportunity. Buster is unique in earnestly seeking a genuine togetherness. If he seems the loneliest of all comedians, it's because he's the one to whom companionship matters the most.

That loneliness is hauntingly conveyed in those distant long shots, typical of Keaton, in which he appears as a tiny figure amid large empty surroundings: in the river town during the storm, or practicing by himself in the college stadium, or—in *The Frozen North* (1922)—coming out of a subway exit into an arctic wilderness. In *The Navigator* he wakes up one morning to find himself adrift at sea on a deserted ocean liner, the epitome of the alien territories the solitary Buster is called upon to master. But he's not there all alone, as he supposes at first; the girl he wants to marry also finds herself aboard the ship. When each becomes aware of the other's presence some-where on board, the two anxiously try to come together, but they keep miss-ing each other in that huge ship. James Agee's description of this extraordi-nary sequence is worth quoting:

> First each walks purposefully down the long, vacant starboard deck, the girl, then Keaton, turning the corner just in time not to see each other. Next time around each of them is trotting briskly, very much in earnest; going at the same pace, they miss each other just the same. Next time around each of them is going like a bat out of hell. Again they miss. Then the camera withdraws to a point of vantage at the stern, leans its chin in its hand and just watches the whole intricate superstructure of the ship as the protagonists stroll, steal and scuttle from level to level, up, down and sidewise, always managing to miss each other by hair's-breadths, in an enchantingly neat and elaborate piece of timing.[6]

"Enchantingly neat," with the boy and girl seeming like pieces in some gigantic clockwork geared to prevent their meeting, this sequence is at the same time a disquieting expression of the need to come together somewhere, somehow, in a forbidding world.

Pretty soon, of course, the boy and girl find each other, or rather they are brought into each other's company by the same mysterious mechanism that kept them apart. Earlier the girl had flatly turned down Buster's pro-posal of marriage, so it's a lucky break for him, in a way, that they have been fortuitously brought together aboard the ship; but that is only the beginning of their relationship, and they still face the formidable task of coping on their own with a drifting ocean liner that certainly was not designed for two. The girl had turned him down because she thought him an ineffectual rich boy, and indeed, when he went to propose to her he had his chauffeur drive him to her house, directly across the street from his. Like the bookworm in *College,* the rich boy in *The Navigator* must prove himself in the unfamiliar arena of action, where, in the case of the deserted liner at sea, sheer survival is at stake. In *College* Buster is responding to the girl's demands, in *The Navigator* to the pressure of circumstances; under that pressure, however, as during the cyclone in *Steamboat Bill, Jr.,* he can measure up in the girl's eyes as earlier he could not. The girl in *The General,* like her counterpart in *The Navigator,* after having rejected Buster, joins him in his undertaking—though in both cases by necessity, not choice. And whether he is on his own or has the girl's help—and she's not much help in either case—he must still carry out that undertaking before the two can have a life together. Whether required of him by the girl or by circumstances or by a conflation of both, that is the test he must pass to secure the place he seeks in the world.

In *The General,* we are informed at the beginning that there are two loves in Buster's life: his girl and his locomotive. He is an engineer on a Southern railroad at the time of the Civil War, so useful to the South in that capacity that the Confederate army won't enlist him; but he's not told the reason, and his girl, who had urged him to be a soldier and now assumes him to be a coward, won't have him either. So he turns to his locomotive, not because, as has been maintained, he prefers it to the girl—he was first in line at the recruiting office after she suggested that he enlist—but as his only consolation. "Keaton's love for his cow, in one picture," wrote Hugh Kenner, "or for his locomotive, in another, was a love transferred from girls diminished to abstraction by inexplicable rituals of courtship, through which alone they are accessible. The locomotive's rituals he could master."[7] He stands to lose his locomotive too, however, when some Northern spies make off with it, and he rushes in pursuit, so intent on the task ahead that he doesn't notice that the Confederate soldiers who were to join him in the chase have been left behind. Once again Buster is on his own. This is, after all, a personal matter: his locomotive has been stolen, and his girl, though he doesn't know it yet, is being kidnapped along with it. What his preference may be between the girl and the machine seems to me a false issue, since the fates of the two are thoroughly bound up together. As in *The Navigator,* it is through his mastery of the machine's rituals that he manages to get the girl.

Buster Keaton in
The General.

His successful recapture of his locomotive accomplishes at the same time his regaining of his girl: not only does he rescue her from the enemy but he brings back information that leads to a Southern victory against a Northern offensive, and after participating in the battle with a borrowed uniform he is enlisted in the Confederate army as a lieutenant, thus ending up as the soldier she initially wanted him to be. Buster never fulfills the girl's expectations in the expected way—his uniform is usually a borrowed one, for he's a visitor, not native—but fulfill them he must, if he is to get her.

The Navigator and The General, Keaton's most celebrated pictures, unfold his two most sustained engagements with the machine. As E. Rubinstein has remarked, in advance of seeing the films one would presume the two titles to refer to a sailor and a soldier, but they are actually the names of the ship and the locomotive that command such central importance.[8] Both pictures indeed enact not so much a human as a mechanical drama, a drama in which, if Buster is the protagonist, the machine is not only the main scene of action but the main force actuating the proceedings. The ship in The Navigator amounts to nothing less than the world for the two characters aboard it, obliged as they are to conduct their lives in accordance to its system. The extended railway chase that takes up most of The General progresses along a single line of tracks, first in one direction as Buster pursues, then in reverse as Buster, having retrieved girl and locomotive, is pursued in turn, the course of the action thus exactly coinciding with that railway line, as if foreordained by it. The arrangements of the inanimate world exert everywhere in Keaton a governing influence on the dramatic development. All his films may be said to enact a dramaturgy of mechanics: the mechanics of a railway chase or of opening and closing an umbrella, a feat that eludes Buster at his high-school graduation in College but one that, to Buster's awe, a man sitting right beside him unfailingly performs; the mechanics of an unmanned ocean liner or of a motorcycle deprived of its driver, in Sherlock Junior, while Buster is riding on the handlebars; and the mechanics not only of machines but of other physical formations, sports, a herd of cattle compounded with city traffic in Go West (1925), natural phenomena such as a cyclone, a waterfall in Our Hospitality, an avalanche in Seven Chances (1925).

Aren't the ways of the physical world the standard business of every silent comedian? Isn't the greatest of them all supposed to be Chaplin, whose comedy is the most human, the most dependent on character and least on the pratfall and the chase? In a review of The Gold Rush (1925) at the time of its first release, Edmund Wilson wrote about Chaplin that "instead of the stereotyped humor of even the best of his competitors, most of whose tricks could be interchanged among them without anyone's knowing the difference, he gives us jokes that, however crude, have an unmistakable quality of personal fancy."[9] Granted, of all the characters, comic or serious, that the silent screen portrayed, none matches the subtlety and complexity of Chaplin's Tramp. But "an unmistakable quality of personal fancy" can be found in the work of such humble practitioners of slapstick as Laurel and Hardy: they set up their own relationship to a physical world they saw as the seat of disorder unamenable to man, disorder they methodically fomented themselves, having evidently concluded that there was no use fighting it. For Keaton, on the contrary, the physical world embodied the strictest order. He was the geometrician of slapstick, at opposite ends from the unruly variety exemplified by Laurel and Hardy or Mack Sennett or the Marx Brothers, in which things can be counted on to get madly out of control. Things in Keaton can be counted on to adhere rigorously to a system, a pattern as imperturbable as a line of tracks. To adopt Hugh Kenner's formulation, Keaton's universe is ruled by the implacable neatness of Newton's laws of mechanics, Laurel and Hardy's by the no less implacable disorganization, the irresistibly rising entropy, of the second law of thermodynamics.[10] It's a mistake to suppose that all slapstick comes from the same bag of interchangeable tricks: a considerable range of attitudes can be expressed through the medium of physical comedy.

Until the rediscovery of Keaton that took place in the sixties—when his films, most of which had been thought lost, started to be circulated again— Chaplin's supremacy among screen comedians was unquestioned. Chaplin was certainly right to feel that the messy farces of Mack Sennett, his first employer in the movies, tended to dissipate his characterization; it was after he left Sennett's Keystone Company, when he became his own director, that he was able to perfect his craft as an actor, and to develop an unerring sense of where to put the camera with a minimum of elaboration, bringing his pantomime comedy to a peak of refinement that seems impossible to surpass. As André Bazin has said, Chaplin used the film medium to turn the low comedy of the circus and music hall into a high art. In films, the closer view permitted by the camera exempted him from the exaggeration that would have been unavoidable on the stage; moreover, he could reshoot a scene as many times as was needed to get a certain gesture, a certain timing, just right. What Chaplin did—and in saying this I don't mean in any way to detract from his achievement—was adapt to the movies a theatrical idiom, an idiom for which, to a large extent, the silent screen was better suited than the stage.

I think it helps explain the readiness with which Chaplin's greatness was recognized—almost from the beginning he was not only immensely popular but widely hailed as a genius by critics and intellectuals—that he was working in a familiar idiom, bringing to fruition on the screen a long tradition of stage clowning. It took much longer for Keaton's greatness to be recognized, and even nowadays it's not so widely accepted as Chaplin's, though many regard Keaton as his equal, and some consider him his superior. Easy as it is to like Keaton the funnyman, it has been difficult properly to appreciate his artistry. "Keaton worked strictly for laughs," wrote James Agee, "but his work came from so far inside a curious and original spirit that he achieved a great deal besides."[11] What he achieved was a body of films that ranks, I believe, with the best work that has been done in this century. If he hasn't been sufficiently appreciated, it's perhaps because that "curious and original spirit" produced a kind of comedy that was wholly new, without any counterpart on the stage or in any other traditional medium.

While admiring Keaton as an actor, Edmund Wilson thought he was misused by Hollywood, forced to do those assembly-line gags that, in Wilson's view, everybody except Chaplin was turning out at the time. Hollywood, in fact, destroyed Keaton's career—Hollywood in some conjunction with the coming of sound that is hard for us to disentangle[12]—but that was after that halcyon period in the twenties when Keaton was able to work with a freedom comparable to Chaplin's. Keaton's gags were his own, done with the assistance of a team, of course, but—before he joined MGM as the silent era was ending and found himself on a real assembly line—everywhere colored with a sense of comedy and of life that is distinctively his. And Wilson praised Keaton's acting in terms more applicable to Chaplin's: "a pantomime clown of the first order."[13] That may have been what Wilson would have wanted him to be, but Keaton, unlike Chaplin, was not chiefly a pantomimist. When expressing emotion—as he often does, contrary to the received idea of his face as an impassive mask—his acting approaches the naturalistic. When in action, he exercises the skills of a consummate acrobat, a mode of acting that in a sense may also be called naturalistic, since the acrobatics were actually done by him, not faked with doubles or clever cutting. Unlike Chaplin, who mostly worked in the studio, Keaton exploited the naturalistic possibilities of film, the impression of reality that the medium can convey with peculiar impact.

This is not to put Keaton in the category of naturalism. Equally he exploited the phantasmal possibilities of the medium of moving shadows. Along with the impression of reality, and with no less impact, his films convey an impression of *un*reality, of inhabiting a hallucination. It's as if the visitor dropped to this earth, unsure that our world is real, were trying to convince himself that it is by recording its strange behavior in actual earthly locations. The evocative power of Keaton's cinema stems in large measure from the way he combines—in a surreal blend of his own that won him the admiration of the surrealists—the actual and the apparitional, lifelikeness and a dreamlike strangeness, the dream made all the more haunting for being so convincingly materialized. Keaton saw the world as a place both real and unreal, and he took to film as a medium both real and unreal: the material ghost.

As if seeking to dispel the ghostliness that haunted him, Keaton showed a concern for verisimilitude singular in a comedian. Especially in his feature-length films (the shorts are zanier), he developed his plots with unfaltering logic, kept all the incidents, however far from the ordinary, scrupulously within the realm of the possible, and took such care over the accuracy of his settings that his recreation of the Civil War in *The General* has been compared favorably with those in *The Birth of a Nation* and *Gone with the Wind*. The physical world he depicts is not a mere pretext for gags but a living milieu, grippingly credible even when verging on the incredible, like a dream disconcertingly become incontrovertible reality. It impeccably adheres, for one thing, to the selfsame mechanical laws that obtain in this place of our occupancy we call the real world.

At one point in *Our Hospitality* Buster is on a cliff, tied by a long rope to a man above him who loses his footing and plummets into the river below. The look on Buster's face, as he registers the inescapable gravitational consequence that he is himself imminently to be pulled down into that river, memorably summarizes his sense of his dealings with the physical universe. The universe, that look acknowledges, dictates its own terms: nothing to be done, at this point, against the pull of gravity. But that pull can on other occasions be put to one's advantage, as Buster demonstrates at the climax of this film by devising a pendulum with that same rope and himself as the suspended mass: swinging on the rope, he leaps forward from a ledge and seizes the girl just as she's being thrust over the brink of a precipitous waterfall, using gravity to overcome gravity, since thanks to the principle of the pendulum he and the girl are now swung back to safety on the ledge. It used to be assumed that Keaton regarded the physical universe as his adversary; some recent commentators have stressed his treatment of it as an ally. Indeed, its forces would often work in his favor, sometimes as a result of his harnessing them, sometimes of their own accord. It's surely going too far, however, for Walter Kerr to maintain that Keaton "trusted" the universe:[14] he only trusted it to be itself, neither for nor against him, but simply and uncompromisingly *there*. As exemplified by the ship in *The Navigator*, the apparatus of the universe was not set up to accommodate him; as exemplified by the climax of *Our Hospitality*, the laws of nature acted both as his adversary and as his ally in a contest from which he could emerge victorious only through an exceedingly precarious maneuver.

He meets the forces of the waterfall by means of a machine, the pendulum, into which he incorporates himself. In that brilliantly resourceful device, calculated to intersect the girl's path at precisely the right moment, he functions as a mere weight, swinging like any other under the joint pulls of gravity and the rope. To prevail against the inanimate world, he contrives the most effective way to make himself part of it. That, generally, was the policy informing Keaton's elaborate acrobatics: to engage a mechanical universe by the strategic use of his body as a piece of the machinery, an implement that the acrobat could wield with the requisite exactitude.

Keaton's comedy of kinetics would appear to illustrate the proposition, advanced by Henri Bergson in his well-known essay on laughter, that the human body becomes comical insofar as it behaves in the manner of a

Our Hospitality.
Buster at the waterfall.

machine.[15] Bergson was thinking, however, of the body as an encumbrance, unfortunately subject to the laws of matter and thus getting in the way of man's higher strivings. For most comedians the body may indeed be that thing which keeps tripping over other things; but not for Keaton. Although he took his share of falls, the body was for him also a means of soaring, of surmounting the obstacles in his way and achieving his objectives. Risky though the trajectories of the acrobat were, they proved to be the most reliable course of action for Buster to follow in his strivings: it was always through some physical feat that he managed to win what had been denied him otherwise.

Such prowess may seem inapposite in a comedian. "In every Keaton story," wrote John Grierson disapprovingly, "the action whoops in reel five to allow Buster Keaton the clown to become Mr. Keaton the romantic achiever of all things. . . . Clowns are the world's incompetents. They are bound to the wheel of incompetence or they cease to be clowns."[16] I don't think there is any inconsistency between Keaton's climactic exploits and his preceding characterization: from the beginning, his most distinctive trait has not been incompetence but perseverance, and his eventual success comes not as a miracle but as an earned victory. Whatever his falterings before he achieves his goal, he has been single-minded in his pursuit of it, a serious man, as his unsmiling face indicates, not the laughable figure of utter incompetence Grierson would have wanted him to be.

Perhaps, then, Keaton nowhere qualifies as a true clown. The physical dexterity of the actor, great as that was, is not what sets him apart, for clowns are usually dexterous, their inveterate art being to elaborate a graceful rendition of perpetual fumbling. Buster applies his dexterity, however, to a practical task, a job he aims to get done, whereas the dexterity we expect of a clown is one that precisely takes delight in its waywardness, its irredeemable impracticality, its unfitness to get any job done: the orchestration of chaos in Laurel and Hardy, for example, or the elfin ballet Chaplin performs around the machines in *Modern Times* (1936). The clown's embellishment of incompetence transforms it from mere inadequacy into a principle of behavior, a defiant alternative to the standards of the competent world. Clowns, one might say, are the world's conscientious incompetents, who formalize their refusal to participate in the world's business. Chaplin's concluding departure down the road, in *Modern Times* and other films, sums up the clown's disposition: better to take the chances of one's own vagrant path than follow the instituted procedures of an uncongenial world. That is not Buster's disposition: his governing drive is to participate, to fit into the world's scheme, and he entertains no alternative.

The laws of mechanics tolerate no alternative. In the Newtonian system, once initial conditions are set, subsequent configurations evolve ineluctably. Keaton the acrobat sedulously maneuvers within the workings of that system, endeavoring to have it reach a desired configuration, such as the one bringing together the girl and himself at the coordinates of the altar. That oddly impersonal amorous approach, which would get him the girl through a mechanical rather than an emotional interaction, is called for by the world he inhabits, in which human relationships are as systematized as celestial bodies. Keaton's girls tolerate no alternative either: it is imperative that he take up sports or join the Confederate army—or, in *Battling Butler* (1926), that he fight a world boxing champion—if he wants anything to do with them. The equation that is made in *The General* between the girl and the locomotive—he loves them both, loses them both, rescues them both in the same action—exemplifies the fundamental identity Keaton posits between the human and the inanimate realms, between the unbending conventions ruling human transactions and Newton's immutable laws. Initial conditions, in Keaton's universe as in Newton's, determine subsequent behavior, and in Keaton's case they extend from the physical—the layout of an ocean liner, the course of railroad tracks—to the conditions of a girl whose mind is made up about the qualities she desires in a fiancé.

Although inflexible, the girl's conditions are not capricious: that her boyfriend should be a soldier or an athlete is not her own predilection but a reflection of the standards prevalent in the community, an instance of the beliefs generally shared by Southerners at the time of the Confederacy or by students at an American college. In courting the girl, Buster at the same time is seeking admission into the community of which she is a representative member. When she rejects him, it's not because she doesn't like him, not for reasons of personal taste, but because, judging him by criteria that every nice girl has been taught to apply to any suitor, she finds him wanting in the qualities sanctioned by general agreement. Buster's problems with the girl, that is, are not a private matter: winning her is tantamount to gaining the acceptance of all, to belonging at long last in the midst of human fellowship. He is the visitor, she the native whose favors will be granted him only if he satisfies the norms of the tribe, as a kind of certificate of naturalization.

Our Hospitality, Keaton's first full-length film—I'm discounting *The Saphead* (1920), somebody else's film in which Keaton was merely an actor, and *The Three Ages* (1923), a feature-length film made up of three shorts strung together—differs in some interesting ways from most of the others. It portrays the world of the rural Old South about thirty years before the Civil War, a setting in which mechanization has barely begun to make an appearance. In order to claim a Southern inheritance, Buster travels down there from New York in a train so primitive that a dog's gait can keep pace with it and a recalcitrant donkey can block its course, necessitating that the tracks be manually displaced to circumvent the immovable animal. These are hardly the tracks in *The General*, which determine the course of the action: by contrast, the machines in *Our Hospitality*—the train, the guns the characters attempt without much success to fire—are pretty ineffectual. Even Buster's rescuing pendulum at the waterfall is a makeshift device just able to snatch the girl from the forces of nature. The interaction between Buster and the girl is also portrayed differently in *Our Hospitality*, perhaps, as Walter Kerr has suggested, because the actress playing her this time, Natalie Talmadge, was Keaton's own wife. This girl, in any case, gives Buster no trouble: she takes to him from their first meeting aboard the train; she invites him to dinner at her Southern home when they arrive at their destination; and she sides with him against her father and brothers, who, as she and Buster learn only after he's come to dinner, aim to kill him.

The reason they aim to kill him is nothing personal; they didn't even know him before his arrival in town. But they've discovered that he is the heir to a Southern family with which their own family has been carrying on a longstanding feud, a feud they feel bound to resume now that he has turned up. So they are after him by convention, because the code of feuding demands it. While he's a guest in their house, however, they're prevented from killing him by another convention: the laws of Southern hospitality dictate that they welcome him, treat him with the utmost courtesy, offer him a plentiful meal. They even put him up for the night when a rainstorm breaks out and Buster, who by now has caught on to the situation, takes advantage of the weather to prolong his stay, knowing that he's safe as long as he remains under their roof. (Most comedians would have played much more on the character's ignorance of such a situation, but Keaton, distinctively, soon makes his character aware of it and plays on the stratagems afforded by that awareness.) The moment he steps outside the house, the well-treated guest becomes the sworn enemy, hospitality ceases and by an automatic switch in conventions feuding assumes jurisdiction. The girl's love for Buster, her pleading with her father and brothers in his behalf, makes no difference in their formularized behavior. Even after he's saved her life they're ready to kill him, and they stop trying only when they find that the girl and Buster have just been married, the feud convention being superseded at this point not by warm sentiments but by yet another convention: marriage into the family. In the preindustrial, pastoral Old South of *Our Hospitality,* where Buster has to strive neither with elaborate machines nor with a girl who holds back her love, the coalition of implacable natural forces and rigid social conventions nonetheless makes for a vast impersonal apparatus scarcely more accommodating than the ship in *The Navigator.*

It may be instructive to compare the South in *Our Hospitality* with the Ireland John Ford depicts in *The Quiet Man* (1952), which is also a comedy about the difficulties of an outsider in a traditional community. Nothing so extreme as a feud threatens Ford's protagonist (John Wayne), an American gone to live in an Irish village, but his situation bears some resemblance to that of Keaton's New Yorker down South. In each case the protagonist has returned to the rural place of his birth, which he hasn't seen since childhood, with a mind to settle there, expecting it to be idyllic. The looks of the place, the natural beauty rendered vividly in both films, would seem at first to fulfill that expectation, but in each case the outsider is soon disappointed. Like Buster, the character played by John Wayne falls in love with a local woman (Maureen O'Hara) who loves him too but with whose family he finds he must contend: her older brother detests him, and according to Irish custom without this brother's consent she cannot be married. The trouble persists even after the couple are married: the brother, when he learns he's been tricked into giving his consent, retaliates by withholding the bride's dowry, which doesn't matter at all to the American but which the Irishwoman feels she must have if she is to be a proper wife; moreover, she feels that the American, if he is to be a proper husband, must prove his mettle, to her and to the entire village, by standing up to her brother and fighting him for the dowry that is due her, so she withholds herself from her husband until he does as she sees fit. Thus summarized, the plot of *The Quiet Man* sounds like the plot of a Keaton movie, with the wife, in the demands she makes as a paradigm of convention, behaving more like the usual Keaton heroine than does the girl in *Our Hospitality.* Ford's slant on this material, however, differs considerably from what Keaton's would have been. *The Quiet Man* is a wonderful traditional comedy, comedy of the kind that shows the social order is all right even as it shows we all have our troubles with it. *Our Hospitality* is something different.

For good reasons of his own, the husband in *The Quiet Man* is unwilling to fight the brother: he had been a professional boxer in America and had quit after killing an opponent in the ring, at which point he vowed to himself never to fight anybody again. He had imagined that Ireland would be a tranquil haven where he could be a quiet man. But his wife has reasons that are more than private for his fighting in this circumstance: in addition to her self-esteem, the esteem of their neighbors—the couple's public standing—depends on it. When he eventually gives in and confronts her brother, Ford treats the extended fight sequence as a kind of dance of celebration involving everyone in the village, a ceremony of the American's initiation into the Irish community. The private reasons, in Ford's view, must give in to the public, the American's romantic notions of Ireland to the realities of his living there with his fellow men. Once he accepts the communal traditions, the established forms of human interplay, his life in that beautiful setting, the film assures us, will be a happy one. So Ford elevates the rituals of the community above the idiosyncrasies of the individual—in contrast with Keaton, who presents the rituals of Southern hospitality and feuding as absurdly conventionalized.

Yet Keaton leaves his character no option except adjusting to such absurd rituals: life in *that* beautiful setting, no less than in Ford's Ireland, necessitates conformity with the traditions of its inhabitants. These traditions may be murderous if one happens to be a member of a rival family, but otherwise they seem hospitable enough, and after the marriage brings reconciliation they may well allow for the reputed ease and amenities of old-fashioned Southern living. They are, in any case, the law of the land, strictly enforced by its unpersuadable inhabitants, and anyone wishing to settle there has no choice but to submit. Neither in *Our Hospitality* nor anywhere else can Keaton be said to celebrate the community: he sees its conventions as arcane dictates, intricate and arbitrary yet somehow accepted by everyone without question, the bizarre social equivalent of mechanical determinism. Any attempt at rebellion or escape, however, seems inconceivable to Buster: who would heed his rebellion? what place can he hope to escape to that he would find more congenial? He must work with the existing situation, try to make the best of it, or else face the dread prospect of irremediable loneliness. So, although Keaton by no means elevates the community above the individual, he still, like Ford, presents it as the individual's only harbor.

Keaton's equation between mechanical systems and human conduct is pointedly illustrated by two gags, one from *The General* involving a railroad car, the other from *Steamboat Bill, Jr.* involving the girl, and both exploiting the same idea. Throughout Buster's pursuit of the Northerners in *The General,* various obstacles are laid in his path, among them a freight car disengaged from the stolen train. Buster shunts the car onto a siding and, believing he's solved that problem, turns his attention to other work that needs to be done, thus failing to notice that the course the car follows on the siding soon rejoins the main track. The next time he looks, he finds the car he thought he had sidetracked again before him. Unable to deal with it at the moment, having yet other pressing matters to attend to, he turns away again and now fails to see that the problem is solved for him by a log laid by the Northerners on the track as another obstacle but serving instead to derail the obstructive car. When he looks once more, prepared to contend with the car that had unaccountably resurged, he finds that, as unaccountably, it has vanished.

The gag in *Steamboat Bill* plays on a similar appearing and disappearing, this time not by an inanimate object, in accordance with the laws of motion, but by the girl, in accordance with her emotions. This occurs when Buster runs into her while on his way to take the next train back to Boston; having alienated both her and his father, he's concluded there's nothing to keep him in the river town. On meeting her, however, he pauses and begins to give her an explanation, diffidently, with his eyes turned downward, assuming that she would listen. So he doesn't see that she chooses to snub him, walks right past him and into a building. The next time he looks, no sign of her is to be found. Puzzled, he proceeds on his way and now cannot see that, behind his back, she's come out of the building and follows him steadily from a distance, no longer wishing to ignore him but hesitating to address him. He doesn't know that she's behind him, and in front of him, moreover, something unexpected happens that takes his mind away from any further pondering of her whereabouts: his father is thrown into jail. Deciding under the circumstances not to leave town but to stay and help his father, Buster turns around to head for home, and the girl behind him, at a loss for what to do, turns around too, so, as it looks from his perspective, she has reappeared out of nowhere with her back to him and briskly walking away. The girl's psychology is as clear to us as the physics of the railroad car, but in both cases the governing mechanism is hidden from Buster, and we can appreciate his perplexity in confronting the manifestations discernible to him. A sense is conveyed of that perplexing process, that generally hidden mechanism, by which things come to be as they appear before our eyes.

In a visual strategy typical of Keaton's style as a director, the entire progress of the sidetracked car, how it runs parallel to the main line and then rejoins it, is shown in the background of an uninterrupted traveling shot, with Buster in the foreground all the while, too busy stoking his engine to mind anything else. This use of deep focus, even as it simultaneously reveals both the car's trajectory and the reason for Buster's inattention, yet conveys the feeling that it's terribly easy for any of us to miss what's important in our environment. The car is right there, visible to us behind him, and if only he'd known to look, a mere turning of the head would have sufficed to apprise him of the situation. Furthermore, the car, though clearly visible in the shot, is pretty far in the background and near the edge of the screen, barely within our field of vision: we feel that we too might easily have missed that crucial detail with only a slight shift in the camera angle. By a similar use of deep focus in *Steamboat Bill*, the girl covertly following Buster appears in the

The similar gags in *The General* and *Steamboat Bill, Jr.:* the sidetracked car rejoining the main track, the girl following Buster.

background of the shot and he in the foreground, his attention again otherwise engaged. In neither case does Keaton cut to reveal to us what's hidden from his character; instead he shows it taking place in the same shot, rather as if the camera had picked it up by happenstance. A cut to a closer view either of the car or of the girl would have been like a nudge signaling to us that this is privileged information, made available for our benefit as spectators while the character remains in the dark; that would have tended to encourage in us a comfortable feeling of omniscience, of our superiority over Buster in being given access to all the pertinent facts unknown to him. As it is, we see more than he does but are kept aware of the difficulty, which we generally share with him, in looking where we need to look, seeing what needs to be seen.

Another gag in *The General*—perhaps the most famous one from that film, beautifully sustained and well worthy of the praise it has received—also depends on a counterpoint between background, where a significant occurrence unfolds, and foreground, where Buster is too busy with other things to pay attention. More than an important detail, what Buster fails to notice this time is positively momentous: whole armies moving behind him, first Southern troops retreating, then Northern troops advancing, while Buster, moving in the opposite direction in his pursuit of the stolen locomotive, has eyes only for the wood he's chopping to use as fuel. Admittedly, it's not easy to miss an army going by in one's vicinity, and E. Rubinstein, in his valuable monograph on the film, calls this an instance of Buster's "myopic absorption with his labors."[17] But Buster's labors are no less than Herculean in his

The General.
Buster chopping wood
as Northern troops
advance.

single-handed endeavor to retrieve his locomotive from the Northern raiders; given all the things he has to do, I wouldn't say he's "myopic" to have no time for an exploratory glance at the surrounding countryside. When he eventually looks up from his task and at the enemy troops around him, it's not behind him, where we've been watching the military movements, that he looks first: he stares before him instead, where, as a shot from his point of view now reveals, there are troops too. We may have thought we had a commanding view of the situation, but now we recognize that there was a whole other side we had not previously seen, a side that had been hidden behind the camera just as the troops within our view were hidden behind Buster's back. There were, so to speak, troops behind our backs too. The soldiers' presence in back of him was something we had expected he'd sooner or later discover, to his surprise; their presence in front we're rather surprised to discover ourselves. Although his surprise is of course greater, his moment of discovery coincides with ours, and he finds out something that we didn't already know. If his perspective is limited, so also, we're not allowed to forget, is ours.

In this instance Keaton cuts, to show us that other side, when most directors wouldn't have: it's standard practice in films to keep the camera as often as possible on the same side of the action, for having it switch sides, unless necessary for the purposes of dramatic exposition, is thought to be undesirably disorienting. Here the troops in front catch us unawares without bringing on a change in the plot—they're not, say, Southern troops coming to Buster's aid—so most directors would have preferred to omit them and arrange for the character to make his discovery by looking behind him, to the territory we're familiar with. Keaton's cut serves no dramatic purpose; rather it acts as a reminder that the world is always larger than any of us can see. More often, as with the sidetracked car or the shadowing girl, Keaton doesn't cut when most directors would have. His procedure, in either case, responds to the same principle: he denies to the camera its usual role as the observer that knows exactly where to look, conventionally endowed with the preternatural capacity to pick out for us at each moment in the film the part that matters, the section of the world we need to see at this point. Keeping the camera on the same side encourages us to discount the possible relevance of the other side, to feel certain that nothing of significance, such as half an army, may be hidden behind the camera; cutting closer to an important detail similarly reassures us that the camera wouldn't fail to notice anything important.

When a director like Hitchcock restricts the point of view to that of one of the characters, the limitation in our perspective does not really strike us as *our* limitation, since we vicariously attribute it to a participant in the story. The withheld pieces of information are a gap in somebody else's knowledge, and their being withheld from us is a premise we are to accept in the interests of dramatic effect. With Hitchcock, the camera may be denied omniscience but is still granted the status of a knowing observer, whose calculated assumption of a character's point of view is posited as the exactly appropriate manner of unfolding the plot. With Keaton, we're allowed to know more than the character does while being made conscious of our own limited perspective, so we cannot attribute that limitation to anybody else, to anything other than our inescapable human finitude. If Buster cannot see in back of his head, neither can we; if Buster must make do with what one pair of eyes can see in this vast world, so must we. At the movies we can of course see with the camera's mobile mechanical eye, but the eye of Keaton's camera is seen to partake of the finitude of our being in the world.

Like Keaton, Hitchcock often portrays characters who find themselves on their own in a perilous environment. The difference in the results— suspense with elements of comedy as opposed to comedy with elements of suspense—derives in part from the way Hitchcock's camera promotes our identification with the character, whereas Keaton's keeps us at a distance, in a frame of mind that more readily permits our laughter. And yet, in a more profound way than Hitchcock's, Keaton's camera shares the character's position in the world. It may not often take the character's point of view, it may not share the particulars of the character's limitation, but it shares the condition of limitation.[18] Hitchcock plays a knowing game with the camera all through the character's difficulties: the character may be at a loss but the director never betrays a moment's hesitation in his cunning moves to elicit from us the response he wants. Keaton's command of film technique is no less assured than Hitchcock's, but he declines to assume such an authoritative posture in his handling of the camera. Rather than as the observer that knows, he treats it as an explorer faced with an uncharted terrain of incalculable dimensions, able to cover only so much ground and liable to miss some significant feature—thus putting the camera on an equal footing with his character, the visitor puzzled by an unfamiliar land yet seeking a place in it.

Lest this suggest anything awkward or desultory about Keaton's camera work, I should stress its distinctive elegance, its geometric finesse. In *Sherlock Junior*, for example, when Buster, the naive would-be detective, follows a suspect so conscientiously that he walks about a foot behind and all but trips over the man, the camera follows as steadily in a brisk, smooth traveling shot that perfectly mirrors the character's single-mindedness and much enhances the comic effect. Or consider another eloquent traveling shot, the first of several in *The General* that show Buster intently chopping wood against the background of unnoticed troops. In all these shots the camera moves in the same direction as Buster, opposite to the troops; in the first one, however, it does not keep pace with him, so that he appears to overtake the camera—he enters frame, passes through the shot, and goes beyond—which conveys a sense of his inadvertent daring in so plunging into enemy territory, faster than the camera seems initially prepared to go.

Keaton developed, no doubt intuitively, an original cinematic style beautifully suited to his purposes. His penchant for deep focus and long takes, his avoidance of close-ups and reduction of cuts—an approach unappreciated by his contemporaries, who were schooled in Griffith's editing and Eisenstein's montage—assisted his rediscovery by film critics in the sixties, when André Bazin's anti-montage conceptions became widely influential. Keaton's work indeed resembles, and more than in his use of this or that similar technique, the work of such later directors as Renoir and Antonioni, who also employ the camera to conduct an inquiry into the world rather than to parcel out the answers. His films differ from theirs, however, in being as much the actor's as the director's: Keaton's inquiry, one might say, is a joint endeavor, a venture undertaken by his character and camera together. The director performs as deftly in his shots as the actor does in his acrobatics, but they both seem precariously poised in their dealings with an uncertain situation.

Keaton and Chaplin are great actors and great filmmakers, and in their work the actor and the filmmaker are one. Both began in the theater, the popular theater, at a very young age (Keaton at three, in his parents' act in vaudeville). Coming to films after a formative experience acting in that integral space, the stage, where no such thing as a cut is allowed to interrupt a performance, both brought to films a respect for the actor's continuity and a wariness of the editor's scissors: in their craft as film directors both take care to preserve on the screen the integrity of the actor's space.

The actor's discomfort with the disjunctions of film editing is expressed in that wonderful sequence from *Sherlock Junior* in which Buster, asleep on his job as a movie projectionist, dreams that he walks up to the screen and into the movie being projected. It's as if Keaton had stepped into a movie directed by D. W. Griffith, and didn't like it: the locale keeps shifting on him, by abrupt cutting, while he remains continuously himself, in the same place on the screen from one shot to the next through all the cuts disconcertingly transporting him from one place to another, his performance uninterrupted even as he finds himself now amid city traffic, now up on a mountain, now by a choppy sea, now surrounded by beasts in the jungle. This sequence is a special case of the visitor's situation recurrent with Keaton: here he's a visitor not anywhere on earth but in the world of somebody else's movie, a movie made in a style, foreign to his own, denying him a unified space for his performance.

Such a unified space for the actor to act in is established on the screen by Chaplin and Keaton alike. Chaplin's peerless pantomimes—his mock sermon on David and Goliath in *The Pilgrim* (1923), for example, or his little dance with the buns in *The Gold Rush*—unfold in such a space, commanding the camera's undivided attention; and in such a space Keaton displays his intricate acrobatics, convincing us that they are actual feats rather than tricks of the cutting room. It is a different kind of space, however, with Chaplin and with Keaton. Chaplin's space recalls the stage not only in its integrity but in its quality of enclosure, in our sense of a demarcated area—the area of a pulpit during the mock sermon, the area of a table during the bun dance— within which each scene is contained. The size of that area may vary, but its boundaries are usually well defined, and the action rarely extends beyond them for the duration of the scene—quite unlike the action in Keaton, which regularly spreads out over a field of indefinite size.

Chaplin's practice of shooting in the studio, and in sets at least slightly stylized, partly accounts for this feeling of confinement; but the studio can be made to yield the illusion of a much larger area, and Chaplin's sets feel nearly as confined as stage sets. Conversely, the use of actual locations by no means ensures the sense of an open space we get in Keaton's films: actual locations can be treated much like a stage backdrop—as indeed Chaplin treats them on the occasions in which he uses them—but Keaton is one of the few directors who truly engages an environment and makes us aware that the screen can hardly encompass the dimensions of the actual place. More than in their choice of settings, Chaplin and Keaton differ in the basic conformation of the space they inhabit, a space corresponding, in Chaplin's films, to the stage, and in Keaton's, to the world.

In both cases the actor's space befits the kind of character he plays. "Chaplin's Tramp," wrote Robert Warshow,

> represented the good-hearted and personally cultivated individual in a heart-
> less and vulgar society. The society was concerned only with the pursuit of

profit, and often not even with that so much as with the mere preservation of the ugly and impersonal machinery by which the profit was gained; the Tramp was concerned with the practice of personal relations and the social graces. Most of all the Tramp was like an aristocrat fallen on hard times, for what he attempted in all his behavior was to maintain certain standards of refinement and humanity, to keep life dignified and make it emotionally and aesthetically satisfying.[19]

The Tramp, then, is the man who stands apart, the exceptional individual misunderstood and rejected by the society around him, a better grade of human being whose unfitness for the tasks of that society only underscores his personal superiority, his interest in higher things. Although Chaplin's films carry a social protest, an appeal for change, he does not propose his character as any sort of revolutionary, for the Tramp would be as unfit to take any action against the society as he is to work within its constrictions; moreover, he is too insular to show much solidarity with the poor and too singular to be regarded as typical of them. We are to side with the Tramp for his intrinsic human qualities, for what he is in himself, apart from anything he does or could do or anything he stands for beyond himself. His strongest bond is with us, the spectators, rather than with any of the other characters in the film: he communicates with us (to borrow Louise Brooks's phrase) "in a kind of intense isolation,"[20] tacitly addressing us with an entreaty for us to recognize his fine qualities and the injustice of a society that does not. Sometimes he gets the girl, but never as a result of his having undertaken any conventional courtship: he gets her because she, like us, is sensitive enough to appreciate his personal worth. (In *The Gold Rush*, the one film in which the Tramp makes good, ending up as a millionaire, the logic of the character demands that he come to his money fortuitously, not through his own efforts, and that the girl, when he runs into her aboard a ship at the end, accepts him *as a tramp*, in a scene arranged so that she thinks he's a stowaway and offers to pay for his passage, before she finds out about his money.)

It would be an exaggeration to say that Chaplin needs no space outside of himself to realize his character: something like a bare stage would not do for the Tramp, who exists in relation to a milieu that Chaplin's sets pithily evoke. In Chaplin's circumscribed space, however, the setting becomes strictly subordinate to the character, and that little fellow scraping through on the outskirts of society assumes on the screen his rightful place at the center of things. That place, due him by virtue of his higher humanity and denied him in a society that has no place for that humanity, must be granted him, Chaplin implies, in a space closed off from the world and constituted for the little fellow's benefit. The man who stands apart from that vulgar milieu deserves, in Chaplin's view, a space set apart for the proper display of his unique attributes. Unlike the Tramp, Keaton's character wants a place in the world, not just in our hearts, and not a special place but one like everybody else's, so Buster accordingly inhabits a space that seems as large as the world and in which he enjoys no primacy over his surroundings.

If the society will not accommodate the Tramp, that is for Chaplin sufficient reason to condemn it, and he concentrates our attention on his character's personal qualities, upholding them against an order that callously discounts them. The world Keaton depicts, though not so inimical to the character, is even more impersonal, even more indifferent to the claims of individuality. Now and again the Tramp comes across a responsive soul—a girl, a kid, men such as the artist who befriends him in *The Immigrant* (1917) or the alcoholic millionaire in *City Lights* (1931), who, when sober, rebuffs him but who at least intermittently takes him to his heart. Nobody in Keaton's world ever departs from the established patterns of behavior; there are no exceptions made in this or that individual case, no exemptions from the rules of courtship granted on account of personal niceness. And Buster has no expectations that things will be otherwise: he accepts the formulistic nature of the world he inhabits and attempts to integrate himself into its formulas, knowing that considerations of personality will have no more effect on the conduct of its inhabitants than on the fall of an apple from a tree.

Even when the Tramp finds himself all alone, rejected by everyone in the film, he still has us, the main recipients of his personal appeal. His directing that appeal to us of course stresses his alienation from his milieu, but it also indicates Chaplin's confidence that the appeal will be heeded, and thus his hope that the established order will be changed. Buster seems to have no thought for us, occupied as he always is with some demanding task at hand—and convinced, we may surmise, that soliciting anybody's sympathy, ours included, is not going to make any difference. (In *The Cameraman* [1928], the first picture Keaton made for MGM after he lost his independence, we can tell that the studio gagmen have tampered with his conception the moment the girl is drawn to Buster because she feels sorry for him.) Keaton's universe is beyond condemnation, and beyond appeal: if it refuses to accommodate personality, there is no point in contesting that, in insisting that things ought not to be so. Whereas the Tramp, above all, projects his personality, Buster suppresses his as much as he can, given that it fits no-where in a set scheme of things. Personal feelings, which Buster has nonetheless, he might as well not be having, and so tries not to display: hence that famous Keaton face, which is not expressionless at all but on which the expression surfaces as if against his will.

Finding himself in a world of inexorable interlocking systems such as Hawthorne describes in "Wakefield," Buster would not risk stepping aside in his pursuit of a place in the scheme of things; any diversion might lead to his falling hopelessly out of step with the world around him. Other people are nicely adjusted to that world; they play their sports, carry on their feuds, wage their wars, go about their daily business with unruffled expertise in the way things are done: as they belong in the world, so too Buster aspires to belong. But they are natives, and their procedures are to him like an arduous and convoluted foreign language that requires his intent application and that, try as he may, he can never master with their sure fluency. Truly to belong in that immense machine that is Keaton's world, a man must conduct himself with the unthinking proficiency of a machine, and that's not something Buster can manage. The impersonal skills of the acrobat, his best resource in dealing with the scheme of things, he yet fails to make wholly impersonal: the movements of his body remain distinctively his own, unmistakable even in extreme long shot. And on his face his thoughts and feelings are equally unmistakable: they persist in showing through that would-be blank countenance.

It is Keaton's genius as an actor to keep a face so nearly deadpan and yet render it, by subtle inflections, so vividly expressive of inner life. His large deep eyes are the most eloquent feature; with merely a stare he can convey a wide range of emotions, from longing to mistrust, from puzzlement to sorrow. A poignant instance occurs in *Sherlock Junior* during a visit Buster pays to the girl he's courting. He has brought her the conventional present of a box of candies, and she responds with the conventional gesture of putting her hand between them on the couch where they're both sitting. Then, not quite daring to hold her hand but stirred by her offering it, he shuts his eyes in a moment of bashful bliss. She doesn't notice this, nor does the camera come in closer to give it emphasis; it's a private moment, and his eyes, by a very little, betray its subdued intensity.

Keaton rightly avoids close-ups in portraying a character who tries so hard to avoid isolation from his environment. Through other means, how-ever, he brings his character's face into prominence. A strategy he often employs, and one of his invention, is the frontal view taken from some distance, the long shot or sometimes medium shot that, while showing Buster in the midst of things, singles out his face by showing him looking almost straight at the camera. In *The General* there are many such shots: when Buster looks up to discover the troops around him, for example; or when, inspecting the tracks ahead, he blinks in astonishment at the disappearance of the reappeared car; or when, giving up his initial attempt to enlist in the Confederate army, he addresses the recruiting officer who has turned him down, and says with a hurt expression, "Don't blame me if you lose this war." At the end of *Sherlock Junior,* Buster and the girl are reconciled in the booth where he's at work projecting a movie, and unsure of how to proceed with her, he seeks instruction in the ways of romance from the lovers in the movie, turning periodically to the screen to see what he should do next. Here too he's photographed head-on, through the booth window as he looks out, which points up his inquisitive gaze—and eventually his bewildered stare when the movie to which he looks for guidance skips all the intermediary steps between a kiss and a marriage with children.

Perhaps the most striking of these frontal shots is the one in *Steamboat Bill, Jr.* that shows Buster changing hats. Brought to a haberdashery by his father, who disapproves of the beret he's been wearing and aims to get him a proper hat, he stands before a mirror while variegated hats are tried on him in succession, each making him seem different, as if he were rapidly donning and discarding a succession of identities, all of them imposed on him from the outside, none of them consonant with the inside we perceive through his

Steamboat Bill, Jr. Buster changing hats before the mirror.

forlorn eyes. Here his eyes are fixed on the camera for the longest stretch of all, since no cuts are needed to show us what he's looking at: the camera takes the place of the mirror, and Buster stares at it as at his own reflection. In each of these frontal shots, it must be stressed, the object of Buster's gaze is clearly established as something specific in his environment, so that his eyes appear directed not at the camera itself but at some point past it that claims his attention. We never get the feeling that he's looking at us: the effect, instead, is of our looking into him.

Before the mirror in *Steamboat Bill*, however, the object of his attention happens to be his own image, and that shot has the quality of an introspective monologue, an apprehensive meditation on his own condition. Literally his view of himself, that shot becomes an epitome of Keaton's view of the self as a foreign entity in the world, a visitor forever having to borrow the world's uniforms, and uncomfortable in any of them. The collegiate outfit that Buster affects at the beginning of this film was the fashion in Boston, but in a Southern river town his father is appalled to encounter an arriving son in a beret and a little mustache who is playing a ukelele and singing and dancing to it. (Buster is trying to pacify a baby he accidentally caused to cry, but his father doesn't know about the baby, and concludes that his son is in the habit of breaking into song and dance in the street.) The steamboat captain proceeds to strip away an outfit he finds offensively effeminate: the beret must be replaced, the mustache he has a barber shave off, the ukelele he crushes under his foot. More than these particular items, the principles on which Buster has based his life till now are thrown into question. At the haberdashery, without the trappings of a Boston collegian, he stares into the mirror and sees for the first time the hopeless discrepancy between his inner being and any of the roles he may have to assume in his dealings with the external world.

Such a dawning of self-consciousness usually occurs early on in Keaton's films, as when the rich boy in *The Navigator*, all dressed up on his first morning on board for a breakfast that nobody is there to serve him, comes to realize that the ocean liner is deserted. In *Sherlock Junior*, the format of a film within the film delays that dawning until the end, when the projectionist is left staring out of the booth window and scratching his head. At that point, in any case, Buster is led to a fearful reappraisal. The unexamined life of the rich boy who expected everything to be done for him, or of the projectionist who looked to the model of fictional detectives, or of the college boy who followed the Bostonian fashion, can no longer continue: Buster comes to the recognition that he must drop his previous assumptions and make a new start, taking nothing for granted in the endeavor, so much more difficult than he thought, of setting up residence in the world. From then on he looks at life with perpetually questioning eyes, knowing he cannot afford to relax his vigilant scrutiny; even amid the urgency of action, while executing some wondrous feat, he retains that perplexed, pondering gaze, which attests to his self-consciousness.

Robert Bresson—another practitioner of the deadpan approach, in a different way from Keaton's but with a similar sense that life is not a matter of personality—once defined originality as the failed attempt to do the same as everybody else, a definition that applies exactly to Buster. For all his efforts to join in, and all his eventual successes in meeting the forces outside, inside he cannot shake off the sense of his singularity. He thinks, therefore he stands alone in a world where no other minds are discernible, only systems of behavior. Ultimately he remains even more isolated than Chaplin's Tramp, since it's not Buster's individual qualities that single him out—these he hardly lets interfere in his transactions with others—but the very fact of his individuality, of his possessing the inner dimension of a self in the realm of the formula.

Buster is not, then, Grierson's "romantic achiever of all things" but a bewildered equilibrist whose mind runs counter to the achievements of his body: a new kind of clown who may not so often trip over physical objects but who, so to speak, keeps tripping over his thoughts. The charming incompetence of the traditional clown was the conception of an earlier time, with more room for eccentricity than has been allowed in our ruthless century. Things were not so good then, of course—things never have been—but at least the clown could thumb his nose at the world and expect the world to let him be. He would puncture our lofty pretensions with his reminder of the claims of the body, of the fact that in our flesh and blood we all fumble our way through life. That conception hasn't lost its validity, and Chaplin can still use it to portray a doughboy in *Shoulder Arms* (1918) or a factory worker in *Modern Times;* but he was looking back to a Victorian humanism that decidedly fails him when portraying a Jew under the Nazis in *The Great Dictator* (1940). Keaton reverses that conception: to our age of increasing mindlessness he offers a comedy of mind. Although he never dealt with contemporary issues as Chaplin did, he accurately depicts the landscape of our time in its vast inhuman organization. He reminds us of the claims of consciousness against a mechanistic order, of the fact that our expert procedures and outward accomplishments take no account of our

inner nature. Whereas the old clowns would assert our right to our idiosyncrasies, he asserts our need to live with one another in a community that
does justice to our individuality. The sadness that emerges at the end of
College underlies all of Keaton's happy endings: it is the sadness of inescapable isolation, of knowing that he does not in the end, any more than he did
at the beginning, belong in a world where happiness is available only as a
convention. Yet Buster has done his best, and leaves us with the haunting
image of his solemn and solitary figure, at once purposeful and detached,
bravely attempting the impossible.

4 : The Deadly Space Between

To pass from a normal nature to him one must cross "the
deadly space between."

HERMAN MELVILLE, *Billy Budd*

Nature, to a classical way of thinking, has its finest development in
culture; human nature, builder of cities, comes to fruition in the city. That is
not the nature or the human nature of the romantics. To a romantic way of
thinking, nature lies beyond the walls of the city, and human nature is
primarily to be found within an individual self not subsumable into the
conventions of culture. Feeling that classicism slights both the outward and
the inward, both nature and the individual self, romanticism would regain
them both in the same movement bringing the self face to face with nature.
The result can be wonderful and it can also be fearful. In expressionism, in
Munch's *Scream* or in *The Cabinet of Dr. Caligari*, romanticism pushes to the
extreme of fear. Expressionism is a romanticism that can no longer bear the
face of nature and retreats into a world of the self's anxious fabrication.

Not a whiff of nature is allowed into the askew spectral sets of *Caligari*,
a paranoiac sketchbook of a world that seems continually on the point of
toppling. Made in the immediate aftermath of the First World War, *Caligari*
allegorizes that war in a tale of insane authority impelling youth to somnam-
bulistic murder. This horror fantasy began in Weimar Germany a cinema of
anxiety and gloom fabricated in the studio. F. W. Murnau's *Nosferatu* (1922),
perhaps the greatest of Weimar films, was another response to the First
World War, a response not to the insane authority that unleashed the war
but to the death that ensued. Murnau's film endures as one of the most
resonant and unsettling responses that have been made in art to the death
that inescapably awaits us.

Nosferatu is singular among Weimar films because it enacts its tale of
horror, the first screen version of *Dracula*, largely in natural settings rendered with emphasis. The texture of *Nosferatu* is infused with dusky skies
and restless seas, trees with branches like flourishing claws, the woods and
mountains and perched castles of the rugged Carpathian terrain, the narrow
cobbled streets and close-packed gabled houses of a town on the Baltic.
Commentators have pointed out the influence on Murnau of the early Swed-

ish cinema with its feeling for landscape and the open air; less often noted is the deeper influence of German romanticism, of E. T. A. Hoffmann, of Caspar David Friedrich's mystical natural landscapes where the human presence makes but a frail mark. Set in the romantic period, *Nosferatu* when seen today gives the uncanny impression of a remnant of that period somehow animately preserved, like a manuscript in a bottle brought to shadow life on the screen. The romantic roots of expressionism are nowhere more evident than in this extraordinary film.

Dreyer's *Vampyr* (1932), which alone bears comparison with *Nosferatu* among the many vampire movies that have come after it, also makes expressive use of natural settings. But nature in *Vampyr* is seen through a glass darkly, the natural dissolves into an atmosphere of the supernatural, everything appears eerily blurred in a no man's land between life and death. One can imagine *Vampyr* done, without great loss, in appropriately misty studio sets. One cannot imagine *Nosferatu* except in natural settings: the face of nature in this film is not an embellishment but of the essence. *Nosferatu* and *Vampyr* alike combine the unreal with a vivid element of reality. Reality in *Vampyr* resides principally in the human face, the naked human face that Dreyer, here as elsewhere, photographs with peculiar intensity as a mirror of the soul. For its reality, its center of gravity, *Vampyr* looks inward. *Nosferatu* looks outward: from the self's window Murnau's camera casts an apprehensive gaze on the world out there, a world that to the recoiling self appears implacably ominous and sinister.

Seen nearly always from a distance, a supernatural figure deeply situated amid the natural world, Nosferatu the vampire is not so much a character as a symbolic personification of that fearful world out there. This vampire is a different conception from the original Dracula of Bram Stoker's novel or the familiar wickedly seductive aristocrat of other stage and screen versions. This is, for one thing, not a sexy vampire—which hasn't kept commentators from offering sexual interpretations of him nonetheless. Loomingly thin, with long predatory arms culminating in claws, the two front teeth protruding like a rodent's, and between pointed ears a pale bald head like a bare skull, Nosferatu monstrously suggests a cross between a human skeleton and a rat. His skeletal aspect, the way his figure evokes the skull and bones beneath the skin, helps establish this vampire as a specter of death. His resemblance to a rat makes more pronounced his association with pestilence: rats he carries with him, in his coffins filled with the Transylvanian earth he needs for his diurnal rest, carry the plague everywhere he goes. Both carrier and specter, a rat assuming the proportions of the grim reaper that will claim us all, Nosferatu is a figure of death ingrained in life, death emerging from the depths of nature.

In *From Caligari to Hitler* Siegfried Kracauer puts an apt question about this vampire. Is Nosferatu an embodiment of pestilence, a symbol of destructive nature, or, conversely, does the image of pestilence serve to characterize him as a bringer of destruction? Does he stand for death, metaphorically, or does death, metonymically, follow in his path? Kracauer argues against the former and for the latter view, which fits in with the thesis of his thesis-bound book: for him Nosferatu is, like Caligari or Mabuse, one of a "procession of tyrants" in Weimar cinema, and pestilence, like the grass that no longer grows where Attila's horse has set foot, one of the attendant traits of this "tyrant figure."[1] A tyrant, however, is a political figure; the reign of death that Nosferatu represents is not a political order because it cannot be changed, it can only be faced; the death that comes to all the living falls outside the political because it is something inevitable. An anxious emphasis on inevitable death, arguably a displacement from afflictions that are not inevitable, doubtless has political significance. But no political persuasion or orientation attaches to Nosferatu, no scheme for gaining or wielding political power. Political power can be resisted; the power Nosferatu wields, though it can be dispelled as the fear of death can be dispelled, cannot be resisted. He is not a political figure, not even in the allegorical way in which the diabolical Dr. Caligari can be seen to represent oppressive political authority. Rather, he is both the agent and the icon of death, the natural cause and the supernatural symbol, metonymy combined with metaphor, at once elemental and unearthly.

As he is pictured in the space he prowls, this vampire appears to dominate that space everywhere around him, to permeate the air with an odor of the grave. Toward his prey he advances with sovereign slowness, at the shivery somber pace of inevitability. In his castle we see him coming out of the dark depths of arches that from the first suggest a crypt and at a key moment in the film become equated with a coffin. On the ship taking him from Transylvania to the Baltic town, he and the plague he carries kill the entire crew. As he approaches the last surviving person on board, the captain tying himself to his ship's helm, we watch not from the captain's perspective but from a camera angle below deck, through a hatch rather like an open grave looking up at the living that remain to die. Within the frame of the hatch, which doubles at a slant the rectangle of the screen, the lines of a spar and rigging look like steeply converging lines of perspective in a foreshortened space where the figure of the vampire looms taller than ever. Space itself seems to buckle under Nosferatu's sway. His claws, seen from below, seem to be creeping up the side of the screen as, moving along the hatch's edge, he hovers at the edge of our view before leaving frame; and after he exits toward the hapless captain, his shadow lingers in our grave's-eye view. In this arresting composition and elsewhere, the power of this deathly figure is felt to reach in all directions within the frame and without.

Much of the vampiric lore that audiences have come to expect—the cross that fends off the vampire, for example, or the way the vampire's victims become vampires themselves—Murnau and his scriptwriter, Henrik Galeen, chose to disregard. The cross in *Nosferatu* serves merely as a marker of death: religion with its consolations for dying, its promises of an afterlife, has little role in a film depicting an unmitigated reign of mortality. And Nosferatu's victims become nothing other than corpses: having them turn into vampires exempt from dying would have discorded with the conception of this vampire as death personified in all its incontestable finality.

In the novel the chief antagonist of Count Dracula is a scientist, Professor Van Helsing. Generally in the horror genre science plays a central part: science sometimes complacently falling short and failing to recognize the danger and sometimes recklessly going too far and bringing on the danger, science sometimes producing the danger in madness or malignity and sometimes, as with Van Helsing in the novel, meeting the danger with brave perspicacity. The battle between the staunch professor and the fiendish count may be seen as a conflict between an ascendant bourgeois order reliant on empirical science and a decaying aristocratic order that yet refuses to be

Nosferatu. The vampire advancing toward the ship's captain: a grave's-eye view.

buried and keeps rising from the grave. By taking science to the limits of its understanding, having it contend with forces outside its purview, the horror genre often enacts a testing of science as a pillar of our cultural and social edifice. In *Nosferatu*, however, the professor plays a greatly diminished part. In his main appearance he lectures to his students on the vampirism of nature, and the film presents his scientific detachment as a response to death scarcely more adequate than another response shown in comparative juxtaposition, the insanity of a real-estate agent who under Nosferatu's sway gleefully joins in that vampirism. Science with its researches into the merely palliative or dilatory, its remedies ultimately powerless before the death that awaits us all, has but a minor role in a film concerned with the irremediable.

"Death is something that stands before us—something impending," writes Martin Heidegger in *Being and Time*.[2] A deathly figure sovereign amid the natural world of our existence, Nosferatu the vampire personifies the existential conception of death as something inherently facing and determining our being-in-the-world. Unique among creatures in our awareness of death, we human beings are for German existentialism creatures primordially informed and oriented in the world by that awareness of our own end to come. *Dasein*, the kind of being distinctive of human being, exists authentically for Heidegger only when freely taking upon itself the condition of "being-toward-death." Even though *Being and Time* first appeared in 1927, five years after *Nosferatu*, surely the ideas of German existentialism were in the air the film breathed.[3] Nosferatu is an allegory of the self thrown into a world where death impends.

If the vampire represents impending death, the film's other characters, all stylized, generalized figures drawn with the broad strokes of expressionism, represent different responses to death, different ways in which the self may approach life as death approaches. At the safe distance of scientific objectivity, treating death as a matter of biology with nothing personal at issue, the professor loses touch with the meaning of death and thus of life; the real-estate agent, taking death so personally that he identifies himself with it, cannot deal with death either and goes raving mad. On the ship the first mate, when the vampire suddenly arises before him, flees and falls overboard in utter disabling fear; the captain, by contrast, faces the vampire's approach with a resigned, baffled dutifulness. And the film's two main representatives of the self responding to death are the figures of a young husband and wife.

The film begins with the husband and wife in a setting of flowers. There are flowers around the wife as she plays with a pet kitten, flowers around the husband as he picks a bunch for her in a sunlit garden, flowers in the wallpaper behind the couple as they embrace and kiss: flowers that symbolize the bloom and also the transience of their youthful connubial love. Intertitles written in the assumed voice of a historian's account tell of the trouble to come. No less telling is a ghostly aura about Murnau's images, a quality, innate to all photographic images and heightened in his, of appearances become apparitions, phantoms of themselves, a sense that these luminous moments rendered on film are in reality soon to evanesce.

Soon the husband, sent by his employer the real-estate agent, takes off on a trip to Transylvania, land of phantoms, where the pets and gardens of nature domesticated give way to nature deathly. There to transact business with Nosferatu, who wants to buy a house in the Baltic town, the husband shrugs off the local people's insistent warnings, the disquieting view from his inn window of frightened horses at twilight, the revelations of a book about vampires he picks up at the inn. A smiling innocent journeying in mortal territory, the husband represents the type of person who would put death out of mind.

For about the first third of *Nosferatu* we follow the husband's path; he is for that stretch a Jamesian center of consciousness leading us through the film. He makes an interesting comparison with another journeying young man who takes us into fearful country, the protagonist of Dreyer's *Vampyr*. The husband in *Nosferatu* starts out disclaiming fear but comes to find himself in mortal danger. The young man in *Vampyr* starts out already frightened but remains all along a spectator to danger much like us in the audience: a singularly passive protagonist, a center of consciousness who is little more than a consciousness wandering around as a double of our own, he is an introspective abstraction of the fear of death—which is always a fear of our own death. The husband in *Nosferatu* embodies an attitude toward death decried by Heidegger, the attitude of those who regard death as something that happens to others, something too far off to worry about. And far off the husband goes to find death staring him in the face. At the very moment this happens the film strikingly shifts point of view from the husband to the wife.

Two strange bites he finds on his neck after spending a night in Nosferatu's castle the husband nervously smiles away. Among business papers the next evening, while settling the purchase of a dilapidated old mansion facing the couple's home in the Baltic town, Nosferatu espies a small framed portrait of the wife, which he beholds admiringly rather like a hero of romance falling in love with a picture. This is the first suggestion of a peculiar bond between the vampire and the wife. Retiring to his room in the castle, the husband kisses his wife's picture; hearing the clock strike midnight, he opens an arched door and sees, in the dark space beyond, the vampire poised for attack like an unearthly beast of prey, hatless for the first time so that the skull of a head is alarmingly unconcealed. The smiling innocent collapses in terror. A helpless child before the death he can no longer evade, he shuts the door and gets into bed with a sheet over his face. But the door opens again of itself, its Gothic arch framing a black patch of abyss more fraught and frightful than the vampire imminently to emerge from the darkness. As the vampire enters the room the arch of the door fits him exactly like a coffin. Here the film brings into decisive alignment two of its central motifs, the arch and the coffin, the one bounding life's passages, the other the final destination, their congruence reverberating throughout with the disturbing recognition that each passage in life is a passage toward death.[4] And on this framed picture of death, at this point when the vampire stands at the door and the arch becomes the coffin, the film shifts from the husband to the wife rising out of her bed in the Baltic town.

From far away the wife somehow senses the grave danger to her husband. She rises in a somnambulant trance from which she awakens crying out his name, her arms thrust forward in an intense gesture of reaching. But her collapsed husband is in no position to respond to her cry. Rather it is Nosferatu she reaches. The vampire halts his mortal advance and looks over his shoulder as if he heard her calling right behind him. Between vampire and wife, pictured on the screen so that each appears to be looking in the

Nosferatu. The vampire at the husband's door: the arch becomes a coffin.

direction of the other, the film cuts alternately as if the two were exchanging glances face to face across the distance that separates them. The vampire backs off from the husband and retreats into the arched darkness. How does the wife manage to face down this figure of the death that faces all of us? An answer to this question must be deferred until the film's end.

With the husband the film travels the path of many horror narratives, from the ordinary to the outlandish. We follow him from happy domesticity in the Baltic town to a Transylvania on the border between the world and the otherworldly. Recognizably actual yet remote from daily experience, nature during the Carpathian journey trembles and turns spectral before a marveling camera that may one moment see a carriage in fitful, breathless speeded-up motion and the next moment see it plunged into the phantom forest of a negative image. This assertive camera artifice has been thought crude, which by illusionistic standards it is; but surely its intent is not to create an illusion but to disrupt a reality. It unsettles the setting of nature, the seeming solidity of trees and hills, by making manifest the flickering incorporeity of their representation on the screen: trees and hills and the ground underfoot are suddenly seen to crumble into the thin imagery that constitutes them. At the heart of this Carpathian darkness lies a phantasmal sense of the images on the screen as shadows of things gone, shimmerings left in the wake of the vanishing, traces of the world's frailty. Because the camera represents things by receiving an imprint of their likeness, André Bazin compared a photographic image to a death mask. Murnau's images carry with peculiar resonance the feeling of a death mask of appearances, an imprint of things disappearing.[5]

Reached through a journey into a strange land that is also a journey into the self, this Carpathian heart of darkness, unlike Conrad's, is not the end of the story. After the wife's preternatural intervention the narrative, no longer centered on the husband but now unfolding along several parallel strands, turns back toward the Baltic town in a return journey from the outlandish to the ordinary. From a high window of the castle we gaze through the husband's eyes at the vertiginous sight of Nosferatu down below, in speeded-up motion, loading a carriage with earth-filled coffins, lying down in one, and covering himself with the lid before taking off. The vampire is departing by carriage on a trip that continues by raft down a turbulent river, and then by ship for the long stretch to his destination in the Baltic town. Meanwhile the husband, bound for home, wends his way on land toward the same destination. These two concurrent journeys, together with the professor teaching his class, the real-estate agent in a madhouse, and the wife awaiting her husband's return, are arranged contrapuntally in a sustained passage of crosscutting that grows progressively more unsettling. Near a graveyard of the drowned marking their memory in the wind-blown reedy dunes, the wife waits by the sea, a shimmering phantasmal sea that brings not her husband but Nosferatu and his coffins.

Crosscutting, as D. W. Griffith developed it, is a rupture looking forward to its mending, a disjunction rhythmically made anticipant of a resolving conjunction. As early as the 1909 *Lonely Villa* Griffith announced both his central theme, the home imperiled, and his characteristic treatment, the cutting back and forth between increasing peril and approaching rescue. A great innovator and a yearning traditionalist, Griffith marshaled his innovations to the rescue of tradition: the cuts that briskly break apart the integrity and continuity of the stage, of the home, also carry the reassurance of an eventual reparative coming together. In Eisenstein and Pudovkin crosscutting, parallel montage, is a rupture that deepens and broadens into the grand rupture of revolution: though no longer rescuing, in their hands the form is still reassuring, for it leads to the desirable, not a mending in their eyes but an overthrowing. Even as it arouses suspense, crosscutting imparts the reassurance of knowledge in a dynamically commanding view of a situation unfolding in two or more places at once. But the form acquires a different meaning and conveys a different feeling in the hands of such Weimar filmmakers as Murnau and Fritz Lang. In Eisenstein's *October* (1928) crosscutting builds up a complex image, with Lenin the knowing leader at its center, of all

Nosferatu. The wife waiting by the sea.

the factors and circumstances that must be orchestrated for triumphant revolution; in Lang's *Spies*, made the same year, a similar parallel montage discloses an intricate conspiratorial network being manipulated by a diabolically knowing master criminal who somehow represents both capitalism (he runs a bank) and communism (he looks like Lenin). In *Spies* as in *Dr. Mabuse the Gambler* (1922), Lang associates omniscience with villainy, the commanding manifoldness of the film's plot with the will to power of a criminal plot to take over the world. Knowledge here is not reassuring but a confirmation of paranoia. Knowledge in *Nosferatu* is not reassuring either, for it is the knowledge of death impending.

As opposed to Griffith and Eisenstein, filmmakers of the cut, Murnau has usually been thought to be a filmmaker of the moving camera. Old histories of cinema would talk about him mainly as the director of *The Last Laugh* (1924), the film that made his reputation and a work much celebrated in its time for two things it didn't innovate but merely handled very well, its avoidance of intertitles and its movement of the camera. The French who rediscovered him around 1950, contesting the emphasis on editing in earlier film theory, championed a cinema of deep focus and long takes and saw him as an exponent of that approach. Murnau was for Bazin a silent ancestor, with Stroheim, of a cinema that does without the fragmentations and disjunctions of montage. Bazin was wrong, however, about both Stroheim and Murnau, filmmakers who may not have cut as abruptly as some but who, in their different ways, cut articulately and with point. Even a passage so remarkably fluid as the trolley ride from the country to the city in Murnau's *Sunrise* (1927) does not proceed without cuts, cuts deftly accelerating the soothing flow of time over the inner turmoil of the characters.

For *Tabu* (1931), which turned out to be his last film, Murnau, seeking not realism but a romantic immersion in nature, enlisted as collaborator the documentarist Robert Flaherty and traveled far to make, under the sun of the South Seas, a film haunted by the shadows of German expressionism. *Tabu* tells a story of lovers on the run, lovers whose precarious union and impending separation the film expresses by crosscutting between them, interweaving their actions and their points of view in such a way that moments of tender conjunction fall continually under the threat of disjunction. This now convergent, now divergent mode of crosscutting builds to a tragic climax in the moonlight, or rather sunlight dimmed through a filter to yield the otherworldly moonlight of the most beautiful day for night ever projected: night as the glistening ghost of sunny day. Swimming desperately after the pale sailboat taking the young woman away into the dark vast sea, the young man clutches a rope dangling from the boat, a rope that another's hand promptly cuts with one smooth stroke of a knife—the definitive cut of this crosscutting, the conclusive irreparable divergence.

If Lang's parallel montage in *Spies* or *Dr. Mabuse the Gambler* unfolds a menacing design that seems to extend everywhere, the menacing design that Murnau's parallel montage unfolds in *Nosferatu,* the design of death, indeed extends everywhere and implicates everything. A design as spectral and yet as natural as the web of a spider that the real-estate agent madly observes, as the tentacles of a polyp that the professor explicates, is in *Nosferatu* writ large by crosscutting and seen to inhere in the fluid ubiquity of water and the air. With ominous omniscience the film cuts between water and water—between the wake of the ship in which the vampire travels and the waters of a stream the husband crosses, between the ship's prow thrusting ahead at sea and waves breaking at the shore. And between air and air—between the wind swelling the ship's sails, which an intertitle identifies with the "fatal breath of the vampire" driving the phantom ship on toward the Baltic town, and the wind blowing through agitated plants around the waiting wife, the wind stirring the leaves of large ramifying trees under which the husband passes, the wind billowing the curtains of a bedroom window. Into an image of the town harbor, with buildings in the background and in the close and middle distance mostly water and air, the phantom ship makes a slow, inexorable, culminant entrance. Death's vessel is seen to be taking over the town's midst.[6]

"He's coming. I must go to meet him . . . ": thus the wife could be referring either to her husband or to the vampire, both of whom are arriving

Nosferatu.
The phantom ship entering frame as it arrives in the town harbor.

in town at the same time. Arch and coffin again conjoin as the vampire, through a Gothic arch framing the ship at dock, enters the town with a coffin in his arms; and again as he passes in front of a Gothic church. In the twilight before sunrise the town sleeps, its streets empty save for the two parallel arrivers, the husband eagerly reaching home, the vampire stealthily taking up residence. Even after the sweet reunion of husband and wife, who embrace on the steps of their house and inside their regained home kiss feelingly—a reunion such as usually would resolve a sequence of crosscutting in the Griffith manner—Murnau continues his crosscutting and breaks the unity of this reunion by shifting back and forth between the couple and the vampire, between their embrace and his approach, their kiss of undying love and his lingering outside their house before proceeding to his dilapidated mansion across the way, coffin in hand. This crosscutting leads to a deepening rather than a resolving of the peril: its outcome is no happy confluence but the plague that spreads in the Baltic town, the death that strikes the site of the everyday.

In the gray light of early morning the arriving vampire, photographed from afar, appears eerily to blend with the town environment. Tiptoeing in the quiet streets, slinking through the deserted squares, this creature capable of breathing ships forward and propelling carriages at fantastic haste now nicely relinquishes Transylvanian flourishes in order not to disturb the town's sleep. The bald rangy monster carrying his own coffin for his own kind of sleep snugly fits into the ordinary actuality of the Baltic town. In

Nosferatu. Nosferatu entering the town: arch and coffin again conjoin.

front of his new home, a massive structure rising ruinously from a canal, he looks up at its high gables and dark arched windows and disappears into its facade by way of a dissolve; and since he does not reappear after this point until the film's conclusion, as pestilence breaks out everywhere in the town, it feels as though he had dissolved into the texture of all the town's cheerless facades, the bricks and cobblestones, the windows and arches, the grain of the very air. From a spooky Carpathian remoteness the film has moved to a horror that dwells in the ordinary, a daunting undifferentiated fusion of the quotidian and the uncanny.

In his essay "On Point of View in the Arts" José Ortega y Gasset argues that proximate and distant vision are two different ways of seeing. "Proximate vision has a tactile quality," he writes, whereas distant vision has a quality of the spectral:

> If we take up an object, an earthen jar, for example, and bring it near enough to the eyes, these converge on it . . . and seem to embrace it, to take possession of it, to emphasize its rotundity. Thus the object seen at close range acquires the indefinable corporeality and solidity of filled volume. We see it "in bulk," convexly. But this same object placed farther away, for distant vision, loses this corporeality, this solidity and plentitude. Now it is no longer a compact mass, clearly rotund, with its protuberance and curving flanks; it has lost "bulk," and become, rather, an insubstantial surface, an unbodied spectre composed only of light.[7]

In proximate vision we don't merely see, we virtually seize hold of an object with our eyes, an object we apprehend as palpably rounded and corporeal against the blurred background of the rest. In distant vision no object stands out and our gaze instead spreads over the entire visual field, so that the central object of attention becomes the space between objects, the hollow space that reaches to our eyes as objects recede into the distance, the air in which all seem to float like a mirage. Ortega sums up the evolution of Western painting as a movement from a proximate to a distant way of seeing, from Giotto's painting of bulk to Velázquez's painting of hollow space. Giotto, and his Italian and Flemish successors of the early Renaissance, paints solid objects; in their pictures everything, whether near or far, seems painted at close range. Velázquez, and the impressionists after him, paints the air; in their pictures everything seems distant and indistinct, a shimmering play of light that vanishes into sheer paint as we come close to the picture. Especially in his late period, in *Las Meninas* and in the less famous but no less extraordinary *Las Hilanderas*, Velázquez composes pictures mainly out of empty space, space between, vibrantly painted.

Cinema, like painting, can seize hold of solid objects, each having a specific importance and each perceived from a specifically suitable point of view; or it can stand back and look at things from a distant point of view that chiefly perceives the space between. Stroheim, Eisenstein, Dovzhenko, Dreyer, and Bergman are filmmakers who favor the solid, a cinema of rounded corporeal individualities; Murnau, Buster Keaton, Max Ophuls, Mizoguchi, and Antonioni favor the empty, a cinema of thin air, of the interval, the passage, the transition. Close-ups are an apt means for a cinema of solid objects, as long shots are an apt means for what may be called a cinema of empty space. Yet of Dreyer's films, insistently though they all focus on the human face, only *The Passion of Joan of Arc* (1928) actually makes insistent use of close-ups. And Murnau will use a close-up—of the young woman in *Tabu,* for example, retreating apprehensively behind the young man's shoulder when a policeman comes into their hut—as a detail inseparable from its context in the surrounding space. There are other means than close-ups for bringing the weight of a face or the body of an object into individual relief; and other means than long shots for rendering the ambient hollow field in which things take place.

A great example of a cinema of solid objects is Dovzhenko's *Earth* (1930). A film of vividly tactile close-ups, *Earth* captures with rooted and ardent poetry the energies of steadfast corporeal life. Yet this film of life is also, like *Nosferatu,* a film about death. It begins with the death of an old peasant, recumbent amid the rich land he long plowed, and it ends with the funeral of a young man, a leader of a new order in the land, murdered at the height of his vitality. But in *Earth,* though there is deep sorrow, there is no fear of death, for death, fearful when looming on the self's subjective horizon, is here not a conclusion each of us must face alone but an occurrence capable of being assimilated into the embracing fabric of life enduring. Nature in *Earth* is seen as a plenitude that incorporates the self and its extinction; nature in *Nosferatu* is seen as a void on whose edge the self totters.

In the medium of moving images Dovzhenko is the poet of immobility. From the transitory he brings forward and holds in place aspects of the essential, embodiments of the abiding. Each of his images feels complete in itself, definitive in its apprehension of a state of being rounded and revealed "like the open face of the rose" (as Adrian Stokes would say).[8] Each image in Murnau, by contrast, feels elusive and incomplete, threatened by the unseen, a composition in transit, an interval expectant of intrusion. "With Murnau," wrote Alexandre Astruc, "each image demands annihilation by another image. Every sequence announces its own end." In the medium of fleeting shadows Murnau is, precisely, what Jean-André Fieschi thinks a vaporous way of characterizing him, the poet of mortality.[9]

A painting puts the visible on view; a film brings into view successive pieces of the visible, and so enacts a continual exchange across the border, impassable in a painting, between the visible and the invisible. A painting exists within its frame; a film image exists amid transaction with what lies out of frame, what cannot be seen at the moment, what has left view and what at any point may enter. Representation in the film medium rests on the out of frame: it's in relation to a space off screen and its implied contents that the images unfolding on screen make sense. The out of frame is not a fact, however, but a convention, a creation of film technique, in most cases not what was actually there out of range of the camera's picturing but what we are to accept as being there in the space off screen. "Il n'y a pas de hors-texte," wrote Derrida: there is no out of text. The out of frame in a film, the *hors-champ*, is not out of text but a construction of the text.

In constructing and construing the out of frame, filmmakers have proceeded in widely different ways. With Dovzhenko the out of frame is but a blurred background to the solid object palpably being displayed on the screen and claiming our full attention. With Murnau the hollow space centrally engaging our attention fluidly continues out of frame: the space between, the air fraught with the impending, becomes one with the space off screen, a boundless restless sea of the invisible from which bits of the visible transiently emerge. Ruffled waters behind the wife in *Sunrise*, embarking in a boat with her husband and starting to recognize that he means her harm, charge the image with the threat of the surrounding unseen in which her husband plans to drown her. Later in the film, after the couple have reconciled and on their way home their boat capsizes in a storm, dark ruffled waters are all we can see for a long moment until the wife, kept barely afloat by bulrushes, enters view at top right, drifts diagonally across the rectangle of the visible, and at bottom left returns to the vast invisible.

By his cutting and his use of entrances and exits in and out of frame D. W. Griffith broke with theatrical enclosure and spread cinematic space beyond the boundaries of the screen, but he still treats the space within the frame as a kind of theater stage, changeable from one moment to the next but at each moment nonetheless containing, if not a whole scene, the part that is important dramatically. Like a theater stage, each shot in Griffith is a container of action, a space of performance constituted for our benefit, exhibiting the significant before our eyes against the background of the space off screen. In *The Art of Describing,* a study of Dutch art in the seventeenth century, Svetlana Alpers draws a distinction between pictures that give priority to the spectator (the Albertian mode) and pictures that give priority to the world seen (the northern mode).[10] Griffith and the mainstream of dramatic cinema after him give priority to the spectator; Jean Renoir, who likes to invoke and to subvert theatrical containers, gives priority to the world seen, which in his films does not address itself to our eyes, does not arrange itself for our benefit, but goes about its business independently of the camera framing and reframing our views. Entrances and exits, which in Griffith advance the plot, in Renoir call attention to what's being left out: the marginal, the distant, and the out of frame have for Renoir as much claim to attention as the prominent. Murnau is closer to Renoir than to Griffith, to the northern than to the Albertian mode.

In Murnau as in Renoir, a certain imbalance, a deliberate incompleteness relates the image inextricably to the world extending beyond the frame. But that surrounding world, which Renoir establishes socially as a concrete milieu of human and material interconnections, Murnau regards as sinister territory encroaching upon the anxious self. Renoir's images seldom feel composed for the camera; rather they come across as open on all sides, mere partial views caught by a roaming camera from the uncontainable flux of appearances. Murnau's images do feel composed, arranged in pause and in movement, but their composition is "an unstable equilibrium" (as Astruc put it),[11] a fugitive attempt at containment that anticipates its own undoing in the face of imminent flux. Composition in Murnau expresses the apprehensive subjectivity of an apprehending consciousness seeking structure in the world and encountering disruption. An eerie sense of the invisible, the hidden from view in the space off screen and in the depths, recesses, and shadows of the image, haunts Murnau's compositions and colors them with foreboding. Entrances and exits, which in Renoir occur easefully, in Murnau generate disturbances in the ambient field of tension, waves of disquiet propagating in the space between.

A ship entering view at the horizon, seen from the top of a tall palm through the eyes of the young man in *Tabu,* portends for the protagonist couple, carefree so far amid the cascades of Eden, paradise lost. A garland of flowers comes down a cascade like a gift from sensuous nature, but the ship brings severe law declaring the young woman sacred to the tribal gods and off limits to human love, and appearing as a shadow, a mournful shadow he casts on the sunlit deck, the young man picks up her discarded garland, his lone reaching hand being all of his flesh that enters frame. If *Nosferatu* begins with the ordinary idyllic and goes on to the marvelous fearful, *Tabu* begins with the marvelous idyllic, the marvelous in nature rather than in the supernatural; and if *Nosferatu* returns to the ordinary now become fearful, *Tabu* watches marvelous nature turn fearful, ghostly. Like the ship in *Nosferatu*, the ship in *Tabu* is a vessel of fatality, a carrier of the irremediable. After the lovers have fled across the sea to an island distant from tribal rule, the moment they begin a dance of celebration, the ship catches up with them. Its sudden, steady entrance into frame, interrupting their dance, is an unsettling image of the inescapable that distinctly recalls the phantom ship's arrival in the town harbor in *Nosferatu*. The lovers withdraw into their hut, which Murnau treats not as a hut open to sweet climate but as their frail refuge against an environment turned inimical, its caressive air now tinctured with menace: their space is no longer in nature but in a privacy under sustained assault from the world outside. The space within the frame in Murnau is always under such assault.

To all appearances the climax of *Nosferatu* is a natural calamity. When pestilence comes to the Baltic town the vampire who with his attendant rats brings it and spreads it is nowhere to be seen. Vividly photographed on location in the clear light of day without the least expressionist distortion or embellishment, the scenes depicting the stricken town have an arresting, stark lifelikeness. Neither the bloodsucking monster nor any of his supernatural concomitants, not even the mark of his bite on the necks of victims, can now be glimpsed; between victims of his bite and victims of rat-borne disease no differentiation is made; from the somber actuality of pestilence we are left to infer his presence and his agency. His presence is felt in the air; his agency is generalized beyond his bloodsucking, beyond the plague even, into a symbol of the inescapable agency of our common mortality.

Just as the arriving vampire yielded to the tone and circumstance of the sleeping town, so now the town environment seems to be echoing in daily grimness the gray dawn that saw Nosferatu's arrival. The coffin he carried with him foreshadowed a ceaseless succession of coffins that are now the principal sight in the town streets. The streets and houses remain nearly as quiet and still as when he crept into their deserted ambiance: not the quiet of sleep now but of death, the stillness of eternal rather than nocturnal rest, the coffin in which the vampire sleeps portending for the whole town the sleep of the grave. It's as if the town's sleep had on that early morning seamlessly turned into death.

A town official goes along a street marking with a cross, one after another, the doors of the dead—tall arched doors each implying a coffin and one actually opening to let out through its arched passage, feet first as is the custom, a coffin being carried to burial. Some of the townspeople panic and scapegoat the mad real-estate agent. Most of them, apparently unaware of the vampire lurking in their midst, receive death with seemly resignation and bury their dead in composed solemnity. No longer an innocent but even now not prepared to face the horror at large in the town, the husband suppresses his knowledge of the vampire's agency for the sake of maintaining composure. The husband's smiling innocence has turned into dim conventionality.

Only two of the townspeople face up to the vampire in their midst; only two, that is to say, recognize for what it is, assess in its true magnitude, the horror of death. These two are the real-estate agent and the wife. In two striking point-of-view shots we share their awful vision. From the top of a steep tiled roof he has climbed, the real-estate agent, escaped from the madhouse and being chased by a crowd, glances at his pursuers scurrying in a narrow alley below: through his eyes the living look like so many swarming insects ready for the spider. From her window the wife, her viewing position emphasized by a window bar in the extreme foreground, gazes at a long line of the dead and their pallbearers proceeding in orderly gloom along the jagged shadow line cast by houses down the middle of a cobbled street:

Nosferatu. The doors of the dead.

through her eyes we see, coming toward us, what we the living are to be-come, an inexorable procession of corpses slowly but surely encroaching upon the window bar marking the place of the beholding self.

Between the distant yet approaching line of the dead, foreshortened into a dark vertical line advancing out of the depths of the image, and the beholder's window bar up close, running horizontally across the image near its bottom edge, yawns space, hollow space that we feel continuing past the bar and the boundaries of the image, reaching to our eyes and drawing us into the scene. This is not an Albertian window displaying for our con-templation and dividing from our reality a self-contained view arranged in a demarcated realm of its own. Like Velázquez's *Las Meninas*, this is an image composed mainly out of empty space, space between rendered in such a way that it affects us as extending forward past the picture plane to include the space between us and the picture, to implicate the space where we stand. In the space before the picture where we spectators stand *Las Meninas* shows to be standing, as Foucault has noted, the king and queen of Spain—which makes literal and at the same time paradoxical the sovereign beholder tacit in the Albertian mode of picturing. The point-of-view shot in film, which attributes the camera's perspective to a character whose eyes we assume for the moment, is a common device. The view from the wife's window in *Nosferatu* is a point-of-view shot of uncommon intensity and implicative resonance. Like the king and queen in *Las Meninas*, the wife occupies a posi-tion outside the image yet central to the configuration of its space: a position that the space between, as if exerting the pressure of a gaping void, seems to

Nosferatu. The view from the wife's win-dow: the advancing line of the dead.

be calling for someone to fill. Rather than, as in the usual point-of-view shot, our putting ourselves in the wife's place and vicariously adopting her subjectivity, here we feel the wife to be bravely embodying in our place a primordial anxious subjectivity that the image expresses: the subjectivity of the self confronting death, answering the pressure of the deadly space between.

"Distant objects please," wrote Hazlitt in his essay on this topic,

> because, in the first place, they imply an idea of space and magnitude, and because, not being obtruded too close upon the eye, we clothe them with the indistinct and airy colours of fancy. In looking at the misty mountain-tops that bound the horizon, the mind is as it were conscious of all the conceivable objects and interests that lie between. . . . We drink the air before us, and borrow a more refined existence from objects that hover on the brink of nothing. Where the landscape fades from the dull sight, we fill the thin, viewless space with shapes of unknown good, and tinge the hazy prospect with hopes and wishes and more charming fears.[12]

For much the same reasons—because we fill the thin, viewless space with our subjectivity, because objects that elude the clear grasp of proximity we clothe with indistinct and airy colors of our projection—in *Nosferatu* distant objects deeply disturb.

Where the vampire appears he typically emerges slowly out of the distance and hovers on the brink of nothing, his lingering far presence dominating all the conceivable objects and interests that lie between, just as, to the existential way of thinking, death for us human beings, who can discern it on the horizon of life, informs every path we may take through the space between. In the plague scenes, with the vampire visible nowhere, the streets and houses of the stricken town are viewed from afar, in persistent long shots that at first glance would seem to reveal everything yet leave everything imprecise, hovering on the brink of nothing, spectrally suffused with what Heidegger calls "the indefinite certainty of death." Declining to single out any telling details, any particulars that may warrant closer inspection, the distant camera disperses attention over a whole that yet lies outside our grasp, open to the projection of our worst fears. Almost documentary in their unblinking naturalism, these scenes are at the same time vertiginously subjective— subjective not from any character's maintained point of view but from the camera's, from our own point of view. There being no object that stands out and holds the consciousness, nothing solid on which the eye can rest or the mind settle, we are tremblingly thrown back on our own subjectivity and our own fear of death. Death seen to dwell at the heart of the everyday, when the false reassurance of the familiar falls apart before our eyes, brings on the anxiety that for Heidegger inheres in our being-in-the-world.

In the moonlit marshes of *Sunrise* the camera at first keeps pace with the husband as he advances toward his clandestine rendezvous with the woman from the city. But then, in a striking move, the camera, allowing the husband to go on past it, swerves to one side and takes a path of its own that feels very much like the path of an individual consciousness traveling through the marshes independently of the husband and arriving before he does at the spot where the woman from the city seductively awaits him. This is a justly famous camera movement; Marcel Carné admiringly discussed it at the time in an article entitled "The Camera, a Character in the Drama."[13] Murnau's camera, however, is less like an unseen character in the drama than like a visual narrator whose point of view makes itself felt as a consciousness distinct from the characters', a consciousness that becomes bound up with our own through the implicative subjectivity of the space between reaching forward to our eyes and drawing us into its compass. When the camera in *Sunrise* follows the husband he fills the space of our view as an object of attention and identification; when the camera departs from him and travels on its own through the misty moonlit air we in our turn are left on our own to fill the space, charged with an enthralling risky sexuality, between us and the obscure object of desire, the darkly captivating woman from the city.

According to Christian Metz and other theorizers, when watching a film we primarily identify ourselves not with the characters but with the camera. Whether or not this is true in general, it applies in particular to our experience of a Murnau film. Space between is the chief thing we experience when watching Murnau's images—the space traversed in the marshes or on the trolley in *Sunrise*, the space around the lovers' hut in *Tabu* or the revolving door in *The Last Laugh* or the rococo staircase in his insufficiently appreciated *Tartuffe* (1925), the space that in the plague scenes in *Nosferatu* the vampire's absence punctuates. In that space left largely empty, incomplete without our participation, we register with heightened awareness the perspective the camera makes ours, the individual viewing point that we occupy outside the image and that informs the geometry and the slant of its perspectival space. The point of view we sometimes share with the characters and always share with the camera commands in Murnau peculiar involvement.

Few other filmmakers have been as influential as Murnau has been. Especially in his treatment of space and of point of view he was a major shaper of visual and narrative form in the film medium. From him Mizoguchi learned much about composing in long shot, John Ford about arranging entrances and exits in interplay with the cutting, Max Ophuls about moving the camera, Hitchcock about managing point of view.[14] In *Shadow of a Doubt* (1943), which with good reason he declared a personal favorite among his films, Hitchcock recalls in significant ways the structure, the movement, and the concerns of *Nosferatu*. Charles and Charlie, the sinister uncle and the wide-eyed niece in *Shadow of a Doubt*, have between them a preternatural affinity reminiscent of the bond between the vampire and the wife in *Nosferatu*. As in *Nosferatu*, in *Shadow of a Doubt* horror comes to the sunlit site of the familiar, horror in the person of the worldly, shady uncle visiting his perfectly average family in a perfectly average American town. And like the wife in *Nosferatu*, the niece in *Shadow of a Doubt* sees through the surface of the ordinary and comes vertiginously face to face with the awful.

Like Murnau and like Mizoguchi, Antonioni often renders things at a ghostly distance, in airy, eerie long shots that call upon the viewer insecurely to fill in what the image falls short of embodying. If Murnau took German expressionism outward, from anxious fabrications of the studio back to a primordial anxiety before the face of nature, Antonioni turned Italian neorealism inward, from the observation of the external world to a self-questioning of the eye's evidence and a reflective emphasis on the subjectivity of the observing point of view. Even more than Murnau, Antonioni leaves spaces between wide open to our apprehensive projections, but his spaces between are those of the estranged self in society, not the self before ominous nature. Antonioni is rather like a materialist Murnau, a Murnau concerned not so much with the primordial as with an anxiety arising out of the concrete relations and circumstances of human society. In the summery yet discomforting Roman suburb of Antonioni's *Eclipse* (1962) Monica Vitti faces something as elusive and as pervasive as the daily death that in *Nosferatu* the wife faces out her window, something no less mysterious and uncanny for being more precisely observed as a social reality. Appearances in Antonioni as in Murnau are viewed with attentive suspicion, not because appearances are deceptive but because they are unclear and incomplete, ambiguous fragments of a whole beyond our purview, glimpses fraught with the invisible.

On appearances *Nosferatu* presents different perspectives: the husband's smiling innocence and the real-estate agent's knowing insanity, the professor's scientific detachment and the ship captain's dutiful resignation, the townspeople's scapegoating panic on the one hand and conventional solemnity on the other, and—most telling and meaningful of all—the wife's perspective of brave awareness. And the film also presents different written texts: the intertitles giving a town historian's account of the plague and its circumstances, a letter the husband writes to his wife from the vampire's castle that she receives by the shivery sea, a newspaper report of the plague's spread in ports along the ship's route, the captain's log found in his cabin in the phantom ship and read with alarm at the town council, the book about vampires the husband picks up at the Carpathian inn and brings home with him but asks his wife never to open. *Nosferatu* exhibits and compares different ways of regarding appearances that harbor the ultimate, different readings of the world that holds death in store.

Considering its prominence not just in Stoker's *Dracula* but in most vampire tales, and not just in vampire tales but in most of our traditional pictures and conceptions of death and ways of dealing with our mortality, religion is remarkably absent from *Nosferatu*. In the banishment of religion as in the downgrading of science and in other significant respects the universe of the film is much the universe of Heidegger's existentialism. The vampire book is as close as the film comes to scripture. Unable to resist her impulse to open it, the wife finds in this book that the vampire is the cause of the plague and that "only a woman can break his frightful spell—a woman pure in heart—who will offer her blood freely to Nosferatu and will keep the vampire by her side until after the cock has crowed." This sounds like an oracular pronouncement calling for an atoning sacrifice to appease the gods so that the plague may cease; but the film knows no divine power that might be propitiated and no crime or sin that might have brought on the plague and requires atonement. After gazing out her window at the line of the dead, the wife feels called upon to sacrifice herself to put an end to the vampire and his frightful spell. Hers is not an atoning sacrifice, however, not a propitiation of the divine, but a bravely human taking upon herself of the death that awaits her.

The vampire awaits her, longingly, at his window across the way. He who has devastated the town and can have access to anyone else must in her case wait for her opening her window and allowing him to come to her. The vampire who reappears in the film's closing sequence no longer seems the sovereign fiend of death but a figure himself vulnerable, aching, the death's head that is his face suddenly a sign of his own impending end.

As the film unfolds the presentation of the vampire shifts significantly. First he is the monstrous lord of a deathly Transylvania; there he most purely represents the fear of death, which is a fear not of the fact but of the idea of death, an idea that appears foreign and ghastly to the smiling innocent led to contemplate it. Then, as he and the husband journey concurrently toward the Baltic town, the vampire represents a horror seen to pervade the fabric of nature. Then, in the scenes of the plague, when death is no longer something foreign but something grimly immanent in everyday life, the vampire dissolves into a phantasmal documentary of a natural calamity. And finally he reappears as a figure more frail than formidable: no longer a figure of the idea of death terrifyingly coming to consciousness, or of the reign of death in nature, he is now a figure of the individual's death, a representation of the death the wife must face. As such the vampire is vulnerable because the wife has the courage to face him.

Women are central in Stoker's *Dracula*.[15] In his Transylvanian castle Dracula does not live alone like Nosferatu but with three women, his brides, who are themselves vampires; and after the predatory count reaches England, his two main victims are young women who under his sway become or threaten to become vampires. The horror of vampires expresses in *Dracula* a fear of sexuality and especially of female sexuality. The lone vampire in *Nosferatu* stands not for the threat of sexuality but for the threat of death. In *Nosferatu*, where there are no woman vampires, a woman is the vampire's chief opponent and eventual destroyer. None of the vampire's victims in the film—none of those shown rather than just implied to be his victims—is a woman until the wife offers her blood to him at the end. The scene in which he comes to her bedroom and she keeps him by her side until daybreak is the only scene in the film that associates the vampire's grip with sexuality, which even here is not the main point. If vampirism in *Dracula* is a metaphor for

Nosferatu.
The courage of anxiety: the wife opening her window for the vampire, making her death her own.

sexuality, sexuality in the final scene of *Nosferatu* is a metaphor for the self embracing, anxiously yet freely, the condition of "being-toward-death." A woman is central in *Nosferatu* not principally as a sexual being but as a figure of existentially authentic human being.

As Nosferatu the vampire personifies death, so the woman who confronts him, and who defines herself as an individual through this confrontation, may be seen to personify authentic *Dasein*. The wife in *Nosferatu* represents what, in the existential view of life, is the best way of being human at the juncture most defining of human being, the juncture with death. In destroying the vampire she certainly does not conquer death: she knows that in the process she must die herself. Unlike her husband in his journey, she is not the smiling type who would rather not think of death; unlike her husband later and unlike most of the townspeople, she is not the solemn type who would subsume death under the conventions of mortuary composure. Neither detached like the professor nor deathly afraid like the ship's first mate, neither resigned to die like the dutiful captain nor welcoming of death like the mad real-estate agent, she meets death of her own free will but in fear and trembling. She has what Heidegger calls the "courage of anxiety" in the face of the end. Her peculiar bond with the vampire and her power over this figure of death may be seen to allegorize the orientation toward death peculiar to human being and the power one gains by making one's death one's own.

If Nosferatu the vampire represents death, it may be asked, how can it be that at the end he dies himself? Surely this cannot mean that death itself dies? Death is seen in different guises in the course of the film: as an otherworldly

Nosferatu. Death's shadow approaching the wife's bedroom.

monster, as a design of nature, as the deadly space between. After the death diffused everywhere in the stricken midst of the familiar, the death personified by the vampire when he reappears at the film's conclusion is not death generally but the death each human being must face individually. By her sacrifice the wife gains for the town relief from the plague. But it is not the death of others that she confronts: it is the death that awaits her. And it is not with the fact of her dying that she contends—as a fact death is invincible—but with the idea of her impending death, with death as a specter haunting the consciousness, a specter she bravely embraces and succeeds in dispelling by making her own. As the plague brings forward the deathliness of everyday life, so the wife comes forward to the human juncture with death.

The shadows of German expressionism attain their most haunting manifestation in Murnau's images. For the film image as itself a shadow Murnau has a special feeling. Physically a shadow, a shadow cast on the screen by film passing through the projector, the image in Murnau becomes charged with the emotional coloring of a shadow, with a poignant and disquieting sense that what we watch moving on the screen is the world's ghost. It is as a shadow, a shadow ascending the stairs and extending its long clawed arm toward the door, that the vampire comes to the wife in her bedroom; and as a shadow he grasps the palpitant heart within her breast. As body yields to ghost in the film image, so her flesh yields here to the specter of death. After this night of spectral rather than carnal knowledge, the rising light of daybreak comes in through the window, the window she opened to let in death's shadow, and kills the vampire. Fittingly, it is light that destroys the vampire, that dispels his shadow; but this, we cannot forget, is the light of the medium of shadows.

5 :   The Meaning of Revolution

Near the beginning of *Boudu Saved from Drowning*, Jean Renoir's 1932 film version (and subversion) of a stage comedy of the time, the tramp Boudu has lost his dog and is looking for it in a park. Various persons, Boudu among them, wander in and out of view in a shot characteristic of Renoir in its openness to the world beyond the frame. Boudu is given no place of prominence in the shot; he remains mostly in the background until at length he wanders off into the space out of view. Even though he is the main character, the camera in no way singles him out for attention from among the other passersby. A policeman does assume a privileged position, however; he walks toward the camera and stands with his back to it in the foreground, surveying the scene from nearly the same vantage point; in his stance of authority, he becomes equated with the camera's point of view. He brusquely dismisses Boudu, threatens to throw him into jail, when the tramp comes forward to ask about his lost dog, but when a well-dressed woman reports the loss of an expensive dog, he gets a search going without delay. This cop embodies an authority we want to question. By equating him with the camera, which in most films assumes authority as framer of the views we are meant to see, Renoir calls into question the camera's authority. We are not to accept the views we are given in a Renoir film as just what we should be seeing, but to recognize them as mere partial views that could have been chosen otherwise from the vast field of possibilities the world offers.

The mainstream tradition of cinema derives from the theater. In the beginning the movie camera was a stationary spectator and the spectacle was presented before it as on a theater stage. After filmmakers started changing camera position and editing the picture, the view was no longer fixed but it was still like a theater stage arranged at each moment so as to present the spectacle before the spectator, a piece at a time, the right piece at the right time. Jean Renoir departs from this tradition. His ironic equation between camera and cop—ironic because he posits it in order to negate it—declares his refusal to employ the camera as a commanding eye, the eye of the spectator, to which each moment is played, each successive view directed, like a staging in the theater. The world in a Renoir film of the thirties is not arranged for our gaze; it is not a spectacle addressed to a spectator. In a film by

Sergei Eisenstein the world is very much so arranged; it is there to make an impact, a spectacle emphatically addressed, designed to arouse the spectator.

Eisenstein began in the theater. He worked in a vein of theater that pursued avant-garde experimentation while embracing elements of popular culture. He apprenticed with Vsevolod Meyerhold, the famous director whose alternative methods of staging challenged the illusionist realism practiced by Konstantin Stanislavsky at the Moscow Art Theater. The art of the avant-garde has usually sought its audience in the appreciative few, but in Soviet Russia in the years after the 1917 revolution an avant-garde flourished that endeavored to combine the experimental with the popular, seeking a grounding and an audience in the people. The building of a new society seemed to call for the making of a new art that wouldn't just appeal to a few but would engage all. Eisenstein the stage designer and director looked to the forms and effects of popular theater; the "attraction," as in the circus or the variety show, was for him the theatrical building block. A dramatically tense scene, for example, he staged by having the actor on a tightrope: "The tension of such an 'act on wire' extends the *conventional* tension of acting," he wrote, "and transfers it into a new level of *real* physical tension."[1] A "montage"—an assembly, a mounting together—of such "attractions," each an "aggressive moment in theater," made for Eisenstein a play. The basic material of theater, the stuff on which the director works, was for him the audience, not the drama or its performance (these were merely the means for working on the audience); theater direction meant for him "the moulding of the audience in a desired direction."[2]

Boudu Saved from Drowning. The ironic equation between camera and cop.

Eisenstein's last theatrical production was a stretch of the medium of theater, a play about factory workers staged in an actual factory during working hours before an audience brought into its midst; the failure of this play—it closed after four performances—led its director to a medium, the cinema, in which actuality would be more amenable to direction. An actual factory provides the setting for much of Eisenstein's first film, *Strike* (1925), but there the factory comes under the control of camera and cutting; rather than distracting the audience, as the actual factory did in the play, the factory in the film serves to impress the audience in the desired direction. At the start the film cuts from a large head-on close-up of a laughing fat capitalist to an overhead traveling shot of the interior of the factory, a space thus seen to belong to the capitalist, to fall under his oppressive dominance. Here, as often in Eisenstein, the close-up, where meaning can be more tightly controlled, slants the long shot. D. W. Griffith and American filmmakers after him use close-ups mainly "to *show* or to *present,*" said Eisenstein, whereas he and other Soviet filmmakers use close-ups mainly "to *signify,* to *give meaning,* to *designate.*"[3]

The space of work does not belong to the workers: they are, in the classic Marxist formulation, alienated. Their meetings, their attempts to organize, must take place covertly, in the recesses and corners, on the margins of the factory—in a lavatory or a junkyard, out on a swim or up on a tower or a roof—and are photographed disorientingly, from odd, oblique or obstructed camera angles serving to underscore this precarious marginality. The suicide of a worker precipitates the strike. Unjustly accused by the management of stealing an expensive tool, this worker leaves the manager's office distraught at being branded a thief; cut to a repeat of the overhead traveling shot already associated with capitalist oppression, a shot in which the belts in the factory machinery figure prominently; as the worker takes off his own belt from his pants, ties it to a pipe above, and hangs himself with it, further cuts point up the connection with the factory belts and palpably imply that the worker was in effect hanged by those belts, by the capitalist machinery of exploitation and subjugation.

The belts in *Strike* signify. They are an example of the way Eisenstein makes objects into vehicles of meaning, tropes and symbols, metaphors and metonymies, visual figures of speech speaking to us in the audience. If theater is the arrangement before an audience of a world addressed to us, invested with meaning meant for us, Eisenstein's films are a theater enabled by cinema to enlist a larger world for its stage.[4] If Renoir's films subvert theater, Eisenstein's enlarge it. Eisenstein's silent films, made in the twenties before Stalinism gained despotic ascendancy, were a revolutionary theater addressed to an audience responsive to the call of revolution. What is the meaning of those films today, now that the Soviet revolution is distant history and the Soviet state a thing of the past?

The pioneer Soviet documentarist Dziga Vertov, who developed the craft of the newsreel into major filmmaking, keenly believed that films, or at any rate the films of nascent socialism, had no business at all with theater. "Film-drama is the opium of the people," he declared. The acted film, the film that stages a fiction, was in his view an obfuscation of consciousness, a form of bewitchment that works on the audience by "stupefaction and suggestion" and betrays "the genuine purpose of the movie camera—the exploration of the phenomena of life." To the sway of this bewitchment— and he numbered Eisenstein among the swayers—Vertov opposed the eye of documentary consciousness, the "kino-eye" that does not fool the audience with illusions but instead presents it with "carefully selected, recorded, and organized facts."[5] "It is not a 'kino-eye' that we need," replied Eisenstein, "but a 'kino-fist.' "[6]

Strike ends in defeat and bloody suppression. Cossacks invade the workers' district; mounted on horses, they go up on the balconies and connecting footbridges over the courtyards of multistory tenements housing the workers; brutal intruding centaurs, they are seen everywhere taking over the workers' own living space and there conducting a massacre. In this sequence as in the later, better-known one on the Odessa steps in *The Battleship Potemkin* (1925), Eisenstein brilliantly manipulates the space of reality for the staging of a theater of bloodshed that makes an indelible impact on the audience. At the finish of the Odessa steps sequence a Cossack, his movement made more striking by being rendered twice over in an abrupt montage of successive close-ups, swings his saber right in our direction; as we wince, the film cuts to a frontal close-up of a woman's bleeding face. In *Strike* Eisenstein cuts, in a famous montage metaphor, between the massacre of the workers and a bull being slaughtered by a butcher. The massacre is equated with the slaughterhouse both in its bloodiness and in its impersonal matter-of-factness: this sort of violence, the juxtaposition implies, is done every day.

Brecht was Eisenstein's exact contemporary—they were both born in 1898—and like him a Marxist artist engaged in changing his art so that it would help change the world. They were both against the make-believe reality of mainstream theater and film and for an art of undisguised artifice. Brecht wanted the audience to be aware that the actor is acting; Eisenstein wanted the audience to register the cut, the break in our perception that conventional editing would smooth over. Yet, though both men diverged from the mainstream, they went in different directions. In making us aware of the actor's acting, Brecht aimed to cool down the heat of the drama and to keep us, certainly not from feeling, but from being carried away by emotion; whereas Eisenstein, in making us register the cut's cutting, aimed to give us a jolt that intensifies our response, to hit us all the harder with his "kino-fist." The slaughterhouse metaphor in *Strike* is not a Brechtian interruption of the drama but a vivid augmentation of it, calling not for critical detachment but for an impassioned response. Mainstream theater and film arrange a world meant for us, a spectacle for our eyes and ears, but dissemble the arrangement so as to foster the illusion of another world. Both Brecht and Eisenstein point up the arrangement, but for different reasons: Brecht so that we may stand back from the illusion, Eisenstein so that the spectacle may affect us more forcefully by having its address to the spectator made explicit.

Like Brecht, Eisenstein was an artist who himself undertook the theory of his art; montage was to him what the alienation effect was to Brecht, his aesthetic position summed up in a word. For the young Eisenstein of the twenties—his later theorizing got vaguer and grander, less polemical and more platitudinous, in its accommodation to the uncongenial aesthetic of Stalinist "socialist realism"[7]—montage meant cutting that brings on a "collision" between the pieces of photographed reality it successively juxtaposes. The rupture makes an impact and the juncture makes a meaning. He compared montage to the Japanese ideogram, a writing system that he saw as also signifying by juxtaposition: the characters meaning "knife" and "heart," for example, joined together mean "sorrow." From the conjunction of two objects arises a concept. From the conjunction of two shots arises an emotion, an idea, a way of thinking. Montage was for Eisenstein "the nerve of film." In his hands it was a potent director of emotion, and it strove for more, toward "directing the entire *thought process.*"[8]

As an example of what he called "intellectual montage" Eisenstein cited the scene in *October* (1928), his movie about the 1917 revolution, in which Kerensky, head of the provisional government the Bolsheviks opposed, is shown again and again going up the same flight of stairs in the Winter Palace, his repeated ascension intercut with titles ("Dictator," "Minister of the Army," "Minister of the Navy," "Prime Minister," "Etc ... etc ... etc ... ") designating the power he gained after the suppression of the uprising of July 1917. The stairs physically symbolize Kerensky's rise to power; the Winter Palace tells us that Kerensky's power is the same thing as the czar's; the repeated ascension and the titles make fun of that power as something pompous and hollow. This is good political theater, intellectual in the sense that all satire is intellectual but not particularly an inducement to inquiring thought. After this, however, comes another, more complex and more resonant example of intellectual montage.

As Kerensky stands before the door to the czar's chambers, the film cuts back and forth between him and a gold peacock seen in isolation from the surrounding space. With no spatial connection established, the connection we are first led to make between Kerensky and the peacock is purely metaphorical, an equation between the two: Kerensky is vain as a peacock. Like the slaughterhouse in *Strike* and like various other instances of metaphorical montage, this is a figure of speech made physical, not a literalization—though the vehicle is physical, the sense remains figurative—but a theatricalization of metaphor. The peacock, a fancy mechanical contraption, spreads its feathers and turns around to display them, its movement fragmented and partly repeated—an Eisenstein specialty—in shots cut together so as to heighten the movement by showing it from different angles and prolonging its duration on the screen. Now a spatial connection is suggested: the opening of the door to the czar's chambers seems geared to the peacock's turning, and after Kerensky enters, this suggestion is strengthened by the cutting between the door's closing behind him and the peacock's turning the other way. The peacock, we might infer, turns at the top of the door as the door opens and closes. Never shown together on the screen, and not in fact linked together in the space of the Winter Palace, the peacock and the door are made to seem so linked in a fictive metonymy constructed by montage. Added to the metaphor—Kerensky is vain as a peacock—the metonymy leads us to see Kerensky as a peacock whose vanity is mechanically activated by the gears of the old regime, a puppet whose illusions of grandeur are part of the machinery of exploitation. From the peacock as it concludes its turning the film cuts to bird claws that for a moment seem to be the peacock's but are in fact clasps on the door of a cell where Bolsheviks are imprisoned: the vain mechanical bird wields the claws of repression.

By a strenuous fragmentation of the world and rearrangement of its pieces Eisenstein makes it speak to the spectator, makes it mean. No other filmmaker has been so intent on interpreting the world for us, on having its every aspect and detail signify. "It was not at all an aesthetic failure that I encountered in these movies," wrote Robert Warshow in a dissenting article about the Soviet cinema, "but something worse: a triumph of art over humanity." Or a triumph of meaning over reality: "What we want most, that cinema rarely gives us: some hint of the mere reality of the events it deals with."⁹ (Vertov's movies, which Warshow didn't see, he probably would have liked better than Eisenstein's, but not much better. His article, left unfinished at his death in 1955, has a clear bias of Cold War anti-Communism. It cannot be discounted on account of that bias, however; its challenge to a purely aesthetic appreciation of the Soviet cinema stands.) But mere reality for Eisenstein would merely ratify the status quo, would let the reigning situation reign unopposed. "No death is without meaning," objected Warshow; "even that baby hurtling in its carriage down the Odessa steps in *Potemkin* is part of the great plan, and the spectacle is exciting but not saddening."¹⁰ The spectacle is not, or not merely, saddening because the Cossack aggression is opposed by an aggressive montage that does not just lament the bloodshed but sounds a call to action. Horrible though it is, the spectacle is exciting because it has a meaning that we can grasp, and grasp in a way that makes us feel empowered to act.

Boudu Saved from Drowning was originally a play that celebrated the universalizing embrace of the bourgeoisie. Renoir reversed the ending and the meaning of the play. The Boudu of the play is a tramp saved from drowning by a bourgeois bookseller and eventually assimilated into the ways of the bourgeoisie; the Boudu of Renoir's film is unassimilable. In the play Boudu ends up happily housebroken and married to the maid; in the film Boudu overturns the boat carrying the wedding party and drifts off down the river at the end, in no need of rescue. As this tramp is not to be contained by the conventions of bourgeois society, so this film is not to be contained by the conventions of bourgeois comedy. Renoir's camera prepares for Boudu's escape from the bourgeoisie by continually drawing attention to the world beyond the frame, vividly bringing into play the world beyond the plot. For this camera and for this tramp the wide world out there breaks the container of bourgeois theater and of bourgeois society. As in his later *Rules of the Game,* in *Boudu* Renoir uses the form of a theatrical comedy ironically, as a form that purposely fails to contain the content. Those who would set apart realism and modernism don't recognize it, but Renoir is more like Brecht than Eisenstein is, for both Brecht and Renoir are artists who call into question the forms of their art and, at the same time, the forms of their society; whereas the young Eisenstein worked in a society of triumphant socialism and in a mood of confidence and solidarity rather than irony and detachment.

The theater of Eisenstein's films contains the world. It employs reality as its setting, not as a backdrop but as a central element, material to the action. It employs the people as its actors, not as extras but in the leading part. "The real hero of these movies is history," observed Warshow. "But," he added, "if there is one thing we should have learned from history—and from the history of the Russian Revolution above all—it is that history ought to be nobody's hero."[11] It's hard to argue with that. The socialism that triumphed cruelly betrayed all the hopes and aspirations it was to have realized. The confidence stirringly expressed in Eisenstein's silent films—the confidence in our capacity to understand the world and to change it, the confidence that history has a meaning and that we the people can make history—gave rein to a revolutionary violence that, it may be judged, continued without respite in the violence of that betrayal. Many years later, his last film, *Ivan the Terrible* (1944–46), enacted a different sort of theater, claustrophobic and paranoid, equally bloody and much darker: "the great Stalinist film," wrote G. Cabrera Infante, "an epitome of terror and total power."[12]

Where does the battleship *Potemkin* go? At the film's end the rebel battleship meets a czarist squadron deployed to subdue it which instead greets it with a cheer of solidarity. In the last shot the ship's prow, seen from below, seems to break forth from the screen and to sweep over us in the audience. This is where the *Potemkin* goes symbolically, but many viewers still have wondered where the ship would have actually gone, as Eisenstein acknowledged in an essay whose title gives the historical answer his film omits: Constanţa, a Rumanian port on the Black Sea, was where the *Potemkin* went and where its mutinous sailors sought refuge after their defiance of

The conclusion of *Potemkin*: where does the *Potemkin* go?

czarist rule.[13] Out of the revolt of the *Potemkin,* an actual incident from the suppressed 1905 revolution in Russia, Eisenstein made a myth of revolution on the rise. Constanţa would have been a letdown; he ended his film, as he explained, at a point when the failed attempt of 1905 looks forward to the triumph of 1917.

Where does the *Potemkin* go, now that the 1917 revolution has itself ended in failure? The vigorous rhythmic montage of the sailors running their own ship as they prepare to meet the squadron endures as a rousing image of the people running their own lives and taking charge of their own destiny. For Eisenstein in 1925 this was an image of what had come to be. For us it is what we like to call "utopian": an image of what we may find ardently desirable but think in all likelihood unattainable.

In Spanish and in French, in Italian and in Russian, silent films are called "mute." When we watch them today, most silent films indeed give us the feeling of their being mute, unable to speak and striving to express themselves by other means. We are now used to sound, of course, but this doesn't quite account for the way we miss it in silent films. We don't get the same sense of a lack when we watch films in black and white, even though by now we are also used to color. The movies are supposed to be predominantly a visual medium, but they seem to require sound more than they require color. Seeing people move on the screen, we want to hear them talk; seeing them react to one another, we want to hear what they say to one another; it's hard for us to accept the convention of their silence. The movies are not only a visual but also naturally a dramatic medium where we can see enacted the interaction between human beings, a peculiar affair when it is conducted without their being able to speak. Physical comedy was the one dramatic mode that thrived in silence; the films of Charlie Chaplin and Buster Keaton have not aged and can be watched today without our having to make an effort of adjustment in their behalf. The comedians seem at home in silence, maybe because a long tradition of silent clowns existed before them on the stage but also, one might argue, because the necessary unreality of silent acting is better suited to the artificiality of a comic mode.

The films of D. W. Griffith and Erich von Stroheim do call for an effort of adjustment. Griffith's films are in an archaic dramatic mode, a transposition of Victorian melodrama into a kind of mute opera in which the images make music and often make the difference between the ridiculous and the sublime. (Melodrama, it will be remembered, originally meant drama with music.) Stroheim's films look much more modern than Griffith's, not only because of their greater physical realism but because of their camera technique, which, perhaps more than that of any other silent films, anticipates the technique of sound films, the reverse angles and point-of-view shots, the breakdown of scenes into many different shots put together in a smooth continuity—the kind of shot arrangement the French call *découpage classique.* (André Bazin was quite wrong to take Stroheim as an exemplar of the kind of filmmaking style that doesn't much rely on editing. On the contrary, Stroheim's films are notable for their fast cutting—almost as fast as Eisenstein's.[14] The difference is that Stroheim cuts smoothly, so smoothly that a sharp observer like Bazin could take little note of his cutting.) But Stroheim's actors, seemingly oblivious to the surrounding realism and the fluent camera technique, go on acting in the operatic and to our eyes overdone manner of serious silent drama. The combination of reality and unreality is more successfully managed in certain films of F. W. Murnau—*Nosferatu, Sunrise, Tabu*—where it becomes the calculated style of a generalizing allegorical mode well suited to the silent screen.

Can't all the visual means of cinema, all the techniques of camera and cutting, make up for the acting, take the place of the spoken word as dramatic means? Surely in opera the music is able to make up for the acting. Yes, but films are (with some exceptions such as *The Cabinet of Dr. Caligari*) a more realistic medium than opera in that they make a more direct reference to the real world. The movie camera reproduces the actual appearance of human beings in movement, and the visual means of cinema can be effective as dramatic means as long as they work together—in concert or in counterpoint—with the interacting human beings we see reproduced on the screen.

The stylizations and exaggerations of serious silent drama are boldly deployed in a film made near the end of that era, Carl Dreyer's *Passion of Joan of Arc* (1928). This film unfolds a mute drama of countenance and grimace enacted against sparse white backgrounds largely in close-ups of great intensity. It strips melodrama to the bone, deprives it of all cliffhanging action and farfetched situation, and plays it with ardent spiritual austerity. If Griffith's close-ups are like operatic arias that arrest the action to dwell on a moment of emotion, Dreyer's close-ups in *Joan of Arc* are the action, which is all emotion, heightened by the music of the aggrandized countenance: a "fugue of faces," this film has been called.[15] The exaggerated acting of Dreyer's actors, unlike that of Stroheim's, works together with his camera technique, which does its own exaggeration: the acting and the camera together bring silent film to a unique unremitting pitch of distilled melodrama.

A film, unless it is made up of abstract shapes, is not a mere arrangement of images; it is also an arrangement of the concrete reality the images reproduce, and must be given a form in accordance with the demands of that reality. A purely visual organization, the form of moving wallpaper, will not do; but a dramatic organization isn't always what is required either. Drama, though a central and an abidingly popular possibility of the film medium, is certainly not the only possibility. *Nanook of the North* takes us out into arctic expanses, *Un Chien andalou* takes us inside a dreaming psyche: two films of widely different persuasions that have in common their departure from dramatic motivation. One deals with the conflict between man and nature, the other with the conflict of forces in the mind; neither deals with the conflict between dramatic characters. Films not dealing with a dramatic situation must devise a formal alternative to the dramatic plot, another kind of structure adequate to the demands of the concrete image and able to give the film its movement and its unity. Silent cinema was able to solve this formal problem; as alive today as the comedies are some silent films that manage an undramatic form.

Some of these are documentaries whose movement is impelled not by a story but by our curiosity about the world. Flaherty made *Nanook of the North* (1922) out of years of acquaintance with the Inuits and never surpassed that first film, which endures as a classic documentary and for which he devised a classic documentary form. Our curiosity, what every documentary depends on, *Nanook* makes its organizing principle: its structure is a process of discovery, our finding out more and more about how an Eskimo lives. Vertov engaged a different kind of curiosity—curiosity not about the exotic but about the current, and the future that may be glimpsed in the current—and he organized it differently. Rather than imitating the perceptions of a human eye, the camera in his documentaries flaunts its status as a mechanical eye; *The Man with a Movie Camera* pictures the city as a vast machine seen by the omnipresent seeing machine that is the camera. The structure of Vertov's films, their aggregate space pieced together in the cutting room out of all the manifold things the mechanical eye can see, suggests the constructions of the engineer so prized in that new Soviet society.

In the same year as *The Man with a Movie Camera*, 1929, but in another country and artistic climate, Luis Buñuel made *Un Chien andalou* from a script he and his associate Salvador Dalí derived from their dreams. *Un Chien andalou* is the quintessential surrealist dream film, in which charged physical images, like the famous slicing of the eye, come before us abruptly, one after the other without any rational connection between them, in a structure based on their sensual association. Abruptly yet smoothly: this film moves like a dream not just in its impossible transitions, its disconcerting liberties with space and time, but in the astonishing fluidity with which it makes those transitions and takes those liberties. *Un Chien andalou* has the disjointedness of a dream and also the flow, the flow that gives us the feeling, as dreams so often do, of compelling sense in this apparent nonsense, inexorable reason in the unfolding of this madness. Buñuel's surrealism availed itself with gripping self-possession of the means of silent film. So, a few years earlier, did Fernand Léger's cubism in his one film, *Ballet mécanique* (1924), a celebration akin to Vertov's, though more abstractly conducted, of the marriage between the human and the mechanical. *Un Chien andalou* stands behind all cinematic surrealism, whether of avant-garde affiliation (Maya Deren, Stan Brakhage) or otherwise (Jean Vigo, Federico Fellini, David Lynch); *Ballet mécanique* is the ancestor of what may be called the geometric avant-garde film (Michael Snow, Ernie Gehr).

Eisenstein avoided the problems of serious silent drama because he was unconcerned with individual character. People aren't individuals in his silent films but members of a crowd, emblems of a class, representatives of historical forces. No acting of any complexity is called for: sweeping strokes, of caricature for the ruling class, of collectivity for the working class, are quite sufficient. It is not in the voices of dramatic characters that his silent films speak but in the overriding address of rhetoric. His is not a dramatic so much as a rhetorical theater.

Soviet filmmakers of the silent period, however they may have differed from one another, all accorded primacy to the assertive, constructive editing they called "montage." Montage lends itself well to rhetoric, to the purposes of persuasion—to Vertov's documentary rhetoric no less than to Eisenstein's theatrical rhetoric. V. I. Pudovkin's brand of montage was closer to mainstream cinema; his theoretical writings were for years read in Hollywood as a manual. His films attend more to the individual; their rhetoric takes a more dramatic form. The drama they enact is precisely a drama of political persuasion, the persuasion of a representative protagonist with whom we in the audience are to identify ourselves as he or she comes to revolutionary consciousness. If Dreyer purified melodrama and made it spiritual, Pudovkin politicized it and made it militant. He was one of the best directors of serious silent acting.

Modernism can be an art of pronounced subjectivity (expressionism, surrealism, the stream of consciousness) and it can be an art of emphatic impersonality (cubism, futurism, the Bauhaus). The montage of Soviet silent films belongs with the impersonal schools of modern art. Vertov and Eisenstein have evident affinities with futurism and cubism and more broadly with a modernism whose enthusiasm for the systematic and eschewal of the subjective fitted in with the spirit of confident Communism, of Marx and the machine, of those years after the revolution in Russia.

My parents were illiterate. Grandmother and Great-grandmother were also illiterate. Grandfather was literate, however, and Father never forgave Grandfather for his own ignorance. My parents had many children—fourteen in all, a variable group of whom two survived, myself and my sister Polina, who is now a doctor. The other children died at different times, hardly any of them reaching working age. Now, whenever I think of my childhood and of my home, in my mind I see crying and funerals. And the first telegram that came to our house told us of the death of my brother, who had been working as a freightloader in Rostov. I still cannot bear to look at funerals, and yet they pass through all my scripts and all my pictures, for the question of life and death affected my imagination when I was still a child and left its imprint on all my work.

ALEXANDER DOVZHENKO[16]

The Ukrainian Alexander Dovzhenko had been a schoolteacher and a diplomat, a cartoonist, illustrator, and aspiring painter, before he decided that films were the art of the future and the work he would pursue. He started a little later and more slowly than the other major figures of the Soviet cinema, and he owed them an appreciable debt. Yet soon enough he found his own voice in the medium of silent film, his own idiom in the language of image and montage. It was not a dramatic idiom. Like Vertov and Eisenstein, he left drama aside out of a refusal to let the individual take precedence over the larger pattern, the collective endeavor; like them, he was committed to Marxism and to an art that brings forward the objective rather than the subjective. But, unlike theirs, his is not a schematic art securing its objectivity through a systematic exclusion of the personal, not an art of hard edges and imposed arrangements either in the engineering manner of Vertov's kino-eye or in the theatrical manner of Eisenstein's kino-fist. His films do not turn people into abstractions, do not subsume the individual into brisk patterns of the mechanical or ready generalizations of the rhetorical. They take a more difficult path between the particular and the general.

None of the other Soviet filmmakers dared represent the pain of revolution, the suffering and death that were entailed, as Dovzhenko represented it. Suffering and death were for Eisenstein the enemy's doing, an outrage perpetrated by the oppressors and moving the liberators to action. Of all the pictures of the revolution projected on the Soviet screen, Dovzhenko's *Arsenal* (1929) alone pictures a tragedy. It is a hopeful tragedy, one that looks forward to a better future, but a tragedy nonetheless in its sense of the dolorous cost and waste and its reverberant sorrow. A dying revolutionary soldier wants to be buried at home after years of being away, and his comrades and their horses, with little time to spare, hurry him across a wintry embattled landscape to his grave on home ground. A flurry of movement leads the man to his final stillness. By an open grave, on a mound of dark earth dug amid the white snow, a woman stands immobile and steadfast, waiting for the man to come home at last. "Revolution," say the horses conveying him with such haste to his eternal rest (horses in *Arsenal* are on occasion moved to speak in the silent voice of intertitles). "We feel it in the air. . . . We are flying with all the speed of our twenty-four legs." The rush of revolution expressed in a rush to the grave, the drive and energy of revolution inextricably combined with the grief: this sequence is saddening at the same time that it is exciting, without at all diluting either the militant excitement or the mournful sadness.

Horses that speak are among the things in *Arsenal* that call to mind the folk tale. "There was a mother who had three sons," an intertitle tells us at the film's opening. We see a peasant woman inside her house in a fixed posture of frustration and dejection. "There was a war." We see a train carrying soldiers. We see women standing desolate and immobile in the streets of a village, their stillness broken by the movement of a one-legged man on crutches, a war cripple with a child in tow. "And the mother had no sons." We see a woman endeavoring to sow a large field all by herself: not, as we may have expected, the same woman we first saw but a different one sharing the same oppressive situation, another individual isolate but not singular in her plight. The mode of narration here—the once-upon-a-time tone of the intertitles, the hieratic, epitomizing use of gesture and immobility in the visual presentation—suggests the manner of a legend, of a folk tale, even though the narrative has to do with events in recent history, the First World War and the harm it brought to the Ukrainian people. In his earlier *Zvenigora* (1928) Dovzhenko had already put together an "astonishing mixture" (as Eisenstein called it) of the legendary and the contemporary. Renoir's *Toni* (1934), also a story of peasants caught up in the modern world, similarly mixes together elements of the ballad, which is the way the peasants would tell the story to themselves, with elements of realism, which is the way the modern world prefers to tell the story.

Modernism is an art born of the modern big city. It belongs specifically, as Raymond Williams has stressed, to the culture and the conditions of the modern metropolis that industrial capitalism built. The experimentation of modern art, its penchant for making new and making strange, its emphasis on its artifice and its medium, Williams saw as the practice of artists who feel themselves strangers in the big city, artists whose only community is in their artifice, their shared medium of expression.[17] The montage of Soviet silent films is such an art of the city, though a socialist city that would overcome the alienation of the capitalist metropolis. Vertov's vision of community is indeed a community of artifice, the artifice of film linked together under socialism with all the other artifice and machinery of modern life. Eisenstein lacked Vertov's faith in an encompassing order of the machine, and his emphasis on artifice is more rhetorical and more aesthetic, one might say more alienated; the community his films picture is a community of the mass, the depersonalized group.[18] Dovzhenko came from the country and remained of it, a rooted Ukrainian, the son of peasants, who made films about his land and his people. The community his films picture is organic rather than mechanical, concretely embodied in its individual members and their interrelationships rather than abstractly conceived as an anonymous mass. He did not turn his back on the past in order to look forward to the future. Yet he resolutely envisioned a vital future in which great changes would come about and the past he cherished would live on. He was not one of the strangers in the city, yet in that future the native was a stranger too. His art makes new and makes strange. It was modernism that gave him the means for his complex picture of tradition, transition, and aspiration in the life of his people.

After *Zvenigora* and *Arsenal* Dovzhenko made *Earth* (1930), one of the last Soviet silent films and perhaps the greatest. *Earth* is a tractor movie, to use a condescending term for what was at that time in the Soviet Union a pressing and fraught topic, the collectivization of agriculture. *Earth* is a tractor movie that Dovzhenko made into a great film poem.

Dovzhenko has often been called a poet, and no other filmmaker better qualifies. Some have objected, though. P. Adams Sitney understandably reproves those for whom poetry just means beautiful images.[19] Dovzhenko's poetry isn't just in his painter's eye—striking though that is, an eye that knew how to compose for the screen—but in his arrangement of the images in expressive concatenation, his way of putting together the pieces of the visible into a montage ensemble. For Vance Kepley, who minds the word's being applied to Dovzhenko, poetry means a focus on the personal that loses sight of the social, the historical; but dividing the personal off from the social and the historical is a mistake that Dovzhenko precisely did not make.[20] It's difficult to define what poetry is in cinema. Maya Deren made a good attempt to define it at a 1953 symposium devoted to the subject; although the other participants (Arthur Miller, Dylan Thomas, and Parker Tyler, three men who treated the one woman with sexist condescension) gave her a hard time, she usefully distinguished between the "horizontal" progression of drama and the "vertical" intensification of poetry.[21] Dovzhenko's films exemplify that intensification, that compression of experience into a manifold moment, a pregnant apprehended juncture. However one may define poetry in cinema, it is what these films are.

What can be more personal than death? Yet deaths in Eisenstein are robbed of their personal dimension, summarily assigned their place in the progress of history. Dovzhenko too sees deaths as taking their place in a larger order; but even when, at the beginning of *Earth*, an old peasant dies in the fields amid the generations of his family and the fruits of the land, in peaceful harmony with the cycles of nature, there is at the same time a sense of the man's death in its awesome, inviolable privacy. "The question of life and death affected my imagination when I was still a child and left its imprint on all my work." Thus Dovzhenko. "A poet of death, as part and parcel of eternal life," wrote Ivor Montagu about him after his death in 1956. "Pantheism? No. Nature worship? Not at all. Sound Marxist dialectic: the union of opposites."[22] *Earth* can be said to be about the meaning of death— personally, socially, historically. The meaning of death and the meaning of change, change deep and irrevocable as death. Kenneth Burke has argued that death functions in art as an image of transformation.[23] The deaths in *Earth*—the old man's death at the beginning, the death of his grandson later on—are an image, a complex embodiment, of the large transformation, hurtful and hopeful, that collectivization, and more generally the revolutionary remaking of the world, brought to the land and its people.

In the same dialectical way that it stresses the common good without slighting the individual, *Earth* puts its faith in the new social order without relinquishing the old faith in the things of nature. In dealing with the political it remains in touch both with the personal and with the natural. It did not please the commissars, who found it insufficiently militant—they wanted a pamphlet, not a poem—and criticized its lyrical view of nature for obscuring the class struggle. It did not please Eisenstein, who found it insufficiently formalized, too concrete where it should have been more symbolic. *Earth* was too many-sided and ambiguous for Eisenstein as for the commissars, its politics combined with too much of the pastoral, its affirmations too qualified by a recognition of human weakness, its generalizations too complicated by an attention to particular experience.

Before a man and a machine Dovzhenko's camera more often than not will frame the man and leave out the machine: a larger system transcends the man but the man himself is to be acknowledged. In *Old and New* (1929, also known as *The General Line*), Eisenstein's own movie about farm collectivization, the tractor is a symbol of progress, the new sweeping aside the old, whereas in *Earth* we are made aware of what the tractor means to different people whose lives are being affected by the changes it brings about. *Old and New* culminates in the abstraction of a vast ballet of tractors that recalls a Busby Berkeley number; in *Earth* it is Dreyer who is called to mind by the weighty close-ups of human faces. But these close-ups, unlike Dreyer's, are not used to concentrate our attention on a few individuals, the main characters in a dramatic situation; rather they take in, at one point or another, virtually everyone in the Ukrainian village that is the setting of *Earth*. *Earth* is undramatic not because it is unconcerned with individuals but because it is concerned with many individuals, all brought to the foreground, all, we are made to feel, equally deserving of attention.

Dramatic movement is generated by the interaction between a few characters to whom any others must be kept subordinate. The movement of *Earth* is managed in a different way, through a structure that can accommodate a greater breadth of attention than is possible in drama. It is a structure based on the interaction between the particular and the general, between what each person is in him or herself and what he or she has in common with others, the place he or she has in a larger system that overrides and contains everyone. The movement of *Earth* is in the assimilation, the synthesis, of the diverse claims of individuality into an objective order in the world.

Earth begins with several shots of wheat fields in the wind. We see nothing but the sky and the wheat; the fields are like a wind-stirred ocean. Then the film cuts to a close-up of a young woman standing, motionless, next to a huge sunflower swaying in the wind. The woman's immobility comes across as the opposite of passivity: it is a resistance to being swayed, an assertion of her intrinsic energy, her own intensity, before the surrounding energies and intensities of nature.

In the next shot the swaying sunflower fills the whole screen: it too has its own intensity. And so have the fruit on the trees, the apples and pears we see next—which we almost reach out and grasp—in an unhurried succession of close-ups. Each cluster of fruit, each apple or pear singled out by Dov-zhenko's camera, is seen in isolation from the others around it, as an object of attention complete in itself. We have little sense, as we watch each shot, of what lies in the neighboring space. It is the same with the shots of people in the sequence that follows. Even though the people we see are all gathered in one area, around the old peasant lying on the ground preparing to die, they are nevertheless shown one at a time, each isolated from the rest, with no establishing shots of the whole group, no clear sense conveyed of where they stand with respect to one another. They are all nearly immobile in their places, and each one, photographed frontally, holds the screen by him or herself: each one has his or her own intensity.

Earth is a film of big spaces, expanses of land seemingly without limit. We get extreme long shots where everything looks tiny beneath a huge sky that takes up most of the screen. Yet individual things hold their own against the vastness of the sky and the land. They are not merely glimpsed, they are virtually gripped when the camera comes close, rendered with the tactility that Ortega y Gasset argues belongs to proximate vision,[24] so that our eyes become like our fingertips in their apprehension of the body of things. Things stand rounded and solid in the tactile individual focus of Dov-zhenko's close-ups. Things are taken out of their context in the space around them: what they are in themselves matters more than where they are exactly within that vast space. Space is fragmented; there is little feeling of its continuity from shot to shot. Even when the camera moves, which happens rarely, it is always to dwell on an object, follow it closely, rather than to

Earth. The young woman and the sunflower swaying in the wind.

explore the surrounding space. Spatial fragmentation was of course not peculiar to *Earth* but generally characteristic of Soviet silent films. The close-up that ruptures space, the cut that juxtaposes things pried from their spatial context, was something Dovzhenko learned from Eisenstein and others in the montage school. For Eisenstein, however, fragmentation was a means of subjugating reality, making its aspects and appearances less resistant to his manipulation; his close-ups serve not so much to show something in reality as to impose a meaning on reality, to assert a slant. With Dovzhenko it is different. In his hands the fragmentation of space helps bring forward the body and individuality of things. His close-ups neither merely show nor simply signify. They serve to enhance, not diminish, the intrinsic reality of the things depicted, the sense of their independent life.

"Clearly outlined, brightly and uniformly illuminated, men and things stand out in a realm where everything is visible," writes Erich Auerbach of the representation of reality in the Homeric poems. In "Odysseus' Scar," the opening chapter of *Mimesis,* Auerbach characterizes the Homeric style of representation as being "of the foreground." Homer, he maintains, "knows no background. What he narrates is for the time being the only present, and fills both the stage and the reader's mind completely." The story of Odysseus's scar, when it comes up in the *Odyssey,* is the story of something that happened in the past, an interruption of what is happening in the main narrative, but it takes over our attention completely—it becomes "the only present"—while it is being told. It takes us back into Odysseus's boyhood and a boar hunt in which he was wounded, just as the old housekeeper, washing the feet of a traveler who is the returning Odysseus in disguise, recognizes him by his scar. Its suspension of the main narrative does not work to generate suspense, as Auerbach argues:

> The broadly narrated, charming, and subtly fashioned story of the hunt, with all its elegance and self-sufficiency, its wealth of idyllic pictures, seeks to win the reader over wholly to itself as long as he is hearing it, to make him forget what had just taken place during the foot-washing. But an episode that will increase suspense by retarding the action must be so constructed that it will not fill the present entirely, will not put the crisis, whose resolution is being awaited, entirely out of the reader's mind, and thereby destroy the mood of suspense; the crisis and the suspense must continue, must remain vibrant in the background. But Homer . . . knows no background.[25]

We are not to keep the present in mind as we go into a past that wholly takes over as its own present. We are not, in Homer, to keep anything in mind other than what is there, clearly and fully related. All is there in the foreground; as long as it is there that is all there is.

Dovzhenko's style may also be said to be "of the foreground." Literally he often puts things in the foreground—he uses plenty of close-ups. But a close-up will almost always create a background as well as a foreground: it will ask us to keep something else in mind while we look at the detail it singles out for our notice. It is not the frequent use of close-ups but the distinctive way he uses them that makes for a foreground style in Dovzhenko, the way the detail his camera singles out for our notice commands our complete attention. A Dovzhenko close-up wins us over wholly to itself for the time of its projection; that bit of the world holds the screen, and while we look at it we have little awareness of anything else. No other filmmaker so excludes from our minds everything not being shown, so leads us to concentrate on what each image contains. Any film may show us a close-up of an apple, but it will show it, say, when one of the characters wants the apple to eat, it will present it from some perspective that takes us outside the apple itself. With Dovzhenko the apple is the only present, the object of our complete attention while it is there on the screen.

A close-up is a synecdoche, it has been thought: a part that stands for a whole. Many close-ups are indeed synecdoches, maybe most. A doorknob turning stands for a door being opened; a full ashtray means that a stretch of time was anxiously spent. Certainly many of Eisenstein's close-ups are synecdoches. The ship doctor's pince-nez dangling from a rope, in a celebrated close-up from *Potemkin,* refers to the fate of its owner, the doctor thrown overboard by the mutinous sailors. The shaking chandeliers in the besieged Winter Palace in *October* stand for the tottering provisional government, and more than that, for a whole world of privilege trembling under revolutionary fire and about to crumble. The turning doorknob, the full ashtray, the dangling pince-nez, the shaking chandelier—the thing depicted in a close-up that is primarily a synecdoche—is not so important in itself: it recedes in favor of the meaning it carries, which is what such a close-up really brings forward. What counts is not what is there but what it refers to. With Dovzhenko, as with Homer, what is there is all that counts, the thing clearly and tangibly in view. A Dovzhenko close-up is a part that stands on its own. It is a part of a whole, a particular thing within a larger order that contains it, but the relation between part and whole, between the particular and the general, is not a simple standing for.

Not only a close-up but every shot in a film is a detail, a section of a larger field extending out of frame, continuing without bounds in the space off screen: a painting is a whole, a theater stage is a whole, but what we see on screen is always a part of a whole. More than any other filmmaker, Dovzhenko makes us forget the space off screen as we apprehend the thing we have before our eyes. Not only his close-ups but every one of his shots is a detail that commands our complete attention, a part that stands on its own. The dying old peasant sits up on the ground and bites into a last pear, in sensual enjoyment of the fruits of a world to which he is saying good-bye: that image in front of us absorbs us totally, its richness and resonance all in the foreground, all in what we see.

As the story of Odysseus's scar is not mere background information, subordinate to the main narrative of the *Odyssey,* but something with a full importance of its own, so in *Earth* the apples and the wheat are not a mere backdrop for the action, and the people of the Ukrainian village are not subordinate to a few main characters: everything that is shown assumes a full importance of its own. This is foreign to the dramatic procedure of assigning importance to things only as they have bearing on the main action. Goethe and Schiller, as Auerbach discusses, contrasted the Homeric mode of narrative—which for them defined the epic mode[26]—with the dramatic mode of the tragic poets. (This contrast lay behind Brecht's conception of an "epic theater" as opposed to a dramatic one.) To put all in the foreground, to bring things forward into a clear light where they stand fully revealed, is indeed to dispense with drama: nothing is dramatic in a realm where everything is visible. Homer—and the same may be said of Dovzhenko—leaves nothing dark or incomplete, no room for things to take on a subjective significance; what he depicts takes place in an absolute present, where things are simply themselves, seen without perspective. Drama requires perspective. It requires that things be seen to some extent as they appear to the characters, that they be seen, at any rate, as they appear in the perspective of the plot, with the present placed in relation to what has happened in the past and to what we anticipate may happen in the future; dramatic tension can be generated only if we keep something else in mind beyond what, at the time being, is objectively there. This is not the case when we read Homer and not when we watch a film by Dovzhenko.

It is not only individual things that are clearly displayed in Homer: the connections between things, their relationships with one another, are also "brought to light in perfect fullness," as Auerbach stresses, "so that a continuous rhythmic procession of phenomena passes by, and never is there a form left fragmentary or half-illuminated, never a lacuna, never a gap, never a glimpse of unplumbed depths."[27] Homer's foreground can accommodate much more than Dovzhenko's. Homer can put before us a whole scene in all its aspects, Dovzhenko merely a part, a detail his camera frames and focuses in an image on the screen. Dovzhenko proceeds image by image, one thing at a time palpably captured. The full clarity he accords to each part does not extend to the connection between the parts and between the parts and the whole. His style depends on a spatial fragmentation that has no equivalent in the Homeric poems and little in common with the flowing continuity of their storytelling. Like Homer's, his is a style of the foreground, but his is a foreground not of the whole but of the part, not of the scene but of the shot, not of the story but of the image. *Earth* is epic in its images, one might say, in the things it represents and the way it represents them, but lyric in the succession of images, in the connections it makes between things and the way it puts them together. This again raises the question of how, lacking in dramatic impetus and lacking also in narrative flow, *Earth* achieves its movement.

Of the Soviet movies he saw Warshow liked *Earth* best. But he objected to both deaths in the film: to the old man's death at the beginning as the clearest example of the sentimentality he saw in the film's pastoral side, and to the young man's funeral at the end as the clearest example of the inhumanity he saw in the film's revolutionary side. For him,

> Dovzhenko's virtues are all connected with a certain passivity. He is most successful in presenting the life of the peasants when he is willing to accept it as something irremediably "given" and devote himself to recording its meaningful appearances; even his sentimentality, though it is partly dishonest like all sentimentality, is not so much an active falsification of the material as a willfully excessive surrender to it. Whenever he assumes a more active posture— which is to say, whenever he becomes fully an "artist" in the sense in which the Soviet film directors understood that term—his work takes on as glassy and inhuman a brilliance as Eisenstein's.[28]

Passivity is not the word for Dovzhenko's fiery respect for his subject; a passive recording of appearances would not convey the potent sense we get in his work of the energies of being, the intrinsic force that people and things possess. *Sentimentality* is a more problematic word, which easily slides from a disapproval of false sentiment to an avoidance of strong sentiment, an avoidance endemic in a culture that has made the word *sentimental* derogatory more often than not. The old grandfather who dies at the beginning of *Earth* was based on Dovzhenko's own grandfather. Here is the scene in Dovzhenko's words:

I remember too that it was a fair summer day and that everything around me was beautiful—the orchard, the vegetable patch, the sunflowers and poppies, and the ripening crop in the surrounding fields. In the orchard, near the dugout that we used for a cellar, beneath an apple tree, among the fallen apples, on an ancient white linen sheet, dressed in a white shirt, himself white and translucent from kindliness and old age, lay my grandfather Semen, once an ox-cart driver. He was a hundred years old. That is, he was probably less, but I am fond of thinking he was a hundred, because this was long ago and beautiful. He was radiant. At least that was the impression I got because he was smiling and it was Sunday and a holiday too.[29]

Undoubtedly this is sentimental. Is it false?

Dovzhenko is perhaps less concerned than any other filmmaker with momentary appearances, incidental particularities that the camera happens to record. He seeks to photograph the essential shape of things, to reveal concrete objects in their enduring aspect. His images seldom give us the elusive impression, the passing glimpse, the oblique view; things, squarely confronted, show us their full face, so to speak, and are held on the screen long enough for our eyes to go beyond the mere appearance and get a grasp of the substance. Movement in his images will sometimes come to a standstill, "transforming," as Siegfried Kracauer wrote, "moving life into live immobility."[30] Standing immobile like statues, maintaining a posture, a gesture, against all the movement that surrounds them, his characters evoke the permanence and solidity—but none of the inertness—of stone. Their stillness is

Earth. The old grandfather preparing to die.

not that of the freeze frame, the moment plucked out of a continuum, the movement artificially arrested; rather it is the stillness of a posture that intrinsically endures, sustained by living energy as time visibly passes, the embodiment, we feel, of an essential state of their being.

Like the painters of the Renaissance, Dovzhenko emphasizes not how things look from a certain viewpoint, under a certain light, submerged in a *mise en scène,* but what Bernard Berenson called "the corporeal significance of objects."[31] Like Giotto, and like his successors in the Italian and the northern Renaissance, Dovzhenko strongly engages the sense of touch in images that vividly render the fullness and self-sufficiency, the rounded steadfastness of solid forms. The settled, stable quality of Dovzhenko's images—one can imagine many of them going on indefinitely—contrasts with the restlessness one finds in Eisenstein or Murnau, filmmakers who, for all their differences, both have a quality of the baroque. Something Adrian Stokes said about Piero della Francesca could as well be said about Dovzhenko: compared with his images, those of all other filmmakers are as sea to land.[32]

Giotto and Piero may be characterized as painters "of the foreground." Everything in their pictures, as Ortega says, seems painted at close range, solidly apprehended whether near or far. Piero combines Giotto's painting of bulk with the perspective of the quattrocento, so that, like Homer, he brings to light in perfect fullness both individual things and the relations between things. Geometric perspective is not used by Piero to express a subjective perspective, a particular point of view that makes some things stand out and others recede in importance; to everything on the picture plane Piero gives an equal stress.

The camera automatically reproduces things as they appear from a particular point in space, which automatically tends to give to some things—those closer to the camera, or in sharper focus—a greater stress than it gives to others. And what the camera reproduces, unlike a painting, is felt to be incomplete, a detail out of a larger space continuing off screen, so that the camera tends to place an uneven stress on the visual field, to create a kind of foreground and background, simply by bringing some things into view, while we are aware that other things around them are left out. A painter like Piero can portray with the same distinctness, the same vividness of color, objects that are close and objects that are well in back, making them all equally present, putting a uniform stress on things in the unified space of the picture. To achieve a similar evenness of stress, a similar effect of all in the foreground, a filmmaker like Dovzhenko must rely on spatial fragmentation. He must often show things one by one, with the equal clarity given by close-ups, in isolation from the context of a larger space that, were we made more aware of it as we watch each shot, would function in the manner of a background for what we see. Stokes wrote that in a painting by Piero, or in a relief by Agostino di Duccio—and this too could as well be said of a film by Dovzhenko—"every part is on some equality with every other part."[33] Every shot in Dovzhenko is on some equality with every other shot; what different shots contain is, so to speak, put on the same plane.

Eisenstein too counters through spatial fragmentation the uneven stress the camera tends to give to the things it reproduces, but this enables him to impose on things another, more aggressively uneven stress of his own. Each of Dovzhenko's shots is a more or less self-sufficient detail, balanced within itself, its center of gravity in the object that is there in view. Eisenstein respects neither the integrity of space nor that of objects, and the bits and pieces into which he takes things apart, the unusual aspects his camera angles press on us, feel fragmentary, imbalanced, parts crying out for a whole that is not there. Eisenstein's shots demand to be balanced by other shots. The relationship between shots in Eisenstein is generally not one of equality but of contrast. His style is based on contrast, "collision," as he himself put it, the yoking together of things often abruptly dissimilar. Dovzhenko, like Piero, prefers to bring out correspondences, connections between things, to juxtapose elements that have some intrinsic similarity. Unlike Eisenstein, Dovzhenko often cuts between similar compositions, different things seen in the same way—just as Piero paints different things in the same way. When, at one point in *Earth*, an older peasant and his progressive son are having an argument with their backs turned to each other, we are shown the back of one and then the back of the other, in separate shots composed so that the two backs look almost the same, suggesting not so much an opposition between father and son as an affinity between them.

One sequence in *Arsenal* cuts back and forth between a peasant woman inside her house and a one-armed man in a field, the woman a war widow with small, hungry children, the man a war cripple with an old horse that shares his inadequacy to work the field. Back and forth, we see the woman and the man each standing still in frustration and each breaking into a violent anger turned on the object at hand; back and forth, in shots that frame the motion of striking and leave out the object being struck, we see the woman beating her children and the man beating his horse. The woman stops, the man collapses, the children cry, the horse speaks: "You're wasting your blows on me, old man. I'm not what you need to strike at." Such parallel editing, done for thematic rather than for dramatic purposes, bringing together separate things not into a plotted action but into a pointed comparison, goes back as far as Griffith's 1909 *Corner in Wheat*. Dovzhenko, like all the other Soviet filmmakers—like all filmmakers everywhere—learned a great deal from Griffith. What is unusual about Dovzhenko is the precise way in which he isolates two individuals and articulates what they have in common, keeps them separate and yet heightens their kinship. Dovzhenko's style is based on sameness, a sameness established in separateness. The space within the frame, which he treats in each shot as a separate and self-contained unit, becomes with him a kind of constant, a common ground that different things, located in different places, successively occupy. What different things have in common is thus enforced; it is as if they were brought, one after another, into the same space.

Fighting is about to start in the city in *Arsenal*. It is dark and the streets are empty; people are staying indoors. One by one, in the stillness of tense waiting, we see a succession of people differently situated spatially and socially—an aproned blacksmith, a woman knitting, some of the workers barricaded at the arsenal, a bald man of the professional class sitting at his desk— all nonetheless in the same situation, all caught up in the same charged atmosphere, all poised to hear the sound of civil war imminently to be heard. Along the bottom edge of the frame a solitary amputee crosses a street. On the long receding wall of the arsenal the shadows of combatants obliquely enter frame as fighting breaks out. After dwelling on the anticipatory suspense, Dovzhenko merely suggests the actual strife. Parallel editing is a common device for generating dramatic suspense. Dovzhenko's suspense, however, is not dramatic but epic in that its eyes are not on what next but on what is, the state of being of the city and its people in the midst of civil war; and not dramatic but lyric in that, instead of leading—horizontally—to a burst of action, it gives an arresting composite image of the moment before action, it intensifies—vertically—the feeling of the situation. Dovzhenko's parallel editing mainly connects, brings together the different people separately inhabiting that moment, sharing that situation.

The tractor is coming to the Ukrainian village in *Earth*. This is another anticipatory situation involving everyone in the community. But the people of the village aren't staying inside their homes, aren't sharing the situation separately: they are all assembled waiting for the arrival of this new machine that is going to change the old ways. And yet Dovzhenko presents them separately, each one in turn brought to the foreground, each one holding the screen in isolation from the others and the surrounding space. Normally a scene such as this, taking place in one area, would have been edited along the lines of spatial connection, with each part placed as a detail belonging to the whole, but Dovzhenko breaks up spatial connection and focuses on each person as a part standing on its own. Parallel editing of any sort—the cutting back and forth between pursuer and pursued in a regular chase sequence, for example—links together shots that are spatially separate; nothing unusual about cutting across a spatial discontinuity bridged by a parallel construction. But it is unusual for a scene taking place in one area to be treated much in the manner of parallel editing. The people of the village are spatially together: they are made separate in Dovzhenko's shots, pried from their spatial context, and then linked together by means of his editing. The community is taken apart into its individuals and then put back together through a kind of parallel construction bridging the spatially adjacent.

We get some long shots of the assembled villagers, but mostly we see them one by one or in clusters of two or three, isolated from the others in the self-contained space of Dovzhenko's screen. An old peasant, distrustful, stands flanked by two oxen; another looks on skeptically; the kulaks, propertied farmers threatened by collectivization, strike hostile attitudes, alarmed or derisive; children run to meet the tractor; there are shots of horses and cattle, roused and waiting like the people; there are many close-ups of young men and women of the village smiling in excited expectation. Seen individually as each one adopts his or her own stance, the villagers are yet seen in terms of what they have in common; each succeeding shot of them is on some equality with the previous shot—taken from a similar angle, showing them in similar groupings, giving them more or less equal weight on the screen. Here as elsewhere in Dovzhenko the rounded presences of people are brought into correspondence by the way they occupy the space within the frame. What brings the people together on this occasion is of course the tractor they all await: they are all looking in the same direction, all oriented toward the point on their horizon where they expect the tractor's arrival. But we are not oriented in relation to that point, we have no clear sense of where the tractor is in the space off screen: no clear sense, in Dovzhenko's images, of anything outside what is there on screen. The villagers all look expectantly in some direction but we look intently at them.

Their gathering on account of the tractor is for Dovzhenko not enough to bring the villagers together into a community meaningfully unified. The tractor is out there somewhere, and we get a few shots of it, but we chiefly attend to the people attending to it, the different sentiments they exhibit, the concern they all share with the machine they regard as bringer and symbol of the new. The spatially discontinuous shots are linked together by their inner arrangement, not by their relationship to some object out of frame in a location not specified, and the feeling conveyed is of people brought together not by some external circumstance but by an inner connection they have with one another, an intrinsic affinity between them. Later on, toward the end of the film, a speaker addressing a crowd of the villagers points up to an airplane flying above them, whereupon they, as one, all turn their heads and look up at the sky; what they are looking at doesn't much matter, and the airplane is never shown.

"Whenever he assumes a more active posture . . . his work takes on as glassy and inhuman a brilliance as Eisenstein's." What Warshow calls "more active" in Dovzhenko is the endeavor of meaning, of synthesis, of putting things together: an endeavor Dovzhenko undertakes in a manner indeed reminiscent of Eisenstein's, through the montage of shots that are disjunct, the arrangement of separate parts into a whole constructed in the cutting room. But the disjunct shots carry an independent weight in Dovzhenko's montage they are not allowed to carry in Eisenstein's. With Dovzhenko the parts retain their autonomy in the order of the whole. With him meaning and synthesis are not to be abstractly fabricated in the cutting room, they are to be won in the face of the concrete reality tangibly depicted in his shots, fragments that, even when arranged into a larger design, breathe an undiminished life of their own. Meaning and synthesis are a construction, not something inherent in things or merely discovered in them but something invented, put together; but with Dovzhenko meaning and synthesis are a construction put together in vital give and take with concrete things. Warshow distrusts a meaning that goes beyond particulars, but meaning always does; he disapproves of a synthesis that overrides individuals, but a social order or a philosophical system, a political regime or an artistic composition, always does. Yet meaning can transact attentively with particulars, synthesis with individuals, and in Dovzhenko meaning and synthesis do. A striving for a larger order, for the general that subsumes the particular, the system that transcends the individual, is not incompatible with an ardent regard for the particularity and individuality of people and things; Warshow wants to draw a line between the two, between what he calls a more active and a more passive posture, but in Dovzhenko the two are combined.

If Warshow criticizes Dovzhenko for "inhumanity," the order dictatorially constructed, Vance Kepley criticizes him for "naturalization," the order that dissembles its own construction and pretends to come from nature. Too assertive for Warshow, *Earth* is for Kepley too self-effacing in its arrangements: neither grasps its dialectical interplay between the parts it defers to and the whole it puts together. Nowadays it is fashionable to frown on "naturalization" as an ideological move promoting a false consciousness. It is true that ideology will often want to pass itself off as nature, but it is also true that an order confident in its appropriateness to the things it encompasses will usually want to emphasize its ties to nature. Aristotle thought the city a natural thing because a thing of human nature. In the modern world such confidence is rare: who would think the modern big city a natural thing? A modernist rooted in the country, a peasant engaged in building the city—the city of the socialist future—Dovzhenko mustered such confidence. Nature for him was in the details, in the parts, not the whole; nature considered as a whole, an order of things, he recognized as a construction like any other order of things. But the things of nature, the concrete particulars, he would not slight for the sake of an order of things; rather he brings the parts vividly into play in a dialectic with the whole. The parts are emphatically nature, the whole as emphatically a construction.

In his deference to the parts, in the autonomy he allows them, Dovzhenko is like Brecht, and like Renoir. Eisenstein adopted in *Old and New* a method of montage he called "overtonal" because it cuts not on the dominant but on the overtones of the shot, and he considered this method "democratic" because it would grant equal rights to all the elements of the shot; but in his hands "overtonal montage" meant not democracy but a more intricate authoritarian control. Not for a moment does Eisenstein's camera relinquish the authority Renoir's calls into question. Renoir negates the hierarchy of foreground and background in a very different way from Dovzhenko, one might say in the opposite way: not by putting all in the foreground but by making the background—the actual background of the shot and the implied background off screen—fully as important as the foreground. Both in Dovzhenko and in Renoir a true equality of the parts, a real independence from the rule of the whole, reigns.

In *Earth* each image is an island, an intense apprehension of being, self-contained and essentially static. But Dovzhenko doesn't leave it an island: he strives to connect and bring together. Chiefly by means of montage, the rupture that is also a juncture, he assembles and arranges a whole out of the parts separately rendered, an order of things out of the things standing on their own. From the very effort to put the pieces together the film gains its forward movement. It is not the movement of pure pattern, as in a musical composition, but the movement to establish pattern against the weight of concrete things, to incorporate into a larger design the individual energy they possess.

Earth is symmetrically divided into two parts, two main movements, each beginning slowly, at a point of stillness, and building up to a culminant synthesis. The first part begins, after the prelude of wheat fields and close-ups of fruit, with the death of the old grandfather, and it culminates in the arrival of the tractor and the fast-cut sequence that follows. In this sequence men and tractor, reaper and thresher and women vigorously binding the sheaves of grain, all join forces in the labors of the land and the wheat, with plowing and harvesting, threshing and breadmaking, all mixed together by Dovzhenko and compressed into a symbolic day's work. Land and tractor, the human and the mechanical, spiritedly marry. But this marriage, this synthesis, is not a *ballet mécanique:* it dances to a rhythm less of the machine than of the body, a brisk rhythm the machine makes possible but does not dictate, a rhythm that feels organic, even erotic, befitting a true marriage in which the men and women at work are not pieces in the machinery but individuals robustly in concert with it. The old is not swept aside but assimilated into this organic rhythm of the new.

The second part of the film begins in the evening of that day. In its montage ensemble of human and mechanical work, the day did not go into the slower workings by which the earth bears fruit. An adagio after the day's allegro, the evening takes up the theme of fruition, the land's fertility and its people's sexuality. The day was not a *ballet mécanique* and the evening is not exactly a pastoral; the day did not portray a people in submission to the machine and the evening does not portray a people in submission to nature. Nature as an order of things is as much a construction as the machine, and pastoral is the genre traditionally devoted to that construction, an idealization of the country from the city's point of view. The country Dovzhenko portrays is not nature but culture, culture made out of nature's materials as culture always is. The grandfather dies in harmony with nature because he and the people around him see it that way: his death is beautiful in the eyes of the community of its beholders. Dovzhenko's adagio on the theme of fertility likewise focuses on a human community and its individuals.

The day's work is done and in the country moonlight lovers stand. We see one peasant couple, then another, standing in perfect stillness, each man's hand on the woman's breast in a steadfast gesture of erotic transport. First the right hand on the left breast, then the left hand on the right breast: the two couples together may be seen as reprising the way the dying grandfather, having eaten his last pear, crossed his hands on his breast in a ritual gesture of readiness for death. Love is as solemn an occasion as death, as much an offering of the self to a larger pattern of being. In the amorous immobility of the couples in this sequence—at closer range we see the first two couples again in reverse order, we see an older couple asleep in bed, we see other young lovers transfixed like flesh-and-blood statues in the summer night—Dovzhenko makes a connection between love and death. But it is not the same connection made in our tradition. Puritan, romantic, bourgeois, our tradition pictures love and death as extreme experiences transcending the social order, breaking its bounds, taking the individual out of the com-

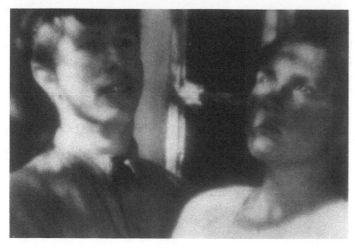

Earth. Lovers in the moonlight.

munity. For Dovzhenko, for the peasant culture he portrays, love and death are experiences integral to the social fabric, transporting yet steadfast, rooted in the earth and rooted in the community. Seen one at a time in isolation from their surroundings, in the privacy and transport of love, the peasant couples are yet seen as joined together in that experience and joined with the world around them.

Immobility in Dovzhenko is the opposite of inanimate: it is a moment of life captured, distilled, with the completion of eternity. The lovers' immobility in the Ukrainian summer night is a distillation ecstatically verging on death of the energy animating all life. The hieratic use of posture and gesture

Earth. Vasyl's girlfriend frightened, the smile they share.

invests this sequence, as it invested the death of the grandfather, with a ceremonial, a sacramental quality. The death of the grandfather was a ceremony of death blessedly at one with life's cycles; this is a ceremony of life exaltedly on the edge of death's oblivion.

Among the lovers we see the grandson, Vasyl, leader of the young peasants working toward collectivization. He stands with his eyes shut and his arm around his girlfriend, her head firm against his breast. Her eyes are open, however, wide open and restless. She is frightened. The moment's intensity frightens her, the feelings powerfully moving her where she is not ready to go, the currents bringing life to a juncture with death. Such fear, at the juncture of love and death, is the stuff of horror movies. But love and death are a horror in horror movies because a threat to the social order, a transgression, whereas in Dovzhenko they are nothing of the kind. Rather than exacerbating the self's fearful subjectivity, *Earth* recognizes it without letting it take over. Vasyl opens his eyes and looks into his girlfriend's. There is no hurry, he reassures her, the time will come for the fruition of their love. They share a tender smile.

Vasyl goes home alone in the encompassing night. Around him everything is dormant and indistinct, glimmering under the moon in the near darkness. Along the dusty road he breaks into a dance, a dance of joy in life and its prospects, a dance of celebration of the day that has passed and the future that lies ahead. Now his subjectivity comes to the fore. The immobile moonlit lovers were at one with the subdued richness of the summer night and the quiescent life around them. Vasyl in his dance is all by himself; the world around him doesn't join in. Unlike the lovers, he is photographed in long shot, an isolate figure the camera does not frame in isolation from his surroundings. With his eyes shut, he dances faster and faster to a rhythm inside him, a vision stirring him, a fruition yet to come. Through a series of jump cuts, he remains on screen from one shot to the next while his surroundings change, a technique that heightens our sense of a dance proceeding on its own excitement without regard for the surrounding world, a dance belonging solely to the dancer. In a horror movie we would be afraid for the lone figure making his way in the night oblivious of his environment. Here all is in the foreground, all in the dance that builds up, the state of being it represents; Dovzhenko builds up no suspense of the sort that would make us fear for what may happen next. But in the dance, in Vasyl's state of being in the world, there is an intrinsic tension between the exultant movement and its impassive setting, between the body swaying to the music of an aspiration and a world in which that aspiration is yet to find embodiment. And there is, in such intense reaching for an objective as yet unrealized, a built-in suspense. What happens next is that, in the midst of the dance, suddenly the dancer drops to the ground, shot dead (as we find out later) by a drunken and vindictive young kulak through whose land, his no longer, Vasyl had driven the tractor that day.

In a film noir, as in a horror movie, love is a transgression that entails death: the *femme* is *fatale*. Robert Mitchum holding Jane Greer in his arms on the moonlit Mexican beach in *Out of the Past* (Jacques Tourneur's 1947 noir masterpiece) is succumbing to a desire that overwhelms him and will destroy him, headily surrendering to a fatality imputed to the woman. Love's offering of the self, as Dovzhenko portrays it, is not self-destructive but life-renewing. None of the lovers in *Earth* is succumbing, none of the men to the woman, none of the women to the man; these transfixed lovers are not surrendering to something larger than themselves, they are embodying it. Vasyl's love is seen in a complex way, not only personally (love for the woman) but also socially and politically (love for the land and its people, love for the emergent new order). And it entails death in a complex way—in the oblivion of the moonlit night, in the murderous bullet of an enemy of the new order hidden in the darkness of that night. The grandfather's death renews life as love's oblivion renews life: the body is offered to nourish the soil or perpetuate the race, the self is offered to fructify the earth. But Vasyl's death? He dies before his personal love could, like his grandfather's, find fruition in new life. And he dies before his social and political love could find fruition in a new life for the land and its people.

Earth. Vasyl dancing alone in the night.

Vasyl lies in his bier, his father broodingly by him, his mother by him in a frozen gesture of grief. His girlfriend comes into the room and, at the sight of his dead body, calls out his name in anguish; in a point-of-view shot singular in this film—a subjective moment departing from the foreground style, for a point-of-view shot refers the image on screen to an observer off screen—we see her dead boyfriend through her distraught eyes. Vasyl's father refuses the officiations of the village priest and decides instead that the body of his son should be buried by the young people of the village with songs of the new life his son did not live to see. In the sequence centered on this funeral the second part of the film reaches its culmination.

Like the coming of the tractor, Vasyl's death is an event engaging the whole village, evoking a response in everyone and a defining response in each one, an event bringing out essential attitudes in the people. But it is harder to come to terms with this event, harder to give it a clear meaning. Vasyl murdered in the prime of life is not something that can be assimilated to the cycles of nature like the death of the old grandfather; and yet the dead young man, in an open coffin, is carried to his grave across the same vast and fruitful fields where the old man died, and the apples on a tree caressingly brush his face as he passes under. The dying old man said good-bye to the earth by eating one of its fruits, and in their turn the fruits of the earth now say good-bye to the dead grandson. Religion is excluded from the burial— the old priest is all alone in his empty church—but not so easily from the minds of the people: an old peasant woman, then another, then an old kulak woman, then Vasyl's mother, pregnant with a new child imminently to be

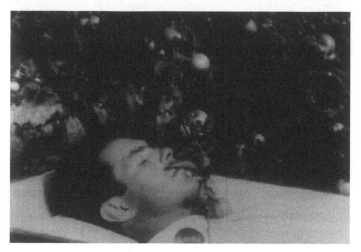

Earth. Vasyl in his coffin.

born, all make the sign of the cross as the funeral procession goes by. Vasyl's father walks in the procession, but he doesn't join in the singing of the young people; he remains apart from them in his private grief and cannot readily be consoled by the invocations of the future. Vasyl's girlfriend seems quite inconsolable, all alone in her house with her clothes off, painfully yearning for her dead boyfriend, screaming his name and throwing herself about the place in despair. Seized with remorse, the young kulak who killed Vasyl likewise becomes frantic: he runs across the fields toward the people at the funeral and shouts his guilt for all to hear, he almost stands on his head

Earth. The naked girlfriend inconsolable in her house.

on the ground he yells is his—a gesture both clownish and reverential—and then, next to graveyard crosses, his lone figure tiny under the immense sky, he performs a mad reenactment of Vasyl's dance on the night of the murder. But his confession fails to get him the attention of the people assembled at the village burial ground: they are all listening to the speech of a young Bolshevik eulogizing Vasyl as a hero who gave his life for the new order.

None of the actions depicted in this sequence impinges on the others. The body being buried and the various responses it evokes are intertwined in the editing, but each is an action complete in itself, taking place on its own. As Vasyl goes to his grave past orchards and sunflowers and young men and women sing about the future, the heartbroken girlfriend is in her house, the forlorn priest in his church, the pregnant mother in her bed after she starts to feel the pangs of birth, the guilty kulak off on his own even after he shouts his confession, the somber father on his own too even in the midst of the proceedings. Between these self-contained pieces, each in turn wholly occupying our awareness, Dovzhenko's parallel editing perceives and proposes many connections, none of them along the lines of dramatic interaction. The pieces don't interact; rather they are, one might say, connected from the inside, by what they intrinsically have in common, brought forward by Dovzhenko's technique, established through the juxtapositions and concatenations of his elaborate intercutting. Without ever encroaching on one another, the various strands interweave into a subtle and mighty tapestry. This is, for a sustained, breathtaking stretch, true *parallel* montage, montage that draws parallels.

Griffith's most ambitious parallel construction was the monumental *Intolerance* (1916), in which four stories, set in four different periods of history, are told not consecutively but alternately, by cutting back and forth between them in parallel fashion. *Intolerance* was the Griffith film the Soviet directors admired and studied the most. In his well-known essay on Dickens, Griffith, and Soviet film, Eisenstein paid his respects to *Intolerance* but criticized it on the grounds that its parallel lines don't come together—just as, he theorized, the haves and the have-nots don't ever come together in bourgeois society. But parallel lines in Griffith (the parallel lines, for example, of a party in peril and a party coming to the rescue) normally do come together in a dramatic resolution (a last-minute rescue). *Intolerance* and *A Corner in Wheat* are exceptions to his usual practice. And in *Intolerance*, while the parallel stories remain separate—and Eisenstein was right to criticize their failure to cohere thematically—the parallel lines in each story do not fail to come together dramatically.

In *Earth* the parallel lines remain separate dramatically but come together thematically. Drama works within an order of things. Implicit from the outset, ratified at the conclusion, the order of the plot knows exactly where things are going and exactly where everything fits in that design: hence the hierarchy of a dramatic scheme, the assignment of greater or lesser importance to each part according to its place in the unfolding whole. *Earth* negates such hierarchy and it defers to the parts even as it constructs a whole: hence its eschewal of dramatic form and its pursuit of another kind of structure. *Earth* does not work within, it works toward an order of things. It proceeds not from the whole to the parts but from the parts to the whole: its movement is not in the unfolding of a design but in the putting together of one.

The montage ensemble of the day's work that was the film's first large synthesis hung together principally through an overriding rhythm of quick cutting. Rhythm is vital to the cohesion of montage, and in its second large synthesis, the ensemble of Vasyl's funeral, the film also makes assertive use of rhythmic cutting for bringing the separate shots into play together. But this is a larger synthesis, weightier, more difficult to achieve. The diverse pieces being put together here have greater emotional charge and wider and deeper import; they are less amenable to meaning because more fraught with significance, and they cannot simply be made to dance together. Synthesis is more complex here, and harder won, won not so much through a ruling rhythm of the whole as through the parallels, the numerous correspondences, drawn by the parallel montage between the individual parts.

A cut, with Dovzhenko, typically serves to establish a bond. His tendency, his guiding principle, is to cut between kindred elements, to bring out, in a juxtaposition, a kinship between different things. Variously juxtaposing one person with another, one action with another, he links together the separate pieces that make up this sequence. He cuts successively between similar close-ups, taken from below, of different young men and women singing at the funeral; he cuts between the excluded priest and the grieving, withdrawn father, both, unlike the young people, photographed from above, two men who have something in common, we perceive, in spite of their differences. We are led to recognize an affinity between the mother giving birth and the girlfriend in her virginal, despairing nakedness, two women both in pain and both handsomely embodying life; between the frenzied girlfriend in private, the space of her lost love, and the crazed kulak out in the fields, the space of his lost land; between the mother and the father, one seeing their offspring into life, the other to the grave; between, even, the kulak and the dead Vasyl, the man he killed, whose stillness confronts him and whose dance he is moved to repeat; between the girlfriend and a young woman like her who is with the others in the procession singing about the future. An intricate pattern of connections is exhibited, like great poetry rich with concentrated, manifold implications. The film then concludes as it started, with a sequence of close-ups of fruit, apples and pumpkins on

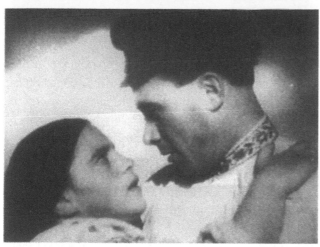

Earth. Apples in the rain, Vasyl's girlfriend with her new-found love.

which rain falls, rain that weeps and washes away, rain that freshens and replenishes—a symbol of natural cleansing and renewal, the assimilation of abrupt change with time passing. At the end, after the rain stops, we see Vasyl's girlfriend with a new-found love.

"More like an ode to life than a requiem for the dead," wrote John Howard Lawson about Vasyl's funeral.[34] But this sequence is both ode and requiem, hopeful and mournful strains in intricate counterpoint; the hopeful strains may rise higher, but the mournful continue to be heard. Lawson was a Communist (and one of the blacklisted Hollywood Ten); the anti-Communist Warshow found the ode to life in this sequence too pat ("one man is dead, another is born") and too propagandistic and depersonalizing ("They carry Vasili's body as if it were a banner. . . . The murderer, like all enemies of the people, simply does not exist; he has become, in Orwell's word, an 'unperson'").[35] But Warshow saw the film as it was circulated for many years, in a version cut by the Soviet censors, who, looking both ways, removed both the priest and the naked woman from this sequence; had he been able to see the complete film, perhaps he would have better recognized the complexity of its affirmations, the compassion of its oppositions.

On the naked woman at least Eisenstein seems to have agreed with the censors. In the course of criticizing *Intolerance* he criticized the naked woman in *Earth* for what he saw as a similar failure to generalize by metaphorical montage:

> A healthy, handsome woman's body may, actually, be heightened to *an image of a life-affirming beginning,* which is what Dovzhenko had to have, to clash with his montage of the funeral in *Earth.*
>
> A skillfully leading montage creation with *close-ups,* taken in the "Rubens manner," isolated from naturalism and abstracted in the necessary direction, could well have been lifted to such a "sensually palpable" image.
>
> But the whole structure of *Earth* was doomed to failure, because in place of such montage material the director cut into the funeral *long shots* of the interior of the peasant hut, and the naked woman flinging herself about there. And the spectator could not possibly separate out of this concrete, lifelike woman that generalized sensation of blazing fertility, of sensual life-affirmation, which the director wished to convey of all nature, as a pantheistic contrast to the theme of death and the funeral!
>
> This was prevented by the ovens, pots, towels, benches, tablecloths—all those

details of everyday life, from which the woman's body could easily have been freed by *the framing of the shot,*—so that *representational* naturalism would not interfere with the embodiment of the *conveyed metaphorical* task.[36]

Eisenstein wanted the ode to life but not the requiem for the dead. He would have turned the woman's body into an abstraction, a metaphor for "a life-affirming beginning," in utter disregard of the concrete woman and her situation. Dovzhenko's image is a metaphor but it is a concrete woman first, and that makes it a richer metaphor, a metaphor for a life-affirming beginning, yes, but also for the human cost of such a beginning, for the suffering involved in such an affirmation. Between rhetoric and poetry it may not be possible to draw a line, but there is a difference, and nowhere is that difference better exemplified than in the disparity between the rhetorical use Eisenstein would have made of this naked woman and Dovzhenko's poetic representation of her both in her pain and in her potential, both in her individuality and in the generality she embodies.

Earth came out in the early spring of 1930, at a time of crucial change in the farm policy of the Soviet government—crucial change for the worse. Lenin's New Economic Policy, which remained in effect until 1928, had relied on individual farming; collectivization would come gradually. In the struggle for power after Lenin's death the farm policy was one of the cards in play. Stalin, who emerged the victor, played that card duplicitously, and it didn't become clear until the winter of 1929–30 that he meant to push for collectivization with coercive haste. *Earth* was being edited when, in December 1929, Stalin announced his intention to "liquidate the kulaks as a class."[37] The result was brutal and disastrous. Dovzhenko couldn't have known the enormous suffering that, as he was finishing *Earth,* was beginning to be inflicted on the villages that are the subject of his film. And yet, alone of the films about the collectivization of agriculture, *Earth* knows suffering. It was denounced as defeatist and counterrevolutionary.

Earth is about the meaning of death. It is not counterrevolutionary but it seeks the meaning of revolution in the meaning of death. Death is universal but its meaning is not; death is given to us but we give it meaning. The grandfather dies in the bosom of a traditional peasant culture that assimilates his death to nature. The grandson dies in the midst of a striving, in the midst of a dance to the music of revolution. The songs of the new life that the young sing at his funeral are very nice but, as the continual intercutting of other responses makes manifest, not enough to give his death the meaning, the sense of completion, that his grandfather's had. The sequence of Vasyl's funeral is a fervent endeavor to construct the meaning of his death, the meaning of revolution for the land and its people.

In *Zvenigora* Dovzhenko portrays an old grandfather, symbol of the traditions of the Ukraine, who has a revolutionary grandson and a reactionary grandson. Although not literally brothers, Vasyl and his kulak murderer are, as Marco Carynnyk observed,[38] inimical yet fraternal doubles of each other, children of the land they both love and both dance to, one revolutionary and the other reactionary yet both alone with their dreams on the moonlit night of the fratricidal murder. In *Old and New* the kulak and his wife are made so fat, so entrenched in their privilege, as to belong not just to another class but virtually on another planet. The kulaks in *Earth* are not so far apart from the peasants, which was the truth but not the view of a regime bent on destroying a class it erected as the enemy. The violence in *Earth* (based on an actual event in which kulaks killed a Soviet activist) is the kulak's doing; the violence in reality was overwhelmingly done to the kulaks, and to the peasants but not by the kulaks. Treating the violence as fratricidal, however, mourning it as the violence that revolution entails, *Earth* is able to deal, if not with the violence that collectivization actually entailed, yet with the tragedy of revolution. *Old and New* is a pastoral comedy of sorts (William Empson mentions it in *Some Versions of Pastoral*);[39] *Earth* is closer to a tragedy, though like *Arsenal* a tragedy that looks forward to a better future. *Earth* is not a pastoral so much as a tragedy that looks forward to a pastoral under construction.

The excision of Vasyl's girlfriend from the montage ensemble of his funeral was surely not just a puritanical but also a political move on the part of the Soviet censors. For she is key to the film's endeavor of meaning, as the choice to end with her makes manifest (an ending excised as well). Of what may be called the dissidents to Vasyl's funeral—those who for one reason or another are not participants in the singing, dissidents very much included in Dovzhenko's ensemble—the kulak and the priest could be cast aside as mere reactionaries, the mother and the father reckoned too old to take full part. The girlfriend is the only one whose dissidence is undismissible. Neither reactionary nor old, she is the figure who most clearly bears both the sorrows of the tragedy and the possibilities of the future. She is the virgin who stopped short of love on the moonlit night of her boyfriend's death, and she represents both the pain of lost love and the potential for love's fruition—personally, socially, politically.

A work of art is the product of a time and place. How can it speak to us, who are not of that time and place? As a materialist who believed that the social existence of human beings determines their consciousness, Marx was concerned with this question, which he addressed in the *Grundrisse* in connection with the art of ancient Greece. "The difficulty," he wrote,

> is not in grasping the idea that Greek art and epos are bound up with certain forms of social development. It lies rather in understanding why they still constitute for us a source of aesthetic enjoyment and in certain respects prevail as the standard and model beyond attainment.
>
> A man cannot become a child again unless he becomes childish. But does he not enjoy the artless ways of the child, and must he not strive to reproduce its truth on a higher plane? . . . Why should the childhood of human society, where it had obtained its most beautiful development, not exert an eternal charm as an age that will never return?[40]

Eternal? Marx seems to have missed the way Greek art, as the revered ancestor of European civilization at a time of colonial expansion, served in its perceived supremacy the interests of European world supremacy. It was, as Marxists like to say, no accident that the Elgin Marbles ended up in the British Museum. But was Marx wrong to enjoy Greek art, wrong to be moved by the freshness and energy he saw in it? The art spoke to him, and if it didn't say the same thing it said to the ancient Greeks—how could it?— neither did it say the same thing it said to the imperialists of his time. If the fallacy of formalism is to presume that form speaks in the same way for all time, the fallacy of historicism is to suppose that historical circumstance allows only one way a work can speak at a certain time.

Earth was the product of a time when, a place where, a great hope lived and a great brutality ensued. It powerfully spoke to me, when I first saw it in the sixties, of an aspiration both personal and political, a reaching toward an order that would bring harmony without sacrificing individuality, a striving aware of sorrow but undiscouraged by that awareness. I didn't fully understand it but I heard it; I think I understand it better now and I hear it more clearly. In Marx's admiration for Greek art there was a nostalgia, which he felt as a modern man sickened by the alienation of the industrial age, for a simpler and more unified time. No doubt my admiration for *Earth* harbors a similar nostalgia. But *Earth* is not itself nostalgic. It conveys a peasant's first-hand sense, vivid to the eye and to the fingertips, of the integral rather than the alienated life: not an idyllic closeness to idealized nature but a concrete interpenetration of nature and culture, a vital fabric of human interrelationships grounded in the material world. And there is nothing retrograde about this peasant, either politically or artistically. *Earth* has no wish to stop time at the stage of the village: rather it draws on a living tradition of village life for its vision of a better life in the socialist city it seeks to build, a city where the communal integrity of the village would more broadly reign. It is a marvel that a work such as *Earth* exists in the art of our century.

6 : Landscape and Fiction

"I set foot in the world of the cinema only in order to make my wife a star," wrote Jean Renoir in his autobiography.

> Dédée was very beautiful. Everyone told her this, and it was difficult for her to ignore it. We went to the cinema nearly every day, to the point that we had come to live in the unreal world of the American film. It may be added that Dédée belonged to the same class of woman as the stars whose appearance we followed on the screen. She copied their behaviour and dressed herself like them. People stopped her in the street to ask if they had not seen her in some particular film, always an American film. We thought nothing of the French cinema. So it was very easy for us to believe that Dédée had only to show herself to be accepted as another Gloria Swanson or Mae Murray or Mary Pickford.[1]

Dédée had modeled for Jean's father, the famous impressionist painter; earlier, she had applied to Matisse, who looked at her and said, "You're a Renoir." She had the kind of beauty, with red hair and a round figure, that Auguste Renoir favored; the kind of beauty, she and Jean thought, that would shine on the silver screen. For her career in the movies she adopted the name of Catherine Hessling. But her husband, the rich boy (rich because his father's paintings were already selling very well) who thought he would merely help his beautiful wife become a star, turned out to be the one who made a success in the movies.

Jean Renoir's career as a filmmaker spanned forty-five years, from 1924 to 1969. It may be divided (as Ronald Bergan suggests in his biography) into three periods corresponding to the three women who shared Renoir's life.[2] First there were his curious silent films with Catherine Hessling, which combined the unreality of mute Hollywood with that of French avant-gardism, and in which the most unreal thing was the actress herself, who seemed masked by her own stylized acting. Renoir put his own money into these films and lost a lot of it. *La Chienne,* which he made in 1931, shortly after the coming of sound, marked his break with Catherine Hessling and his breakthrough into the commercial film industry. (She was to have played the female lead, but the producers insisted on another actress, and when Renoir consented and went ahead without her she felt betrayed, and that was the end of their relationship.) It was also his first masterpiece, and a film as realistic, as grounded in a social and material reality, as his earlier ones had been unreal. *La Chienne* began a remarkable period of social realism and searching innovation in Renoir's career: realism that demanded formal innovation, innovation that responded to concrete reality.

This period coincided with the decade of the thirties and with Renoir's involvement, personal and professional, with a woman he described in his autobiography just as "my friend and film-editor," Marguerite Houllé, who, even though she was never married to him, took the name of Marguerite Renoir. She came from the working class (as did Auguste Renoir, whose father was a tailor) and from a family and a milieu of trade unionists and left activists; she was herself an activist for women's suffrage in France—where women couldn't vote until 1944—and a member of the Communist Party. If his infatuation with Catherine Hessling inspired Jean Renoir to make movies, his association with Marguerite Houllé disposed him to make his movies more socially probing and more politically oriented; although he never joined the Communist Party himself, during his years with Marguerite he became the leading filmmaker of the French Left. It would be too simple to say that he became involved in politics because he was involved with her; it could as well be said that he was drawn to someone like her because he was drawn to social and political concerns. Certainly he wasn't the only artist who moved from aestheticism in the twenties to politicization in the thirties. Yet it's interesting to note that in his case the move was bound up with a change from one woman to another as partner both in his life and in the practice of his art.

Jean Renoir found himself as an artist when he found the world. His art went out into the streets, into the arena of what is, and developed the means for rendering and interpreting the world's situations in their concrete complexity. If Griffith's technical innovations dramatized cinematic space, if Murnau's made it subjective and Eisenstein's made it rhetorical, Renoir's innovations may be said to have socialized cinematic space. "His deep-focus shots, tracking camera and multiple action within the image," wrote Eric Rhode, "have the effect of socializing space"; in *The Social Cinema of Jean Renoir* Christopher Faulkner picked up this apt phrase and developed its implications, especially with regard to *Toni* (1934).[3] Multiple action in Renoir, one might add, unfolds not only within the image but also without, in the space off screen, which he treats not as a mere implied background in the usual manner but as an area of action no less important than the image on screen.

When Legrand, the retiring petit-bourgeois protagonist of *La Chienne*, arrives unannounced at the apartment where he keeps his beloved mistress Lulu and finds her in bed with another man, the pimp to whom all along she has been in thrall, virtually any other director filming the scene would have promptly come in for closer views of this dramatic confrontation. Renoir holds a view from the landing outside the apartment door as Legrand walks in and opens the door to the bedroom, where Lulu and the pimp can be glimpsed in the far background; then he cuts outside the bedroom window and, past the flowerpots on the ledge, through the sheer embroidered curtains, like some curious neighbor looking in on the scene, the camera catches another glimpse of the couple in bed and moves sideways to frame an obscured distant view of the stunned Legrand. No mere stylistic flourish, this camera technique serves to refer the inside to the outside—the drama coming to a head inside that bedroom to the material circumstances that have governed it, the emotions stirring inside the characters to the social existence that has shaped their consciousness. The personal in a Renoir film of the thirties is always seen to be a function of the social. Whatever takes place inside—inside a room, inside a person's mind, inside the frame of a film image—takes place in relation to the world outside.

Sensitive and soft-spoken, Legrand in *La Chienne* is the kind of person who leads more of an inner than an outer life. His tragedy is that the inner life is determined by the outer—that the inner life he would shelter from the outer world has from the start been thoroughly penetrated by that world. His is a petit-bourgeois tragedy, as Christopher Faulkner observes;[4] for Legrand is characteristically petit bourgeois in the way he delusively identifies himself with the bourgeois he is not, the way he defines himself in terms of a false consciousness that keeps him from recognizing his real situation in the world. When Legrand comes to recognize that situation, he kills: the quiet man with the inner life had it in him to kill. And Renoir accordingly presents the murder as he presents the discovery of Lulu with the pimp that shatters romantic and domestic illusion: by referring the inside to the outside, the bedroom to the street; by socializing the space of the inner life and seeing it in relation to the outer world.[5]

Neither *La Chienne* nor his other great films of the early thirties— *La Nuit du carrefour, Boudu Saved from Drowning, Toni*—gained Renoir a secure position in the film industry. None of these films was much of a commercial success. (None was distributed in the United States for many years, and *La Nuit du carrefour* still hasn't been.) Renoir was regarded as an amateur in spite of what he was accomplishing—or precisely because of it, because he was accomplishing something new and breaking the rules of the professionals. But this defier of convention wanted to reach a popular audience. In an article from the mid-thirties he wrote:

> Film directors are the sons of the bourgeoisie. They bring to this career the weaknesses of their decadent class. The public of the exclusive cinemas, who often decide the success of a film from the beginning, is also a bourgeois public. It's only after they have sanctioned a film that the cinemas of the poorer quarters hurry to pick it up. . . . Without delay, the cinema of France must be restored to the people of France.[6]

In 1935 the Comintern softened its hard line and the Communists joined the Socialists and other parties on the Left in an antifascist alliance, the Popular Front, which won elections in Spain and France. That year Renoir made the extraordinary *Crime of Monsieur Lange*, his first explicitly political film and a film deeply of the Popular Front both in the story it tells and in its style of representation.[7] But it still was not a popular success: for that Renoir had to wait until *Grand Illusion* (1937).

In the story it tells, about workers at a print shop who gain freedom from capitalist subjection and organize themselves into a cooperative that happily prospers, *The Crime of Monsieur Lange* celebrates socialism. In its visual arrangement, centered on a courtyard that the camera identifies with the community, it socializes space in a spirit of populist solidarity. And it is in this spirit, underscored by an amazing camera movement all around the courtyard as he takes his decisive action, that Monsieur Lange commits his crime: killing the unscrupulous entrepreneur Batala, exploiter of workers and women and enemy of the cooperative. Lange is a dreamer, a concocter of stories of the American West, which the cooperative publishes with great success, and he kills Batala as his fictional hero Arizona Jim would kill the villain.

Lange is a figure of the artist, and like other such figures in Renoir's work—a trouper with the commedia dell'arte in one film, a stager of the cancan in another—he is a popular rather than a highbrow artist. This too was in keeping with the Popular Front, which broadened not only political but cultural allegiances and embraced popular forms often viewed with disdain. *The Crime of Monsieur Lange* is high art embracing popular art with a certain irony but quite without condescension. The irony comes from the recognition of fantasy, the fantasy of Lange's stories, of course, but also the fantasy of the film's own story of the working class airily rising to self-rule. Not condescension but solidarity is the posture adopted toward the fictions of Lange the dreamer by a film declaring itself a fiction, a dream of socialist sweetness and light, enacted in response to a reality but not to be taken as something realized. Just as the cooperative prospers by publishing Lange's stories, so the cause of socialism will have been served by the film's happy fantasy, undeceived and undeceiving, improbable yet indelible. Fantasy in *The Crime of Monsieur Lange* is not an escape from reality but part of the endeavor to change reality.

Following the sweetly radical *Crime of Monsieur Lange* Renoir made two films of more militant temper that were produced outside the established commercial system: *La Vie est à nous* (It's Our Life, 1936), commissioned by the Communist Party for its electoral campaign; and *La Marseillaise* (1938), sponsored by the C.G.T., the left-wing labor federation, and financed by public subscription ("the first film made for and by the people," Renoir wrote at the time).[8] *La Vie est à nous* combines fiction and documentary not in a seamless but in a dialectical fashion. A little-known film, often slighted as a work of propaganda—which it is, but not to its detriment—it has been extolled by some who would want Renoir to be more like Eisenstein; but if Eisenstein manipulates reality into political theater, Renoir brings theater out into political reality. *La Marseillaise* looks back to the time of the French Revolution, as *Grand Illusion* looks back to the time of the First World War, so as to arouse the spectator's historical consciousness and encourage a comparison between the past and the present. The present was the time of the Popular Front and of belligerent fascism, a time of hope on the brink of calamity. The great dream could turn out to have been the big illusion.

Grand Illusion was halted in the middle of a showing when the Nazis entered Vienna in March 1938. That spring the French Popular Front was crumbling, and that fall it was finished after the Munich agreement. France mostly cheered the appeasement of Nazi Germany. Renoir was one of the few who spoke out against it. He was making *La Bête humaine,* which opened in December and did well at the box office, only the second hit of his career. He updated Zola's novel from 1869 to 1938 without doing much to brighten its gloomy picture of the working class. For his next film he turned to comedy in an upper-class setting but wanted to use again the same actors, Jean Gabin, Simone Simon, and Fernand Ledoux. They were not available, and neither was his famous older brother, Pierre, whom he also wanted for a leading role he ended up playing himself. Nothing about *The Rules of the Game,* the last of Renoir's films of the thirties and one of the great works of the century, turned out as planned. An independent production that ended up costing far more than any other French film made that year, *The Rules of the Game* opened in July 1939 and "rubbed most people up the wrong way," as Renoir wrote in his autobiography. "It was a resounding flop, to which the reaction was a kind of loathing."[9]

It may seem surprising that a film so lively and delightful, a comedy of love in society that calls to mind Marivaux and Beaumarchais—and Beaumarchais's musical refashioner, Mozart—should have met with so hostile a response from the public. But *The Rules of the Game* is a tragedy cast in the form of a comedy. If the portrayal of the working class in *The Crime of Monsieur Lange* employed popular forms with good-natured, hopeful irony, the portrayal of the upper class in *The Rules of the Game* employs the form of classical comedy with an irony grown mordant, devastating, despairing. Tragedy is traditionally the form of singularity, comedy the form of community. *The Rules of the Game* is a tragedy of community. Its fatality resides not in the singular individual, the hero with a tragic flaw—its characters have the flaws of common humanity, the flaws of comedy—but in the order of a society that does violence to nature and human nature, a society that fails to accommodate its individuals into a sustaining community. If *The Crime of Monsieur Lange* was the comedy, the romance of the Popular Front, the celebration of its vision of community, *The Rules of the Game* turns the comedy into tragedy. It is one thing to tell a tragic story, which *La Bête humaine* did to great popular success, and quite another to tell a comic story that turns tragic through the very ways of comedy, the paths that traditionally would lead to a happy resolution. *The Rules of the Game* enacts the tragedy of a society no longer capable of comedy.[10]

This time the artist figure—Octave, the character played by Renoir himself—is a highbrow artist, a classical musician, but he is a failed artist. Renoir felt like a failed artist himself after the public reaction to *The Rules of the Game*. No sooner had the public at last embraced him, with *Grand Illusion* and *La Bête humaine,* than it crushingly rejected his wonderful ensuing film. "I tried to save the film by shortening it," he recollected, "and to start with I cut the scenes in which I myself played too large a part, as though I were ashamed, after this rebuff, of showing myself on the screen. But it was useless."[11] In mid-August, barely a month after the film's opening, Renoir took off for Italy, leaving Marguerite behind. He had declined to go to fascist Italy two years before when *Grand Illusion* won a prize at Venice; now he accepted an invitation to film *La Tosca* in Rome. His leftist friends were upset; they didn't know that another leftist awaited him in Rome, Luchino Visconti, who had been his assistant in France and was again to be on the Italian film; but they weren't wrong to perceive that Jean Renoir was abandoning ship.

A new woman in his life, Dido Freire, accompanied him to Italy. The working-class Marguerite had been his companion in his years of political involvement, and now Dido, a diplomat's daughter from a well-to-do Brazilian family, became his companion in his retreat from politics, a retreat that was to last for the rest of his life. As Visconti was showing Jean and Dido around Rome, the Nazi-Soviet pact was signed, which appalled Renoir and abashed the Communist disapproval of his presence in a fascist country—but this was the sort of embarrassment that does not make for conciliation. In early September the Second World War broke out, and Renoir quickly returned to France, but the French government, which banned *The Rules of the Game* as "demoralizing," sent him back to continue with *La Tosca* as part of the effort to keep Italy out of the war. He didn't get beyond the opening sequence. In June 1940 France surrendered, and six months later, on New Year's Eve, Jean and Dido arrived in the United States.

After that tangled juncture of the personal and the political, art and its fortunes and history and its vicissitudes, nothing was ever the same again for Jean Renoir. The wartime émigré became a lifelong expatriate. He married Dido Freire and settled in Beverly Hills. Not that he took to Hollywood, where his way of working did not find favor, and where he made some films worth attention but none to put beside his French films of the thirties. For years he couldn't go back to France because his California divorce from Catherine Hessling wasn't recognized there and he feared being arrested as a bigamist; but even after he could go back he did not return to live there. His exile fed the antagonism of French leftists who thought of him as a deserter from their ranks. Admirers such as Eric Rohmer and François Truffaut, proponents of the *politique des auteurs* and politically conservative, viewed Renoir as never very political, an artist above the struggle, a warm-hearted humanist too affectionate toward his characters to take sides. Renoir himself said in 1952:

> Before the war my way of participating in the universal concert was to try and raise a voice of protest. I do not think that my criticism was ever very bitter. I love humanity too much, so that I hope my sarcasm was always mixed with a little tenderness. Today, the new being that I am realizes that this is not the time for sarcasm and that the only thing I can bring to this illogical, irresponsible, and cruel universe is my "love."[12]

The "new being that I am" had been born not only in American exile but also through his encounter with India, where he went to make *The River*

(1951), an unassumingly profound film about death and rebirth on the river of life that was his first major work since his departure from France. Like *La Vie est à nous, The River* unconventionally combines fiction and documentary; but *La Vie est à nous* was a propaganda film, and *The River* is rather like a home movie. It is a movie about home, except that since it portrays a British family in India, home is a foreign country (surely a reflection of Renoir's own exile); the home movie is also a travelogue, beautifully done but with no pretension of offering anything other than a visitor's perspective. Fiction, seen in *La Vie est à nous* as an intervention in a world we should remake, becomes in *The River* a meditation on a world we did not make. *The River* is about our foreignness in the world, our foreignness and our dailiness. This film has been construed as mystical and as preaching submission to nature. But if the river in the film is nature, it is the humanly inflected nature we call culture, very much a populated river, a river where people work and pray and dream and are unhappy; and the film is about people not surrendering to the cosmic but reconciling themselves to the daily business of living in the world.

The River has been taken to task for its avoidance of politics. Writing in praise of the film at the time it came out, Renoir's best critic, André Bazin, saw the objection:

> What has become of the tender, mocking skepticism, the social satire of *The Rules of the Game*? *The River* describes the life of two English families someplace in Bengal. They are wealthy and without material worries. Renoir never subjects this colonial bourgeoisie to antipathy, to the slightest critical irony. Of course, the characters of *The Rules of the Game* had his sympathy too, but the tenderness they inspired in him did not in any way mitigate his mercilessly lucid appraisal of them.[13]

The River does not dissemble the social situation of its characters, their colonial privilege in a country under imperial rule: it does not dissemble it but neither does it dispute it. "Melanie, what do we do?" asks the one-legged Captain John, at a fraught moment in the film, of the half-caste young woman infatuated with him. "Consent," she replies with troubled serenity: consent to our limitations. The greatness of *The River*—and the same can be said of the three major films Renoir made after it, *The Golden Coach* (1953), *French Cancan* (1955), and *The Elusive Corporal* (1962)—is inseparable from its modesty, its humility, its consent to limitation. It places itself not above but below politics, at the level of everyday life. *The Golden Coach* and *French Cancan* are celebrations of art that cherish its pleasures without pretending they will fix our troubles or transcend our sorrows, without aggrandizing them into anything more than a good time. (Christopher Faulkner thinks the films of Renoir's late period espouse art for art's sake, what he calls an "ideology of aesthetics."[14] This seems to me in error. Renoir's late films remain socially aware even if they no longer contest the social order. They don't elevate art above society, they see it as working within the conditions of society: they are unassuming about the art they celebrate. Faulkner is an Althusserian and *his* ideology rules out an art that can make its peace with a social situation it neither endorses nor presumes to transcend.)

In Renoir's postwar films some see the same Renoir of the thirties and some see a different Renoir. Those who see the same Renoir see the lover of humanity; those who see a different Renoir miss the critic of society. The social criticism never mattered as much as the humanism, some say: look at the marquis in *Rules of the Game*, the presiding figure of a decadent society and yet a charming and well-meaning man, personally the most likable character in the film. But the marquis can be likable as an individual precisely because his personal qualities are almost irrelevant to the social situation in which he plays a quite dislikable role. He didn't arrange to have his wife's lover killed, as the general approvingly supposes at the film's end: he didn't arrange the killing as an individual, but he effectively did in his social role. Not being personified—not being moralized—the criticism is not softened but sharpened, more clearly focused on its social target. Humane though he is, Renoir is not exactly the humanist he is often taken to be, for he does not give primacy to the individual as humanism proposes. He treats individuals with sympathy and affection but doesn't see that they make much difference in the course of things. "Why is it that, in a world so free of malevolence as is that of Renoir's films," asked William S. Pechter, "things seem almost always to end so sadly?"[15] There may be no bad guys in Renoir, but that doesn't make things much better. His films of the thirties tend to violence and harbor a hope for change. His later films are gentler and more accepting but perhaps sadder for that very reason.

In his book on his father Renoir warns us at the outset that history is subjective. The reflections on his art and his career we have from Renoir come mostly from his later years. Critics, and especially auteur critics, have tended to take the older Renoir as the measure of the younger. It is curious, as Bergan notes, that the older Renoir, whether in his autobiography or in his interviews and other statements, says so little about Marguerite Houllé. Maybe, as some have suggested, he was afraid Dido would be jealous; but his relationship with Marguerite was not only personal but artistic and political as well. After Renoir left her, Marguerite married a man with whom she was not happy and whom she came to kill in self-defense; she was detained for a month, and the case against her was dropped. She pulled herself together and resumed her work as a film editor, notably on the films of Jacques Becker, Renoir's longtime friend and assistant in the thirties.

A man who limps because he lost a leg in the war, Captain John in *The River* calls to mind Renoir himself, who limped all his life because of a wound he suffered in the First World War. It is tempting to see the three young women who become infatuated with Captain John as figures of the three women in Renoir's life: Melanie as Dido, thin and dark and (as Bergan characterizes Dido) spiritual; the beautiful redheaded Valerie as Catherine Hessling; and, as Marguerite, Harriet, the film's narrator and informing sensibility, its figure of the artist. Perhaps this was Renoir's way of telling Marguerite, secretly and for all the world to hear, that she was his figure of the artist.

In the summer of 1936, following *La Vie est à nous* and the advent to power of the Popular Front, Renoir went out to the country and back into the past. He made *A Day in the Country* from a story by Maupassant, a story from the time of the impressionists set in the countryside near Paris they so often painted. In 1936 he had to go farther away from Paris to find suitable impressionist countryside. He shot the film on the banks of the Loing River, near the village of Marlotte by the Forest of Fontainebleau, a landscape painted by Corot and the Barbizon school before Monet and Auguste Renoir sojourned there in the early years of impressionism. (It was in the Forest of Fontainebleau that Monet painted his *Déjeuner sur l'herbe* in the mid-1860s, following Manet's more famous treatment of the subject.) This was a landscape Jean Renoir knew very well himself: he owned a house there and he had made his first film there with Catherine Hessling. Sylvia Bataille, who had played in *The Crime of Monsieur Lange*, played the lead in *A Day in the Country*; Renoir, a director as responsive to the actor's special qualities as he was to the concrete surrounding world, felt that period costumes would be right for her and that the sound of her voice would be right for the film.[16]

A Day in the Country was planned for sunny weather but during the filming it rained a lot. Renoir changed the script accordingly as he would always change a script according to the actualities of making the film. But the rainy weather caused delays, and at length the production was interrupted when the director had to leave for another project. Marguerite made a cut of the almost finished film, but it was less than feature-length and the producer wanted a longer picture. The film was shelved. During the German occupation the producer, Pierre Braunberger, while hiding from the Nazis on an island in the middle of a river, had a vivid recollection of *A Day in the Country* as Marguerite had cut it, and he decided it could be shown that way.[17] Marguerite's cut had been lost but the negatives survived, and she cut the film again. It was finally released in 1946.

If previous ages looked to Giorgione or Claude, our version of pastoral landscape was painted by the impressionists. True, that version is over a hundred years old by now, but nobody has painted a newer one to replace it in our cultural imagination, and when we look at the country through the city eyes of pastoral, which see in it an idealized sweetness and peace, it's still an impressionist picture that we tend to see. Pastoral is always a fiction, a fantasy of the country, but the impressionists, in keeping with their time—and ours—made it a more realistic fiction, not a mythical Arcadia but something they constructed out of the actual passing appearances— the impressions—of the world we all know. And theirs was a more democratic fiction, something that relates to the experience of anybody who can get a glimpse of a stretch of water or a piece of greenery once in a while. Made halfway along the hundred years and more since Monet and Renoir took their paints to the Forest of Fontainebleau, *A Day in the Country* looks back to the time of the impressionists and evokes their pastoral in all its enduring appeal; but it looks back inquiringly, not just nostalgically, leading us into reflection rather than mere surrender to that appeal.

"In landscape painting I like pictures which make me want to wander about inside them," said Auguste Renoir. R. H. Wilenski commented:

> When painting landscape he [Renoir] never took a point of focus . . . and he never used the defined foreground of the classical-picturesque tradition which closed as it were the picture at the bottom and provided a point where the spectator himself could stand. . . . The entrance to the landscape depicted in his pictures is always open at all sides; and the spectator is thus tempted to enter and "wander about inside them."[18]

In impressionist painting generally, the picture, rather than seeming contained within the frame, enclosed by it, gives us the feeling of an open field where we can imagine wandering about, inside and outside the boundaries of our view. We get much the same feeling in a Jean Renoir film. In films the frame does not mark, as it does in painting, the boundaries of the visual field: a space off screen is always implied, an indefinitely larger field of which at the moment we are seeing only a section. But most films ask us to regard that section as all we need to see for the moment, so that the frame nonetheless conventionally functions as a boundary mark enclosing, not the whole, but the part that matters. Rarely have the movies moved, the camera and its subjects wandered about, with the openness of Renoir's work of the thirties; in his different medium, he accomplished a liberation from the conventional enclosures similar to that of his father and the other impressionists. In a Renoir film, as Bazin wrote, "the action is not bounded by the screen, but merely passes through it."[19] Jean Renoir needs no prestige by association, and he has been compared to Auguste Renoir perhaps too often, but the artistic kinship between son and father is not to be slighted. *A Day in the Country* explicitly looks back to the father's work and evidently encourages the comparison.[20]

No less than the similarities, however, this film brings out the differences between the two Renoirs. It employs the period setting not so much to recapture the impressionists as to bracket them in their own time, to help put them at a distance from which it examines their vision in a spirit at once affectionate and critical. The Maupassant story it adapts certainly regards the impressionist countryside in a critical spirit. "The two men were friendly enough but frankly admitted they had nothing in common," wrote Jean Renoir of his father and Maupassant. "Renoir said of the writer, 'He always looks on the dark side'—while Maupassant said of the painter, 'He always looks on the bright side.' "[21] *A Day in the Country* is usually taken to brighten the writer with the painter, to answer critical detachment with a sensuous immersion in nature, but it can as well be taken to darken the painter with the writer, to answer the impressionist pastoral with an incisive social awareness. It generates a dialogue between the beauties of nature and the conditions of society. It is not exactly a pastoral but a film about pastoral.

Maupassant's story begins with a Parisian family—Monsieur and Madame Dufour and their daughter, together with an old grandmother and a yellow-haired young man whose apprenticeship in the family's hardware business entails an expectation of marriage to the daughter—on their way to lunch at some country restaurant near the city in the milkman's wagon they have borrowed for the day. "Here we are in the country at last!" announces Monsieur Dufour, and as they all admire the distant landscape, Maupassant describes the industrial wasteland stretching around them with its factory chimneys and its unpleasant smell. Argenteuil, the town where Monet lived in the 1870s and where Manet and Renoir also went to paint, can be seen in the distance; but the Dufours get barely past Bezons and its rubber factory. They cross a bridge and on the other side of the river, where the air is purer, they find a country restaurant that suits them.

The petite bourgeoisie on an outing to what was not really the country but more like an illusion of it: Maupassant depicts a country excursion such as had become common in the later nineteenth century, and he takes toward it a disenchanting stance such as observers at the time frequently adopted. The impressionists were well aware of the disenchanters when they painted the enchantment. "When painters went out to the countryside round Paris in the 1870s—in search of a landscape, say, or a modern *fête champêtre*—they would have known they were choosing, or accepting, a place it was easy (almost conventional) to find a bit absurd," wrote T. J. Clark in his book on Manet and his followers.[22] The impressionists gave us a pastoral of the country outing. They chose, they accepted, the excursionist's countryside near the city, and their way of painting highlights the transient, the fluid, the casual, the impression rather than the permanency—which suggests the visitor's way of seeing and makes felt the momentariness of the enchantment they painted. (Monet in particular liked to give his painting the look of off-handedness and labored to dissemble his labors.) The impressionists painted leisure, not the leisure of the upper class but of the ordinary people: "a day off, a trip to the country, boats, smiling women in sunlight, flags, trees in flower—the impressionist vocabulary of images," wrote John Berger, "is that of a popular dream, the awaited, beloved, secular Sunday."[23] Why is it that left-wing art critics like Berger or Clark wish that impressionist painting had more of the solidity of Renaissance painting? The Renaissance emphasis on the corporeal, the tactile, expressed the outlook of a rising bourgeoisie that felt it could lay its hands on the world; the impressionist emphasis on the passing moment, the colorful delight of light, expressed the outlook of a rising petite bourgeoisie that felt much less secure in the pleasures it could lay claim to.

"It is remarkable how many pictures we have in early impressionism of informal and spontaneous sociability," wrote Meyer Schapiro in a 1937 essay,

> of breakfasts, picnics, promenades, boating trips, holidays and vacation travel. These urban idylls not only present the objective forms of bourgeois recreation in the 1860's and 1870's; they also reflect in the very choice of subjects and in the new aesthetic devices the conception of art as solely a field of individual enjoyment, without reference to ideas and motives, and they presuppose the cultivation of these pleasures as the highest field of freedom for an enlightened bourgeois detached from the official beliefs of his class. . . .
>
> As the contexts of bourgeois sociability shifted from community, family and church to commercialized or privately improvised forms—the streets, the cafés

and resorts—the resulting consciousness of individual freedom involved more and more an estrangement from older ties; and those imaginative members of the middle class who accepted the norms of freedom, but lacked the economic means to attain them, were spiritually torn by a sense of helpless isolation in an anonymous indifferent mass. By 1880 the enjoying individual becomes rare in impressionist art; only the private spectacle of nature is left.[24]

At the beginning of his book Clark quotes this passage more fully and with great admiration. But he wonders "how informal and spontaneous is the sociability depicted already in Manet's *Déjeuner sur l'herbe*, or for that matter in Monet's."[25] For informal and spontaneous sociability he should have gone to Renoir. Sociability in Manet is always uneasy. Looking is what matters in Monet, the sheer sight of something, the view from which the viewer stands back to look. Renoir brings us in. He may be said to have socialized the space of impressionist painting as his son socialized the space of the movies.

Yet informal and spontaneous sociability is rare in the son's work. Perhaps only in the utopian *Crime of Monsieur Lange* does it prevail. Certainly not in *A Day in the Country*. Moving the setting deeper into the country, to the banks of the Loing rather than the Seine, makes it less a site of community and more the setting for an individual's private encounter with nature. And this individual—the Dufour daughter, Henriette—is just the imaginative member of the middle class Schapiro describes, reaching for freedom but lacking the economic means to attain it.

A Day in the Country begins on the bridge the Dufours cross into the pleasanter stretch of countryside. There are no factory chimneys anywhere around, no signs of the city other than the Dufours themselves. (A shot of them on the road from Paris is among the rushes the Cinémathèque Française recently compiled for showing but not in the finished film as Marguerite cut it.) If the film's countryside is "a bit absurd," it is the Dufours who bring the absurdity. On the other side of the bridge nature stands unspoiled and lovely. Most of all it is the presence of nature—and the presence of Sylvia Bataille as Henriette—that sets Renoir's film apart from Maupassant's story.

From the bridge the film cuts to a lyrical traveling shot that takes the point of view of the arriving Parisians. The ambient trees sweetly float by as the visitors, and we with them, approach a country inn they have spotted for their lunch on the grass. (Marguerite, who along with Jean Renoir plays a small part in the film, can be seen coming out the inn door and down the front steps as the camera goes past.) This first impression of the place feels indeed like an impressionist picture, both in the mobile camera's sensuous response to appearances—which provides a sort of equivalent, in black-and-white film, for the bright impressionist palette—and in the conveyed sense of their fluidity and impermanence. No less than his father would have on canvas, Renoir celebrates this first impression, relishes this prolonged moment when nature seems to extend us an embrace. That he attributes the view to the petit-bourgeois visitors does not deny its validity but does signal its one-sidedness.

Identification is something much talked about but insufficiently understood. As in any point-of-view shot through a character's eyes, in this traveling shot we identify ourselves with the Dufour family whose point of view we share. But how do we identify ourselves with them? Not as individuals. We have only just met them and they are as yet scarcely individualized. We share their point of view as a group. But even as a group they are as yet scarcely particularized. Unlike the conventional point-of-view shot—which Renoir seldom uses—this traveling shot proceeds without any inserted shots of the characters looking at the scene and reacting to it such as normally would mark the view as belonging to those characters. This view does not belong to the Dufours either as individuals or as members of a particular family. It belongs to them as members of a whole social class. And it is as members of a class, the urban middle class seeking the pleasures of a day in the country, that we identify ourselves with them. That family's perspective on the inn could have been the perspective of any Sunday excursionist, could have been ours if we had been there, arriving for a *déjeuner sùr l'herbe* at that pretty country spot. Renoir implicates himself, and implicates us, in the excursionist's point of view. But he still wants us to recognize it as a point of view, a certain way of regarding things, a slant on the sights of nature rather than a universal human response.

This is made further manifest when, without having given us a closer view of the Parisians, the film cuts inside the inn to a perspective looking out from its door, the country people's reverse angle, one might call it—a reverse angle not attributed to anyone in particular but, like the angle it reverses, construed collectively. From a visitor's perspective the film switches to an insider's, from one side of things to quite another. Inside is of course where the country people eat, lunch on the grass being a Parisian penchant on which two local young men—two *canotiers*, boatmen such as are often depicted in impressionist painting—comment derisively.

In Maupassant's story these bare-armed *canotiers* are indistinguishable from each other; in Renoir's film they are the first characters individually drawn, Rodolphe as the more frivolous, Henri as the more serious of the two. As the two sit at table, Rodolphe opens a window that lets in, with a sudden brightness, another lovely impressionist picture of the outdoors. Mock the Parisian pastoral though these men may, nobody could resist, we feel, the charm of that light and air, that view pouring in through the window of the visiting mother and daughter on swings. But the two men have different reactions, Rodolphe leaning out to watch, Henri taking hardly a glance outside; and the window frame intrudes to remind us that the alluring sight within its edges is after all only a picture, literally a picture for us in the audience and for the two men only a spectacle with which they have made no real connection.

For our first close look at any of the visitors Renoir singles out the daughter, Henriette, whom we see swinging on her swing, exulting in the open air, the camera empathetically following her from a low angle that enhances the sense of her soaring. And it adds to the exhilarated feeling that the camera doesn't follow her quite steadily through the air, so that its movement seems to partake of her excitement, and doesn't frame her quite stably on the screen, so that her excitement seems uncontainable within the bounds of the image. Like the brush strokes in impressionist painting, and like much else in Renoir's film technique, this unsteady following and unstable framing could be deemed awkward or coarse, an unseemly showing of the artist's hand, by received standards of polish, to which in truth this is a considered alternative, capable of nuance and elegance as well as expressive force.

Henriette on her swing puts commentators in mind of an Auguste

A Day in the Country. Rodolphe opens the window and leans out to watch.

Renoir painting, *La Balançoire* (The Swing, 1876), which depicts a young woman standing on a swing. But the young woman in the painting is not swinging, and right beside her, in the spotted sunlight shining through the trees, are two men and a child sociably arranged. (Another group can be discerned in the background by her face and arm.) Henriette is with her family, and when she gets on the swing she attracts onlookers—Rodolphe at the window, boys gazing over a hedge, a group of seminarians passing by— but she is essentially alone as she swings up in the air. In her openness to the outdoors, her surrender to the pastoral of the country outing, she is by herself, enjoying a private experience of immersion in nature.

The woman on a swing often appears as a subject of art in the eighteenth century, a subject represented with amatory purport.[26] Fragonard's 1767 painting *The Swing*, for example, depicts a young woman swinging before a young man lying in the bushes under her and looking straight up her skirts, a plain enough representation of her giving herself to him sexually (plain enough to us, but hidden from the older man behind her who pulls her swing). This is not Auguste Renoir's swing, which evokes middle-class contentment rather than aristocratic love play. Henriette's swinging in *A Day in the Country* has none of the salaciousness of Fragonard's swing but it carries an unmistakable sexual energy and a feeling of delighted awakening, of liberation rather than contentment. (The lonely wife's swinging on her garden swing in Satyajit Ray's *Charulata* [1964], after her husband's attractive younger brother has come to the house, expresses a rather similar delighted awakening.)

A Day in the Country. Henriette on her swing.

In an article comparing *A Day in the Country* with Maupassant's story, Seymour Chatman sees a problem and ponders how the film solves it: "the problem of communicating the innocent yet seductive quality of Henriette's charms."[27] This is, one might think, a problem solved by Sylvia Bataille's performance, which splendidly renders both the character's innocence and her emergent sexuality, but Chatman sees it as a problem for the camera. Henriette on her swing figures this way in Maupassant's story:

> Mademoiselle Dufour was trying to swing herself standing up, but she could not succeed in getting a start. She was a pretty girl of about eighteen, one of those women who suddenly excite your desire when you meet them in the street and who leave you with a vague feeling of uneasiness and of excited senses. She was tall, had a small waist and large hips, with a dark skin, very large eyes and very black hair. Her dress clearly marked the outlines of her firm, full figure, which was accentuated by the motion of her hips as she tried to swing herself higher. Her arms were stretched upward to hold the rope, so that her bosom rose at every movement she made. Her hat, which a gust of wind had blown off, was hanging behind her, and as the swing gradually rose higher and higher, she showed her delicate limbs up to the knees each time, and the breeze from her flying skirts, which was more heady than the fumes of wine, blew into the faces of the two men [not the *canotiers*, who haven't entered the story yet, but the father and the yellow-haired apprentice], who were looking at her and smiling.[28]

Talk about the male gaze. This narrator eyes Henriette with lust. Innocent though she may be, in this description she is seductive. Chatman remarks on the ambiguity of her "showing" her legs up to the knees—the word leaves it undecided between her showing innocently and showing with intent, leaves it open to seductive construction—and he thinks the camera incapable of conveying that ambiguity. So, he argues, the camera must adopt the point of view of a character who eyes Henriette with lust, the point of view of Rodolphe, in order that we may see the innocent young woman as seductive.

But the fact is that for most of this sequence Renoir's camera does not adopt Rodolphe's point of view. Rodolphe opens the window and looks out, but the camera remains at some distance behind him and frames Henri as well on the other side. Then the film cuts to an angle quite detached from Rodolphe's perspective and holds a long shot of the Dufour family ordering lunch, the mother sitting on her swing, the daughter standing on hers. By the time we cut to the exhilarating close view of Henriette swinging, the onlooking Rodolphe little enters our minds. "Suddenly we are very much identified with Henriette's feelings: Rodolphe's voyeurism is forgotten," Chatman grants. But if Rodolphe's voyeurism is forgotten, Chatman's argument is in trouble. In the close view Henriette takes over: she stands apart from the others in her ride through the air and she alone matters, her feelings, her consciousness, not Rodolphe's or anybody else's. Chatman seems to think that her sexuality can only reside in the eye of a male beholder, but Renoir vividly presents it as her own.[29]

Twice during this sequence we return to the close view following Henriette on her swing. But no single point of view governs our perception, certainly not Rodolphe's but not her own either. She is the center of this sequence and we feel with her but we also stand back and observe her from various points all around. We see her from below and also from eye level and from above; from close and also in long shots taken from different sides; moving with her through the air and also standing still as she swings forward and swings back; through the eyes of the passing seminarians and also through those of her most devoted watcher, the lustful Rodolphe. After the last close view following her movement, we cut to him at the window, the window that framed her like a picture or a performer when he initially opened it, and now we see *him* framed by that window like a theatrical performer. In connection with *The River*, William Rothman noted Renoir's sense of the "theatricality of viewing."[30] Rodolphe sees Henriette as performing for his benefit on a stage he intends to join as seducer, but it is his viewing rather than her swinging that strikes us as theatrical, a conventionalized performance. A frame confines; Rodolphe is confined by a role, whereas

A Day in the Country. Rodolphe watching Henriette: the theatricality of viewing.

Henriette on her swing precisely rejoices in her freedom from confinement. And yet, natural and spontaneous though she may feel, when observed from Rodolphe's point of view she can be seen as theatrical, as vulnerable to theater. How real is her freedom? we may ask ourselves. How significant her naturalness? Rodolphe's point of view is introduced not to convey Henriette's sexuality but to qualify it. The ambiguity of her swinging is not so much between innocence and seductiveness as between freedom and convention, naturalness and theatricality.

"Wonderful invention—swings!" says Rodolphe as we watch Henriette and her mother from his point of view. "But you can't see a thing!" comments Henri. "Because she's standing," admits Rodolphe. "If she *sat*, it would be more interesting." In a moment, she sits, and we cut to a closer shot from the ground below, looking up her skirts as she swings toward us, the young man's position in Fragonard's picture. Cut to a closer shot of Rodolphe watching from the window that frames him, leering like a stage seducer and stroking his mustache, thinking of himself as the director of this show. It is he, not she, who makes theater; and yet he makes of her a theater, theater in the eye of the beholder. Now the two men start discussing amatory matters, and Henri says he's not interested in a fling. "Suppose that little one fell in love with you?" he warns Rodolphe. "You know you'd leave her . . . ruin her life." Cut to a shot of trees in the wind, and after a moment, from above the frame, Henriette swings back into view: this is the angle looking up her skirts, but now invested with a poignant sense of her vulnerability. "Enough, Henriette, come down!" we hear her mother call. As she gets down from the swing, we cut to a shot in which the window, as it did initially, frames the two women.

(The editing of this sequence, and of this film generally, is extraordinary. Renoir was fortunate to have Marguerite as his editor; what she did in his absence with *A Day in the Country* attests to how much he owed her in his other films of the thirties. His predilection for long takes and avoidance of the conventional shot breakdown have led commentators to neglect the editing of his films. This is a mistake. His style called for a different kind of editing that required special skill. Marguerite had that skill. It is time that her talent and accomplishment be recognized.)

Henriette on her swing acts out a sense of freedom inseparable from a sense of nature. Freedom, to a way of thinking we inherit from the romantics, arises from nature: in nature we are born free, and in nature we gain freedom from the constrictions and conventions of society. On a Sunday outing we get a taste of nature and a taste of freedom and we go back to the city renewed: the "re-creation myth," as Clark calls it, the brief immersion in nature from which we are to emerge replenished.[31] Henriette is young and naive and she takes her taste of nature and her taste of freedom quite seriously, as if these wouldn't just enable her to go back and go on with her life but would change her life. Her sense of awakening has to do with her sexuality, but something larger is involved: to reduce her feelings to the merely sexual as Rodolphe does—and he's not a villain but only typical of what people will do—is to threaten the larger promise, the larger impulse she embodies. Thus his theater endangers her naturalness; but his isn't the only theater she has to fear.

In *The Crime of Monsieur Lange,* as Bazin observed, Jules Berry plays the slick Batala in a stylized manner purposely at odds with the other actors:[32] the theatricality of the capitalist exploiter threatens the naturalness of the workers. Eisenstein did a similar thing with his caricatured capitalists and workers out of a newsreel. Mixing styles of acting is not uncommon on stage or screen. In the Astaire and Rogers musicals, for example, Fred and Ginger are less comically stylized than the other actors, so that they strike us as the only normal human beings around, and therefore as right for each other. In *Boudu Saved from Drowning* Michel Simon as the tramp Boudu gives an aggressively physical performance so at odds with the conven-

A Day in the Country. Henriette on her swing: a sense of freedom inseparable from a sense of nature.

tionalized gentility of the bourgeois characters as to make palpable the impossibility of the tramp's domestication into their household. Fred and Ginger belong with each other but they comfortably inhabit the same world as the other characters. Not so Boudu: in the precincts of the bourgeoisie he is an irreconcilably foreign presence.

In *A Day in the Country*, as in *Boudu*, Renoir mixes acting styles with uncommon discordance. The father and the apprentice, the petit-bourgeois patriarch and the heir apparent, are bumbling figures of farce. The apprentice is pale and thin and the father is rotund—Laurel and Hardy in the impressionist countryside. Henriette is the daughter of this father, the woman promised to this apprentice, but no character in comedy: she is portrayed with touching conviction in a naturalistic style that would seem to belong in a different universe from this Laurel and Hardy's. The mother is somewhere in between the father and the daughter, comically stylized but not broadly farcical like the father, affecting in a way but not a serious character like the daughter. The portrayal of Rodolphe matches the mother's portrayal: these two belong together in their playfulness and their conventionality. And, as the names indicate, the portrayal of Henri matches that of Henriette: these two belong together in their seriousness and their sentiment (some have said sentimentality).

Sitting by the window that looks out on the swinging mother and daughter, Henri thinks Rodolphe irresponsible for wanting to seduce the daughter but he considers the mother fair game and he agrees to join his friend in a pursuit of the two city women—a pursuit in which, as things develop, the couples sort themselves out for the afternoon seduction into Rodolphe and the mother and Henri and Henriette. After the Parisians have had their *déjeuner sur l'herbe*—which the film portrays not lyrically but farcically, an occasion for gluttony rather than sociability, the father and the apprentice drunkenly recumbent in the aftermath—Rodolphe and Henri approach the mother and daughter. The women love the idea of going boating on the river, and the *canotiers* lend fishing rods to the father and the apprentice to keep them occupied and out of the way. In a held deep-focus shot we see Henriette and the four men, the two designing boatmen both with designs on her and the two bumbling city men with their borrowed fishing gear, farce and romance jostling each other on the screen. As the city men wander off into the background, toward the river, and the boatmen and Henriette follow—each *canotier* in turn grabbing her hand—all the while in the foreground the two swings, with nobody on them now, gently sway in opposite directions, slowly coming to a halt. The swings and their swaying may be taken as a metaphor for the two suitors and their pulling the young woman in opposite directions; but the swings are also Henriette herself, a reminder of her ride through the air, and their winding down suggests the impending coming down to earth of first impressions. Just as, by a law of nature, the swings slow down, so the hopes and exhilarations of the air are inevitably to meet the ground of reality.

The arrival at the country inn is enchanting, the *déjeuner sur l'herbe* a disenchantment. Nature is lovely, the father and the apprentice more than a bit absurd. *A Day in the Country* holds to no single mood or mode of representation, no settled way of seeing the landscape and the human beings in its midst. Rodolphe and the mother in one rowboat, Henri and Henriette in another, travel along the river and get off at an island where, in very different fashions, parallel seductions ensue. Unlike the story, which stays with the daughter and lets the mother recede into the background, the film cuts back and forth between the two couples. While Henri and Henriette are romantically in earnest, Rodolphe and the mother perform a parody of a classical pastoral seduction in the woods, Rodolphe impersonating a satyr and the mother playing along as a matronly nymph.

The two couples clash, and yet each colors our impression of the other. The daughter is earnest and the mother is playful, but isn't the one's palpitant sensitivity to a nightingale's song comparable to the other's giggling delight in a nymph's role? Henri is sentimental and Rodolphe is contriving, but doesn't the one behave as irresponsibly with an ingenuous young woman as he thought the other would have? And isn't Henri's reticence, rather than Rodolphe's forwardness, just what that ingenuous young woman would fall for? One couple acts naturally and the other acts artificially, but aren't both couples guided by the fantasy rather than the reality of nature? In Renoir's parallel arrangement, the two seductions make no simple contrast but call for an inquiring comparison.

Brecht has been much discussed in connection with films but seldom in connection with Renoir. Yet the playwright famous for his alienation effect and the filmmaker celebrated for his humane sympathy (aside from the fact that they were friends) shared important artistic concerns. In their work they both endeavored, each in his own medium and with his own outlook, toward what Brecht called "complex seeing": not a single focus but a multiplicity of perspectives that invites from the audience active reflection rather than mere acquiescence. Mixing modes, shifting representational gears, bringing together what isn't supposed to go together, served both Brecht and Renoir as a principal means to complex seeing. Breaking the consistency of a style or a tone they might have asked us to accept, they encourage us, instead, to keep in mind different ways of doing things, of regarding things. Such a mixture is difficult to bring off; it's always easier to maintain consistency than to manage diversity. *A Day in the Country* succeeds so well, with so little apparent effort, that to inattentive watchers it has seemed a simple small picture, Renoir and his actors on a Sunday outing themselves. The film is simple only in its plot, small only in its short running time, effortless only because it has the technique to take the risks it takes. Its complexity is not in the tale but in the telling—in the seeing.

Just as Henri feared, the susceptible Henriette falls in love with a se-

A Day in the Country.
The parallel seduc-
tions: crosscutting
between the serious
and the comic.

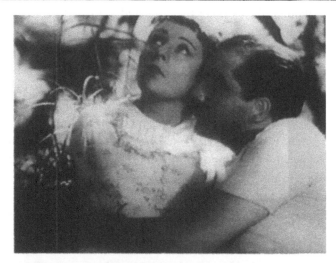

ducer, himself as it turns out; and just as he feared, her love, even though he susceptibly reciprocates it, comes to nothing after the day in the country. She goes back to the city and marries the pale apprentice: Romeo and Juliet foiled by Laurel and Hardy. The tale may be simple but the interpretations have been conflicting. According to Leo Braudy, Henri and Henriette are too serious: they suffer from a "sentimental view of nature" and "melancholic self-indulgence in emotion," while Rodolphe and the mother, with their "pagan exuberance," know how to have a good time.[33] According to Alexander Sesonske, Monsieur Dufour is to be commended as a family man, Rodolphe is an innocent like Henriette, and Henri is the villain of the piece, the cynical seducer he accused his friend of being, albeit a clumsy one who has no feeling for love play and a gloomy one who infects Henriette with his self-pity.[34] According to Tag Gallagher, Henri is the hero of the piece—the tragic hero—a morose young man awakened from despondency by a beautiful woman who brings him love one Sunday afternoon but abandons him for someone else.[35] These are all misreadings, but all have some basis in the film—misreadings that impose a simple slant on complex seeing.

Deftly balancing naturalism and farce, parody and tragedy, the film allows us no stable response. Neither a serious drama with comic relief nor a comedy with serious touches, it asks that we entertain the serious and the comical on equal terms and generates between the two a continual give and take. Of the parallel seductions one may say, after Marx, that what occurs the first time as tragedy, in the daughter's youth, occurs the second, in the mother's middle age, as farce; and Renoir, setting the farce and the tragedy side by side, insists that we keep both in mind together. Such is the give and take he later sets up in *The Rules of the Game*, where comedy and tragedy mix in a similarly unsettling way. In *A Day in the Country* the different modes are kept more separate, however, not so much mingled as juxtaposed. Henriette and Anatole, as the apprentice is called in the film, she a wholly serious character and he a clown, make the film's most incongruous juxtaposition, whose full impact is saved for the end, when we see the two married and realize with a shock that his farce is her tragedy.

Place in the movies is usually but background to the fiction staged there. Sometimes place is made prominent by being deployed theatrically, as the Odessa steps are deployed in the action Eisenstein staged there, or as city streets may be deployed for the excitement of a car chase: place as spectacle rather than background. In a Renoir film of the thirties place is neither background nor spectacle.

Natural landscape is an agreeable movie performer. It will lend itself to the pretty pictures of a love story and to the spooky atmosphere of a gothic story, to the grand vistas of a Western and to the thrilling sights of a cliff-hanger. Yet landscape in these roles is not engaged as an actual place, a stretch of the world we inhabit. Whether relegated to a background or brought forward as a spectacle, it is made to play a part in a fiction and made subservient to that fiction. The landscape may assume prominence but only within the fictional requirements; the love story or the cliffhanger will set the terms of our response. *A Day in the Country* is a rare film that gives primacy to the landscape and lets it have a life of its own. It does not assign it a role and a meaning defined by the fiction. Rather it has the fiction define itself and its characters against the character of a landscape that was there first.

Normally a film will start with a story and then arrange for the setting, whether in the studio or out on location. Renoir may have started with Maupassant's story but he went out to a location that for him was there first—a place that was part of his life, a landscape with a painterly past—and the film he brought back makes that primacy felt. Landscape is a sovereign presence in *A Day in the Country,* fiction an uncertain undertaking that takes variable forms. What sort of fiction is to be enacted here? asks the film through its mixture of modes. Are we to stage a farce with the father and the apprentice and make fun of the petit bourgeois and their country outing? Are we to have a lighthearted romp in the woods with the mother and Rodolphe? Or are we to be serious and sentimental with Henriette and Henri? No mode of fiction being dominant, the landscape takes center place; each mode of fiction seeing the landscape in a different way, the landscape gains independence from any way of seeing it. Rather than a mere background to the fiction, the landscape becomes an enduring ground on which the fiction sketches tentative figures; rather than assigning meaning to the landscape, the fiction becomes a foray in quest of meaning. Setting in most films is put to the service of fiction; landscape in *A Day in the Country* puts the fictional venture to the test. Renoir makes fiction into a trope for the human attempt to connect with nature, endow it with meaning, feel at home in it or at least feel welcome in our outings.

A sovereign presence and yet also an absence. For in a work of fiction, a story, a painting, a film, landscape can only be apprehended through fiction, and fiction in *A Day in the Country* is seen to have no secure claim on landscape. Nature cannot appear on the screen, only its representation in necessarily reductive images, but films will usually promote the impression that the images represent nature, capture it, with perfect adequacy. *A Day in the Country* declines to give us that impression and instead makes us aware of the fiction in any view of nature, any picture of it. Nature in this film, though represented with rich vividness, is yet perceived to be always in excess of its representation. Nature is there first and yet not there.

When Rodolphe opens the window, Henriette on her swing is but a picture for him, a piece of theater; when we move with her through the air, we share her feeling of freedom and forget the theatricalizing voyeur; but at the end of her swinging, our view of her is again bordered by the window frame. This not only shows her as threatened by the seducer's picture of her, it suggests that her feeling of freedom, of communion with nature, is itself a picture, an illusion, a fiction. For the window, with the reminder that we're watching a picture that its borders provide, can now be seen to frame the entire swinging sequence from beginning to end, and all the diverse views and points of view we have been getting, with Henriette at the center, become retroactively bordered by our awareness of fiction. And Henriette is especially vulnerable because, though the way she pictures herself in nature is not her own invention but a social construction, she is all alone in that picture.

She is with Henri when they go off together on their boat ride. We see them in an overhead shot of their boat gliding on the water, from which we cut, movement to movement, to a shot traveling along the river and showing the grasses and trees going by on the shore. This is not a point-of-view shot— it is neither preceded nor followed by a character looking, and the characters in any case are facing backward, toward the stern of their rowboat, while the camera moves forward—but it does give us the sense of looking at the shore through the eyes of someone riding in a boat. This sense is stronger in another, more extended traveling shot that soon follows, a shot in which we gaze at the other shore, the trees overhanging the river and their reflections on the water, from what indeed feels like the perspective of a slow-moving, gently rocking rowboat. In the story the perspective is Henriette's and the sensuality of the river and the trees is attributed to her subjectivity:

> The girl, who was sitting in the bow, gave herself up to the enjoyment of being on the water. She felt a disinclination to think, a lassitude in her limbs and a total enervation, as if she were intoxicated, and her face was flushed and her breathing quickened. The effects of the wine, which were increased by the extreme heat, made all the trees on the bank seem to bow as she passed.[36]

In the film we feel the subjectivity of an individual taking in the river scenery from a boat, but Henriette (not affected by wine that we can see) is not sitting in the bow, and though she could be turning her head toward the front, the camera moves forward along the river without any inserted shots attributing the point of view to her. (Or to Henri, who might be glancing at the shore too if he could take his eyes off her.) Here as in the arrival at the country inn, Renoir's camera, while adopting the position of traveling in the same vehicle as the characters, travels without bracketing or interruption by their glances or reactions, so that the camera's point of view, while associated with theirs, is not equated with it. Inserted glances and reactions are a means, which normally would have been employed here, of assimilating the setting to the fiction, making us see it in the fiction's terms—as the characters see it, as it pertains to them and their situation and only to that—but Renoir grants the fiction no prerogative to dictate terms.

Freeing the landscape from the dominance of fiction, Renoir at the same time frees the camera from its customary role as agent of that dominance, provider of views and perspectives that center on the characters and impose the priorities of the plot. Whereas the camera in most films takes its prompting from the dramatic fiction, Renoir establishes his camera, in this film and elsewhere, as an autonomous narrative agency that conducts its own transaction with the world. The normal point-of-view shot, which gives the camera over to a character's fictional eyes, he mostly avoids; but he often employs what may be called the loosely attributed point of view, which proposes, instead of an equation, varying degrees of correspondence between the camera's perspective and a character's. Renoir deserves his reputation for sympathy; his autonomous camera—and this registers as a choice, a well-felt gesture, rather than a dramatic necessity—remains attentive to the characters, in tune with their perceptions and sentiments; but his is a sympathy combined with detachment. He wants us to feel with Henriette on that boat ride—the point of view, if not quite hers, is not quite apart from hers either—but he also encourages us to keep our distance from her so that we may look at things with our own eyes. Just as his camera takes a path of its own, so we, rather than simply deriving a vicarious response from the dramatic fiction, are to consider our own response, the ways we have of relating to that landscape along the river and to nature more generally—the ways in which we are and the ways in which we are not in the same boat as the characters.

In Maupassant's story we identify with the tipsy young woman being rowed over the water by a young man who finds her pretty. But in this identification our own position isn't at stake: these are her feelings, and we can relate to them, but they're not our feelings. Our identification with Henriette in Renoir's film is of a different kind. The scene is not presented from her perspective, which isn't ours, but from a perspective akin to hers that, imagining ourselves in a boat on that river, we feel could well be ours. We are in a way more detached from her than we are in Maupassant's story and in another way more identified with her: we're not seeing through her eyes but, from a position we recognize as our own, we have much the same response as she has to the beauty and sensuality of nature in summer.

In the traveling shot toward the country inn, we identify with the arriving Parisians not as individuals but as members of a class. On the river we identify with Henriette as an individual, but an individual conditioned by her society to regard nature in a certain way, a way that, precisely, isolates the individual from society in the experience of nature. In the traveling shots along the river we are all on our own—inserted glances and reactions would have been company—for a sustained imbibing of nature that affects us like wine. It is enchanting, this immersion in nature, and it is isolating in its enchantment. We put ourselves in Henriette's place, see that her place could be ours, as individuals likewise conditioned by our society to look to nature for this kind of private experience. She is with Henri on the river, and he may share her experience, but the experience shared by two is scarcely less private. The experience these two share cannot endure beyond the day in the country because it can only endure in society. To blame Henri for seducing Henriette, or Henriette for throwing over Henri, is misguided. Renoir doesn't moralize, doesn't put the blame on individuals—not because he loves them too much but because he sees the social picture that blaming them would obscure, because he tells the social story that determines their stories. It was in the cards, the cards society deals, that the romance of Henriette and Henri would amount to no more than a moment.

"How beautiful! I've never seen anything so beautiful!" says Henriette when she and Henri disembark on the river island. The sweet trill of Sylvia Bataille's voice matches the sound of a nightingale they hear in the woods. The camera starts moving, as if itself responding to the nightingale's call and leading the characters into the woods rather than merely following them. "All enclosed . . . like a house," notes Henriette of the surrounding verdancy. A crooked branch, rectangularly shaped, comes into view from above and marks the spot. "I come here often," says Henri. "I call it my 'private den.'" They sit down on the grass and listen to the nightingale up in a tree; he puts his arm around her waist and she removes it. Cut to the mother and Rodolphe and their parodic romance. Cut back to Henriette and Henri: she wipes a tear from her cheek while looking up at the romantic bird perched above them. Cut to Rodolphe and the mother as satyr and nymph. Cut back to Henri pressing close to Henriette: he tries to kiss her and she resists but in a moment she gives in to him, "tremblingly, like a captured bird," as Pauline Kael wrote.[37] Cut to a very tight close-up of Henriette that, Henri's hand on her cheek as she lies under him on the grass, her face cropped by the top edge of the frame so that we see only one tearful eye as she turns toward us, indeed compares her to a captured bird. Not that she is being coerced into sex, as some have thought: she is captured by her own feelings as well as his advances. She cries the tears of a virgin losing her virginity, and perhaps also the tears of a woman who knows that this romance she so wants cannot last. Her looking at us, however, signifies that she feels alone in this romance and in these tears.

In the aftermath of the two seductions, right after Henriette has yielded to Henri with passion and tears, the film switches away from the characters altogether. Unpeopled nature takes over in the ensuing images, first the wind-blown plants and dark clouds of a gathering rainstorm in a series of quick static shots, then the rain falling on the river and its banks with the camera backing away. This may seem an instance of the pathetic fallacy, a projection of Henriette's feelings or even, in Sesonske's plausible interpretation, a "sexual metaphor" in which the tension before the storm and the release when rain falls stand for the emotions she experiences as she resists and then surrenders to sexual passion.[38] If we switched to nature from the tight close-up of Henriette, or if we returned to her after the views of nature, this interpretation might be more convincing. But from the close-up the film dissolves to a long shot of Henri and Henriette after lovemaking, and as they

A Day in the Country. Henriette like a captured bird.

look away from each other, their passion spent, the film cuts to the plants and the clouds and the rain. Nature here offers no clear correlative for Henriette's emotions, whether during or, more likely, after her first experience of sex; and besides her, three other characters, each with emotions not to be discounted, have been sexually engaged at the same time. Landscape in this film is no serviceable vehicle for the meanings of fiction.[39] At first we expect that we will soon enough return to the characters after a digression into the landscape, but gradually it dawns on us that Henriette and Henri, the mother and Rodolphe, the father and Anatole, all are being left behind. As the rain breaks and the camera retreats down the river, this sequence continues and concludes without people: the time that passes without even a glimpse of the characters works to dispel any direct associations we may entertain between their feelings and nature. Nor is this a case of nature presented as grandly impervious to the concerns of humanity (as in, say, Werner Herzog's Amazon films); to see nature as uncaring is but another form of the pathetic fallacy, to see it as meaningless but another way of assigning it a precise meaning. Nature here becomes neither too closely associated with the characters nor too far dissociated from them and the human standpoint they represent.

But the human standpoint, as Renoir here and elsewhere reminds us, is nothing universal, nothing eternal. It varies greatly according to the individual's situation, the class outlook, the premises, the conditions, the constructions of a culture and society, the sense and circumstance of a time and place. It always differs between a spectator or reader, situated outside, and a character inside a work's proposed world. Renoir brings forward this difference dividing us from the characters—rather than induce in us the kind of identification that would dissemble it—as well as the differences dividing the characters themselves. Despite the moment of love Henriette and Henri share, her feelings and his are not truly at one; the two part ways after their encounter, not to meet again until years have sealed their mutual isolation and her unhappy marriage to Anatole. The mother and Rodolphe may be better matched in their parallel encounter, but only because neither of the two harbors any notion of oneness. Among these four individuals who all make love on that river island that summer afternoon, feelings and attitudes are split four ways.

Without hurry, savoring the appearances of summery nature, *A Day in the Country* has moved toward that river island and the moment of communion it holds for the characters. But no sooner is that consummation reached than, briskly, at an increasing pace, in three successive shots that are the film's most assertive visual maneuver, the camera travels backward as the country outing comes to an abrupt rainy end. A meandering, exploratory progression is suddenly broken, reversed, by this decisive traveling "over the rapidly receding face of the river," as Sesonske writes, "pierced by the myriad needles of the rain":[40] unpeopled images reverberating with a sense of loss, separation, togetherness fleetingly reached and now swiftly, in a few moments that seem to constitute a lifetime, left behind. Not only the speed and direction, the time scale is switched here in one bold stroke: from the scale of a day, a few hours lingered over, suspended in sensual apprehension, to a few moments whose movement evokes the rush of years ceaselessly passing.

"Swiftly the years, beyond recall. / Solemn the stillness of this spring morning." In *Seven Types of Ambiguity* William Empson discusses these two lines from a Chinese poem and their juxtaposition of two different time scales—the large scale that "takes the length of a human life as its unit" and the small scale that "takes as its unit the conscious moment":

> Both these time-scales and their contrasts are included by these two lines in a single act of apprehension, because of the words *swift* and *still*. Being contradictory as they stand, they demand to be conceived in different ways; we are enabled, therefore, to meet the open skies with an answering stability of self-knowledge; to meet the brevity of human life with an ironical sense that it is morning and springtime, that there is a whole summer before winter, a whole day before night.[41]

The Chinese poem shifts from the years to the day; *A Day in the Country* shifts from the day to the years, the moment to the lifetime. In the film as in the poem the two time scales come together in our minds. "The *years* of a man's life seem *swift* even on the small scale," writes Empson; "the *morning* seems *still* even on the large scale."[42] Disconcertingly swift on the scale of the day, the camera's retreat down the river evokes the scale of the years and seems swift on that scale too; and conversely, the exhilaration on the swing, the imbibing of nature on the boat ride, the tender verdant privacy on the river island, are moments that seem suspended even on the scale of the lifetime. But the film's shift from the moment to the lifetime is a shift from promise to loss, from a feeling of oneness to a sense of alienation: not the serenity the poem conveys with its juxtaposition.

Autonomous but not godlike, declining to assume a superior point of vantage, Renoir's camera meets the world from a position that is always recognizably concrete, on a human plane. If it traveled up river in a rowboat, it backs away down river—as becomes significant because we register its concrete position in both cases—with the speed of a motorboat, a vehicle in which the nineteenth-century characters couldn't have been traveling. Although the vehicle isn't shown, the departing backward views were evidently taken from an unsteady small boat, which could be the same one that traveled up river, one in which we can imagine ourselves riding on a Sunday and hurrying back when it starts to rain, but whose propelling drive in the retreat would have been unavailable to the characters. This rapid motion, especially in comparison with the leisurely progress up river, makes us note a speed beyond mere rowing, a plane of human experience attainable only since the advent of motorboats and cameras endowed with mobility to match that of an age just being born when the impressionists were painting. At the close of an excursion it has made its own—and ours—Renoir's camera detaches itself not only from the characters but from the whole period of the fiction: its departing motion belongs unmistakably to our century. The sense of years passing, a long span compressed into those retreating moments, extends from the characters' lives to the lives of all of us, in all the years that have passed since that time of impressionist picnics on the grass and virginal daughters tremulously surrendering to love by the waterside. It's as if the day in the country, having begun in the nineteenth century, were ending in the twentieth—as if that river we're leaving behind were the last version of pastoral receding from our twentieth-century motorboat. Incitingly, Renoir omits the characters from this visual cadence that, no mere ornament to the story, is the film's culminant sequence, rich in associations with them but essentially addressing us, drawing us into a reflective look at things from where we stand outside the fiction.

Besides picturing a dramatic fiction enacted before it, the movie camera enacts the fiction of a perceiving eye, an apprehending consciousness. The dramatic fiction imitates an action; the camera imitates a gaze, a point of view, an act of perception and of consciousness. The movies are a representation both of the world and of an apprehension of the world. But usually the camera, made subservient to the drama, does little more than unfold the plot, the characters' actions and perceptions and the pertinent attendant circumstances; caught up in the movement of plot, we scarcely register the camera's point of view, the choice to look at things in this manner and succession, as a directed act of consciousness, a movement of mind. Imagine a shot that, in conventional fashion, presents something dramatically significant from a suitable angle and distance, then imagine that shot held for a moment longer than necessary to make the dramatic point: that extra moment, such as we're normally denied, would arrest the movement of plot long enough for us to gain the sense of an apprehending mind behind the camera. Renoir often gives us such extra moments, either after or before the dramatically significant thing, to which he characteristically pays no privileged attention. His camera, with its distinctive autonomous gaze, everywhere enacts an unmistakable movement of consciousness.

Rather than determining in usual fashion the point of view and the meaning, the dramatic fiction in *A Day in the Country* proposes different ways of seeing that, along with the camera's ways, partake in a complex apprehension of a landscape that seems to extend the invitation of pastoral but conforms to no settled way of seeing it or giving it meaning. The film's movement of consciousness begins with the arriving perspective of a generalized visitor, the petit bourgeois from the city come for a pastoral day in the country. A discrepancy in points of view then starts to be made manifest, a discrepancy not only between the visitors and the locals but among the various individuals, their differences accentuated by the different acting styles, and, moreover, a discrepancy between the characters and the autonomous camera. In such difference lies no oneness. These discordant points of view belie the harmony with nature that pastoral promises. We're made aware of a separation between nature and the consciousness that apprehends it and attempts to invest it with meaning, between a landscape that can be regarded from many different perspectives and the different perspectives from which we may regard it. Vividly represented yet always in excess of its representation, nature in *A Day in the Country* is in excess of our consciousness, of the mind's capacity to apprehend it with any conclusive adequacy. The rainstorm strikingly frustrates pastoral expectations, not only for the day but for the years swiftly receding, and not only for the characters but for all of us who joined them in the sunny arrival and now look upon stormy nature from the departing perspective of a visitor no longer identifiable with them, generalized beyond their circumstances and their century. That uncannily rapid departing motion of the camera—rapid like our passage through this world where we're all mere visitors—evokes the movement of a consciousness that recognizes its own foreignness amid the trees and the river and the rain, its own apartness among the things of nature.

From an imaginary plenitude, a Lacanian might say, we retreat here to the recognition of loss—loss of what was lost already, always already lost, the trees and the river that were never there on the screen, the ever unattainable oneness felt at the mother's breast once upon a time and sought in vain thereafter. Indeed the film here pulls us back from its fiction and throws us back on our own situation as viewers of that fiction. But the Lacanian reading assumes that there was nothing there to begin with, that there can be nothing there. Taken literally, this is merely obvious: we never thought the trees and the river were actually there on the screen. Taken in its implications, it tells us we can make no real connection with the material world around us, only an imaginary connection. Henriette (incarnated, as it happens, by a woman Lacan married) was deluded from the start: just as the nature we watch on the screen can only be an illusion, so the nature that seemed to offer her freedom and tenderness was only in her head. We are all deluded from the start if we seek freedom and tenderness in the world. Alienation in this view becomes something inalterable, all but metaphysical, not a social condition but a given of the human condition.

Between consciousness and nature, illusion and reality, where Lacanians and other theorists posit an irrevocable breach, Renoir sees a complex interplay. The famous ending of *Grand Illusion* shows the two escaped French prisoners crossing the border into Switzerland, saved from German bullets by a border quite undiscernible in the unbroken stretch of snow ("an invention of man," says one of the characters; "nature doesn't give a damn") yet quite real nonetheless. Stanley Cavell comments on

> the two figures bobbing through a field of snow, away from us. Somewhere under that one white is a mathematical line, a fiction men call a border. It is not on earth or in heaven, but whether you are known to have crossed it is a matter of life and death. The movie is about borders, about the lines of life and death between German and Frenchman, between rich and poor, between rich man and aristocrat, between officer and soldier, between home and absence, between Gentile and Jew. Specifically, it is about the illusions of borders, the illusion that they are real and the grand illusion that they are not.[43]

Henriette's view of nature is as much a fiction as that border and as much a matter of life and death. Just as for the men crossing that border, freedom for her hangs on that fiction. The border is a fiction made real by nations acting on it, and the men reach freedom because the German patrol honors that fiction and lets them go. If Henriette fails to reach freedom, it's not because she pursues a fiction but because she acts alone on that fiction, because the society that constructed that fiction by and large doesn't act on it.

A hundred years before the impressionists painted the version of pastoral that is still ours, the romantics framed the conception of freedom that is still ours: freedom as natural, freedom as a regaining of nature. The impressionist version of pastoral, a naturalistic rather than a conventionalized pastoral, responded to that naturalistic conception of freedom and its democratic extension to the petite bourgeoisie. If nobody has painted a newer version of pastoral to replace the impressionists in our cultural imagination, surely that has to do with the fact that nobody has framed a newer conception of freedom to replace the romantics in our political imagination. The camera that retreats from nature in *A Day in the Country*, the consciousness that recognizes its own apartness from nature, is calling into question the pastoral the impressionists painted and the natural freedom the romantics conceived.

In *Earth* Dovzhenko combined that romantic conception—which Marxism modified but did not discard—with a peasant sense of community in nature. Tenderness is rooted in community for the virginal girlfriend in *Earth*, whereas the virginal Henriette can only achieve her moment of tenderness away from community. The view of nature expressed in *Earth* is no less a fiction than Henriette's view and, moreover, a fiction Soviet society flagrantly didn't honor, but it is a fiction Dovzhenko saw as sanctioned by a society that would act on it. For Renoir in the days of the Popular Front the freedom we would achieve in nature is a fiction as yet never realized in action. He is not prepared to discard that conception: hence our identification with Henriette, hence the sweetness and enchantment of much of the day in the country. But he is prepared to question it: hence our detachment from her, hence the retreat that pulls us up short, hence her tragedy.

It is as a fiction we're being invited to act on, not merely a fantasy and not yet a reality, that *The Crime of Monsieur Lange* presents socialism. Jacques Prévert collaborated on the script and commentators such as Dudley Andrew have given him much of the credit for the film's "wonderfully farfetched" quality. But the genius of the film lies in the way that—unlike the just as wonderfully farfetched *Drôle de drame* (Bizarre, Bizarre, 1937), which Prévert wrote and Marcel Carné directed—its farfetchedness engages an actual world. *The Crime of Monsieur Lange*, as Andrew says, "explicitly inserts itself between fantasy and reality as a truly imaginative representation of the possibilities of social life."[44] Its farfetchedness expresses a dream we are to share, a striving we are to join. And at the same time it expresses the difficulty of that striving, the distance between that dream and the world as it exists. Wonderfully hopeful though it is, *The Crime of Monsieur Lange* is also quite aware of what its hopes are up against. Lange's killing of Batala—with which the film does not endorse cold-blooded murder as some have thought, but allegorizes revolutionary violence—endangers the cooperative even as it saves it, for Lange and his Arizona Jim stories have been key to its success and he must now run away. The cowboy hero who rights wrongs with his gun and rides off into the distance is a fantasy the film knows doesn't square with reality. The cooperative we warm to we recognize as an unlikely and precarious arrangement; the cherished dream of socialist community would be difficult to attain, the film acknowledges, and still more difficult to sustain. The circle of the courtyard, the circle that stands for community in the film's symbolic scheme, is at the end broken by a straight line traced by footsteps across a frontier.

Even at their most hopeful Renoir's films of the thirties enforce no singleness of vision but keep to their complex seeing, and the same holds true even at their grimmest. In an unstressed yet breathtaking sequence from *La Chienne* the middle-aged Legrand is in his apartment, lathering his face for shaving by a window open onto a courtyard, and on the point of stealing some money from his domineering wife for the sake of his young mistress. The sound of a piano is heard, coming from somewhere nearby. This isn't conventional, disembodied background music; that convention hadn't been established in the early years of sound, and especially not in the work of Renoir, who even on location, where he preferred to film, insisted on having sound recorded direct rather than postsynchronized. Sound in *La Chienne* always comes from a revealed source within the world of the film, and on this piano we hear a beginner playing exercises, though we are yet to see it and its player. In one uninterrupted take, casual in its manner yet unerring in its execution, the camera follows Legrand as he silently, furtively moves toward the linen cabinet where his wife keeps her savings and as, the theft accomplished, he moves back to the window and happily resumes shaving. On returning to the window, the camera looks out, as if by happenstance, from a somewhat different angle that allows us to see into another window across the courtyard, and after a slight adjustment of focus, through this other window we finally observe—independently of Legrand, who isn't looking in this direction but at his own face in his shaving mirror—a little girl playing the piano we've been hearing all along. Our seeing this little girl, who has no dramatic role in the film, evidently a neighbor to whom Legrand pays no mind and whom we just glimpse, is a curiously affecting and gladdening revelation.

For the most part in counterpoint, then finally in unison, this sequence sets up an interplay between sound and image that conveys the excitement of trying out what was at the time a new technique, sound, which Renoir welcomed and which enabled his full development as an artist—sound no longer separately played, in the fashion of silent cinema, but incorporated into film. Like a piano player at a silent movie, the little girl provides a musical accompaniment to Legrand's silent theft, but we feel her presence in his vicinity, not in ours, and the camera, in the course of following him, ends up finding her, and integrating the sound of her piano with her image playing it. As the sound testifies, she is there, and even if she has nothing to do with the plot, we must take account of her. Formally the sequence moves from an unresolved separation to a resolving fusion of image and sound; thematically it suggests the interconnection, and potential coming together in harmony, of such disparate individuals as Legrand and the little girl—or ourselves and the strangers who live next door to us in the towns of our modernity.

Legrand and the little girl are in their own worlds as it seems to them and yet in the same world as it looks—and sounds—to us. Their separate privacies come together with delicate eloquence. The inside where he shaves and steals and she plays the piano is seen to be open to the outside, to the existence and possible community of others. The camera that follows him and finds her might equally have followed her and found him. Their association through form—the musical accompaniment she unknowingly provides for him, the camera movement linking them together in a continuous path of gaze, and joining the image with the sound that has been proof of her existence—disposes us to regard them in terms of connection and what they have in common. As the little girl is a beginner at the piano, so is Legrand a beginner and even an innocent at cheating on his wife and stealing from her; as the little girl is an incipient musical artist (the exercises she plays were composed by Leopold Mozart for his son Wolfgang), so is Legrand a man of feeling and, on his free time from his job as a cashier, a talented amateur painter; as the little girl is a learner at the piano that is a petit-bourgeois pretension, so is Legrand a petit bourgeois pretending to his mistress that he is a successful painter while in fact lacking adequate funds to support her; and so on. Disparate yet interconnected, alienated yet akin, at cross-purposes yet bound up together: thus are the characters in Renoir's films of the thirties. Although the disparateness and the cross-purposes may win out, as sadly happens in La Chienne, the sense of coming together this sequence imparts, the feeling of kinship and connection in spite of alienation, nonetheless keeps open other possibilities.

Another middle-aged married man who painted on the side one day left for Tahiti. But Legrand's Tahiti is Lulu, and when he leaves his wife for her he finds her in bed with the pimp. The pimp has been selling Legrand's paintings in the art market just as, in effect, he has been selling Lulu to Legrand and taking the paintings in payment—selling all the love, all the beauty in Legrand's life. After killing Lulu and letting the pimp be guillotined for it, Legrand becomes a bum but not a bum artist like Gauguin, for he has killed his Tahiti, killed the beauty he loved when he saw it was for sale, and he has no interest left in the art he made for love. Legrand is a figure of the artist as the petit-bourgeois lover of beauty. Henriette in *A Day in the Country* is not an artist but she is a lover of beauty. The excursionist's experience of nature is an aesthetic experience, and nature's beauty on that summer day means the world to her. Too young to have recognized quite yet what there is to escape from, she doesn't dream of a Tahiti to escape to, she dreams of bringing that beauty into her everyday life. Henriette and Legrand are alike sensitive children of the petite bourgeoisie who erroneously hope for a personal, sentimental answer to their longings.

Maupassant's story has a brief scene in Paris two months after the day in the country. Henri is in the city and goes into the Dufour hardware store, where he talks to the mother and learns from her that Henriette has married the apprentice. Renoir had planned to film such a scene but never got around to it, and in its place the film makes use of a title. From the camera retreating down river in the rain we fade out to these words: "Years have passed. Henriette is married to Anatole. The Sundays are now as sad as the Mondays. And on this Sunday . . . " On this Sunday we see Henri rowing alone to the river island and finding Henriette there too, drawn independently by the same sentimental memories the place holds for him.

A Day in the Country. Henri by the river at the end.

Nostalgia is an emotion allegedly soft and silly, but what else are Henri and Henriette to feel on this occasion? On this Sunday the mood is not summery but autumnal. The camera follows Henri along the same path he and Henriette followed when the nightingale sang; he pauses at the spot marked by the crooked branch and the camera pauses with him for a moment, then swiftly moves ahead to find Henriette where he has noticed her, sitting on the grass with Anatole napping beside her; and this long take continues uninterrupted as she in turn notices Henri, gets up and walks toward him, and the camera now moves with her back to him. But this continuous path of gaze—which may be described as a double following and finding, first from his side and then from hers—leads to no togetherness except a shared yearning for what might have been. In a gesture of sentimental sympathy, the moving camera traces the form of a coming together that only underscores the missed togetherness in the lives of these two. Those who would frown on them for being sentimental shouldn't exempt Renoir. But who are we to frown on Henri and Henriette? Who can presume to feel superior to their longing for tenderness and freedom? Renoir does not presume.

Anatole calls out, and Henri withdraws, the camera alongside him as, from a distance, he watches Henriette leaving with her clown of a husband, who compounds his ridiculousness with a petty tyrannical manner he apparently believes is the way to treat a wife. Then Henri goes over by the river and, leaning on a tree overhanging it, wistfully smokes a cigarette. As he throws away the cigarette, the camera turns in that direction, panning leftward in a movement more or less identified with his glance but interrupted by a striking cut—a cut breaking the conventional rules of smooth editing—to another panning movement starting again from the tree he leans on but turning rightward this time, and continuing in an unhurried look at the river and its shore. A pan is like a turning of the head, and here the camera first turns its head leftward, in sympathy with Henri, and then rightward, away from him in the direction opposite to his glance. In its rightward panning the camera observes Henriette rowing away with her husband—she doing the rowing—whereupon its gaze moves down to Henri's empty boat by the shore, and on sideways to the unruffled, rippling water. These paired panning shots conclude the film. The cut between them feels like a bouncing back, with the tree as a point of stability, from Henri's melancholy contemplation, which projects onto nature an understandable but fruitless nostalgia, to an open, lingering view of nature's unceasing countenance.

7 :   American Tragedy

The two most successful creations of American movies are
the gangster and the Westerner: men with guns.

ROBERT WARSHOW

THE POLITICS OF THE WESTERN. In the first movie Western,
Edwin S. Porter's 1903 *Great Train Robbery,* one image stands out from the
rest. It's an image apart from the story—exhibitors at the time were free to
show it first or last or, for good measure, both first and last—and whether as
overture or as finale it may be taken as a kind of distillate of the experience of
the film. It's the only close-up in a film that otherwise keeps the camera at the
considerable distance that was normal in early cinema. And it's a startling
image of violence: a Western bandit faces us, points his gun straight at us,
and opens fire. The thrill of this image stems from the fear it elicits by
putting us in the position of target to the bandit's violence. A fear promptly
dispelled: as the image clouds with gun smoke, we smilingly regain our
awareness that a bandit in a movie can do us no harm. The camera reassures
us, one might say: its shot of the bandit counters the bandit's shot.

The Western is a drama of violence, certainly not the only such that has
bloodied our stages but one that for a long time occupied a central if always
pretty disreputable position in our culture. When Porter's bandit fires at us,
the only issue is whether it will hurt, and we're reassured that it will not. The
more developed Western deals with violence not just as something that hurts
but in relation to moral and social issues and as a component both of
savagery and of civilization.

The pain and also the excitement—the pleasure—of violence break
forth disconcertingly in the extraordinary opening sequence of *The Wild
Bunch,* made in 1969 by Sam Peckinpah and perhaps the last Western of
major sweep and stature. The violence unleashed in this sequence is ghastly
and prolonged and it comes upon us without the moral orientation, the
alignment of good and bad guys, that the Western traditionally sets up. As
William Pechter wrote at the time, "The bloodshed is witnessed as morally
indiscriminate."[1] Yet it is not witnessed with the astounded passivity of an
uncomprehending bystander; rather it is arranged with consummate asser-

tiveness by a filmmaker whose intricate command of camera and cutting matches an Eisenstein's.

Like the violence on Eisenstein's Odessa steps in *Potemkin,* the violence that opens *The Wild Bunch* is shocking and exciting at once. On the Odessa steps, however, the shocking bloodshed belongs to the Cossacks, to the other side in a scheme of good and bad sides as clear as a conventional Western's, and the excitement is in the sense of mastery conveyed by Eisenstein's technique. If Porter's camera reassures us bodily, Eisenstein's camera reassures us politically: its bold angles and forceful cutting impart confidence in our ability to come to grips with the forces of history and take action against the kind of brutal oppression we are witnessing. As assertive as Eisenstein's, Peckinpah's camera is not reassuring. It implicates us in the bloodshed. It comes forward and takes responsibility for a violence it doesn't merely observe but dynamically orchestrates, and it presses us to recognize that we are no innocent bystanders either. It unsettles us by making us face, at unsparing length and without the intermediation of a moral or political scheme, the mixed feelings of pain and pleasure, powerlessness and mastery, horror and exhilaration, that the spectacle of violence arouses in us.

In 1954, when the Western was in its heyday, Robert Warshow wrote an essay on the genre in which he argued that it gained its special hold on our imagination

> because it offers a serious orientation to the problem of violence such as can be found almost nowhere else in our culture. One of the well-known peculiarities of modern civilized opinion is its refusal to acknowledge the value of violence. This refusal is a virtue, but like many virtues it involves a certain willful blindness and it encourages hypocrisy.

"The values we seek in the Western," he maintained,

> are in the image of a single man who wears a gun on his thigh. The gun tells us that he lives in a world of violence, and even that he "believes in violence." But the drama is one of self-restraint: the moment of violence must come in its own time and according to its special laws, or else it is valueless.

The Western hero, that is to say, offers an image, a style, of responsible, of *civilized* violence:

> He is there to remind us of the possibility of style in an age which has put on itself the burden of pretending that style has no meaning, and, in the midst of our anxieties over the problem of violence, to suggest that even in killing or

being killed we are not freed from the necessity of establishing satisfactory modes of behavior.[2]

The style of the Western hero has a meaning: it signifies the appropriateness of his violence, its justice and necessity.

An image of civilized violence is an image of politics, of the management of power. The Western was for many years the chief, if unacknowledged, popular political drama of America. Warshow himself failed to recognize this. He thought social issues didn't belong in the Western. But the Western is almost always about social and political issues, though it treats them not in the manner of social realism but of romance or allegory. By the time of *The Wild Bunch*—the time of the Vietnam War—the Western could no longer present with conviction an image of American violence that was civilized rather than savage: the civilized violence in Peckinpah's film is in the hands of Mexican revolutionaries.

Warshow's essay is paid little attention in recent studies of the Western. In Richard Slotkin's lengthy *Gunfighter Nation* it gets no mention at all.[3] In *West of Everything* Jane Tompkins mentions it only in the acknowledgments, where she says that it "spurred me on by making me angry."[4] She was angry, one gathers, because she takes Warshow to be an apologist for violence, as she takes the Western genre as a whole to be a justification of violence. And for her no justification of violence can be just: it can only be an incitement to bloodshed and a rationalization of cruelty. Warshow is disregarded, it seems, because "modern civilized opinion," as he put it, "refus[es] to acknowledge

The Great Train Robbery. The bandit shooting at us.

the value of violence. This refusal is a virtue, but like many virtues it involves a certain willful blindness and it encourages hypocrisy." Another way of putting it would be to say that righteousness, often these days in the form of political correctness—on the left or on the right—usurps the place of politics.

The politics of the Western are for Jane Tompkins almost exclusively sexual politics. In her view the Western is an embattled masculine genre that "struggles and strains to cast out everything feminine." It isn't really about the West or the frontier, she maintains, but "about men's fear of losing their mastery, and hence their identity."[5] Its rise as a literary and cinematic genre in the early years of this century she sees as a concerted retaliation on the part of men against what Ann Douglas has called the "feminization of American culture" in the later nineteenth century.[6] In Tompkins's view of literary history, the feminine sentimental novel reigned until the masculine Western took over and shifted the stress from the inner to the outer, from the domestic and the spiritual to the public and the physical. Meekness reigned in the nineteenth century, Tompkins would appear to believe, until the twentieth, with the Western as a guide, invented violence and its justification.

In 1902 Owen Wister published the best-selling novel that has been considered, as Lee Mitchell writes, "responsible all by itself for the emergence of the soft-spoken, sure-shooting cowboy hero."[7] Besides its unnamed eponymous hero (later portrayed on the screen by the resplendent young Gary Cooper), *The Virginian* delineated other characters and situations that became classic features of the genre: the fallible friend, the schoolteacher from the East, the climactic shootout with the villain on the main street of town. That year Henry James wrote to Wister an admiring letter about the novel that expressed one cavil about the portrayal of the hero:

> I find myself desiring all sorts of poetic justice to hang about him, & I am willing to throw out, even though you don't ask me, that nothing would have induced me to unite him to the little Vermont person, or to dedicate him in fact to achieved parentage, prosperity, maturity, at all—which is mere *prosaic* justice, & rather grim at that. I thirst for his blood. I wouldn't have let him live & be happy; I should have made him perish in his flower and in some splendid sombre way.[8]

James would have wanted, it seems, a Virginian more in the tradition of Leatherstocking, a lone figure of the wilderness unassimilable to civilization, but Wister's scheme of things called for his hero's marrying the schoolmarm from Vermont and achieving parentage, prosperity, and all. Through this fruitful union of West and East, as John Cawelti has noted, Wister was able to resolve the governing antithesis of the Western—laid out in Fenimore Cooper but there not resolved satisfactorily—the antithesis between wilderness and civilization.[9] Leatherstocking was a noble country bumpkin, but the Virginian is a natural aristocrat, a gentleman and a knight in the rough; if Fenimore Cooper remained bound to established social hierarchy even in the encounter with the wilderness, Wister believed that from the encounter with the wilderness a truer hierarchy would emerge, which he embodied in the natural superiority of the Virginian and sanctified in the union between the cowboy and the schoolmarm.

Wister dedicated *The Virginian* to his friend Teddy Roosevelt, another Easterner who looked West for a renewal of the American spirit at a time when many feared the dilution of that spirit by the immigrants arriving in large numbers on the Eastern shore. On the Western frontier Wister envisioned, a natural ruling class would assert itself and gain ascendancy over the rest. The coming together of the Virginian and the Vermonter—persons of "quality" as opposed to "equality," in the terms the novel sets up—surely carries an import of Anglo-Saxon supremacy.

No less surely it performs a demonstration of male supremacy. The cowboy's courtship of the schoolmarm proceeds as a kind of contest that the cowboy decisively wins. His victory is crowned when, in a situation re-enacted in Westerns many times since, she pleads with him not to fight the villain but, even at the cost of estranging her, he feels he must, and after the gunfight, relieved that he has come out of it alive, she accepts that he was right to have gone through with it and they are reunited. But his victory over her is not (as Tompkins thinks) simply a victory of violence over language, of the tough laconic male over the sensitive articulate female. The Virginian, as Lee Mitchell observes, is not only skilled with a gun but also a master of words who bests the schoolteacher in her own domain of language. We may think of the Western hero as the strong silent type and we may be sure he's not garrulous, but generally he's not uncommunicative either.

The reason the Western has the classic showdown between hero and villain take place on the main street of town is that the matter at stake is not a merely personal but a public, a social matter. Good and bad in most Westerns are not metaphysically given or personally inherent but, as is said nowadays, socially constructed, and constructed, moreover, in the terms of a society that is not established but itself under construction. Although the terms may vary as Westerns have varied in political slant, usually what is seen as good is what is seen to foster—and what is seen as bad is what is seen to threaten—the burgeoning social good. Even in *Shane* (George Stevens, 1953), which aims at a kind of metaphysical essence of the Western, the social conflict between homesteaders and ranchers is what defines the good and bad guys. The Western hero may be a rugged individualist but he's not the self-contained isolate figure he's cracked up to be. If he represents individual freedom, his is an individuality engaged in transaction with the claims of community; if he characteristically roams the wilderness, just as characteristically he enters into the give and take of an incipient social contract.

In adventurous departure from the mode of narration in the rest of the novel, the climactic gunfight in *The Virginian* is depicted through a technique of abrupt shifts from one character to another that feel like cuts in a movie. As the schoolmarm hears three shots in the distance, we switch back in time to the villain just before the gunfight in his worry and whisky and nervous movement; as the villain draws out his pistol, we again switch back in time to the Virginian. In the movies such a technique, native to the medium and a natural for scenes of showdown, has served the Western well. Retarding time as the action comes to a decisive juncture is a device that film cutting can bring off with suspenseful verve. Furthermore, the technique of orchestrated cutting from one character to another, one perspective to another, has the effect of making us see the different individuals as an ensemble and heightening the import for the social group of the action on which the different perspectives all impinge.

No better scene of showdown exists in the Western than the final sequence of John Ford's 1939 *Stagecoach*. Ford's arrangement and emotional coloring of this sequence, however, take the emphasis significantly away from its usual center in the climactic gunfight. Another walk down the streets of the frontier town assumes at least as much prominence. The Ringo Kid (John Wayne in the role that made him a star) is to face the Plummer brothers in the imminent showdown, but more affecting and no less important is another, quieter confrontation that gradually presents itself as—the camera following with steady gaze and steadily mounting sympathy—he walks the woman he wants to marry home where he hadn't known she lived, in the red-light district of town. The tremulous inner realm of sentiment, the alleged feminine domain that the Western is supposed to exclude, is here movingly brought forward and conjoined with the outer realm of action. From Luke Plummer brutishly shoving aside a saloon girl who tries to hold him back from the gunfight, Ford tellingly cuts to Ringo walking side by side with Dallas (Claire Trevor), the saloon girl he loves. Earlier Dallas had pleaded with Ringo not to fight the Plummers, and Ringo, unlike the Virginian in this situation, had allowed himself to be persuaded. But her motive was not only to avoid violence, the confrontation with his past, but also to avoid the confrontation with *her* past; and neither confrontation was to be avoided. In Ford's scheme of things the man and the woman meet on a plane of equality. A birth is a central event in *Stagecoach,* and the newborn baby is a girl. As major a shaper of the Western as Owen Wister and a far greater artist, John Ford reconceived and revitalized the genre and he may be said to have feminized it.

Ford's feminization of the Western is indicated by the title of his film about Wyatt Earp and Doc Holliday and the gunfight with the Clantons at the O.K. Corral, *My Darling Clementine* (1946). "A soft and beautiful movie," Warshow called it with disapproving intent in the course of arguing his opinion that Ford went astray from the Western genre.[10] Ford's darling Clementine is his reimagining of the schoolteacher from the East, perhaps not at the center of the plot (she has nothing to do with the Clantons or the gunfight at the O.K. Corral) but certainly at the heart of the movie, which allegorizes the winning of the West in her winning the heart of Wyatt Earp as the two happily dance together in an unfinished church frailly open to the Western sky. Linear narrative, with its drive toward a finish, its harnessing of character and situation to the forward movement of action, its thrust toward a climax, is a mode many feminists consider intrinsically masculine. If that is so, then Ford's style of narrative—relaxed, digressive, episodic, prone to dwelling on character and situation in disregard of action—can only be called feminine. The finish in *My Darling Clementine,* the anticipated show-

Stagecoach. Ringo walking with Dallas.

down with the Clantons, for long stretches fades from the mind; the dance matters more to Ford than the gunfight and carries more resonance.

Linear narrative establishes a hierarchy: it assigns greater or lesser importance to persons and things according to their place in the order of the advancing plot. The digressive and episodic narrative Ford favors goes against such hierarchy: it displaces the ostensibly central and emplaces the usually marginal. In social content as well as narrative form the Ford Western is for equality and against hierarchy. *Stagecoach* likes best the least conventionally reputable of its characters, and its figure of the ruling class is a pompous, thieving banker. Rather than a natural aristocracy, a supremacy of the fittest such as Wister promoted, the Ford Western celebrates a democracy emergent on the frontier. Through the encounter with the wilderness, civilization in Ford undergoes a breakdown of classes and snobberies and a renewal of the democratic spirit.

In his staunch egalitarian allegiance and his picture of the frontier as the place and the process formative of American democracy, Ford is in the line of Frederick Jackson Turner and his famous frontier thesis. Turner first set forth his thesis in 1893, in an address that began by declaring the closing of the frontier and the ending of an era.[11] On the open frontier, he went on to assert, a frontier that was not a boundary like those in Europe but an edge of freedom, the distinctive character of the American nation was forged. "American social development has been continually beginning over again on the frontier," he said. "This perennial rebirth, this fluidity of American life, this expansion westward with its new opportunities, its continuous touch with the simplicity of primitive society, furnish the forces dominating American character."[12] Not in a simple advance on the wilderness, but in a dialectic of advance and return enacted again and again, Turner saw the making of American civilization. If a natural inequality would triumph on Wister's frontier, in Turner's—and in Ford's—dialectic of the frontier a continual new beginning gives rise to a natural liberty and equality.

Stagecoach was Ford's first Western in sound, and it inaugurated his major reconception of the genre. It epitomizes the Ford Western of equality as *The Virginian* epitomizes the Wister Western of "quality." It tells the story of a journey. The story has a beginning, a middle, and an end, just as the journey has a point of departure, a path of travel, and a point of destination. There is reason to leave the point of departure: the stagecoach sets out from a town where civilization has grown straitened and intolerant. There is trouble to be faced along the path of travel: Apaches threaten the stagecoach as it traverses the wilderness and eventually they attack. So far this sounds like a classic journey story. But now the film does something unusual for which it has drawn criticism. After building up to a dramatic climax in the Indian onslaught and resolving that with the cavalry's coming to the rescue, it proceeds not to a conclusion but to a second dramatic climax in the show-down with the bad guys. Two full-fledged climaxes one after the other have been thought awkward supererogatory dramaturgy; certainly they don't make for a classical plot structure. Yet audiences don't complain, only pedants do. For the film's two climaxes satisfy the logic and the expectations of another kind of structure, informed not by classical notions of closure but by a dialectic of the open frontier.

The narrative development of *Stagecoach* corresponds to the dialectic of Turner's "perennial rebirth" on "the outer edge of the wave—the meeting point between savagery and civilization."[13] From one climax, one crest, the wave moves on to another; no climax can settle things once and for all. The point of destination in a classic journey story is a point of trouble overcome and harmony reached, a place where one wants to stay. Not so in *Stagecoach:* the town at journey's end is sinister and corrupt, not a desirable place to live. Even after Ringo has killed the Plummers and he and Dallas are to be married, they must move on and begin over again. Unlike the lone cowboy riding off into the wilderness, these two head for the horizon with the aim of settling down; they leave civilization behind in order to build it anew. *Stage-coach* ends at a new beginning.

Whether in endorsement or distaste, many regard John Ford as a nostalgic conservative. Many regard the Western in general as a conservative genre. Yet Westerns have run a gamut of political persuasions. And in his political persuasion Ford was actually one of that endangered species, a liberal populist. His nostalgia did not yearn for something that was once in place or is imagined to have been. He looked back to a past that looked forward to a future. He cherished a prospect, an aspiration, a striving. He celebrated something open and unfinished, like the church where Wyatt Earp will forever dance with Clementine.

Turner's emphasis on the frontier has often been taken as an agrarian emphasis, and indeed it owed much to the conception of yeoman democracy advocated by Jefferson and others in the American tradition. But the land, the expanse of wilderness, was only one side of Turner's dialectic of the frontier, in which democracy does not simply grow out of the land but arises from the encounter, the give and take, between wilderness and civilization. Critics of Turner such as Henry Nash Smith miss the dialectical character of his thought and posit nature and civilization as static abstractions rather than as the dynamically, materially interacting pair Turner had in mind.[14] It was not a return to nature that Turner saw on the frontier but a continual new beginning of civilization. Civilization would tame nature, and nature would keep civilization from hardening into hierarchy.

The landscape of the frontier, as we chiefly picture it, is the desert of the Southwest. Although everywhere in America was once frontier country, the frontier we tend to imagine is not the forest of Daniel Boone or Fenimore Cooper but the sparser wilderness farther to the west. As the site of the last American frontier, that desert left a lasting impression on the national imagination. It is the characteristic setting of the movie Western. Neither a green world nor a lifeless one, the desert of the Southwest lends itself peculiarly well to the myth of the frontier because it is a landscape of inchoation, a world where green seems to be making a beginning. Like the ocean or the sky, it is sublime in its awesome immensity, a sight that dwarfs the beholder and defeats the attempt to contain it; unlike the ocean or the sky, and unlike the dead desert, it is a sublime that allows human beings to inhabit and cultivate it, that offers a field of human possibilities and potential growth: an image of the open frontier. The buttes and mesas of the Southwest are in their shapes as fanciful as clouds, as amenable to the eye that would see things in them, but these are clouds made of solid earth, fanciful projections embodied in enduring stone. The landscape of the Southwest seems to bring the sky to the ground and to invest the ground with a reaching for the sky. It blends together the ideal and the material, the palpable and the potential.

My Darling Clementine. The dance in the unfinished church.

The landscape of the Southwest as an image of the frontier found its epitome in the Monument Valley pictured in John Ford's Westerns. Monument Valley as an American icon, as the spirit of the frontier materialized in landscape, was a creation of Ford's first seen in *Stagecoach* and continued in several of his postwar Westerns, including *My Darling Clementine, Fort Apache* (1948), *Wagon Master* (1950), and *The Searchers* (1956). Ford was a tribal poet, however, a popular and deeply social artist endowed with the power of bringing to fruition images that belong not to him individually but to the collective imagination, images that say "we" rather than "I": his Monument Valley is not his but ours.[15] Its natural formations have an architectural quality that evokes sacred structures, churches or temples elementally sculpted, a sacredness that Ford often augments with ceremony and with such structures as the church being built in *My Darling Clementine* and yet a sacredness that remains alien to us like the beautiful but strange land where it inheres.

The agrarian imagination envisions the pastoral, the land fruitful and contained; the imagination of the frontier contemplates the sublime, the uncontainable field of possibilities, the unrealized that lies ahead. Turner's— and Ford's—conception of the frontier parallels the idea of the avant-garde in the arts: the notion that art gains its vitality and its point through the continual venture into new territory. Like the avant-garde, the frontier these days is largely out of fashion.

In *Gunfighter Nation,* the third in his trilogy of books on the myth of the frontier, Richard Slotkin puts beside Turner's another frontier thesis,

My Darling Clementine. Monument Valley: the spirit of the frontier materialized in landscape.

Teddy Roosevelt's, and slights the big differences between the two. Roosevelt's view of the frontier—expressed in his multivolume history *The Winning of the West* (1885–94) as well as in his political career—was steeped in a mystique of violence quite foreign to Turner but well in keeping with Slotkin's construction of the frontier myth as centrally involving "regeneration through violence." Roosevelt was racist and imperialist; Turner was neither. Although he recognizes these differences, Slotkin blurs them in his disapprobation of what he lets Roosevelt define as *the* frontier. "Savage war" and "bonanza economics" are for Slotkin the governing principles of the frontier myth; but they are not what governed the Turner frontier. The frontier, as the founding myth of the American nation, has been enlisted for diverse purposes and persuasions; if it has served the cause of American racism and imperialism, it has also served the cause of American liberty and equality.

In *Regeneration through Violence,* the first of his three books on the frontier mythology—and the most manifestly Jungian in its approach—Slotkin put forward the myth of the frontier as a variant of the myth of the hunter who gains vitality and power from the violence of the hunt and the blood of the prey.[16] This view of violence emphasizes the mystical and deemphasizes the political. It sees killing as something ritual and sacramental, something primarily motivated by the exalted, redemptive experience. (*The Wild Bunch* is both an expression of that exaltation and a critique of it. So is Peckinpah's later *Straw Dogs* [1971], not a Western yet a kind of companion piece to *The Wild Bunch* in theme as well as style, and a film that almost everyone—William Pechter was the notable exception[17]—misunderstood as a glorification of violence as a rite of passage into manhood.) Violence in this view is not justified by what it gets done, by some purpose it serves—feeding the hungry by killing an animal, defending the threatened by fighting off an assailant, supporting a social order deemed desirable or opposing a social order deemed undesirable—but something done for its own sake as a blood-stirring act of blood. Slotkin is taken in by the mystique of violence he righteously condemns. To see violence chiefly as a blood myth and ritual, whether one upholds it or condemns it as that, is to mystify all the violence that has a practical or a political motivation, a social or an economic purpose.

Gunfighter Nation centers on the Western movie as the prime twentieth-century expression of the frontier myth. It knowledgeably examines the history of the Western in relation to the history of America in this century. But it treats the Western as if it had fallen from the big sky of the American West. It does not properly situate it in relation to other genres and it especially neglects those of foreign provenance—the Homeric or the medieval

epic[18] or the Soviet revolutionary movie, to mention other epic genres dealing in myths of formative violence. And it little considers the history of
America in relation to the history of other nations. It suffers from American
exceptionalism not because it believes in American preeminence—rather the
contrary—but because it nonetheless assumes the singularity of American
history and American mythology.

In a chapter called "Killer Elite" (after a Peckinpah film that goes un-
mentioned) Slotkin discusses the gunfighter hero of the Western as a figure
of entitled violence. An interesting if debatable case could be made—Slotkin
almost makes it—that the Western portrays the violence of the ruling class
and views it approvingly, whereas the gangster movie, whose hero is usually
an immigrant, portrays the violence of the upstart lower class and views it
disapprovingly. The Western, in any case, has for its hero a man of violence
that does good, whereas the gangster movie has for its hero a man of violence
that does no good. The professional gunfighter, as opposed to the man
merely skilled with a gun, didn't become a hero of the Western until the early
fifties, with such movies as *The Gunfighter* (Henry King, 1950), *High Noon*
(Fred Zinnemann, 1952), and *Shane*.[19] The Western hero is often a loner, but
the gunfighter is a loner to the point of alienation, a specialist in violence
whose violence calls for a special justification.

What entitles the gunfighter to violence, in Slotkin's view, is not a social
allegiance but a personal superiority. *Shane* tells the same story as *The Virginian*, the story of the Johnson County War,[20] but takes the other side:
Shane is a knight on the side of the homesteaders as the Virginian was a
knight on the side of the ranchers. For Slotkin, however, it is not the homesteaders' cause that justifies Shane but his own chivalric nobility and lofty
expertise in the gunfighter's art: "Shane is never part of the community, and
his superior values are not seen as belonging to the community. He is an
aristocrat of violence, an alien from a more glamorous world, who is better
than those he helps and is finally not accountable to those for whom he
sacrifices himself." That Shane is not part of the community, that he is
superior with his gun, doesn't make him superior to the community. His
antagonist is equally an "aristocrat of violence": what, then, distinguishes the
gunfighter hero from the gunfighter villain he typically faces? Very little,
according to Slotkin, and that is the problem: might makes right, might
exercised with the commanding elegance and precision of the superior man.
This reading goes against one's entrenched sense that in a movie such as
Shane right makes might, the hero wins because he is on the side of the
angels. Shane may look more like an angel than the homesteaders do but it is

they who make him one, who entitle him to his golden violence in their be-half. He is an outsider to their community rather as a union organizer is an outsider, someone more skilled in conflict who can help the good guys win.[21]

Not only does Slotkin cede the frontier to Teddy Roosevelt, he cedes him progress as well. Roosevelt was a "progressive" in a particular sense of the word pertaining to the politics of his time: what he advocated in the name of progress was the advancement of capitalism and imperialism and the rule of the wealthy. "Progressive" in this sense is the opposite of "popu-list," which in this context means a resistance, of democratic conviction and backward-looking agrarian bent, to the forward-looking dominance of in-dustrial capitalism. This dichotomy of "progressive" and "populist," current in American politics circa 1900, Slotkin freezes and applies to everything that comes under his scrutiny: "progressive" for him always means advancing the interests of the capitalist ruling class, interests to which the only alternative he sees is a "populist" nostalgia for an agrarian past that cannot be recap-tured. Turner escapes this dichotomy: he was neither a "progressive" nor a "populist," and he was both a populist and a progressive. The same is true of Shane, which seems to trouble Slotkin because its populism looks forward rather than backward and, instead of lamenting a lost cause, wins by taking effective action. And the same is true of John Ford.

In 1939, the year of Stagecoach, two other Westerns were made, Dodge City by Michael Curtiz and Jesse James by Henry King, that for Slotkin exem-plify the "progressive" and the "populist" outlooks in the "town-tamer" and the "outlaw" variants of the genre. "The 'town-tamer' Western," he writes, "offered a 'progressive' answer: social injustice is imposed by powerful crim-inals; the hero must defeat them and thus empower the 'decent folks' who bring progress to the Frontier. The 'outlaw' Western proposes a critique of this model by locating the source of injustice in the powerful institutions (railroads) that are also the agents of 'progress.'"[22] The sheriff who cleans up a town, Slotkin implies, is making it safe not so much for the ordinary "de-cent folks" as for the big greedy concerns of capitalism. The outlaw repre-sents a popular rebellion against those concerns but a rebellion that cannot win: he is a frontier version of the gangster hero, a nobler figure perhaps but as much a tragic figure. In this scheme the winners can only be bad and only the losers can be good. In Shane as in a Ford Western like Stagecoach, My Darling Clementine, or the unassuming, magnificent Wagon Master, the win-ners are good but what they win is only a start, a hope for the future.

My Darling Clementine is a town-tamer Western but one that doubles the hero and so becomes a kind of outlaw Western as well. In this film the town-taming sheriff, Wyatt Earp (Henry Fonda), and the chief town felon, the gambler and saloon keeper Doc Holliday (Victor Mature), are not enemies but good friends; rather than hero and villain, they are both heroes of the story, one happily and the other tragically. At paired key moments in the film each looks at his reflection in the mirror and sees a changed man: Wyatt Earp is the Westerner adopting civilization, Doc Holliday the Easterner embracing the wilderness. Each is the mirror image of the other: they are doubles like Jekyll and Hyde except that they represent, not a struggle between good and evil within a split psyche, but an interplay between civilization and wilderness unfolding out in the social and material world. They enact the dialectic of the frontier that, in Ford's conception as in Turner's, was the making of America. This dialectic enables the portrayal of a tragic hero in Doc Holliday together with, in Wyatt Earp, a hero of the pursuit of happiness. Clementine is the Eastern woman Doc Holliday forsakes and Wyatt Earp fancies; she goes West after the one, dances with the other, and stays. *My Darling Clementine* has the movement both of a tragedy—it fittingly incorporates the soliloquy from *Hamlet,* recited in a frontier tavern by a drunken actor who forgets his lines and turns for help to Doc Holliday— and of a formative epic.

The frontier makes for dualities—East and West, past and future, feminine and masculine, European and Indian, order and freedom, garden and wilderness, civilization and savagery, culture and nature—dualities often dramatized through a pairing of characters that leads us to regard them in comparison with each other: Natty Bumppo and Chingachgook, the Virginian and his fallible friend Steve, Shane and his gunfighter antagonist. Such frontier dualities, and their representation through such character doubling, Ford's Westerns develop into a vital dialectic.[23] East and West in *My Darling Clementine* come to a sweet synthesis when Clementine and Wyatt Earp dance together that sunny Sunday morning in the unfinished church amid the gathered townspeople before the numinous buttes of Monument Valley— a mere prospect, not an achieved thing, but a prospect that soars.[24]

In Ford's next Western, however, the extraordinary *Fort Apache,* the dialectic of East and West admits no such happy synthesis. It is strained to the breaking point, perhaps past it, and the West's concluding espousal of the East only points up the problem in the guise of resolving it, so that the film closes with an open question. The celebration of the frontier as the cradle of American democracy—"The life of Fort Apache is one of Ford's richest creations," wrote Robin Wood, "a miniature civilization in its own right founded on the traditions of the cavalry but with its disciplines made flexible and humane through adaptation to the wilderness"[25]—is held in check by an incisive critique of American imperialism. This is a remarkable turn for a work of popular culture made at the height of the American empire in the genre that gave America its national epic.

In *Fort Apache* Ford again doubles the hero, and has the paired figures of Colonel Owen Thursday (Henry Fonda) and Captain Kirby York (John Wayne) represent East and West on the frontier. Colonel Thursday, the commanding officer at a Western outpost of the U.S. Cavalry, is a martinet and a careerist, a snob and a flagrant racist; Captain York is a good soldier and a friend of the Indians. It is not unusual for a Western to show sympathy for the Indians, but *Fort Apache* shows such sympathy with unusual whole-heartedness. Brave and wise and strong, the Indians in *Fort Apache* assert themselves as the rightful owners of the land on whose countenance the camera dwells; moreover, they win. They are the land's and so is their victory, secured in close alliance with the terrain, the earth that seems to swallow up the defeated paleface intruders in immemorial dust the natives command. Thinking the Indians an inferior race and an unworthy opponent he will easily vanquish, Thursday foolishly leads his men into an attack that

The dance in *My Darling Clementine:* East and West come to a sweet synthesis.

results in their complete destruction. Thursday dies with his men; York survives because he voiced his objection to the attack and was ordered aside. Yet the aftermath is that Thursday—plainly a character modeled on the historical Custer—is enshrined as a national hero whose last stand with his men serves as a rallying symbol for the intensified warfare against the Indians.

In an arresting epilogue we see York, now the commanding officer of Fort Apache, publicly concurring with the picture being painted of Thursday as a great man. And this, Ford makes clear, is not just what York says to the press but what he acts on. Next we see him putting on Thursday's hooded cap and marching off with his men into a campaign against the Indians that vigorously carries forward the policy of aggression Thursday stood for. This epilogue purposely invites two contradictory readings: we may regard York's taking over Thursday's mantle as a frontier synthesis of West and East that makes for a better Thursday, a renewed and improved American version of European civilization; or we may regard York as an even worse Thursday precisely because he is better equipped to implement the hateful policies of his predecessor.

This epilogue has troubled many who have not seen that it is intended to be troubling. For Wood it is a confused sudden reversal of all that has preceded it: "The film has thoroughly exposed the falseness of the legend it ends up affirming."[26] But what the film affirms is not the legend it knows to be false but the community the legend helps bind together. And what is deeply troubling about the epilogue is its undeceived recognition of the loss as well as the gain the legend abets.

For Slotkin the epilogue is telling us "to believe in our myths despite our knowledge that they are untrue," calling on us to enter into "a deliberate and consensual falsification of history."[27] But myths, though sometimes presented as the truth—in which case they become lies generally don't elicit belief that way. Their conviction resides not in factual veracity but in their interpretive, their rhetorical, their poetic power, their ability to capture and structure the imagination of a people. Myths are not true or false but helpful or harmful, sustaining or damaging. The myth of Thursday and his last stand is disturbing not because it is false but because it is harmful—both sustaining and harmful. *Fort Apache* does not tell us to set aside the truth so that we can accept the myth; rather it sets the truth beside the myth, and it asks us to examine with open eyes the nexus of myth and history and politics. Ford's films are perhaps the most sophisticated political works of art America has produced because they understand, with a lucidity that has no time either for cynicism or for moralizing, the way myth and rhetoric, image and ideology, function in a society and a polity. They know that a community needs myth for its cohesion and that a democracy needs to bring myth under the light of critical reason. The epilogue of *Fort Apache* dramatizes both needs at a point of their conflict.

Progress on Ford's frontier, as on Turner's, was not a simple onward course but a double movement toward nature and toward culture, toward freedom and toward order, a wave of successive new beginnings that at each stage would newly empower the people. The dialectic of the frontier reached toward a synthesis of East and West that would entail a synthesis of culture and nature, order and freedom, the progressive push and the populist pull. If in *Fort Apache* that dialectic comes to a quandary, it is largely because that push and that pull can here come to no satisfactory resolution.

Captain York starts out as a populist and a progressive, an exemplar of the frontier democracy that the men and women of the fort can achieve without the extraneous presence of Thursday. Fort Apache is mostly a community of immigrants—Irish who historically served in the U.S. Cavalry and serve Ford to represent the ethnics in American society—immigrants whom the racist and hierarchical Thursday holds in almost as much disdain as he holds the Indians. The trouble is that Thursday is both extraneous to the local fort community and representative of the national community the fort exists to uphold. Whereas the inchoate town in *My Darling Clementine* stands on its own as the germ, the promise of a nation, the fort community is in the service of a nation run on principles other than its own.

Besides Thursday, York has another double, the Apache chief, Cochise, with whom he has a bond.[28] At a resonant juncture the two meet in the heart of the landscape and make a peace that Thursday subsequently betrays. York's solidarity with the Indians is of a piece with his populism. Rather than being cast as the enemy in whose face Americans overcome their differences, the Indians in *Fort Apache* are seen as kindred with the immigrants in a way that heightens the racial and social differences dividing both groups from the ruling class and the exponents of official "progress." When York changes from a friend to a killer of the Indians he in effect renounces his populism (or retains it merely nostalgically) and becomes a "progressive" in the Teddy Roosevelt mode. *Fort Apache* is a tragedy, not the tragedy of an individual but of a community, of two communities: the fort and the Indians.

Fort Apache is a *political* tragedy. The allegiance to the fort community that makes York a good man entails an allegiance to a national community that makes York an agent of imperialist aggression. Ford, said Jean-Marie Straub, is the most Brechtian of filmmakers: he lays bare the contradictions.[29] In *Fort Apache* he pushes the dialectic of the frontier to its limit and exposes its limitations: it yields a better Thursday but that means a better killer of Indians. Ford sorrowfully takes the view that York acts as he must under the circumstances. One may want to take issue with this view. But one cannot feel superior to it. Righteousness will not do in the face of this political tragedy.

"Westerns," asserts Jane Tompkins in an odd characterization of the genre, "satisfy a hunger to be in touch with something absolutely real." By that she means something that affects her bodily, that gives her "the titillation you get from reading books where excitement is so acute it becomes a physical sensation."[30] But the sheerly physical she takes the Western to be about makes an alarmingly unreliable guide to the world of the social and political, to the circumstances and possibilities of history. The lesson of *The Wild Bunch* lies precisely in the way it leads us to reflect on our alarming bodily responses to the experience of violence and to consider the part our savage impulses play in the processes of history, processes inescapably violent but not necessarily wholly savage. Slotkin and Tompkins are not so far apart. He takes the Western to be about a myth of the sheerly physical. What she thrills to he mystifies. What gives her titillation gives him grounds for moralistic condemnation. Two sides of the same coin, a coin that misses the politics of the Western.

THE GANGSTER'S ENTERPRISE. "The initial contact between the film and its audience," wrote Warshow about the gangster film, "is an agreed conception of human life: that man is a being with the possibilities of success or failure." "The Gangster as Tragic Hero" first appeared in *Partisan Review* in 1948; half a century later that agreed conception of human life remains in force—so much so that it may be a bit startling to see it stated as an assumption we make about life rather than just the way life is—and the gangster film remains popular, changed but not very much changed from the classic form Warshow analyzed. "The whole meaning of [the gangster's] career is a drive for success," he maintained. "At bottom, the gangster is doomed because he is under the obligation to succeed, not because the means he employs are unlawful. In the deeper layers of the modern consciousness, *all* means are unlawful, every attempt to succeed is an act of aggression."[31] The gangster is a tragic hero because the very success that is his meaning is his undoing:

> In the opening scene of *Scarface*, we are shown a successful man; we know he is successful because he has just given a party of opulent proportions and because

he is called Big Louie. Through some monstrous lack of caution, he permits himself to be alone for a few moments. We understand from this immediately that he is about to be killed. No convention of the gangster film is more strongly established than this: it is dangerous to be alone. And yet the very conditions of success make it impossible not to be alone, for success is always the establishment of an *individual* pre-eminence that must be imposed on others, in whom it automatically arouses hatred; the successful man is an outlaw. The gangster's whole life is an effort to assert himself as an individual, to draw himself out of the crowd, and he always dies *because* he is an individual.[32]

Another representation of business as murder and the successful man as killer, Chaplin's *Monsieur Verdoux,* had come out not long before and been the subject of Warshow's previous essay for *Partisan Review.* It must have colored his thinking on the gangster film. Not that Monsieur Verdoux is a gangster: he is a split man like many another, a genteel family man at home and a ruthless businessman out in the world. But like the gangster, Monsieur Verdoux does business by murder, making literal the killer instinct of the successful man: while keeping his wife and child secluded in some suburban haven, he marries rich women and kills them for their money. Aristotle said that tragedy represents characters better than we are and comedy characters who are worse. Monsieur Verdoux is a comic hero, a little man like Chaplin's Tramp, who becomes a successful man—that is, a killer—because he cannot survive any other way. The gangster is a tragic hero because he reaches all out for success. He may be lower than we are in social standing but he is higher in ambition. "He is what we want to be," wrote Warshow, "and what we are afraid we may become."[33]

If the classic gangster films of the early thirties—*Little Caesar, The Public Enemy, Scarface*—established the genre, the most popular and most celebrated of all gangster films has been *The Godfather* (1972), which gave the genre a new orientation. A new *double* orientation, for *The Godfather,* set mainly in the forties, has one eye on the past, on the traditional family, and one eye on the future, on the world of corporate capitalism. This double orientation is made fully explicit in the alternate narrative structure of the 1974 *Godfather, Part II,* which switches back and forth between the careers of the immigrant Vito Corleone and his son and successor Michael decades later. But it already informs the first *Godfather,* where Vito and Michael already make a dual hero, one representing the familial past and the other (educated at a top school, groomed for the power elite) the corporate future. Neither one is the classic gangster; the character cast in that mold is the impetuous older brother Sonny who briefly heads the family and who, in a way that puts one in mind of Scarface and seems to declare the choice not to have that kind of hero, meets his death halfway through the film. The classic gangster film tells a story of individual enterprise, the self-made man, the success story of entrepreneurial capitalism taken to its terrible logical conclusion and turned into tragedy. *The Godfather* tells the story not so much of an individual as of a group, a group alternately, contradictorily defined as a family and a corporation, and a group that in either case relieves the individual from shouldering on his own the obligation to succeed. Guy Debord has commented on the curious way in which that remnant of preindustrial backwardness, the Mafia, which once seemed quite outmoded in an era of enlightenment and progress, has now come to epitomize our world of organized dishonesty and secrecy.[34] It's the genius of *The Godfather* to bring together the backwardness of the Mafia, the nostalgia it arouses for a bygone world of familial wholeness, and its brutal corporate modernity.

The theme of the family in gangster films is present from the beginning. One sees it in Scarface's attachment to his sister (similar to Sonny's in *The Godfather* and similarly leading to his downfall). One sees it especially in *The Public Enemy*, the richest in social texture of the early gangster films and the one that most vividly portrays the gangster as a street kid. (William Wellman directed and James Cagney is Tom Powers in the performance that made him a star.) Tom Powers has an indulgent mother, a rival virtuous brother, and a policeman father who beats him; he finds a truer brother in his street buddy and he seeks a truer father in a gang leader. One gang leader proves a false father, and in the event the truer father he does find still cannot save him from being brought back home as a corpse. *The Public Enemy* fits Warshow's thesis less well than *Scarface* or *Little Caesar:* it is less the tragedy of the successful man than of the boy looking for a family. What happens in *The Godfather* is that the street kid's dream of family comes true.

Capitalism may pay lip service to the family but it tends to undermine it. Monsieur Verdoux personifies that contradiction: he says he is in business for the sake of his family but—in an irony made more resonant because we cannot be quite sure whether Chaplin fully intended it—we perceive that his family is but a rationalization, a pretext languishing in its suburban haven, for the ruthless business that really brings him to life. But in *The Godfather,* as William Pechter said in his review of the film, Vito Corleone is not a mere pretender like Verdoux but a genuine family man.[35] He is a ruthless businessman, to be sure, but he is not a split man: his zeal in business is at one with his love of his family. Business and family are one, and that is a rare thing in a world that would divide them. Therefore the family is one, and that is a rare thing in a world that would dismember it.

In John Ford's Westerns the family centers on the woman. Ford's main concern is not the family but the larger community, the polity, and he sees the woman as a civilizing figure, kind and steadfast, enlightened and egalitarian, the center of a family that promises to open out into a liberal and democratic polity. In *The Godfather,* as in most gangster films, the family is strictly patriarchal. It is aggressive and authoritarian and, though quite an extended family, so walled in that it cannot open out into any larger community, certainly not any democratic polity. It is like a feudal fortress in the modern world. It may have all the appeal of togetherness but it has all the drawbacks of tyranny. And yet that feudal fortress not only prospers in the capitalist world but heralds the new form of corporate capitalism.

Vito Corleone is not a tragic hero but, despite such blows as the loss of Sonny, a fulfilled man. What "most distinguishes *The Godfather* from other gangster films," wrote Pechter, "is that Don Corleone isn't a doomed overreacher but a man who dies, in effect, in bed."[36] The classic gangster believes, and his story belies, the ideology of the individual in the land of opportunity. He is a doomed overreacher because he represents the ambition of the unprivileged, the drive for success of those—which is to say, most of us—not marked for success. Vito Corleone doesn't believe in the individual, he believes in the family. And the same goes for Michael Corleone, except that in his case, and under his rule, the family becomes the corporation. The smoothness of the transition is chilling. *The Godfather, Part II* wants to stress the contrast between the family and the corporation, but it is the continuity that is more disturbing. *Part II* and the much later and much inferior *Godfather, Part III* make Michael into a split man, a kind of corporate Monsieur Verdoux, but that a feudal and a capitalist order should come into conflict is not so interesting as their sinister congruence.

The same year as the third *Godfather,* 1990—the year we saw in the news that other story of corporate gangsterism, the savings-and-loan scandal—Martin Scorsese made *GoodFellas,* a gangster film that brilliantly reconceives the genre. Based on a true story, *GoodFellas* is more realistic than other gangster films, closer to the actual facts of criminal life. Scorsese told an interviewer that whereas *The Godfather* is "epic poetry, like *Morte d'Arthur,*" his own film is more in "the spirit of a documentary. As if you had a 16 mm camera with these guys for 20, 25 years."[37] From the extraordinary, the level of tragedy or epic, *GoodFellas* brings the gangster down to the level of ordinary greed-is-good suburban America—a street kid's version of greed is good. Like Tom Powers in *Public Enemy*, Henry Hill (Ray Liotta) in *Good-Fellas* is a kid whose father beats him and who looks to the street—in his case right across the street, which is where the local mob gathers—for an alternative family he might better fit into. But Henry Hill's alternative offers no true fellowship but the fellowship of cash, no true sense of belonging but material belongings—a hoodlum's version of the consumer society. Here the drive for success just means the pursuit of money. Here the will to power just means the cheap superiority of not having to wait in line for a table at the Copa. This is the gangster as comic hero.

"Funny how? I mean, what's funny about it?" asks the truculent Tommy De Vito (Joe Pesci) at one point in *GoodFellas*. "Funny like I'm a clown, I amuse you? I make you laugh, I'm here to fucking amuse you?" Tommy has been sitting in a bar with some fellows and telling them an amusing story. "You're a funny guy," says Henry as he laughs out loud with the others, and now Tommy unaccountably turns on him. Suddenly the laughter stops and violence impends. *GoodFellas* is a comedy of sorts but serious violence is never far away. "Funny how, what's funny about it?" is the question its comedy keeps tacitly asking. *GoodFellas* works as comedy, without the comic exaggeration that would have detracted from its everyday realism, chiefly through its use of voice-over narration. This narration, a first-person account given by Henry and sometimes by his wife Karen (Lorraine Bracco), is in itself no more comic than the action, but the interplay between action and narration yields the uneasy comic effect characteristic of the film.

The narration in *GoodFellas*, the voice-over narration together with the visual narration of camera and editing, is something remarkable. It freely dispenses with the conventional division between enacted scene and narrated summary, the usual clear separation between parts that are fully dramatized and parts that are compressed and accompanied on the soundtrack by a voice-over account. In *GoodFellas* the enacted and the narrated complexly intermingle with amazing ease and fluency. The film is based on the memoirs of the real Henry Hill, a lifelong gangster who made a deal with his captors and told on his associates, as recounted by Nicholas Pileggi in his book *Wiseguy*. Pileggi collaborated with Scorsese on the screenplay, and the dramatized journalism of *Wiseguy*, its rendering of Henry Hill's first person, no doubt influenced the narrative style of *GoodFellas*. But film is not writing, and narrative on the screen has problems and possibilities different from the page. The narrative of *GoodFellas* is an extraordinary formal achievement, of the kind that would deserve being hailed as pathbreaking avant-garde experimentation except that it was done in a work of popular art. Sometimes what we see on the screen corresponds to what we hear Henry saying, sometimes not. As the story progresses and Henry loses control of events, the visual account will get ahead of the verbal account, will even give it the lie. Finally Henry can regain control only as witness for the authorities, but that is to relinquish control, and the film switches from voice-over narration to Henry speaking to us from the screen, diminished from the role of narrator to that of mere performer.

In *Casino* (1995), Scorsese takes the narrative experimentation of *Good-Fellas* further. *Casino* is again a gangster film based on a true story recounted in a book by Pileggi, who again collaborated on the screenplay. But nothing in the book would lead us to expect what we see and hear in the film. If *GoodFellas* has Karen Hill at times take over from Henry as narrator, *Casino* employs a dual narration throughout (and at one point a third narrator comes in). "It takes two to tango," we hear on the soundtrack—Ray Charles and Betty Carter singing, the music being another significant part of the film's narration—when the gangster Nicky Santoro (Joe Pesci) arrives in Las Vegas to join his boyhood friend the gambler Sam Rothstein, called "Ace" (Robert De Niro). Ace and Nicky take turns telling the story. "I was given paradise," Ace tells us of his days running a big casino operation in Las Vegas. "But it turned out to be the last time," Nicky tells us, "that street guys like us were ever given anything that fucking valuable again."

Ace and Nicky have different points of view, and their first-person accounts complement and sometimes contradict each other. The more quarrelsome Nicky often interrupts Ace on the soundtrack, as if the two were sitting together watching the movie we're watching and jointly commenting on it in the narration we hear. This is not the relation of the voice-over to the image we expect in a fiction film, where the convention is that the voice-over must not refer to the image on the screen but that both voice-over and image should refer to the story, take us into the world of the story. "These old greaseballs may not look it," Nicky tells us as we watch the mob bosses gathered in the back of a grocery store in Kansas City, "but these are the guys who secretly control Las Vegas." Nicky's voice-over words are talking about the image we have before us, as if he too were watching this image, which is not a fictional narrator's way of talking but more like the way the narrator of a documentary may comment on the image we are being shown: "This is the Strip in Las Vegas, where fortunes are won and lost every day." Just as it moves between the enacted and the narrated, *Casino* moves with nimble freedom between the world of the story and the commentary that stands back from the story. At the end, the Nicky who stands back is suddenly brought back in with a vengeance, the narrating Nicky who often interrupts is himself interrupted not by another narration but by the action, which cuts his voice-over account short with a blow to his person that begins a brutal onslaught on him and his brother by mobsters who meet them in a cornfield and murder them there.

Just as these fictional voices tell the story with the liberties of a documentary narration, so the story in *Casino* takes the liberty of shifting into a kind of documentary. The traditional gangster film, as Warshow noted, emphasizes sheer criminality and shows us little of the actual business the gangster does, the enterprise that regularly yields him profit. *The Godfather* is no exception, bringing forward the family but not so much the business activity. *GoodFellas*, with its documentary sense of the gangster's daily business, changes that, and *Casino* continues this change with its vivid picture—enabled by a narration that feels free to digress from the event to the explanation, the story to the mechanics behind the story—of the business of running a casino. Ace tells us that even he isn't allowed into the count room, but the camera smoothly goes in and gazes at all that cash and comes out with a man carrying a suitcase full of skimmed money for the mob bosses in Kansas City. We see the mob's business and we see Ace's business in the daily operation of the casino: how he keeps an eye on all the details, how he arranges for a big winner to be detained in town and tempted back into losing, how he spots cheaters at cards—here the film pauses like a documentary and gives us a diagrammatic picture—and punishes them so that they'll never try it again. Ace is a man who enjoys his work, is very good at it and makes very good money. And in his work he meets the stunning Ginger McKenna (Sharon Stone, in a splendid performance), falls in love and marries. Surely paradise is not too much of a hyperbole.

Ace Rothstein is a merit boy. It is fitting that we should see him doing his work because his professional ability has been his road to success. "He made his first bet when he was fifteen and he always made money," Nicky tells us over a shot of red dice we see Ace carefully calibrating: gambling is not a matter of chance to him but of calculation, of expertise and intelligence. Ace rose in life by his expertise and intelligence. He made a lot of money for the mob bosses and they gave him paradise. Back home they had assigned Nicky to protect him, make sure nothing happens to him. Ace is not a man of violence. It takes two to tango: Ace is the brains and Nicky is the muscle. Nicky is the classic gangster in *Casino*, the overreaching street kid with a gun, and he could have been made into a tragic hero like Scarface or

Little Caesar. Ace is the overreaching street kid with a mind, and though he falls from paradise he is not made into a tragic hero either. There can be no tragedy in the first person, not in the protagonist's first person. No man is a hero to his valet, and no man can be a tragic hero in his own account.[38]

Rather than a mere background to the rise and fall of Ace and Nicky, the documentary picture of the casino business is a frame to their story, a way of subsuming it in a larger story of the mob and enterprise in America. If the classic gangster film tells the story of an individual, and *The Godfather* the story of a family, *Casino* tells the story of a business, a bigtime enterprise, in which our heroes the gambler and the gangster did their bit. Theorists may say that narrative rests on causality, but the verbal and visual narration of *Casino* moves along other lines than simple cause and effect. Ace the merit boy, the stickler for detail, fires an incompetent subordinate with connections in the local government and consequently gets into trouble over his gambling license: a story of meritocratic hubris, it would seem, except that this trouble is not the cause of Ace's downfall, which comes about through no fault of his own, no tragic flaw, when the FBI puts a wire in that grocery store in Kansas City for some other reason and finds out about the mob connection to his Las Vegas casino. Ace may have risen by his ability, but only because the mob was making a profit from that ability: he owed his rise to the mob, and he owes his fall to the mob. The merit boy may think he rises on his own, but he rises at the sufferance of the powers that be.

Sharon Stone in
Casino: the woman
of his dreams.

The mob bosses in *Casino* rule from afar, and there isn't much sense of the mob as a fellowship, not even the fellowship of cash there was in *Good-Fellas*. Ace in Las Vegas would rather have nothing to do with his old friend Nicky from back home: he wants to pretend the mob is not there, the brains doing without the muscle, the merit boy getting ahead without the powers that be. Ace wants his own family. On the casino floor, when he sees her throwing a man's chips up in the air—in a scene rendered like a memory so often returned to it becomes a dream, the woman of his dreams—he falls for Ginger. But his marriage is a marriage of cash. This is not because Ginger is (as one reviewer called her) "an opportunistic party girl." She is no more opportunistic than Ace—if anything, she is more of a tragic figure than he—and Scorsese treats them both with equal questioning sympathy. It is because those are the terms that are set up, Ace's terms as well as Ginger's, the terms of the world in which they live. Ace wants his own family and it can only be a family of cash.

The gangster film, as Warshow said, is not about real gangsters but about a figure of the imagination, a mythical gangster who "in ways that we do not easily or willingly define . . . speaks for us."[39] That gangster is a metaphor for success in America, success as crime. If the gangsters in *Good-Fellas* and *Casino* come closer to real gangsters, this isn't finally a documentary concern but a way of reimagining the myth, recasting the metaphor. Evidently Scorsese no longer feels able to tell the gangster's story as the doings of an individual, an overreaching street kid or even an overmastering don, a protagonist whose actions we can follow in cause-and-effect unfolding. That no longer speaks for us, no longer expresses, in corporate America, our imagination of success and failure. The mob bosses in *Casino* are old, and by the time the FBI brings them to justice they are on their last legs. But the organization they head is practically a corporation, and after they're gone something much like it will stay in place. Only it won't give street kids much of a chance any more.

8 :   History Lessons

Poetry, therefore, is a more philosophical and a higher
thing than history: for poetry tends to express the universal,
history the particular.

ARISTOTLE, *Poetics*

I tried to give the impression that the mud sticks when you
walk in the mud and that the fog blocks your view when you
walk in the fog.

JEAN RENOIR, talking about *La Nuit du carrefour*

Modernism is thought to be the opposite of realism. That once influential champion of the modern, Clement Greenberg, said as much: "Realistic, naturalistic art had dissembled the medium, using art to conceal art; Modernism used art to call attention to art."[1] And much the same view is expressed in Peter Bürger's recently influential *Theory of the Avant-Garde*, which theorizes that modernism was essentially synonymous with art for art's sake.[2] The autonomy of art, the institution of art in bourgeois society, reached its logical conclusion according to Bürger in the sheer aestheticism that for him was modernism. Unlike Greenberg, who used the terms more or less interchangeably, Bürger draws a line between modernism and the avant-garde—the "historical avant-garde," as he calls it—which he sees as a revolt against the bourgeois institution of art and especially against its culmination in the heightened autonomy of modern art. Greenberg has long been out of fashion, but though his taste may no longer prevail, his characterization of modernism still does. Champions of postmodernism have sought to connect Bürger's historical avant-garde—which lasted barely more than a decade, the years of vintage dada and surrealism and the Soviet and Weimar twenties—with the postmodern revolt against the modern. The modern was formalistic, this story goes, whereas the postmodern is political: the modern was all wrapped up in its own concerns, its own aesthetic territory, whereas the postmodern engages the concerns of society, the surrounding territory of history. The modern, in this view as in Greenberg's, is the art that turns its back on the representation of reality.

At the dawn of modernism the poet Stéphane Mallarmé took a different view. "The search after truth, peculiar to modern artists . . . enables them to see Nature and reproduce her, such as she appears to just and pure eyes," he wrote in an 1876 article on the artists who began modern painting, "The Impressionists and Edouard Manet." "The scope and aim of Manet and his followers," affirmed Mallarmé, "is that painting shall be steeped again in its cause, and its relation to nature."[3] Quoting this sentence in his book on Manet and the impressionists, T. J. Clark stops at "its cause," which he takes as an emphasis on the medium similar to Greenberg's, and leaves out "its relation to nature."[4] But the emphasis on the medium, on the means of art, was only half of Mallarmé's emphasis, and the other half was no less important: the emphasis on nature, on putting the means of art toward the end of representing the face of reality.

The emphasis on the means stems from the difficulty in achieving the end. The search after truth peculiar to modern artists is a search that can assume no higher ground from which to look at reality, no divine system or scheme of things that has the key to the truth. An art that dissembles its means wants us to accept the perfect adequacy of its access to the truth; an art that calls attention to its means wants us to recognize it as a construction, a matter of choice rather than necessity, an order of human making rather than a higher order of things. A higher order would supply the answers; an order of human making must put things in question, put itself in question. Modern art declares its means not because they are its only subject but in order to put them in question, because it feels it cannot take its assumptions for granted in its search after truth.

Manet and the impressionists were at once naturalistic and formalistic. They endeavored to paint actual appearances as they had never been painted, to render on canvas the way things really look to the eye that perceives them; and at the same time, as part of the same impulse, they made palpable to the viewer the means of their rendering, the paint they applied on canvas and their way of applying it.

Literature in the nineteenth century was ahead of the visual arts in the endeavor to depict the particulars of actual experience. A whole new literary form, the novel, came into being just for that purpose and was already in full flower when that new visual form invented for a similar purpose, the photograph, was scarcely getting started. Although the novel has assumed central place in our literary tradition and we may often speak of the "classic realist" novel, we must keep in mind that at the time of its development, the realism of the novel was a revolutionary break with the conventions of classicism. Critics may like to draw a line between the "realist" and the "naturalist" novel, but naturalism was a further development of the modern search after truth and an extension of it into new regions of actual experience. Naturalism only intensified what Ian Watt has called the "formal realism" of the novel, its "circumstantial view of life," its attention to particulars and mistrust of generalities, its insistence on getting down to specifics rather than relying on the idealizations, the universals of classicism.[5] Those who would have an opposition between realism and naturalism—Georg Lukács is a notable example—hold a classicizing conception of realism that runs counter to its original impulse. And the modernist novel did not turn its back on naturalism or give up the search after truth. Flaubert and Conrad had one foot in naturalism and the other in modernism; the full-fledged modernism of Joyce and Faulkner kept strong ties with naturalism all the same. These modern novelists didn't renounce the formal realism of the novel but brought forward its forms: their work, like that of Manet and the impressionists, is naturalistic and formalistic at once.

Film, which sets in motion the photographic look into the actual appearance of things, has been the preeminent art form of the twentieth century as the novel was of the nineteenth. The dominant form of film, however, has been neither realism nor modernism but, reining in the naturalistic possibilities of the medium, a species of classicism. If a classical style in art is a style that settles comfortably within the norms and forms of its own artifice, a style that follows convention with confidence in the adequacy of its own conventions to express all that needs to be expressed, then it makes sense to call the style of film Hollywood made dominant after the coming of sound a classical style.[6]

Yet film's naturalistic possibilities seem insuppressible. Ever since the Lumière brothers took their movie camera out into the streets, naturalism has kept coming back into the art of film. And where naturalism appears modernism is not far behind. As in impressionist painting, so in the Soviet films of the twenties, in the work of Vertov, of Eisenstein, of Dovzhenko, a naturalistic emphasis combined with an assertive formalism into a modernist style. In France in the thirties, the surrealism of Buñuel and Vigo, the searching realism of Jean Renoir, likewise brought together a vigorous naturalistic impulse and an equally vigorous impulse toward formal innovation and the challenge to convention. In the films of the forties the emergent naturalistic style was Italian neorealism, and it didn't take long for that naturalism to turn, without much of a break, into the modernism of Antonioni and Fellini, Rosi and Pasolini and Bellocchio. Something similar happened with the French *nouvelle vague* of the sixties and also with the Brazilian *cinema nôvo* of Nelson Pereira dos Santos and Glauber Rocha. And at present something similar is happening in the work of the Iranian filmmaker Abbas Kiarostami.

Kiarostami's *Close-Up* (1990) begins with a reporter and two policemen getting into a taxicab and going to the scene of a crime. The crime, as the reporter tells the cab driver on the way to the scene, is a curious kind of fraud: someone has been impersonating a famous film director (Mohsen Makhmalbaf) and has been gaining entry into the home of a prosperous family under the pretense of making a movie with them. In the Iranian film industry, one gathers, the directors are the stars and the actors are often recruited nonprofessionals in the neorealist tradition. *Close-Up* reconstructs a true story and has the real persons involved playing themselves on the screen: the family may not have gotten to act in a Makhmalbaf movie, but they got to act their story for Kiarostami.

This is going to be a big story, the reporter feels sure, and as we ride with him in its pursuit we assume he is going to be the character taking us into it, the film's figure of the storyteller. When the taxicab arrives at the family's home we expect we will go inside with the reporter. But the film frustrates our expectations: we remain outside with the cab driver and the two policemen, and even after the two policemen are called inside to make the arrest we still remain outside, with the driver we took for a secondary figure, subordinate to the reporter we thought would be giving us entry into the story. By frustrating our expectations, keeping us outside the gate to the family's house in a neighborhood where all the houses are walled with gates, the film makes us aware that the actual world does not grant us special entry into the stories under way any more than it grants us entry into the houses of the privileged. This is how naturalism leads to modernism: in the actual world we inhabit, where we can have no privileged access to what goes on, no ideal place from which to apprehend what takes place, we must acknowledge the means by which we actually manage our access, we must put in question the means our art employs for representing the world.

The waiting driver turns the car around in the dead-end street where the family lives. He gets out of the car and (a former flier) he looks up at an airplane leaving its white trail in the blue sky. From a pile of leaves on the street he picks out some flowers, and in so doing he sets loose an aerosol can he now kicks gently and watches roll down the sloping street and across to the other side, where it comes to rest at the curb. That rolling aerosol can may be taken as a witty epitome of the naturalistic approach. It may be seen to represent the detail of everyday life on which naturalism dwells: we thought we were in pursuit of a big story and we find ourselves watching the course of an insignificant can down a suburban street. And the course of that can may also be seen to represent the iron rule of cause and effect in narratives of the naturalistic school: we watch, and keep watching until eventually it comes to rest, the inexorable effect of a cause, the perhaps trivial but nonetheless ineluctable consequence of the driver's actions of picking out the flowers and kicking the can he set loose. Kiarostami calls attention to the forms of formal realism he is employing: the attention to detail, the unfolding of cause and effect.

As the driver brings to the car the flowers he picked out, the reporter and the two policemen briskly emerge from the family's house and get into the taxicab with the man they came to seize for the crime of impersonating a film director. We've been kept waiting long enough, we feel, and surely now we're getting down to the story. But the reporter needs a tape recorder. He gets out, pays the large cab fare, and lets the car go off without him; we stay with him as he rings the bells at the gates of the family's neighbors, asking if they have a tape recorder he might borrow. We had expected to go inside the family's home with the reporter and instead we waited outside with the driver; now we expect to ride with the driver and the policemen and the man they have arrested, the protagonist of the story, and instead we are left behind with the reporter. Our expectation each time is for the narrative to follow the character placed closer to the center, the stage where things are happening, but this narrative seems to want to stay on the margin of things, and each time it shifts away from the character who has the better access to the story. We are kept in suspension but not exactly in suspense. The point is not merely to tell us the story but to make us aware of our path to the story.

Cause and effect: we watch the reporter going down the street in quest of a tape recorder as we watched the aerosol can rolling down the street in the same direction. But the reporter doesn't come to rest, he starts moving faster once he gets his tape recorder, and as he scampers off after his story he kicks the aerosol can, not gently as the driver kicked it but spiritedly, so that it starts rolling much faster than before. This time we don't stay with the can on its rolling course but cut to a printing press (the sound of the can rhyming with the sound of the press) putting out the paper with the reporter's story, not a connection of cause and effect between can and press but a metaphor: the unremarkable detail of everyday life given the kick, the spin of publication. Or the resonance of art: in Kiarostami's hands that aerosol can becomes remarkably expressive. It becomes expressive not so much within the story as in what it tells about the telling of the story, as a representation of the means of representation: expressive in the characteristic manner of modernism. The detail of naturalism is treated with the self-consciousness of modernism and turned into a metaphor for the means of art.

✻ Naturalism and modernism are forms of European art, it may be objected, terms that shouldn't be applied to the art of a country such as Iran. But the novel, with its circumstantial view of life and its formal realism, is a European form that has spread and taken root all over the world. The same may be said of film, and of the naturalistic possibilities of film; like Satyajit Ray in India or Pereira dos Santos in Brazil, Kiarostami has acknowledged his debt to Italian neorealism. Modernism is a more problematic matter, and even within the orbit of European art it is not quite clear what it is. But its influence beyond that orbit is clear, its effect not just on art that would imitate European models but on art as locally implicated, as specific to the place of its making, as the novels of Gabriel García Márquez or the painting of the Mexican muralists. Modernism is thought to be Eurocentric, but the art it has inspired internationally has considerable variety and local specificity; by contrast, the international art one sees exhibited under the rubric of postmodernism all looks pretty much the same. *Modernism* and *postmodernism* are in any case terms sure to come in for future reconsideration. And as we rethink our notions we must recognize the nexus between naturalism and modernism, a nexus neglected by theorizers and critics yet long vital to the work of artists, and currently the nexus where Kiarostami's films can be seen to have their life.

The art of modernism is supposed to be a difficult art. In his famous essay on the modern, "The Dehumanization of Art," José Ortega y Gasset argued that it is an art difficult on purpose, an art that makes demands of its audience so as to divide it into the appreciative few and the uncomprehending many, an art that creates, is meant to create, an aristocracy of taste.[7] The modernism even of a work of revolutionary socialism such as Vertov's *Man with a Movie Camera*, which would hope to reach the many, still appeals only to the few, the heroic few who seek the good of the many and hope the many will join them. A taste for modern art used to be a badge of distinction, but today people see it as a mark of elitism, and take the badge of distinction to lie in the disapproval of elitism. The populist modernism of artists such as the Mexican muralists is, because populist, not even recognized as modernism either by champions of the elitist modern like Greenberg or Theodor Adorno or by champions of the allegedly populist postmodern.

There is nothing pretentious or abstruse about Kiarostami's films. They are unaffected and uncomplicated, they make no such demands on their audience as would divide the knowing from the unknowing. Theirs is a modernism that children can understand. Children in fact are often their subject and an audience they are intended for; Kiarostami helped set up, back in the days of the shah, a cinema division at the state-supported Center for the Intellectual Development of Children and Young Adults, where he has worked for most of his career. *Regular or Irregular* (1981) is a short film that sets out to teach an elementary lesson: by showing a number of things done in an orderly and in a disorderly fashion—children getting into a school bus in neat sequence, for example, as opposed to children in free-for-all contention to get in first—it shows that order is the quicker and better way. On the soundtrack we hear the filmmakers commenting on the images, not just on their content but on their form: over a shot of the school bus from across the street, a shot held while the children messily struggle to get in, we hear the filmmakers saying that this is a long take, a really long take, then that this distant shot doesn't give a good view of what's going on, whereupon they cut to a closer view of the children all stuck struggling at the bus door. The lesson, then, is not just on how best to get into a bus but on how to make a film about it.

And more than a lesson, *Regular or Irregular* is a reflection on order, the order of life and the order of art, the arrangement of order in art and in life. The film's final example of order and disorder is a busy intersection where pedestrians cross the street at random and traffic gets stuck chaotically like the children at the bus door. It is easy for the filmmakers to show us the intersection in a state of disorder. But order is a much more difficult proposition, and after several tries they cannot manage, either by their own efforts of arrangement or by enlisting the authority of a traffic cop, to bring the chaotic irregularity of that intersection into any kind of regularity. This is a good joke and a wonderful undercutting conclusion to the lesson on the virtues of order. Order how? we are prompted to ask, order by what manner achieved, by what agency imposed on unruly life? In a review of Kiarostami's films in the *Chicago Reader,* Jonathan Rosenbaum rightly calls this "the most philosophically profound of the shorts"; but Rosenbaum stresses the film's laying bare of the lies of art, the way the "hilarious offscreen critiques of the chaos make brilliantly clear how much everyday deception is involved in fashioning documentaries—in the preparatory work as well as in the cut-and-paste editing."[8] It seems to me that Kiarostami is after bigger game than the cheating regularly (or irregularly) practiced in documentaries.

The greatest of Kiarostami's documentaries is *Homework* (1990). Like all great documentaries—like *Nanook of the North* and *The Man with a Movie Camera* and *Land without Bread,* in whose company it belongs—*Homework* acknowledges the artifice of its making, the fiction that enters into it. Kiarostami shows himself and the equipment and technicians that flank him as he interviews working-class children at their school; he shows the camera, the mechanical eye that stares at the children like an exacting schoolmaster as they answer the questions being put to them. He shows the means of representation plainly, without fuss, not to make a show of artifice but—and here again naturalism leads naturally to modernism—because they are part of the reality represented. The children respond to the camera and we must see the camera they see if we are to understand their response. Their lies, for example: they all say they like doing homework, the heavy load of homework they are assigned every day, better than they like watching cartoons on television. The children are intimidated, not because Kiarostami is particularly intimidating but because these working-class children are already intimidated by authority, and they answer what they think is expected of them. The exacting eye of that camera exacts lies.

Yet it is also an instrument of truth. The stress on the lies of art, the lies of that purported medium of truth the documentary film, neglects the capacity for truth that, amid all its feigning and fabrication, art possesses nonetheless. "We can never get close to the truth except through lying," said Kiarostami, and Rosenbaum, who quotes this statement, takes it as a call for exposing the lies; but Kiarostami does not rest content with that. He may expose the lies, he may lay bare the constructions of art, but he also employs them in the search after truth, and if he lays them bare it is because that way he can better employ them.

The children in *Homework* may lie, but their lying is part of their truth. They cower before the camera's authority as they cower before all the authorities that rule their lives. On their faces we often see bruises; shyly, without presuming to complain, mumbling at times so we can hardly hear them, they talk about the punishment they receive from their teachers and their parents and their older siblings. This is the time of the war with Iraq—when Saddam Hussein was as officially demonized in Iran as he was here during Bush's Gulf War—and we see the kids assembled in the school yard beating their chests and militantly intoning chants of religious war; at one point, ostensibly claiming that the martial religious chants are not being executed with the proper ceremony but slyly implying that we could do without them, Kiarostami turns off the sound. Documentary is supposed to be direct, but *Homework* proceeds obliquely and even metaphorically, as no doubt it must in order to work under an authoritarian system that rules not over kids alone but over filmmaking as well. The camera the children see as an authority we come to see as itself under the authority the children fear. Kiarostami acknowledges not only what the camera does to the children but what the context does to the camera, an acknowledgment specific to his situation yet pertinent to all documentary situations, for the camera at any time and place always does something to its subjects and the context of any time and place always does something to the camera. And what Iran does to its children, which Kiarostami's camera penetratingly renders in the process of itself doing something to those kids standing before it, likewise pertains to what we all do to our children.

In the form of a documentary about schoolchildren and their homework and the educational system in Iran, *Homework* gives us a moving and implicative depiction of a society that terrorizes its children. One of the kids interviewed is so afraid of the camera, so terrified of a punishing authority, that he can scarcely answer questions without bursting into tears, and he keeps asking that a friend stand beside him for protection. Even with the friend by his side, he still pleads tearfully with the interviewer to let him go, until finally he calms down by reciting a prayer, not a warlike prayer this time but a prayer to God the creator and bringer of comfort and joy. Kiarostami ends his film with this prayer he makes his own. He concludes on a freeze frame, an arrested and arresting image, of this boy barely able to hold back his tears as he prays with his friend beside him.

If fiction always enters into documentary, documentary, the camera's

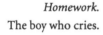

Homework.
The boy who cries.

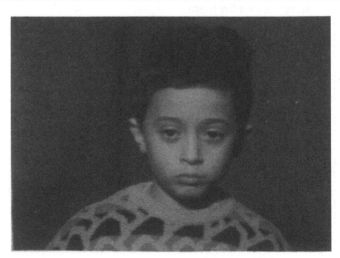

record of actual appearances, always enters into the fictions of the film medium. As if to declare how film combines fiction and documentary, Kiarostami makes documentaries that own up to fiction and he also makes fiction films in the documentary vein descending from neorealism. In a mode of neorealist picaresque, his first feature-length film, *The Traveller* (1972), follows a boy's determined endeavor to get to Tehran for a big soccer game. Also in that picaresque mode, *Where Is the Friend's House?* (1987) follows a boy's errant attempt in a village in northern Iran to bring a school notebook back to a friend whose house he tries to find. The extraordinary *Life and Nothing More . . .* (1992), a film that looks at disaster with rare self-possession—without despair and equally without the facile resignation its other English title, *And Life Goes On,* would suggest—returns to that region of northern Iran after the devastating earthquake of 1990. Once again this is a kind of neorealist picaresque, but now the main character is a filmmaker, a stand-in for Kiarostami, who drives with his son to that devastated region in search of the boy who played the lead in *Where Is the Friend's House?* He finds the boy who played the friend and at the end, in an extreme long shot that evokes both the puniness and the grandeur of human strivings, we see his car failing and then succeeding in the attempt to go up a steep hill on the road to the other boy's village. Kiarostami's next film, *Through the Olive Trees* (1994), has another stand-in for the director and takes as its central situation the filming of a scene in *Life and Nothing More . . .* and the courtship that actually developed during that filming between the young man and the young woman locally recruited to play newlyweds in the scene. Kiarostami's twist on neorealism brings the filmmaker into the film, visibly involves him in the reality being represented, as none of the films of the Italian neorealists and few of the films of their modernist successors ever did. Kiarostami makes with remarkable naturalness the move from naturalism to modernism, from the representation of reality to the representation, as part of reality, of the means of representation.

In *Life and Nothing More . . .* and *Through the Olive Trees* two different actors impersonate a film director, the crime for which the protagonist of *Close-Up,* an unemployed printer named Hossein Sabzian, is arrested and brought to trial. Partly a documentary of Sabzian's trial and partly a reconstruction of events leading up to his arrest, *Close-Up* makes us aware of the construction in the documentary and of the documentary in the reconstruction. It is Kiarostami's most complex reflection so far on reality and its representation. For Rosenbaum it is his most uncompromising exposure of misrepresentation:

Beginning with one lie, Sabzian's impersonation, Kiarostami proceeded to generate several other lies—or at best half-truths—by getting all of the people to impersonate themselves. . . . The reporter, Sabzian, and Kiarostami are playing three different versions of the same game, each capitalizing on the awe and intimidation ordinary people feel about movies; by the time the film is over, every participant—including the family, the judge, Makhmalbaf, and the audience—has agreed to become an active part of the boondoggle.[9]

For Rosenbaum impersonation is indeed a crime of which everybody here is guilty, though Kiarostami wins acquittal because he is seen to plead guilty. This is a postmodern view of the matter, the view that everybody lies, artists and politicians, institutions and individuals alike, that there's no such thing as the truth and even if there were you couldn't get to it anyway, that the only thing to be done is a critique, an assertion that you're not being taken in. This may be the view we've come to in our society of the spectacle, but it is not the view Kiarostami expresses in his film.

(It would not be fair to impute this complacent postmodern skepticism to Jonathan Rosenbaum, a humane critic and a seeker of truth. But this skepticism is so much in the air these days that it seeps into his article even if he doesn't subscribe to it himself. There have been times when skepticism and cynicism could be a resistance to the established order, but this isn't one of those times: skepticism and cynicism are practically the official philosophy of late capitalism.)

When Kiarostami first interviews Sabzian, first gives us the close-up from which the film takes its title, Sabzian sends a message to Makhmalbaf: "Tell him his last film is my life." Sabzian impersonated Makhmalbaf out of admiration, love of art and especially of art that tells the truth about life; and it was a similar love of art that led the family to be taken in by the impersonation and allow this stranger into their home. The family may be naive, though they object to the reporter's having so characterized them in his article; Sabzian too may be naive in his love of art, or he may be lying, putting on an act as the poor man sensitive to art as he put on an act as Makhmalbaf to impress a rich family sensitive to art. The close-up is not necessarily the truth, and Kiarostami wants us to be aware of that; but he does not want us to discount it as necessarily a lie. For Kiarostami, for the society in which he works, art counts, and counts not just as a critique telling us to discount it. Art is a construction, and must be recognized as such, but that doesn't mean that the only thing to be done about it is deconstruction.

Close-Up ends with a sequence done in long shot. Sabzian comes out of jail and, in an encounter arranged by Kiarostami, meets the real Makhmalbaf and rides with him on his motorbike to the family residence where he impersonated him. At the trial one of the family's sons recounted how Sabzian swindled him out of a fair amount of money when, riding with him on his motorbike, he pretended to have lost his wallet and, playing the film director, said he had an idea for a sequence in which two men ride on a motorbike, one loses his wallet, the other lends him money, and the two become friends. Now Sabzian rides with the real film director and borrows money from him to buy flowers for the family he deceived; whether the two will become friends, whether they and the family will become friends—the poor man and the rich family and the artist who brings them together—is at least a possibility. Kiarostami shoots this sequence in the style of a documentary rather than a neorealist reconstruction, but not a documentary in the close-up style he has been employing; instead he adopts the long-shot style of a camera and microphone taken out into the streets to capture as best they can the sights and sounds of ongoing life. He presents the meeting between Sabzian and Makhmalbaf as if he and his crew were eavesdropping on it, and by creating the illusion of unrehearsed actuality, with a distant camera tracking the two men from a van and faulty sound recording letting us hear their conversation only intermittently, by a paradox of art he creates the aesthetic distance fitting for this scene, the room our imagination needs for its flight.

The flowers Sabzian and Makhmalbaf pick up on their way to the family refer us back to the flowers the cab driver picked out right outside their gate in the opening sequence. Picking out those flowers, we remember,

Close-Up. The director, the impostor, and the flowers.

set the aerosol can loose on its rolling course. If the aerosol can represents truth, the truth naturalism seeks in the details of life, the flowers represent beauty. As the can may be taken as a metaphor for the means of naturalistic art, so the flowers may be taken as a metaphor for what art can do, what the experience of art can do for us, what art can make happen. If in quest of beauty the cab driver set truth loose to roll on its course, in quest of truth Kiarostami sets beauty free to soar in our minds. The flowers Sabzian and Makhmalbaf pick up become the focus of the camera tracking them from its van, and on the soundtrack their faultily recorded conversation gives way to music. Their faulty rapport with each other, our faulty connection with them, gives way to the promise of happiness that for Stendhal defines beauty. This does not signal a happy ending but a happy beginning on which we end, having reached no settled harmony but only the possibility that harmony might be reached: art cannot make us happy, cannot make us live happily with one another, but it can give us a taste of what that might be like. Kiarostami believes in beauty as he believes in truth, not as a conclusion but as an undertaking.

There is another, earlier book with the same title as Bürger's but with a different point of view, Renato Poggioli's *Theory of the Avant-Garde*. For Poggioli, whose book appeared in the sixties, the art of the avant-garde spans a century and more, beginning in the aftermath of romanticism and continuing into the present and the foreseeable future. What Poggioli calls avant-garde is what others (not he) call modernism, and includes the historical avant-garde that Bürger sees as a break with modernism and others (not he) relate to postmodernism. Bürger's historical avant-garde was a short-lived fusillade, a failed attack on the bourgeois institution of art from movements like dada and surrealism, whereas in Poggioli's view the art of the avant-garde is the art of alienation and will last as long as alienation lasts in bourgeois society. The revolt against art of Bürger's historical avant-garde is for Poggioli but an episode in the longstanding avant-garde revolt against official culture—"the genuine art of a bourgeois society," he says, "can only be antibourgeois"[10]—a revolt that can be traced back to the romantic rebellion against the classical norms of aristocratic culture.

The alienation of avant-garde art Poggioli theorizes is not only alienation from official culture; it is also—and in his view this sets it apart from the romantic movement with its populist tendency—alienation from popular culture. For many others besides Poggioli, alienation from the popular, not merely disdain but a more embattled opposition, has been central to the avant-garde impulse. American avant-garde film, for example, has largely defined itself in opposition to Hollywood. The Hollywood movie is deemed the epitome of the popular pseudoculture, or kitsch, that Greenberg, in "Avant-Garde and Kitsch," the 1939 essay that launched his intellectual career, saw as the antithesis of the "only living culture we now have," the culture of the avant-garde. "Simultaneously with the entrance of the avant-garde," he wrote,

> a second new cultural phenomenon appeared in the industrial West: that thing to which the Germans give the wonderful name of *Kitsch:* popular, commercial art and literature with their chromeotypes, magazine covers, illustrations, ads, slick and pulp fiction, comics, Tin Pan Alley music, tap dancing, Hollywood movies, etc., etc. . . . .
>
> The peasants who settled in the cities as proletariat and petty bourgeois . . . did not win the leisure and comfort necessary for the enjoyment of the city's traditional culture. Losing, nevertheless, their taste for the folk culture whose background was the countryside, and discovering a new capacity for boredom at the same time, the new urban masses set up a pressure on society to provide them with a kind of culture fit for their own consumption. To fill the demand of the new market, a new commodity was devised: ersatz culture, kitsch, destined for those who, insensible to the values of genuine culture, are hungry nevertheless for the diversion that only culture of some sort can provide.
>
> Kitsch, using for raw material the debased and academicized simulacra of genuine culture, welcomes and cultivates this insensibility. . . . Kitsch is mechanical and operates by formulas. Kitsch is vicarious experience and faked sensations.[11]

Commenting on Greenberg's essay, Poggioli stresses the modernity of the concept of kitsch, of the notion that the derivative, the formulaic, the ersatz, makes for inferior art. Classical art saw nothing wrong with the imitation and repetition of norms and models of beauty; it was the romantic movement, and after it the avant-garde, that prized novelty and originality and gave them aesthetic primacy. The Hollywood movie is another descendant of romanticism, but one that sees nothing wrong with imitation and repetition and the adherence to norms. In the dichotomy of avant-garde and kitsch it can only be kitsch. But *classical* would be another term for it, romantically classical, popularly rather than aristocratically classical.

What Greenberg calls "avant-garde" in "Avant-Garde and Kitsch"—and in "Towards a Newer Laocoon," a companion essay he published the next year—later he would more often call "modernism." The shift in vocabulary does not reflect a shift in taste—over the years Greenberg remained pretty consistent in the kind of art he liked—but a shift in political position. *Avant-garde* was originally a political term, and even after it came to be applied primarily to art it has kept something of a militant connotation, a sense of the subversive. Not that he ever saw the avant-garde as revolutionary, but the earlier Greenberg was a Marxist who saw bourgeois culture as decadent and the avant-garde as a vital response to that decadence; his championing of avant-garde against kitsch, undertaken from a Trotskyist standpoint of opposition to Stalinism and to the cultural politics of the Popular Front, belonged in a context of revolutionary aspiration. The later Greenberg belonged in a different context, one of Cold War anti-Communism, and in the art he admired he tried to downplay as much as possible any suggestion of the militant and the subversive. The earlier Greenberg was no less an aesthetic purist than the later, no less a believer in the autonomy of art, no less an exponent of the "modernist" principle that art should concern itself above all with its own means and medium. Earlier as later, Greenberg espoused abstraction in art, but later he tended to regard art in abstraction from society as he had not earlier.[12]

In the area of cinema, some have attempted to affix the term *modernism,* following the sense of the later Greenberg, to the kind of avant-garde film that renounces representation and gives itself over to the formal problems of the medium.[13] Presumably the term *avant-garde* would then be reserved for alternative cinema of a more political kind. But the term *avant-garde* as applied to films has too long been associated with formal experimentation and a bent toward abstraction to be available for use in a different sense. The later Greenberg may have preferred the term *modernism,* but he continued to use *avant-garde* as an equivalent term. Neither in cinema nor in the other arts can a sharp and stable distinction be drawn between the two terms.

Bürger's *Theory of the Avant-Garde* attempts to draw such a distinction. On modernism Bürger invokes not Greenberg but Adorno, whose conception parallels Greenberg's. (Adorno started from modern music, Greenberg from modern art, and they reached similar conclusions about modernism; what each may have owed the other, or whether each developed his conception independently of the other, isn't clear.) What, according to Bürger, distinguishes the historical avant-garde from the preceding modernism is the avant-garde attempt to break down the institution of art that had fostered modernism. But what, exactly, is the institution of art? Bürger goes into no details about ministries or museums, academies or the art market. He gives no answer more precise than this: the institution of art is the autonomy of art in bourgeois society.

Art as a blanket term for poetry and painting, music and architecture, was a bourgeois invention. As this notion of art came into being, in the later eighteenth century, so did the notion of its autonomy from the church and the state and all the practical purposes of life. In aesthetic experience, said Kant, we find "purposiveness without purpose," a purposiveness that engages our faculties and a lack of purpose that allows them free play. Kant maintained that aesthetic experience is disinterested, by which he meant its indifference as regards the existence of its objects: its autonomy from the concerns of actual existence. Bürger argues that this autonomy, which for him constitutes the bourgeois institution of art, reached its full development in the aestheticism of the late nineteenth century, which for him constitutes modernism, and that the historical avant-garde reacted against such aestheticism and sought to bring art out of its autonomy and into the concerns and purposes of life.

For Bürger bourgeois art culminates in aestheticism; but if the aesthete is a bourgeois type, so also is the moralizer who looks to art for edification and uplift. And surely the moralizer better typifies what art has represented in bourgeois society. In "The Dehumanization of Art" Ortega y Gasset hailed the new art of the early twentieth century as a turning away from the moralizing bourgeois art that had dominated the previous hundred years. Writing in the twenties, at the time of Bürger's historical avant-garde, Ortega saw the new art in a way diametrically opposed to Bürger's, as a reaction not against an art that was too detached from life but against an art that was too involved with it. For Ortega it was nineteenth-century art that "asked to be placed in connection with dramatic social and political movements, or else with profound philosophical or religious currents"; he admired in the new art precisely the reverse of what Bürger theorizes. "To the young generation," wrote Ortega,

> art is a thing of no consequence. . . . I do not mean to say that the artist makes light of his work and his profession; but they interest him precisely because they are of no transcendent importance. For a real understanding of what is happening let us compare the role art is playing today with the role it used to play thirty years ago and in general throughout the last century. Poetry and music were then activities of enormous weight: nothing less was expected of them than the salvation of humanity. . . . It was a remarkable sight, the solemn

posture with which the great poet or the musical genius appeared before the masses, the posture of a prophet or founder of a religion, the majestic pose of a statesman responsible for the fate of the world.

An artist of today would be terrified, I suspect, to be entrusted with so enormous a mission and thus obliged to deal in his work with matters of such great consequence. Something begins to taste like art to him precisely when he notices that the air loses seriousness and things start skipping lightly, free of all formality. . . . . If it can be said that art saves man, it is only because it saves him from the seriousness of life.[14]

Ortega may go too far in stressing the "dehumanization" of the new art, its detachment from life's concerns, but he accurately characterizes nineteenth-century art in its deep involvement with life. It is true that the movements of Bürger's historical avant-garde disclaimed any privileged aesthetic realm, that the surrealists, for example, sought a new interpenetration of art and life, but surely the surrealists were heir to the romantics and their subversive and redemptive aspirations. The notion of art's autonomy we inherit from Kant means that art is not to be governed by outside interests or dictates; it is a mistake to suppose it means that art is to have nothing to do with life.

The repudiation of art's autonomy that defines the historical avant-garde for Bürger as a break with modernism is for many a mark of postmodernism.[15] But the historical avant-garde wasn't a break with modernism except in the way modernism was continually breaking with itself, in revolt against established convention including its own, what Harold Rosenberg called the "tradition of the new." Rather than a break, it would be better to say that the historical avant-garde was the last phase of European modernism—and that postmodernism is a specifically American phenomenon. The United States rose to world power at the time of modernism, and after a history of mistrusting and marginalizing art, at the height of its power the high art it institutionalized was the art of modernism, the poetry of T. S. Eliot, the painting of Picasso, the architecture of Mies van der Rohe—and the homegrown modernism (with Greenberg as a house critic) of the New York school. This was, in the years between the Second World War and the Vietnam War, the American equivalent of Racine and Poussin and Versailles in the France of the Sun King. Postmodernism emerged as a reaction against the institution of modernism in the United States. But it is not anti-institutional. From its inception postmodernism was fostered by institutions, by the academy and the media, the museum and the market, the cultural agencies and the givers of grants.

Some postmodernists deem modernism too negative, too critical, too austere, too exclusive: less is less, they say, and they want more, they want to have more fun. Other postmodernists, who think of themselves as radical, deem modernism not negative enough, not critical and oppositional enough: they want no fun at all, it seems, only the gratifications of puritanism, the pleasure that can be derived from the righteous exclusion of pleasure. Modernism as an oppositional art has worked under a contradiction: not only has its opposition to bourgeois culture depended on bourgeois patronage but, sooner or later and more often sooner than later, its works have been incorporated into the bourgeois culture they would oppose, recuperated for the established order. Postmodernists of the righteous sort conclude from this that the negations of modernism have been bogus, an opposition coopted from the start. What about, it may be asked, the negations of their own postmodernism? Have these escaped dependence on bourgeois patronage and recuperation by bourgeois culture?[16]

Postmodernists of the fun-loving sort want to dance to rock music and learn from Las Vegas, to tap into the energies of the popular culture they think modernism wants nothing to do with. One of the distinguishing traits of postmodernism, we hear, is that it does away with the hostility to the popular characteristic of modernism. That hostility has indeed been characteristic of theories of modernism like Greenberg's and Adorno's, but the actual artistic practice of modernism tells a different story. A different story from the beginning: "Manet's *Olympia*," wrote Thomas Crow, "offered a bewildered middle-class public the flattened pictorial economy of the cheap sign or carnival backdrop, the pose and allegories of contemporary pornography superimposed over those of Titian's *Venus of Urbino*."[17] From the beginning, and again and again in the course of its development, from the impressionist pastoral of popular leisure to the cubist collage bringing in pasted bits of vernacular graphics, from *Madame Bovary* and *Ulysses* to *The Threepenny Opera* and *Waiting for Godot*, modernism has been actively engaged with the popular.

Adorno and Greenberg were wrong in their sweeping dismissal of popular culture. Adorno's essay against jazz is hard to forgive, not for being mistaken but for the arrogance of its ignorance.[18] Around the time Greenberg was writing "Avant-Garde and Kitsch," Hollywood was making, along with plenty of stuff warranting dismissal as kitsch, such films as *Swing Time* and *History Is Made at Night*, *Stagecoach* and *Young Mr. Lincoln*, *Mr. Smith Goes to Washington* and *His Girl Friday*, to name a few of the high points attained by a popular art in its classical style. And Adorno and Greenberg were wrong in their belief that the modernism they championed depended on a rejection of the popular as haughty as their own. Although Adorno and Greenberg—the earlier Greenberg, at least—valued the avant-garde as a contestation of bourgeois culture, their rejection of popular art in the name of high art pointed the way to the recuperation of the avant-garde as high art enshrined by the bourgeois culture it intended to contest.

Popular movies may be institutional, and they may sometimes be high art, but even if they have been received into the academy and the museum, they are still not institutional high art. The movies as an institution offer distraction, an opiate for the masses; high art as an institution confers prestige, flattery for the privileged and intimidation for the unprivileged. Many—all those who feel insecure about their position, and that probably includes most of us who have a stake in these matters—walk the line between such flattery and such intimidation. Postmodernists of the righteous sort are mistaken if they think they can escape such flattery and intimidation by renouncing the aesthetic claims of high art, for that renunciation carries its own flattery and intimidation, surely no less strong. The distraction of the culture industry and the prestige of high culture may work to similar ideological effect, but they work through different institutional channels. Hollywood movies and (as Serge Guilbaut has argued) the modernist high art of the New York school may alike have served the national purposes of the United States during the Cold War, but the movies and the art reached different publics and reached them in different ways. For all the talk, not to mention the fact, of movies as art, the powers that be for some reason have not seen fit to institutionalize them as art. The popular media construct them as mere popular entertainment, and so, by and large, do those who teach them in the academy. This means that, at least, a taste for the movies is still relatively unburdened either by the flattery of belonging to an aristocracy of taste or by the intimidation of not belonging.

" 'The one thing that can ruin everything revolutionary,' said Lenin in April 1917, 'is the phrase—this flattery of the revolutionary people.' " This is Meyer Schapiro in the *Marxist Quarterly* of October–December 1937, quoting Lenin in a review of a book about Mexico with paintings by Diego Rivera and text by Bertram D. Wolfe. Rivera's murals, wrote Schapiro, "produce a powerful impression of the density of historical life, the struggles, heroes, festivals, labor and slogans of a whole people. No other painter of our time has been so prolific and inexhaustibly curious about life and history. With all its limitations, Rivera's art is the nearest to a modern epic painting." But these murals were done under the patronage of a Mexican state that, in Wolfe's account, only pretended to revolutionary socialism. Are they then, asked Schapiro, since their revolutionary content may be seen to have served the false pretenses of a pseudorevolutionary government, to be judged politically reactionary? Are the criteria of the political character of a work of art, he inquired,

> to be found in the intentions of the artist or in the interests of the group which pays for the work? In the work itself, in what is represented or conveyed, or in the momentary effects on those to whom the work is addressed, effects which largely depend on changing circumstances? And can these effects be prejudged from the doctrines and actions presented imaginatively in such art? (There are also the criteria of revolutionary sensibility and "nourishment" which Rivera has mysteriously applied to the "revolutionary" Cézanne: "even if he painted a loaf of bread there was in it the reflection of the character of the revolutionary artist," he wrote in 1933.) It is conceivable that an art which avows a socialist doctrine may support attitudes dangerous to the working class. It may idealize violence, leadership, or national tradition in a manner congenial to fascism; it may lull its audience with reassuring images of the expected change, creating an agreeable atmosphere of revolutionary security and converting the issues of action, the stubborn obstacles and shortcomings, into ordered images of triumph. The sculptures of the Last Judgment on the portals of the cathedrals often show bishops and kings in hell, and offer to the worshippers discontented with the feudal hierarchy the guarantee that the Church has listened to their charges and is on their side. The ease with which slogans of socialism are appropriated by the fascists indicates how great is the gulf between slogans and action, between general assertions and effective tactics. And in so far as the revolutionary work of art projects slogans, phrases and their counterpart images, in so far as it forms a spectacle rather than determines an action, its effect in stirring the imagination may be manipulated in contrary ways. "The one thing that can ruin everything revolutionary," said Lenin in April 1917, "is the phrase—this flattery of the revolutionary people." On the other hand, works without political intention have by their honesty and vigor excited men to a serious questioning of themselves and their loyalties; they have destroyed the faith in feudal or bourgeois values and helped to create the moral courage necessary for revolutionary action and will.[19]

If art is to be judged by its political effects, so should anti-art. To the flattery of aesthetic revolutionism, to the self-congratulation of the avant-garde, the flattery of anti-aesthetic revolutionism, the self-congratulation of the righteous Left, is scarcely to be preferred. If aesthetic revolutionism partakes of bourgeois aestheticism, anti-aesthetic revolutionism no less partakes of bourgeois moralism.

The problem with judging art by its political effects is not that this measure is too crude but, on the contrary, that it is too fluid and fraught with imponderables. That is what the autonomy of art means, not that art is above politics but that it cannot be so easily subsumed politically. Devotees of the avant-garde feel that the art they like is an act of resistance to the established order. Devotees of kick-ass action movies no doubt feel likewise. The avant-garde set looks down on the kick-ass crowd as mindless; the kick-ass crowd looks down on the avant-garde set as useless. It may be that both that crowd and that set feel the same discontent with bourgeois society, that both avant-garde art and action movies give expression to that discontent, and that by giving it expression they help channel it into some kind of movement toward change. Or it may be that by making their audiences feel they are resisting the system, they just make them feel better about themselves and thus help perpetuate the way things are. Contrary to what Adorno and the earlier Greenberg thought, one cannot found a preference for the avant-garde over popular culture on the basis of an opposition to the established order. But then, contrary to what some current practitioners of cultural studies seem to think, one cannot found on that basis a preference for popular culture either.

If, in the older arts, it is not quite clear what the avant-garde, what modernism is, in the art of film it is even less clear. If the avant-garde characteristically strives to "make it new," if that defines the art of modernism, then it may be concluded either that the art of film, because new, is automatically modern, or that it is automatically not modern because, being new to begin with, it cannot be part of the striving to make it new. For some devotees of the avant-garde, film is an inherently modern art betrayed by Hollywood into the ways of traditionalism, whereas for others, devotees of the Hollywood movie, film has been exempted from the imperatives of the modern and enabled to flourish as the last traditional art. And for still others, film started becoming modern when it ceased being new, when the forms and conventions of classical cinema started losing their vitality and their viability. For these last the key figure in the rise of a film modernism was Jean-Luc Godard, who came to filmmaking with a self-conscious awareness of what had been done in the past and a readiness to ransack it, and who more boldly and broadly than anyone before him took apart the diverse artifice of the medium while rescuing it for his purposes until, around 1968, he apparently decided it was beyond rescue.

Watching Godard's films when they were coming out in the sixties gave me, at an impressionable age, my first experience of modernism in art. The modern literature I had read, the modern painting I had seen, was art already recognized, art hanging in museums, and though I have always liked going to museums, as Gertrude Stein said about the Museum of Modern Art, you cannot be a museum and also be modern—not in the way modernism wants to be modern, not in the way Godard's films impressed me as modern in the sixties. "Godard's films haven't yet been elevated to the status of classics or masterpieces," wrote Susan Sontag in February 1968. "They retain their youthful power to offend, to appear 'ugly,' irresponsible, frivolous, pretentious, empty."[20] Keeping up with his films as they were coming out, one or two, maybe as many as three beautiful and bewildering films a year, films by turns or even at once frustrating and exhilarating, flippant and moving, uncouth and exquisite, films one often didn't know quite what to make of and argued about and changed one's mind about, films that engaged one on many shifting levels and refused to stay put in one's response— keeping up with those films was a heady experience of the kind of art that pulls the rug from under one's feet, the kind that will not allow one a settled ground for one's experience of it.

Godard's modernism promiscuously embraced popular culture. Virtually all the "popular, commercial art and literature" on Greenberg's kitsch list, the "magazine covers, illustrations, ads, slick and pulp fiction, comics, Tin Pan Alley music, tap dancing, Hollywood movies, etc., etc." found its way into Godard's work—above all the "Hollywood movies, etc., etc.," the forms, the characters, the genres of popular film, the gangster and the fallen woman, the private eye and the outlaw couple, film noir and science fiction, the musical and the war movie, the thriller and the television documentary, all called into question yet all pressed into service. Those who posit an opposition between the modern and the popular may see Godard's embrace of the popular as heralding the postmodern. But if we recognize the long-standing commerce between modern art and popular culture, we can see that Godard's films of the sixties were in the modernist line of the impressionist pastoral and the cubist collage. The Godard involved with popular culture was a modernist; a better candidate for a postmodern Godard, postmodern of the righteous sort, was the drearily politicized Godard who emerged around 1968, the Godard who gave up on the popular and on almost everything that would engage the public in favor of the kind of critique that appeals exclusively to the converted, the theoretically converted postmodernists who are fighting political battles in their heads. Still another Godard emerged in the eighties, a post-postmodern Godard who is again a modernist, though not so popularly involved a modernist as the Godard of the sixties.

Modernism is not a style. Cubism and impressionism are both forms of modernism and yet, stylistically, they are as far apart from each other as Renaissance and baroque. Modernism is not a style but a stance, not a stance against realism or against the popular, not any settled stance but a stance against the settled, a stance of questioning, of self-questioning. What, then, can postmodernism be? It can be a stance of acceptance, postmodernism of the fun-loving sort, or it can be a stance of certainty, postmodernism of the righteous sort. But things have been more confused than that. In America, where for a spell modernism became the established high art, postmodernism has been for many a vague slogan of dissent, serviceable for a variety of postures and purposes, from whatever is thought to be the establishment. And Europeans have offered their own versions of the postmodern that see it more as an aspect of the modern than as a departure from it. Slavoj Zizek sees artists like Kafka and Hitchcock as postmodern. Jean-François Lyotard sees the postmodern as marking the moment after one phase of modernist innovation has gained acceptance and before the next phase begins: the postmodern not as a break with the modern but as the moment between modernist breaks. If the modern is a succession of breaks, what kind of break

History Lessons. The young man driving.

can the postmodern be? We can be sure, as I have said, that in the future, the not too distant future, our notions of modernism and postmodernism will be significantly recast.

For long stretches in *History Lessons,* a film made in 1972 by Jean-Marie Straub and Danièle Huillet, the camera is inside a car a young man drives around the streets of Rome. As the little car wends its way through the city streets, in the wider avenues and the narrower alleys, the emptier and the more crowded places, as accordingly it speeds up or slows down, as it makes turns and gets caught in traffic and sometimes stops or backs up, the camera all the while maintains a fixed position in the back seat looking out toward the front. Without any cuts or pans or even the slightest wavering, the city is photographed from that fixed viewing point inside the moving car, through a kind of compositional grid constituted by the two side windows on the left and right of the screen, the windshield at the center, and an open sunroof at the top. Built into the photographic image are the rectangular frame and the perspective of an individual viewing point conventional in Western painting since the Renaissance, and here our attention is called to that construction, basic to any picture, moving or still, made with a camera. Here the camera is both moving and still: moving with the car and quite still within it. What appears in the picture may move and shift all it wants but the manner of picturing it stays put: the camera always works in the same way, and here we are made aware of its way of working. We are made conscious of the perspective imposed from that single viewing point in the back seat, as we are made conscious of the unchanging frame and the gridlike partitioning of our view: it is like watching the set pictorial scheme of a Renaissance painting carried around the city streets and applied to the diverse actualities there encountered.

Here we can plainly see why some say the painters invented photography "by bequeathing it their framing, the Albertian perspective, and the optic of the *camera obscura,*" as Roland Barthes wrote.[21] But at the same time we get a vivid sense of the documentary image, of the city streets and the people in them and the young man driving his car in their midst. Seldom has the camera been taken out into the streets with such concreteness, such utter specificity of time and place. Not only the camera but the microphone as well: Straub and Huillet are sticklers for direct sound, and we hear the actual sounds of the city recorded on the spot. And so we can as plainly see why Barthes says it was not the painters but the chemists who invented photography by enabling it to capture directly the actual look (and here also the sound) of things: "From a real body, which was there, proceed radiations which ultimately touch me, who am here."

For Greenberg photography could not be a modernist art because its interest was "literary," extrinsic to itself, in what it tells about reality rather than in its own resources as a medium; but the reality represented, the real body that was there before the camera, is not extrinsic to photography but intrinsic to its medium of representation. For Barthes too the interest of photography lay not so much in its form as in its content, and especially in the kind of content that breaks through the form of a picture, the detail that sticks out, the element that does not fit into the arrangement, what he called the *punctum*: "A photograph's *punctum* is that accident which pricks me (but also bruises me, is poignant to me)."[22] Barthes did not think of the *punctum* as "literary" but on the contrary as unnameable, unamenable to meaning: "What I can name cannot really prick me. The incapacity to name is a good symptom of disturbance."[23] In *History Lessons* the perspective from the back seat and the framing through the windshield and windows and sunroof are the form, the container photography inherits from the tradition of Western painting; the content is all we see out there, all we can glimpse in the city streets, a content uncontainable by the form, spilling out of it like liquid through a sieve. All that comes into view in the streets of Rome is a *punctum* that breaks through the form of the picture, a detail unamenable to meaning, a disturbance to the arrangement. Those who find these sequences boring, who say that nothing happens when so much is happening out there, are bored not for lack of action but for lack of a scheme of meaning that would subsume all that action going on in the streets. In modernist fashion, Straub and Huillet are acknowledging the conditions of photographic representation, the camera's encounter with the contingent, both the artifice and the reality that go into the photographic image. This is another example of the nexus between naturalism and modernism, but here that nexus resides in the very constitution of the photographic image, its invention both by the chemists and by the painters, its direct derivation from reality and its built-in application of forms of pictorial construction handed down from the Renaissance.

Because the photographic image is peculiarly close to reality there is a tendency to take it as a transparent window on reality, as if the camera could bring before our eyes the very appearance of things in the world. A photographed tree is a real tree that was there before the camera, but what we have before our eyes is not the real tree but a picture, an image framed and flat. And yet it is a documentary image: not the real tree but a trace it has left us, something like its shadow preserved in the form of a picture, a construction that yet carries something of the tree's reality. If those who stress the peculiar realism of photography tend to slight its artifice, those who stress the illusoriness of the image tend to slight its source in reality. In *History Lessons* the artifice and the reality get equal stress. We are denied the illusion of reality without being allowed to forget the fact of its photographic reproduction— the fact that this is a picture taken of reality, a construction but not a pure fabrication, not a firsthand experience of the streets of Rome but not a self-contained design apart from life either. Rather than dematerializing the image before our eyes, as if watching it were just like being there ourselves, or the reality before the camera, as if the image constituted a realm of its own, Straub and Huillet materialize the commerce between the image and reality peculiar to a medium both pictorial and documentary. The image in *History Lessons* is to be recognized both as an image, a piece of artifice, and as the imprint of a piece of reality: as a documentary image.

"The greatness of film is the humbleness of being condemned to photography," Straub and Huillet believe. In his book on their work Barton Byg quotes this statement and maintains that their films "evoke the photographic immediacy of the early cinema" and that "this acceptance of photography as a baseline clearly distinguishes Straub/Huillet from the avant-garde."[24] But only some avant-garde films renounce photographic representation. If mainstream cinema often borders on the documentary from the side of the dramatic, avant-garde cinema often borders on the documentary from the side of the abstract or the visionary. The comparison to early cinema is apt: the work of Straub and Huillet indeed conveys a sense of seeing the world pictured on the screen as if for the first time, letting the world be as the camera captures what was there. But "photographic immediacy" seems wrong: this is what *was* there, we always feel in their work, not what is there on the screen before us, which is but an image, a remnant of what is *not* there. Photography is an art of the remnant. Photography gives us what has been, said Barthes, who thought that cinema gives us something quite different, the past of the photographic image animated into a present. But cinema is not as simple as that. Straub and Huillet rigorously give us a cinema of what has been, a deeply photographic cinema but not at all a cinema of immediacy.

In *The Country and the City* Raymond Williams quotes from Virginia Woolf's *Orlando:*

The Old Kent Road was very crowded on Thursday, the eleventh of October, 1928. People spilt off the pavement. There were women with shopping-bags. Children ran out. There were sales at drapers' shops. Streets widened and narrowed. Long vistas steadily shrunk together. Here was a market. Here a funeral. Here a procession with banners upon which was written 'Ra-Un', but what else? Meat was very red. Butchers stood at the door. Women almost had their heels sliced off. Amor Vin—that was over a porch. A woman looked out of a bedroom window, profoundly contemplative, and very still. Applejohn and Applebed, Undert ——. Nothing could be seen whole or read from start to finish. What was seen begun—like two friends starting to meet each other across the street—was never seen ended. After twenty minutes the body and mind were like scraps of torn paper tumbling from a sack and, indeed, the process of motoring fast out of London so much resembles the chopping up small of identity which precedes unconsciousness and perhaps death itself that it is an open question in what sense Orlando can be said to have existed at the present moment.

"This fragmentary experience," Williams comments,

> —now accelerated by "motoring fast"—has remained a perceptual condition. It is deeply related to several characteristic forms of modern imagery, most evident in painting and especially in film which as a medium contains much of its intrinsic movement. There is indeed a direct relation between the motion picture, especially in its development in cutting and montage, and the characteristic movement of an observer in the close and miscellaneous environment of the streets.[25]

The car rides through the streets of Rome in *History Lessons* are in the line of this characteristic modern imagery, this characteristic modern experience, the shifting and opaque surface of the city, the rush and diversity of particulars one can neither fully assimilate nor safely disregard. But there is no cutting in these sequences, no montage: no attempt to shape or interpret the experience, merely the camera's fixed stare from the back seat. Straub and Huillet see no reason to embellish that documentary stare. Photography, after all, was invented for just the purpose of recording the particulars of modern life; it became important to record them faithfully precisely because their meaning is uncertain, elusive; one has to pay more attention to the surface when it isn't so clear what lies behind.

All that is left out of our view from the back seat of the car, all that we see distantly and partially and might have seen more clearly and more fully, is brought to our awareness as we ride around Rome with the young man. Except for the color and sound, the direct sound picked up in the city streets, these sequences—there are three of them in the film, each lasting about ten minutes—recall the technique of early cinema; with a camera freed from a fixed viewing position, with cutting and montage, we would have seen more and seen more clearly. But we still wouldn't have seen enough, we still wouldn't have seen all that needs seeing; we might have gotten the illusion of a full picture but only if we consented to shut out of our minds all that would still be missing. By limiting us to what we can see from the back seat of the car, Straub and Huillet make us notice what we are not seeing and lead us to recognize the inescapable limitation of our view. The camera is equated with that other machine to which it is affixed and with which it moves around, the car, bodily there in the world's midst, moving as the world allows and limited in its access, which is our access, to what the world allows. Obviously the camera need not have been limited to the particular path followed by the car, but any other course the camera might have followed would still have yielded only a particular sequence of partial views.

Long thought a higher thing than history, poetry in the nineteenth century began to seek a ground in history. Poetry, said Aristotle,

> should have for its subject a single action, whole and complete, with a beginning, a middle, and an end. It will thus resemble a living organism in all its unity, and produce the pleasure proper to it. It will differ in structure from historical compositions, which of necessity present, not a single action, but a single period, and all that happened within that period to one person or to many, little connected together as the events may be. For as the sea fight at Salamis and the battle with the Carthaginians in Sicily took place at the same time, but did not tend to any one result, so in the sequence of events one thing sometimes follows another, and yet no single result is thereby produced.[26]

As opposed to the disunity of history, Aristotle valued the unity of poetry, the pleasure that comes from seeing something whole, the satisfaction of a beginning, a middle, and an end. But in the streets of our modernity nothing can be seen whole, what is seen begun, as Virginia Woolf tells us, is never seen ended. This fragmentary experience, which some postmodernists seem to think was born with television, goes back at least as far as the London of Blake and Wordsworth at the turn of the nineteenth century.[27] It is the characteristic experience of the city of industrial capitalism, and the characteristic imagery of the art of modernism. Whereas the poet of Aristotle's day was licensed to leave out that sea battle if it seemed irrelevant, to set aside mere particulars in pursuit of the essential, the modern poet can no longer decide with the old confidence that the sea battle need not be taken into account, that any of the world's innumerable particulars may not after all be relevant to the matter at hand. Poetry can no longer trust the old universals and seeks a ground in the shifting particulars of history.

One must put everything into a film, Godard once said; nothing can be left out with impunity, everything in the complex world of our modernity may pertain to the story one is telling, the picture one is painting, the film one is making. Beginning in the nineteenth century, and more and more as we move through the twentieth, events all over the world must be reckoned as possibly having a bearing on any matter at hand. But of course one can't put everything into a film: one can only acknowledge all that is left out, one can only make the viewer aware of the omission, aware of the choice to picture this in this way rather than that in that way, aware of the means and the medium one employs to represent things and the slant one brings to them.

If, in Alberti's famous metaphor, a Renaissance painting is a window, an ideal window through which the viewer sees the scene with perfect clarity, in *History Lessons* the metaphor is changed to the material windows of a car out in the streets, subject to all the limitations of our concrete existence, our immersion in the world's circumstances. The car is the young man's means of access to the reality of the city, not an ideal but visibly a material means, a means that can gain no privileged access and afford no perfect clarity, a means stuck in the world as we are all stuck and a means to which the world sticks as the mud sticks when you walk in the mud.

As we watch the streets of Rome from our perspective in the back seat, at the center of the screen is the rear-view mirror, where we see reflected the young man's eyes. Perspective is a system of representation that depicts the way things look to an individual observer, that refers the look of things to the eye of an individual implicitly observing them, and here, right at the center of this picture calling attention to the perspective system, we see the eyes of an individual explicitly depicted. It is the individual driving the car that stands for the camera, for the machinery of perspective.

But it is not the young man's perspective that we share in this picture. The young man is at the wheel, in the left front seat, and our viewing point is in the back seat on the right-hand side. The side windows and the sunroof are like an armature of lines of perspective that the car carries around the city streets and imposes on everything out there; the vanishing point at which these lines converge is the mirror image of the viewing point and is on the lower right-hand side of the windshield. If a mirror were there we would see reflected in it the eye of the camera; when we look in a mirror the lines of perspective always converge at our eyes, just as the line of moonlight on the water always comes toward our eyes; this is subjectivity.[28] Even if the subjectivity here is not exactly the young man's, it is his eyes we see reflected in that central rear-view mirror and he may be said to be a figure of the individual observer, a figure of subjectivity, the subjectivity central to the perspective system, driving the perspective car.

What perspective is to a picture, point of view is to a narrative. The young man whose eyes take up the center of the picture is the center of consciousness of the narrative. *History Lessons* is based on an unfinished historical novel by Brecht, *The Business Affairs of Mr. Julius Caesar,* which Byg describes as the narrative of a young man who "sets out to write a biography of Caesar some forty years after his death" and who "represents a consciousness to which all the contradictory evidence about Caesar's life is presented."[29] Straub and Huillet turn the young biographer of Brecht's novel, who speaks to several old men who knew Caesar, into the contemporary young man who drives the car around modern Rome and who, in sequences alternating with the car rides, speaks to the old men from ancient Rome. These are of course impossible conversations, and when we see the young man in his modern suit next to some ancient Roman dressed in a toga we are certainly not being asked to suspend our disbelief. It is quite evident that this is a fiction; any illusion of the reality of these ancient Romans is indeed dispelled. The narrative, if you like, is deconstructed. But, as Byg rightly

History Lessons. The young man driving: the lines of perspective the car carries around the city streets.

insists, it is not destroyed, it is still a narrative and the film depends on it. In however distanced a way the film still tells us a story, and the young man takes us through the story as he takes us through the streets of Rome. In however distanced a way he is still the narrative center of consciousness.

Both perspective and narrative have generally had a bad name among the avant-garde and other detractors of convention and illusion. Perspective brings the viewer into an illusory space, narrative into an illusory time and an illusory story. Perspective is what traditional painting did, dissembling the flatness of the medium with the illusion of depth; narrative is what Hollywood does, dissembling any number of realities with any number of illusions. For Lacanian-Althusserian film theory, perspective and narrative serve to promote all the deceptions that go by the name of "bourgeois ideology": perspective with its individual viewing point and narrative with its portrayal of individual characters allegedly conspire not only to instill in us the ideology of bourgeois individualism but also to give us, through our identification with the image on the screen, our illusory sense of individual identity in illusory relation to a world whose real workings are being systematically obscured from us. The unity of an image, according to Lacanian-Althusserian theory, fosters an imaginary sense of unity in the perceiving subject that makes for subjection to bourgeois ideology. In his essay "Narrative Space" Stephen Heath theorized how narrative combines with perspective to construct on the screen the unity that serves to subject us: perspective begins by giving the image the perceptual unity of a Renaissance painting, but the image moves and its movement disturbs its unity, and in order to reassert that unity narrative enters the picture and ties things together.[30] Even if one grants the Lacanian-Althusserian premise that unity is a bad thing, one cannot accept this account of the way the movies manage their unity. Like others, Heath supposes that narrative requires the deep space of Renaissance perspective, but actually the flatter space of medieval painting suits narrative better, for it better accommodates the arrangement of one thing at a time, one thing after another, the narrative sequence.

It is curious that the film theory of the seventies should have combined derogation of narrative with admiration for Brecht, the very playwright of an "epic" or *narrative* theater. But illusion was deemed the enemy, and Brecht was deemed the enemy of illusion. Brecht's alienation effect was held up as the model for what art should do: destroy illusion. It was not recognized that Brecht put a curb on dramatic illusion in order to generate a kind of narrative illusion, a kind of theater that would report rather than enact characters and events, that would represent a story no longer in the form of action but of narrative. Moreover, the alienation effect was taken as the model for political art: since the established order was thought to rest on illusion, the destruction of illusion was taken as tantamount to political subversion. No distinction was made between illusion in art and in life: the illusions art creates in its spectators were assumed to be the same thing as ideology, as the illusions a social and political order creates in its subjects. This politicizing of art was actually an aestheticizing of politics, an aestheticizing that took the negative form of a critique, an aesthetic critique believing itself to be political in its blithe equation of aesthetic effects with political effects. Aesthetically as well as politically Brecht was much cannier. He called a stage a stage; he brooked no confusion between the space of art and the space of life. His theater certainly engaged the space of life, or else it wouldn't have been a political theater, but it engaged the space of life from a space clearly marked out as a theater stage, the site of illusion rather than reality, the autonomous space of art. Maybe the autonomy of art is an illusion, but an illusion that allows space for standing back from what is and entertaining the alternative, constructing not just fantasies but the possible realities to which fantasies may lead. Brecht's was the theater, the political theater, of entertaining the alternative.

People often say they found a Brecht play moving "in spite of his intentions." They take Brecht's theater to have been against emotion and they think the alienation effect was a means of extinguishing it. But Brecht's plays are clearly intended to be moving, and the alienation effect was meant not to extinguish emotion but only to temper it, to cool down the heat of emotion the plays generate. Brecht's was a theater of consciousness, a theater that aimed to raise the spectator's consciousness. It was not a theater against emotion but only against emotion sweeping the spectators away and keeping them from thought; it was not a theater against illusion but only against illusion holding the spectators in thrall and keeping them from reflection. In the old days this needed to be said to defend Brecht against detractors devoted to the traditional theater of illusion and emotion; these days it needs to be said to defend Brecht against admirers who swear by the alienation effect and cheer at the prospect of destroying illusion and extinguishing emotion. Merely as a destroyer of illusion and extinguisher of emotion the alienation effect would do nothing that simple incompetence would not do as well. The alienation is only effective as a check on illusion, a curb on emotion, a brake on involvement. Little purpose is served by pulling us back where nothing is drawing us in.

In a poem addressed to his fellow theater workers Brecht wrote:

Leaning back the spectator
Should see
How cunningly you prepare for him
Should see
The tin moon come swaying down
And the cottage roof brought in.
Do not disclose over much
Yet disclose something to him.
Friends
Let him discover
You are not conjuring
But working.[31]

Show enough, says Brecht, for the spectator to see that art is work, not magic, but do not show so much that the illusion of art breaks down altogether. How much to show in each case—enough to reveal the workings of art but not so much as to keep art from working—is the technique of the alienation effect. Lacanian-Althusserian theory fails to grasp this. It assumes that illusion is complete, that we wholly accept as reality the representations of art or ideology, and that the alienation countering the illusion must accordingly be complete as well; it can only throw out the baby with the bath water. But as Eric Bentley said in a defense of Brecht against his illusionist detractors, "illusion is a matter of degree,"[32] and the alienation effect is a matter of degrees of illusion, degrees that can become kinds.

The view from the back seat of the car in *History Lessons* is an alienation effect pulling us back from the illusion of reality and making us conscious of the artifice of the image, of the perspective and the framing that rule the construction of the photographic image. But illusion is a matter of degree, and we retain a vivid sense of the reality of the streets even though we are quite conscious that watching the image is not the same thing as being there in reality. Having the young man meet with those old men from ancient Rome who tell him about Caesar—he speaks to a banker, a peasant, a jurist, and a poet—is again an alienation effect making unmistakable the fact that we are watching a fiction. And yet, implausible though they may be as ancient Romans meeting the young man across the ages, those old men are quite convincing as persons of a particular class and occupation, the actor's appearance and gestures and way of talking palpably evoking in each case a banker, a peasant, a jurist, and a poet we can imagine meeting in life. Alienation is a matter of degree: we may not believe this fiction but we believe something about it, something about it grabs us, something convinces us, and in that way, to that degree, we are drawn into it. If we were not drawn into the fiction there would be no point to the alienation.

"Do not disclose over much / Yet disclose something to him." By equating the camera with the car, *History Lessons* discloses to us the machinery of the camera, with its built-in framing and perspective, but it does not disclose the camera itself, which would have been to disclose over much, to make us so conscious of the picture machinery that we might have lost sight of the picture. The car is a visible means of access to the reality of the streets but the camera remains invisible, imperturbable in its alignment with the path of the car and thus imperceptible, so perfectly fixed in its position in the back seat that nothing in the picture we watch betrays its separate presence in the actual world where the car travels. The car materializes our access to that world but the camera traveling with the car, the picture machine picturing that world, is itself dematerialized. Not only do we recognize both the artifice and the reality that go into the camera's image—the car serves as a metaphor for that—but we also recognize the curious dematerialization that the image on the screen, the projector's image, undergoes. The camera is not the only picture machine picturing that world we watch on the screen. There is also the projector. The camera was there to take the picture but the projector was not there, and when the film is shown on the screen the projector takes over from the camera. If the visible car in *History Lessons* is a metaphor for the camera that was there, materially involved with the world being pictured, the invisible camera—visibly invisible, noticeably dematerialized in the projector's moving images, where for so long the camera's movement coincides so exactly with the car's—is a metaphor for the projector, the picture machine that was not there. In *History Lessons* we are made aware that the film image is both the camera's and the projector's, both material and dematerialized: the material ghost. And this awareness prepares us for our encounter with those material ghosts from ancient Rome.

On a shaded garden bench the young man sits next to the banker from ancient Rome. We see them from an oblique overhead angle behind the bench, the banker in profile and the young man from the back as he turns toward the banker, who looks straight ahead. Quickly, without changing the angle, we cut to a closer view of the banker, as if the camera couldn't wait to inspect this curious apparition in a toga; then we cross to the front of the bench for a close-up of the banker, held on the screen for a long time but still taken from an oblique overhead angle. The next shot is more frontal and nearer to eye level and shows the banker from the waist up—a more conventional view, as if the camera were now more comfortable with him. This shot of the banker is the first so far that by conventional standards could passably alternate with a reverse shot of the young man, though here the banker is not looking at the young man, and no reverse shot interrupts this long-held shot. At one point during it, however, the banker, as he disparages those generals who boast that the grass no longer grows where their legions have set foot ("You know, from one of these grasses bread is made"), suddenly glances at the young man for the first time. With the darting of this glance, off screen to the left, the implied place out of frame where the young man sits, a flash of life comes to the banker's hitherto impassive face. If the alienation effect works against our involvement in the fiction, this implied first meeting of the eyes, this glimmer of an exchange between the young man and the banker, works against our alienation from the fiction and has on us what may be called an *involvement* effect. For a moment, we are less detached, more drawn into this impossible encounter with an apparition from ancient history.

On the banker's glance, a cut to the young man's reaction would have involved us further by confirming the scarcely established eye contact. But instead the banker resumes his vacant gaze straight ahead, and we may well question why we should even assume that the young man, who so far hasn't said a word, is still there, off screen, still looking at the banker from the same place on the bench where we saw him briefly in the initial shot. We may well question, that is, why we should accept the convention of the shot, the basic convention of dramatic cinema, the convention that asks us to look at just

History Lessons. Our first view of the young man and the banker.

this, the section of space being shown on the screen, and to grant the existence of the rest, the unseen rest that lies implied in the space off screen, to grant its existence while agreeing that at least for the moment we don't need to see it.

The young man who has been driving us around modern Rome is our point of entry into this peculiar conversation with ancient Rome. He is like an interviewer speaking to the ancient past, like a young student getting lessons in Roman history from old teachers who took part in that history. He is the representative of our modernity in this encounter with antiquity, and we identify ourselves with him. We don't wholly identify ourselves with him, of course; our identification with a character is never complete. Identifica-

History Lessons. The banker and his glance at the young man.

tion is a matter of degree, and *History Lessons* wouldn't work if we didn't to some degree identify ourselves with the young man. Straub and Huillet do not want to break that identification but they do want us to take the distance from it necessary for reflection. For a long while after our initial view of the young man and the banker we are denied any further glimpse of the young man, any sense of his response on which we might base ours, so we are left on our own to find our bearings as the camera, circling around the banker, looks into him from a succession of different perspectives, seemingly no more sure than we are of what angle to take on this ancient Roman tranquilly recollecting Caesar in his days as an ambitious young lawyer.

Having gone around from the banker's right profile to an oblique three-quarter view to a nearly frontal view, the camera keeps circling him in three more held shots, each a successively closer view from an angle successively higher and more sideways—which symmetrically reverses, on the banker's left side, the progression in the three previous shots. This is the side away from the young man, and the camera angles are now far enough removed from his perspective that we may come to forget about his presence out of frame as we concentrate on the banker, who seems to be addressing no one in particular and who has many interesting things to say about the man he calls "C." Our alienation from the ancient character lessens as we become less aware of the modern character by his side and more involved in all he is telling about the Julius Caesar he knew. As the banker goes on talking, we are drawn, though not exactly into suspending our disbelief in the character or even our mistrust in the truth of his statements, at least into listening with puzzled fascination to this insider's account of Caesar's career. Evidently a fiction, evidently not a character we are to accept as a real ancient Roman, this banker is nonetheless a character we come intermittently to regard as a possible ancient Roman, or a possible banker, a modern counterpart suggesting what a banker might have been like back then. The actor playing him sure looks like a crafty banker—an actual one, not a caricature in the manner of Eisenstein. A measure of the degree of our involvement is that when the camera gets all the way around to an overhead close-up of the banker's right profile, the reappearance into frame of the young man's hands and part of his body comes as something of a surprise, striking us anew with the incongruity of his sitting right beside the ancient character. So the young man is still there, after all. Now the camera pulls back, without changing the angle, to an oblique overhead view of the two characters seated on the shaded garden bench, a view diametrically mirroring our initial view of them.

The young man now speaks for the first time. Underscoring this break with what so far has been the banker's monologue, the camera breaks with the high angle it has so far maintained and shows the young man in a close-up taken from below. He asks the banker a question about the young Caesar and his affiliation with the democratic party of those days. We cut back to an eye-level close-up of the banker, who now steadily returns the young man's gaze. This is a shot/reverse shot. But the shot of the young man lasts only five seconds, and the reverse shot of the banker goes on for two minutes, with no further shot of the young man even as he asks several further questions. And both in the shot of the young man and in the reverse shot of the banker there is a noticeable empty space, not, as convention prescribes, on the side of the screen leading toward the other character, signaling his presence off screen in

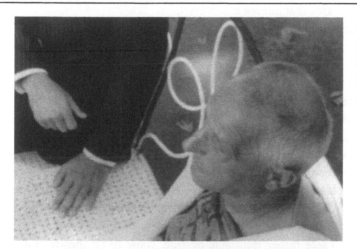

History Lessons. The young man's reappearance into frame, his face in close-up as he asks the first question.

that direction, but on the side leading away from the other character. The young man glances off screen to the right, a glance that points in the direction of the banker, but with an empty space on the left of the screen that tends to direct our attention away from where the banker sits. This empty space in the wrong direction—wrong according to convention—has the effect of opening up the space of the conversation so that we may wonder what else there is to see besides these two characters, what else there is to know besides what they are saying to each other. With the naive idealism of a student, the young man's questions want to establish Caesar's democratic orientation, but the knowing old banker stresses Caesar's orientation toward money. Behind the young man, back there in the empty space opened up in the direction away from the conversation, we may notice a sumptuous villa bespeaking the rewards that money has to offer.

After this brief shot of the young man and sustained reverse shot of the banker, we now get a sustained shot of the young man and no reverse shot at all of the banker as the two characters take a stroll in the garden. The camera steadily follows the young man—steadily leaving an empty space on the wrong side of the screen, the side away from the other character—while the banker remains off screen, out of view for so long as to strain our acceptance of the convention that he is there walking alongside and listening to the young man recite at length, like a student answering the teacher, the story told in the history books about Caesar's kidnapping by pirates. After their stroll together the banker sits down on the bench again, but the young man enters and leaves frame in the foreground (which signifies his freedom, as Byg interprets it) and takes a seat on a chair opposite. Now the two characters, sitting face to face rather than side by side, come to be shown in a shot/reverse shot approaching the conventional, the young man screen-left looking off to the right, the banker screen-right looking off to the left, as if each character, having taken his time, were now settling on his assigned side of the screen (screen-left is the young man's position in the driving sequences). But we see the young man for only a few seconds, as he speaks once more before falling silent for the remainder of the scene, and from then on we focus on the banker, who sets straight the story of Caesar and the so-called pirates, actually slave traders from Asia Minor competing with Roman slave traders, and expands on the larger story of the slave business and its politics in the ancient Mediterranean. As the banker talks on, his gaze directed at the young man off screen to the left, several momentary blackouts—not fade-outs, just inserted frames of black film—keep returning to the same shot at an indeterminate later point, with a slight abrupt change in the light suggesting a later time of the day, a slight abrupt change in the banker's face and a discontinuity in his statements suggesting perhaps a response to some remark we haven't heard or some expression we haven't seen on the young man's face. It is as if once the two characters have come to be shown in a conventional shot/reverse shot, the shot of the young man might as well be skipped and black film inserted instead.

The reverse angle is a staple film technique. Usually it pivots on a character's glance: it brings into view the space before the character's eyes, the space of our point of view in the previous shot, the space lying implied

History Lessons. The shot/reverse shot near the end of the young man's first conversation with the banker.

toward and past the camera. The reverse angle may give us the character's point of view—in which case it is what we call a point-of-view shot—or it may be taken from beside or behind the character. And no character at all need be involved: we may see the front of a house in one shot, for example, and then cut to a reverse angle looking at the street through the front pillars. The shot/reverse shot involves two characters. We cut back and forth between two characters looking at each other, each standing in the implied space before the other's eyes, so that each shot is the reverse angle of the other shot. Each shot implies the other and each shot completes the other; the shot/reverse shot sets up two interlocking reverse angles in the kind of perfect balance that belongs to classical art.

Straub and Huillet purposely throw the shot/reverse shot off balance in modernist fashion and break up its interlocking completeness so that we may entertain the alternative. In *Modernist Montage* P. Adams Sitney takes the reverse angle to be the "cornerstone of narrative continuity in films," and since he takes modernism to be against both narrative and continuity, the avoidance or subversion of the reverse angle becomes for him the hallmark of modernist cinema. It is true that the reverse angle, and the shot/reverse shot even more, have, as Sitney says, "the implicit effect of erasing the presence of the camera," because the camera in the reverse angle comes to be placed where it was shown not to have been only an instant before in the previous shot.[33] But any cut to a different camera position puts us where the camera was not in the previous shot and where it could not have moved in the space of an instant. Generally the projector's images tend to have in their ghostly continuity "the implicit effect of erasing the presence of the camera." And for avoidance of the reverse angle one need look no further than D. W. Griffith, the founder, if anyone was, of what Sitney calls "narrative continuity in films."

Griffith was the founder of dramatic film technique. If a theater stage is a bounded whole where a complete action unfolds, the movie screen after Griffith does not exhibit a whole but a succession of parts, parts whose succession yet makes a whole, details selected and arranged one after the other so as to unfold a complete action. A painting is an image complete within the frame, but film images make sense—the shot/reverse shot is an obvious example—only as fragments of an implied larger field, only if we keep in mind at each moment what lies unseen out of frame. Yet what lies unseen is not something we should miss seeing; rather we should accept it as an offscreen background to the image on screen, the detail that by virtue of being brought into view is being designated, by the convention of the shot

Griffith instituted, as just the part we should be seeing at the moment, the detail that matters. The shot/reverse shot is again an obvious example: the character being shown at the moment, whether saying something or reacting to what the other character is saying, is for the moment to be regarded as the character that matters, the character whose utterance or expression most significantly advances the action.

In a chase or last-minute rescue Griffith quickly cuts back and forth between the different places where the action unfolds, but when the action unfolds in one place, on one stage, Griffith cuts less frequently, and then he tends to keep the same angle in the closer view, the perspective of a theater spectator using opera glasses for the significant detail. In the theater the stage is an area divided from the spectator, set apart for the performance, an area where we are not invited for the duration of the play; and Griffith's camera, though empowered with the mobility of the movies, usually adopts the perspective of a spectator who remains outside the stage. The reverse angle invites the spectator inside, invites us to take a character's place, to step into the space of the action. Griffith held to theatrical tradition and preferred to avoid the reverse angle and its invitation to trespass onto the stage where the action is taking place.[34] But the reverse angle is no less dramatic than Griffith's more theatrical technique. In extending us that invitation, it merely extends the convention of the shot into a kind of drama that encourages the spectator vicariously to enter the space the characters inhabit.

Velázquez's *Las Meninas* is a painting that contains its own reverse angle. Like people posing for a photograph, figures in a painting often look out in our direction, but usually they look out in the manner of figures on a stage addressing the spectator. The figures in *Las Meninas* are looking out toward the front but they are not looking at the spectator: rather they are looking at other figures in their own space, figures we can see reflected in a mirror at the back and make out to be the king and queen of Spain.[35] That mirror could be said to represent the painting's reverse angle, or better, the painting could be said to represent the reverse angle of that mirror, the point of view of the king and queen of Spain, the field of vision lying before their eyes. In the essay on this painting that opens *The Order of Things*, Michel Foucault takes *Las Meninas* to be representing classical representation by rendering explicit the construction of the picture from the perspective of a viewer who commands the view, a sovereign beholder who stands before the picture and for whose eyes everything depicted is meant.[36]

Inspired by Foucault on *Las Meninas*, Jean-Pierre Oudart came up with a theory of the film image as the field of vision before the eyes of a sovereign beholder, the reverse angle of an implied viewer who commands the view. According to Oudart, the film image will leave an open gap, a gaping incompleteness, unless that implied commanding viewer is seen to be a character in the film, shown in the next image on the screen just as the sovereign beholder of Velázquez's painting is shown in the mirror at the back. Every shot in a film is for Oudart a reverse angle in search of a character to occupy the viewing angle: every shot calls for completion in a reverse shot, for closure of the gap that the viewer's absence leaves in the view with a character's appearance in the next view, for what the Lacanian-Althusserians call "suture."[37]

This theory can be refuted with a simple example. A character is alone in a room and suddenly we cut behind the character's back to a shot of the doorknob turning and the door starting to open. This shot is no one's reverse angle; its effect depends precisely on its showing us something the character is not positioned to see. That this kind of shot is a cliché of the suspense film only illustrates how common it is for a shot to show us something that is not before the eyes of anyone in the film. Trina kisses McTeague in *Greed* (Erich von Stroheim, 1924), and we cut to a close view of her feet as she stands on his and even so stands on tiptoe: a view that belongs to no viewer in the film, a significant detail meant for us. Most film shots are significant details meant for us, larger or smaller details, details sometimes presented as a character's view and gaining significance for that reason.

The system of classical representation that *Las Meninas* makes explicit sets up the picture as a stage meant for the eyes of a spectator who stands outside it; the space in front of the picture where the spectator stands is a space outside the boundaries of the picture stage. In *Las Meninas* the space of the picture stage is seen to extend in front of the picture, and in that implied extension the sovereign spectators, the king and queen of Spain, are seen to be standing. In making explicit the picture stage of classical representation, *Las Meninas* at the same time makes a breach in it, breaks through its boundaries and opens it up in our direction. From the moment that Lumière's arriving train came at those spectators who got out of the way, the movies have broken through the traditional picture stage and opened up in our direction the space of representation. The reverse angle is one means by which that breach is contained: we don't get out of the way because the space in front of the picture is appropriated by the picture stage, assimilated to the dramatic fiction, seen to belong not to our world but to the world before the characters.

The fragmentary view characteristic of our modernity has been, Raymond Williams says, especially characteristic of film. Film is indeed an art of fragments: a painting is a whole, a theater stage is a whole, but on the movie screen we see merely a part, a piece of a larger field extending indefinitely beyond our view. Lacanian-Althusserian theory supposes that, like babies at the mother's breast, we first see the film image as a plenitude and become alarmed when we recognize it as a fragment, so that we need to have our feeling of incompleteness patched up with the stitching operation of suture. This theory may be wrong, but the perception is not wrong that some kind of stitching together is being performed. The nostalgia for the mother's breast is a nostalgia for a time when things could be seen whole. And film takes the fragments we recognize from our experience and arranges them into an ensemble. Film is an art of fragments but of fragments pieced together, parts put together to make a whole. Thus it has been both a modern art and a classical art in our time.

Doors in Griffith's earlier films are usually aligned with the edges of the screen, so that a character entering or leaving a room is also entering or leaving frame. It looks rather funny today, that exact coincidence between the boundaries of a room and the boundaries of our view, between the stage and the picture stage, but it makes clear the practice that has been followed in most movies to this day, the treatment of the picture as a stage. The picture stage of the movies is not static like a painting and not set like a theater stage for the duration of a scene. It is a stage that represents fragments, details picked out from a scene larger than we can see, a stage capable of changing at any moment from one place to another, one detail to another, one perspective to another; and yet we are to take it at each moment in the same way we take a painting or a theater stage, as the space containing just what we should be seeing, displayed for our benefit, meant for our eyes. It is by this convention of the shot, which asks us to regard each fragment as a part lacking nothing essential to the whole, fitting exactly into the unfolding scheme of a complete action, that the movies are able to marry their modernity with their classicism, to render their fragmentary view and also achieve their rounded completion.

It may be that the marriage of fragmentation and completion, the parts into which our experience is broken and the whole into which they appear to be unified, promotes a false consciousness. It is here that one may detect the workings of ideology: our experience is actually in pieces and we are given the illusion of unity. But this is a far cry from the notion prevalent in postmodern theory that unity is necessarily a bad thing because necessarily a false consciousness serving the established order and the ideology by which it keeps itself in power. The corollary to this notion is a cheerful embracing of fragmentation, the "postmodern subject" as the self fallen to pieces and glad of it, which truly does serve the interests of the ruling order that has brought on the fragmentation in our lives. Along with its blanket condemnation of unity, postmodern theory tends to make a blanket equation between the unity of art and our sense of unity in life, and the work of art that suits the theory, the postmodern work of art, is the work fallen to pieces and glad of it. But art is not the same thing as life, it is an alternative to life, and the unity that a work of art proposes does not necessarily pretend to be a unity that can be found in actual existence. The feeling of unity that a work of art gives us, which may be an illusion in many cases and even a deception, is in other cases better described as an aspiration.

The shot/reverse shot imitates, in an exchange between shots on the screen, the exchange taking place in the scene between two characters. For some it imitates what an observer in the scene would see, a bystander whose attention switches back and forth between the two characters. This "idea that editing simulates the change of glance of an observer," writes David Bordwell, "makes shot/reverse shot a kind of heightening of our ordinary perception of an event involving participants." Bordwell contrasts this older "naturalist position" with the view, which "dominates film studies today," that the shot/reverse shot is merely "a stylistic convention . . . an arbitrary device, having no privileged affinities with natural perception," and he wants to stake a middle ground between the two.[38] He is right to say that the shot/reverse shot gives us neither an equivalent of natural perception, what we would see as an observer ideally positioned in the scene, nor a piece of screen artifice without any basis in nature. He is right to dispute the notion, which structuralist and poststructuralist theory derives from the arbitrariness of the sign posited in Saussure's linguistics, that a convention is always something quite arbitrary. But he disputes that notion by invoking a universality that loses sight of the specifics of history, of the way a convention, though often not arbitrary, is always not arbitrary for the reasons of a time and place, the motives of a certain human group and its circumstance, a culture and society with a history. Otherwise it is not a convention, an agreement that things be done in a certain way, but simply the way things are done. The shot/reverse shot, Bordwell argues, is based on "contingent universals"—contingent because they didn't have to be so but universal because most human societies so have them in place—such as the face-to-face encounter between two persons, the way they will take turns speaking and listening, the centrality of the human glance as director of attention. All these are conditions of the shot/reverse shot, they enter into it and make it possible, but whether or not they are as universal as Bordwell thinks, they are not what makes it a convention.

The shot/reverse shot does not give us a bystander's view: it has us stand in turn where each character stands. That people engaged in conversation will face each other, that they will speak and listen in turn, does not adequately account for a device that puts us not in the ideal but in the unreal position of switching back and forth between one point of view and its opposite. That we should accept that unreal position—and accept it we do, with remarkable readiness—is the convention. Usually we are only asked to stand approximately, but sometimes we are asked to stand exactly where each character stands, so that we look into the other character's eyes. The shot/reverse shot can be done with the actors looking straight into the camera. Stroheim, an early master of the device, often did it that way, already in *Foolish Wives* (1922) and especially in *Queen Kelly* (1928). One recent director who often does it that way is Jonathan Demme, for example in *The Silence of the Lambs* (1991), where the encounters with Hannibal Lecter in his cell gain much of their creepy hypnotic effect from that gaze fixed in our direction. Having the actors look straight into the camera is thought to strain the convention, for we are to accept the fiction that the characters are looking at each other as if the camera weren't there; but as Stroheim and Demme do it, we have no trouble accepting our position—no more unreal, really, than in the usual shot/reverse shot—right on the line of eye contact, looking straight into the eyes of one character and then, switching to the reverse angle, into the eyes of the other.

That identification is a matter of degree is nowhere more evident than in the shot/reverse shot. We couldn't switch back and forth between two characters, we couldn't accept the convention asking us to switch, if our identification were all with one character and not at all with the other, if we didn't to some degree identify ourselves with both of them. How much we identify ourselves with each of them, and in what way, depends, among other things, on how the shot/reverse shot is done. It may be done in close-ups, making the characters close on the screen even if in the scene they are not that close together. It may be done from a fair distance, as in the wonderful shot/reverse shot at the end of *Bringing Up Baby* (Howard Hawks, 1938) in which we look up at Cary Grant on a scaffold and look down at Katharine Hepburn on a ladder and a huge dinosaur skeleton about to collapse stands between them. Or one character may be shown in close-up and the other character in long shot: neither the distance nor the angle need be the same for both characters, and often there is a significant difference, a character the camera distinguishes from the other in a closer or more frontal view. A shot/reverse shot may depict the characters separately, one at a time on the screen, or it may depict each character, or just one of the two characters, over the opposite character's shoulder. Often the arrangement will change in the course of the scene. In a romantic scene it may be deemed appropriate to keep both lovers together in the frame throughout the exchange of shots, and show each character in three-quarter view next to the other in back profile. Two characters having an argument, however, are likely to be shown separately, maybe in closer and closer views that express the growing intensity of the argument more than they reflect the changing position of the characters. A police officer interrogating a suspect, a reporter conducting an interview, will often be shown in profile while the suspect or person interviewed is shown full-face, for the profile will seem like an arrow, an appropriate representation of the one putting the questions, aimed at the target of the full-face, an appropriate representation of the one facing the questions. The shot/reverse shot is a special case of the convention of the shot, which always asks us to accept the appropriateness of the angle and distance to the thing being shown.

Appropriateness rules out arbitrariness. Classical art dwells in appropriateness, and the shot/reverse shot is nothing if not classical: it dwells in the appropriateness of an exchange of shots nicely corresponding to an exchange of glances and an exchange of words, in the appropriateness of each shot to the character and the dramatic situation, the thing being said and the accompanying or answering expression. Modernism challenges the sense of appropriateness with the recognition of arbitrariness. But it cannot dwell in arbitrariness: no successful work of art can. The art of modernism, a precarious art, lies in finding the appropriateness of its arbitrariness, the appropriateness that will hold at bay, hold in suspension—maybe just for a moment, and that moment is the work of art—an arbitrariness that cannot be ruled out. Postmodern theory merely celebrates arbitrariness.

It is arbitrary for Kiarostami at the beginning of *Close-Up* to keep us waiting outside with the cab driver while the reporter and the policemen go inside the house where the story is happening. The appropriateness of that arbitrariness comes from the reflection it elicits on our access to the story and on the means and ends of art as embodied in the flowers and the aerosol can we encounter while we wait. It is arbitrary for Straub and Huillet all through the car rides in *History Lessons* to keep the camera fixed in the back seat of the car, and the appropriateness of that arbitrariness likewise comes from the way it makes us aware of our path to the story, of the inescapable limitation of our point of view; aware of our identification with the young man who drives the car—an identification held in check by our awareness but still in place— the young man who leads us into the story and whose eyes are at the center of our view; aware of the means of photographic and cinematic representation as embodied in the car stuck in the streets of our modernity.

It is arbitrary for the camera to circle the old banker sitting next to the young man on the garden bench and telling him about the business affairs of Mr. Julius Caesar. Here the film has shifted from a documentary of modern Rome to a dramatic fiction about ancient Rome, and the arbitrariness of circling the banker finds its appropriateness as a way of negotiating the shift, the path to a fiction involving implausible face-to-face encounters across the ages that the conventional shot/reverse shot could not plausibly depict. (Such encounters might have been depicted with the blatant implausibility of a comedy, but *History Lessons* is not a comedy.) Even after the stroll in the garden, the film would not settle into a conventional shot/reverse shot, and the arbitrariness of inserting sections of black leader where shots of the young man might have been finds its appropriateness in the film's insistence that we not settle in any assigned position but instead question our standpoint.

After he finishes telling about the slave trade, the way it was taken over and enlarged by Roman businessmen and the ruinous effect this had on peasants and artisans who could not compete with slave labor, the banker falls silent and stares into space. Suddenly we cut to the rush and noise of a small stream, the camera panning upstream and bringing us to a long shot of the young man facing an old peasant who stands at the door of a small wooden water mill. As the young man talks to this Latin peasant, a veteran of conscripted service in the Roman army under both Caesar and Pompey—it was his bad luck that he fought on Pompey's side in the civil war—the film cuts back and forth between the two characters in the manner of a shot/reverse shot. But in this exchange of shots the distance and especially the angle on each character change disconcertingly. First we see the peasant in profile and the young man full-face, and then each successive shot of the peasant becomes more frontal and each successive shot of the young man becomes more sideways, until at the end of the conversation we see the peasant full-face and the young man in profile. From profile to front, from front to profile, the camera circles each character by 90° and each time it shows the character from an angle different by 90° from the previous shot of the opposite character. No shot/reverse shot is ever done like this. The angle or distance on one or both characters may change appreciably in the course of a shot/reverse shot but it will change appropriately, which is to say in accordance with the unfolding action, as when two characters having an argument kiss and make up. Here the appreciable change does not seem motivated dramatically but generated by an arbitrary geometry. What is the appropriateness of this arbitrariness?

Talking to the banker, the young man was deferential, like a student learning from a teacher who knows the story, but when he talks to the peasant his attitude is a bit patronizing, as if he knew the story better than the old man. The young man has democratic ideas, he sides with the little man in theory and he supposes Caesar took that side too, but toward this little man standing before him the posture he tends to assume is of a certain class condescension. Yet the little man holds his own; he has spirit, like the little mountain stream rushing by. At first the young man is shown full-face, as if he were the one giving the answers, but gradually the roles shift and the young man is shown more and more in profile, more and more as the one asking the questions, and the peasant more and more full-face, more and more as the one who really knows the story.[39] The changing camera angles suggest the shifting roles the characters assume in this exchange. This is an unconventional shot/reverse shot but a shot/reverse shot all the same.

Cutting back and forth between two characters expresses a connection between them, a rapport of some sort even if it is the rapport of contention. The encounter with the peasant is the most dramatic exchange in *History Lessons* and the exchange of shots back and forth is the quickest in the film—as if the young man, across the distance of the centuries and the difference in social class separating him from this peasant, were somehow developing a rapport with him, more of a rapport than he has with the banker or with the jurist or the poet he later talks to.

Relatively dramatic though it is, the exchange with the peasant is still not quite an exchange made present on the screen. The cinema of Straub and Huillet is a cinema of the past, of history, not just the history of Julius Caesar and his time but the history of Brecht and his unfinished novel, the time of his writing about Julius Caesar and his time, and the history of the making of this film based on that novel, the time of the young man's driving through modern Rome and of the actors' enacting passages from Brecht's novel before Straub and Huillet's camera and microphone. Documentary is always of the past, of a moment now past even if it was only a moment ago, and the cinema of Straub and Huillet, even when most flagrantly fictional—as when actors in togas pretend to be ancient Romans and speak in Brecht's German to a contemporary young man—is strictly a documentary cinema.

History Lessons. The young man's conversation with the peasant.

Every book, every film, every object that comes down to us from the distant or the near past, may be regarded as a document of its own time. Straub and Huillet's films are consciously made as documents of their own time and set in a kind of dialogue with documents of earlier times, the time of Caesar and the time of Brecht, as well as in a dialogue with future times, the times when audiences will be watching the film. *Fortini/Cani* (1976) is not about ancient history but about the conflict between Arabs and Israelis, history currently in the news. Yet Straub and Huillet deal with this current history by focusing on a document from the past. They could have interviewed the Florentine writer Franco Fortini and asked him to express his views at the time the film was made, but instead they have him read aloud in the film from his book of ten years before, *I Cani del Sinai* (The Dogs of the Sinai), which was a response to the Arab-Israeli Six-Day War of 1967.[40] So the Fortini in the film enters into a kind of dialogue with the Fortini who wrote the book, which in turn evokes earlier Fortinis; and we in the audience are brought to reflect on our own time and our own relation to Fortini at various points in his life and to the situation in the Middle East and its history past and present. Straub and Huillet always use preexistent works in their films—Brecht's novel or Fortini's polemic, the music of Bach or Schönberg or Haydn or the fiction of Böll or Pavese or Kafka, the drama of Corneille or Hölderlin or Sophocles or the poetry of St. John of the Cross or Mallarmé or the painting of Cézanne—works treated not as something to be adapted and made present on the screen but as something given, handed down from the past, to be quoted or excerpted rather than adapted, a piece of another time to be juxtaposed rather than blended with other elements, themselves fragments of history, documents of what has been.

What is past, asks Heidegger in *Being and Time,* about things from the past? Surely the things are not past, since we encounter them in the present. If they are no longer what they once were it is not because they are past but because their world is past. It is their world that is past, the world to which they once belonged, the whole of which they were part, the context in which they existed. They no longer exist in that context, they are no longer part of that whole, and that context is their past, that whole no longer in place where they once had their place. It is not the parts that are past, it is the whole. It is a whole world that is past, not the things, the parts of that world that survive in the present. What is past about things from the past is a world that no longer is.[41]

A film is a piecing together. The pieces may come from different places and different times, but arranged into a whole they will be seen as parts of that whole, things in the world the film constructs on the screen. The context the film gives them, the whole of which it makes them part, completely takes over. It is not that their world no longer is, it is as if it never was, now that they have their place in the world that comes into being on the screen. Over the documentary details, the things that were there in the world before the camera, the fiction constructed on the screen reigns. The pieces brought together in a film by Straub and Huillet are not put together that way. No such fiction is constructed, no such whole that wholly takes over, no such world whose coming into being wipes out what has been. The documentary details captured by Straub and Huillet's camera and microphone are not turned into what is but remain what has been, retain the mark of their provenance in a world prior to the film. They are things from the past and are to be recognized as such, recognized as pieces that come from different places and different times, different wholes of which they once were part, different worlds that no longer are.

"Under the Aristotelian system of constructing a play and the style of acting that goes with it," wrote Brecht in his journal,

> the audience's deception with regard to the way in which the incidents shown on the stage come about and take place in real life is helped by the fact that the story's presentation forms an indivisible whole. Its details cannot be compared one by one with their corresponding parts in real life. Nothing may be taken "out of its context" in order, say, to set it in the context of reality. The answer lies in the alienating style of acting. In this the story line is a broken one; the single whole is made up of independent parts which can and must be compared with the corresponding part-incidents in real life.[42]

To the indivisible whole Aristotle prescribed, the world of a work of art, Brecht opposes an autonomy of the parts, parts that may readily be taken out of their context in the world of the work and set in the context of the real world, compared with reality. Bürger quotes this passage and relates it to his conception of the historical avant-garde, which he characterizes both as an assault on the autonomy of art and as an assertion of the autonomy of the parts that make up a work of art, the autonomy of the parts, as he sees it, acting against the autonomy of the whole. "A theory of the avant-garde must begin with the concept of montage that is suggested by the early cubist collages," he writes: "the insertion of reality fragments into the painting . . . means the destruction of the unity of the painting as a whole."[43] He rightly takes issue with Adorno's view, which is not only Adorno's, that the fragmentary form of avant-garde art of itself carries a political statement, a contestation of the established order; but what he proposes instead is pretty weak: the notion that a broken form allows the insertion of a political statement into the work, something like a commercial break on television. The politics of Brecht's political theater was not in the form alone nor in the mere insertion of content. It was where politics in art must be, in the representation of reality. A broken form, a montage of scenes and elements of scenes, would serve in Brecht to prevent the simple acceptance of the representation and provoke its comparison with reality.

Neither theater nor painting is a documentary medium. A document is an index in Peirce's sense, a sign that has a direct connection with its object. A play or a painting may give us a document of its time—anything that comes from a particular time has a direct connection with that time, and the signs it exhibits of that connection constitute a document—but it does not give us a documentary representation such as we get in a photographic image. In a photographic image reality is part of the picture, the index enters into the representation, the light from things in the world received into the camera and imprinted in the image. In a play or a painting the index may enter into the work—the brushwork is always an index of the painter's activity—but it does not enter into the representation as an index of the reality represented. The reality represented in a play or a painting has no direct connection with the picture, does not come into the picture except through the artist's rendering and interpretation. Even in a cubist collage it is not exactly "reality fragments" that come into the picture but pieces of paper, bits of other graphic design brought into the design of the painting, not the artist's own rendering but fragments of other renderings rather than a direct record of reality.

A broken form, a montage of scenes and elements of scenes, serves in Straub and Huillet to keep from being turned into fiction, from being subsumed in the world of a fiction, the documentary details the camera and microphone have recorded. Moreover, it serves to turn into a document the fiction of a preexistent work, to make us regard a piece of theater or painting, of prose or poetry or music, as a remnant of the past, a trace history has left us, a document of what has been. The cinema of Straub and Huillet is a thoroughly documentary cinema.

A document of its time, of its author and his times, *I Cani del Sinai* is a Marxist critique of Zionism and a personal and political memoir that goes into how the author came to this position from his own background as an Italian Jew. Fortini's father had spoken out against Fascism at the time of its coming to power in the twenties, had been beaten and arrested, but later he hoped the Fascists would forget about that past and he signed his son up in their youth organization, the Avanguardisti, at whose gatherings the boy would see the two sons of his father's old partner, the lawyer Consolo, who on an October night in 1925 had been killed by the Blackshirts right in his home, in front of his children. As we hear Fortini's voice recounting this on the soundtrack we see the Florentine Via dei Servi on the screen; we are not told, but perhaps it was here that the lawyer Consolo was killed, or here that the Avanguardisti gatherings took place, or here that Fortini's family lived on the floor above Consolo's widow and children but did not visit them, out of prudence. Our view begins above eye level, at the street sign on the rusticated wall over a corner bar, then pans along the facades until a perspective opens down the street and our eyes can travel into the depth. But at the far end of the street the huge dome of the cathedral brings the perspective to a halt, and the camera now tilts down to eye level and holds the view of the street and its traffic and passersby. If the dome looms large in back, the iron bars of a window now loom large in front, armoring the privacy of a house; if the dome (built by Brunelleschi, inventor of Renaissance perspective) is what we cannot see beyond, the limit of our perspective on public things, the window is what we cannot see into, the limit of our perspective on personal things. We are not told, but perhaps it was here: the story of what happened in the past, what may have happened here, hovers over the present but does not take over, does not appropriate this street as the site of that past. The street keeps its autonomy from the story yet the story resonates in the street, resonates as a possible missing context for these details we have before us, these parts without a whole, these things without a world.

Fortini/Cani.
The street in Florence.

Cut to a long shot of the city of Florence seen from one of the surrounding hills. "All this was a waste of time. The past was too recent—only
thirteen years since 1925," we hear Fortini reading on the soundtrack, referring to his father's efforts to ingratiate himself with the Fascist regime:

> Nothing doing, he had always been "beige," as the Florentines said, that is an
> anti-Fascist: and what's more, he was Jewish. In Rome he was classified by the
> Department of Demography and Race as a "dangerous Jew"—which got him
> arrested, as soon as the Duce had declared war, in June 1940. Now it was
> necessary to save the son. The horizon was blocked. But it would be a passing
> storm. Some trick ought to suffice. As the son of a Jewish father and an "Aryan"
> mother, I could be "Aryan." . . . If only I had had the tranquil opportunism, the
> healthy cynicism needed to conform. . . . But no. All the terms of my culture
> exalted the "seriousness" of the Spirit, of morality . . . and for years now my
> relations with the protestants in Florence, and the Waldensians in particular,
> had been, without my being aware of it, the way out I had been seeking from
> my provincial, petty-bourgeois world to look towards the European grand
> bourgeoisie, past rather than present. . . . I can recall the painful seriousness
> with which, in May 1939, I received the baptism which—back-dated by ten or
> twelve months—was supposed to rescue me. . . . But no way, the Fascists weren't
> that stupid . . . . "Filthy anti-Fascist Jew!", these words, accompanied by a fist
> and the taste of blood on the teeth; and the fist was that of a Senior in the
> Militia, the brother of an acquaintance of mine whom I had "led astray" with
> my Judaism; and mine the teeth—in a street in the center of Florence, in the
> crowd, early November 1939, Italy not yet at war: these words were intended to
> fix me, identify me.[44]

We hear all this and much more read aloud on the soundtrack, and we
cannot take it all in. We are purposely put in the position of not catching
everything, a position that many seem to resent but surely not an unusual
position for us to be in; what is unusual in the work of Straub and Huillet is
that they make us quite aware that we are not catching everything. Politics
especially is an area in which people often have strong opinions about things
they don't know enough about, and it serves a useful political purpose just to
make us aware of all that we don't know.

The word we hear in films most of the time is the word acted out,
dramatized, made present by characters in action. The word we hear in
Straub and Huillet is the word merely spoken, recited from a past text: the
word merely spoken but spoken at length. Straub and Huillet give the word
rather than the image center stage, some say, as if this were something

unusual, when actually the word dramatized, the characters' dialogue, takes center stage in films most of the time—not to mention documentaries where the voice-over narration rules. The word in Straub and Huillet may take center stage but does not take over, does not appropriate the image as an illustration, an accompaniment subordinate to the word. The image in Straub and Huillet is not treated as the surface to the word's depths. The word is not the answer but is itself a question, itself a document we endeavor to decipher. Word and image are both treated as documents, traces of the past, parts without a whole, fragments of history juxtaposed before our ears and eyes.

Fortini reads alone in *Fortini/Cani*. There is no young man listening to him and asking him questions, no other character with whom he has an exchange, only the former self that wrote the book and the other former selves and characters from the past the book evokes. There is no shot/reverse shot in the film, nothing like it, but at one point there is something like a point-of-view shot, a point-of-view shot that is a kind of exchange with the past.

From the long shot of the city of Florence the film cuts to Fortini sitting in a terrace in a country house and reading from his book. We see him in profile, screen-right, against a green hill in the background, his gaze fixed downward on the book below the bottom edge of the frame; and we keep returning to this shot through a series of momentary whiteouts—not fade-outs to white, just inserted frames of clear film—marking transitions to his reading of different passages. Over the street and the long shot of the city we heard him read passages about his father and his own personal experience, but now that we see him personally he reads passages more generally political:

> It seems to me that to affirm the universalist vocation of the Jewish people it is not necessary to have recourse to the authority of the Scriptures. The Jews *have been* the "figure" of that universalism, the "witnesses of God among the nations." And if then to be Jewish means a certain synthesis of behaviors, movements and situations, a certain destiny in a certain measure undergone and chosen, then several human communities can be this. The attribute "Jew" is acquired and is lost, is concentrated and dissolved....
>
> There remain the political and military affairs of the state of Israel and the Arab countries. That state was born by force and war, and force and war can maintain it or destroy it. I am convinced that the world as a whole can expect great benefits from the existence and development of the state of Israel. The greatest is probably—and many people have said this—that of its potential function of revolutionary mediation between the so-called West of liberal-

Christian and socialist inheritance and the Third World, a function so far not fulfilled. Revolutionary mediation—in other words expressed in a struggle for an end to national states, to private profit, and to exploitation, particularly neo-colonialist. I can see no other rights to national survival, or at least none that are different from the rights of any other national or ethnic group. . . .

Men, groups, peoples are not equal; but they are not different just because their past is different and determines them differently. They are not, they must not, they cannot be equal, and indeed they must be, and they are forced to be, different, because here and now their actions are different, because they occupy different places in the complex of historical forces, in the simultaneity of the world. Their past has placed them where they are, but it is the future which makes them move. And they are different in relation to you because, with their action in the present, they implicate *your* difference, *your* action. My closeness to you, your distance from me, are measured by what we both do, by how and where we do it, in the context of a confrontation, of a struggle both immediate and universal.[45]

At a pause in his reading Fortini looks up and stares straight ahead. He seems to be looking at something off screen to the left, and the empty space screen-left helps draw our attention in the direction of his glance, as in a conventional shot preparing us for a cut to a point-of-view shot through a character's eyes. Cut to the base of a monument on the Lungarno in Florence, on which we can read the inscription commemorating the patriots who fell at Mentana for the cause of Italian liberation in the nineteenth century: a monument to a national struggle, and we may think of the struggle for the Israeli nation, the struggle for Palestinian liberation, and of the way Fortini, though "well aware that we are living through a revival of nationalisms," has been stressing the traditional Marxist, and Jewish, internationalism. The base is seen from eye level, not quite head-on but from an angle a little to the right, and with an empty space screen-right, as in a conventional point-of-view shot indicating the presence off screen to the right of a character shown looking from that direction in the previous shot. Although we may get that impression for an instant after the cut, this monument in the city could of course not be what Fortini is looking at from the terrace where he sits in a country place. The expectation is raised and then frustrated that we would share his perspective in this shot.

The shot is held on the screen, and Fortini's voice is heard over it as he resumes his reading, which now returns to the subject of his father and comes in time to the monument we have been seeing: "It must have been my father

Fortini/Cani. Fortini reading from his book, the monument on the Lungarno, the mark of the Masonic triangle in the stone.

who made me pause in front of that monument on the Lungarno. . . ." At this moment the camera starts to move toward the foot of the monument, where the mark of a triangle can be seen incised in the stone step. "And later I noticed in the stone the trace left by a Masonic triangle which the Fascists had torn out." The downward movement of the camera so precisely imitates a movement of the eyes that it virtually inscribes on the screen a gesture of looking—as if that ghostly stretch of projected light were material enough to bear an inscription—a gesture of looking through the eyes of someone stand-ing in front of that monument and taking notice of that triangular dent at the foot. And so the point-of-view shot we had expected comes after all: not what Fortini is looking at now, not a flashback to the boy who went there with his father long ago, not even the memory, the image that remains inscribed in Fortini's mind of his going there then, but something like the inscription of that memory, that recollected point of view, in the image on the screen.

Danièle Huillet and Jean-Marie Straub have been together since the fifties and have been making films together since the early sixties. They have pursued a solitary path in their art; they belong to no school or move-ment, not even to a nation. They were born in France (Straub in Lorraine, on the border with Germany), and they might have been associated with the *nouvelle vague* had they not moved to Germany at the time and begun making films there. The majority of their films have been in German, but they have also worked in French and Italian, and since 1969 they have lived in Rome and have shot most of their films in Italy.

For some modernism means austerity, the art of less is more—as if the sensuous Matisse were not as much a modernist as the austere Mondrian. Straub and Huillet are often supposed to be of the party of less is more. That austere modernist Robert Bresson is thought to have been a major influence on their work. To an interviewer who asked him about Bresson's influence Straub replied that he greatly admired *Les Dames du Bois de Boulogne* (1945) and *The Diary of a Country Priest* (1951) but not so much Bresson's later work and that in any case Jean Renoir had influenced him no less[46]—Renoir the modernist seldom recognized as such because he was a realist rather than an abstractionist. What Straub and Huillet most of all learned from Bresson, the Bresson who adapted Diderot in *Les Dames du Bois de Boulogne* and Bernanos in *The Diary of a Country Priest*, was the refusal of a conven-tional screen dramatization of a preexistent work and the pursuit instead of a method of juxtaposition.[47] But juxtaposition, the montage of elements rather than their blending, does not serve in Bresson the kind of documentary purpose it serves in Straub and Huillet. And in Straub and Huillet the refusal of dramatization does not yield a paring down but a surplus, not too little but too much. Films are surely not of the party of less is more that keep offering us more than we can assimilate.

It is not clear how the disinterestedness characteristic of aesthetic experience according to Kant, the indifference as to the actual existence of the thing experienced, would apply to a documentary art, an art predicated on the record of things in actual existence. Although Kant never saw a photographic image, his conception of the aesthetic embraced not just things made but things in nature, and he might have said that photography enhances our capacity for aesthetic experience of things in nature. But things in history are another matter, and the art of Straub and Huillet is a documentary art predicated on the record of things in history. This is not an art that calls for our disinterestedness, not an art that solicits our indifference as to the actual existence of the things it represents. It is a modernist art—an art that calls attention to art, an art that declares the artifice of its means and its medium—but certainly not an art of sheer aestheticism. It calls attention to art, its own art and the art of the past it enlists, as an activity taking place in history, a human activity performed under the existing circumstances of history just as the young man drives his car under the existing circumstances of the city streets. Its declaration of artifice is a way of inscribing itself in history just as the mark of that missing triangle is inscribed at the foot of that monument on the Lungarno.

The mark left in the stone by that Masonic triangle the Fascists removed, the memory in Fortini's mind of his father taking him to that monument, the account given of that memory in the book Fortini wrote in response to the Six-Day War, the sound of his voice reading that passage from the book in the film made a decade later, the image on the screen of that triangular dent still there: all these signs of that missing triangle, in various contexts and with various connotations, are brought to our attention together at one moment in the film. We are led to compare them with one another, the image on the screen with our sense of the mental image from Fortini's boyhood, the words read aloud on the soundtrack with our sense of the words at the time of their writing, the printed or the spoken words with the remembered or the photographed image. The signs of the past are seen to take on a new meaning in each new situation in the present, including our own situation at a showing of the film as spectators invited to make our own connections. I thought of my own father taking me when I was a boy in Havana to the monument commemorating the dead at the sinking of the

Maine, and of his explaining that the Spaniards surely did not sink that ship as the Americans claimed, that they had enough trouble contending with the Cuban war of independence and that the last thing they wanted was to provoke a war with the United States: another father taking another son to another waterside monument having to do with a struggle for national liberation. Possibly Straub and Huillet know the poem by José Martí with the lines about the poor of the earth and the mountain stream that the peasant in *History Lessons* made me think of. Maybe they intended that connection, maybe not, but either way it belongs in a film that would not restrict its spectators to the connections its makers intended. Certainly Straub and Huillet do not know about my father taking me to that *Maine* monument by the bay of Havana and giving me a history lesson: this connection is peculiar to me, but not irrelevant to a film that wants each one of us in the audience to consider what we bring to it, to place ourselves in relation to it.

The traces of history, the marks left by the past in the present, are central to the work of Straub and Huillet. Straub characterized *Moses and Aaron* (1975), the film he and Huillet made of Schönberg's unfinished opera, as a comparison between three concrete historical periods: the time of the biblical events, the time in the early thirties when the opera was written, and the time when the film was made. He might have added the time, each of the times, when the film is seen and heard. Every film by Straub and Huillet may be characterized as a repository of documents, a juxtaposition of traces from different times in the past, concrete pieces of evidence to be compared with one another in the present.

In *The Chronicle of Anna Magdalena Bach* (1967) the actor playing Bach is a musician mostly playing the music that is the chief trace Bach left us of his existence. Rather than the man in some dramatization of what he was like, some reenactment of his life and times, the music is the rightful protagonist, the music performed by musicians today and recorded direct, grounded in this particular performance taking place before the camera and microphone. Unlike a concert, however, the film demands that we also consider the original ground of the music in the life and times of the man who composed it in eighteenth-century Germany. Even though we remain aware that the players are contemporary musicians, they wear the wigs and costumes and play the instruments of Bach's time in actual old churches and rooms; even though not much is reenacted of Bach's life outside the musical performances, the narrated chronicle of his second wife Anna Magdalena tells about family matters, money problems, the endeavors and frustrations of her husband's job as a musician. The film becomes a kind of dialogue between Bach as he survives in his music and Bach as he lived and worked. We get a sense of the materials Bach worked with, the difficulties he faced, the concrete circumstances under which he composed the music we are hearing, even as we recognize that this enduringly beautiful music somehow transcends those often troublesome circumstances. This is a dialogue between our aesthetic experience of the music and our sense of the musician's historical situation, between the autonomy of art and its embedment in history.

The Bridegroom, the Comedienne, and the Pimp (1968) opens with an extended traveling shot along a street on the outskirts of Munich where prostitutes line up at night, waiting to be picked up by customers driving by. The image is underexposed in the darkness and for nearly two minutes it remains silent; then suddenly we start to hear Bach's Ascension Oratorio on the soundtrack, a strikingly incongruous musical accompaniment that continues through the second half of the traveling shot. The silent shot documents the sordid reality of the street; the addition of the exalted music does not change the street we go on seeing, but it registers as an assertive choice exercised by the filmmakers against that reality, a refusal to let it stand as it is. At the end of this short film, a young woman who may have been one of the whores we saw in the street begins a new life married to a black man; he speaks to her in lines of poetry, a German translation of the Spanish mystic St. John of the Cross. When the couple arrive at their new home, her pimp (played by R. W. Fassbinder) is there waiting, but she takes his gun from him and shoots him straightaway. Then the camera follows her to a window, and the film closes with the brightly overexposed image of the trees outside, accompanied on the soundtrack by more of St. John's poetry, which she recites, and by a section of Bach's music played again.

The film begins with the darkness of prostitution and ends with the light of redemption, but the prostitution is a documented reality and the redemption a manifest contrivance, a fiction the film does not ask us to accept as a reality. The shooting of the pimp is made implausible on purpose, so we cannot take it as an accomplished fact; the light that shines at the end is plainly the artificial light of the projector shining through overexposed film. The film does not presume that the beauty of the trees cancels the ugliness of the whores' street, or that Bach's music and St. John's poetry, those remnants of the past, provide an answer to the problems of the present. A feeling of redemption is nonetheless evoked, but redemption as a hope, a goal we must work toward, something we must make happen rather than something that has taken place. The pimp, we are led to recognize, has not yet been shot, nor is the whore yet married: the shooting and the marriage are not realities but

The Bridegroom, the Comedienne, and the Pimp. The dark street of prostitution, the shooting of the pimp, the light and the trees at the conclusion.

symbols of the kind of action that must be taken against an intolerable reality. *The Bridegroom, the Comedienne, and the Pimp* is an allegory. The reality of prostitution, of the oppression and exploitation of women, stands for all the real oppressions and exploitations of our time. The shooting of the pimp stands for revolution, the trees and the light and St. John of the Cross and Bach stand for redemption, the revolution and the redemption that have not yet come about. The aesthetic experience the film offers us, the beauty of Bach's music and St. John's poetry and the light at the end and the trees in the wind out the window, is not offered as an answer to our problems but enlisted in opposition to our prevailing reality.

Straub and Huillet acknowledge that art cannot change the world, that Bach's music cannot change the reality of the whores' street, that the change the world needs, the revolution and the redemption, art cannot make happen. But this does not mean that art can make nothing happen. That conclusion leads either to aestheticism, the enjoyment of art for its very irrelevance to what happens in life, or to philistinism, the disparagement of art for its inability to make happen in life what one would like to see happen. What art can make happen is not in the realm of what actually happens in life but in the realm of what one would like to see happen, the realm of consciousness: art may not be able to change what actually happens but it may change what one would like to see happen. *The Bridegroom, the Comedienne, and the Pimp* is an allegory of revolutionary consciousness.

As much as with the remnants, the marks of the past, Straub and Huillet are concerned with the things that no longer remain, the marks that have been effaced, the past that has been buried or forgotten. In *Fortini/Cani* the camera inspects the landscape of the Apennines near Florence in a series of slow, prolonged panning shots around places where the Germans massacred large numbers of Italian partisans during the Second World War, pretty landscapes where no trace can be seen now of the blood that once was spilled here. That blood may have left no mark in these places but the camera marks them with its deliberate panning, marks them but does not appropriate them, lets us know but lets them be, for people died in these places but people go on living here too. When the last of these panning shots, taken at the village of Marzabotto where hundreds were killed, goes around full circle and keeps going over the same ground we have just seen, enough time has passed since we saw it, owing to the slowness of the panning, that we have to make an effort of recognition: after only a few moments we have already started to forget. *Not Reconciled* (1965) deals with the effort Germans must make to remember their history in this century, with their general failure to recognize that they are going over once again the same ground they went over before, at the time of the Nazis and of the Kaiser before that. In this film too the camera pans slowly around the space of the present, searching for traces of the violent past. *Not Reconciled* is based on Heinrich Böll's novel *Billiards at Half Past Nine* and set in an unnamed German city that on the screen is recognizably Cologne. One of the main characters in the story is Schrella, a militant anti-Nazi in his youth who is now returning from exile after many years, and who in one scene goes back to the street where he once lived. The camera pans full circle around the utterly changed street and stops in front of his old house, where, as a child who lives around there now tells him, no family named Schrella ever lived.

Straub and Huillet construct no world on the screen, no whole of which the things we see and hear are part—neither the past world in which a village in the Apennines was the site of a massacre nor the present world in which people go on with their lives, neither the past world in which a street in Cologne was where Schrella lived nor the present world in which a child who lives in that street denies Schrella's existence. A world may have gaps but gaps that can be filled in; a whole may have parts missing but parts that can be put in place. A "lacunary" film is what Straub called *Not Reconciled* and what every film by him and Huillet may be called, a film in which the gaps cannot be filled in to make a world, the parts missing cannot be put in place to make a whole. It is not that we are called upon to complete the work ourselves: how can we, if its makers cannot? It is that the gaps, the parts missing, are to become ours as well as the work's: the work of putting the parts together, the parts without a whole, is one in which we must take part.

Billiards at Half Past Nine tells the story of a family, three generations of a family of architects brought to a focus, with various retrospections and interior monologues, delvings into the past and into the mind, on the eightieth birthday of the family patriarch in 1958. The abbey that made Heinrich Fähmel's name as an architect in the days before the First World War was destroyed in the last days of the Second World War, and his son Robert has kept it secret that it was he who destroyed it, acting under orders from a deranged general but acting willingly, and seeing the destruction as a kind of monument, or countermonument, to the dead in the Nazi reign. *Not Reconciled* may itself be seen as such a countermonument. Its "destruction of Böll's narrative parallels Robert's demolition of his father's church," asserts Paul Coates; and to Barton Byg the film "suggests the Holocaust 'countermonuments' of which James E. Young has written. The countermonument does not seek the permanence of stone but instead documents its own fragility and disappearance."[48] Fragility and disappearance: the face of Edith, Schrella's sister and Robert's wife, a face that haunts the narrative like the spirit of their youth, Edith killed by bombing in the war, the face commemorated above all others in the destruction of the abbey, is seen in *Not Reconciled* for only a few moments. Straub and Huillet, who can dwell on things for longer than most filmmakers would, know perhaps better than anyone else the power of showing something just briefly on the screen.

It is not things that are past, it is their world. In *Not Reconciled* the remnants of the past, of the various pasts, are not clearly placed in those pasts; with disconcerting abruptness the film shifts between different periods, between different actors playing the same characters in different periods, and so the things from the past are not experienced as past but as things with the same claim as anything else to belonging in the present. Precisely the point: the German past is not over and done with, it continues in the present. But in *Not Reconciled* things do not exist in a world of the present either. They are things without a world, things the German people must make into a world. Easy to make them into a false world, but this the film will not do: it breaks Böll's narrative into pieces that are purposely difficult to put together. "Tell what, boy?" asks Robert Fähmel in the abrupt opening line: tell what about his experience under the Nazis, when he was about as old as the adolescent boy he is addressing? Tell what about the German past, in what connection to the concerns of the present? asks the film tacitly throughout; the question is built into the fragmentary, dislocated arrangement of the largely retrospective narrative. Out of a long story spanning half a century we get a tangled agglomerate of fragments, bits and pieces of the past recounted by the characters or reenacted in flashbacks to Nazi and to Kaiser Germany, with no connections made, no cohesion established among the different pieces that can be readily grasped. Hence the missing pieces carry as much weight as the things included, the weight, we feel, of all in the past that has been forgotten or repressed and yet continues to bear upon the present.

Robert's countermonument is a private one: everybody knows the abbey was destroyed, but nobody knows he did it and nobody knows what it meant to him. His father Heinrich figures out he did it and approves of his action; his son Joseph finds out he did it and decides to give up his own architectural studies and his own part in the rebuilding of the abbey being planned. But all this remains private in *Billiards at Half Past Nine,* all in the interior of characters who do not talk to one another about it. The novel's interior monologues, or such parts as the film retains, are spoken out by the characters in *Not Reconciled,* brought out into a public sphere. The personal stories, the family story that Böll's characters would keep to themselves, Straub and Huillet make into the story of a nation. But the novel's words are not dramatized in the film, they are merely spoken, excerpted rather than fully enacted, brought out into a public sphere but deposited as fragments, pieces of evidence demanding our attention but not yet integrated into a cohesive national story, not yet articulated in a shared public discourse, not yet assimilated into a public order of things. Telling the story of a nation is something no artist can do alone. *Not Reconciled* unfolds an effort of collective recall, with all its actors reciting their bits of text, offering their pieces of evidence, doing their part in the work of putting together a story that can belong to all. And the missing pieces, all the lacunae in this lacunary film, imply that the work is not yet done and call for our effort as well. Telling the public story is work in which the public, all of us in the audience but especially the German public, must here take part.

The one of the Fähmels who brings things out into the open is in a mental institution for it. This is Johanna, Heinrich's wife and Robert's mother, who during the First World War publicly called the Kaiser a fool and during the Second World War went to the trains and asked to be sent away with the Jews. She was put away as a madwoman to save her life and has been in an asylum since. "Don't think I'm mad, I know exactly where we are," she reassures her son Robert while she talks about the war as still happening, the dead as still living, the past as still present. Her sense of where we are, the way she mixes up past and present in her mind, is much the same as the film's. Her long monologue in the novel, where "precisely because she is supposed

Not Reconciled. Johanna entering the greenhouse: her penetration into the depths yields a gun.

to be a little mad, Böll spends less time 'justifying' the movements of her thought back and forth from present to past," wrote Richard Roud, "most resembles Straub's treatment in its somewhat cryptic but extremely effective palimpsest of fifty years of German life."[49] The discourse of the mad usually gets translated into the exacerbated subjectivity of expressionism, but *Not Reconciled* renders it with cool objectivity as the discourse closest to the truth. Rather than Heinrich, Robert, or Joseph, the three generations of Fähmel architects, Johanna (played by Huillet herself in the flashbacks to Kaiser Germany) is the character with whom Straub and Huillet most identify themselves and the figure of the artist in *Not Reconciled*.

A frontal view of the outside of a greenhouse, with the door shut, gives an impression of flat space, but then Johanna opens the door and walks inside the surprisingly deep greenhouse, going way into the background, into the unsuspected depths of a space that feels as if she were excavating it. This madwoman who sees the past as living is better able than the other characters to perceive the pattern of continuation underlying German history—better able, as the image of her entering the greenhouse implies, to penetrate the surface and get to the bottom of things. Her penetration into the depths yields a gun. She goes into the greenhouse to get a pistol the gardener keeps there, and she wants to shoot a certain Nazi in order to free her son Otto from his bad influence. Her son Otto was killed at Kiev during the war, but the Nazi is not only alive, he is now chief of police. There he is, on a white horse at a parade of war veterans, and from a balcony Johanna takes aim with the gardener's pistol. Behind her stands the cathedral of

Not Reconciled. Johanna taking aim with the gun against the background of the cathedral.

Cologne, which, in another impression of flat space, seems to be pressing right against her, symbol of the obdurate reality the gun is aimed against.

But there is not only the fat man on the white horse, there is, as her husband points out, another reinstated Nazi at the parade perhaps even more deserving of being shot, and there is, on the next balcony, a government minister courting the military vote, "your grandson's murderer," as Heinrich calls him because he represents the future. Expecting to plead insanity, Johanna shoots the minister, but he is not seriously wounded. "I hope the great look of astonishment will not disappear from his face," says Heinrich in the film's last line, spoken at the family party for his eightieth birthday, a party that becomes a celebration of Johanna's act of protest. The camera pans over the members of the Fähmel family, all now (except for Johanna) gathered together for the first time in the film, and continues to a window, to the bright closing image of trees by the Rhine outside, accompanied on the soundtrack by the music of a Bach suite. This Bach suite was heard before, when Johanna called the Kaiser a fool, and her act of violence has not accomplished much more now than her act of defiance accomplished half a century before: she only managed to put a look of astonishment on the enemy's face, not much of a change in the reality the gun was aimed against. But now as then she has made things manifest in a public act. Johanna has done all that art can do. Art cannot change the world but it can change our consciousness of the world. Art cannot kill the enemy but it can commit symbolic violence, aesthetic terrorism. In this ending, as in the similar ending of *The Bridegroom, the Comedienne, and the Pimp*, we breathe an air of redemption even though we are quite aware that nothing has changed in reality: an air of hope, resistance to what is, not redemption achieved but a reaching for redemption. That is cause enough for celebration.

After his conversation with the peasant the young man in *History Lessons* takes another drive through modern Rome. Then he talks to the jurist and to the poet. The jurist has great admiration for Caesar, whatever his flaws, as a champion of democracy in the tradition of the Gracchi:

> We have forgotten that we are plebeians. You are, Spicer [the banker] is, and I am. Don't say that it doesn't matter any more today. Precisely that is what was achieved: that it doesn't matter any more today. That's Caesar for you. Compared to that, what are the couple of old-style battles, the couple of shaky contracts with a couple of chiefs of native tribes that he may have made! . . . It was the ideas of the Gracchi that Caius Julius took up. The fruit was: Imperium.[50]

Democracy as empire: sound familiar? If talking to the banker is like reading the *Wall Street Journal*, talking to the jurist is like reading the *New York Times*. After that, the poet, from his position of privilege, reclining on a chaise longue on a terrace by the sea, expresses disdain for the whole dirty business of politics and for the robbers that make up the Senate. In his conversation with the poet the young man is not shown even for a moment, merely implied as a listener off screen. After another drive through the streets, he goes back to the garden of the sumptuous villa for a second conversation with the banker.

This second conversation with the banker concludes *History Lessons* and differs significantly from the first in treatment and implications. The

History Lessons.
The young man and
the jurist, the poet by
the sea.

setting is the same as before, with the banker seated on the garden bench again and the young man on a chair across a table, which is how they remain throughout the scene, steadily facing each other, on the table a pitcher of red wine the two are sharing in an afternoon drink. The scene begins with an exchange of shots close to the conventional: first the banker full-face, screen-center, looking off to the left, and then the young man in profile, screen-left, looking off to the right.[51] Moreover, the exchange of full-face and profile is a mode of shot/reverse shot conventional in this kind of situation in which one character, the banker, is giving the answers, and the other one, the young man, is asking the questions. The profile tends more to direct our attention

History Lessons. The young man's second conversation with the banker.

off screen, the full-face to become more the center of attention. "The demo-cratic cause had really gone to the dogs," says the banker as he tells the story of the civil war between Caesar and Pompey, the story the young man heard briefly from the peasant now recounted at length from the point of view of an insider. But if the young man starts out in profile, the position of the one seeking information, the interviewer he resembles, step by step he comes to be shown full-face, not the position of the one asking but of the one facing the questions. And on his side the banker comes step by step to be shown in profile, as if he were not the one telling the story but the one putting the questions, as if he and the young man were gradually exchanging roles as interviewer and interviewed.

Just as in the conversation with the peasant, so in this second conversa-tion with the banker we begin with one character in profile and the other one full-face and gradually the angle on each character changes—each time dif-fering by 90° from the previous shot of the opposite character—until we end with the character who started out in profile coming to be shown full-face and the character who started out full-face coming to be shown in profile.[52] The geometry is the same but the pace is much slower now, so that with the banker the exchange of shots becomes more thoughtful and lacks the sense of rapport that was established with the peasant. And the same geometry is now applied in reverse: the camera circles the young man from profile to front and the opposite character from front to profile, rather than the other way around as before. What is the appropriateness of this arbitrariness?

The young man's conversation with the peasant was his most active exchange with another character. He was quieter in the first conversation with the banker, more the listening student deferring to the teacher, but he still asked several questions and (aside from the stroll in the garden, when it was his turn to answer a question) he was never shown more than briefly. Now he asks no questions, says nothing at all. And yet he is shown as regularly as the banker, held on the screen for as long, given the same em-phasis or perhaps even more, since the gradually more frontal view brings his face more and more to the center of attention. Even though he listens in silence he is shown with insistence, progressively more insistence; and even though he listens in silence he no longer looks like the listening student deferring to the teacher. He looks no less keenly interested in what he is hearing about Roman history, but his expression seems stern now, his gaze probing rather than trustful.

Talking to the peasant, the young man at first thought he knew better than the uneducated old man but was gradually put in his place as the interviewer, the one learning from the other. Listening to the banker in this second conversation, he is gradually put in his place as the one facing the questions, the one who must decide what to do about what he has been learning from the other. By the end of the scene, as he listens to the banker relating with relish a particularly dirty business—Caesar's subjugation of rebellious Lusitanian mountaineers whom he brought down in large numbers to work as slaves in profitable silver mines—we may read something like anger on the young man's face. "My confidence in him had proved well-founded," says the banker about Caesar in the film's last line. "Our small bank was no small bank any more." Right after the first conversation with the banker, the young man talked to the peasant; right after the jurist, to the

History Lessons. The last four shots of the young man and the banker.

poet: in each case one account was opposed by another from a different point of view. No account follows the second conversation with the banker, but he is not really allowed to have the last word: his account is opposed by the barely contained anger we detect in the young man's stare at him. This is again an unconventional refashioning of a conventional device, the reaction shot, the prompting of a response in the audience by cutting to the reaction on a character's face.

The reaction on the young man's face, however, is not so easy to read. Our response here cannot be the simple sharing of a character's feelings that the reaction shot normally asks for. The young man is the narrative center of consciousness but we are given no ready access to his consciousness; he is the

Our small bank was no small bank any more.

central figure of identification but our identification is complicated and held in check by a detachment calling for our reflection. We cannot be sure of what he is feeling, we can only surmise, which leads us to examine our own feelings about the situation, to take stock of our own consciousness and bring it into play. The unconventional shot arrangement, the gradual exchanging of the positions of interviewer and interviewed in the initial shot/reverse shot, does more than simply direct our attention to the young man's reaction: it implies that he must react, it turns the banker's narrative into a kind of question put to the young man. He started out as the student confronting history, and history ends up confronting him, challenging him to take a stand on the basis of what he has learned. His reaction does not determine ours but, from our own perspective, we are called upon to react just as he is called upon.

No representation of an action, of a world, can make its spectators part of the action, of the world represented. But *History Lessons* is a representation of consciousness, of a coming to consciousness, and it asks its spectators to take part in the process of that coming to consciousness, a process in which the protagonist, the center of consciousness, is the young man. He starts from a democratic position, and during his last car ride we may have noticed the recurrence of Communist posters on the walls of buildings along that route, perhaps an indication that he may be on the road to a Marxist consciousness or somewhere in the neighborhood ("I am not a Marxist—not as far as I know," Straub has said). However that may be, his face exhibits a new look of understanding in his final encounter with the banker, and his stance toward him seems clearly to have changed. Our having to ponder the young man's reaction, in the uncommon context given it by the unfolding shot/reverse shot, presses us to ponder our own reaction, to decide where we stand ourselves. Rather than just sharing the young man's anger vicariously, we must develop our own anger at the banker, the film implies, for, as Mother Courage explains to a young soldier in Brecht's play, a long anger is required, an anger based on reflection rather than on the emotion of the moment.

The young man's silent anger could be our projection, but his loss of innocence and gain of responsibility are a certainty. Nothing is more seductive to a young man interested in politics than the kind of insider's account the banker has been giving him. And besides the seduction of being in the know, one form of privilege or the illusion of privilege, there is all the privilege of wealth and power that the banker represents. Taken into the banker's confidence over sips of a doubtless excellent wine, the young man is invited into a complicity with the ruling class that he appears to repudiate—

about which, in any case, he is called upon to make up his mind, whether to throw in his lot with the mountain stream or the sumptuous villa. As the camera circles to the banker's profile, in the background of one shot the fountain of his villa comes into view and then the mansion itself makes a distant but imposing appearance. There are flowers all around in the garden, flowers that represent the seduction of beauty, the beauty that wealth and power will afford us.

As it circles to the young man's full face, the camera comes in for a close-up, screen-center, of the young man in three-quarter front view, but in the next, still more frontal shot of him, the last view of him in the film, instead of coming still closer the camera pulls back and shows him on the lower right of the screen, leaving an empty space above and on the left side, the wrong side of the screen according to the rules. Or rather, a space full of flowers, flowers stirred in the wind as the banker talks about all the money Caesar made for himself in his Iberian campaign. The camera's pulling back when we would have expected it to come closer gives the impression that the young man is recoiling from the banker, putting distance between himself and the exploiters. The flowers stirred in the wind are rather like the shaking chandeliers in Eisenstein's besieged Winter Palace, the beautiful accouterments of privilege trembling under fire, in this case the fire of the young man's silent anger. But the flowers in *History Lessons* are a more complex image of agitated beauty. As flowers in a rich man's garden they represent privilege, seductive beauty, and their trembling in the wind represents the young man's resistance to that privilege and that seduction, the readiness to blow up that beauty we may detect in his stern countenance. But the flowers are beautiful in a way that does not belong to the ruling class alone.[53] As the camera lingers on their beautiful agitation, they seem themselves to partake of the winds of change, and they come to represent the beauty of nascent revolution. Like the beauty of Kiarostami's flowers in *Close-Up*, this is beauty as an undertaking.

We may almost expect, by the end of the film, that the young man will get up from his chair and shoot the banker—the burst of Bach music on the soundtrack following the banker's last statement feels indeed like a shot—but we are aware that this ancient Roman has long been dead, that now the enemy is to be found in his modern counterparts, lurking in the streets of contemporary Rome.

9 :   The Signifiers of Tenderness

The inventor of the motion picture bore the appropriate name of Lumière. Photography, as its name implies, is inscription by light, light that the camera receives from its subjects and retains in its pictures. And out of light the film image is twice made: light inscribes the image in the camera and light projects the image on the screen. In the movie theaters of my childhood people smoked, and the smoke in the air would allow one to see the rays of light reaching across the dark auditorium and, like a long spectral brush, painting the pictures on the screen. Lumière's original movie camera doubled as a movie projector: light went into the machine and light came out.

The light of the *nouvelle vague*—the "new wave" in French cinema that crested in the early sixties—was special. It was the light of available light on black-and-white film, and on the screen it made for a striking combination of naturalness and artificiality. The light that went into the machine was uncorrectedly natural, the light that came out unmistakably artificial. The dazzling *Lola* of Jacques Demy (1961; his first film, one of the many first films brought into being in the brief reign of available opportunity that was the *nouvelle vague*) made that special light into a medium of enchantment. Another first film shot by the same cameraman, Raoul Coutard, stays in the collective memory as an epitome of the *nouvelle vague:* the brisk and audacious *Breathless* of Jean-Luc Godard (1959). If the light of *Lola* was magical, the light of *Breathless* was existential: the undimmed light of the immediate moment, lived dangerously.

The filmmakers of the *nouvelle vague*—Godard and Demy, Truffaut and Rivette, Rohmer and Varda—liked to take the camera out into the world and film on location not only out in the streets but also in the rooms and corridors of real life. Available light is the actual light of an actual place, the light of day or the lamps of a room or the city lights of night, the world's light uncorrected by additional lighting concealed from the viewer such as is usual in filmmaking. When a scene in *Breathless* required such additional lighting, Godard contrived to have it take place in a photographer's studio so that the studio lights would be unconcealed. Available light gave the images of the *nouvelle vague* a look of documentary spontaneity. In a lecture at the time, Slavko Vorkapich, a Hollywood montage specialist who later in his life took it upon himself to theorize about the movies, complained that the rather rough documentary look was all right for filming in the streets but certainly not for a bedroom scene: what, asked Vorkapich rhetorically, would a newsreel camera be doing in a bedroom? For available light, natural and spontaneous though it may look, tends at the same time to call attention to the camera, to the artifice of film, to the fact that what was the world's light is now the projector's light casting the images on the screen.

Uncorrected by additional lighting the world's light will often overexpose or underexpose the image. In life our eyes readily adjust to bright sunlight coming in through a window, but on film, unless studio lights or reflectors compensate for the discrepancy between the light of day and the dimmer light indoors, the outside will appear overexposed and the inside will appear underexposed. Such deviations from normal photographic exposure, which traditional filmmaking had disallowed because they call attention to the artifice of the image, the filmmakers of the *nouvelle vague* not only allowed but welcomed and thematized and embroidered. The newsreel look of *Breathless,* central to its sense of life as improvisation in the midst of action—in the midst of a bedroom no less than in the streets—was itself not an improvisation but a calculated effect for which Godard and Coutard took pains to get the right film stock.

This was not the first time that the reputedly amateurish was made into a successful style in art. Out of a like disregard of conventional finish the impressionist painters likewise made a style with their blunt bright colors and undisguised brush strokes; pursuing a similar aim of rendering the actual sparkle and play of natural light, they similarly called attention to the artifice of their medium, and so achieved a like combination of naturalness and artificiality. Impressionism sought to capture the fleeting in a medium of the lasting; the *nouvelle vague* sought to capture the present moment, the feel of the here and now, in a medium that unfolds before our eyes a world elsewhere, a world that (as both Godard and Stanley Cavell see it) has already taken place.

A Godard film gives the impression not of the complete but of the ongoing, a world in the process of taking place, "a film in the process of being made" (as his 1966 *Masculine Feminine* declares itself). Most films are like most novels, Godard has said, recountings of what has passed and come to an end, whereas he attempts instead to account for the pressing inconclusive present, and he compared himself to a journalist rather than a novelist. Following *Breathless* he made the much less famous but even more remarkable *Le Petit Soldat* (1960), which for three years the French government suppressed: again a film about life lived in the moment but now both the personal and the political moment.

The burning political issue in France at that moment, the Algerian war, *Le Petit Soldat* addressed with an implicative urgency summed up in the image of a hesitant assassin walking behind his victim with a large pointed pistol along a crowded street without attracting anybody's notice: a startling image of the daily unbelievability of political violence. As the protagonist and narrator, the central consciousness of this spy thriller taking over the space of real life, Godard purposely chose a character on the wrong side of the struggle, Bruno Forestier, an opinionated young man working for the right-wing French as a terrorist against the Arabs and their sympathizers: the existential hero as a callow intellectualizing thug. Neither likable nor simply dismissible, a figure who leads us into the story but does not command our allegiance, this protagonist is Godard's way of putting the questions to us, leaving us on our own to find our bearings in a critical situation. *Le Petit Soldat* is a rare political film that takes sides (by the film's end it is clear that its sympathies lie with the cause of Algerian liberation) but does not pick sides for us. Attacked from the right and from the left as well, the film conformed to nobody's prejudices and made everybody uncomfortable. Politics is the tragedy of our time: so, as quoted by a character in the film, said Napoleon.

Le Petit Soldat remains Godard's best political film. This is heresy for those who hold that Godard found himself, artistically as well as politically—and for these people it is the same thing, the artistically and the politically correct—only after 1968. As late as the 1966 *Two or Three Things I Know about*

Le Petit Soldat.
Political violence.

Her, wrote Colin MacCabe in *Screen* in the days when that magazine was setting the pace of English-speaking film theory, Godard was "still offer[ing] an aesthetic position to the viewer," still "hesitating between the art cinema and the political cinema."[1] MacCabe represents the view of what he later called the "class of '68," the view that pleasure must be renounced for knowledge and that art must be renounced for politics. But in that case, why bother with art? For several years after 1968 Godard didn't much bother with art but he kept making it, making it for those who thought that not bothering with art made for militant politics. Among other things, the protagonist of *Le Petit Soldat* is an aesthete, and though his aesthetic orientation is connected with his right-wing politics, it is his sense of beauty—the beauty of Anna Karina in her ravishing first appearance in Godard's films, playing the part of a woman working for the cause of Algerian liberation—that awakens him to the error of his political ways. It is not true that beauty is truth, but neither is it true that, as the likes of MacCabe assume, beauty is the opposite of truth.

Godard, the Godard that from *Breathless* on kept taking the breath away in the years before 1968, was the most playful and the most serious of the filmmakers of the *nouvelle vague,* the most renewing and the most enduring. Longer and more profoundly than any of the others, he sustained the challenge to convention, the readiness to take risks, the spirit of excited exploratory possibility. A prime artist of the sixties and shaper of the temperament of those years, he remained all through the decade a very controversial figure, much admired by some and as much detested by others; all through the decade he continued to make people uncomfortable. Godard's importance, said the theater and film director Peter Brook at the time, is that he gives the cinema not just mobility of camera but mobility of thought:

> he liberates the picture from its own consistency, so that at one second you are genuinely looking at a photograph of three people in a bar, then you are half alienated, then three-quarters alienated, then you are looking at it as a film, then as something made by a filmmaker, then you are reminded that it is made by actors, and then you are thrown right back into believing it. This is the changing relationship that you have in Shakespeare.[2]

Paris impersonates Alphaville in Godard's 1965 film of that title the way his actors impersonate his characters. Alphaville is the capital city of a totalitarian interstellar future, but the city we see on the screen is plainly contemporary Paris. As Paris plays the part of Alphaville while remaining manifestly itself, so Godard's actors play their parts while remaining manifestly themselves. Like Alphaville, Godard's characters are a declared fiction, one in which we are *not* to suspend our disbelief; like Paris, his actors signify that fiction but are kept distinct from it and assert on the screen the traits of their own reality. And yet, though Godard makes us quite aware that Paris is not Alphaville, the actors not the characters, he wants us to recognize Alphaville in Paris, the characters in the actors, the deliberately unbelievable fiction in the presented reality signifying it. Paris plays the part of Alphaville without disguise because, Godard suggests, it needs none to be seen as the embodiment of a dehumanized, computer-ruled future; in a sense, Alphaville *is* Paris

Anna Karina in
Le Petit Soldat: photographing beauty
and talking about truth,
twenty-four times
a second.

because much of that science-fiction future already exists in our actual present. In a similar sense, Godard's characters *are* his actors, who bring to their implausible parts the conviction of their own documented characteristics.

Like Brecht before him, Godard sets up a marked separation between the actor and the character. Brecht's "alienation effect" is usually discussed as an effect on the spectators—it keeps them at a distance from the drama, keeps them from identifying themselves with the characters—but it is first of all an effect on the drama and its performance: it keeps the performance at a distance from the drama, keeps the actors from being identified with the characters they play. As Roland Barthes put it, Brecht's is a "theater of the signifier," by which he meant a theater that brings forward its means of representation—its words, actors, sets, costumes, lights, music—and exhibits them doing their work as signs, to be seen not as constituents of drama but as referring to a drama that is not to be equated with its representation on the stage. As Brecht himself said, his theater breaks with the dramatic to become "epic," by which he meant a *narrative* theater that, instead of performing a drama, tells about it through the performance, gives an account, making clear that this is but one among many possible accounts, of the characters and the action by means of these words, these actors, this stage. Aristotle drew a distinction between epic and tragedy, narrative and drama, between a medium that tells about things and one that enacts them before an audience; Brecht's quarrel with Aristotle was the quarrel of a man who made enactment into a medium of telling.

The alienation effect is pointless except in conjunction, in interplay, with a generated involvement that it holds in check. In Brecht it sets off against each other two pulls to involvement that are usually merged: involvement in the drama and involvement in the live performance. Working with a distinction intrinsic to the medium of theater—between the fiction of drama and the reality of live performance—Brecht accentuates it and makes it into a structural principle. In a movie what takes the place of live performance is the organized reproduction of sights and sounds. The movie audience becomes involved in the camera's observation of appearances, appearances that, projected as images on the screen, make no clear distinction between fiction and reality, just as in a verbal account the same words may tell about a fiction or about a reality, or the same passage may describe fictional characters and real circumstances. For this reason the movies and the novel are thought to be more realistic than the theater.

The stage is an actual space made fictional by convention, by the audience's agreement to regard the performance before it as representing another world; the screen is a fictional space made to seem actual by convention, by the audience's agreement to regard the images being projected before it as tantamount to views of the world. As long as a movie secures that agreement, the actors on the screen—though these aren't the actors but merely their traces in light and shadow—can seem more immediately real, more vividly present, than any actors who are in fact present on a theater stage. No device or mode of performance in the theater elicits the intimacy of a movie close-up. It is a fictional intimacy, an illusory proximity that nonetheless gains a peculiar hold on the audience: a face not there at all and yet insistently there, its lineaments filling the screen like the flesh of an apparition.

Owing to this potent illusion of presence, of intimacy with the figures on the screen, the movie actor, to a greater degree than the stage actor, tends to become identified for the audience with the character he or she plays. Or rather, in the case of a movie star, each character in turn becomes identified with the actor, who from movie to movie remains by and large a constant presence, an icon that is primarily "Greta Garbo" or "John Wayne" and only secondarily a particular character played by Greta Garbo or John Wayne. Although they give that impression, such stars do not exactly play themselves: they play their icons, a compound of themselves and camera and screen that can accommodate a range, even if not a wide range, of particular characterizations. Other kinds of movie acting also encourage and depend on the audience's identification of actor and character. There is the "typage" method practiced by Eisenstein, the striking face, seen maybe for a moment but in arresting close-up, that succinctly personifies a social type. There is the neorealist nonprofessional, the real person picked off the streets of Rome or the villages of Sicily for the part of a Roman worker or a Sicilian fisherman, an icon of authenticity that, supposedly the opposite of a movie star, more thoroughly gives the impression of someone playing himself, being himself on the screen. There is the nonactor in Bresson's films, the severe and subdued performer who, allowed very little emotive externalization, acts by sheer presence, by a certain unyielding look, a way of being on the screen that intimates the interior. Films are an art of appearances, faces whether of people or of things, surfaces displayed on the surface of the screen. Generally in movie acting the actor's appearance, the surface of personal features he or she presents for close observation, distinctively establishes the character's perceived identity. Appearance as a signifier of character leads the movie audience to identify the actor, who supplies the face, the voice, the perceptible features, with the character being portrayed.

Certainly we go to the movies to watch performers we like, but we go to watch *them*—for the convincing illusion that we're watching them on the screen—not so much to watch them *perform*. When a movie makes us take note of the actual situation of its performance—the camera, the technical crew, the usually brief, often repeated takes—it brings on by that an "alienation effect." In a home movie, where the camera creates and records an evident situation of playacting, no effect of alienation occurs because the playacting is part of the ordinary reality of people we know: we're interested in the people, not in their performance except as it reveals them to the camera. A fiction movie, which normally dissembles the playacting for the camera, generates a similar involvement in what the camera reveals about people, in what, without distinguishing between the actors and the characters they play, we perceive as a human reality on the screen. "Every film," Godard has said, "is a documentary of its actors." This is more strictly true of a home movie. A fiction movie constructs the fiction of characters from the documentary of actors. It is the documentary of a fiction enacted before the camera; and it is the fiction of a documentary of characters merged in our minds with their incarnation in the actors.

Foreign to the medium of theater—which cannot observe or record, only perform—documentary enters into every film save an animated cartoon or a visual abstraction. It enters even into such a blatantly theatrical film as W. C. Fields's sardonically phony version of the frozen North, *The Fatal Glass of Beer* (1933), whose theatricality gains much of its satirical impact from being measured against the possibility of documentary. It enters centrally into the flagrant science-fiction secret-agent fantasy of *Alphaville*, a fantasy made more flagrant by the incongruity of its documentary enactment, the reality of Paris and of the actors vividly on the screen, and yet a fantasy resonating with that reality and somehow made real.

If every film combines fiction and documentary, a Godard film characteristically clashes them together. Already in *Breathless* he does not seek to blend fiction and documentary in the usual fashion but treats them as separate, discordant modes, opposite directions in which he pushes at once. *Breathless* is not a gangster movie made more credible by the use of real locations: this gangster fiction, though not exactly a parody, is presented within virtual quotation marks, and made not more but still less credible by the atmosphere of actuality, the unpolished, improvised, here-and-now look that the film assumes. It's as if a newsreel camera were urgently capturing on the spot an action transplanted there from the fantasy lots of Hollywood. The newsreel aspect of *Breathless* expresses a sense of life as improvisation, self-definition in the midst of existence, and the film has been cogently interpreted as an existentialist statement; but the fantasy aspect acts as a critique of existentialism, for the hero's self-defining improvisations are modeled on the figure of the Hollywood tough guy, a make-believe essence that does precede the hero's existence. And not just a critique of Hollywood existentialism: *Breathless* leads us to recognize that the existential hero is a fiction, whether a tough guy on the Humphrey Bogart model or a less evident fiction. Through its clash between documentary and fiction *Breathless* makes us see the fiction of authenticity, the fiction one acts out when defining oneself in action, as well as the authenticity of fiction, the way a fiction one acts out may all the same be what one authentically is.

At the theater, if we sit too close to the stage we likely notice details not actually meant for display, not part of the performance; whereas at a movie everything we notice about the actors is there to be observed. The camera knows no dividing line between the person and the impersonation. Godard draws such a line. He divides the actors from their characters by a twin emphasis on the reality of the actors and the fictionality of the characters they play. On the one hand, he points up the characteristics belonging to the actors themselves, their peculiarities of aspect and gesture, speech and demeanor, what the real persons in front of the camera bring to the film; and on the other hand, he has them impersonate characters pointedly fictional, conceived so as to invite disbelief. "I ask the actors to be themselves," he has said, "in structures that are not their own." The structures he devises for his actors encourage them to be themselves, enlisting their personal traits on the documentary side of the break he induces between the reality the camera reproduces—"the truth, twenty-four times a second," as his garrulous hero puts it in *Le Petit Soldat*—and the declared artifice of his fictional constructions.

To separate actor and character, whose merging comes about differently in films and in the theater, is in each medium a different undertaking. Simply to separate them is very easy: incompetence does that, miscasting, bad acting, bad writing or directing. It is another matter to separate them articulately, in an artful interplay between alienation and involvement such as Brecht and Godard arrange. Theater is founded on representation by performance, film on representation by documentary. The first signifying act of theater is to mark out a stage, set an area apart from the surrounding world for the purpose and the duration of a performance. The first signifying act of film is to train a camera on a subject, a piece of appearances to be documented. Although there may be much preparation beforehand, each medium starts with a fundamental act of pointing: pointing to a stage as the area of performance, pointing a camera at something in the world that claims its documenting attention. Both Brecht and Godard induce a break between signifier and signified—between the means of representation and expression and the things being represented and expressed—but each does it in a different way, each along the grain of his medium, so to speak. If Brecht sets up a dialectic between performance and drama, Godard sets up a dialectic between documentary and fiction.

Documentary is usually thought of as content, factual content, the actual existence of the things represented. And documentary in this common usage is the kind of film that represents fact—nonfiction film, as some prefer to say. But documentary also resides in the form of the photographic image, in the way it is constituted, in its means of representation. The sense of fact peculiar to the photographic image (a sense that may be vanishing with the increasing facility of its computer reconstitution, in which case it will no longer be the photographic image we know but a different kind of image) comes from its incorporating into the picture something of the very appearance of the things represented, from the way the camera receives their light directly from them and lets it draw the picture. Documentary is a means as well as a result, a means whose mark the result distinctively bears. And a means common to all films, fiction as well as nonfiction: the fictional world a film represents it constructs out of bits and pieces it takes from the actual world.

Documentary in a fiction film, documentary whether of place or of persons, serves as a means for the representation of fiction. Just as performance in the theater is a signifier of drama, so in a fiction film documentary is a signifier of fiction. The landscape of the West stands, in Westerns, for a fictional past; in 1903, when the old West was still a present, the landscape of New Jersey did service for a fictional West in *The Great Train Robbery*. It's essentially no different with a movie taking place in contemporary Paris and photographed on location: the sights of the actual city, chosen according to the requirements of a fiction, are made to stand for the world of that fiction. The movie actor of course acts, gives a performance of a character; but the performance shades into a documentary of the actor's own characteristics that also, and often more expressively, portrays the part he or she plays. In the same way that he splits Paris from the science-fictional Alphaville, Godard splits the documentary of the actor, the person, from the characterization of the fictional being he or she impersonates.

"To photograph a face is to photograph the soul behind it. Photography is truth. And the cinema is the truth, twenty-four times a second." Photography is truth, says Bruno, a character given to spouting half-truths, while photographing beauty. He utters those lines in *Le Petit Soldat* while photographing Anna Karina—or Veronica Dreyer, the first of several parts that Karina, who became Godard's wife, played for him—a woman Bruno falls for in about the time it takes to snap a picture. So, we may surmise, did Godard. On Anna Karina as a photographic subject, as beauty and truth but not in the Grecian urn's simple equation, he fashioned his own sustained essay, enchanted yet reflective, in the form of his 1962 movie *Vivre sa vie*.

Here, as in *Le Petit Soldat*, Godard links his portrayal of Karina with her fellow Dane, Carl Dreyer, a filmmaker who would reveal the soul, and the souls of women especially, in the intently photographed face. Apart from the credits, the first close-ups of Karina's face in *Vivre sa vie* come in a scene where her character, whose name is Nana, goes to see Dreyer's famous 1928 film about Joan of Arc, famous most of all for its close-ups, and Godard cuts between her tearful face in the audience and the tearful face of Falconetti as Dreyer's exalted heroine. But Nana, an ordinary young woman who has trouble paying the rent and drifts into prostitution, surely does not live an exalted life, nor does she die an exalted death when she gets caught in the middle of a gunfight between rival pimps. Her death scene is notably unbelievable: rather than at each other, both pimps aim straight at her, which, almost diagrammatically, represents a concept, not a plausible reality. And yet this scene echoes, visually and in its emotional impact of sudden arbitrary tragedy, the memorable neorealist death, gunned down by Nazis in the street, of the Anna Magnani character in *Open City* (1945). The reference to Dreyer's film and this less explicit reference to Rossellini's are acknowledgments of artifice—of the fiction that depicts a woman crying in a movie, a woman dying in a movie—and also of the power such a fiction can have to move us deeply nonetheless. Between Karina as Nana and Falconetti as Joan of Arc, Karina as Nana and Anna Magnani as a victim of Nazi bullets, Godard proposes both a parallel and an ironic contrast, a parallel and a contrast that involve the actresses as well as their characters, the form of expression as well as the content expressed. While he holds up the sordid ordinary story of Nana as a tragedy, worthy like any other of high pathos, he calls into question the premises and the telling of that story, the evocation of that pathos.

Dreyer's is the pathos of the close-up, the suffering soul that transcends circumstances; Rossellini's is the pathos of the long shot, the individual caught in unfortunate circumstances. The point of view in *Vivre sa vie* strikingly shifts between the close-up and the long shot. Besides documentary and fiction, Godard's fundamental opposition, his films will clash together close-ups and long shots, abrupt cutting and long takes, the natural light of a scene and the artificial light of the image, the unrehearsed and the composed, the unexpected and the predictable, words and pictures, sounds and sights. Like Brecht, Godard separates elements that are usually blended together and discordantly juxtaposes them, so that, in an effect of reciprocal alienation, by their discordance they make one another strange. More intricately, more radically than Eisenstein, that theorist and practitioner of "collision," he orchestrates conflict, the unstable mixture, the interruptive shift, the give and take of dialectical discrepancy.

According to Godard's advertisement for *Vivre sa vie*, Nana "gives her body but keeps her soul." She is, to compound the cliché, a whore with a heart of gold and as such has virtual quotation marks around her like Belmondo's gangster in *Breathless*. But in what serious sense, beyond the clichés of movies or of piety, does she keep her soul, a soul that transcends her giving her body, the unfortunate circumstances in which she's caught? In one episode—the film is divided into a disjunct twelve in a manner reminiscent of Brecht, with titles in between announcing what's to come—she maintains that, though she sometimes forgets it, she is responsible for her life, "responsible . . . and free." She is, however, manifestly an actress saying lines that are not her own, delivered with a certain earnest, smiling awkwardness that the director responsible for them—responsible in fact for the whole course of Nana's life, and calling this fact to our attention—makes plainly visible in close-up. In her films with Godard, Karina is an inspired amateur actress; he turns to his advantage her inadequacies as a performer, which he frankly displays and brings into his structures.

All fictional constructions, digressive or open-ended though they may be, are at bottom deterministic; the characters may appear free, but everything that happens to them has been arranged with forethought by the author who created them. Diderot's outrageously digressive novel *Jacques le fataliste* designedly plays with the fact of the author's design; while the fatalist Jacques believes everything to have been divinely foreordained, "written up yonder," in fact everything is written right here, on the pages of this novel the reader holds, whose outcome he or she can skip forward to find out. If in modernist fictions a sense of the arbitrariness of exercised choice replaces the old necessities, this is because a modern artist can no longer comfortably assume the godlike role that falls upon an author. A modernist fiction declaring its maker's arbitrariness, *Vivre sa vie* designedly entertains its heroine's notions of responsibility and freedom within the countering, undisguised determinism of its fictional design. The foretelling titles, as William S.

Pechter has noted, serve to underscore that determinism. In his essay "For
and Against Godard" Pechter dissents from Susan Sontag's reading of the
film, which takes Nana as indeed responsible and free,[3] and he argues that
the "main force and extreme poignancy" of *Vivre sa vie* derive from the
"contradiction between how the heroine conceives herself and what happens
to her."[4] Neither the heroine nor what happens to her, however, is presented
as a reality soliciting our belief. What chiefly carries conviction and generates involvement is the actress herself, the documented reality of Karina. As
an actress playing a part, she gives her body to the camera and is not
responsible for the fiction; but insofar as she remains herself, distinct from
the part and from the fiction, she keeps her soul.

Vivre sa vie is about the making of a film, about the contriving of a
fiction, about fiction and documentary, about Godard's enchantment with
Karina; but it is also about Nana the prostitute, who is not merged with
Karina the actress but set beside her for a reflective comparison. As in the
later *Two or Three Things I Know about Her*, Godard treats prostitution here
both as an actual occupation—one episode adopts the form of a factual
report on prostitution, with voice-over narration—and as a sort of allegorical figure standing for all our occupations, all our dealings with the society
around us—a "radical metaphor," as Sontag calls it, for the dissociation of
the outside we offer to others from the inside we would keep for ourselves.
(The film carries an epigraph from Montaigne: "Lend yourself to others; give
yourself to yourself.") Alongside this metaphor, doubling it and complicating it, is another large metaphor the film develops from an occupation:
acting, more specifically the acting of women in movies, quite particularly
Karina's acting for Godard. Both acting and prostitution are occupations
that deal in the body, offering the very person as goods, the person surrendered to the expectations of others; both make familiar metaphors for the
lending of ourselves to others, the turning of ourselves into an object for
others. Of all of us it may be said that, to some degree at least, we are actors in
our transactions with others, prostitutes in our occupations. Is it possible,
the film inquires, for us to be the actors and the prostitutes that our society
demands and still keep our souls, still remain responsible and free? Can any
of us preserve an inside that somehow endures, perhaps even thrives, even
though we surrender the outside to others? For the figure of Nana the
prostitute, victimized by death when she tries to escape the victimization of
her life, the answer would have to be no. But for the figure of Karina the
actress, entangled with Nana but distinct from her, the answer the film
articulates is a qualified, a tentative yet hopeful yes.

Before she turns to prostitution, Nana is caught attempting to steal and brought to the police station. There, as Nana faces the interrogation of a not unsympathetic police officer, Karina faces the probing gaze of the camera. The episode begins with a frontal, off-centered shot of her against a window. Her face, the inside, appears dim in the image because underexposed against the overexposed bright white of the window, the outside that is the source of light. As has been his consistent practice, Godard shoots with natural, or "available," light but makes us aware of how this becomes in the image an artificial light. This and two further frontal shots of her, each held at length, convey a sense of looking into, bringing to the light of day, the dim recesses of her face: the camera gets successively closer, the framing successively more centered, the inside (as her face takes up more of the image and the window less) more clearly exposed. Intercut with two brief, well-lit, also frontal views of the policeman at his typewriter, these three shots, culminating in an extreme close-up, compose the episode, whose sustained frontal viewpoint heightens the feeling of confrontation. It is Nana's, and Karina's, confrontation with the other, with the gaze of the other that (as Sartre represents it in a well-known passage from *Being and Nothingness*) brings on shame. The other is embodied for Nana in the interrogating policeman writing on his machine his report on her, and for Karina in the intently, intimately witnessing camera, the machine whose report on her appears on the screen. Visibly not at ease before the camera's unswerving frontal stare, Karina sometimes returns the gaze but more often averts her eyes downward or glances aside, showing in any case the effort it takes her to hold her own. The character's shame at being exposed to the law parallels the actress's shame, her sense of self-exposure, at being photographed from so close and at such length.

A convention of the fiction film asks the actors to pretend not to notice the camera photographing them. That same convention asks us in the audience to see nothing remarkable in the camera's being able, at any chosen moment and for any chosen duration, to observe people at a proximity that in real life they would normally grant only to a lover or the like. In the Biograph films that pioneered, among other things, the dramatic use of the close-up, D. W. Griffith hardly ever used it in what was soon to be the area of its greatest appeal and acclaim—the human face. There were by 1910 or 1911 not infrequent close-ups of objects in his movies, but of faces, which one would suppose would have come first, there were few if any until later. Why did the founding innovator of dramatic film technique hold back from the face? Griffith must have, I surmise, felt reluctant to intrude on so personal an area, felt shy of violating its privacy. Later, when he did intrude, and focused his camera on the face of Lillian Gish, he composed close-ups that are perhaps the most beautiful in existence. Whereas close-ups nearly always take their proximity for granted, these don't; rather they treat it as something indeed remarkable, a privilege, a gesture of genuine intimacy. By 1920, when he made *Way Down East,* close-ups of the face were common in movies and already pretty much taken for granted, and yet in his movie the camera views Lillian Gish's face with the awed tenderness of a first lover. For some it's a fault, the founding innovator faltering in his technique, that his close-ups here aren't visually matched with the other shots in a smooth continuity such as was by then already becoming conventional; but in my judgment that's what he was after, close-ups that stand out from the rest like arias in an opera. It was, I think, because Griffith still felt shy of violating the privacy of the face, because he regarded it as a lover's privilege to come this close to a woman, that he invested his close-ups of Lillian Gish with their unique tremulous lyricism.

Despite his citing Dreyer, Godard's close-ups of Karina remind me more of Griffith. Dreyer's close-ups of Falconetti have nothing amorous in their spiritual intensity. Rather they have something merciless and inquisitorial about them: Dreyer's camera, though siding with Joan of Arc against her judges, adopts toward her something like their unyielding stance of authority, and shows its sympathy by holding onto her naked face through the ordeal and letting her inner triumph shine through her suffering. The relentless proximity of Dreyer's camera registers as an imposition rather than an earned intimacy, the privilege not of love but of power. A director always has power, authority, over the actor, a power and authority exercised most plainly in the close-up, by the camera's taking visual possession of the face. In the episode at the police station, Godard, comparing his camera with the policeman, expressly putting them both in the position of the shaming other, acknowledges his exercise of that power and authority; but at the same time he allows the actress to respond to the camera's gaze with her own affecting human power, her own authority as a person, gathered in a visible exertion of self. To allow that reciprocal power to assert itself is to bestow love, to exhibit—if you'll pardon the sentimental phrase—the power of love.

Nobody can recapture the innocence of those Gish close-ups. I don't mean the sexual so much as the technical innocence, the conveyed excitement of learning to speak, and speaking with surprised eloquence, the camera's language of love. Godard is, in effect, asking us to pardon his sentimental phrases as he attempts to relearn a language grown unduly facile, to give the signifiers of tenderness, hackneyed from long, mostly unexamined and unfeeling use, a fresh significance, a renewed eloquence. In a love scene by the sea in *Pierrot le fou* (1965), as the couple, Karina and Belmondo, embrace tenderly, Godard enhances the romantic atmosphere by means of a device conventionally put to such uses, the "day for night," the day photographed through a filter that turns it into a night of soft, glowing darkness. He lays bare the device, however—he baldly shows us the sun becoming a moon under the filter's effect—and thus declares his fabrication of this romantic scene; and yet, while challenging, he also rescues the convention of the soft artificial night by employing it with unusual beauty, a beauty managed through an old device that seems to have been invented anew just for this scene. Tenderness is a precarious, precious thing, he implies, not to be gained with a filter's ease, the moments of its enjoyment, even if illusory, still to be cherished as an aspiration.

In Griffith's time an incipient convention that could well accommodate his employing it idiosyncratically, the close-up was by Godard's time a long-entrenched one that, like the day for night and various other received conventions and procedures of cinema, he felt it necessary to challenge and make over for his purposes. His close-ups of Karina neither ask her to ignore the camera's proximity nor ask the spectator to accept the camera's entitlement to that proximity: they earn their intimacy and gain their tenderness by a displayed reciprocity between a possessive yet deferring camera and an actress who lends her face but maintains her own humanity.

A performer frankly conscious of the camera, self-conscious before its gaze, wouldn't challenge or disrupt normal usage in a home movie. Like all Godard's work of the sixties, *Vivre sa vie* has about it something of the home movie: a movie celebrating the filmmaker's wife, giving her license to playact for the camera, half-seriously drawing parallels with famous actresses, a personal song to her and a song made as enchanting as it is enchanted. But Godard holds to no consistent mode or mood. Another kind of movie, a dramatic fiction about a prostitute, disrupts and is disrupted by the personal song, whose lyricism comes into conflict with the pathos of the prostitute's story: side by side, the song to Karina and the story of Nana have an alienation effect on each other, each putting a curb on the emotions the other generates. The song opens up possibilities that the grim story seems to close; the story brings up difficulties that the sweet song tends to disregard. These are, in short, the possibilities of love and freedom, the difficulties of power and prevailing circumstance. In the end the film, song and story and everything else, asks to be taken figuratively, allegorically: the lyricism celebrates the triumph, the pathos laments the defeat of the soul that would assert itself, the tenderness that would gain embodiment, the freedom that would achieve realization on the ground of recognized necessity. Not in abstract terms but through the concreteness of art—through an art reflecting on its means as it wields them to engage the senses—*Vivre sa vie* addresses large matters with dispassionate intensity.

Actors have different ways of being themselves on the screen. Besides differing in their individual traits, they differ in the kind of presence they manifest, the style they assume, not just of acting, but of selfhood. If Greta Garbo and John Wayne are hard to imagine together in the same movie, it's not because they're incompatible as individuals are in life—in life incompatible individuals often find themselves together—but because their star presences conjure up different movie universes. Movie actors may be variously associated with big pictures, with grade B pictures, with distinct genres; they may be nonprofessionals of the Eisenstein, the neorealist, the Bresson kind, the home-movie variety. *Vivre sa vie* is mainly a solo performance by Karina, or rather, a duet for actress and camera. *Contempt*, which Godard made the following year, assembles an unlikely mixture of performers: Brigitte Bardot, sex icon of the French kitten species; Michel Piccoli, a splendid actor but not a star; Jack Palance, the heavy, imported from American movies and here a crass American movie producer; and Fritz Lang, literally playing himself, the renowned director of *M* and Hollywood exile from Nazi Germany, except that here he inhabits a fictional context. All these performers are "themselves" in *Contempt*, but themselves in different styles of selfhood that clash with one another significantly—Fritz Lang directing a movie produced by Jack Palance and meeting with his interference, Michel Piccoli married to Brigitte Bardot and having troubles encapsulated in the conflicting figures of the ordinary man and the sexy movie star.

Already in *Vivre sa vie*, and more so three years later, by the time of *Alphaville* and *Pierrot le fou*, Anna Karina was a movie star—of sorts. Not exactly a star—not even of the special sort Monica Vitti became in four movies with Antonioni—Karina remained the inspired amateur while, in paradoxical combination, assuming a star selfhood. A cross between the home-movie player and the screen goddess, she was at once a star and a critique of stardom. In *Alphaville* she's incongruously paired with a B-picture professional, Eddie Constantine as Lemmy Caution, secret agent, a role in which this American actor had starred in a series of French thrillers. Karina is the incarcerated princess of Alphaville, the daughter of Professor Nosferatu, alias Von Braun, the city's mastermind. Born in Nueva York but brought to Alphaville by her father, she scarcely remembers her past, for the past is outlawed in a city that, more than books, bans words from the language: the word *tenderness*, for example, which used to be one of her favorites. *Tenderness* and *conscience* are among the dying words of Henry Dickson, an agent who, like Dick Tracy and Flash Gordon, failed in his mission to Alphaville. As befits a secret agent in a movie, Lemmy Caution triumphs over Alphaville and rescues the princess, in actions less incredible than the way this poker-faced, comic-strip tough guy reawakens her to the humanity that the city has suppressed. To the question, "What transforms darkness into light?" put to him by the master computer Alpha 60 in an interrogation, Lemmy Caution curtly replies: "Poetry."

In the star selfhood she assumed with Godard, Karina is an emblem of the soul, a signifier of tenderness, a concrete manifestation of unsuppressible beauty and humanity. Surely Lemmy Caution is not the man to bring that out in her, and yet he does, she being his secret weapon against Alphaville, this secret agent out of cheap fable becoming still more fabulous as the agent of poetry. "Think of the word love," he tells her as they're trying to find their way out of the collapsing Alphaville, whereupon, without delay, she points them in the right direction. The word *love*, the word *tenderness*, the word *conscience* (or *consciousness*, the same word in French): these, Godard emphasizes, are words, signifiers, not the things signified: pointers in the direction of things sought, calling them to mind but not to be equated with their actual attainment.

Barthes called Brecht's theater a "theater of the signifier" because it is a theater that takes us through the process of signification, the play of the signifier, without arriving at an end product, a signified where the process stops and meaning is settled: a theater that moves toward meaning but "suspends this meaning as a question (a suspension we encounter in the particular quality of historical time represented in Brecht's theater, a time of the not-yet)."[5] Godard's cinema may likewise be called a cinema of the signifier, a cinema that leaves a gap open between the signifier it presents and the signified it suspends, the signified not yet reached that evokes "a time of the not-yet."

The day for night in *Pierrot le fou*, like the words in *Alphaville* a declared signifier, signifies a tenderness we can neither take as real nor dismiss as phony, a tenderness that is phony as an actuality but real as an aspiration, a "not-yet" tenderness. An allegory of tenderness, we may call it, as we may call *Alphaville* an allegory of beauty in trouble and of its rescue from dehumanization; allegory is a traditional mode that separates literal and figurative levels. But traditional allegory settles the meaning at the figurative level, whereas in Godard's and in Brecht's kind of allegory the meaning is open, suggested but not settled, a not-yet meaning. Lemmy Caution in *Alphaville* is a signifier of action but manifestly not of any credible sort of action that may be adequate against the organized forces of dehumanization. Although very much needed—Lemmy Caution stands for this need, giving it satisfaction in primitive fantasy—that sort of action, Godard implies, is yet to be properly conceived, let alone taken.

In a movie what transforms darkness into light is, literally, the projector. *Alphaville* begins with a close-up against a dark background of a round light intermittently shining at us, calling our attention to the projector's light that, here as always at the movies, bringing the actors into being and the world they inhabit, bounces at us from the screen. The light flashes according to some pattern or code unfamiliar to us: this is a signifying light, as always at the movies, but here the messages it transmits are not to be readily readable. On the soundtrack we hear intermittent thriller music and then an odd narrating voice talking about fiction and reality—not the voice of the author as we may at first suppose but, as we later ascertain, the voice of the computer, Alpha 60. Laying bare, in this movie about the machine society, the material elements of his machine medium and the way it produces sights and sounds, Godard hints at a connection between the movie's author and the sovereign machine that its fiction erects as the villain. The next narrating voice we hear is that of Lemmy Caution as he arrives in Alphaville; the protagonist's narration, a familiar device, alternates throughout this movie

Alphaville. The arriving Lemmy Caution.

with the computer's narration. Like a digital computer, *Alphaville* is an artifact of alternations.

Illuminated by the flame with which he lights a cigarette, the arriving Lemmy Caution's face emerges from darkness, before going dark again, for a vivid moment that wittily epitomizes a tough guy from film noir, that off-shoot of German expressionism in American soil. A black-and-white movie of strong blacks and whites, *Alphaville* is, as Jonathan Rosenbaum has observed, a critique of expressionism,[6] calling forth its anxious shadows and ominous atmospheres and, without exactly dispelling them, declaring these signifiers of fear to be shadows cast not by doom but by a strip of film running through the projector. Flashing, blinking lights, at various rates and of various sorts, pulsate throughout *Alphaville*, all reminders of the swiftly flickering projector's light that materializes the moving images. Here the effects of light and darkness, which traditional expressionism fabricated in Caligari's studio, are obtained instead with available light as this is rendered in the artificial light of the projected image. Rather than a studio gloom, we get the underexposed night of Paris streets illuminated by cars, neon, lit windows, street lights, reflections on wet pavement; replacing the usual concealed lights of studio chiaroscuro, in one scene a low-hanging lightbulb is set swinging right in the foreground, so that we can plainly see how it generates long, oscillating shadows. The source of light in every scene is made manifest, and so is the change into the different light of the image being projected before us. At times the image switches into negative film, and back again into positive; in traveling shots along hotel corridors, the uneven illumination from spaced ceiling lamps causes alternating changes in exposure as the camera moves, so that the image turns now brighter, now darker. The signifiers of fear become in a way more fearful, because more real, when their source is recognizably in the lights of actuality. Godard's dialectic between documentary and fiction includes not only the fiction of story and characters but also the fiction that, even when derived from actuality, the image itself is.

As Lemmy Caution, facing the computer, upholds poetry's transformative power, the pulsating light of Alphaville, accentuated during the interrogation, shines on him. And, bounced from his image on the screen, it shines on us too: if the computer's narration sounds rather like the author speaking in machine guise, the light of Alphaville, literally issuing from the projector, is associated with its light thematically as well, implicated with the machine bringing the author's images into animate existence. As plainly as it is Paris, Alphaville is the projector's city, whose days and nights come into being on the screen that brightens and dims. A modernist artist, Godard acknowledges the facts of his medium, its conditions of being and meaning, and enlists these acknowledged facts into his signifying practice.

Returning to his hotel in the morning, Lemmy Caution finds the princess, who has been forbidden to see him, awaiting him in his room. Like a vision, a dream—though he's not the dreamer type—she appears three times in a row behind doors he successively opens. The doors open into the film's sunniest sequence: the sun shining through the windows suffuses the images with a light that has the feel of an actual bright morning and also the overexposed resplendence of a vision. It is this light, both the sun's and the projector's, lifelike and dreamlike at once, that radiantly illuminates Karina, herself at once real and a fantasy, as the tough guy implausibly reawakens the princess to poetry and love.

"Love, what is it?" she asks him, glancing out of a window and noticing in the street below the arrival of the police. Seemingly undisturbed by this threat, she answers her own question in a passage of great beauty, lyrical and majestic, a strange entranced ceremony suspended from the film's action—as if the imagination of love, even though not the actuality, could afford to take its time in disregard of the police—and the only passage narrated in her voice. In this poem of love rescued, the author speaks in the voice and mental images of his beloved. It begins with a close-up of her eye, on which, like an eye blinking, like the round blinking light that began the film, a flashing light shines. Then, in a held close-up of her face that continues with a slow pan to

Alphaville. The sunlit princess who asks what love is.

a formalized kiss, the light flashes from behind her, giving her face a blinking nimbus of back-lit hair. As in the rest of the film, in this passage set apart from it, hieratically celebrating love's rebirth in the beloved's mind, the light of Alphaville pulsates unabated. Before the film switches back to the sunny morning, and the police intrude into the hotel room, the passage ends with the room at night, underexposed, the lights of Paris outside the windows, the night not of fear now but of love. The princess, we may say, must imagine even love in the light of Alphaville, since she is its citizen, its prisoner. But, Godard implies, we are all citizens of Alphaville, children of technology's capital city, certainly including the author who has associated himself and his medium with the artifacts of that city: we all must imagine love, and attempt to realize it, from our present situation amid a technology that may be dehumanizing but could be otherwise, depending on what we make of it. The same light that evokes fear can be made to evoke tenderness.

Declared for what they are, the means and materials of expression—the signifiers of fear or of tenderness—are kept distinct from the things expressed in such a way as to hold these in abeyance, the fear as something conquerable, the tenderness as something attainable—the world as something changeable—but not yet. How the one is to be conquered, the other to be attained—how the world is to be changed—is left open. Evidently we're not to look to Lemmy Caution for the answer, not as a figure of the fearless, still less as a figure of the tender. Besides him, the film proposes another, more significant signifier of action, of consciousness acting upon resistant matter, in the very activity that went into its making and gave it shape. In Godard's work, as in much modernist art, the undisguised formative process through which the artist arranges the materials of a medium—words on the blank page, paint on the flat canvas, images made with the world's light and made over with the projector's light shining on the screen—comes to stand for the endeavor to find, the striving to construct, an order in the world: the making of art, not as art's chief subject, but as an allegory of the ordering of life.

It is the projector, and it is poetry—it is the poetry Godard makes of the projected images and accompanying sounds, builds with his medium's technology of reproduction and rearrangement—that transforms darkness into light. As he has exercised his and his medium's transformative capabilities, so, he suggests, we must exercise ours and build with our materials and our technology an order more humanly satisfying than the one that prevails in our world. "My aim," whispers his narration in *Two or Three Things I Know about Her*, is "as much political as poetic": words heard over the image of tender, trembling leaves reflected on the shiny metallic red of a car hood.

Frankly artificial and grounded in actuality at the same time—like all his work—this intricately arranged sequence from *Two or Three Things,* centering on a prosaic car wash, constructs a lyric poem out of the tawdry accouterments of the consumer society. A poem allegorizing, not abstractly but in the concrete form it gives to its materials, the aspiration to change the world, this is perhaps Godard's most eloquent pointer from what is to what may yet be, what we may yet make of the materials around us.

Leaving Alphaville for good, the princess and the tough guy get into his car—which he calls a Ford Galaxie but is in fact a Mustang—and set out on the long drive home through interstellar space. Bright overexposed points, stars that shine in the underexposed night, the tall, bowing street lights along

Alphaville. The light that evokes tenderness.

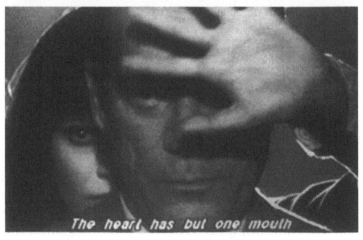

The heart has but one mouth

the highway, extending far into the distance and coming toward us as the camera moves following the car, make an image, no less haunting for being witty, of infinity in the mundane. Reflected on the windshield, in frontal shots first of the tough guy and the princess, then of her alone in sustained close-up, the street lights seem like flashing, rising stars, the light of Alphaville now a fireworks of rescued love and triumphant humanity. (A still more glorious windshield fireworks, in color and wide screen, occurs in *Pierrot le fou*, which Godard made next, but there that is a beginning, and tragedy is the end.) Very slowly, with halting effort, the princess speaks the redemptive concluding words: "I love you." In this final view of her face, the inspired amateur actress, her large eyes moist and poignant at the edge between light and shadow, plays in earnest but betrays some uncertainty that maybe she should be playing in jest: an uncertainty quite in keeping with the uncertain tone of an ending that elicits sentiments no less stirring for being mixed. For Godard's conclusion remains inconclusive: his closure of the form does not pretend to have settled the content. Without asking us to suspend our disbelief in the fiction, he draws us into the undeceived wonder, the sense of sought possibility, expressed in this light-lined ending—but without asking us either to see in this beautiful formal resolution, on the highway that doubles as interstellar space, the figurative road to a proposed actual solution. Figuratively construed, the unbelievable fiction implies the unlikelihood of an actual solution, which, as allegorized in the incongruous pairing of Lemmy Caution and Karina, would require an improbable combination of tough violence and tender love; and yet this unreal happy ending, not

Alphaville. The highway that doubles as interstellar space.

merely ironic, has about it a genuine hopeful happiness. Godard's allegory does not put forward an answer but a flashing, inciting question. The tough guy has rescued the princess from the capital of dehumanization; Godard has rescued the signifiers of tenderness from their common sentimentalization; the real rescue is yet to be accomplished.

In May 1973, after the *nouvelle vague* had for the most part run its course, Godard wrote a letter to his old friend and colleague François Truffaut in which he started by calling him a liar:

> Yesterday I saw *La Nuit américaine*. Probably no one else will call you a liar, so I will. It's no more an insult than "fascist," it's a criticism. . . . Liar, because the shot of you and Jacqueline Bisset the other evening at Chez Francis is not in your film, and one can't help wondering why the director is the only one who doesn't screw in *La Nuit américaine*.

La Nuit américaine, or *Day for Night* (in French as in English the title refers to that trick of movie magic by which a filter dimming the light of day creates on the screen the illusory "American night"), is a film about filmmaking that was a big hit for Truffaut; it went on to win the Oscar for best foreign film. But Godard was quite right: it is the film of a liar, and not just because the director in it, played by Truffaut himself, a notorious womanizer who at the time was involved with the star, is made chaste and sweet to the point of saintliness. This dishonesty Godard accurately considered symptomatic of the film's larger dishonesty. *La Nuit américaine* wears the flat sentimental smile of a dissembler and is as phony and empty as it is eager to please.

In the same breath, however, that he put down Truffaut and his dissembling film, Godard, with some effrontery, asked him to invest in a project of Godard's own: "you ought to help me, so that the public doesn't get the idea we all make films like you." By "we all" Godard no doubt meant the filmmakers of the *nouvelle vague;* he was reminding Truffaut that once they had both been part of that gang of the innovative young. Truffaut had long since given over to a safe-playing gentility; after three or four good films he tamely devoted most of the rest of his career to making just the sort of "well-made" film that as a young critic he had passionately denounced. The commercially compromised received a letter from the politically uncompromising. Godard had become radicalized since 1968 and now made films no longer as an individual artist but as a member of the militant Dziga Vertov Group; he had more or less given up the attempt to reach an audience beyond the converted—the converted not only to a politics but to a regimen of un-pleasure in art seen as the right way to communicate that politics. The fluffily agreeable received a letter from the rigorously disagreeable.

The reply was angry and lengthy. In its inventory of all that was wrong with Godard it never got around to explaining why the director is the only one who doesn't screw in *La Nuit américaine.* Together with the arousing letter it is included in the published *Correspondence* of Truffaut, who died in 1984; a mellowed Godard wrote a foreword to this collection of his friend's letters.[7] Showing no such mellowness, however, two reviewers, one in a leading neoconservative, the other in a leading liberal organ of our culture, make these letters that are about many other things the occasion for attacks on Godard enlisting the anger Truffaut vented against him. Both John Simon in the *New Criterion* and Julian Barnes in the *New York Review of Books* relish every item in Truffaut's enumeration of Godard's flaws and failings.[8]

Why this animosity? Simon's animosity goes back to the sixties, when, in his posture of cultural bully, he railed against Godard for pages on end of uncomprehending invective.[9] Barnes tells us how impressed he was by *Breathless* when he saw it in his youth, but now, having grown wiser as he assures us, he has come to see Godard's film as "a tremendous display of style desperately searching for content." (Searching, questioning, Godard has in-deed been, but Barnes seems to think of content as something that ought to be comfortably settled, like warm water in a bathtub.) "The closeness of Truffaut and Godard at the time . . . was deceptive," Barnes continues: "Truffaut was, as it were, just trying on the bell-bottoms; Godard was laying in a lifetime's supply."[10] Truffaut trying on the bell-bottoms made his best film (so thinks Simon, and in this I agree with him), *Shoot the Piano Player.* But Barnes's animosity has something to do with bell-bottoms; evidently it is an animosity against the sixties. If one filmmaker were to be singled out as emblematic of the sixties, which was a great period for films, Godard would have to be the one.

In associating Godard with bell-bottoms Barnes means to dismiss him as a mere fad of the sixties; in having bell-bottoms stand for the sixties Barnes means to belittle the whole period as just a phase we have been wise to outgrow. Barnes writes from England but he fits in with the American tradition of expunging the leftist past, the tradition that has managed to wipe out any American tradition of the Left. The specter of the sixties looms largest not for the nostalgic but for those who, in a kind of fierce inverse nostalgia, obsessively regret them and blame them and condemn them, for those who lastingly resent all the fun they did not have, for all those threatened by the sixties and afraid to let go of them lest they might rise again. The much overrated Truffaut is being praised as the nice well-behaved kid among the bunch of sixties hoodlums epitomized by Godard. An attempt is being made to dispose of Godard and all that he represents artistically and politically. It suits Godard's detractors to reduce him politically to the trendy, tiresome politicizing of the Dziga Vertov Group; but the "Ursula Andress of militancy" as Truffaut called him, the preacher to the converted who much of the time seemed to be trying by rote to convince himself, is by no means the only political Godard. From the beginning his work has carried a political charge, and most of the many attacks on his art over the years have been to a significant degree politically motivated.

For some the sixties began in 1968; but in 1968 in this country, with the assassinations of Martin Luther King and Robert Kennedy and the election of Nixon that started us on the road to Reagan, the hopeful sixties received a fatal blow. In France the rebellion of May 1968, which one can see coming in Godard's splendidly attentive *La Chinoise* of the year before, enacted a revolutionary aspiration that swept along Godard and many others. In 1968 Godard's sixties ended: the period of open-eyed questioning and spirited path-breaking exploration that began with *Breathless* ended with *La Chinoise* and the first half of *Weekend*. What followed was a Godard wholly politicized but impoverished politically as well as artistically. This Godard—co-director of such films, seldom shown commercially, as *Wind from the East* (1969) and the insufferable *Letter to Jane* (1972)—has been a favorite with certain teachers and theorizers of film. The earlier Godard is too complex and shifting and paradoxical; the doctrinaire Godard, the exponent of militant unpleasure, may be hard to take but he is not hard to teach. This Godard did not last that long, however—the Dziga Vertov Group disbanded in 1973, shortly after the letter to Truffaut—but a newer Godard has been slow to take shape.

With *Sauve qui peut (la vie)* (Every Man for Himself, 1979) Godard returned to commercial filmmaking eccentrically pursued. Deemed by some a return to form and by others a new breakthrough, this film is impressive in stretches but on the whole rather morose and unengaging, a work Godard has saddled with a boring and disagreeable central character representing the director—boring and disagreeable on purpose, no doubt, but a drag for the viewer all the same. By the mid-eighties, however, Godard was getting back something like his former edge and excellence: with *First Name: Carmen* (1983) and *Hail Mary* (1985), women fatal and germinal, films put together as tremulous mosaics; with the somberly resplendent *Detective* (1985) and the brusquely elegiac contemporary *King Lear* (1987). And most mysteriously consummate of this newer wave in Godard's work is the 1990 film he titled *Nouvelle Vague*. *Nouvelle Vague* played at the New York Film Festival but was badly reviewed and failed to be picked up for American release. The audience he was precariously recapturing in the early and mid-eighties Godard seems to be losing even as his work is regaining its artistry. No one making films these days makes films more beautiful than Godard's. But beauty has become suspect in our current cultural climate.

Black-and-white film is more phantasmal than color film, more the mere shadow of things, more purely an affair of light projected on the screen; color film compounds light and shadow with color, which tends to carry more of the texture and complexion of things. Already in his color films of the sixties—*Contempt, Pierrot le fou, Two or Three Things I Know about Her*—Godard, by an emphasis on whites and primary colors and an insistence on letting the sources of light shine on the screen, managed a sheerness of projected light akin to the scintillant black and white of the *nouvelle vague*. His palette is more somber in *Detective*, which is a film noir of sorts set in a grand hotel, and yet in the gloomier images of this film, in the chandeliers in the hotel lobby or in the neon signs across the street, the distinctive light of film—a light that one misses in Godard's work on video—shines with much the same resplendence.

Obscure yet luminously beautiful, *Nouvelle Vague* unfolds as a kind of pastoral in a Swiss lakeside landscape that for the director, who grew up in Switzerland, holds memories of childhood. In the sixties Godard made films of the present that were principally films of the city; recently he has gravitated to the country, which tends to entail a retreat from the present and a longing for harmonies of the past. Rather than the rush and temper of the here and now, the light of *Nouvelle Vague* carries the ghostly dimming beauty of vanishing summer, the time when autumn begins to cast its shadow on the brightness whose season is passing. Perhaps the great visual beauty of *Nouvelle Vague* is not enough to make it a great or even a good film, but one cannot begin to deal with the film unless one can see that breathtaking beauty. Vincent Canby of the *New York Times* couldn't see it: "pretty as a feature-length lipstick commercial," he wrote in a review so damning that (like his review of Antonioni's *Identification of a Woman* on its showing at the New York Film Festival several years before) it left the film without much chance of finding a distributor, such being the power of a review in the *Times* over the fate of a foreign film within these shores.[11]

Beauty nowadays is largely out of fashion. Postmodernists mostly disown it. As a quality men see in women ("Beauty is pleasure regarded as the quality of a thing," said Santayana)[12] feminists largely discountenance it. The Thatcherite aesthetician Roger Scruton thinks it too imprecise a notion for meaningful consideration; but an aesthetician who cannot talk about beauty had better find another line of work. On the left beauty is suspect both of being elitist, the plaything of a privileged few, and of being a whore seductively selling the ideology of the ruling class. In the puritanism of today, a puritanism on the right and on the left, beauty is to be approached with the protective crucifix of (Right or Left) political correctness.

Nouvelle Vague is a thing of beauty and at the same time a critique of that beauty, of the conditions of that beauty: a critique that unsettles our response and disallows our complacency but does not diminish our enraptured appreciation. The film's main setting is a luxurious country estate that provides a luxuriant pastoral of encroaching autumn. Better go to Vermont for the turning foliage, Canby advised readers of the *Times:* have your autumn pastoral unperturbed by a recognition of the privilege enabling your pleasure. For the film's pastoral is darkened and complicated, not just by an awareness of the transience of all things—that mood is as central to traditional pastoral as the celebration of nature's endurance—but by a continual scrutiny of the privilege, the unfeeling exploitative privilege, by which the feelingful pleasures of pastoral usually come to be secured.

Pastoral is a mode that presupposes access to a privileged space and time allowing the leisurely contemplation of nature as an object of delight. Sidney's *Arcadia,* as Raymond Williams reminds us in *The Country and the City,* "was written in a park which had been made by enclosing a whole village and evicting the tenants."[13] In *Nouvelle Vague* the exploitative privileged are of the particularly unfeeling contemporary corporate ilk, who relegate the feelingful admiration of nature and the architecture to their women and their servants—a maid partial to Schiller, a philosophical gardener—and whose business deals and personal relations, in Godard's mordant *mise en scène,* transpire in unseemly cohabitation.

The main characters are a woman and two men who may be one. The woman, played by Domiziana Giordano, is an aristocratic beauty with green eyes and long curly hair the color of red autumn leaves. (Godard calls her Contessa Torlato-Favrini, the title Ava Gardner acquired in *The Barefoot Contessa* by a fatal marriage to a handsome but impotent aristocrat.) The two men, both played by Alain Delon, are twin brothers—or twin selves of the same man—and successive lovers of the woman, one soulful and unshaven and tiresome to the point that she lets him drown in the lake, the other a smooth and dynamic businessman (reminiscent of the stockbroker the young Delon played in Antonioni's *Eclipse* [1962]) who turns up after his brother drowns and who eventually has to save *her* from drowning in the lake. In *The Good Woman of Setzuan* Brecht reversed the Jekyll-and-Hyde scheme of the double by having the *good* side of a person be the self that must be repressed in society. Godard does something similar here: the sensitive and sentimental brother fails and gives way to his double, the successful wheeler-dealer. But the sentimentality and wistful self-pitying passivity of the first brother are offered as no answer to the prevailing corporate ruthlessness, certainly not in the realm of action but not in the realm of consciousness either. Soulful self-absorbed laments for the passing of the good old days won't do.

Pastoral is a nostalgic mode. Yet *Nouvelle Vague* is a pastoral that drowns its figure of nostalgia and resurrects him as a figure of enterprising activity, exploitative enterprising activity such as makes for the privileged conditions of pastoral. We are confronted with a contradiction between stirring beauty and the ugly privilege enabling that beauty. At the end, after the enterprising brother shows he harbors in him enough of the sentimental brother to be moved to save from drowning the aristocratic autumn-haired beauty, there is a happy hint that the man may have been playing the ruthless capitalist while secretly siding all along with kindness and tenderness—a hint of poetry beneath the ruthlessness, ruthlessness as the secret agent of poetry, that may recall secret agent Lemmy Caution as the champion of poetry and rescuer of beauty in *Alphaville*. This is no more credible here than that poetic tough guy was in *Alphaville*; it surely does not resolve the contradiction between feelingful beauty and unfeeling privilege; but it gives us a glimmer, a precious glimmer, of energies of renewal that may yet change our circumstance.

Autumn leaves might seem to belong outside the realm of politics, but, lyrically though he contemplates them, not for Godard. He makes us quite aware of the conditions, the social and material conditions, making that lyrical contemplation possible. Yet that awareness does not lead him to discount that lyricism as the plaything of the privileged. It is not the privileged but their servants that are lyrical in *Nouvelle Vague:* is lyricism then the consolation of servants, of all of us servants of the ruling class? Godard the member of the Dziga Vertov Group, the righteously postmodern Godard, would have scorned such lyricism. The frequently lyrical, modernist Godard of the sixties would not have settled for such a consolation. The post-postmodern Godard of *Nouvelle Vague* seems to be telling us that the consolations of lyricism are not to be discounted: we may all be servants of the ruling class, but we can at least take pleasure in the beauty of the autumn leaves in their gardens.

But the post-postmodern, the again modern Godard does not leave it at that. The beauty of *Nouvelle Vague* is too stirring for mere consolation, the conflict between that beauty and its enabling privilege too pointed for mere resignation. Beauty that comes from privilege, as the film tacitly yet keenly puts to us, can be enlisted to uphold but also to defy and disrupt the premises of that privilege. By embodying an aspiration, a reaching for an alternative to the existing order, beauty can challenge the present; but that challenge to the present can only come from a beauty as cognizant as the beauty of *Nouvelle Vague*, as aware of where it comes from in the present, a beauty that acknowledges rather than dissembles the activity and the conditions that make for it. The sense of beauty in Godard is not the disinterested, not the universalizing sense of beauty that Kant posited. Rather it is a partial beauty, partial to the ruling class that pays for it as their property, yet better recognized, better appropriated, by those who would resist their rule, so that its very partiality—and at the same time its communality, not the universality Kant claimed for it but the power to bring people together—may be turned into an instrument of that resistance.

10 : The Point of View of a Stranger

Antonioni's *Eclipse* (1962) begins at the end. It is the end of a love affair that has lasted for some time and the end of a long night of quarreling between the lovers who are breaking up. In the light of an unreassuring dawn that is Antonioni's starting point, the man and the woman are exhausted and have little left to say to each other. We in the audience have missed the main drama and come in on the aftermath. As always with Antonioni, but to especially striking effect in this beginning, we're given no preparatory information about the characters, no explanatory dialogue such as conventionally would serve to clarify them for us. About these lovers we know nothing beyond what can be gathered, discovered, from the appearances of this particular situation into which we're plunged: we observe the man and the woman from the point of view of a stranger who somehow has come upon them during the last moments of their relationship. And yet this stranger that is Antonioni's camera observes them and their situation with a keen interest, a searching intentness.

Every work begins with an ellipsis, since it omits all that happened before the beginning, but Antonioni's use of ellipsis, at the beginning of *Eclipse* and elsewhere, differs significantly from normal practice. Normally an ellipsis is an omission of what, because implied, need not be stated or shown: the reader or viewer can be counted on to supply what's being omitted, as when, in an ellipsis that used to be standard in movies, a love scene would fade out during a kiss. "Ellipsis is an important formal property of modernist plots," writes Seymour Chatman in his recent study of Antonioni,[1] who indeed makes notable use of ellipsis in a modernist manner. Unexpected, unexplained, and unresolved, the disappearance of Anna in *L'Avventura* (1959)—where Antonioni presents her as the main character until she perhaps runs away, perhaps dies in an accident or by suicide—is a memorable instance of a hole in the plot that serves to give it shape. But Chatman fails to draw a distinction between the classical ellipsis, the omission that can be filled in without reasonable doubt, and the characteristically modernist ellipsis, the omission that cannot. We don't know what happened to Anna in *L'Avventura*; we wonder what's been happening before the beginning of *Eclipse*; but nobody except Buster Keaton, as the projectionist in *Sherlock Junior*, is left in doubt about what happens after the fade-out during a kiss. An ellipsis in Antonioni typically marks an uncertainty. We cannot supply the missing piece with confidence: about the gap that's left open we can only speculate. The missing piece is truly missing, not merely a rhetorical omission but a felt lack in our knowledge.

What the characters are like counts for less in a work of fiction than the way they are presented, the way we come to know them. We feel we know the characters in a John Ford film, from our first, distinct impression of them, as if we had known them all our lives: a style of characterization, a way of knowing people, that belongs to the village, the small city, the cohesive community. "The face of every one / That passes by me is a mystery," wrote Wordsworth in the seventh book of *The Prelude*, "Residence in London": "Even next-door neighbours . . . yet still / Strangers." "At every meeting we are meeting a stranger," says the psychiatrist in T. S. Eliot's *Cocktail Party*. Partially, gradually, inconclusively, as we come to know people in a modern big city, so Antonioni presents his characters: a style of characterization true to the uncertainty and estrangement of modern life.

An Antonioni film weaves a texture of incompleteness, partial views of arresting partiality, empty spaces, narrative pauses, spaces between imbued with heedful disquiet, pieces missing in the story and characterization and, image by image, sequence by sequence, in the camera's unfolding picture of appearances. "By a flawless and quite personal feeling for the *interval*," wrote Vernon Young of Antonioni, "he infuses his films with steadily mounting suspense. *Suspension* would be as apt a word: the moments hang, the passages of an hour are gravid with expectation; waves of emotion crest but never break; each image threatens to disclose a monstrous withheld truth or to discharge an act of violence forever hinted but always suppressed—heat lightning without thunder."[2] Antonioni's missing pieces should be distinguished not only from the classical ellipsis but also from the withholding of information in conventional narratives of mystery and suspense, a withholding that bespeaks knowledge of the answer—as when the criminal's face is teasingly kept out of view—and merely postpones a resolving disclosure. Asked about what happened to the missing Anna in *L'Avventura*, Antonioni, no better able than his film to answer that question, replied that he didn't know. Mystery and suspense in his kind of cinema, which offers an idiosyncratic modernist variant of that genre, stem from the resonantly uncertain, the hauntingly unknown, not the knowingly withheld and in due time disclosed.

Talk of the modern may sound old-fashioned in these days of the postmodern. Antonioni was a late modernist in a medium that, because new, was late to the renewing dynamic of modernism. Today he is out of fashion. Yet his concerns are still ours and his articulation of those concerns has lost none of its renewing energy. Without proposing to recast him in the fashion of today, I suggest that we reconsider him in the light of the postmodern recasting of those concerns. His art endures as one of the sharpest and most pregnant renderings we have of our troubled age.

Like other modernist works, an Antonioni film designedly disorients us, not to promote confusion but in the recognition that our accustomed ways of making sense are no longer reliable, our received assumptions about the world no longer adequate, and in the attempt to find new bearings amid uncertainty, new ways of apprehending and ordering our experience. As seen through Antonioni's camera, our everyday world gives us pause: we're kept from presuming familiarity and made to look with fresh inquiring eyes. At once tentative and arresting, anxious and measured, intense and detached, Antonioni's distinctive visual style is no mere decoration. Much as Heisenberg's famous principle doesn't just declare but mathematically formulates uncertainty, and thereby enables its comprehension, so Antonioni's images render the uncertainty of modern life with elegant exactness, and thereby assert, in the face of a puzzling and precarious world, the endeavor of an arranging consciousness.

Antonioni is a great artist of doubt. No contented skeptic, he is a seeker, a seer, though not a seer of visions but one devoted to the visible, attentive to the nuance and transience of actuality, an unhurried yet eager and alert explorer of (to use Chatman's apt title) the surface of the world. Unsettlingly contemplative, everywhere prepared to revise impressions, suspend conclusions, Antonioni doubts not because he mistrusts appearances but because he trusts nothing else. Asked about the inconclusiveness that disturbs—is meant to disturb—viewers of his work, he responded by quoting an ancient natural philosopher, the poet Lucretius, whose words pertain well to our time: "Nothing appears as it should in a world where nothing is certain. The only certain thing is the existence of a secret violence that makes everything uncertain."[3] Even if nothing appears as it should—that is, clearly, fully, without concealment—Antonioni declines to assume access, the access that fiction conventionally provides, to a truth behind appearances. Truth for him is to be sought in appearances themselves, not behind or beyond them but in their shifting, elusive, equivocal, yet material realm. Neorealism, which after the years of Fascism and war gave Italian cinema a vital fresh start and to which his own early documentaries marginally contributed, taught him to eschew studio fabrications and train his camera on actuality. But the neorealists were more confident that the truth would reveal itself before the camera's direct mechanical mimesis, whereas Antonioni sees the quest for truth as a problematic and necessarily a partial, provisional undertaking. Trained on actuality, his camera, instead of giving us a purportedly straightforward account of the way things are, conducts a watchfully circuitous, probingly dilatory, eye-opening interrogation of the opaque face of things. If the neorealists (in André Bazin's words of praise) "put their faith in reality," Antonioni puts any perspective on reality, any account of it, in doubt. Observed with precision yet fraught with uncertainty, the world's appearances as Antonioni renders them seem under threat, as if that secret violence were always about to break out into his suspensive images.

Place rather than action, situation rather than event, is Antonioni's chief concern. Sicily, Milan, Rome, all three in summer, are the locales, vividly pictured, whose complexion and circumstance inform *L'Avventura*, *La Notte*, *Eclipse*, the trilogy that in the early sixties won Antonioni fame as the maker of films short on incidents and long on the spaces between. "Nothing will have taken place but the place": in him those lines from Mallarmé's *Un Coup de dés* may be said to have found their cinematic exponent. Action in the theater is abstracted from place; space in painting is abstracted from time; in the movies, which are a dramatic and a pictorial medium, action and place, space and time, can be integrated. Although he's more of a painter than a dramatist, the picture of place in Antonioni is not static or merely descriptive but animated by a sense of action, action that may not be occurring at the moment but whose wake—as at the beginning of *Eclipse*—or whose impending or potential occurrence reverberates through every moment.

Time in Antonioni is a time of the moment, a time that dwells on the space of the moment, not the dramatic time that in most films subordinates the moment to the overriding arrow of plot. Time in Antonioni is not a time of the what next but a time of the what now, not a linear but a lingering time that views each moment as a point of intersection of many lines of actuality and possibility. This suspensive time, in no hurry to move ahead to the next thing, often gives us the sense of our sharing with the characters an unabridged interval in the passage of their lives. Feeling immersed in the flow of their own time, we feel we inhabit a piece of their experience alongside them; and this may be a duration of little dramatic consequence, an aftermath, a wait, an abeyance, an uneventful space between, which heightens the sense of our sharing a personal, a private experience—something that wouldn't mean much to anybody else. The shared interval in Antonioni invites us into a curious intimacy with the strangers who are his characters, of whose privacy we partake without feeling we know them well and without being able quite to put ourselves in their place: an intimacy combined with an inquiring detachment. Such a pull and push is characteristic of modernism: a pull to involvement, an aroused impulse to empathy, and a concomitant push holding back that impulse and keeping us, not at an equable, comfortable aesthetic distance, but in an unsettled position both involved and estranged.

Drawing things out and cutting them short is the distinctive Antonioni rhythm, lingering and interruptive, suspensive and elliptical, a crisp deliberate pace, a restless, syncopated movement of unhurried attention. Normally a shot in a film will be held for just as long as it takes to show something with adequate clarity and make a dramatic point or an impression deemed appropriate. Almost every shot in Antonioni is held for at least a moment longer than that so as to invite us to look again, reflect on the image, revise our first impression; but then, before we've had time to settle on a revised impression, a cut or move will shift our perspective. Antonioni's dwelling on his images serves, not merely to insist on their composition or content, but to encourage a perceptual questioning, a questioning that their succession alertly articulates. If we get into the rhythm of his observation, the pace of his films will seem fast rather than slow. A rhythm similar to that which animates his editing informs his plotting: the plot of *Eclipse* lingers and meanders and then, before we can reach conclusions, is cut short. Time in the closing sequence moves with a clipped expectancy that feels at once hopeful and ominous.

A kind of still life, nicely composed and held for a few moments, opens *Eclipse:* a row of books cut off by the right and bottom edges of the frame, a shaded lamp cut off by the left and top edges, and, blankly resting on the books, a white shape revealed to be, after its stirring prompts a slight panning movement of the camera to the right, a man's white-sleeved arm. Such compositions, momentarily harmonious within the frame yet incomplete, unstable, subject to revision from without, are typical of Antonioni; and so is the stillness that turns into movement that leads to discovery. The man in the white shirt looks glum and stares mutely at the younger woman in his company, who is not saying anything either and not glancing back at him. Through the alternate, disparate perspectives of these two unknowns we abruptly enter the scene, and gradually we piece together the setting, a modern, well-appointed suburban house belonging to the man, and what we can surmise of the drama from an ending that for us is a beginning.

It transpires that the young woman, Vittoria (Monica Vitti in her third

Antonioni incarnation, acted with her engaging diffident verve), has decided she no longer loves the man and is gathering the resolve to leave him. He gazes at her hands, her face, her legs amid the legs of a table and chairs, as at a possession he sourly resists losing. Hurtfully he makes a show of not showing his hurt and maintaining his dignity. Regarded with a gentle edge of humor, he is throughout the sequence a study in male pathos, his sincerity inseparable from his posturing. Rather like the vanished Anna, this man, after an opening sequence that presents him as a main character, plays almost no part in the film except as a memory. "People disappear every day," to quote an exchange of lines from a later Antonioni film, *The Passenger* (1975). "Every time they leave the room."

The opening onto a view, the window, mirror, picture, is a theme on which Antonioni plays many variations in the opening sequence of *Eclipse*: the window or picture and also its bounding frame, the opening along with its enclosing edges, which delimit the view and divide it from the viewer. When we first see Vittoria she is holding an empty picture frame and arranging objects within it, taking out a full ashtray, a remnant of the sleepless night, and centering a small sculpture, an instance of the modern art and design decorating the man's house on the outskirts of Rome. Like a film director, she arranges signs within a frame, an empty picture frame that brings to mind the frame of moving pictures, of this picture: a set rectangle movable anywhere but able to include within its edges only a small piece of the world at a time, and ready to be emptied and filled according to the director's choice. Within the frame of nearly every shot in this opening

Eclipse. Vittoria looks out a window.

sequence a frame of some sort appears, often a combination of frames. Pictures, large and small, abstract and representational, abound on the walls of this house, whose modern rectangularity and impeccable partitioning everywhere provide hard edges to frame a view.

An electric fan whirring, the lights still on, the curtains still drawn: nature seems shut out of this house until Vittoria parts a curtain and peeks at some trees in the morning light outside, the windowpane dividing her from the trees yet superimposing on them the reflected image of her face looking to their dawning verdancy. She proceeds to open curtains and look out of windows, large modern windows—picture windows, we say—whose transparency to the outside encloses the inside within a glassed prospect of freedom, a bounding display of apparent openness and possibility; especially after she turns off the lights inside, the prospect outside looks like a picture being projected on a movie screen. (*La Notte* [1960], which begins with the camera incessantly descending the glass exterior of a skyscraper in Milan, is Antonioni's sharpest reflection on the architecture of glass.) Finally bringing herself to break free from the cage of a moribund romance, Vittoria backs away toward the dark wooden front door, which flatly fills the screen except for her cropped figure hovering at the left edge. The door opens like a curtain as she leaves; cut to the man, downcast, framed by a large abstract expressionist painting behind him, the light on him dimming as the door closes behind her. Outside, as she goes toward and through the gate, a horizontal opening at the top, framed by the camera across the middle third of the screen, frames trees in the distance.

Eclipse. Vittoria leaves.

Near the end of his life—his career had ended long before—D. W. Griffith remarked that the cinema wanted what it had in his day, the beauty of the wind in the trees. Nowhere in cinema are trees more beautiful than in the Roman suburb pictured in *Eclipse,* not even in the luxuriant countryside of a Griffith pastoral such as *True Heart Susie* (1919), where trees with leaves trembling in the wind evoke a permanence through change, a frailty that endures, like the frailty of Lillian Gish's Susie. The trees of pastoral are trees that, no less staunch for their trembling, reliably weather the storm and blossom after winter, symbols of the mutable endurance of nature. The suburban trees in *Eclipse,* vital though unsettled, their beauty colored with a fearful undertone, tremble in a wind that seems to carry not just nature's mutability but a more terrible uncertainty, and their agitated leaves evoke a precariousness unallayed by summer and the sun, a frailty that may or may not endure, like the frailty of Monica Vitti's Vittoria.

In her own world, among its inhabitants, Vittoria feels as if in a foreign country. Like Antonioni's camera itself, she views the world with probing detachment, with perplexed, reflective curiosity, the type of character in his films that Chatman calls a "witness." But the camera keeps its independence from her: though it often approximates, as often it diverges or departs from her perspective. From outside, through a window, we observe Vittoria, after she leaves the man's house, arriving alone in the early morning at her apartment in a glassy modern building nearby. The camera pans leftward with her, past a wall, so that we now observe her through a second window as, her gaze at right angles to ours, she looks out of a third at some trees in the wind that are framed for us, as if through a fourth window, by the edge of a wall and the screen's left edge. Through windows that repeat the window of the screen we look at her, the Antonioni witness who repeats our position as viewers, and at the disquieted trees at which she looks through another window. An epitome of the witness's position in Antonioni, and of our own analogous yet separate position of felt separation, this concluding shot of the opening sequence sums up the film's point of view. From the point of view of a stranger we observe Vittoria as well as the environment she observes from the point of view of a stranger.

Views framed apart from their viewers, pictures at least since Alberti—framer of Renaissance perspective—have been compared to windows on a reality divided from ours. Although more involving than most pictures in their representation of reality, movies nonetheless picture things through the window of a screen that, as Stanley Cavell says, screens. By calling our attention to the frame, to the fact of our being divided from the world pictured, Antonioni acknowledges in modernist fashion the medium and its mediation. In different ways he declares both the rectangular frame and the perspective of an individual viewing point, the two formal principles pictorially constitutive of the film image, inherited from the tradition of Western art since the Renaissance and mobilized by the movie camera. If a marked surface defines a painting, a movable frame and perspective pictorially define a movie.

In his films of the fifties Antonioni set in motion a technique of long takes, with few cuts and fewer close-ups, his camera fluidly moving about, framing and continually reframing, the space off screen activated, the evolving viewing point asserted as an autonomous, searching consciousness.[4] A typical Antonioni camera movement may start out following one character, then turn to another encountered along the way who after a bit will go on past the camera, which may now pause before proceeding in some other direction and coming upon a third character, while the first will perhaps reenter view in the far background of the continuing shot. Such an arrangement of shifting attention, of entrances and exits and paths variously crossing the camera's own path of gaze, will often make the dramatically central visually marginal and the dramatically marginal visually central. Antonioni's direction of attention calls into question where attention should be directed. We note his choice, note that at any moment it could have been otherwise, of a particular succession of framings and perspectives leading our eyes along this rather than an alternative path of gaze. From *L'Avventura* onward, his films combine the searching move with the terse cut, the fluid with the abrupt perceptual shift, the reflective pause that makes us look again with the interruptive concatenation of sharply different aspects that makes us keep looking anew.

In bringing to our awareness his means of representation and expression, Antonioni isn't concerned only with matters of form: like all great modernists, he renders the acknowledged means of the medium themselves meaningful, metaphorical. The experience of empty space on the barren volcanic island of Anna's disappearance becomes in *L'Avventura* a guiding formal metaphor: empty space delineated and shaped, in a choreography of disparateness, by the crisscrossing paths of a camera and characters looking for the missing woman all over the island. Applied elsewhere in the film, this distinctive way of shaping empty space, sensing the space between, suggests an equation with the island as a site of absence and disparateness and of search for the missing.

The frames within the frame, salient in the opening sequence and recurrent throughout *Eclipse*, signify the characters' estrangement and make the frame itself, that formal constant of the medium, into a metaphor for our own estrangement. In *Cronaca di un amore* (1950), a tale of illicit love that was Antonioni's first fiction movie, the lines of perspective, the receding parallels pictured as convergent at a vanishing point, are accented in compositions that not only lead our eyes into the represented deep space (as Chatman notes) but also call our attention to the lines themselves and their pattern of pictured convergence, by which linear perspective represents that depth. Lines that appear to meet but in fact endlessly recede, leading away from here to a vanishing point nowhere, symbolize the situation of the illicit lovers in this film, who brood over the past and worry about the future while enacting in the present a drama of powerlessness and inaction.

Modernism is an art of estrangement, in content and in form. It began with Baudelaire, Flaubert, Manet, citizens of the capital of the nineteenth century, painters of modern life who met its estrangement with their own. An alienated subject, in *Madame Bovary* or in *Mother Courage*, in Manet's painting of a barmaid at the Folies-Bergère or in *L'Avventura* or *Eclipse*, modernism renders through an alienating form. It portrays estrangement through the calculated estrangement that Brecht called an "alienation effect," not adding insult to injury but answering injury, and complicating sympathy, with the critical vision of a reflective art. The alienating form modernism sets up, the division it accents between artifice and reality, brings about a divided response to the alienated subject. As Flaubert both did and did not identify himself with Madame Bovary, and his novel articulates the split, so Brecht with Mother Courage, so Manet with his barmaid, and so Antonioni with his Monica Vitti characters. Rather than asking us simply to identify ourselves with alienation, modernism puts it at a distance that calls it into question—but not a comfortable distance, so that we cannot simply detach ourselves from it either. "On to an alienated world," wrote Raymond Williams, "Brecht turned an alienated consciousness."[5] The questioning activity of an alienated consciousness is chiefly what, in modernism, the acknowledged means of expression themselves express.

Although supposed to be objective because it directly captures the look of things, the camera is in a sense always subjective because it depicts in each image the way things look from the viewing point of an individual observer. Whether or not this observer is represented as a character in the film, the imitation of an individual's perspective and perceptions is built into the camera. The conventional subjective camera, taking its cue from a character's glance directed at something off screen, turns to the object of the glance by way of a cut, and gives us a point-of-view shot through the character's eyes, a shot designated as subjective by the glance that leads to it and that usually, after another cut, follows it as well. This conventional demarcation between subjective shots, inserted within the brackets of a glance, and the rest, the presumably objective shots, Antonioni's practice artfully disestablishes.

In one scene in *Eclipse* a curious Vittoria follows a short bald man with reading glasses who has just lost a fortune in the stock market. He goes to a drugstore for a tranquilizer and to a café for a glass of water to drink it with; she follows him to the drugstore and to the café and, from her inquisitive glance off screen toward the front, the film cuts to the reverse angle and gives us her point of view on the man sitting at an outdoor table and ordering mineral water from the waiter. This begins as a conventional point-of-view shot, but instead of cutting back to the onlooking Vittoria as convention prescribes, the film holds the view for an extra moment until she enters frame from behind the camera, intruding into her own designated field of subjective vision. Advancing well into the middle distance near the table where the man sits, she now assumes in our view much the same place as the object of her curiosity, who, as she discovers after she picks up his scrap paper, has been drawing flowers. What began as a point-of-view shot through her eyes becomes without a break—except a break in convention—a shot turning her inquisitive eyes on her, so to speak, no longer a subjective shot from her perspective but a shot in which the impression of an observing subjectivity remains. Initially signaled by the character's glance and the ensuing cut, this subjectivity now belongs to the camera's own inspective gaze. Modified, qualified, revised point-of-view shots are many in Antonioni; conventional point-of-view shots are few.

The impression of subjectivity arises when one senses the partiality of a view, the particularity of a point of view, when an incompleteness makes itself felt, an insufficiency in what the eye apprehends that leaves room for the play of sentiment and surmise. Normally a film will convey such a sense of partiality and insufficiency only when attributing it to a character in a point-of-view shot. Like a line of dialogue in a novel, a character's words set apart from the narrator's governing words, the conventional point-of-view shot is a character's view set apart as a subjective moment from the views that govern the storytelling. Pasolini compared Antonioni's technique in *The Red Desert* (1964), his first color film and a work colored by the disturbed consciousness of its neurotic protagonist, to the technique in prose fiction known as free indirect speech: a character's words, not quoted as direct speech and marked off from the rest, but incorporated into the very narration and infusing it with the language and consciousness of that character.[6] Antonioni's film language articulates a subjectivity freed from the convention that restricts it to certain bracketed views directly representing what the characters see. Declining the governing stance of superior knowledge usual in storytelling, his camera explores rather than governs, inquires rather than tells, from a point of view that feels as subjective as any character's—without consistently reflecting, however, any character's subjectivity. *The Red Desert*, a work verging on expressionism in the way it largely gives itself over to its protagonist's anxiety, is a special case for its director, whose more typical technique will switch, with deft unexpectedness, between passages of closer involvement with the characters and passages of dispassionate distance.

Eclipse. The world looks back. Successive frames: Vittoria and her friend looking out at the neighbor, cut to the neighbor's distant perspective on them.

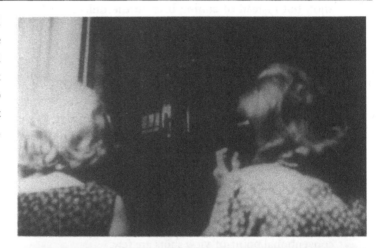

Often more or less aligned with a character's perspective, and acquiring from that a staying subjective hue, Antonioni's camera arrestingly shifts in and out of such alignment in a process of perceptual reassessment that keeps drawing our awareness to the limited individuality of each viewing point. Whether approximating or not what a character perceives within the film, each of the perspectives this camera unfolds conveys the impression of subjectivity. Sometimes associated with, sometimes dissociated from the point of view of the characters, this pervasive subjectivity resides primarily in the camera's own point of view.

Home in the evening after the love affair ended at dawn, talking with a woman friend who has dropped in, Vittoria gets a phone call from a neighbor she hardly knows, a colonial woman from Kenya. She and her friend go over to a window from which they, and we with them, can see the neighbor at her balcony across the dark street; cut to a distant, haunting point-of-view shot, unmoored, unbracketed by any shots of the observer, from the neighbor's inferred perspective: the point of view of a stranger on Vittoria and her friend, now diminutive silhouettes at the lit window amid the darkness. From the window they subjectively look out at the world, and now the world, as subjectively, looks back at them. The effect is of our suddenly seeing ourselves as the world distantly sees us.

One pull to involvement in an Antonioni film is his keen documentary sense, his strikingly lifelike rendering of the look, the feel of things. Films are a pictorial and a documentary medium, a medium of pictures taken directly from a reality before the camera, but few filmmakers have been at once so concerned with pictorial arrangement as Antonioni and so attentive to the appearances of our reality. *Eclipse* is of his films perhaps the richest in vivid documentary perceptions. For the sequences at the stock market, the Borsa in the center of Rome, Antonioni hired real stockbrokers and brought them to their place of work on their day off; with the actors mingled among them, the fiction shades into a sheer documentary of the hectic workings of finance. Some find these sequences too long: "I got the point right away," complained Dwight Macdonald; but the point he got reduces to a simple indictment of unbridled greed Antonioni's open-eyed look, critical yet not scornful but interrogative, at capitalism in action. Action, fast-moving and aggressive, is certainly not lacking in these sequences, which, if a background to Vittoria's story, set off the sparse foreground with a welter of partially comprehended incident that we, like her, view from the perspective of a curious outsider. On the day whose dawning opens the film

Vittoria goes to the stock market looking for her mother, wishing to talk to her about the love affair that has just ended. But her mother is too absorbed in the financial to talk about the personal, and amid all the market activity the main thing that happens in Vittoria's personal story is her briefly meeting Piero (Alain Delon), a young stockbroker with whom she's to start a new love affair.

Dawn, day, evening at home and on a visit to the neighbor from Kenya: in this film we feel the movement of the sun. Its title inspired by a solar eclipse that Antonioni filmed but decided not to include, *Eclipse* palpably "reminds us," as Cavell wrote, "that half the world is always eclipsed by the world itself."[7] The sun, the time of day and the time of year, the warm days and sweet evenings of summer, the trees, the sensate air: in this film we feel the rhythms, the fabric of nature in the life of the city and the suburb. Instead of erecting a dichotomy between nature and culture, Antonioni exhibits their interpenetration, their interplay. Nothing natural is not also cultural, for it is through culture that we apprehend nature; nothing cultural is not also natural, for it is with nature that we construct culture. In a film, and *Eclipse* keeps us aware that it is a film we're watching, we apprehend nature through the artifice of pictures, documentary pictures constructed directly from nature. Film's combination of documentary and picture, both equally heightened in his images, Antonioni makes into a metaphor for the commerce between nature and culture.

The many photographs and other objects from Kenya in the neighbor's apartment, traces of Africa arranged into a suburban setting, motivate Vittoria to do an impersonation of an African native, with black makeup and a spear and records as accompaniment, a bit of playacting that expresses her sensuality and her fantasy of a simpler, more natural life. Her pretend native is for some a symbol of natural man in contrast to the stock market's civilized man. But the reverse is more nearly the case: the stock market brings out tremendous if misplaced human energy, and Vittoria's impersonation sets forth the idea of a return to nature as a fabrication of civilized man. Afterwards, while looking for the neighbor's escaped black poodle in the suburban summer night, Vittoria comes upon a row of tall, clattering flagpoles shaking in the wind against the dark sky, thin inanimate verticals that seem weirdly animate, pale lines trembling against black that suggest a ghostly, skeletal negative image of trees in daytime, a modern abstraction of trees in the wind.

Its edge parallel to the screen's left edge and at right angles to the descending horizontal of the runway in the background, the wing of a departing small airplane brings the film abruptly forward to the next day. In a form of plotting typical of Antonioni, a now lingering, now elliptical arrangement of time, the film follows Vittoria more or less in her own time through a segment of her experience, then skips forward to another segment like a stranger encountering her anew. She feels at ease on this airplane ride, up in the clouds—nature viewed through the means of culture—and at the somehow agreeable nondescript provincial airport where she lands; she turns this uneventful excursion into a kind of private pastoral, the camera weaving in and out of her point of view as she subjectively fashions another version of a return to nature from the materials of civilization. Sitting contentedly at the airport's outdoor café, she glances at something off screen, and on her glance the film cuts, not to the expected point-of-view shot, but to Piero and his boss arriving at the stock market some days later.

So far the film has stayed with Vittoria, but now it switches to Piero and goes into a second, longer, more frenzied market sequence, which comes after the stillness of the peaceful airport as the first came after the stillness of the concluding love affair. Although this time an insider, Piero, takes us into the market, our perspective remains that of an outsider, immersed in the turbulent proceedings without knowing quite what to make of them. We miss Vittoria, whose position as the witnessing outsider would have provided something of an anchor in this sea of finance. This digression from her story continues until it becomes a story in its own right: it's as if the film were beginning again, with Piero instead of Vittoria as protagonist.

Vittoria's mother arrives as, on this day in the life of Piero, the market is taking a turn for the worse. Navigating this choppy sea, the camera in one shot follows the mother as she walks on after talking to Piero and nervously bites her lip; then he reappears in the background, dashing in the opposite direction and prompting the camera to veer back and follow him at his quick pace until, in the extreme foreground, an unknown woman with straining puzzled eyes behind glasses comes into view and brings the shot to a pause. By the time Vittoria herself turns up, her mother, among many others, has lost a fair sum of money. Vittoria's trailing outside the market the man who draws flowers seems by now less like a return to her story than like a digression from Piero's. The movement of Antonioni's plots is as digressive as the movement of his shots, as prone to shifts of attention, ruminative distractions from the central to the marginal that may become the central. If his films have been thought wanting in plot, this is largely due, as William S. Pechter wrote, to "their sense of 'found' narrative, of discovering their stories almost at random amid a number of other narrative paths not taken."[8]

Distractive and exploratory, suspensive and peregrine, Antonioni's paths of plot have much the same quality and shape, on a larger scale, as his camera's paths of gaze around the local space of scenes.

Eclipse is a modern middle-class picaresque with two independent protagonists, a heroine and a hero whose differently motivated, winding trajectories, perhaps complementary, perhaps incompatible, happen to intersect. Piero's accompanying Vittoria to her mother's place after the bad morning at the market may be seen either as the tentative beginning of a story of romance or as a lunchtime interlude in the story of his day. Back at work, a young man tirelessly astir, he deals with peevish customers at the office, the losses they suffered, the money they owe his firm, in a briskly good-natured manner that is rather endearing. Past ten that evening, finally done with the day's work, he impulsively drives out to Vittoria's neighborhood and walks along her street, looking for her place. A woman leaving Vittoria's building attracts his attention for a moment; cut to a view from Vittoria's upstairs window, a shift to her perspective before he sees her and as she also observes the woman, who gets into a car and drives off. This sudden cut from his side to hers pivots on a stranger who transiently brings together their separate glances into a point of intersection. A second such meeting point of their attention, before she lets him see her, is a bearded, drunken man who staggers by and waves to Vittoria at her window, leading Piero's attention to her: these lovers-to-be come face to face through he oblique intermediation of two passersby who might have diverted the narrative elsewhere. And now the drunk does divert the narrative: like the woman, he gets into a car and drives off, but this is Piero's sports car, and he drives it off into a lake in the neighborhood, killing himself, as Piero and Vittoria learn the next day when they watch the car and its driver being retrieved from the water. Antonioni had planned to have them go to the lake that night and observe in the darkness the car's headlights continuing to shine underwater, but the circumstances of shooting did not allow it.

The paths of strangers in Antonioni, the paths of the stranger that is his camera, are an unsettling relativistic geometry mapping the space and time of modern life, a web of lines of orientation and disorientation that come together at unexpected meeting points and drift apart in directions unforeseen. Openness to distraction is for Antonioni not the failing people take it to be but a responsive way of dealing with the diverse implicative claims, which may be extraneous or may be decisive, continually made on its inhabitants by a modernity that confounds distinctions between the central and the marginal, the important and the incidental, the story and the digression.

Errant and episodic, picaresque narrative follows the wanderings of a protagonist across an expanse of space and time. Like Joyce's *Ulysses,* another modern picaresque with two independent protagonists—an incipient father and son rather than an incipient couple—*Eclipse* compresses the space and time of traditional picaresque while retaining the journeying spirit, the sense of an exploration of life's possibilities, a charting of its terrain. From a frontal traveling shot of Vittoria, arriving at the lake the next day for an odd rendez-vous at the scene of the accident, the film cuts far behind her and above and shows her meeting Piero in a sudden overview of the area that accents the road she has taken to meet him, no doubt the same road the drunk took with the car the night before. The road of life, as Bakhtin says, is a metaphor made real in picaresque narrative.[9] Evergreen branches, one of which Vittoria briefly grabs as she passes under, go by like markers of a progress in the foreground of an overhead shot traveling with her and Piero as they stroll away from the lake. At an intersection they come to, a corner distinguished from the others by nothing special, Piero tells Vittoria that he will kiss her when they get to the other side. Cut to an overhead camera movement following them from behind and showing, on the pavement ahead, the white stripes of a pedestrian crossing, another set of markers of a progress that she further punctuates by pausing in the middle of the street and saying, part flirta-tiously, part gravely: "We are halfway across." A casual wandering combines in this sequence with a feeling that the couple, without their planning it, are advancing toward a destination along a course observable from high per-spectives, an all but fateful if meandering course leading to this intersection.

Eclipse. White stripes on the path to a kiss.

On the other side of the street is an unfinished building covered with straw matting and, it seems, no longer or not currently under construction. Leaves stirred in the wind, their green rendered in luminous, shaded tones of rippling gray, suddenly fill the screen before Vittoria turns to Piero by the unfinished building, inviting the kiss he hesitates to give her. But now *she* hesitates and shrinks from the kiss he twice attempts; the kiss suspended, she awkwardly departs, dropping a bit of wood in a metal barrel full of water as she turns the corner. In a movement that suggests the lingering perspective of Piero watching her go, the camera follows her from behind, pausing as she halts and, with something more to say, turns around to address him. Cut, not to a view of him at the corner from her perspective, but to a startling image of absence: the camera's own about-face keeps her in view as she faces the corner where she and we expect to find him, and we, who thought we had been sharing his perspective on her, are perhaps more startled than she to discover that he is gone. Her blond hair and white blouse, bright in the afternoon light, contrast with the dark trees fringing the corner and casting deep shadows about it while on her and elsewhere the sun shines: an eerie conjunction of light and darkness, the empty corner perceived as a pocket of night within the summer day, something like a Magritte painting of trees and houses at night with a daytime sky. Cut to Vittoria at home alone in the evening, dark against the electric light of a modernly designed lamp.

For her next meeting with Piero Vittoria arrives at the corner early and regards the place alone. Her arriving early bespeaks both an impatience to

Eclipse. The empty corner as a pocket of night within the summer day.

meet and a wish to wait and allow herself a private preamble to the meeting. Behind a pile of bricks at the building site, she enters view from the left and moves toward the right, the camera panning with her past the bricks, which look like a modern city of Lilliputian scale and jutting, jumbled rectangularity. After she exits right the film cuts to the sky, a clear afternoon sky lined by the airy profiles of streetlights and slender trees, her head reentering view at the bottom left and moving along the bottom edge of the screen until she again exits right. Crossing the line of her movement,[10] which on the screen appears flipped toward the left as suddenly she's the one that looks Lilliputian, the film now cuts to our first encompassing view of the unfinished building, a queer outsize box with bare scaffolding at the top and concealing curtain walls

Eclipse. Vittoria's early arrival at the corner: the pile of bricks, the unfinished building.

of straw and attendant trees. The relation of figure to landscape, the unfinished landscape of a modernity that seems always somehow under deferred construction, keeps changing under Antonioni's interrogative beholding.

Turning the corner and stooping over the water barrel, Vittoria is pleased to find the bit of wood she dropped, a tiny mark of her presence she left on water like the mark a more assured young lover might have incised on bark. She looks up toward the building, and we see from her perspective the straw covering gently waving in the breeze; she moves back a few steps and leans against a tree, the camera panning with her and bringing into view the white stripes of the pedestrian crossing. Poetry, said Novalis, makes the familiar strange and the strange familiar. This ordinary suburban corner becomes suffused with a hovering strangeness, a coloring of the uncanny, but begins to gain a new familiarity as Vittoria and the camera return to its aspects and details. And now Piero, as if recalled by those crossing stripes that were the path to his announced kiss, returns too: from behind the tree, Vittoria turns to look at a harness racer with horse and sulky trotting along the street, and the camera follows this distractive passerby past the tree and the crossing stripes, whereupon the arriving Piero comes into view. He's surprised to find her already there, for he too has arrived early for their meeting. Both of them, it seems, want to settle the corner sentimentally, to make its alien though quotidian space their own. They would make its familiarity their strangeness and its strangeness their familiarity.

The anxiety of disappearance, the reassurance of return: gone from the corner when Vittoria last looked in his direction and found a hollow of

Eclipse. Disappearance and return: Piero turns up at the crossing of a stranger's path and the path to a kiss.

shadows, Piero comes back at the crossing of an incidental stranger's path and the path to a kiss. In *Beyond the Pleasure Principle* Freud gives a well-known account of a little boy's assiduously played game in which the child would throw something out of sight and say, "Gone," and then retrieve it and say, "There." This visual game punctuated by words seems to have been the child's way of compensating for his mother's frequent absences by symbolically enacting a mastery over absence and presence, disappearance and return. Films enact a similar interplay between the seen and the unseen.[11] Whereas a painting makes a world visible, a film leaves most of its world invisible in each image on the screen. In a painting or on a theater stage anything outside the space of representation is not merely unseen but incapable of being seen, outside the realm of the visible. Painting and the theater are arts of presence but not of absence, since each wholly displays before us the realm of the visible, the place of presence. In the theater Anna could not have disappeared but only left the stage, the only place where she could have been found. Film is an art of absence, of partial views, an art that hides more than it shows. Usually, however, a film will satisfy our expectations of presence, much as the child in his game would return into view what he caused to disappear. When D. W. Griffith cut from an actor leaving a room to that actor entering a hallway, he established both the possibility of absence—because he was creating on film a space larger than the camera's range of vision—and a gratifying continuity of presence. An absence in a film, an emptiness, an incompleteness, a pointing to the unseen, is conventionally to be resolved by a presence. Antonioni is a master of the unresolved absence. Like the island in *L'Avventura,* the corner in *Eclipse* is a place of absence and of search for the missing, the missing that Vittoria and Piero seek in a quest not so much physical as sentimental, but the sentimental dwells in the physical and their quest dwells centrally in this unlikely suburban crossroads they would romantically appropriate.

Piero takes Vittoria not to his own place but to his parents' large, ponderous apartment, shut in but seemingly no longer lived in, a gloomy enclave of the familial past. Neither his place nor hers is at any point in the film a place where the couple spend time together. Earlier they went to her mother's, now they go to his parents', their old homes where they don't feel at home. The corner is their space if anywhere is. It represents their unfinished endeavor to make a place for themselves at the intersection of their errant paths.

On arriving at the foreign inner space of Piero's family, Vittoria looks out a window and sees a woman across the way who quickly retreats into the darkness of *her* window, like a ghost vanished into a homely gloom. A window frames a view of the outside for an observer inside; here two windows, two observers, two dark insides, face each other like mirror images and cancel the outside view. Withdrawing into dim parental rooms after her dress gets amorously torn, Vittoria opens the shutter of another window and looks to the sunlit outside. Her leaning forward prompts two successive point-of-view shots: the white square tables of an outdoor restaurant, a lone soldier at a corner, distantly seen through her eyes in the near empty small piazza below. Again she leans forward, but now, in an astounding shift away from her perspective, the film cuts, first down to the piazza, then to a view of her at the window as distant as her view of the piazza and as subjective, through the eyes, we feel, of someone out there, some unseen stranger watching her watch. Like the sudden long shot from the inferred perspective of the neighbor telephoning, this strikes us as the distant viewpoint on ourselves of an unmoored subjectivity: the world's reverse angle on the self. Cut to the self's answering angle, abstracted, unbracketed by the observing Vittoria, in two further point-of-view shots, the second a lingering glimpse of a few persons coming out of a baroque church: what Vittoria sees from the window and the stranger's glimpse of her at the window face each other like mirroring outsides and cancel the inside viewpoint. Denied the advantage that an insider's vantage point usually has, her perspective is as much as the other the point of view of a stranger, an outsider. Cut to the dark interior of the parental apartment, a constituted inside no more accommodating to the self than the otherness of the outside world.

Eclipse. The woman across the way.

The clarity and completeness of a Renaissance painting imply the vantage point of a privileged inside, an inside enabled to gain, through the Albertian window, a commanding view of the world pictured outside. Expressionism, which turns the insider's look into a frightened stare, nonetheless presents it as a privileged viewpoint from which to apprehend the essential expressionist truth, the anxious irreparable breach between the injured self and a fearful world. Neither classical nor expressionist, Antonioni's art waives an insider's position of advantage and conducts an outsider's troubled, fascinated inquiry, adroitly disorienting and reorienting, into the perplexing appearances of our reality.

Poised at the window between a cavernous inside and an outside bathed in emptiness, Vittoria turns to Piero's embrace in quest of love as the pres-

Eclipse. Vittoria looks out a window, the world looks back: the outdoor restaurant from Vittoria's perspective, Vittoria at her window from as distant a perspective.

ence that will dispel absence. "Romantic love, in the modern sense," wrote John Berger, "is a love uniting or hoping to unite two displaced persons," a love seeking to overcome "the displacement, the homelessness, the abandonment" of modern life.[12] If *L'Avventura* is about love's weakness, and *La Notte* about love's failure and love's ghost in a modern marriage, *Eclipse* is about love's chances of success. Vittoria and Piero are Antonioni's most appealing, most hopefully depicted couple. The brisk stockbroker and the tentative young woman moodily emerging from a long love affair, his nervous energy manifested in the impatience of doing, her nervous energy manifested in the impatience of pondering, are not a bad match: he gives her motion and she gives him pause. He may be thought insensitive, she may be thought tiresome, but Antonioni presents them both with a sympathy that recognizes their shortcomings.[13]

Eclipse is a boy-meets-girl—or girl-meets-boy—story, but one with a curious shape. It may be divided into four parts: Vittoria; Piero; Vittoria and Piero; neither Vittoria nor Piero. For more than half its length it follows first the girl, then the boy, before the two start meeting as a couple; and soon after their becoming lovers, it ends without them, in a mysterious cadence of suburban dusk, leaving their future together an open question. If *Eclipse* begins at the end, it ends at the beginning.

Every work ends with an ellipsis, since it omits all that happens after the end, but the ellipsis that ends *Eclipse* leaves everything in haunting suspension. This ending is Antonioni's boldest and most resonant unresolved absence. Several commentators, Chatman among them, have attempted to

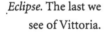

Eclipse. The last we see of Vittoria.

fill in this final ellipsis with the unwarranted conclusion that the young lovers will be seeing each other no more. To be sure, this is a disquieting, not a happy ending; Vittoria and Piero's relationship may be over, or may not last much longer; but the last time we see them, in Piero's otherwise empty office during lunchtime—the long lunchtime of Mediterranean countries, with a summer breeze blowing in through the open windows—the two seem pretty happy, a lively and playful if still tentative couple. As she's about to go and he to return to work for the afternoon, their mood turns pensive and rather somber; embracing, they promise to see each other tomorrow, and the day after tomorrow, and the day after that—and tonight. All we know for certain about their future together is that neither she nor he keeps their appointment—maybe they called it off, maybe they changed it to another time or place—to meet that evening at the corner. The camera keeps the appointment.

Picaresque narrative, from its ancient ancestor in the *Odyssey* to a modern rendition such as *Ulysses*, typically ends with a homecoming: the wanderer on the road of life eventually finds home. Home in *Eclipse*—or the closest thing to it, a home as yet unfinished and precarious, no more than a potential for a home, but a home that draws the camera even if not the characters—is the suburban corner, the dubious and lonesome intersection that Vittoria and Piero have made their meeting place. This is a home outside, a sentimentally invested piece of common ground, the inside represented by the concealed unfinished building: the inward as well as the outward remains under construction.

As if at once impatient for the expected appearance of the lovers and wishing to wait and allow itself a private preamble to their meeting, the camera is hours early for the appointment, though its waiting time, compressed by Antonioni's stunning montage, takes less than ten minutes on the screen, starting at mid-afternoon and, the couple having failed to turn up, ceasing as night falls. A film that began at dawn, and that all along has kept us in touch with the circling of the sun, fittingly ends at dusk. A concluding dawn and an inconclusive dusk: the beginnings and endings of nature guide but do not dictate the beginnings and endings we make. The subjectivity of Antonioni's camera, the sense of its gaze, its point of view, as belonging to a distinctive individual eye, an autonomous percipient mind arranging our awareness, makes itself felt with peculiar eloquence in this extraordinary closing sequence in which the camera at day's end comes to a home that seems to have no other dwellers.

On arriving at the corner, the camera looks, not for Vittoria and Piero, who wouldn't be there yet, but for the familiar sights of their previous meetings there. Again the unfinished building, the pile of bricks, the water barrel, the camera panning to where Vittoria stood beside it and, from the place that was hers, cutting to a view of the building with its straw covering from the same angle that was her perspective. Again the harness racer passes by, and the camera follows him just as before, but now there is no Piero at the juncture with the pedestrian crossing. Now a stranger, an unknowing usurper, we feel, of that path to a kiss, crosses the street at a slight diagonal, with a casual disregard for the lines on the pavement that marked a progress. Again the luminous, shaded leaves ripplingly fill the screen. In a personal, a private experience that wouldn't mean much to anybody else, we share with the camera a recollection of the lovers through a beholding of things associated with them, things that for the camera, for us, carry their memory and at the same time point up their absence.

The camera wants to see the corner as the lovers' place, and looks for the imprint of their past there, yet recognizes that this setting of unfinished modernity, this site of absence even with them present, consorts oddly with a retrospective, rather elegiac mode of beholding. Without straying far from the corner or from the mood of anticipation of the lovers' appearance, the camera turns its searching attention to other things, other people in the neighborhood at the day's end. Nothing unusual happens at the end of this day. A view of the neighborhood from high above, its sparse stretch all calm except for a lone car moving in the tree-lined distance, slowly pans toward the corner and centers it on the screen as crossing diagonals within a rectan-

Eclipse. The corner from high above.

gle. In quick, still succession, two separate women are seen standing, waiting. Its movement taken apart into three shots concatenated like distinct stages of a wave's breaking, a bus turns the corner and stops, letting off two passengers, a man and a woman who go in different directions. A newspaper the man reads talks about the prospect of atomic war, a subject much in the news then, around the time of the Cuban missile crisis. The water barrel has started to leak, and the camera gazes in wonderment at the water running out as at an abstract pattern that probably has no meaning. Children play in the background of a sprinkler watering the grass; we recall that Vittoria and Piero played with this sprinkler, which is now turned off; leaves drippingly fill the screen. All the things we see in this sequence, little and large, are incitingly poised between a possible symbolic reading—the draining water barrel, for example, as the draining energy of a relationship unlikely to continue—and a precise documentary rendering of the detail and circumstance of a particular time and place.

Nature perceived and arranged by an active, reflective consciousness: a daily movement of nature, the gradual and inexorable onset of night, the eclipsing of half the earth by the turning earth itself, Antonioni's camera dissects into charged fragments of the uneventful and articulates as an expectant, apprehensive movement of mind. Each shot in this sequence pins down a moment; each cut crisply makes palpable the passing of time as afternoon gives way to evening, daylight to twilight, twilight to darkness. Culture and nature: a modern building, pale and rectangular, with a serrated edge of balconies, divides the screen with the foliage, rounded and quivering, of dusky trees. Cut closer to the balconies, still closer; as persons watch the sunset from the roof, a long thin cloud being left in the wake of an airplane lines the darkening sky. A thin curving streetlight, which seems to grow out of the rounded dark top of a tree, like a cross between tooled metal and organic nature, electricity rising from foliage, glimmers and brightens with the artificial light of modern night. As trees get dark, streetlights, their partners in lining the suburban streets, shine. In this film we feel a correspondence, an exchange, between nature's light and dark and the answering light and dark of culture.

In the near darkness, another bus turns the corner and stops, letting off several passengers, none of them Vittoria or Piero. For a hovering moment the camera follows these strangers walking away, all no doubt headed home in the suburb at the day's end, but doesn't keep up with them and instead anxiously glides toward its own sought home in the corner. Cut to a long shot of the tenebrous empty corner, the unfinished building dimly lit by a single light bulb that yet saves it from seeming quite abandoned; pan to an intersecting street lined on one side by trees now scarcely visible and on the other by a row of streetlights shining like stars and receding into the obscure distance. Cut to the final image: a blinding close-up of a streetlight, like a staring into the sun, the sun of the projector that shines on the artificial days and nights of the screen. Called by some a paradoxical eclipse by light, taken by others as suggesting an atomic explosion, this sudden dazzling halt of the progressing gloom may also be construed as a bright new day that our artifice may yet bring about.

Besides marking an uncertainty, an ellipsis in Antonioni poses a generalizing question. Why are these lovers breaking up? we wonder at the beginning of *Eclipse,* and lacking acquaintance with the specifics of this case, we're led to ponder more generally the troubles of unsettled modern love, the sentimental homelessness of our time. It doesn't matter so much whether Vittoria and Piero will or will not stay together after the film ends; if they drift apart, other unforeseen romantic intersections will surely detain her path and his; but on the quest for home the two enact and represent, not a private haven fending off the world outside but a humanly satisfying place we can all inhabit and make our own, hangs the fate of our culture, our nature.

"One might compare the art of photography to the act of pointing," proposed John Szarkowski. "Surely the best of photographers have been first of all pointers—men and women whose work says: I call your attention to this pyramid, face, battlefield, pattern of nature, ephemeral

Eclipse. The passengers off the bus, headed home at the day's end.

juxtaposition."[14] Surely not just the best of photographers but all wielders of the camera use it to point to bits of the world they find deserving of attention. Surely all photographic images, whatever else they may say, say first of all: look at this as I saw it.

Isn't that true, one might ask, of handmade pictures as well? Doesn't every image that depicts something point to what it depicts? The rectangular frame that painting bequeathed to photography serves, in painting no less than in photography, as a pointer, a means of directing attention to what is to be seen in the area whose boundaries it marks: ornately or plainly the frame tells us to look at this within its four edges. But in a painting what is to be seen is another world, apart from ours and enclosed within its boundaries, a world that may recognizably resemble ours but whose only encounter with our circumstances was through the eye and hand of the painter who put it together. A photograph, by contrast, is the record of a piece of our circumstances; what is to be seen within the frame was not put together in a separate domain of the image but picked out from the multitudinous realm of actual appearances. The frame of a painting points to the picture; the frame of a photograph points to the piece of actual appearances depicted.

Anything that points, anything that functions as an index finger, is an index in Peirce's sense. The photographic image is an index because it is an imprint taken directly from the things represented; and it is also an index because, like a pointing finger, it tells us to look at those things. The imprint, the remnant, the trace, is the kind of index most often talked about these days but not the only kind. A plumb bob is an index and so is a proper name;

Eclipse. The corner as night has fallen at the film's end.

a spotlight on the stage is an index and so is a knock on the door. "Anything which focusses the attention is an index," wrote Peirce.[15] The frame is an index that photography took over from painting and takes out into the world so that it serves to call attention to life's details, to aspects and moments arrested from life's flux. The camera is an indicative instrument, a means of picking out and bringing to awareness: pointed at things, it points at them by receiving the imprint of their light and framing it into their image. As their delayed light reaches us, our gaze follows the camera's indicative gaze and focuses on their relayed appearance. The photographic image is doubly an index, then, because both receptive and indicative: it registers waves like a seismograph and it points like an index finger at something chosen for attention.

The frame divides us from the world of the picture; it marks the border between life and the image. The photograph, however, is an image taken from life; the world of its representation is the same world we inhabit. "A painting *is* a world," wrote Stanley Cavell; "a photograph is *of* the world."[16] It is not another world we see in a photograph but another time, another place; what divides us from the scene represented is merely distance—the passage of time, the stretch of space—or merely absence: we are not there, it is not here. If the frame of a painting is traditionally ornate and that of a photograph usually plain, it is not only because traditional taste ran to the ornate and modern taste runs to the plain. It is also because the frame of a painting bridges a greater gap: at the four edges of the picture a world ends, and the embroidery of those edges works to set up that world, as a kind of stage, in the context of our world. The frame of a painting, like the proscenium arch in the theater, is an index that designates the arrangement within its compass of a domain of representation set apart from the surrounding reality. The frame of a photograph is an index that designates not the edges of a world but the extent of a choice.

Linear perspective, another heritage from painting built into the camera and applied by it directly to life, also comes in photography to significantly different use. Perspective was invented in the Renaissance as a means for representing depth, for making three dimensions out of two. Lines of perspective in a painting serve mainly to construct on the picture plane a fictive receding third dimension. Photography inherits painting's perspective but applies it in reverse. Whereas a painter starts with the picture plane and on it composes a world, a photographer starts with a piece of the world and from it derives a picture. Perspective works in photography to make two dimensions out of three: not to deepen the plane into a world but to flatten the world into a picture.[17] Lines of perspective in a photograph serve not so much to represent depth as to lead the attention back there, to steer the eye along a certain path into the distance, to point in a certain direction. In photography lines of perspective are mainly indicative. A camera angle is a line of pointing.

Anything that focuses the attention is an index, and the camera is a machine armed with a focus: literally, by the physical agency of a lens, it focuses the attention. Not a heritage from painting but a technique native to photography, the camera's focus is another means of photographic pointing. Bringing something into focus points to it, selects it for our notice; bringing something into sharper focus than something else in the picture is a gesture of pointing, of singling this out rather than that, as visible as an aimed index finger.

The child learns language with the indispensable assistance of pointing. Pointing at things and saying what we call them first teaches us the meaning of words. Those who believe that words refer only to other words, as in a dictionary, must have forgotten about pointing; a dictionary is useless unless one already knows the language well enough to follow a definition of words by other words that depends on pointing for bringing words and things together. Pointing is an act of drawing attention, a first person's index finger drawing a second person's attention to a proposed shared object of consciousness; a word learned, red, tree, signifies such a shared object. But the proposed object may be too particular for the generality of words—not any red but *this* red, not any tree but *that* tree—in which case we rely on pointing as the chief signifier. The adult usually points when words are less than adequate to the occasion.

Photography points. From among the world's innumerable number the camera specifies a particular sight it captures for our looking. Still photography's index finger freezes into an image the object it proposes to our consciousness. The movable index finger of the movies unfolds before our eyes a succession of images that are so many pointings.

Unlike a still photograph, and like a painting, a fiction movie *is* a world. A still photograph has its life as a fragment taken from life. A movie may take fragments from life but it arranges them into a fiction; the world of its representation is not the world we inhabit but another world put together on the screen. Yet it is a world presented a piece at a time, so that each image is to be regarded as *of* the world, a detail picked out from an indefinitely larger world of the movie that the movie treats as tantamount to the world. The movie camera proceeds *as if* the sights it frames and brings into focus were being selected for our notice from among the world's innumerable number. Central to the fiction of a fiction movie is the convention that the movie camera is like a still camera endowed with access and mobility in a world like our own where it can go about successively pointing to the significant detail.

An unknown man encountered on the outskirts of a city stands with his legs apart, his right arm tensely raised, his finger resolutely pointing. Pointing at what? This man figures in one of the short stories Antonioni has published, one of his "tales of a director"[18]—verbal sketches, "narrative nuclei" that he relates as observer and sometimes as participant, recollected or invented points of departure for films that this too often unemployed director will probably never make.[19]

For looking at things, his vocation and avocation, Antonioni has his own technique, "which consists in working backward," he writes, "from a series of images to a state of affairs."[20] Whereas most filmmakers start with a state of affairs, a story that determines their choice of images, Antonioni works backward from the images to the story rather as a detective works backward from the evidence to the crime: instead of following a story line, his images point toward different possible stories, different paths the attention may pursue. Such a series of images, fraught with the undiscovered, even at the end of the masterly *Eclipse* holds a conclusion in stirring abeyance.

The unknown man points with anxious emphasis at nothing discernible, the indicative line of his raised arm and finger leading to "an empty passageway between two buildings, empty of everything but emptiness." Maybe, the onlooking Antonioni wonders, this man is "one of those people who point to something that only they see," his intent gesture an idiolectic drawing of attention to no object of consciousness that can be shared.[21] The index finger seems to find its target, however, when an opened door in one of the buildings catches the man's reflection and casts it back toward Antonioni, rebounding the line of pointing his way and, like a recruiting poster, aiming the finger at him. Suddenly the object of consciousness, as if subjectivity were being called upon to fill the absence of an object, becomes the conscious self.

This sketch of the man pointing may be taken as a little parable of film direction. If a camera angle is a line of pointing, a reverse angle, which brings the facing area into view in the next image, is like a rebounding of that line. In *Strangers on a Train* (1951), a film about doubling, about symmetry and its sinisterness, Hitchcock cleverly likens the exchange between angle and reverse angle to the bouncing back and forth of tennis; when at a tennis match the villain looks, not back and forth like the other spectators, but straight ahead at the hero who is his double, his gaze tells that the ball is in the hero's court in an exchange of murders. The pointing man's reflected reverse angle, surprising and implicative, similarly puts the ball in Antonioni's court. Angle and reverse angle in turn point off screen, each the object of the other's pointing, but here the director, the viewer, is pulled into the exchange as if he were the pointing man's double.

In a film not only the camera points. The actors too, with their glances and their gestures, their words and their movements, lead the attention toward things within view and without. A film often points to what lies without, off screen. A film image exists in the context of a space off screen, an unbounded field of the unseen that is not merely implied but continually impinges on what is being shown. A still photograph may point outside our view but it can only suggest what lies there; a film can bring it into view in the next image. When a film image points outside our view—by showing an actor going out a door, for example, or looking out a window—the next image will likely bring into view the object of the pointing—where the actor goes through the door, what he or she is looking at from the window. In a sequence of film images a pointing to something unseen creates an expectation of seeing it.

An absence in a film creates an expectation of presence. When something off screen draws our interest, or when something on screen seems incomplete, what is missing from our view is apt to be brought in. A pointing to an emptiness is common in a sequence of film images, creating an expectation that the emptiness will be filled, as when an actor's entrance into frame fills the expectant image of an empty room—or as when, in a startling variant, the image of the man pointing at an emptiness enters the frame of the opened door, meeting in this unexpected way the expectation created by his own pointing. To meet expectations created by his or her own pointing is the task of a film director; to meet them in unexpected ways is Antonioni's characteristic practice. Antonioni's expectant images, the absences that haunt them, the intervals on which his camera lingers, are seldom filled by a conventional resolving presence. After Anna, the initial main character, disappears in L'Avventura, the expectation that she will be found, that at the least what happened to her will come to be known, gradually in the days of search gives way to another story—or perhaps the same one with another character in her place—a story resonant with her felt absence.

At the end of The Passenger, in a breathtaking long take oblique to the resolving action that leads, off screen, to the protagonist's death in a Spanish hotel room, Antonioni's camera moves from inside the room out into a dusty sunlit square right through a window whose bars fail to impede the smooth outward movement, which continues around the square and in time gets back to the window, the camera now looking in from outside at the inside from which it started looking out. Earlier, when conducting an interview in his capacity as a television reporter, a purveyor of the outside for the inside of our living rooms, the protagonist found himself before rather than behind his camera: an African rebel leader, the intended subject, seized the position of framer of the picture and pointed the camera at him. In *L'Avventura* the missing Anna and the searching Claudia who virtually takes her place may be regarded as doubles of each other; in *The Passenger* the missing person and the searcher are combined in a protagonist who exchanges identities with a dead stranger who resembles him. *The Passenger* is a story of the other self, the doppelgänger, in which the two sides of a split self become the inside and the outside. It is the story of a missing person in search of himself not so much within as without: the protagonist tries to find himself in the external world by assuming the identity of a gunrunner, taking on the part of a man of action rather than a man covering that action in the news. In this version of the doppelgänger story the other self is the self as it appears from outside to the other that is the world, the self as seen from the world's distant reverse angle. The moral of the story, traditional in stories of the doppelgänger, is that the split is fatal: Jekyll and Hyde, the self and the other self, come together in death, which is when, in *The Passenger,* the inside and the outside are seen to be seamlessly one. The interplay between inner and outer that Antonioni's camera always enacts, the subjectivity of an outsider's gaze, the outward movement of an introspective consciousness, *The Passenger* makes into an allegory of the self and the world.

The camera in most films points where the story line leads, so that the objects of interest, the created expectations, are mainly dramatic. But the story of Anna in *L'Avventura*, like the pointing man's finger, leads to an emptiness, a search for the missing: a search calling upon the subjectivity, the outsider's gaze of Antonioni's camera to fill the absence of an object on which consciousness can settle. Endowed with exploratory autonomy, free to linger or to wander outside a line of dramatic development, Antonioni's camera points and maneuvers along paths of its own, attentive to the characters but as attentive to the space around them and often digressive, catching the stray aspect, dwelling on the incidental circumstance that may lead to another story. "Every time I start working on a film," says this director in his book of tales, "another one comes to mind."[22] "Every movement is a succession of asides," wrote Joseph Bennett of *L'Avventura*,[23] and this is true of Antonioni generally. Met with a visual elegance no less arresting for being unsettled, the expectations his pointing creates are mainly about looking, the tension and curiosity of seeing, the searching gaze, the visible pondered. More than a director of actors and dramatic scenes, Antonioni is, with uncommon acuity, a director of attention. As Bresson called himself not a *metteur en scène* but a *metteur en ordre*—rather than staging scenes, he puts their fragments in strict order—so Antonioni may be called not a *metteur en scène* but a *metteur en conscience:* a bringer into consciousness, an arranger of awareness.

The plot of *Blow-Up* (1966) proceeds as a succession of asides, of interruptions, distractions in a day in the life of a smart London photographer, distractions that tangentially, through the glancing contact of pictures taken with something quite other in mind, happen to cross paths with a murder. *Blow-Up* is not so much a murder mystery whose solution is never found as a film that finds its story to be a murder mystery. *Eclipse* takes more than half its length to find its story in the incipient romance between Vittoria and Piero: first it follows her over two days in her life, then him for a day in his, until, their paths intersecting, they start seeing each other. On a rendezvous with him she notices something off screen and moves ahead, out of view; cut to another young man walking by, a stranger whose good looks have attracted her attention and whom the camera, diverging from her perspective as she pauses to observe him, follows in a frontal movement in which she recedes. For a moment Vittoria, hesitant about her involvement with Piero, contemplates the alternative, the distractive passerby who points the narra-

Eclipse. The distractive passerby.

tive away from its unsettled center in the love story; for a moment the film pursues a narrative path it might have taken.

Description, as Roland Barthes has discussed (in his essay "The Reality Effect"),[24] tends to be in excess of narrative meaning; the described aspects and details surpass their function in setting the scene, fleshing out the characterization, motivating and grounding the story. That excess, maintains Barthes, signifies the real in realistic fiction, the real perceived as a resistance to meaning. Put another way, realistic fiction likes to exhibit a pointing to meaning, a focusing on the significant picked out from a larger space of the real. By no mere coincidence, realistic fiction and photography were invented around the same time.

In cinema, a medium able to enact realistic fiction photographically, the canonical style of realism has been that established in postwar Italy. A sense of the resistance that reality offers to meaning marks the films of Italian neorealism, especially the films of Rossellini. The novelty of Rossellini's neorealism, manifested in certain passages that "remain in one's consciousness with the particularity of real experience," as Robert Warshow wrote about *Paisan* (1946),[25] lay not in his letting reality speak for itself—for reality doesn't speak unless interpreted—but in his letting it *not* speak by presenting it from the viewpoint of an outsider able to grasp the unfolding situation no better than partially, a camera that declines a position of interpretive advantage and registers with astonished reticence the outward particularity of things. Rossellini was an important if inconsistent precursor of Antonioni's use of a camera not empowered to interpret the world with an insider's privileged adequacy of perception. But Antonioni combines Rossellini's reticence with Hitchcock's exacting fluency in camera and cutting and the management of point of view: he is the master of the suspense of looking, with an articulate interrogative gaze, at a reality that resists the attempt to make it speak.

"The strange thing is this," writes Antonioni about the empty spot where the pointing man directs the eye, "that you don't have the sense that at that point the outskirts proper begin, as in fact they do. You have the feeling of emptiness."[26] How does one articulate the city's emptying out as it shades into the outskirts? The pointing man enables Antonioni to punctuate absence, to make sharp an experience of the diffuse, bring out the alarming in the taken for granted. In a sequence at once leisurely and alert, meandering and crisply rhythmic, a sequence punctuated by a counterpoint between her pointings and the camera's, her glances and entrances and exits and its lingering angles and terse cuts, Jeanne Moreau's character in *La Notte* walks around the streets and into the outskirts of Milan, enabling Antonioni to articulate

those broadening, sprawling spaces between. Monica Vitti's characters likewise enable him to articulate the spaces of the Roman suburb in *Eclipse* and
the industrial outskirts of Ravenna in *The Red Desert*. These are instances of
the "witness," as Chatman calls the character in an Antonioni film who
parallels the camera's searching apprehension of things and looks at them
with a similar outsider's gaze, detached, intent, perplexed, anxious, probing.

To make us see was for Conrad the novelist's undertaking, for D. W.
Griffith the filmmaker's; Antonioni's undertaking is to make us see and, once
we have seen, to make us look again. The point of view of an Antonioni
witness is not the same as the film's: the director sets up a counterpoint, not a
congruence, between the perspective and perceptions of the witness and the
camera's own. Doubling the camera's gaze, the witness is one of the means
Antonioni employs for making us look again, making us aware of the different perspectives from which a situation may be regarded. When staging a
play in the theater, the director has said, he found it frustrating that he could
not show the audience a scene's other side. In his films Antonioni typically
cuts from a lingering inspective view to a suddenly revised, renewed perspective. From one side of a scene he will cut abruptly across to the other side,
breaking the convention that rules out, because momentarily disorienting,
cuts that "cross the line." Shifting our perceptual bearings, he sharpens our
looking. Watchfully looking again and looking anew, he unfolds an exploration of a scene's various sides, an inquiry into the countless different aspects
of the visible.

Without Jeanne Moreau's character, the sequence in *La Notte* wandering around the streets and outskirts of Milan would have yielded but a series
of impressions, a vignette of everyday life; with her, the series of images
points toward an ongoing state of affairs and articulates a narrative sequence, expectant and suspensive, digressive and uncertain yet precisely
focused and charged with implications, a sequence that evokes a narrative
consequence yet to be discovered. Without the anticipation that the young
lovers will turn up for a rendezvous they miss, without the resonance of their
absence, the final sequence of *Eclipse* would likewise have been a little descriptive essay on an ordinary suburban corner where life winds down as
usual at day's end, instead of the large, troubled, eerie reflection it is—hopeful and fearful at the same time, an arrangement of fragments of suburban
dusk that implicates all of us dwellers amid the spaces between, the missing
pieces of our modernity. Uneventful as his films are for long stretches,
ruminative and reverberant intervals, Antonioni is not only a highly visual
but also very much a narrative filmmaker. If the import, the sensate circum-

stance of his images exceeds their narrative meaning, that is because they suggest the telling not just of one but of many possible stories.

The first of four characters in a row that Monica Vitti played for Antonioni, Claudia in *L'Avventura* is a friend of Anna's who accompanies her and her lover, Sandro, on a yachting excursion in the sea north of Sicily with a group of the wealthy. Claudia is an outsider to the group and a lively young woman, bright, pretty, a bit ingenuous; she brings to mind an innocent abroad in a tale by Henry James. Initially a secondary character, she is a narrative path that Antonioni, who keeps drawing, or distracting, attention toward her, is eventually to take. Claudia is an observant outsider, an Antonioni witness, alert and receptive to the impressions of an environment that she regards, paralleling Antonioni's camera, from the point of view of a stranger. Antonioni's sharpest witnesses are women.[27]

Beginning with Anna and Sandro, couples, all in some way mismatched, disjoined, bored, or unhappy, are a frequent subject of Claudia's observation, not because she pries into the lives of others but because such couples present themselves as a recurrent feature of this environment, like the barren volcanic islands dotting the sea. As she moves from a marginal place in the narrative to the center that Anna has vacated, Claudia becomes more and more involved in what she has been witnessing with a certain questioning detachment. By the film's end, with Anna gone, vanished on one of those islands and found nowhere, and the distant volcanic pinnacle of Mount Etna looming over the two human figures in the closing image—a sudden, sustained long shot that

L'Avventura. Claudia on the volcanic island where Anna disappeared.

asks *us* to look with questioning detachment—Claudia is no longer the observer, the vital outsider to barren territory, but a partner, with Sandro, in one of those unhappy couples. Now more involved with the characters, now more detached from them, Antonioni's camera maintains the outsider's gaze, the point of view of a stranger. "To the extent that Antonioni's imagination is a moral one," wrote William S. Pechter about *L'Avventura*, "he sees all his characters as the same, lost in their similarity . . . united in [their] common weakness . . . all missing persons."[28] Claudia's story is the story of an outsider become an insider out of love's empathy, which is part of her vitality and potentially a strength but is here the weakness that unites her with Sandro and the rest of the missing persons.

To astonish us with the outlandish isn't difficult; Antonioni will astonish us with the commonplace, the strangeness of nothing much, the ostensibly trivial or incidental yet undismissible detail. An instance of Claudia's astonishment, and ours, at such latently telling detail occurs on the first morning aboard the yacht. During an edgy exchange with Anna, in a shrugging sarcastic gesture that Claudia doesn't see, Sandro throws overboard the pages of a newspaper he has been reading. Cut to the pages blowing away behind him, toward the yacht's wake, the camera panning in their direction until Claudia, sitting aft, enters frame; viewed from the back, she sits up, startled at the sight of those printed pages fluttering in the wind and descending into the sea, pages whose source, though known to us, is mysterious to her. Although we don't share her surprise, her astonishment from her witness's perspective leads us to wonder how much we really know about the source of those pages, which we saw Sandro throw away but which point to some obscure trouble plaguing his relationship with Anna; then, with the view of Claudia still held, further fluttering pages enter frame, startling us now much as the earlier pages startled her. Antonioni's use of the witness, in this passage and elsewhere, avoids the "reaction shot," the cut to a character's expression that prompts us into responding to a scene in the way signaled by that expression. Not a character whose perspective or response we exactly share, an Antonioni witness serves to make keener our own apprehension of things. Claudia provides us not so much with a point of view on those pages as with a point of comparison for our response.

Anna soon follows the pages overboard in an impulsive immersion that foreshadows her disappearance. Impatient when the others are slow to decide on a spot for swimming—a small indecision that for her seems to connote a large one—she brusquely dives into the sea without waiting for the yacht to stop. The camera pans along her trajectory and holds on a view, from the back—as Antonioni often photographs the witness, showing us not the expression but the observant posture—of Claudia gazing at her friend swimming away as she gazed at the pages blowing away. The similar manner of presentation, in each case a rightward panning toward the yacht's wake ending on a nonplused witnessing Claudia, connects Anna's plunge and Sandro's pages through a visual parallel that proposes a simile.

Against the notion of Antonioni as contriver of heavy symbols and metaphors—symbols and metaphors grandly communicating our modern inability to communicate with one another—Chatman puts forward the also mistaken notion that Antonioni relies not on metaphor but on metonymy to express his meanings. This deems the director a realist rather than a symbolist, a documenter rather than a poet, but he is an idiosyncratic mixture of both.

Metaphor and *metonymy* are terms that Chatman, like many others nowadays, uses in Roman Jakobson's sense, which makes all association or signification metaphorical that proceeds by comparison (knife and sword, dawn for beginning, characterizing Juliet as the sun) and all association or signification metonymical that proceeds by contiguity (knife and fork, moonlighting for working at a second job, characterizing a man by a description of the clothes he wears or the neighborhood he inhabits). Contrast as well as similitude Jakobson subsumes under metaphor; synecdoche, the part for the whole, he subsumes under metonymy, along with all other relations of context in space and time.[29]

If metaphor is the prime idiom of poetry, metonymy is the prime idiom of realistic fiction; if metaphor leaps, metonymy points. By metonymy detail points to character, aspect to scene, situation to story; here points to there, before to after, cause to effect, and vice versa. A detail or aspect resistant to meaning may be reckoned a metonymy arrested. Although Chatman, a simplistic interpreter in semiotic garb, seems impressed by the term, *metonymy* refers not only to artful but also to quite ordinary matters, a view of smoke to signify fire, a close-up of a laughing face to signify mirth. Indeed a master of the pregnant metonymy, Antonioni is as subtle and evocative a practitioner of metaphor. Taken separately, Sandro's pages and Anna's plunge, each a movement overboard pointing to character and story, are metonymies; but the visual parallel brings them together into a metaphor. A metaphor for what? Metaphor as much as metonymy enacts in Antonioni a quest for meaning that meets with resistance.

Like poetry, painting exhibits an order of comparison, a bringing together of things rhymed with one another, measured against one another.

Metaphor is the prime idiom of painting as of poetry. Painting's meanings result chiefly from the arrangement of likenesses and unlikenesses, correspondences and complements, parities and disparities; pictorial composition leads the eye to see similarity in difference and difference in similarity. Antonioni is among the most painterly of filmmakers, painterly not in a static but in a deeply cinematic manner. As a painter may compare the shape of a raised arm to that of a rising branch, the color of the sky to that of the Virgin's mantle, so Antonioni, through the parallel arrangement of moving images, compares the movement overboard of printed pages in the wind to that of a restless woman impatient for a swim.

Eclipse begins at dawn on one day and ends at dusk on another, and throughout it compares the sun's light and dark, the sunlit and the shadowy, the natural light of day and dark of evening, with the artificial, the cultural light and dark of our electrical modernity, which is, this film reminds us, the light and dark of film images being projected on the screen. At one point Vittoria, seen through her apartment windows as she arrives home in the evening and turns on her lights, makes bright little screens within the dark screen, little artificial days within the dark of evening that, after the film cuts inside her apartment, become as bright as day in the artificial light of the image. Sitting in bed and talking with a friend from the building, she casually raises a black shawl over her head; cut to a disconcerting momentary darkness, an artificial night or eclipse within the artificial day as the shawl, suddenly viewed from close, blackly fills the screen. The reverse occurs at the end, when suddenly the film cuts from the encroaching suburban darkness to the final blinding close-up of a streetlight. The light and dark of *Eclipse* is both literal, the light and dark of the senses, and metaphorical, the light and dark of the sentiments, of the mind that seeks meaning through the constructions of culture.

Antonioni has "a proper feeling for meaning," wrote Roland Barthes in an open letter of appreciation addressed to the director: "you do not impose it, but you do not abolish it. This dialectic gives your films . . . a great subtlety: your art consists in always leaving the path to meaning open, one might say undecided, on principle."[30] Among books on Antonioni in English, Chatman's tends solemnly to impose meaning while Sam Rohdie's tends cheerfully to abolish it: neither is comfortable with the dialectic and the subtlety Barthes speaks of. Filmmakers who pursue the painterly in most cases similarly attempt either to impose meaning (by expressionist distortion) or to abolish it (by sheer decoration). Rivaled perhaps only by Mizoguchi as a pictorial artist in movies, Antonioni avoids both the sheerly decorative and the assertively meaningful pictorial composition. His painterly meanings, his metaphors of pictorial comparison, are advanced but tentatively, tried out, with a deft eye-opening allusiveness that refrains from conclusions, against the claims of a state of affairs and its vividly depicted detail and circumstance. Neither heavily symbolic nor reliant on metonymy rather than metaphor, Antonioni's meanings, suggested yet held in resonant suspension, hover between metonymy and metaphor, between the observed reality and the proposed symbol. The imprint and the image conjoined in photography, the recorded appearance and the arranged picture, enact in his films a mutual questioning and a joint anxious quest.

A rather witty visual rhyme at the beginning of *L'Avventura* links the bald head of Anna's father with the dome of St. Peter's behind him, sitting oddly and majestically on the flat horizon. This metaphor (which Chatman, pressing his argument, calls a metonymy) associates Anna's father, a wealthy, retired diplomat, with the imposing yet obsolescent structures of church and tradition; but his old-fashioned outlook and stately manner are clear enough otherwise, and the visual rhyme would be a bit redundant were it not for the evolving composition, arranged so that Anna herself comes to appear against the dome, which has the effect of trying out whether *her* head in some way rhymes with that round structure associated with her father and signifying tradition. More than to make a comment, the visual rhyme serves to pose a question. The question thus posed pictorially—the unclear issue of Anna's relation both to her father and to the traditional structures of her culture and society—cannot be pictorially answered. A filmmaker more assertive of meaning might have presumed so to answer it, but Antonioni doesn't presume that Anna's abundant dark hair, just because it differs visu-

L'Avventura.
The father's bald head
and the dome on
the horizon.

ally from the churchly shape behind her, should be construed to signify her rejection—even if it inclines us to doubt her acceptance—of father, church, tradition. Her placement against the dome instead raises an issue, a question left open, to be further considered later in the film. After Anna's disappearance a Bible is found among her belongings, and her father, arriving on the scene, says hopefully that her reading the Bible means belief in God and rules out the possibility of her suicide. Claudia draws back in tearful silence. The question remains open.

A head of abundant dark hair measured against a dome rising on the horizon like the reared head of tradition, hairless and disembodied: this pictorial composition symbolically intimates a conflict, which may account for the tension visible on Anna's face, between the sensual and erotic and the beliefs of a culture perhaps outmoded but not so easily buried. In one scene later on, some time after Anna's disappearance, Claudia, her scruples giving way to a readiness for romance with her vanished friend's lover, dons a dark wig over her blond hair. Claudia and Sandro become lovers right after a visit to an abandoned modern town in the hills of Sicily with a shut modern church in a main square without a soul. He proposes marriage to her on the roof of a church in Noto, where they have gone in search of Anna, and Claudia, at a loss for a response, pulls on a rope before her that to her surprise rings a church bell and to her delight gets a response from other church bells nearby, which enter into a chimed exchange: marriage bells, as it were, that the church rings anyhow for this uneasy couple. A dark-haired whore who attracts a large crowd of ogling Sicilian men is compared with Claudia, who similarly attracts a group of ogling men in Noto; and at the end the whore too takes Anna's place: fearing that the missing Sandro may be with her returned

L'Avventura. Anna's abundant hair and the dome on the horizon.

missing friend, Claudia finds him instead on a couch with the dark-haired whore. The associations ramify, metonymically and metaphorically.

Two movements of disjoining that alike point to the trouble disjoining this couple, Sandro's pages and Anna's plunge make a metaphor for disjunction, disparateness, breaking or drifting apart. The visual parallel between the two movements overboard suggestively heightens our sense of the trouble without accounting for the cause: another question posed pictorially and left unanswered. Are we to surmise, from the discarded pages fluttering away, that Sandro's treatment of Anna has been likewise thoughtless and inconstant? But isn't Sandro the one who wants to marry—his motives thrown into doubt only when he later turns to Claudia with equal seeming sincerity—and Anna the one reluctant? Only in retrospect can we see in her plunge something of the suicidal impulse, or the impulse to vanish, and in his pages something of his tendency, while professing love and proposing marriage, to flutter in his affections from woman to woman. If the painters of the Renaissance used the idiom of pictorial metaphor to portray an elucidated world, Antonioni uses that idiom to interrogate the world's appearances. If the Renaissance was an age of clarity, ours—as testified by the enduring appeal, undiminished a century and a half after its inception, of the genre of mystery and suspense—is an age of mystery.

Antonioni's style of characterization takes the form of a mystery under investigation by his camera's detective eye. Presented without the sort of dialogue and acting and knowing camera angles that usually would have spelled them out for us, his characters are like strangers we encounter *in medias res* and come to know in provisional bits and pieces, glimpses often sustained but as often interrupted and never conclusive, as puzzling as they are telling and always to be continued. Well into the film we discover that the apparently self-possessed Sandro is not at ease with himself. Wandering alone in Noto, he comes upon an ink sketch that an architectural student is making of a baroque niche in the cathedral square; feigning distraction, he purposely swings his keys and knocks over the ink bottle, spilling black ink on the white paper and spoiling the architectural drawing. This signifies, by metonymy, the regret and resentment that Sandro feels when encountering the youthful aspiration, which was once his own, to become an architect and build beautiful buildings such as the ones in this square. No longer young but not so old as no longer to entertain that aspiration, Sandro now makes good money at commercial contracting.

After the metonymy comes an arresting interrogative metaphor. As

Sandro tries to avert a fight with the indignant young man whose drawing he spitefully ruined, the two pause to look at something past the camera that catches their attention. A long stream of schoolboys and priests, all dressed in ecclesiastical black, emerges from the cathedral into the square and strikingly resembles the spilled ink leaving on the paper its black trail. This parallel between the churchly and the inky black was construed by John Simon as a satirical "anticlerical touch" reminiscent of Fellini, and indeed the schoolboys and priests are seen as an ink spreading across the square, a blot on its architecture. Yet, as the architectural drawing depends on ink for its making, so did the beautiful baroque architecture of this square depend on the church for its building, ecclesiastical black in a sense being the ink with which its plans were drawn: the churchliness that may seem like a blot today was the designing ink of this architecture, the practical purpose and the spiritual principle of its construction. The irruption of the clerical group, spoiling the aesthetic view as the ink spoiled the drawing, reminds us that beautiful architecture does not arise from aesthetic concerns alone. It is as though, on this grand baroque drawing, the cathedral square of Noto, Antonioni were spilling ink, its own, so that we recognize what went into its making and what separates us from its makers. These buildings we admire we could not build today for want, not of talent—individual talent there always is—but of a church, a society, an informing culture able to inspire and sustain such architecture; and whatever beautiful buildings we may build ourselves will likewise depend on an informing culture, our own, for their inspiration and sustainment. The metonymy conveyed Sandro's personal weakness, his petty resentful regret; the metaphor deepens and broadens

L'Avventura.
Ecclesiastical black
and spilled ink.

that regret, takes it out of the realm of an individual's shortcomings and generalizes it into a question put to our culture. Certainly Sandro will not build beautiful buildings: will any of us?

The eighteenth century coined the word *aesthetic* and divided the aesthetic, the disinterested appreciation of things of beauty held at contemplative arm's length, from the practical, the spiritual, the moral, the social, the political, all the *interested* domains of human experience. Antiquity, the Middle Ages, the Renaissance, knew no such division. The beautiful was for Plato the surest intuition of the desirable, the best the senses could do to perceive the good. In the Middle Ages the beautiful blended inseparably with the spiritual, the most interested thing there was in an age of faith; oriented toward the sky and letting in its light through stained glass, a Gothic cathedral aims to evoke, not beauty at aesthetic arm's length, but a heavenly beauty ultimate to earthly life. In the Renaissance the sense of beauty merged with a confident sense of life as amenable to human measure and order; oriented toward human eyes, a Renaissance or baroque church founds its spirituality on a soaring humanism.

Of all the arts architecture is the one necessarily interested: a style of architecture embodies a culture's manner of arranging the conduct of life. And the one necessarily affirmative: to build something is to uphold it, and what a culture builds, cathedral or shopping center, expresses its values and beliefs with solid sanction. In the later eighteenth century, however, European architecture started vacillating in the stylistic affirmation of its own time and turning restlessly to the styles of the past for aesthetic spoils, which dominated nineteenth-century building through an assortment of period revivals flourishing between the rococo and the next new style of architecture, the modern international style of the twentieth century. If modernism is in its nature critical, an art that takes an adversary position toward its culture and society, architecture, an art form that must be constructive, is a special case within the modern movement. Disdaining to imitate the past, the modern international style at its most vital affirms not the present but the future—and not merely an imagined or adumbrated future but, as things must be in the medium of building, a future to be embodied in a piece of built actuality. In architecture modernism is a utopian undertaking, bravely visionary but impossible to achieve, for a future cannot be built by building alone. Postmodern theorizers have generalized without warrant from this special case, however, and would characterize all modernism as utopian. Anything in any way hopeful, anything that suggests a reaching toward something better, has come in postmodern parlance to be called *utopian,* a word that may be used admiringly but almost always carries a slighting sense of the impracticable, the unattainable, what may be nice to dream about but can never come about. Evidently our current postmodernism has retreated from the hopes modernism harbors even in its anxiety, the aspirations it expresses even in its criticism. The sense of beauty is nothing if not hopeful, nothing if not a reaching, if not the sparkle of an aspiration.

Antonioni in his films is a student, a critic of architecture, an attentive observer of place, constructed or natural, designed or haphazard, as it becomes invested, architecturally, with the practical and symbolic motives of human occupancy. The journey to Sicily in *L'Avventura* feels by and large like a journey into the past, the Mediterranean, the churchly baroque, the sites and contours of traditional life. In Sicily, in that past, the Italian characters are as foreign as tourists from abroad. "Antonioni's tacit subject, first announced in the short film he made about street sweepers (*Nettezza Urbana,* 1948)," wrote Vernon Young, "is the nature of the space that man inhabits."[31] The much disliked *Zabriskie Point* (1969), a flawed but impressive work, captures with baffled accuracy the bluff surface of American life, West Coast, late-sixties style: the activist student meetings; the billboards like painted backdrops setting the giant stage of L.A.; the desert as a site of hippie freedom commingling sand and flesh in the sun; the dim and lonely bars of an older generation; the final wishful blowing up, entrancingly repeated, of an emblematic modern house of plenty into the sweet smithereens of a flower child's fantasy of revolutionary violence. Disliked both by those who saw it as extolling the counterculture of the sixties and by those it was supposed to extol, this film, like all of Antonioni's, is an outsider's incisive investigation of place and its occupancy.

The medium best equipped for a critique of architecture, cinema can articulate anew, in movement and in give and take with an unfolding narrative and its characters, the architectural articulation of place. "What figure of today aesthetically best suits our streets, what figure aesthetically is best framed by our doorways?" asked Adrian Stokes in the thirties, and he took his answer from the "*mise-en-scène* of any good gangster film": "the man in a long overcoat with hand within pocket holding a revolver on which his fingers tighten. There is no gainsaying the aesthetic appropriateness of the thug in our streets and in our interiors. The idea of him saves our town environment from a suggestion of vacuum."[32] Antonioni's recurrent subject is a suggestion of vacuum, the pointing man's emptiness, suffusing the space, the spaces between, that we inhabit.

On the way to Noto following a clue to Anna's whereabouts, Sandro and Claudia come to the abandoned modern town and stop to look around the place, built under Fascism and, they find, now quite deserted. As they drive away, "the camera remains at middle distance from the uninhabited area . . . inching forward almost imperceptibly," as Vernon Young wrote. "After the couple have left, the lone camera continues to creep stealthily forward—as if a presence were covertly watching. . . . From here on in the film we sense that the terms of the pursuit have shifted. Sandro and Claudia are no longer looking for something. A something is looking for them. . . ."[33] Predictably, since she's joined him in the search after retreating from his advances, the two will be lovers before long; abruptly, from that void of a town and that camera lurking toward them the film cuts to Claudia as, with glad sensuality, she embraces Sandro in a field. Through their stop in the abandoned town the camera's maintained distance from them points at, points up, an emptiness not filled until the sudden close views of the two making love, having recoiled into each other's arms from the emptiness and abandonment. The distant views of the town create an expectation of close views of the characters; a place in a film is conventionally to be the setting for an action; but this town is the setting for an action that happens not there but elsewhere, not until after the couple have driven away. Most striking as they depart and already disturbing upon their arrival—when a slowly panning camera gazes at their car from a high terrace—the sense of a presence watching them in the town insinuates the missing Anna they're about to betray: "Is this where Anna disappeared?" asked Pechter. As the thug humanizes our town environment, so the sense of that presence, as of a lone lurking inhabitant of that uninhabitable pocket of the modernistic amid the traditional, strangely humanizes the deserted town's forbidding architecture: an architecture for missing persons.

For the incident or interval, the expectation, transition, discovery, aftermath, the precise turn or suspension of events that will animate a place and bring its spirit into commerce with consciousness, Antonioni has a keen sensibility. A great filmmaker of the spaces between, he made in *Eclipse*, which centers on a time of sentimental abeyance between a love affair ended and a new one beginning, the great film about the suburbs. A time of introspective uncertainty, particular to one young woman yet generally implicative, he turns outward onto that blurred sparse mix of asphalt and trees, the modern suburban, neither city nor country, the architecture for missing persons that has found its occupants. The main setting of *Eclipse*, a neighborhood on the outskirts of Rome called E U R, was designed in Fascist days like the modern town in Sicily, though not abandoned by the local population. Like Buster Keaton's drifting, deserted ocean liner in *The Navigator* (1924), the suburb in *Eclipse* is seen, not in disdain but in alert bewilderment, as an epitome of the alien daily territory of modern life. Amid the Sicilian past of *L'Avventura*, Claudia and Sandro's visit to the modern town, the closed exterior of an abandoned future, precipitates their becoming lovers; amid the suburban present of *Eclipse*, Vittoria and Piero become lovers during their visit to his old home, the enclosed interior of an abandoned past. Both couples embrace romance as the antidote for emptiness and abandonment.

The century that invented the aesthetic also invented the romantic. In the eighteenth century trees started being planted in cities; the cult of nature

L'Avventura. The abandoned town, the romantic antidote to abandonment.

got going; the organic, distinguished from the mechanical, became central to conceptions of beauty and unity; and people started falling romantically in love. Only people who feel separated from nature develop a cult of it; when Vittoria impersonates an African native in *Eclipse,* she acts out both her longing for nature and her distance from it. Classical art assumed an adequacy of form to content; only an art worried about the relation between form and content insists on their unity in the romantic manner. Like the organic unity sought in aesthetic experience, romantic love attempts to repair a felt disunity with the world. A descendant, like the rest of us, of the aesthetic and the romantic, Antonioni makes films about love's attempt to bring us together in an alienated world, sentimental journeys, sentimental educations, pictured in images that arouse a sense of beauty at a distance from the things being viewed.

Yet beauty at a distance need not be a disinterested beauty. The outsider's gaze in Antonioni, the point of view of a stranger, is the troubled gaze of an engaged outsider, the vigilant point of view of a sharply interested stranger. The split between the aesthetic and the interested, though with us for so long that it may seem axiomatic, has not sat comfortably with art. If romantic art would anxiously mend it or transcend it in a will to unity, modernist art such as Antonioni's makes the split into an articulate tension between form and content, a dialectical give and take between beauty and its objects. Classical art, not knowing the split, knew neither formalism nor realism in the modern sense, but much of the best modernist art combines both in fruitful discordant interplay: a conflict between beauty and truth perhaps resolvable but little in keeping with the Grecian urn's serene equation. An intuition of the desirable, distant because uncertain, unsettled, questioning, the beautiful in Antonioni expresses an apprehensive search for the good in our age of mystery.

Notes

Introduction: Film and Physics

1. In his book about his career in cinematography, Néstor Almendros gives a similar account of a somewhat earlier period of Havana moviegoing:

> My father had settled in Cuba. [Almendros's father, Herminio Almendros, a republican in exile from fascist Spain, was a friend of my father's and I would see him on occasion when I was a kid, but I only met his son once, and that was many years later in New York.] As soon as he was able he sent for us, those who had remained in Spain. In 1948 I took a ship for Havana. There I studied philosophy and letters at the university, more to please my family than myself, for cinema was what interested me. But in Havana there were no cine-clubs. There was nothing like those in Barcelona, and no magazines specializing in film either, outside of the fan magazines from North America. On the other hand, paradoxically, Cuba was at that moment a privileged place to see films. First, in Cuba, unlike Spain, dubbing was unknown: all the movies were shown in their original versions with subtitles. Second, since there was an open market, with hardly any state controls, the distributors bought all kinds of movies. There I was able to see all the American productions, even the B pictures, which did not readily get to other countries. I was also able to see all the Mexican cinema and a lot of the Spanish, Argentine, French, and Italian cinemas. Around six hundred films a year were being imported, including titles from the Soviet Union, Germany, Sweden, etc.
>
> At that time, before the dictatorship of Batista, censorship, in comparison with Spain and even with the United States, was very tolerant. Keep in mind that Havana and not Copenhagen was the first city in the world where pornographic films were shown legally. Furthermore, in their double bills the commercial movie houses would run old films such as Dreyer's *Vampyr*, which I came across in a neighborhood theater. Havana was the cinephile's paradise, but a paradise without any critical perspective.

Néstor Almendros, *Días de una cámara* (Barcelona: Seix Barral, 1982), 37–38, my translation. A rather different version of this passage may be found in the English translation of the book published as *A Man with a Camera*, trans. Rachel Phillips Belash (New York: Farrar, Straus & Giroux, 1984), 26–27.

2. Pauline Kael, "Trash, Art, and the Movies," in *Going Steady* (Boston: Little, Brown, 1970), 102.

3. G. Cabrera Infante, *A Twentieth Century Job*, trans. Kenneth Hall and G. Cabrera Infante (London: Faber & Faber, 1991).

4. Orson Welles and Peter Bogdanovich, *This Is Orson Welles,* ed. Jonathan Rosenbaum (New York: HarperCollins, 1992).

5. Griffith's ad appeared in the *New York Dramatic Mirror* on 3 December 1913.

6. This is the title of a book by Thomas Schatz, *The Genius of the System: Hollywood Filmmaking in the Studio Era* (New York: Pantheon, 1988). Schatz took his title from André Bazin: "The American cinema is a classical art, but why not then admire in it what is most admirable, i.e. not only the talent of this or that filmmaker, but the genius of the system, the richness of its ever-vigorous tradition, and its fertility when it comes into contact with new elements" (André Bazin, "La Politique des auteurs," *Cahiers du cinéma,* no. 70 [1957], reprinted in English in *The New Wave,* ed. Peter Graham [New York: Doubleday, 1968], 154). By "the genius of the system" Bazin did not exactly mean the Hollywood studio system, which is the subject of Schatz's book, but something larger, the conjunction of a medium, its practitioners, and its public, the social, cultural, historical juncture that allowed Hollywood's classical art to flourish. Schatz's book is mainly about the Hollywood producer, whom he sees as a neglected creative figure and studies in useful detail. As patron saint of the kind of cinema he most admired Bazin nominated Erich von Stroheim, and it is a little ironic that his phrase should have been used as the title of a book whose patron saint is Irving Thalberg, the producer who took Stroheim's *Greed* away from him and had it drastically cut.

7. Andrew Sarris, "Notes on the Auteur Theory in 1962," *Film Culture,* no. 27 (winter 1962–63), reprinted in *Film Culture Reader,* ed. P. Adams Sitney (New York: Praeger, 1970), 128.

8. Pauline Kael, *I Lost It at the Movies* (New York: Bantam, 1966), 280.

9. Christopher Faulkner, *The Social Cinema of Jean Renoir* (Princeton: Princeton University Press, 1986), 3–16.

10. Robert E. Kapsis, *Hitchcock: The Making of a Reputation* (Chicago: University of Chicago Press, 1992).

11. Alfred Hitchcock, quoted in ibid., 20.

12. Cabrera Infante, *A Twentieth Century Job,* 278–79, 281.

13. Kapsis, *Hitchcock,* 149.

14. Graham Greene, review of *You Can't Take It With You,* in *Graham Greene on Film: Collected Film Criticism, 1935–1940,* ed. John Russell Taylor (New York: Simon & Schuster, 1972), 203–4.

15. Pauline Kael, *5001 Nights at the Movies* (New York: Holt, Rinehart & Winston, 1991), 383.

16. Welles and Bogdanovich, *This Is Orson Welles,* 137.

17. James Harvey, *Romantic Comedy in Hollywood, from Lubitsch to Sturges* (New York: Knopf, 1987), 113.

18. Ibid., 112–13.

19. Stanley Cavell, *Pursuits of Happiness: The Hollywood Comedy of Remarriage* (Cambridge: Harvard University Press, 1981).

20. Frank Capra, *The Name above the Title: An Autobiography* (New York: Macmillan, 1971).

21. Joseph McBride, *Frank Capra: The Catastrophe of Success* (New York: Simon & Schuster, 1992).

22. Richard Griffith, "The Film Since Then," in *The Film till Now: A Survey of World Cinema*, by Paul Rotha, with an additional section by Richard Griffith (London: Spring Books, 1967), 452–53.

23. William S. Pechter, "American Madness," in *Twenty-four Times a Second* (New York: Harper & Row, 1971), 123–32.

24. Eric Bentley, *The Life of the Drama* (New York: Atheneum, 1966), 314.

25. Christian Metz, "The Cinema: Language or Language System?" in *Film Language: A Semiotics of the Cinema*, trans. Michael Taylor (New York: Oxford University Press, 1974), 31–91.

26. John Ellis, *Visible Fictions* (London: Routledge & Kegan Paul, 1982), 59–61.

27. Both signifier and signified are for Saussure psychological rather than physical things, but the signifier is the more material of the two and the signified the more mental: "The linguistic sign unites, not a thing and a name, but a concept and a sound-image. The latter is not the material sound, a purely physical thing, but the psychological imprint of the sound, the impression that it makes on our senses. The sound-image is sensory, and if I happen to call it 'material,' it is only in that sense, and by way of opposing it to the other term of the association, the concept, which is generally more abstract" (Ferdinand de Saussure, *Course in General Linguistics*, ed. Charles Bally and Albert Sechehaye with Albert Riedlinger, trans. Wade Baskin [New York: McGraw-Hill, 1966], 66).

28. Diane Stevenson discusses the inadequacy of the Saussurean model when it comes to images in her essay on Magritte and Foucault, "This Is Not a Pipe, It's a Pun" (unpublished).

29. Christian Metz, *The Imaginary Signifier: Psychoanalysis and the Cinema*, trans. Celia Britton, Annwyl Williams, Ben Brewster, and Alfred Guzzetti (Bloomington: Indiana University Press, 1982).

30. Noël Carroll, *Mystifying Movies: Fads and Fallacies in Contemporary Film Theory* (New York: Columbia University Press, 1988), 42–43.

31. Sigfried Kracauer, *Theory of Film: The Redemption of Physical Reality* (New York: Oxford University Press, 1960), 305.

32. In *The World Viewed*, enl. ed. (Cambridge: Harvard University Press, 1979), Stanley Cavell lays stress on the difference between the automatism of the photographic image and the human-made representations of painting and the theater. In view of that difference, he thinks we should consider film a "projection" of reality rather than a representation. I agree with Cavell on the importance of that difference but I would not express it by saying that a photographic image is something other than a representation. Cavell felt a need to justify the photographic image to the way of thinking (the modernism of Clement Greenberg and Michael Fried) that saw representation as something modern art had to forgo; but modern art (in Manet or Cézanne or Matisse or Picasso) did not forgo representation.

33. I owe to the psychologist David Lichtenstein the link between Lacan's obscurity and his youthful surrealism and the notion that the obscurity was a calculated surrealist tactic.

34. In the Lacanian system the imaginary gives us plenitude but the symbolic—the realm of language, the realm of law and convention, the realm of meaning and also the realm of lack, of castration—takes it all away. And what does the real do? The real is defined as what resists symbolization, as a gap in the symbolic order, a blind spot. Lacan's concept of the real seems to have derived, maybe not directly but through some route that must have included Peirce—Peirce because the real seems to be some kind of an index—from Kant's notion of the thing in itself. Lacanian-Althusserian theory concerned itself exclusively with the imaginary and the symbolic, but more recent Lacanian theory puts emphasis on the real and the relation between the symbolic and the real. A leading figure in this newer Lacanian wave is Slavoj Zizek, who has written several books; see, for example, his *Enjoy Your Symptom! Jacques Lacan In Hollywood and Out* (New York: Routledge, 1992).

35. Laura Mulvey, "Visual Pleasure and Narrative Cinema," *Screen* 16, no. 3 (1975): 6–18.

36. Miriam Hansen, *Babel and Babylon: Spectatorship in American Silent Film* (Cambridge: Harvard University Press, 1991), 1.

37. David Bordwell and Noël Carroll, eds., *Post-Theory: Reconstructing Film Studies* (Madison: University of Wisconsin Press, 1996).

38. Noël Carroll, "Prospects for Film Theory," ibid., 61–67.

39. Judith Mayne, *Cinema and Spectatorship* (New York: Routledge, 1993), 58.

40. In two essays on the cinematographic apparatus that have been central to Lacanian-Althusserian theory, Jean-Louis Baudry holds the apparatus itself, its machinery of illusion, generally responsible for the ideological effects of cinema. The ideological effects are allegedly built into the apparatus, no matter what one does with it. Baudry's two essays, "Ideological Effects of the Basic Cinematographic Apparatus" (1970) and "The Apparatus: Metapsychological Approaches to the Impression of Reality in Cinema" (1975), are both reprinted in *Narrative, Apparatus, Ideology: A Film Theory Reader*, ed. Philip Rosen (New York: Columbia University Press, 1986), 286–318. Judith Mayne writes:

> Near the conclusion·of the 1975 essay "The Apparatus," Baudry makes one of many sweeping statements concerning the desires embodied in the cinema. A wish prepares, says Baudry, the "long history of cinema: the wish to construct a simulation machine capable of offering the subject perceptions which are really representations mistaken for perceptions." If the cinematic apparatus holds its subject in a state of hypnotized fascination, of subjugated fantasy, then surely one of the most decisive markers of the power of the cinematic institution is precisely this confusion of perception and representation. This supposed equation points not only to a powerful system of representation, but to a spectator so caught up in the illusions of this system that all perceptual activity is, if not suspended, then at the very least subjugated to the regressive desires instigated by the machine.

Mayne, *Cinema and Spectatorship*, 55.

41. Carroll, "Prospects for Film Theory," 42–43.

42. Raymond Williams, *Drama from Ibsen to Brecht* (New York: Oxford University Press, 1968), 13.

43. Raymond Williams, *Politics and Letters: Interviews with New Left Review* (London: NLB, 1979), 330.

44. Saussure, *Course in General Linguistics*, 68.

45. Carroll, *Mystifying Movies*, 248.

46. Béla Balázs, *Theory of the Film: Character and Growth of a New Art*, trans. Edith Bone (New York: Dover, 1970), 62–63.

47. André Bazin, *Jean Renoir*, ed. François Truffaut, trans. W. W. Halsey II and William H. Simon (New York: Dell, 1974), 87.

48. André Bazin, *What Is Cinema?* trans. Hugh Gray (Berkeley: University of California Press, 1967), 14.

49. Kracauer, *Theory of Film*, 163.

50. Ibid., 164.

51. Bazin, *What Is Cinema?* 16, tranlation somewhat modified. For the original see André Bazin, *Qu'est-ce que le cinéma?* vol. 1, *Ontologie et langage* (Paris: Editions du Cerf, 1958), 18.

Chapter 1: The Documentary Image

1. André Bazin, *What Is Cinema?* trans. Hugh Gray (Berkeley: University of California Press, 1967), 13.

2. Christian Metz, *The Imaginary Signifier: Psychoanalysis and the Cinema*, trans. Celia Britton, Annwyl Williams, Ben Brewster, and Alfred Guzzetti (Bloomington: Indiana University Press, 1982), 44.

3. Bazin, *What Is Cinema?* 89.

4. Roland Barthes, *Camera Lucida: Reflections on Photography*, trans. Richard Howard (New York: Hill & Wang, 1981), 80–81.

5. Bazin, *What Is Cinema?* 13.

6. For Roger Scruton not only can photography not be art, it cannot even be representation. His argument is a raiment of sophistry dressing up the simple old prejudice against mechanical reproduction as something mindless and unfeeling (Roger Scruton, "Photography and Representation," *Critical Inquiry* 7, no. 3 [1981]: 577–603).

7. Joel Snyder, "Photography and Ontology," in *The Worlds of Art and the World*, ed. Joseph Margolis (Amsterdam: Rodopi, 1984), 21–34.

8. James Agee, *Agee on Film*, vol. 1 (New York: McDowell Obolensky, 1958), 301.

9. André Bazin, *What Is Cinema?* trans. Hugh Gray, vol. 2 (Berkeley: University of California Press, 1971), 78, translation somewhat modified. For the original see Bazin, *Qu'est-ce que le cinéma?* vol. 4, *Une Esthétique de la réalité: le néo-réalisme* (Paris: Editions du Cerf, 1962), 91.

10. Eric Rhode, *Tower of Babel: Speculations on the Cinema* (London: Weidenfeld & Nicolson, 1966), 67.

11. Roland Barthes, "The Face of Garbo," in *Mythologies*, trans. Annette Lavers (New York: Hill & Wang, 1972), 56–57.

12. Roberto Rossellini, interview by Fereydoun Hoveyda and Jacques Rivette, *Cahiers du cinéma*, no. 94 (April 1959).

13. Bazin, *What Is Cinema?* 24.

14. Luis Buñuel, *My Last Sigh*, trans. Abigail Israel (New York: Knopf, 1983), 225, translation somewhat modified on the basis of the Spanish version, *Mi último suspiro* (Barcelona: Plaza & Janes, 1982), 219.

15. Siegfried Kracauer, *Theory of Film: The Redemption of Physical Reality* (New York: Oxford University Press, 1960), 257.

16. Robert Flaherty, quoted in Paul Rotha, *Robert J. Flaherty: A Biography*, ed. Jay Ruby (Philadelphia: University of Pennsylvania Press, 1983), 31.

17. Andrew Sarris, *The American Cinema: Directors and Directions, 1929–1968* (New York: Dutton, 1968), 42–43.

18. Erik Barnouw, *Documentary: A History of the Non-Fiction Film*, 2nd rev. ed. (New York: Oxford University Press, 1993), 39.

19. Tom Gunning has written several articles on early film and the cinema of attractions. See, for example, Tom Gunning, "The Cinema of Attractions: Early Film, Its Spectator and the Avant-Garde," in *Early Cinema: Space, Frame, Narrative*, ed. Thomas Elsaesser (London: British Film Institute, 1990), 56–62.

20. William Rothman, *Documentary Film Classics* (Cambridge: Cambridge University Press, 1997), 6.

Chapter 2: The Narrative Sequence

1. In ordinary language *narrative* can mean both a story and the telling of a story. Theories of narrative usually want to distinguish between the story and the telling. The Russian Formalists distinguished between *fabula* and *syuzhet*, or story and plot; Gérard Genette made a tripartite distinction between *histoire, récit*, and *narration*, or story, narrative, and narration. But ordinary usage reminds us that such distinctions cannot be hard and fast, that a story does not exist unless told or represented in some form.

2. Victor Shklovsky, "Sterne's *Tristram Shandy*: Stylistic Commentary," in *Russian Formalist Criticism: Four Essays*, ed. and trans. Lee T. Lemon and Marion J. Reis (Lincoln: University of Nebraska Press, 1965), 57.

3. Émile Benveniste, *Problems in General Linguistics*, trans. Mary Elizabeth Meek (Coral Gables: University of Miami Press, 1971), 209.

4. Pointing is an index in Peirce's sense. So are the words *I* and *here*, which for Benveniste mark an enunciation. Rather than a theory of enunciation, which imposes on the film image a linguistic model, it would be better to have a theory of pointing, and more generally of the index, in film. For further discussion of the camera and pointing see chapter 10 below.

5. Charles Musser, *Before the Nickelodeon: Edwin S. Porter and the Edison Manufacturing Company* (Berkeley: University of California Press, 1991); idem, *The Emergence of Cinema: The American Screen to 1907* (New York: Scribner's, 1990).

6. In the distant camera and disjointed continuity of Porter's movies Noël Burch saw the technique of an artist who was Brechtian before Brecht (see Burch's

"Porter, or Ambivalence," *Screen* 19, no. 4 [1978–79]: 91–105). On an audience today Porter's style of representation indeed has something like a Brechtian alienation effect. But surely this was not the intended effect of a movie in 1903. The calculated alienation that Brecht proposed only makes sense as a check working against the sway of an involvement. Surely in 1903 Porter was working on involving his audience—though he may not have cared so much to involve it in the story as in the show.

7. André Bazin, *The Cinema of Cruelty: from Buñuel to Hitchcock,* ed. François Truffaut, trans. Sabine d'Estrée with the assistance of Tiffany Fliss (New York: Seaver, 1982), 7. Bazin wrote this in 1949. For a more recent statement of a similar notion see André Gaudreault, "Narration and Monstration in the Cinema," *Journal of Film and Video* 39 (spring 1987): 29–36.

8. Edward Branigan, *Narrative Comprehension and Film* (London: Routledge, 1992), 148.

9. Walter Benjamin, *Illuminations,* ed. Hannah Arendt, trans. Harry Zohn (New York: Schocken, 1969), 247.

10. Susan Sontag, "Spiritual Style in the Films of Robert Bresson," in *Against Interpretation* (New York: Farrar, Straus & Giroux, 1966), 181, 183.

11. To quote Bresson more fully: "Each shot is like a word, which means nothing by itself, or rather means so many things that in effect it is meaningless. But a word in a poem is transformed, its meaning made precise and unique, by its placing in relation to the words around it: in the same way a shot in a film is given its meaning by its context, and each shot modifies the meaning of the previous one until with the last shot a total, unparaphrasable meaning has been arrived at" (quoted in Sontag, ibid., 185).

12. In chapter 3 of the *Poetics.* The quoted translation is by S. H. Butcher (New York: Hill & Wang, 1961), 53.

13. Ibid., chap. 6, p. 53.

14. David Bordwell, *Narration in the Fiction Film* (Madison: University of Wisconsin Press, 1985), 4.

15. Ibid., 62.

16. Tom Gunning, *D. W. Griffith and the Origins of American Narrative Film: The Early Years at Biograph* (Urbana: University of Illinois Press, 1991), 10–30 and passim, quotation on p. 24.

17. The concept of the implied author was advanced by Wayne Booth in his *Rhetoric of Fiction* (Chicago: University of Chicago Press, 1961). Gunning says explicitly that "D. W. Griffith" is to be regarded as an implied author in Booth's sense, the quotes making clear that this is not to be confused with D. W. Griffith the actual person. But Booth's concept is to be understood in its difference not only from the actual person but also from the narrator. Gunning confuses the implied author and the narrator.

18. A. Nicholas Vardac, *Stage to Screen* (Cambridge: Harvard University Press, 1949), 135–51.

19. In his book on Antonioni—the best I know on the subject—Lorenzo Cuccu warns against the "temptation of erecting . . . a positive distinction between two

different film forms" on the model of Aristotle's distinction between drama and narrative. "The error," says Cuccu, "consists in mistakenly transposing onto the plane of the historical phenomenology of forms an opposition that has exclusively methodological value" (Lorenzo Cuccu, *La visione come problema: Forme e svolgimento del cinema di Antonioni* [Rome: Bulzoni, 1973] 121, my translation). Cuccu understandably objects to the tendency to impose on actual works of art, imputing to them as their positive properties, what are just ways of talking about them. But Aristotle's distinction was founded on what art actually does, the actors acting on a stage, the storyteller telling a story. Strictly speaking, film is neither drama nor narrative, neither the actors nor the storyteller. Strictly speaking, the subatomic entities of quantum physics are neither particles nor waves. But it is useful to talk about them in those terms because it relates them to our experience of particles and waves, and it is similarly useful to talk about film in terms of drama and narrative. And just as subatomic entities sometimes look more like particles and sometimes more like waves, so film sometimes looks more like drama and sometimes more like narrative. I'm not proposing to distinguish between drama and narrative as different film forms, but as different aspects the film medium shows us, different ways it works on us. We gain insight into the workings of film when we grasp how on some occasions it works as drama and on other occasions it works as narrative.

20. In two articles on Renoir, Stephen Tifft discusses this shot in analogy with the hunt scene: "As Schumacher moves to the right along the corridor, appearing to our laterally tracking vision in a succession of doorways, he seems again to be initiating the hunt, 'starting' various game." This analogy seems to me rather forced. In the two tracking shots that follow Schumacher and the beaters he leads in the hunt scene, the camera movement is steady and impersonal, as befits the task of starting game for the masters to shoot; there is none of the stopping and starting and quality of surprise that inform the camera movement with him during the danse macabre. In the party sequence the gamekeeper is anything but impersonal and he is the one who will be doing the shooting. Tifft wants to attribute the incompleteness of our view of the characters in *The Rules of the Game*—he remarks on Christine's "fleetingly inscribed" motives in particular—to the "wild activity of farce," which he thinks "incommensurate with intelligible motives." But farce does not usually make motives unintelligible: it makes them simple. The unusual thing about *The Rules of the Game* is that it combines complexity of motives with the wild activity of farce. See Stephen Tifft, "Theater in the Round: The Politics of Space in the Films of Jean Renoir," *Theater Journal* 39 (October 1987): 328–46; and idem, "*Drôle de Guerre*: Renoir, Farce, and the Fall of France," *Representations* 38 (spring 1992): 131–65.

21. *Poetics* 23. That a work of art should have unity—like a living organism, said Aristotle, and the romantics insisted that unity be organic as opposed to mechanical—is a notion that has lately come under challenge. The unity of a work of art, it is maintained, is an ideological construct serving to foster that other false consciousness, the unity of the self. Whether of a work of art or of a self, unity is indeed a construct, a fiction, something that exists in the mind; but it is something the mind

seems to require, even if only provisionally, in the act of apprehension and the task of comprehension. We cannot do without unity. "If a fiction is necessary enough, it is not a lie," as Iris Murdoch put it (*Metaphysics as a Guide to Morals* [Harmondsworth: Penguin, 1993], 1). But unity is not something set and given, it is a field of possibilities; best when achieved in diversity, it admits of wide variety. What needs to be challenged is not unity itself but narrow conceptions of unity erected and imposed as the norm.

22. These remarkable paired shots in *Letter from an Unknown Woman* have been much discussed. George M. Wilson brings them up at the outset of his chapter on the film in *Narration in Light* (Baltimore: Johns Hopkins University Press, 1986), 103–4. He sees them as central to the film's presentation of Lisa "as a consciousness who is crucially closed off to the significance of her experience." I disagree. As I am now going to argue, Lisa is a consciousness—maybe not the Lisa arriving with the pianist, but the Lisa writing the letter to him and looking back on her experience— well aware of the poignant irony these shots express.

23. On their romantic evening together, Lisa and the pianist take a simulated train ride at an amusement park and watch painted scenery rolling by their window in an illusion of traveling in exotic lands. Here Ophuls is drawing a parallel with the movies and calling attention to the machinery of illusion—the Vienna around 1900 depicted in his atmospheric *mise en scène* is just such an illusory exotic land—and as he declares his own artifice he also makes clear Lisa's consciousness of her own investment in illusion. "There, in an amusement-park attraction," wrote Charles Affron,

> Lisa and the emotion-filled movements of this film resonate in the flatness of painted vistas behind the lovers' stationary carriage. Lisa describes to Stefan [the pianist] the workings of her imagination; the mechanical, illusionistic scene-changing procedures (the Venetian panorama rolls to its conclusion, the Swiss one replaces it when an old man operates a set of levers and gears) are meticulously revealed. Lisa is utterly aware of the value of illusion and fantasy in the depth of her fiction, as moving to her as the artifices of depth are to us when we go to the movies.

Charles Affron, *Cinema and Sentiment* (Chicago: University of Chicago Press, 1982), 102–3. For other discussions of *Letter from an Unknown Woman* that recognize Lisa as an aware rather than a deluded character see Tania Modleski, "Time and Desire in the Woman's Film," *Cinema Journal* 23, no. 3 (1984); or, in a reading that sees Lisa as a masochist and as such in control of her own experience, Gaylyn Studlar, "Masochistic Performance and Female Subjectivity in *Letter from an Unknown Woman,*" ibid. 33, no. 3 (1994).

24. In an article on Ford's *Stagecoach* Nick Browne examines the sequence at a way station in which the passengers sit down at table for a meal. He attempts to establish this sequence as an example of the effacing of narration by having the camera placement and editing seem to issue from the point of view of a character in

the scene, in this case Lucy, the proper Southern lady who sits at the head of the table and looks disapprovingly at the prostitute Dallas and the outlaw Ringo. One point Browne makes is certainly well taken: although we look at Dallas from Lucy's perspective, we identify ourselves with Dallas against Lucy's censorious gaze, which shows how the holder of the gaze is often not the character a film sides with. In the terms I have been proposing, what Browne wants to establish is that this is a dramatic rather than a narrative sequence; but the evidence doesn't bear him out. He selects for his analysis only part of the sequence, and even in this part he neglects a crucial shot: as Lucy gets up from her seat near Dallas and along with the gambler and the banker moves to the other end of the table, the whole table is shown from the point of view of the seat she has vacated at the head. This shot from the point of view of an empty seat is pointedly not from any character's perspective. Leaving that place empty and putting us in that position, it invites us to ponder who should be sitting at the head of the table, and it implies that no one should be sitting there passing judgment on others. In this shot Ford shows his narrative hand and asserts the film's egalitarian point of view. The subsequent shots of Dallas and Ringo at table are frontal, freed from the slant of Lucy's or anybody else's perspective. Ford proceeds to a comparison of Dallas and Ringo with Lucy and the Southern gambler, a comparison that respects both couples and brings forward their similarities even as it recognizes their differences and prefers the frontier couple as a better version of the Southern couple. This comparison is neither part of the action in the scene nor the perception of any character in it: it is a narrative rather than a dramatic move. In his book on Ford, Tag Gallagher takes issue with Browne's analysis in the name of Ford's authorship; but authorship is not the issue here. The author is not the narrator, and one can be a film author, an auteur, without employing a film narrator (see Nick Browne, "The Spectator-in-the-Text: The Rhetoric of *Stagecoach*," *Film Quarterly* 29, no. 2 [1975–76]: 26–38; and Tag Gallagher, *John Ford: The Man and His Films* [Berkeley: University of California Press, 1986]: 153–61).

25. Dudley Andrew understands Mizoguchi's camera as a kind of performer enacting a visible response to the action taking place before it, a response that constitutes "another action . . . operative throughout the film, that of the filmmaker's sympathetic reading of the destiny of his characters." Andrew compares the role of Mizoguchi's camera in this "cinema of responsiveness" to the role of the *benshi* in silent cinema, the live narrator popular with Japanese audiences of that era who would provide a running commentary on the film being projected on the screen (see Andrew, *Film in the Aura of Art* [Princeton: Princeton University Press, 1984], 172–92).

26. In the chapter on *Shadow of a Doubt* in his study of Hitchcock, William Rothman discusses this shot and the complicity it intimates between the camera and Charles, a complicity with the villain he deems typical of Hitchcock's camera (see Rothman, *Hitchcock: The Murderous Gaze* [Cambridge: Harvard University Press, 1982], 183 and passim).

27. In the seventies, when I was beginning to teach film at Princeton, an art historian on the faculty joined me in pleading the case for building a film collection

at the university. "As film historians," she said, "Gil and I know which would be the first film to get for the collection." Since I didn't know, I asked her which film she had in mind. "Why, of course, *The Man with a Movie Camera*," she answered. I said I would rather have *The Rules of the Game*. "That's fine," she replied with a smile, "if you like that kind of nineteenth-century realism." For her realism meant illusion, a market on which she assumed the nineteenth century had a corner. No film, not even the most artistically conservative, can be called a work of nineteenth-century realism, and *The Rules of the Game* is one of the most daring of films, no less daring artistically than *The Man with a Movie Camera* and more daring socially and politically, its realism, like that of Brecht's plays, decidedly a realism of the twentieth century.

28. George M. Wilson is among the few to recognize Renoir's style as a singular form of narration in film:

> Many people, when they see *The Rules of the Game* for the first time, come away with the feeling that its narration is somehow in a state of disarray. The idea is wrong, but it is not an unreasonable first response to a style that is designed to acknowledge the limitations of film or any other finite apparatus of observation set up to watch comprehensively and with comprehension a process as intricate as the breakdown of the lives of these characters. The film assembles the fragments of a spectacle that almost no one in 1939 was prepared to see. The film's governing attitude is *not* a blanket skepticism about human knowledge and perception, and the fragments it assembles tell a great deal. But the narration declares its responsibility to the thesis that any overview of events such as the ones in this film will be slightly off center, in dubious epistemic focus, explanatorily disconnected, and, in various ways, incomplete. The audience sees that these fragments cannot honestly be joined into a well-shaped whole and, in some respects, they see why. In accomplishing this, *The Rules of the Game* discovers a new form for narrative film.

Wilson, *Narration in Light*, 92–93. Wilson stresses rather more than I would the fragmentation and disarray in Renoir's film, which does manage to bring its unruly complexity into a felicitous unity in diversity even if not a conventional well-shaped whole. But he points out much that is important and seldom noted about the kind of narrative form the film achieves.

29. Bertolt Brecht, quoted in Klaus Völker, *Brecht Chronicle*, trans. Fred Wiek (New York: Seabury, 1975), 79.

30. If the phrase *narrative space* puts anyone in mind of Stephen Heath's essay of that title (in his *Questions of Cinema* [Bloomington: Indiana University Press, 1981]), I trust it will be clear that I mean by it something quite different.

31. In *Mists of Regret: Culture and Sensibility in Classic French Film* (Princeton: Princeton University Press, 1995), Dudley Andrew sees Renoir as more "theatrical" than the *réalisme poétique* of Duvivier or Carné and Prévert, which he sees as more "novelistic." His concerns are different from mine. His notion of the "novelistic" is predicated on the Jamesian center of consciousness, the point of view of the Gabin hero in *Pépé le Moko* or *Quai des brumes* or *Le Jour se lève*. He doesn't consider how

much this *réalisme poétique* relies on dramatic film technique and a theatrical *mise en scène*. And he doesn't recognize as narrative the *social* point of view of *Boudu Saved from Drowning* or *The Crime of Monsieur Lange* or *The Rules of the Game*.

32. Cuccu, *La visione come problema*, 34–35, 125–27, 134–38, and passim. I was unaware of Cuccu's book on Antonioni when I published the first version of this chapter, "The Narrative Sequence," *Hudson Review* 30, no. 1 (1977). I was still unaware of it, with less excuse, when I published my essay on Antonioni's *Eclipse*, "The Point of View of a Stranger," ibid. 44, no. 2 (1991) (most of that essay, along with other material, has gone into chapter 10 below). Cuccu may not have influenced me but he significantly anticipated me, and I am glad to acknowledge him.

Chapter 3: The Bewildered Equilibrist

1. Walter Kerr, *The Silent Clowns* (New York: Knopf, 1975), 242.

2. Hugh Kenner, "In Memoriam: Buster Keaton," *National Review* 18 (22 February 1966): 167.

3. Ibid., 181.

4. Ibid.

5. Robert Warshow, *The Immediate Experience* (New York: Atheneum, 1970), 207.

6. James Agee, "Comedy's Greatest Era," in *Agee on Film*, vol. 1 (New York: McDowell Obolensky, 1958), 19.

7. Kenner, "In Memoriam," 167, 181.

8. E. Rubinstein, *Filmguide to The General* (Bloomington: Indiana University Press, 1973), 22.

9. Edmund Wilson, "The New Chaplin Comedy," in *The American Earthquake* (Garden City, N.Y.: Anchor, 1964), 69.

10. Hugh Kenner, "Stan, Ollie, and the Universe," *National Review* 19 (14 November 1967): 1277–78.

11. Agee, "Comedy's Greatest Era," 16.

12. Keaton's alcoholism is another factor that needs to be taken into account. See the biography by Tom Dardis, *Keaton, the Man Who Wouldn't Lie Down* (New York: Scribner's, 1979).

13. Wilson, "The New Chaplin Comedy," 73.

14. Kerr, *The Silent Clowns*, 143.

15. Henri Bergson, "Laughter," in *Comedy*, ed. Wylie Sypher (Baltimore: Johns Hopkins University Press, 1980).

16. John Grierson, *Grierson on Documentary*, ed. Forsyth Hardy (New York: Harcourt Brace, 1947), 32–33.

17. Rubinstein, *Filmguide to The General*, 38.

18. "I understand Buster Keaton, say in *The General*," wrote Stanley Cavell, "to exemplify an acceptance of the enormity of this realization of human limitation, denying neither the abyss that any time may open before our plans, nor the possibility, despite that open possibility, of living honorably, with good if resigned

spirits, and with eternal hope. His capacity for love does not avoid this knowledge, but lives in full view of it. Is he dashing? He is something rarer; he is undashable. He incorporates both the necessity of wariness in an uncertain world, and also the necessary limits of human awareness; gaze as we may, there is always something behind our backs, room for doubt." Stanley Cavell, "What Becomes of Things on Film?" in *Themes out of School: Effects and Causes* (San Francisco: North Point, 1984), 175.

19. Warshow, *The Immediate Experience*, 207.

20. "The great art of films does not consist of descriptive movement of face and body, but in the movements of thought and soul, transmitted in a kind of intense isolation" (Louise Brooks, quoted in Kenneth Tynan, *Profiles*, ed. Kathleen Tynan and Ernie Eban [New York: HarperCollins, 1989], 436).

Chapter 4: The Deadly Space Between

1. Siegfried Kracauer, *From Caligari to Hitler: A Psychological History of the German Film* (Princeton: Princeton University Press, 1947), 79.

2. Martin Heidegger, *Being and Time*, trans. John Macquarrie and Edward Robinson (New York: Harper & Row, 1962), 294.

3. In her essay "Martin Heidegger at Eighty," in the *New York Review of Books*, October 1971, Hannah Arendt tells us that Heidegger's fame in Germany was first spread by his students at Freiburg and Marburg and predated the publication of *Being and Time* by about eight years.

4. In his articles on Murnau (in *Film Comment* 7, no. 2 [1971] and 12, no. 3 [1976]) Robin Wood notes the motif of arches in *Nosferatu* but links it to his interpretation of the vampire as a figure of the id, of the animal side of human nature repressed by civilization, so that for Wood the vampire emerging from arches symbolizes the return of the repressed.

5. Dudley Andrew brings up Bazin (and Roland Barthes) on photography and death in connection with Orson Welles (see Andrew, *Film in the Aura of Art* [Princeton: Princeton University Press, 1984], 152–71). But Welles is not so much preoccupied with death as with the past; he looks back in nostalgia, whereas Murnau looks forward in anxiety. Murnau is a filmmaker of the end, the movement toward the end; Welles is a filmmaker of the beginning, the yearning for the beginning. Both *Citizen Kane* and *The Magnificent Ambersons* are narratives of oedipal desire for the irrecoverable, the lost childhood, the bygone age, the haunting receding mother.

6. This is one of several shots from *Nosferatu* that Werner Herzog replicates in his 1979 remake of Murnau's film. In Herzog this shot, though copied well enough as an individual composition, has nothing like the impact it has in Murnau because it lacks the context of Murnau's cutting. The brisk rhythm of Murnau's cutting builds up to the shot as an arresting point of confluence, whereas in Herzog the shot is preceded by a leisurely helicopter shot circling the ship at sea that generates little impetus or anticipation. In Murnau the ship entering frame as it arrives in the town harbor carries the accumulated charge of all that has been transpiring.

7. José Ortega y Gasset, *The Dehumanization of Art and Other Essays on Art, Culture, and Literature* (Princeton: Princeton University Press, 1968), 109–11.

8. This simile is dear to Stokes, and he uses it more than once in his writings on art. It occurs early in his first book, *The Quattro Cento* (see Adrian Stokes, *The Quattro Cento*, in *The Critical Writings of Adrian Stokes*, ed. Lawrence Gowing, vol. 1 [New York: Thames & Hudson, 1978], 34).

9. Alexandre Astruc, "Fire and Ice," in *Cahiers du Cinema in English*, no. 1 (January 1966), 70; Jean-André Fieschi, entry on F. W. Murnau in *Cinema: A Critical Dictionary*, ed. Richard Roud, vol. 2 (New York: Viking, 1980), 704.

10. Svetlana Alpers, *The Art of Describing* (Chicago: University of Chicago Press, 1983), 26–71.

11. Astruc, "Fire and Ice," 71.

12. William Hazlitt, "Why Distant Objects Please," in *Selected Writings*, ed. Ronald Blythe (Baltimore: Penguin, 1970), 148.

13. Carné's article "La Caméra, personnage du drame" is cited in Lotte H. Eisner, *Murnau* (Berkeley: University of California Press, 1973), 86, 280.

14. Murnau's reputation, high though it was in his day, unwarrantably declined after his untimely death (in an automobile accident in California shortly before the opening of *Tabu*) and was not revived until two decades later, when in France Lotte Eisner and the group at *Cahiers du cinéma* made a case for him as one of the greatest of all filmmakers. For many years the mainstream of English-speaking film history—Paul Rotha, John Grierson, Richard Griffith, Siegfried Kracauer—tended to be anti-pathetic to Murnau. That he went to Hollywood was held against him; the films he made there, beginning with *Sunrise*, Rotha in *The Film till Now* deemed a deplorable surrender to the commercial. More covertly, Murnau's homosexuality, which one gathers was something of a hushed scandal in Hollywood, may have also been held against him; Grierson's disparagement of him (in a review of *Tabu*) not only mistakenly considers him a thoroughgoing studio director but smacks unmistakably of homophobia: "Murnau was a studio product, a manipulator of artificial effects, a manager of exaggeration, introspective, perverse: an artist who never smelt an honest wind in his life" (*Grierson on the Movies*, ed. Forsyth Hardy [London: Faber & Faber, 1981], 73). *The Last Laugh*, the Murnau film Kracauer treats best in *From Caligari to Hitler*, he treats less as the work of Murnau than as the work of the writer Carl Mayer. In his *Theory of Film* Kracauer dismisses *Nosferatu* as a figment of camera trickery, just the kind of thing he thinks film should not be. It's hard to forgive him that dismissal. Had he looked at the film with open eyes and an open mind, he would have seen that *Nosferatu* is a work lending unaccustomed support to his theory of film as a medium best equipped not for fabrication but for the revelation of physical reality.

15. In *Woman and the Demon* (Cambridge: Harvard University Press, 1982), 7–34, Nina Auerbach maintains that the women in *Dracula* are more important than the count, and she reads the novel as a "fin-de-siècle myth of newly empowered womanhood." In "Dracula in the Twilight," an article comparing *Dracula* and *Nosferatu* (in *German Film and Literature*, ed. Eric Rentschler [New York: Methuen,

1986], 25–39), Judith Mayne reads the novel as a struggle over the contested terrain of woman's body, which the "good patriarchal figure," Professor Van Helsing, would rescue from Dracula, a figure of wicked sexuality, so as to return it to "its 'normal' functions of marriage and child-bearing." Mayne's article interestingly sees *Nosferatu* as a work tending to deconstruct the polarities of *Dracula* and taking place "in the twilight," in the space between.

Chapter 5: The Meaning of Revolution

1. Sergei Eisenstein, *Film Form: Essays in Film Theory*, ed. and trans. Jay Leyda (New York: Harcourt, Brace, 1949), 175.

2. Sergei Eisenstein, *Writings, 1922–34*, vol. 1 of *Selected Works*, ed. and trans. Richard Taylor (Bloomington: Indiana University Press, 1988), 34.

3. Eisenstein, *Film Form*, 238.

4. In *Signs and Meaning in the Cinema* (Bloomington: Indiana University Press, 1969), 19–70, Peter Wollen similarly points out Eisenstein's theatricality, but he wants to distinguish the more theatrical (which he prefers: *Strike, October,* and *Ivan the Terrible*) from the more cinematic of Eisenstein's films, whereas I propose no opposition between the theatrical and the cinematic and I see all Eisenstein's films as theatrical in their address to the audience. In *The Cinema of Eisenstein* (Cambridge: Harvard University Press, 1993) David Bordwell looks into Eisenstein's theatrical roots and his special connection to theater.

5. These quotations from Vertov are from *Kino-Eye: The Writings of Dziga Vertov*, ed. Annette Michelson, trans. Kevin O'Brien (Berkeley: University of California Press, 1984), 71, 63, 69, 66.

6. Eisenstein, *Writings, 1922–34*, 64.

7. Such scholars as Jay Leyda and David Bordwell do not agree that the later Eisenstein accommodated to an uncongenial aesthetic and stress the continuity between the early Eisenstein and the late. Bordwell in particular makes a persuasive case that Eisenstein's aesthetic position evolved organically over the years. But I remain unpersuaded.

8. The comparison to the Japanese ideogram may be found in Eisenstein, *Writings, 1922–34*, 138–50, and (the same essay in a different translation) in *Film Form*, 28–44. The quotations are from *Writings, 1922–34*, 163, 180.

9. Robert Warshow, "Re-Viewing the Russian Movies," in *The Immediate Experience* (New York: Atheneum, 1970), 269–82.

10. Ibid., 270.

11. Ibid., 272.

12. G. Cabrera Infante, *A Twentieth Century Job*, trans. Kenneth Hall and G. Cabrera Infante (London: Faber & Faber, 1991), 181.

13. Sergei Eisenstein, "Constanța (Whither 'The Battleship Potemkin')," in *Writings, 1922–34*, 67–70.

14. See David Bordwell, Janet Staiger, and Kristin Thompson, *The Classical Hollywood Cinema: Film Style and Mode of Production to 1960* (New York: Columbia University Press, 1985), 61.

15. Vernon Young, "Fugue of Faces: A Danish Film and Some Photographs," in *On Film: Unpopular Essays on a Popular Art* (Chicago: Quadrangle, 1972), 44–50.

16. Alexander Dovzhenko, "Autobiography," in *Alexander Dovzhenko: The Poet as Filmmaker*, ed. and trans. Marco Carynnyk (Cambridge: MIT Press, 1973), 3.

17. Raymond Williams, "Metropolitan Perceptions and the Emergence of Modernism," in his *The Politics of Modernism*, ed. Tony Pinkney (London: Verso, 1989), 37–48.

18. "The struggle with individualism resulted in the elimination of the individual," wrote the Soviet critic Ivan Anisimov in an article on Eisenstein published in 1931. Anisimov took Eisenstein to task for failing to think dialectically about the particular and the general, the individual and the group. He saw Eisenstein as a petit bourgeois who, aligning himself with the proletarian revolution and striving to overcome bourgeois individualism, went to the other extreme of denying individuality and depersonalizing the proletariat. Anisimov has a point. His article is excerpted in Marie Seton, *Sergei M. Eisenstein* (New York: Wyn, 1952), 494–503.

19. P. Adams Sitney, entry on Alexander Dovzhenko in *Cinema: A Critical Dictionary*, ed. Richard Roud, vol. 1 (New York: Viking, 1980), 290.

20. Vance Kepley Jr., *In the Service of the State: The Cinema of Alexander Dovzhenko* (Madison: University of Wisconsin Press, 1986). Kepley's book, as its title announces, attempts to show that Dovzhenko's films were the product of social and historical factors rather than an individual's creation—all his films, those whose audacity still astonishes as well as the later ones made under tighter state control. Kepley sets up a simple opposition between individual creation and social and historical factors, a rigid scheme that allows no give and take between the personal and the social, imagination and history. Art comes out of such a give and take. Dovzhenko's own avowal of the personal sources of his films Kepley treats with skepticism: "Dovzhenko's assertion that his films represent the direct cinematic transcription of personal visions [Dovzhenko did not say direct transcription of visions, which sounds like something out of a séance] certainly leaves the impression that the accumulated fictional worlds of his work constitute a private, imaginary idyll, a mythical terrain as fully subject to sole ownership and proprietorship as Faulkner's Yoknapatawpha County" (4). Kepley's scheme allows nothing between the land of Oz and the hard ground of historical determinism. Could anyone suppose that either Dovzhenko's Ukraine or Faulkner's South, though each bears the stamp of an artist's individuality, is a "private, imaginary idyll"?

21. "Poetry and the Film: A Symposium," in *Film Culture Reader*, ed. P. Adams Sitney (New York: Praeger, 1970), 171–86.

22. Ivor Montagu, "Dovzhenko: Poet of Life Eternal," *Sight and Sound* 27, no. 1 (1957): 47.

23. Kenneth Burke, *A Rhetoric of Motives* (Berkeley: University of California Press, 1969), 3–20.

24. Ortega on the tactility of proximate vision (and the ghostliness of distant version) is quoted and discussed in chapter 4.

25. Erich Auerbach, *Mimesis*, trans. Willard R. Trask (Princeton: Princeton University Press, 1968), 4.

26. For Goethe and Schiller, not for Auerbach. Auerbach contrasts the Homeric mode with another mode of narrative he sees as equally epic, that of the Bible, a mode in which only certain things are brought to light, the rest left in obscurity, much calling for interpretation, everything "fraught with background."

27. Auerbach, *Mimesis*, 6–7.

28. Warshow, "Re-Viewing the Russian Movies," 281.

29. Alexander Dovzhenko, quoted by Marco Carynnyk in his introduction to *Alexander Dovzhenko*, xlii–xliii.

30. Siegfried Kracauer, *Theory of Film: The Redemption of Physical Reality* (New York: Oxford University Press, 1960), 44.

31. Bernard Berenson, *The Italian Painters of the Renaissance* (Ithaca: Cornell University Press, 1980), 59 and passim.

32. Adrian Stokes, *Stones of Rimini*, in *The Critical Writings of Adrian Stokes*, ed. Lawrence Gowing, vol. 2 (New York: Thames & Hudson, 1978), 197.

33. Ibid., 1:247.

34. John Howard Lawson, quoted by Marco Carynnyk in his introduction to *Alexander Dovzhenko*, xx.

35. Warshow, "Re-Viewing the Russian Movies," 282.

36. Eisenstein, *Film Form*, 242.

37. For an account of this historical situation see Paul E. Burns, "Cultural Revolution, Collectivization, and Soviet Cinema: Eisenstein's *Old and New* and Dovzhenko's *Earth*," *Film and History* 11, no. 4 (1981): 84–96.

38. Marco Carynnyk, introduction to *Alexander Dovzhenko*, xliv–xlv.

39. William Empson, *Some Versions of Pastoral* (New York: New Directions, 1960), 6.

40. Karl Marx, *The Grundrisse*, ed. and trans. David McLellan (New York: Harper & Row, 1971), 45.

Chapter 6: Landscape and Fiction

1. Jean Renoir, *My Life and My Films*, trans. Norman Denny (New York: Atheneum, 1974), 49.

2. Ronald Bergan, *Jean Renoir: Projections of Paradise* (Woodstock, N.Y.: Overlook, 1994), 210. Bergan's biography is shallow and gossipy, and it lacks critical acumen for the discussions of Renoir's films it insists on offering. It mostly leans on other writings on Renoir, and at times it borrows phrases and passages in brisk application of scissors and paste. It relies especially on Célia Bertin, *Jean Renoir: A Life in Pictures*, trans. Mireille Muellner and Leonard Muellner (Baltimore: Johns Hopkins University Press, 1991). Bertin's biography is more serious and thorough, but it suffers from a certain piety toward the great man. Bergan is less concerned with smoothing over blemishes and putting things in a good light. His book contains some information and insight not found elsewhere, and, for all its flaws, it is a useful book to have.

3. Eric Rhode, *A History of the Cinema* (New York: Hill & Wang, 1976), 325; Christopher Faulkner, *The Social Cinema of Jean Renoir* (Princeton: Princeton University Press, 1986), 50.

4. Faulkner, *Social Cinema of Jean Renoir*, 17–30.

5. Ten years later, in exile, Renoir thought about doing an American remake of *La Chienne*, which a producer was proposing apparently because Cary Grant was interested. In a letter to one of his closest Hollywood friends, the writer Dudley Nichols, Renoir describes the film in some detail and says that normally he's against remakes but that *La Chienne* is a special case: its *naturaliste* style was much imitated in France and he wonders whether it would have the same influence in America (see Jean Renoir, *Letters*, ed. David Thompson and Lorraine LoBianco, trans. Craig Carlson, Natasha Arnoldi, Michael Wells, and Anneliese Varaldiev [London: Faber & Faber, 1994], 122–25). In the event, *La Chienne* was remade, as *Scarlet Street*, with a screenplay by Nichols and direction by Fritz Lang. *Scarlet Street* could be looked upon as extending to the American film noir of the forties the influence of *La Chienne* on the French film noir of the thirties, which is what Renoir seems to have meant by the *naturaliste* style. But *La Chienne* does not really belong to that fatalistic genre. It may be sordid and sad but it is not enclosed in a mood of ruination: it is a notably open work, open to contradiction and possibility.

6. Jean Renoir, quoted in Faulkner, *Social Cinema of Jean Renoir*, 81.

7. Elizabeth Grottle Strebel explores the relation between *The Crime of Monsieur Lange* and its political context in "Renoir and the Popular Front," *Sight and Sound* 49, no. 1 (1979–80): 36–41.

8. Bertin, *Jean Renoir*, 142.

9. Renoir, *My Life and My Films*, 172.

10. Spike Lee's *Do the Right Thing* (1989) is another film cast in the form of a comedy yet turning into a tragedy because its society—which is to say, our contemporary American society—cannot manage the ways, cannot muster the sentiments, of comedy. A society capable of comedy is capable of recognizing human weakness with humor and aplomb, capable of coming to terms with the flaws of our common humanity through the laughter of a sustained community. The central human weakness in *Do the Right Thing*, the flaw of common humanity that ought to be a flaw of comedy, is racism. But our society wants to deny our common racism and so can only make our racism tragic. *Do the Right Thing* pointedly vacillates between comedy and tragedy and wishes it could be a comedy, for it sees that we would go a long way in dealing with our racism if we could treat it as a common human weakness, a subject of comedy.

11. Renoir, *My Life and My Films*, 172.

12. Jean Renoir, quoted in Faulkner, *Social Cinema of Jean Renoir*, 170.

13. André Bazin, *Jean Renoir*, ed. François Truffaut, trans. W. W. Halsey II and William H. Simon (New York: Dell, 1974), 111.

14. "An Ideology of Aesthetics" is the title of Faulkner's chapter on *The River*, *The Golden Coach*, and *French Cancan* in *Social Cinema of Jean Renoir*, 162–98.

15. William S. Pechter, *Twenty-four Times a Second* (New York: Harper & Row, 1971), 196.

16. Jean Renoir, *Renoir on Renoir: Interviews, Essays, and Remarks,* trans. Carol Volk (Cambridge: Cambridge University Press, 1989), 250. At the time Sylvia Bataille was married to Georges Bataille; later she married Jacques Lacan. When she was fifteen "she stopped Jean Renoir in the street" after seeing his *Little Match Girl* (1928) "and told him she wanted to be in movies" (Bertin, *Jean Renoir,* 73). Subsequently she joined the October Group, a left-wing theater company that came together in the early thirties around Jacques Prévert, who collaborated with Renoir on the script of *The Crime of Monsieur Lange.* She is wonderful in *A Day in the Country* but she argued with Renoir during the filming and never worked with him again after he took off and left the film unfinished.

17. Braunberger told Célia Bertin about this experience. See the account of the making and editing of *A Day in the Country* in Bertin, *Jean Renoir,* 125–28.

18. Renoir's remark and Wilenski's comment are quoted in Adrian Stokes, *Monet,* in *The Critical Writings of Adrian Stokes,* ed. Lawrence Gowing, vol. 2 (New York: Thames & Hudson, 1978), 292.

19. Bazin, *Jean Renoir,* 89.

20. In the view of some, no great artistic prestige issues from Auguste Renoir. The most popular of the impressionists—and they are the most popular school of painting—he is often condescended to by those who like their art less popular and regarded as a prettifier, complacent and crowd-pleasing, superficial and sentimental. At his worst Renoir may answer to some such characterization, but at his best he was a great painter—perhaps the only one of the impressionists, wrote Clement Greenberg, "who was a master painter in point of craft and in joy of artisanship." The disparagement of Renoir has surely to do with a distrust of pleasure. "What a profusion of pleasure there is [in the Renoir paintings on exhibit]," marveled Greenberg at the end of his article, "and how ungrateful it is to carp at it: a foaming, pouring, shimmering profusion like nothing else in painting; pictures that are spotted and woven with soft, porous colors, and look in themselves like bouquets of flowers . . . pictures whose space is handled like a fluid that floats all objects to the surface; pictures in which our eyes swim with the paint and dance with the brush-stroke" (Clement Greenberg, *The Collected Essays and Criticism,* ed. John O'Brian, vol. 3, *Affirmations and Refusals, 1950–1956* [Chicago: The University of Chicago Press, 1993], 22–26).

21. Jean Renoir, *Renoir, My Father,* trans. Randolph Weaver and Dorothy Weaver (San Francisco: Mercury House, 1988), 189.

22. T. J. Clark, *The Painting of Modern Life: Paris in the Art of Manet and His Followers* (New York: Knopf, 1985), 148. Clark's chapter "The Environs of Paris" documents the disdain many contemporary observers felt toward excursionists in the countryside the impressionists were painting.

23. John Berger, "The Eyes of Claude Monet," in *The Sense of Sight,* ed. Lloyd Spencer (New York: Pantheon, 1985), 190.

24. Meyer Schapiro, "The Nature of Abstract Art," in *Modern Art: Nineteenth and Twentieth Centuries* (New York: Braziller, 1978), 192–93.

25. Clark, *The Painting of Modern Life*, 5.

26. See Donald Posner, "The Swinging Women of Watteau and Fragonard," *Art Bulletin* 64, no. 1 (1982): 75–88.

27. Seymour Chatman, "What Novels Can Do That Films Can't (and Vice Versa)," in *Film Theory and Criticism*, 4th ed., ed. Gerald Mast, Marshall Cohen, and Leo Braudy (New York: Oxford University Press, 1992), 412.

28. Guy de Maupassant, "A Country Excursion," in *Sur l'eau and Other Stories*, trans. Albert M. C. McMaster et al. (London: Standard, 1922), 4.

29. In a footnote to his article Chatman discusses the response it elicited when he read it at a conference. Several participants charged him with sexism in the identification he proposes with Rodolphe the voyeur. After defending himself by insisting that he does not at all approve of Rodolphe but only identifies with him for the purposes of a fiction, Chatman notes that to one participant (Roy Schafer) the close view of Henriette swinging "conveyed . . . something of *her* sexual pleasure." "Sexual pleasure" is too strong for her incipient sexuality, though the emphasis on her pleasure is apt, and the sexual does enter into her feelings for nature. See Chatman, "What Novels Can Do That Films Can't (and Vice Versa)," 418–19.

30. William Rothman, *The "I" of the Camera* (Cambridge: Cambridge University Press, 1988), 146.

31. Clark, *The Painting of Modern Life*, 199.

32. Bazin, *Jean Renoir*, 46.

33. Leo Braudy, *Jean Renoir: The World of His Films* (Garden City, N.Y.: Anchor, 1972), 35.

34. Alexander Sesonske, *Jean Renoir: The French Films, 1924–1939* (Cambridge: Harvard University Press, 1980), 241–56.

35. Tag Gallagher, talk at Sarah Lawrence College, Bronxville, N.Y., 10 April 1995; idem, "Jean Renoir: The Dancers and the Dance," *Film Comment* 32, no. 1 (1996): 64–66, 72–76.

36. Maupassant, "A Country Excursion," 10.

37. Pauline Kael, *Kiss Kiss Bang Bang* (Boston: Little, Brown, 1968), 254.

38. Sesonske, *Jean Renoir*, 252.

39. In a sequence from *Picnic on the Grass* (1959) Renoir uses views of unpeopled nature as a metaphor for sexual intercourse. But landscape as he treats it in that film—albeit a landscape shot on location at Les Collettes, the farm in the south of France where Auguste Renoir spent the last years of his life—is mere theatrical spectacle, not the independent presence it is in *A Day in the Country*.

40. Sesonske, *Jean Renoir*, 252.

41. William Empson, *Seven Types of Ambiguity* (New York: New Directions, 1966), 24.

42. Ibid.

43. Stanley Cavell, *The World Viewed*, enl. ed. (Cambridge: Harvard University Press, 1979), 143–44.

44. Dudley Andrew, *Mists of Regret: Culture and Sensibility in Classic French Film* (Princeton: Princeton University Press, 1995), 287.

Chapter 7: American Tragedy

1. William S. Pechter, *Twenty-four Times a Second* (New York: Harper & Row, 1971), 92.

2. Robert Warshow, "Movie Chronicle: The Westerner," in *The Immediate Experience* (New York: Atheneum, 1970), 135–54.

3. Richard Slotkin, *Gunfighter Nation: The Myth of the Frontier in Twentieth-Century America* (New York: Atheneum, 1992).

4. Jane Tompkins, *West of Everything: The Inner Life of Westerns* (New York: Oxford University Press, 1992), viii.

5. Ibid., 45.

6. Ann Douglas, *The Feminization of American Culture* (New York: Knopf, 1977).

7. Lee Clark Mitchell, "'When You Call Me That . . . ': Tall Talk and Male Hegemony in *The Virginian*," *PMLA* 102, no. 1 (1987): 66–77.

8. James to Wister, quoted in Carl Bode, "Henry James and Owen Wister," *American Literature* 26, no. 2 (1954): 250–52.

9. John G. Cawelti, *Adventure, Mystery, and Romance: Formula Stories as Art and Popular Culture* (Chicago: University of Chicago Press, 1976), 215–30.

10. Warshow, "Movie Chronicle: The Westerner," 149.

11. "The Significance of the Frontier in American History" was a originally a paper that Turner, a young historian from Wisconsin, read on 12 July 1893 at a meeting of the American Historical Association held in Chicago at a world's fair celebrating the discovery of America. It is the lead essay in Frederick Jackson Turner, *The Frontier in American History* (New York: Henry Holt, 1962), 1–38.

12. Ibid., 2–3.

13. Ibid., 3.

14. See Henry Nash Smith, *Virgin Land: The American West as Symbol and Myth* (Cambridge: Harvard University Press, 1978), 250–60.

15. James Agee called D. W. Griffith a "tribal poet" in an article paying homage to the director when he died in 1948 (see *Agee on Film*, vol. 1 [New York: McDowell Obolensky, 1958], 313–18). "He was a great primitive poet," wrote Agee of Griffith, "a man capable, as only great and primitive artists can be, of intuitively perceiving and perfecting the tremendous magical images that underlie the memory and imagination of entire peoples." There lay for Agee "the clearest and deepest aspect of Griffith's genius": "As a primitive tribal poet, combining something of the bard and the seer, he is beyond even Dovzhenko, and no others of their kind have worked in movies." Agee failed to recognize that another of their kind, and in their class, was working right before his eyes.

16. Richard Slotkin, *Regeneration through Violence: The Mythology of the American Frontier, 1600–1860* (Middletown, Conn.: Wesleyan University Press, 1973).

17. William S. Pechter, *Movies Plus One* (New York: Horizon, 1982), 66–73.

18. For a look at the Western in relation to the medieval epic see Rémy G. Saisselin, "Poetics of the Western," *British Journal of Aesthetics*, 2, no. 2 (1962): 159–69.

19. The professionalization of the gunfighter in the Western movie came about at the time of the Cold War, when it came to be felt that the defense of the polity could no longer be entrusted to its citizens but had to be given over to the agency of professionals—to professional agencies such as the FBI and the CIA. For example, in Leo McCarey's notorious anti-Communist film, *My Son John* (1952), the figure of the father, the individual patriot, is portrayed as a fool (albeit a fool who stands for the values the film upholds), so that the role of the hero who saves the situation and can be entrusted with the defense of democracy falls on an FBI agent. The gunfighter hero of the Western differs significantly from the FBI agent, however, in remaining very much the individual who stands on his own. The gunfighter is thus a figure of tension, tension between individualism and professionalism.

20. *Heaven's Gate* (1980) tells that story too, and slants it against the capitalist ruling class—apparently not the way America at the outset of the Reagan era wanted that story told. The success of *The Deer Hunter* enabled Michael Cimino to make this ambitious film, whose well-publicized failure put an end to the brief vogue of the auteur director in the film industry.

21. *A Place in the World*, a fine recent Argentinian film made by Adolfo Aristarain, invokes *Shane* in its picture of social conflict in the land: the boy whose point of view we share, the small farmers up against a rich and powerful landowner, the glamorous stranger in town who is a professional for hire but takes the side of the good guys, the mother who falls for the stranger but remains loyal to the father. In *A Place in the World*, however, the rootless stranger has become more cynical in his years of work for the multinationals, and it is the father, himself a stranger in town but with his roots growing there—this is his place in the world—who is the union organizer. In *A Place in the World* the good guys lose.

22. Slotkin, *Gunfighter Nation*, 379.

23. A useful schematic analysis of such dualities in Ford, from an auteurist and structuralist perspective that was yesterday's fashion, may be found in Peter Wollen, *Signs and Meaning in the Cinema* (Bloomington: Indiana University Press, 1969), 94–102.

24. The dance scene in *Clementine* has been criticized for its exclusions, and it is certainly true that not all the townspeople are there dancing that Sunday morning—not Doc Holliday, not his girlfriend Chihuahua or any of the other Mexicans in town, not the Indians. But such criticism seems to assume that Wyatt Earp and Clementine are insiders, part of an exclusive establishment, whereas in fact they are outsiders to a community not established as yet, and the movement of the scene is toward the *inclusion* of these two outsiders, one from the wild West and the other from the civilized East, in the community being built. Ford tends to include rather than exclude, and if we want to build a more diverse community than the one he pictures, his inclusive tendency will still serve us.

25. Robin Wood, entry on John Ford in *Cinema: A Critical Dictionary*, ed. Richard Roud, vol. 1 (New York: Viking, 1980), 380.

26. Ibid.

27. Slotkin, *Gunfighter Nation*, 342.

28. Wyatt Earp also has another double in *My Darling Clementine:* Pa Clanton. Or rather, the Earps as a wilderness family of men without women are doubled in the Clantons, their savage mirror image. In *The Man Who Shot Liberty Valance* (1962), where once again Ford doubles the hero into two figures representing East and West, he again further doubles the hero representing the West and has him paired not only, on the one hand, with an alter ego who represents refinement (again his rival for the girl's affections, except that the girl in *Liberty Valance* is not Eastern but Western and is not won by the West but by the East, embodied in a hero who is himself the civilizing schoolmarm) but also, on the other hand, with an alter ego (Liberty Valance) who represents Western savagery. Like *Fort Apache, The Man Who Shot Liberty Valance* deals explicitly with the issue of truth and myth and with the role of the press and more generally of representers of truth and myth in the public sphere. "This is the West, sir," says a newspaperman in the film. "When the legend becomes fact, print the legend"—a line often cited and often taken to express Ford's own sentiments. But as Tag Gallagher has noted in his study of the director (*John Ford: The Man and His Films* [Berkeley: University of California Press, 1986], 409), Ford does *not* let the legend stand but prints the truth alongside it.

29. Jean-Marie Straub and Danièle Huillet, "Straub and Huillet on Filmmakers They Like and Related Matters," in *The Cinema of Jean-Marie Straub and Danièle Huillet,* ed. Jonathan Rosenbaum, booklet for a retrospective at Film at the Public (New York City, 2–14 November 1982), 6.

30. Tompkins, *West of Everything*, 3, 208.

31. Robert Warshow, "The Gangster as Tragic Hero," in *The Immediate Experience*, 132, 133.

32. Ibid., 132–33.

33. Ibid., 131.

34. Guy Debord, *Comments on the Society of the Spectacle,* trans. Malcolm Imrie (London: Verso, 1990), 63–67.

35. William S. Pechter, "Keeping up with the Corleones," in Pechter, *Movies Plus One,* 86–93.

36. Ibid., 90.

37. "Martin Scorsese interviewed by Gavin Smith," *Film Comment* 26, no. 5 (1990): 28.

38. *Menace II Society* (1992), directed by Albert and Allen Hughes from a screenplay by Tyger Williams, is an exception to this rule—maybe the exception that proves the rule. It is a tragedy, and it is narrated in the first person by its protagonist, a young black man who, like the classic gangster, meets his death in the end. But at the end, at the suspended moment of the hero's death, his voice-over narration, which all along has been rather sparse, not so much a telling of the story as a punctuation of it, speaks to us more as a dramatic soliloquy, the tragic hero's soliloquy expressing his consciousness of his fate, than as a narration of the action. The first-person voice-over narration in *Menace II Society* may thus be construed retro-

actively as a soliloquy spoken from the moment of death that resonates throughout the whole story and can be heard at various points in it.

39. Warshow, "The Gangster as Tragic Hero," 130.

Chapter 8: History Lessons

1. Clement Greenberg, "Modernist Painting," in his *Collected Essays and Criticism*, ed. John O'Brian, vol. 4, *Modernism with a Vengeance, 1957–1969* (Chicago: University of Chicago Press, 1993), 86.

2. Peter Bürger, *Theory of the Avant-Garde*, trans. Michael Shaw (Minneapolis: University of Minnesota Press, 1984).

3. Stéphane Mallarmé, "The Impressionists and Edouard Manet," originally published in *Art Monthly Review* 1, no. 9 (1876). This essay has come down to us only in this English version. It is excerpted in *Modern Art and Modernism: A Critical Anthology*, ed. Francis Frascina and Charles Harrison (New York: Harper & Row, 1982), from which I have quoted, 42, 44.

4. T. J. Clark, *The Painting of Modern Life: Paris in the Art of Manet and His Followers* (New York: Knopf, 1985), 10.

5. Ian Watt, *The Rise of the Novel: Studies in Defoe, Richardson, and Fielding* (Berkeley: University of California Press, 1957), 31–33 and passim.

6. To my knowledge, André Bazin was the first to call the American cinema a classical art (see the introduction, n. 6). The most sustained endeavor to characterize the ways of the old Hollywood as a classical style is David Bordwell, Janet Staiger, and Kristin Thompson's *The Classical Hollywood Cinema: Film Style and Mode of Production to 1960* (New York: Columbia University Press, 1985).

7. José Ortega y Gasset, *The Dehumanization of Art and Other Essays on Art, Culture, and Literature* (Princeton: Princeton University Press, 1968), 3–8.

8. Jonathan Rosenbaum, "Lessons from a Master," *Chicago Reader* 25, no. 36 (1996): 45–47.

9. Ibid., 46.

10. Renato Poggioli, *The Theory of the Avant-Garde*, trans. Gerald Fitzgerald (New York: Harper & Row, 1971), 120.

11. Clement Greenberg, "Avant-Garde and Kitsch," in his *Collected Essays and Criticism*, ed. John O'Brian, vol. 1, *Perceptions and Judgments, 1939–1944* (Chicago: University of Chicago Press, 1986), 11–12.

12. On the earlier and later Greenberg see T. J. Clark, "Clement Greenberg's Theory of Art," in *The Politics of Interpretation*, ed. W. J. T. Mitchell (Chicago: University of Chicago Press, 1983), 203–20.

13. See Peter Wollen, "The Two Avant-Gardes" and " 'Ontology' and 'Materialism' in Film," in *Readings and Writings: Semiotic Counter-Strategies* (London: Verso, 1982), 92–104 and 189–207.

14. Ortega y Gasset, *The Dehumanization of Art*, 49–50, translation by Helene Weyl here somewhat modified.

15. See Andreas Huyssen, "Mapping the Postmodern," in *After the Great Divide:*

Modernism, Mass Culture, Postmodernism (Bloomington: Indiana University Press, 1986), 178–221.

16. The term *postmodern* has come to be applied not so much to a kind of art as to a kind of theory, poststructuralist theory, and this seems apt. Modernism, whatever it may be, was first of all a creation of artists; postmodernism is mainly a conception of academics.

17. Thomas Crow, *Modern Art in the Common Culture* (New Haven: Yale University Press, 1996), 3. The first chapter of Crow's book, "Modernism and Mass Culture in the Visual Arts," was originally a paper that "aimed to document the richness of the modernist tradition in precisely those attributes so confidently arrogated by a born-yesterday postmodernism" (263). In this chapter Crow characterizes modernism as a "resistant subculture" that has repeatedly turned to the popular, to low culture with its "repertoire of potentially oppositional practices," in the endeavor to unsettle the official high culture. "From the beginning, the successes of modernism have been neither to affirm nor to refuse its concrete position in the social order, but to represent that position in its contradiction, and so act out the possibility of critical consciousness in general" (29).

18. Theodor W. Adorno, "Perennial Fashion—Jazz," in *Prisms,* trans. Samuel Weber and Shierry Weber (Cambridge: MIT Press, 1983), 119–32.

19. Meyer Schapiro, "The Patrons of Revolutionary Art," *Marxist Quarterly,* October–December 1937, 464–65.

20. Susan Sontag, "Godard," in *Styles of Radical Will* (New York: Farrar, Straus & Giroux, 1969), 147–48.

21. Roland Barthes, *Camera Lucida: Reflections on Photography,* trans. Richard Howard (New York: Hill & Wang, 1981), 80.

22. Ibid., 27.

23. Ibid., 51. Margaret Iversen (in "What Is a Photograph?" *Art History* 17, no. 3 [1994]: 450–64) has related Barthes's *punctum* to Lacan's real, with which it shares an "uncoded, unassimilable quality" (455).

24. Barton Byg, *Landscapes of Resistance: The German Films of Danièle Huillet and Jean-Marie Straub* (Berkeley: University of California Press, 1995), 22.

25. Raymond Williams, *The Country and the City* (New York: Oxford University Press, 1973), 241–42.

26. Aristotle, *Poetics* 23, translation by S. H. Butcher, 105. In his book on the *Poetics* Michael Davis comments that "Aristotle's example of the disunity of action in history is strange." For the example comes from Herodotus, whose historical account makes a connection between the two simultaneous battles Aristotle uses to illustrate a lack of connection in historical events (see Michael Davis, *Aristotle's Poetics: The Poetry of Philosophy* [Lanham, Md.: Rowman & Littlefield, 1992], 131).

27. See Williams, *The Country and the City,* chap. 14, "Change in the City," 142–52.

28. I owe to the writer Chuck Wachtel this definition of subjectivity as the light on the water always coming toward you.

29. Byg, *Landscapes of Resistance*, 117.

30. Stephen Heath, "Narrative Space," in *Questions of Cinema* (Bloomington: Indiana University Press, 1981), 19–75.

31. Bertolt Brecht, "The Curtains," in *Poems on the Theatre*, trans. John Berger and Anna Bostock (Lowestoft, Suffolk: Scorpion, 1961), 12.

32. Eric Bentley, "The Stagecraft of Brecht," in *In Search of Theater* (New York: Vintage, 1959), 140.

33. P. Adams Sitney, *Modernist Montage: The Obscurity of Vision in Cinema and Literature* (New York: Columbia University Press, 1990), 17–20 and passim.

34. Griffith does use the reverse angle sometimes, not only later in his career, when everybody else was using it, but already in such films from his early years at Biograph as *A Drunkard's Reformation* and *Brutality,* which depict characters at a play within the film and cut between the characters in the audience and reverse angles of the performance on the stage. It is interesting, however, that in these uses of the reverse angle the characters are literally spectators at a performance, so that the reverse angle does not so much bring us into the space of the action as bring together two different spaces of action, the action performed on the stage and the reaction of the characters in the audience (which in these films is the main action). Griffith still draws a clear line of demarcation between the stage and the space outside the stage where the spectator sits.

35. What we see reflected may not be the king and queen but their portrait, which may be the canvas we see Velázquez painting within the painting; the king and queen are still there in the space in front, however, and Velázquez and the infanta and other figures in the painting are looking at them.

36. Michel Foucault, *The Order of Things* (New York: Vintage, 1973), 3–16.

37. Jean-Pierre Oudart, "La Suture," *Cahiers du cinéma,* nos. 211 (April 1969): 36–39 and 212 (May 1969): 50–55, reprinted as "Cinema and Suture" in *Cahiers du cinéma, 1969–1972: The Politics of Representation,* ed. Nick Browne (Cambridge: Harvard University Press, 1990), 45–57.

38. David Bordwell, "Convention, Construction, and Cinematic Vision," in *Post-Theory: Reconstructing Film Studies,* ed. David Bordwell and Noël Carroll (Madison: University of Wisconsin Press, 1996), 87–107.

39. The next to the last shot of the peasant is a three-quarter front view and the closest shot in the scene (also the one that lasts the longest, more than a minute). Given the geometry that has been set up, we would expect the last shot of the peasant to be even closer and more frontal. More frontal it is but not closer: rather it is taken from farther away, and this is another arbitrariness that has its appropriateness. For this last shot of the peasant leaves a large empty space on the "wrong" side of the screen—the side away from the young man—and in that space the little mountain stream can be seen in the distance. So the association of the peasant with the mountain stream, a metonymy and a metaphor, is now appropriately reasserted. The banker's sumptuous villa, we may recall, was also seen in the background on the "wrong" side of the screen and was made more noticeable by its placement on that wrong side. The scene with the peasant then concludes as it began, with a view of the

rushing stream. I was put in mind of lines from a poem by the Cuban writer and revolutionary José Martí: "Con los pobres de la tierra / Quiero yo mi suerte echar: / El arroyo de la sierra / Me complace más que el mar" [With the poor of the earth / I want to throw in my lot: / The mountain stream / Pleases me more than the sea].

40. Franco Fortini, *I Cani del Sinai* (Bari: De Donato, 1967).

41. Martin Heidegger, *Being and Time,* trans. John Macquarrie and Edward Robinson (New York: Harper & Row, 1962), 431–32.

42. Bertolt Brecht, *Journals, 1934–1955,* trans. Hugh Rorrison, ed. John Willett (New York: Routledge, 1993), 83, capitalization added.

43. Bürger, *Theory of the Avant-Garde,* 77. Bürger sees montage as central to the avant-garde but he excludes film from the avant-garde for the very reason that montage is native to film, "part and parcel of the medium." He makes no mention of avant-garde cinema and he takes no notice of the remarkable fact that a characteristic technique of the avant-garde should have been as characteristic a technique of the popular art of film.

44. Jean-Marie Straub and Danièle Huillet, script of *Fortini/Cani,* trans. Geoffrey Nowell-Smith, *Screen* 19, no. 2 (1978): 27–28.

45. Ibid., 30–33.

46. Jean-Marie Straub and Danièle Huillet, "Straub and Huillet on Filmmakers They Like and Related Matters," in *The Cinema of Jean-Marie Straub and Danièle Huillet,* ed. Jonathan Rosenbaum, booklet for a retrospective at Film at the Public (New York City, 2–14 November 1982), 5.

47. The best discussion of Bresson's method of juxtaposition, and one the young Straub must have known, is the essay by André Bazin, "*Le Journal d'un curé de campagne* and the Stylistics of Robert Bresson," in *What Is Cinema?* trans. Hugh Gray (Berkeley: University of California Press, 1967), 125–43.

48. Paul Coates, *The Gorgon's Gaze: German Cinema, Expressionism, and the Image of Horror* (Cambridge: Cambridge University Press, 1991), 216; Byg, *Landscapes of Resistance,* 95.

49. Richard Roud, *Jean-Marie Straub* (New York: Viking, 1972), 47.

50. Jean-Marie Straub and Danièle Huillet, script of *History Lessons,* trans. Misha Donat in collaboration with them, *Screen* 17, no. 1 (1976): 69–70.

51. We may notice that the pitcher of wine is cut off halfway by the left edge of the frame in the shot of the banker and halfway by the right edge in the shot of the young man, so that the two shots, with the pitcher of wine marking a boundary between them, can be seen to divide space neatly between the two characters, with no area of overlap, a hint that the young man and the banker may share little in common but the wine. We may of course not notice: this kind of detail, carefully calculated but easily missed, giving us the feeling that everything counts but that we could not possibly be catching everything, is characteristic of Straub and Huillet.

52. In his useful analysis of these sequences Martin Walsh sees the parallel between them but observes that whereas the young man faced the peasant head on, he sits at right angles to the banker, so that the difference of 90° is no longer in the camera angles but in the position of the characters in the scene. The angles of our

view on the screen still differ by 90°, but now we may see this difference as stemming from the position, the slant on the banker, that the young man himself has assumed (see Martin Walsh, *The Brechtian Aspect of Radical Cinema*, ed. Keith M. Griffiths [London: British Film Institute, 1981], 74–77).

53. The flowers are nature, cultivated nature but still nature, a decoration in a rich man's garden but a decoration that evokes the energies of nature like the poor man's mountain stream. Just as the flowers are shown on the wrong side of the screen (which calls more attention to them) in the last shot of the young man, so the mountain stream was shown on the wrong side of the screen in the last shot of the peasant. See n. 39 above.

Chapter 9: The Signifiers of Tenderness

1. Colin MacCabe, "The Politics of Separation," *Screen* 16, no. 4 (1975–76): 53. "It is impossible to understand for what audience *History Lessons* was made," wrote MacCabe in the same article; "to understand *History Lessons* you have to know the Brecht novel and the Roman history independently of the film" (51–52). When I first saw *History Lessons* I hadn't even heard of the Brecht novel (I still haven't read it because it hasn't been translated, aside from the passages included in the film) and what I knew of Roman history was what I had learned in high school. Yet the film held me even as people around me were walking out (this was at the New York Film Festival in 1973); certainly I didn't understand all of it but I understood enough to be gripped. That it is not clear for what audience *History Lessons* was made is part of its political statement. There is little point in refuting MacCabe's article at this late date, but it remains an interesting document of its time; it is, for one thing, an article in which the phrase "politically correct" is used approvingly and quite without irony.

2. "Shakespeare on Three Screens: Peter Brook Interviewed by Geoffrey Reeves," *Sight and Sound*, 34, no. 2 (1965): 69.

3. Susan Sontag, "Godard's *Vivre Sa Vie*," in *Against Interpretation* (New York: Farrar, Straus & Giroux, 1966), 196–208.

4. "This [is] intensified," Pechter continues, "by our being deliberately deprived, in the manner of the *nouveau roman*, of any psychological interpretation of character and event through which this contradiction might have been reconciled" (William S. Pechter, "For and Against Godard," in *Twenty-four Times a Second* [New York: Harper & Row, 1971], 245). In this essay Pechter calls into question the trendy way in which people were calling Godard "Brechtian." He aptly points out that "when the actors in *Masculine Feminine* turn to the camera and begin to speak to us, the action is interrupted and our interest in it temporarily distracted, but the sense achieved is of a *cinéma-verité* interview in which the subject reveals itself, and, while the critics may go on about the paradoxes of art and life thus embodied as they will, the immediate effect is of an *increased* involvement with the characters' 'reality.' " I agree: rather than an alienation effect as people were calling it, this is an *involvement* effect. Pechter is right to say that Godard is quite different from Brecht. But Godard has in common with Brecht the *interplay* between alienation and involvement that he

sets up, though he works in a different medium and in his work the alienation and the involvement come from different places.

5. Roland Barthes, "Literature and Signification," in *Critical Essays*, trans. Richard Howard (Evanston: Northwestern University Press, 1972), 263–64.

6. Jonathan Rosenbaum, "Theory and Practice: The Criticism of Jean-Luc Godard," in *Placing Movies: The Practice of Film Criticism* (Berkeley: University of California Press, 1995), 21.

7. *François Truffaut: Correspondence, 1945–1984*, ed. Gilles Jacob and Claude de Givray with a foreword by Jean-Luc Godard, trans. Gilbert Adair (New York: Farrar, Straus & Giroux, 1990).

8. John Simon, "François Truffaut: Saved by the Cinema," *New Criterion*, 9, no. 1 (1990): 35–43; Julian Barnes, "Night for Day," *New York Review of Books* 37 (11 October 1990): 14–16.

9. John Simon, "Godard and the Godardians," in *Private Screenings* (New York: Macmillan, 1967), 272–96.

10. Barnes, "Night for Day," 14.

11. Vincent Canby, review of *Nouvelle Vague*, *New York Times*, 29 September 1990.

12. George Santayana, *The Sense of Beauty: Being the Outlines of Aesthetic Theory* (New York: Dover, 1955), 31.

13. Raymond Williams, *The Country and the City* (New York: Oxford University Press, 1973), 22.

Chapter 10: The Point of View of a Stranger

1. Seymour Chatman, *Antonioni; or, The Surface of the World* (Berkeley: University of California Press, 1985), 79.

2. Vernon Young, *On Film: Unpopular Essays on a Popular Art* (Chicago: Quadrangle, 1972), 188–89.

3. Antonioni quoted Lucretius in an interview at Cannes after *L'Avventura* was shown (and booed) at the film festival in 1959. The passage from Lucretius I give as worded in the translator's preface to a volume of Antonioni's stories, *That Bowling Alley on the Tiber: Tales of a Director*, trans. William Arrowsmith (New York: Oxford University Press, 1986), xix.

4. Antonioni's work of the fifties, which Chatman slights undeservedly, includes such remarkable films as *Cronaca di un amore*, *La Signora senza camelie*, and *Le Amiche*. It does not do justice to the achievement of these films to regard them as an apprenticeship on the road to *L'Avventura*.

5. Raymond Williams, *Drama from Ibsen to Brecht* (New York: Oxford University Press, 1968), 290.

6. Pier Paolo Pasolini, *Heretical Empiricism*, ed. Louise K. Barnett, trans. Ben Lawton and Louise K. Barnett (Bloomington: Indiana University Press, 1988), 175–80.

7. Stanley Cavell, *The World Viewed*, enl. ed. (Cambridge: Harvard University Press, 1979), 142.

8. William S. Pechter, *Movies Plus One* (New York: Horizon, 1982), 158–59.

9. M. M. Bakhtin, "Forms of Time and Chronotope in the Novel," in *Dialogic Imagination*, ed. Michael Holquist, trans. Caryl Emerson and Michael Holquist (Austin: University of Texas Press, 1981), 243–45. Taking my cue from Bakhtin's discussion of the chronotope of the road in picaresque narrative and in the novel more generally, I use the term *picaresque* in an extended sense referring not just to the story of a *pícaro* or rogue, Lazarillo de Tormes or Tom Jones, but to the story of any wanderer on the road of life.

10. Here, as often in his films, Antonioni breaks the "180° rule" disallowing cuts that "cross the line." The line not to be crossed if smooth continuity is to be maintained is the line of a movement (Vittoria's movement here) or of a character's glance (especially a glance exchanged between two characters, as in a shot/reverse shot), for a cut across that line will reverse on the screen the apparent direction of the movement or glance, which may disorient the spectator for a moment, something deemed undesirable in conventional filmmaking. But such disorientation, the slight abruptness of the transition, may be just what suits the purposes of a filmmaker like Antonioni. Years ago one of my students at Princeton wrote a paper on Antonioni's crossing the line that I liked very much and suggested he try to publish, but the film journal to which he sent it rejected it as a misguided attempt to analyze what he was told could only be a technical error. The student, Rick Feist, has since become a film editor. I met Antonioni once, on my first visit to Rome in the spring of 1981, at a studio on the Via Tiburtina where he was shooting *Identification of a Woman*. I asked him about crossing the line, and he replied that he did it "deliberately and instinctively."

11. Psychoanalytic film theory has been much concerned with presence and absence and often invokes Freud's account of the little boy's game. But it has not paid much attention to the interplay between the seen and the unseen enacted in the images unfolding on the screen and central to the workings of cinematic representation. Instead its main interest has been in the "illusionism" of the image, in the apparent presence and actual absence of reality on the screen. Lacanian-Althusserian theory assumes that when we watch a film we "misrecognize" the image as a reality present before us and so get caught between an illusion of presence and the fact of absence, between our being taken in by the image, believing it to be reality, and our feeling betrayed by it because it is not reality. Critics of illusionism often erroneously suppose that audiences are mere dupes of illusion—as if the little boy playing with his toys in Freud's story actually believed them to be his mother rather than signs standing for his mother. The interplay I am proposing to consider takes place in the realm of images, signs, representations of presence and absence.

12. John Berger, *And our faces, my heart, brief as photos* (New York: Pantheon, 1984), 65–66.

13. Chatman treats this couple with platitudinous condescension: "How different is a motor intersection from a square or piazza, the traditional meeting place for lovers! The intersection evokes what is most transitory, casual, and ephemeral in our society. . . . In the age of the sports car, people go through lovers like water through

sand on a beach. The beginning of a relationship (the very word suggests preprogrammed triviality) is already the middle, and the end is clearly in sight. We do not
need to be shown how things end" (Chatman, *Antonioni*, 108, 110). Uncomfortable
with Antonioni's use of ellipsis, Chatman keeps explaining away the gaps left open in
our knowledge and telling us that we don't need to be shown the things omitted. In
Antonioni's rich and strange portrayal of Vittoria and Piero's corner Chatman sees
nothing but a boring barrenness, to which he imputes a determinant effect on the
outcome as if Antonioni's settings were in some simple theatrical correspondence
with what happens in them—a cozy piazza for a romantic scene, an old dark house for
a ghost story, a barren corner for a relationship doomed to failure. The word *relationship*, by the way—a word signifying, as Raymond Williams says, both a relation and
the parties involved in that relation—should be defended against the frequent snobbish attacks it has received from self-appointed guardians of our culture. Perhaps the
most interesting thing about Chatman's discussion of *Eclipse* is his managing to
admire a film that in his view is ponderously devoted to a preprogrammed triviality;
one would have expected him to concur with Pauline Kael's philistine dismissal: "I
wouldn't go see *Eclipse* again unless I was tied down and gagged . . . "

14. John Szarkowski, "Atget and the Art of Photography," in *The Work of Atget*,
by John Szarkowski and Maria Morris Hambourg, vol. 1, *Old France* (New York:
Museum of Modern Art, 1981), 11.

15. Charles Sanders Peirce, "Logic as Semiotic: The Theory of Signs," in *Philosophical Writings of Peirce*, ed. Justus Buchler (New York: Dover, 1955), 108.

16. Cavell, *The World Viewed*, 24.

17. Peter Galassi, a believer in photography's invention by the painters, has
argued that the reversal in perspective's application was not a consequence of photography but a development in painting that preceded photography and led to it. See
his catalogue essay in *Before Photography: Painting and the Invention of Photography*
(New York: Museum of Modern Art, 1981), 11–31.

18. Michelangelo Antonioni, *That Bowling Alley on the Tiber*, 93–96.

19. Against all odds, the odds of a commercial film industry loath to give him
backing and the odds of his own advanced age and partly disabled condition from a
stroke of a few years ago, Antonioni succeeded in making a film out of four of these
stories. He had help from his wife Enrica and from Wim Wenders in making *Beyond
the Clouds* (1995) but it is unmistakably an Antonioni film and a lovely farewell work,
a film about desire unattainable not because desire is always anxiously unattainable
(as Freud and Lacan and all their followers think) but because desire is finally,
serenely unattainable to an old man who knows what he will be missing as the world
slips away from him. Antonioni has had a difficult career in cinema. Nearly forty
when he got to direct a feature film, nearly fifty when he gained an international
audience, he was in fashion in a decade when the art of film was in fashion, the
sixties, after which money for his projects has been scarce, and persons unequal to
the demands of his art have felt licensed to make little of it. His art is by its nature not
of wide appeal; the big commercial success of *Blow-Up* is something he shouldn't
have been expected to repeat. Since the failure of the undervalued *Zabriskie Point* at

the close of the sixties he has been able to complete only four feature films. It is wonderful that at eighty-three, almost from beyond the clouds, he got to make *Beyond the Clouds*.

20. Antonioni, *That Bowling Alley on the Tiber*, 71.

21. Ibid., 93–94.

22. Ibid., 3.

23. Joseph Bennett, "The Essences of Being," *Hudson Review* 14, no. 3 (1961): 436.

24. Roland Barthes, "The Reality Effect," in *The Rustle of Language*, trans. Richard Howard (New York: Hill & Wang, 1986), 141–48.

25. Robert Warshow, *The Immediate Experience* (New York: Atheneum, 1970), 251.

26. Antonioni, *That Bowling Alley on the Tiber*, 93.

27. "I especially love women," Antonioni has said. "Perhaps because I understand them better? I was born amongst women, and raised in the midst of female cousins, aunts, relatives. I know women very well. Through the psychology of women everything becomes more poignant. They express themselves better and more precisely. They are a filter which allows us to see more clearly and to distinguish things" (quoted in Sam Rohdie, *Antonioni* [London: British Film Institute, 1990], 183).

28. William S. Pechter, *Twenty-four Times a Second* (New York: Harper & Row, 1971), 49.

29. Roman Jakobson's key essay on metaphor and metonymy, "Two Aspects of Language and Two Types of Aphasic Disturbances," first appeared in Roman Jakobson and Morris Halle, *Fundamentals of Language* (The Hague: Mouton, 1956). Variously reprinted, it can be found in Roman Jakobson, *Language in Literature*, ed. Krystyna Pomorska and Stephen Rudy (Cambridge: Harvard University Press, 1987), 95–114.

30. Barthes's letter to Antonioni was written on the occasion of a prize, the Archiginnasio d'oro, with which in 1980 the city of Bologna honored the director. The French text, "Cher Antonioni . . . ," appeared in *Cahiers du cinéma*, no. 311 (May 1980); the translation is mine.

31. Young, *On Film*, 279.

32. Adrian Stokes, *Colour and Form*, in *The Critical Writings of Adrian Stokes*, ed. Lawrence Gowing, vol. 2 (New York: Thames & Hudson, 1978), 13.

33. Young, *On Film*, 189. This sequence is perceptively discussed as well in Geoffrey Nowell-Smith's article "Shape around a Black Point," *Sight and Sound*, 33, no. 1 (1963–64): 15–20.

Permissions

The author published earlier versions of parts of this book as follows: parts of the introduction appeared in *The Nation* (January 4/11, 1993) and in *Raritan* 16 (spring 1997); parts of chapter 2 appeared in *The Hudson Review* 30 (spring 1977) and in *The Nation* (November 4, 1991); parts of chapter 3 appeared in *The Hudson Review* 34 (autumn 1981); parts of chapter 4 appeared in *Sight and Sound* 36 (summer 1967) and in *Raritan* 13 (summer 1993); parts of chapter 5 appeared in *The Hudson Review* 28 (spring 1975); parts of chapter 6 appeared in *The Hudson Review* 42 (summer 1989) and in *The Yale Review* 83 (October 1995); parts of chapter 7 appeared in *The Nation* (September 14, 1992, and October 25, 1993) and in *The Yale Review* 84 (July 1996); parts of chapter 8 appeared in *Artforum* 17 (October 1978) and in *The Yale Review* 85 (January 1997); parts of chapter 9 appeared in *Raritan* 6 (summer 1986) and in *The Nation* (February 18, 1991); parts of chapter 10 appeared in *The Hudson Review* 44 (summer 1991) and in *The Yale Review* 82 (July 1994).

Name and Title Index

Subject Index

The Library of Congress has cataloged the
hardcover edition of this book as follows:

Perez, Gilberto, 1943–
    The material ghost : films and their medium / Gilberto Perez.
    p.   cm.
    Includes bibliographical references and indexes.
    ISBN 0-8018-5673-6 (alk. paper)
    1. Film criticism.   2. Motion pictures—Philosophy.   I. Title.
PN1995.P397   1998
791.43'01'5—dc21   97-16877   CIP

ISBN 0-8018-6523-9 (pbk.)

Lightning Source UK Ltd.
Milton Keynes UK
UKHW01f2021310818
328139UK00001B/180/P